Social Problems

CH 6/24

2

6

7

8

SECOND EDITION

SOCIAL PROBLEMS

A BRIEF INTRODUCTION

James William Coleman

California Polytechnic State University

Harold R. Kerbo

California Polytechnic State University

Prentice Hall

UPPER SADDLE RIVER, NEW JERSEY 07458

Library of Congress Cataloging-in-Publication Data

Coleman, James William
      Social problems: a brief introduction/James William Coleman.—2nd ed.
        p. cm.
      Includes bibliographical references and index.
      ISBN 0-13-028300-2
        1. Sociology.   2. Social problems.   3. Social institutions.   4. United States—Social conditions—1980–
      I. Title.

HM586 .C65   2003
361.1—dc21

2002152272

AVP, Publisher: Nancy Roberts
Managing editor: Sharon Chambliss
Senior marketing manager: Amy Speckman
Marketing assistant: Anne Marie Fritzky
Editorial/production supervision: Kari Callaghan Mazzola
Prepress and manufacturing buyer: Mary Ann Gloriande
Electronic page makeup: Kari Callaghan Mazzola and John P. Mazzola
Interior design: John P. Mazzola
Director, Image Resource Center: Melinda Reo
Interior image specialist: Beth Boyd-Brenzel
Manager, Rights and Permissions: Zina Arabia
Image permissions coordinator: Debbie Hewitson
Photo researchers: Jane Sanders and Elaine Soares
Cover art director: Jayne Conte
Cover design: Joseph Sengotta
Cover art: Linda Bleck/Stock Illustration Source, Inc.

This book was set in 10/12 Novarese by Big Sky Composition
and was printed and bound by RR Donnelley & Sons Company.
The cover was printed by Coral Graphics.

© 2003, 1998 by Pearson Education, Inc.
Upper Saddle River, New Jersey 07458

Printed in the United States of America
10 9 8 7 6 5 4 3 2 1

ISBN 0-13-028300-2

Pearson Education LTD., London
Pearson Education Australia PTY, Limited, Sydney
Pearson Education Singapore, Pte. Ltd
Pearson Education North Asia Ltd, Hong Kong
Pearson Education Canada, Ltd., Toronto
Pearson Educación de Mexico, S.A. de C.V.
Pearson Education—Japan, Tokyo
Pearson Education Malaysia, Pte. Ltd
Pearson Education, Upper Saddle River, New Jersey

Contents

CHAPTER 5   HEALTH AND HEALTH CARE   134

PREFACE

Like its longer sibling, this book was written for students. Its objective is not only to familiarize undergraduates with the most trying problems of their times, but also to stimulate them to think in a critical, scientific way. It tries to challenge the half-truths and pat answers that many people accept simply because they have heard them repeated so often, and to get students to participate in the dialogue about these issues rather than merely stand back and observe.

This brief introduction to social problems is based on the eighth edition of the *Social Problems* text we authored with the assistance of Linda L. Ramos. It may seem like a relatively simple task to cut an eighteen chapter book down into twelve, but it proved to be a real challenge. Of course, we could have just eliminated six chapters and updated the rest, but that would have produced a poorly organized book with significant holes in its coverage. So the original challenge was to combine material in ways that would allow coverage of all the key points in less space. But as the work progressed, we realized that the demands of this new format encouraged us to make new connections between problems in ways that should, we hope, provide valuable new insights to students. For example, Chapter 2 in the brief edition combines the chapters on political and economic problems into a single chapter that we think does a better job of laying out the fundamental framework of our political economy. Much of the material in the main text's chapter on sexual behavior is included in the chapters on gender and family, and the discussion of warfare and international conflict is now integrated into the chapter on global inequality, which clearly lays out the inevitable linkage between these two problems in a way that has become particularly useful in light of the September 11 terrorist attacks. Population and the environment are covered in a single new chapter that makes the effects of the population explosion on our environmental crisis even clearer.

We have tried to continue all the features that have helped make the main text so successful—the strongly worded debates on controversial issues, informative graphics, a consistent theoretical organizational that includes a section on the major theoretical perspectives in each chapter, and a clear, straightforward style of writing that does not talk down to the reader or oversimplify complex issues. Also continued are the "Lessons from Other Places" boxes that use the experiences of other nations to shed light on the social problems we face in North America. Although this brief edition is based on the main text, which only came out a year before, social problems is a rapidly changing field of study, and each chapter also had to be thoroughly updated and revised. We should also make it clear that while the length of coverage of the various problems differs from the main text, no major topics have been omitted. All in all, we are extremely pleased with the way this brief edition came out, and we hope the readers will feel the same way.

SUPPLEMENTS

FOR THE INSTRUCTOR

Instructor's Manual with Tests   This essential instructor's tool includes detailed chapter outlines, teaching objectives, discussion questions, classroom activities, and additional instructor's resources. Also included are multiple-choice, true/false, and essay questions keyed to the text.

Prentice Hall Test Manager   This computerized software allows instructors to create their own personalized exams, to edit any or all test questions, and to add new questions. Other special features of this program, which is available for Windows and Macintosh, include random generation of an item set, creation of alternate versions of the same test, scrambling question sequence, and test preview before printing.

ABC News/Prentice Hall Video Library for Social Problems   Selected video segments from award-winning ABC News programs such as *Nightline*, ABC *World News Tonight/American Agenda*, and 20/20 accompany topics featured in the text. Please contact your local Prentice Hall sales representative for more details.

FOR THE STUDENT

Companion Website™   In tandem with the text, students can now take full advantage of the World Wide Web to enrich their study of social problems through the Coleman Companion Website™. This resource correlates the text with related material available on the Internet. Features include chapter objectives, study questions, and links to additional material that can reinforce and enhance the content of each chapter. **Address:** www.prenhall.com/coleman

The New York Times Supplement   *The New York Times* and Prentice Hall are sponsoring *Themes of the Times*, a program designed to enhance student access to current information of relevance in the classroom.

Through this program, the core subject matter provided in the text is supplemented by a collection of time-sensitive articles from one of the world's most distinguished newspapers, *The New York Times*. These articles demonstrate the vital, ongoing connection between what is learned in the classroom and what is happening in the world around us. To enjoy the wealth of information of *The New York Times* daily, a reduced subscription rate is available. For information, call toll-free: 1-800-631-1222.

Prentice Hall and *The New York Times* are proud to cosponsor *Themes of the Times*. We hope it will make the reading of both textbooks and newspapers a more dynamic, involving process. This supplement is supplied free to students and is updated twice per year. Please contact your local Prentice Hall sales representative for more details.

Evaluating Online Resources, Sociology, 2003   This guide provides a brief introduction to navigating the Internet, and encourages students to be critical consumers of online resources. References related specifically to the discipline of sociology are included. This guide is free when packaged with any Prentice Hall textbook. Included with the Evaluating Online Resources guide is a free access code for **Research Navigator™**.

Research Navigator™ is the easiest way for students to start a research assignment or research paper. Complete with extensive help on the research process and three exclusive databases of credible and reliable source material—including EBSCO's **ContentSelect™** Academic Journal Database, *The New York Times* Search by Subject Archive, and "Best of the Web" Link Library—Research Navigator™ helps students quickly and efficiently make the most of their research time.

ACKNOWLEDGMENTS

Space permits the mention of only a few of the many people who contributed to this book. First and foremost are the hundreds of students who have given countless invaluable suggestions over the years. We would also like to thank the numerous professors who have sent us comments or reviewed various versions of the book. The work of Sharon Chambliss, Nancy Roberts, and the other members of the Prentice Hall team who have labored on this project is also greatly appreciated.

James William Coleman

CHAPTER 1

SOCIOLOGY
AND SOCIAL PROBLEMS

Questions to Consider

What is a social problem?

What are the sociological perspectives that are used to analyze social problems?

How do sociologists study social problems?

How can we evaluate the claims made about social problems?

> It was the best of times, it was the worst of times, it was the age of wisdom, it was the age of foolishness, . . . it was the season of Light, it was the season of Darkness, it was the spring of hope, it was the winter of despair. . . .

These are opening words in Charles Dickens's famous novel A *Tale of Two Cities*, and they apply as well in the twenty-first century as they did when he wrote them in the nineteenth. On the one hand, we are healthier, live longer, receive better education, and enjoy more technological conveniences than in any other period in human history. On the other hand, perennial problems such as poverty, discrimination, and violence show no sign of fading away, and the specter of terrorism and environmental catastrophe looms menacingly on the horizon. Indeed, the list of our social problems is so depressingly long that many people just throw their hands up and believe there is nothing they can do to help. But is that really true? The sociological study of social problems is founded on the belief that something can indeed be done if we first make the effort to study our problems systematically and then act on our understanding.

Politicians and community officials spend much of their careers trying to solve social problems that include everything from double parking to the threat of nuclear war. Voters select candidates who claim to have the best solutions, but the public's ideas about many social problems are distorted or confused. While the serious study of social problems can clear up much of this confusion and misunderstanding, beginning students often have the uncomfortable feeling that the more they read, the less they understand. There are so many conflicting viewpoints, and even the results of objective, scientific research may appear to be contradictory.

Sociology (the scientific study of society and social behavior) provides a framework for sorting out all these facts, ideas, and beliefs. It provides the perspective and the tools we need to make sense of our social problems. Using this perspective, we can develop programs to deal with our problems and evaluate their results once they have been put into effect. This is not to say that all sociologists agree on the exact causes of our social problems or how we should solve them, but fortunately, such disagreements can result in a richer understanding for the student who is willing to examine all sides of the issues involved.

What Is a Social Problem?

Most people think of a **social problem** as any condition that is harmful to society; but the matter is not so simple, for the meanings of such everyday terms as *harm* and *society* are far from clear. Conditions that some people see as social problems harm some segments of society but are beneficial to others. Consider air pollution. On the one hand, an automobile manufacturer might argue that government regulation of free enterprise is a social problem because laws requiring antipollution devices on cars raise costs, decrease gasoline mileage, and stimulate inflation. On the other hand, residents of a polluted city might argue that the government's failure to outlaw noxious automobile emissions is a social problem because the smog created by such emissions harms their health and well-being. One person's social problem is another person's solution. Clearly, most people define a social problem as something that harms (or seems to harm) their own interests.

A more precise sociological definition holds that *a social problem exists when there is a sizable difference between the ideals of a society and its actual achievements.*[1] From this perspective, social problems are created by the failure to close the gap between the way people want things to be and the way things really are. Thus, racial discrimination is a social problem because, although we believe that everyone should receive fair and equal treatment, some groups are still denied equal access to education, employment, and housing. Before this definition can be applied, someone must first examine the ideals and values of society and then decide whether these goals are being achieved. Sociologists and other experts thus decide what is or is not a problem because they have the skills necessary for measuring the desires and achievements of society.

Critics of this approach point out that no contemporary society has a single, unified set of values and ideals. When using this definition, sociologists must therefore decide which standards they will use for judging whether or not a certain condition is a social problem. Critics charge that those ideals and values used as standards are selected on the basis of the researcher's personal opinions and prejudices, not objective analysis.

Another widely accepted sociological definition holds that *a social problem exists when a significant number of people believe that a certain condition is in fact a problem.*[2] Here the public (not a sociologist) decides what is or is not a social problem. The sociologist's job is to determine which problems concern a substantial number of people. Thus, in this view, pollution did not become a social problem until environmental activists and news reports attracted the public's attention to conditions that had actually existed for some time.

The advantage of this definition is that it does not require a value judgment by sociologists who try to decide what is and is not a social problem; such decisions are made by "the public." However, a serious shortcoming of this approach is that the public is often uninformed or misguided and does not clearly understand its problems. If thousands of people were being poisoned by radiation leaking from a nuclear power plant but didn't know it, wouldn't that still be a social problem? Another shortcoming of this approach is that relatively powerless groups with little money or political organization will not be able to get their problems recognized as social problems.

All the topics discussed in the chapters that follow qualify as social problems according to both sociological definitions. Each involves conditions that conflict with strongly held ideals and values, and all are considered social problems by significant groups of people. The goal of every chapter is to discuss these problems fairly and objectively. From time to time, we will also consider the problems of the powerless that have not been widely recognized by society. It is important to understand, however, that even selecting the problems requires a value judgment, whether by social scientists or by concerned citizens, and honest disagreements about the nature and importance of the various issues competing for public attention cannot be avoided.

The social issues that concern the public change from time to time, and a comparison of the numerous surveys of public opinion that have been done over the years reveals some interesting trends. War and peace and various economic issues

Social movements create public awareness about social problems and push the government to take action to resolve them. The young women shown here are part of a 1999 Seattle protest against the World Trade Organization.

have consistently ranked high on the public's list of social concerns. Interest in other problems seems to move in cycles. Thus, concern about taxes, foreign policy, illegal drug use, or lack of religious belief and morality is high in some years and low in others. Still other social problems are like fads, attracting a great deal of interest for a few years before dropping from public attention.[3]

These changes have many different causes: shifts in ideals and values, the solution to an old problem, the creation of new ones. One of the most important forces affecting changes in public opinion is **social movements** (groups of people who have banded together to promote a particular cause). For example, none of the polls in the 1930s and 1940s showed civil rights or race relations to be significant problems, even though racial discrimination was widespread and openly practiced. It was not until the civil rights movement began in the late 1950s that polls began to reflect an interest in this problem. The problem of racial discrimination would probably have remained buried if a powerful social movement had not developed to demand that society change its ways.

QUICK REVIEW

What are the two common definitions of social problems?
What are the advantages and disadvantages of each?

LESSONS FROM OTHER PLACES

THE AMERICAN VALUE SYSTEM

I was in Germany a few years ago during national elections, and I saw a rather striking contrast between German and American voters. It was 1998 and Chancellor Helmut Kohl was running for reelection during a particularly bad economic time. Unemployment was very high (about 12 percent), and the economy had been stalled with little growth for several years. Taxes in Germany are quite high compared to taxes in the United States (then over 50 percent for the average German compared to about 25 to 30 percent for the average American), with welfare spending much higher in Germany. German workers, for example, are guaranteed about 80 percent of their wages for two years after becoming unemployed, and about 60 percent of their wages for life if they still don't find a job.

Considering the very strong economy in the United States with low taxes and little welfare spending during 1998, some German politicians were calling for Germany to follow the U.S. model. So Chancellor Kohl (of the Christian Democratic Party) began running for reelection on a platform of cutting taxes and welfare spending in Germany, while his opponent, Gerhard Schroeder (of the Social Democratic Party), pledged to protect the welfare state. Gerhard Schroeder won the election in September 1998 primarily on this pledge of keeping high taxes and welfare. My first thought was, "this is not America."

As we begin our study of social problems in the United States, we need to recognize that there are important differences in value orientation between Americans and the people of other industrial nations,* and that these differences have an enormous impact both on the causes of social problems and on their potential solutions. Polls show that Americans have less trust in government, more dislike of taxes and welfare programs, and greater tolerance for poverty and inequality. These differences are in large part a result of the stronger belief in rugged "individualism" among Americans. In the United States, most people see each individual as an autonomous actor who is responsible for his or her own destiny. Americans don't support welfare programs or high unemployment benefits because they see such problems as the result of the personal failure of the individuals involved. In most other industrialized countries, however, the family and community are seen to be far more important in determining our fate.

—Harold Kerbo

*For opinion poll data on contrasting American values, see Evertt Ladd and Karolin Bowman, *Attitudes Toward Economic Inequality*, Washington, D.C.: American Enterprise Institute, 1998, and the annual Gallup Poll. Also see Harold R. Kerbo and Hermann Strasser, *Modern Germany*, New York: McGraw-Hill, 2000.

FOUNDATIONS OF THE SOCIOLOGICAL APPROACH

Over the years sociologists have built up a body of basic knowledge about society and how it operates that can help us get perspective on conflicting claims and counter-claims about our social problems. A great deal of this book is devoted to helping students develop this kind of sociological understanding of the world. Before we can proceed, however, we must look at some basic concepts that provide the foundation on which the sociological approach is built. (A wide variety of sociological concepts are included in the glossary at the end of the book, so if you run across an unfamiliar concept while you are reading, be sure to check the glossary.) As we go though our daily lives dealing with our friends, relatives, and acquaintances, most of us see a group of unique individual people, but the sociologist also sees a set of social roles. In the theater or the movies, a role is the part a particular person plays in the show. Sociologists use the term in much the same way, except that the role is played in real-life social situations. A **role** is usually defined as the set of behaviors and expectations associated with a particular social position (often known as a status). All roles—daughter, son, student, automobile driver, and countless others—offer certain rights and duties to the player. A student, for example, has the right to attend classes, to use the school's facilities, and to be graded fairly. The student also has the duty to read the texts, complete assigned work, and behave in an orderly manner. However, the way people actually carry out their roles often differs enormously from such idealized expectations.

Roles are one of the basic building blocks of our social world, and every society has countless positions with roles attached. Roles are interwoven in complex ways, so it is often impossible to understand a particular role apart from the social network in which it is embedded. How, for example, can the role of wife be defined without reference to the roles of husband, daughter, son, mother, and father? This interdependence stems from the fact that the rights of one position (wife, for example) are interlaced with the duties of other positions (husband, daughter, son). Each of us is judged by our performance as we carry out our roles. The negligent mother, the abusive father, the incompetent professor, and the disruptive student are judged harshly because they fail to meet our role expectations.

The standards we use to make such judgments are known as **norms**. A norm is simply a social rule that tells us what behavior is acceptable in a certain situation—and what is not. Every human group, be it a small circle of friends or an entire society, generates norms that govern its members' conduct. An individual who violates a group's norms is often labeled a **deviant** and given some kind of formal or informal punishment. A person who violates the norm against taking the lives of others may be tried and formally punished with a prison term, whereas a person who violates the trust of his or her friends is informally punished by ridicule or exclusion from the group. Just as the various roles we play may place conflicting demands on us, so the norms of various groups may conflict. Thus, we are sometimes placed in the uncomfortable position of being forced to violate the norms of one group in order to meet the norms of another.[4]

Although some of the roles we play involve nothing more than a small group or a single individual, social roles tend to be woven together into larger units. **Social institutions** are relatively stable patterns of roles and behavior centered around particular social tasks. The family, for example, is a basic institution in all known societies.

It usually handles many of the duties of child rearing and provides emotional and sometimes economic support for its older members.

Social class is one of the most useful of all these basic sociological ideas. Although everyone has some idea of what it means, few of us use the concept in a very clear or consistent way. Sociologists define **social class** as a category of people with a similar position in a society. People of the same social class have a similar chance in life: a similar opportunity to get an education, to receive health care, to acquire material possessions, and so on. Thus, the people you see sleeping on the heating grates outside an office building are from one social class, and the executives who speed past them on their way to the parking lot are from another.

Many nineteenth-century thinkers, including Karl Marx and his followers, defined social class solely in economic terms.[5] Today, most sociologists use a broader definition taken from the work of the German sociologist Max Weber.[6] According to Weber, the valuables a society distributes include social status and power as well as money, so to accurately assess the class positions of individuals or groups, we must know where they stand on all three. Status rests on a claim to social prestige, inherited from one's family or derived from occupation and lifestyle. Power is the ability to force others to do something whether they want to or not, and it is another key to understanding the class system—and for that matter, social life in general. Power is often associated with politics in the public mind, and high political position certainly brings a large measure of power with it; but power has many other sources as well, such as wealth or control of the means of violent force.

Sociologists use several different schemes to describe the class system in contemporary societies, but the most common divides these societies into four different classes (see Figure 1.1 on page 8). The *upper class* is composed of individuals with great wealth, who often hold key positions of corporate power. Next comes the *middle class*, comprised of an upper segment of highly paid professionals, successful executives, and entrepreneurs, and a much larger group of middle-level managers and white-collar (nonmanual) workers. The *working class* is about the same size as the middle class, but its members are mainly blue-collar (manual) workers and lower-level service workers who would traditionally have been defined as white-collar workers but actually have the low pay and low prestige associated with working-class jobs. Although the best-paid blue-collar workers earn more money than many white-collar employees, average members of the working class earn far less than their middle-class counterparts. At the bottom of the social hierarchy is the *lower class*, whose members live in conditions of poverty or very close to them. There is a popular belief that most Americans are middle class, perhaps because the majority of the people we see on television and in the movies are from that class, but the truth of the matter is much different. Of every 100 people in the United States, only 1 is from the upper class, 15 to 20 are from the lower class, and the remainder are more or less evenly divided between the working class and the middle class (see Figure 1.1).[7]

The most all-encompassing concepts in sociology are those of society and culture. In everyday speech, **culture** refers to the refinements of civilization, such as art, music, and literature; but to sociologists, culture is the way of life of the people in a certain geographic area, and particularly the ideas, beliefs, values, patterns of thought, and symbols that make it possible. A culture provides individuals with a

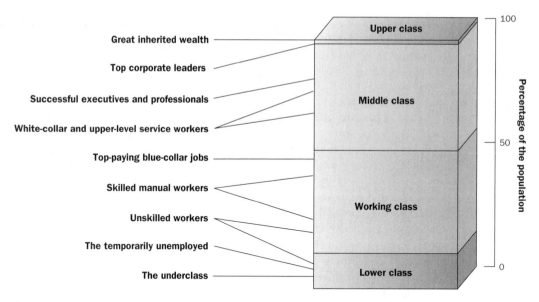

FIGURE 1.1   THE CLASS SYSTEM

Source: Harold R. Kerbo, *Social Stratification and Inequality*, 4th ed. (New York: McGraw-Hill, 2000) and current reports of the U.S. Bureau of the Census.

way of understanding the world and making it meaningful. A **subculture** is a culture that exists within a larger culture that influences it, but has its own distinctive ideas and beliefs; for example, the gang members who cover our cities with graffiti are part of a subculture that places its own special meaning on such symbols.

Although culture and society cannot be separated in real life, sociologists sometimes distinguish between the two so that each can be studied more easily. **Society** refers to a group of people in a particular geographic area who share common institutions and traditions, while culture refers to the physical and mental products of those people. All societies have an overall **social structure**, which is simply an organized pattern of behavior and social relationships. They also have many more focused social structures, such as a particular pattern of family life, social class, and government.

QUICK REVIEW

Look at the list of key terms at the end of this chapter and make sure you can define each one.

SOCIOLOGICAL PERSPECTIVES ON SOCIAL PROBLEMS

All sociologists use the concepts discussed in the preceding section, but there are significant differences in their perspectives and approaches (see Table 1.1). Although the profusion of different theories and opinions can be confusing, there are a few broad theoretical perspectives that underlie many of these differences. Aside from

TABLE 1.1   SOCIOLOGICAL PERSPECTIVES

THE FUNCTIONALIST PERSPECTIVE	Macro level
	Society is held together by shared norms and values.
	Society is a joint effort of many institutions working together for the common good.
	The primary causes of social problems is social disorganization, which often results from rapid social change.
THE FEMINIST PERSPECTIVE	Macro and micro levels
	Gender is a basic organizing principle of contemporary society.
	The social position of women is not only different from that of men but also unequal.
	The primary cause of social problems is the exploitation of women by men.
THE CONFLICT PERSPECTIVE	Macro level
	Society is held together by power, authority, and coercion.
	Society is a struggle for dominance among competing social groups.
	The primary cause of social problems is the exploitation and oppression of some groups by others.
	International conflicts between rich and poor nations help explain persistent world poverty.
THE INTERACTIONIST PERSPECTIVE	Micro level
	Individual behavior is based on the symbols and shared meanings we learn.
	This learning occurs during interactions between individuals and other people and groups.
	The primary cause of social problems is the way we define ourselves and our social situation.

helping make sense of the theories themselves, knowledge of these basic perspectives leads to a better understanding of our social problems by drawing our attention to important social forces often neglected by the media and politicians when they discuss these issues. These general sociological perspectives (and other more narrow theories, as well) tend to focus on one of two different levels. Theories of society (macro theories) try to make sense of the behavior of large groups of people and the workings of entire societies, while social psychological theories (micro theories) are concerned primarily with the behavior of individuals and small groups. Of course, society depends on its individual members, and those individuals depend on society; in the last two decades, sociologists have increasingly come to recognize that a complete understanding depends on the integration of these two different levels of analysis.

Supporters of one theory often have harsh criticisms of other theories. But even though some theories are clearly more effective than others in analyzing a particular problem, none of the broad perspectives can be said to be all right or all wrong. Not only can many different theories be applied to the same problem, but in most cases the deepest understanding comes from combining the insights gained from different theoretical perspectives. In this book, for example, some chapters draw more heavily from one theoretical perspective and some from another, depending on the nature of the problem under discussion, but all the problems are examined from many different standpoints. The objective is always to keep an open mind and draw insight wherever it can be found.

Most sociologists divide the macro-level theories of society into two broad perspectives—functionalism and conflict theory—and we will begin with those two approaches. Next we will look at feminist theory, which combines both macro and micro levels of analysis, and then at interactionist theory, which is by far the most influential of the social psychological (micro) theories in sociology. When reading the following explanations of these approaches, remember that they are only broad summaries. There are many theoretical differences among functionalists, conflict theorists, feminists, and interactionists, and many sociologists combine elements from all these theories into a more integrated approach.

THE FUNCTIONALIST PERSPECTIVE

Many early theorists who held a **functionalist perspective** saw society as something like a living organism. Just as people have a heart and circulatory system, muscles, blood, and a brain, a society has a set of economic, political, religious, family, and educational institutions. And just as all the parts of a living organism work together to keep it alive, so all the parts of society must work together to keep it going. Each institution has a set of **functions** it must perform in order to keep society healthy; for instance, the function of the economic institution is to provide the food, shelter, and clothing that people need in order to survive, while the functions of the government include coordinating the activities of other institutions, dealing with unmet social needs, and protecting society from foreign aggressors. These various institutions make up a balanced whole, so changes in one institution are likely to require changes in another. Thus, from the functionalist perspective, we all have a common stake in helping to maintain society, and all of a society's institutions work together for the common good.

However, societies, like machines and biological organisms, do not always work the way they are supposed to work. Things get out of whack. Even when things are going well, changes introduced to correct one imbalance may produce other problems. An action that interferes with the effort to carry out essential social tasks is said to be **dysfunctional**. For example, educators may train too many people for certain jobs. Those who cannot find positions in their area of expertise may become resentful, rebelling against the system that they feel has treated them unfairly. Thus, "overeducation" may be said to be a dysfunction of our educational institutions. Functionalists also realize there are sometimes unintended consequences from our efforts to change society. For example, the effort to reduce the amount of drugs available on the streets may work to push up the crime rate. As the supply of illegal drugs is reduced, the street price of drugs goes up, and addicts may have to commit more crimes to pay for their drug habit. Therefore, the functional perspective warns us that we must make a systemic analysis of functions and dysfunctions within a society before we attempt a program of social change.

Functionalists see a common set of norms and values as the glue that holds groups, institutions, and whole societies together. Small tribal societies in which everyone is in constant close contact usually have little difficulty in maintaining these common ideals, but as the great French sociologist Emile Durkheim pointed out, as societies have become ever larger and more complex, it has become increasingly difficult to maintain a social consensus about basic norms and values.[8] Thus, one of the major sources of contemporary social problems is the weakening of the social consensus. Functionalists can cite considerable evidence to show that when the social rules lose their power to control our behavior, people become lost and confused and are more susceptible to suicide, mental disorders, and drug problems.

Functionalists also feel that social problems arise when society, or some part of it, becomes disorganized. This **social disorganization** involves a breakdown of social structure, so that its various parts no longer work together as smoothly as they should. Functionalists see many causes of social disorganization: Young people may be inadequately socialized because of problems in the institution of the family, or society may fail to provide enough social and economic opportunities to some of its members, thus encouraging them to become involved in crime or other antisocial activities. Sometimes a society's relationship to its environment may be disrupted, so that it no longer has sufficient food, energy, building materials, or other resources. However, in modern industrial societies, one cause of social disorganization—rapid social change—promotes all the others.

Social disorganization is particularly severe in the modern era because more changes have occurred in less time than during any other period of human history. Basic institutions have undergone drastic changes with technology advancing so rapidly that other parts of the culture have failed to keep pace. This cultural lag is one of the major sources of social disorganization. For instance, when knowledge about nutrition, public health, and medical technology began spreading through the world in the nineteenth century, many lives, especially those of infants, were saved. Yet traditional attitudes toward the family have not changed fast enough to adjust to the fact that more children survive to adulthood. The result has been a worldwide population explosion.[9]

Although functionalism has been a standard theoretical approach to social problems for many years, it has numerous critics. Despite its claims of objectivity, many sociologists see functionalism as a politically conservative philosophy that too quickly assumes that society is fine just the way it is and should be preserved without major changes. Functionalism sometimes blames social problems on individual deviance or temporary social disorganization while seeming to ignore what some view as more basic deficiencies in the structure of society. The critics of functionalism claim that it is often impossible to say whether or not a particular social phenomenon is functional for society as a whole because such phenomena usually have different impacts on different groups. For example, a law that forbids sleeping in the lobbies of public buildings would benefit wealthy people who may be disturbed by such behavior but hurt the homeless, who have nowhere else to go. Critics charge that what the functionalists often really mean when they say something is functional is that it works to the benefit of the status quo.

THE CONFLICT PERSPECTIVE

When theorists with a **conflict perspective** look out at contemporary society, they see a very different world. Where the functionalists see a more or less integrated whole working to maintain itself and promote the common good, conflict theorists see a diverse collection of social groups, all struggling for wealth, power, and prestige. While functionalists emphasize the importance of shared values, attitudes, and norms in holding society together, conflict theorists insist that social order is maintained more by authority backed by the use of force. For example, functionalists hold that most people obey the law because they believe that it is the right thing to do. Conflict theorists, on the other hand, say that most people obey the law because they are afraid of being arrested, jailed, or even killed if they don't. Another important difference between the functionalist and conflict perspectives is seen in their assumptions about social change. Functionalists tend to view a healthy society as being relatively stable; they assert that too much change is disruptive and that society has a natural tendency to regain its balance whenever it is disturbed. Conflict theorists see society in more dynamic terms: Because people are constantly struggling with one another to gain power, change is inevitable. One individual or group is bound to gain the upper hand, only to be defeated in later struggles.

Neither the conflict nor the functionalist perspective can be said to be a single unified theory. Rather, each consists of a number of related theories that share many common elements. One of the most important differences among conflict theorists

Contemporary society has huge inequalities in the distribution of wealth, power, and prestige, and conflict theorists hold that fact to be one of the most basic causes of our social problems.

concerns the type of conflicts they see as most central to modern society. Karl Marx, the famous nineteenth-century scholar and revolutionary who had so much to do with the origins of conflict theory, placed primary emphasis on **class conflict**. For Marx, the position a person holds in the system of production determines his or her class position. In a capitalist society (see Chapter 2 for a discussion of the nature of capitalism), a person may be in one of two different positions. Some people own capital and capital-producing property (for example, factory owners, landlords, and merchants) and are therefore members of the *bourgeoisie*. Other people work for wages as producers of capital (for example, factory workers, miners, and laborers of all kinds). Marx called this class the *proletariat*. He asserted that these two classes have directly opposing economic interests because the wealth of the bourgeoisie is based on exploitation of the proletariat. He thought that workers would develop an increasing awareness of their exploitation by the bourgeoisie and that this awareness, combined with growing political organization, would eventually result in violent class conflict. Marx believed that the workers would overthrow their masters in this great revolution and establish a classless society. Private property and inheritance would be abolished; steeply graduated income taxes would be introduced; education and training would be free; and production would be organized for use, not profit.[10]

Modern conflict theorists continue to see class conflict as a central fact of life in contemporary society. Even though Marx's ideas have had an enormous impact on the world, many conflict theorists look at the class structure in very different terms than Marx did, instead preferring the approach of another famous German sociologist, Max Weber, which we have already discussed. And even many contemporary Marxists have come to see the vision of a popular revolution that will establish a just society without class distinctions as something that will occur only in the distant future, if at all.

Although virtually no conflict theorists would deny the importance of class conflict in modern society, some place greater emphasis on other types of conflict. In the wake of the civil rights and ethnic power movements in the United States and the worldwide epidemic of ethnic strife, some have come to place more importance on ethnic conflict—the struggle for power, wealth, and status between the members of different ethnic groups. Conflict theorists influenced by feminism place greater emphasis on gender and the inequalities based on it.

But whether they emphasize class, ethnicity, or gender, conflict theorists generally agree on some basic criticisms of the functionalists. Conflict theorists deny that our most serious problems arise primarily from a weakening of social values or the unintentional problems created when an important social institution becomes disorganized. Rather, most social problems are the result of the intentional or unintentional exploitation of weak groups by powerful ones. For example, conflict theorists argue that the serious problems faced by Latinos and African Americans in the United States are caused not by the disorganization of the social system that makes it difficult to fully integrate these minorities into the mainstream of society, but rather by exploitation by whites who profit from the economic and political subordination of minority groups.

A conflict perspective is also well suited to move from an analysis of individual nations to a global level. Modern **world system theory**, for example, is a variety of conflict theory that helps us understand the differences between rich and poor nations. Conflict theorists argue that there is something like an international class system in which the rich nations, having more power and wealth, are able to exploit poor nations for their own advantage. From this global conflict perspective we can see how poor nations may sometimes be forced to remain poor because it is in the interests of richer nations to keep them that way, in order to exploit their resources and their labor.

At the same time, a global conflict perspective can help us understand the impact of the **globalization** of the world economy on individual nations like the United States. For example, globalization may be of most benefit to the rich people in the advanced nations because the exploitation of the poor nations can produce fat profits. On the other hand, globalization can hurt the workers of the rich nations as their jobs move overseas to places with cheaper labor. Global conflict theorists argue that one reason that poverty has remained high and wages have shown little growth—despite the longest economic boom in American history (which began in the early 1990s)—is that working class Americans have faced ever-increasing competition for jobs with poor people from around the world.

Just as functionalism has been criticized for being too conservative, the conflict perspective has been criticized for being too radical. Critics say that conflict theorists overemphasize the role of conflict, arguing that if there were as much of it as these theorists claim, society would have collapsed long ago. Moreover, they charge that conflict theorists are too one-sided in their approach. The critics say that while conflict theorists see nothing but the bad side of capitalism, capitalist nations actually do a much better job of dealing with their social problems than other kinds of societies do.

THE FEMINIST PERSPECTIVE

Like the other approaches examined here, **feminist theory** is not a single theory but a group of theories that share a concern with the same basic questions. In their analysis of contemporary feminist theory, Patricia Madoo Lengermann and Jill Niebrugge-Brantley hold that the two most important of those questions are "And what about the women?" and "Why is woman's situation as it is?"[11]

Throughout most of its history, sociology, like the rest of the humanities and social sciences, saw human experience from a male perspective. While there was certainly much in this approach that applied to both genders, women's experience was often ignored or given a decidedly secondary importance. So when feminist theory began to emerge as an influential force in sociology in the 1960s, the first question it posed was "What about the women?" In other words, these thinkers set out to describe the world and women's place in it from a female perspective to counterbalance the male-oriented view of the traditional sociological theories. Feminist theory emphasizes the idea that women's lives are markedly different from men's because women are given the primary responsibility for child rearing and are socialized to care for the emotional and physical needs of others. But the position of women is not just different from that of men; it is unequal as well. On average, women have less wealth, less power, and lower status than men. Thus, feminists often describe contemporary society as a **patriarchy**—that is, a society dominated by men and run in their interest.

In an attempt to explain why a woman's situation is the way it is, feminists tend to split into different theoretical camps. The largest group is probably the *liberal feminists*. Liberal feminists see social activity in our society divided into two separate spheres—the public sphere, which is man's central concern, and the private sphere, which is woman's realm. Liberal feminists view the private sphere as an endless round of demanding, undervalued tasks, such as housework and child care, while the real rewards of life—power, money, and prestige—are to be found in the public sphere. They generally accept the American values of freedom and individualism, but they argue that women have been confined to the private sphere and denied a fair opportunity to compete. The fundamental cause of this exclusion is **sexism**—stereotypes, prejudice, and discrimination based on gender. The solution to this injustice is therefore to attack the sexist traditions that have been handed down from previous generations and to allow everyone to develop their own unique abilities and pursue their interests regardless of their gender.

To the *socialist feminists*, liberals take a far too rosy view of contemporary society. In their view, the roots of the exploitation of women are to be found in the capitalist economic system and the feudal system from which it evolved. Capitalism is based on the exploitation of labor, and women are the most exploited group of all. They are exploited by their husbands, providing unpaid labor for child care and housework, and they are exploited by the larger economy, providing a reserve pool of low-wage industrial labor to be used when necessary and then cast out. To the socialist feminists, a mere attack on sexist stereotypes will have little real impact on women's oppression unless the capitalist system itself is fundamentally transformed to free both women and men.

The *radical feminists* go a step beyond the others, arguing not just that the women's world is different from the men's world but that it is better. Men created and sustain our current social order, which is an oppressive patriarchal system that exploits and represses women, and their primary tool has been violence against women—rape, spouse abuse, incest, and murder. The radical feminists call for a "woman-centered" society that separates women from the oppression of men.

Critics of feminist theory fall into three different camps. One group argues that the feminists are completely wrong when they charge that society, and especially the family, oppresses women. In this view, the family fulfills and enriches women, and feminists are leading a misguided effort to make women become more like men. Another group of critics accepts the idea that women are indeed oppressed, but argues that most men are oppressed too. These critics assert that feminists foster the same kinds of stereotypes of men that our culture has created of women and that feminists try to blame men for injustices that are actually caused by impersonal historical forces. Finally, feminist theory, as well as the feminist movement, have been criticized for assuming all women have the same experience as white, middle-class women. Much attention has been given to rectifying this problem, but it is still important to ask whether or not women who are poor, women who are older, women of color, and women whose sexual identities are not heterosexual are being included in current feminist perspectives.

THE INTERACTIONIST PERSPECTIVE

The sociological approach to social psychology is dominated by a single broad perspective known as **interactionism**. In fact, many of the ideas of the interactionists have become so widely accepted that oftentimes they are not even seen as part of a separate theory, but simply as a standard part of basic sociology. Interactionism explains our behavior in terms of the patterns of thoughts and beliefs we have and in terms of the meaning we give to our lives. To understand individual behavior, the interactionist tries to look at the world through the eyes of the actors involved, to see how they define themselves and their environment. This understanding of the conditions in which we find ourselves, known as the **definition of the situation**, is learned through interaction with other people and is the foundation on which we base all our behavior. For example, a gang member who sees the police as the storm troopers of a racist society will respond differently to an officer's calls for help than a banker who sees the police as the defenders of law and order. Our interactions with others, however, teach us far more than how to define a particular social situation or even how to define the world in general. They are also the basis for the ideas we develop about who and what we are, and such an understanding, in turn, tells us what to expect from other people and how to act in a particular social context.

To the interactionist, reality is not something out there in the world waiting to be discovered. Reality is a socially created agreement constructed by the efforts of people acting together in social groups. Meanings are created as we struggle to define ourselves and the world around us and then share those meanings with others. In interactionist theory, human culture is nothing more than a complex system of shared meanings, and those meanings, in turn, determine our behavior.

The work of American philosopher George Herbert Mead was the original force behind interactionist theory.[12] Mead argued that the ability to communicate in symbols (principally words and combinations of words) is the key feature that distinguishes humans from other animals. Children develop the ability to think and to use symbols in the process known as **socialization**. At first, young children blindly imitate the behavior of their parents, but eventually they learn to "take the role of the other," pretending to be "mommy" or "daddy." From such role-taking, children learn to understand the relationships among different roles and to see themselves as they imagine others see them. According to Mead, the key to a child's psychological development is the creation of a **self-concept** (the relatively stable mental image we all have of who and what we are). This self-concept is created out of the responses a child receives from the important people in his or her life. For example, if a girl's parents constantly tell her how smart she is, she is likely to formulate a concept of herself as an intelligent person. This concept of self is not a fixed, unchanging structure, however. If later in life her teachers and friends begin to treat her as if she isn't really very bright, her self-concept is likely to change. The concept of self is one of the most important in social psychology, for it influences almost every aspect of our behavior. Another important influence on behavior, according to Mead, is the generalized other, the idea we form of what kind of behavior people expect of us (in other words, our conscience).

After Mead's death in 1931, his ideas continued to gain stature among sociologists and social psychologists. Those who adhered most closely to Mead's original ideas became known as *symbolic interactionists*.[13] They have been very active in the study of social problems and have contributed a great deal to our understanding of critical social issues. For example, differential association theory, an important explanation of delinquency and crime, is a direct offshoot of Mead's theories, as is the labeling theory that is used to explain mental disorder and crime (see Chapters 5 and 10). But over the years, interactionist theory has grown far beyond Mead's original vision and has absorbed insights from many other approaches.

Despite its enormous influence, interactionist theory has many critics. The most common complaint is that interactionism is vague and difficult to substantiate scientifically. A more telling criticism is that interactionism has an overly intellectual view of human nature. Classic interactionism sees human behavior entirely in terms of ideas and thoughts; it leaves out feelings and emotions. As a result of such criticism, interactionists have begun to direct more attention to the way our ideas and definitions are linked to emotions and to the role emotion plays in social life.[14]

OTHER SOCIAL PSYCHOLOGICAL PERSPECTIVES

Like sociologists, psychologists have long been involved in the study of social psychology, and they have developed their own perspectives to explain it. One of the most influential approaches is known as **behaviorism**. Originally, behaviorists felt science should investigate only observable behavior and that it is a waste of time to explore thoughts, feelings, or anything else that cannot be directly measured. They argued that all behavior is learned as the result of the patterns of rewards and punishments we receive from our environment.[15] Obviously, this approach is quite different from that of the interactionists, with all their emphasis on thoughts and symbols. However, both perspectives see human behavior as learned, not inherited, and more recent behaviorist thinkers who are more willing to look at the subjective side of behavior actually end up with conclusions that are quite compatible with those of the interactionists.[16]

Among the most popular psychological perspectives are the **personality theories**. **Personality** refers to the stable characteristics and traits that distinguish one person from another. Personality theorists believe it accounts for most differences in individual social behavior. Psychologists usually see personality differences as the result of a child's interactions with parents and other early experiences, although some hold that personality has an inherited component as well. Various ideas about personality have often been used to explain social problems. For example, criminals are sometimes said to break the law because they have "sociopathic personalities" (impulsive, unstable, and immature), and racial prejudice is attributed to an "authoritarian personality" (rigid and insecure, with repressed feelings of guilt and hostility; see Chapters 7 and 10).

One of the most basic and long-running disputes in the social sciences is sometimes called the "nature versus nurture" controversy. Those who support the "nurture" side of the debate, including most sociologists, feel that the majority of human behavior is learned. Those on the "nature" side argue that most human behavior is determined by our inherited biological makeup. The **biosocial perspective** comprises a loose grouping of "nature" theories that emphasize the role of biology in determining human behavior. Originally, biological theorists saw virtually all human behavior as caused by inherited patterns of action they called instincts. Given the enormous range of human culture and behavior, few contemporary scientists still claim that all behavior is inherited.

Contemporary biosocial theorists therefore emphasize the importance of the interaction between biological predispositions and the social environment. For example, many criminologists who argue that there is a hereditary predisposition toward crime see the problem as being as much with society as with genetics. They argue that people with low intelligence, which they hold to be a biological characteristic, are rejected by teachers and more competent students because they do poorly in school. As a result, they are more likely to become rebellious and antisocial (see Chapter 10). Many biosocial theorists focus their studies on the evolutionary process in hopes that an understanding of the forces that shaped the development of humankind will enable us to get a clearer picture of behavioral predispositions that have been passed down from our ancestors.

APPLYING THE SOCIOLOGICAL PERSPECTIVES: AN EXAMPLE

At first, these abstract theoretical perspectives may not seem to have much to do with all the pressing problems facing our society. If we take a concrete example, however, it is easy to show how these perspectives work to help us build an understanding of the issues at hand. Suppose, for instance, that you often stop at a small market on your way home from class. One day you realize that the woman who is sitting in the park across the street with her three children is there every time you come in. You ask the clerk about it, and she tells you that they are all living in their van, which is parked in an alley around the corner. A few weeks later, you go to the market and notice that a police car is parked on the street. You see two officers talking with the woman, and after that you never see her or her children again.

Of course, we would need much more information before we could come to any firm conclusions about why this particular family is in such trouble, but the sociological perspectives can help us learn about the general causes of homelessness and poverty, and that is really the more important question if we are to deal with the roots of the problem. The macro-level approaches lead us to take a broad perspective and to link the family's problem with powerful sociological forces that operate throughout our society. The functionalists see the origins of this kind of problem in the social disorganization that plagues so many parts of modern society. They are particularly likely to see such problems as the product of the weakened family institution. Some functionalists argue, for example, that the growing strength of the ideals of individualism and freedom are leading us to neglect our community obligations. In the past, people were expected to stay in a marriage, even a difficult one, for the sake of the children and society as a whole. But the weakening of such norms has resulted in more and more husbands and wives splitting up, often leaving a weakened family unit in serious financial straits.

Feminists, on the other hand, see this problem in far different terms. To them, this family's problems are far more likely to be the result of sexism and discrimination. Society expects this woman to assume responsibility for her children and to sacrifice her future for their sake. Yet when a marriage breaks up, the mother is likely to face a job market that discriminates against women, offering only jobs that pay less than the cost of the child care, transportation, food, shelter, and clothing her family requires.

While most conflict theorists are likely to agree with the feminists, they would also point out that this mother also suffers from exploitation by the classes above her in the social hierarchy. The reason there are no decent jobs available is that powerful business interests intentionally work to keep wages low so they can maximize their profits. Similarly, welfare benefits are kept at the lowest possible level: just enough to prevent the underprivileged from rising up and disrupting the system, but far less than would really be needed to lift them out of poverty. When the homeless become a nuisance to affluent neighbors, the police force the homeless to move on.

Interactionists are more likely to seek the origins of this family's plight in the way family members see themselves and their social world. They point out that people from disadvantaged backgrounds often come to define the world in ways that make it difficult to escape poverty. For example, research shows that poor people are more likely to see their lives in fatalistic terms and feel that there is little or nothing they can do to change their situation. Moreover, the way poor people talk, act, and define the world is likely to be very different from the way people from a higher-class background do, and their attitudes and behavior may shut poor people out of many occupational and social opportunities. Interactionists are also likely to see this family as a victim of labeling. The people they interact with near the park are likely to label them as bums or riffraff and then treat them on that basis—excluding them from jobs, social contacts, and support. Eventually, the members of the family are likely to start believing those labels are really true, and they will develop an increasingly negative image of themselves and their place in the world. Such beliefs soon become a self-fulfilling prophecy as the mother gives up hope of finding a good job and increasingly avoids the company of "respectable" people. As an early interactionist, W. I. Thomas, put it: If people "define situations as real, they are real in their consequences."[17]

After reading these explanations of the woman's problem it is tempting to ask which theory is actually the correct one. The answer quite often is, they all are. If we knew more details about this particular woman and her children we might say one theory better explains her particular situation. But when we consider the poor and homeless in general, each theory helps us understand some aspects of their social problem that could be missed by using only one theory.

If you were interested in taking the next step and actually doing something about the problem of poverty and homelessness, each perspective could also suggest some possible courses of action. For example, some functionalists believe that we must work to strengthen our family system and to reinforce the values that place family obligations ahead of individual self-interest. Liberal feminists call for tough new laws to fight occupational discrimination and for better welfare benefits. Conflict theorists and socialist feminists call for the poor and underprivileged, women, and minorities to band together with their supporters from other groups and demand fundamental structural changes to reduce inequality and make this a more just society. Taking conflict theory to a global level suggests that something must be done about the ability of big corporations to move their operations to poor countries, thus reducing jobs and wages for American workers. Interactionists advocate education and training programs, not only to teach the disadvantaged new skills but also to help them redefine their world and the way they see themselves. Interactionists would also say that the family needs more supportive contacts with members of the larger community. Of course, these approaches are not mutually exclusive, and just as we can combine their theoretical insights to gain a more complete picture of the problem, so we can combine various proposals for change into a more comprehensive response.

QUICK REVIEW

Briefly describe the main points of the functionalist, conflict, feminist, and interactionist theories.

What are the strengths and weaknesses of each theory?

DOING SOCIOLOGICAL RESEARCH

The theoretical perspectives discussed so far serve as a guide and a point of reference for the student of social problems. Theories are of little value, however, unless they deal with facts, and in the study of social problems, people often disagree about what "the facts" really are. Because their task is so difficult, sociologists give a great deal of attention to the study of **methodology**—that is, how to do research. Volumes have been written on this subject, yet no one can say that any particular technique is better than all the others. The decision about which research techniques to use must be based on the nature of the problem being studied and the skills and resources of the researcher. Among many possible alternatives, the four most common sources of sociological data are public records and statistics, case studies, surveys, and experiments.

PUBLIC RECORDS AND STATISTICS

Governments and organizations such as the United Nations and the World Bank publish a wealth of statistics and information. A look through the references in this book will reveal numerous citations to data from the Bureau of the Census, the Bureau of Justice Statistics, the United Nations Development Programme, and similar organizations, for such information is vital to sociologists' efforts to understand today's social problems. One of the oldest and most reliable sources of statistics is the U.S. Census, which is taken every 10 years. The goal of the census is to count all the people in the United States and determine such characteristics as their age, gender, and employment status. Such an effort to get direct information about every person in the country is obviously a massive undertaking, so most of the information we have comes from surveys that question only a sample of the total population. There are periodic government surveys of selected groups, such as the elderly or the unemployed, as well as general surveys designed to measure, for example, the number of people who have been the victims of crime. Other important sources of data are the bureaucracies that register births, marriages, divorces, and deaths, and the official records of government agencies, such as the federal budget and the *Congressional Record*.

Despite their importance to the sociologist, such data still have serious shortcomings. Almost every researcher has had the experience of spending long hours looking through official publications searching for a particular figure that is nowhere to be found. You might, for example, be interested in comparing the income and educational levels of Chinese Americans and Filipino Americans, only to find that the Bureau of the Census lists only whites, blacks, Hispanics, and "others." More serious is the problem of bias and distortion. For example, it has long been known that many African American males from the underclass vanish from census reports in their early years of adulthood only to reappear in middle age. Government statistics may also be biased by political considerations. Such things as the rates of poverty, unemployment, and crime are often hot social issues, and many sociologists have charged that the standards and procedures for calculating those figures are slanted for political reasons.

THE CASE STUDY

A detailed examination of specific individuals, groups, or situations is known as a **case study**. There are many different sources of information for such investigations, including the official records just discussed, histories, biographies, and newspaper reports. *Personal interviews* and *participant observation* are two of the most direct ways of gathering information for a case study.

Suppose you were interested in studying juvenile delinquency. To do personal interviews, you might locate a gang of delinquent boys and ask each boy why he became involved in the gang, what he does with the other gang members, what his plans for the future are, and so on. You would then study the replies, put them together in some meaningful way, and draw your conclusions. To do a participant observation study, you would actually take part in gang activities. You might disguise yourself and work your way into the gang as a regular member, or you might tell the boys your purpose and ask their permission to watch their activities. One problem with the interview technique is that we can never be sure the subjects are telling the truth, even if they think they are. Although the participant observation technique avoids this problem, it is difficult and sometimes even dangerous to study people in this way, for they often resent the intrusion of nosy outsiders. Then, too, people often act differently when they know a sociologist is watching them.

When compared with other research methods, the case study has the advantage of allowing researchers to come into close contact with the objects of their study. Interviews and direct observation can provide rich insights that cannot be obtained from statistics, but the case study method has its limitations, especially when the cases selected for study are not typical. For instance, a researcher might unknowingly select a group of delinquents who are strongly opposed to drug use while all the other gang members in the same area are heavy drug users. Another common criticism of the case study method is that it relies too heavily on the ability and insights of the person doing the study. Although this problem is common to all research methods, it is especially troublesome in case studies because all the "facts" that are gathered for examination are filtered by the researcher.

THE SURVEY

Rather than concentrating on an in-depth study of a few cases, the **survey** asks more limited questions of a much larger number of people. It is seldom possible to question everyone concerned with a certain social problem; therefore, a **sample** is used. For instance, suppose you were interested in the relationship between people's age and their attitudes toward the abortion issue. You might select an appropriate city for your study and randomly select a sample of 500 names from the city directory. If the sample is properly drawn (that is, each person in the city's population had an equal chance of being selected), it will usually be representative of all the adults in the city.

The survey, in which a sample of people are asked a series of questions about their opinions or behavior, is one of the most common methods of sociological research.

Each person in the sample would then be interviewed to determine his or her age and attitude toward abortion. Next, you would analyze the responses statistically and try to determine the relationship between the two variables.

The survey is an invaluable tool for measuring the attitudes and behaviors of large numbers of people. The Gallup and Harris polls that gauge public opinion about dozens of topical issues are good examples of the way the survey method can be used effectively. However, because most surveys gather answers to only a limited number of fixed questions, they are not as effective as the case study approach in developing new ideas and insights. Another problem is that people do not always answer the questions honestly, particularly if the survey deals with sensitive issues such as sexual behavior or crime. A third difficulty is that surveys are expensive and time consuming. When conducted properly, however, a survey ensures that the people studied are not misleading exceptions; case studies can seldom provide this assurance.

THE EXPERIMENT

The **experiment**, in which the researcher performs some activity and watches the results, provides an opportunity for the most carefully controlled type of research. Although there are many types of experimental design, experimenters usually divide their subjects into an experimental group and a control group. Then the experimental group is manipulated in some way, but the other group is not. By comparing the two groups at the end of the experiment, researchers try to discover the effects of what was done to the experimental group. To illustrate, suppose you were interested in the effects of violent programs on television viewers. You might select two groups of people and show one, the experimental group, a number of violent television programs and the other, the control group, nonviolent programs. You would then test the two groups to see whether the violent programs caused any increase in violent behavior or attitudes.

A major problem arises because most experimental studies of human behavior must be conducted in laboratory settings. Watching violent television programs in a laboratory is likely to have different effects from watching the same programs at home because the conditions in the two settings differ so greatly. True "social experiments," in which a social change is introduced into real-life settings to determine its effect on a social problem, are rare because few social scientists have the authority or the money to carry out such research. Another problem with experimental research is that the subjects may be inadvertently harmed by the experimental manipulations; many potentially valuable experiments cannot be done for ethical reasons.

QUICK REVIEW

Discuss the advantages and disadvantages of the use of surveys, case studies, experiments, and public records in doing sociological research.

INTERPRETING CLAIMS ABOUT SOCIAL PROBLEMS

Even those of us who never do research on social problems sooner or later will have to interpret claims about them. Politicians, journalists, and sociologists, as well as an assortment of cranks and oddballs, constantly bombard the public with opinions and "facts" about these problems. Each person must decide whether or not to believe these claims. Many of them are patently false, but some are presented with impressive-sounding arguments. Reasonable skepticism is an important scientific tool; it should be practiced by anyone who is interested in knowing how social problems arise, persist, and change.

Some people find it easy to believe almost anything they see in print, and they even accept the exaggerated claims of television commercials and newspaper advertisements. In addition, the ability to speak well may be taken as a sign that the speaker is trustworthy and honest. The belief that those who lie in public are usually sued or even put in jail adds to the credibility of public speakers, but there are many ways of telling lies without risking trouble with the law. One technique is to lie about groups rather than individuals. While someone could get in trouble saying, without some proof, that John Jones is a drug addict, a speaker could say that college students or musicians are addicts. Another technique is to imply guilt by association. Consider, for example, the difference between these two statements:

> Mary Jones, the Communist party, and international terrorists agree that there are great injustices in the American economic system.

> Mary Jones, the National Council of Churches, and Supreme Court justices agree that there are great injustices in the American economic system.

Another way of conveying a misleading impression is to quote out of context. This sort of misrepresentation has been brought to the level of a fine art by the merchandisers of paperback books. For example, a reviewer in the *New York Times* might say something like this: "This book is somewhat interesting, but certainly not one of the greatest books of the decade." And the reviewer might end up being quoted like this:

Interesting . . . one of the greatest books of the decade.
—*The New York Times*

It is essential to carefully read claims about social problems and their solutions. Wild propaganda and intentional distortions are usually self-evident. However, most people who are concerned about social issues do not intentionally lie or distort the truth. They may merely be vague, using phrases such as "many people believe" and "it is widely thought" because their knowledge is incomplete. People also tend to unconsciously distort their perceptions to fit their own biases, and misleading statements are hardest to detect when the speaker is sincere. There are a number of standards that can be used to measure the validity of a statement, but none of them is foolproof.

THE AUTHOR

One of the best places to begin evaluating an article or speech is with the author. What are his or her qualifications? Why should the speaker or writer know anything more about the problem than the audience? Titles and academic degrees in themselves do not mean very much unless they have some clear relation to the problem under consideration. For instance, a professor of physics might be qualified to talk about nuclear power, but her opinion about the influence of international politics on our oil supplies could well be of little value. A professor of sociology might be qualified to comment on the causes of crime but might know little or nothing about the fine points of criminal law. An impressive title does not always guarantee authority or expertise.

It is also helpful to know an author's biases. They will often become clear through a look at the author's other work. For example, suppose that an economist who has always supported the Social Security system publishes a study concluding that the system has been a failure. These findings should be given more weight than the same conclusions published by a longtime opponent of Social Security. The same is true of articles published by people with special interests. An article concluding that criminals have been mistreated by the police is more persuasive if it is written by a police officer than if it is written by a burglar.

THE SUPPORT

Scientific research projects are expensive. If the authors say their assertions are based on research, it is important to know who paid for the research and what, if anything, its supporters stand to gain from its conclusions. Few organizations, including the federal government, will fund a study that is likely to arrive at conclusions harmful to their interests. It is not surprising to find that a study funded by an oil company asserts that oil drilling will produce little environmental damage or to find that a study funded by a tobacco company says smoking cigarettes is as safe as playing badminton. However, a study funded by an oil company that concludes oil drilling will cause serious damage to the environment merits attention.

THE DISTRIBUTION

Where an article is published or a speech is given can be another important clue to the reliability of the statements made. You can usually assume that articles published in recognized journals, such as the *American Journal of Sociology* or *Social Problems*, meet some minimal professional standards. But an article on race relations published in a newspaper affiliated with the Ku Klux Klan, an article on the minimum wage published in a trade union weekly, or a speech on gun control before the National Rifle Association are likely to contain few surprises.

THE CONTENT

There are no firm rules for judging which conclusions are reasonable and which are not. Some research papers are so technical that only an expert can judge their value. But most books, magazine articles, and speeches about social problems are not directed at expert audiences, so readers and listeners need no special qualifications to judge the accuracy of what is said. Asking the following questions is a good way to assess the value of an article or speech.

Does the Article or Speech Make Sense? It is important to get involved with what is being said rather than just passively accepting it. Are the author's arguments logical? If a person says that drug addiction is widespread because enemy agents are trying to weaken the country by enslaving its youth, ask yourself whether it is reasonable to claim that such things could be done in secret. It is also logical to ask why those who are being enslaved by drugs are the least powerful people in the population. Do the author's conclusions seem to follow from the evidence presented? There is good reason to reject an argument that, for example, asserts that college students who smoke marijuana do so because of poverty. Subtler gaps in logic can also be detected by the attentive listener.

Why Does the Writer or Speaker Use a Particular Style? A book or speech need not be boring to be accurate. Nevertheless, there is a difference between a calm, thoughtful analysis and demagoguery. Skillful speakers who give emotion-packed examples of human suffering may only be trying to get an audience's attention, or they may use such examples to cloud the issue. Most articles, speeches, and books necessarily contain some vague claims or assertions. One should always ask whether the vagueness is necessary because some facts are unknown or because the author is trying to obscure the subject or conceal information. Conversely, a collection of numbers and statistics does not guarantee that conclusions are valid. An old saying holds that figures do not lie but liars figure.

Do an Author's Claims Fit in with What Others Say about the Subject?   The truth of a proposition is not decided by democratic vote. Majorities can be wrong and minorities right. Even an individual who strays far from what most people—including experts—accept as true is not necessarily wrong. In scientific work, a successful experiment by a lone researcher can challenge truths that have long been accepted; but if an author's claims differ greatly from those of others who know something about the subject, there is reason to be skeptical. The question to be asked is whether the author presents enough evidence to justify rejection of the old ideas and accepted beliefs.

QUICK REVIEW

What are the best ways of evaluating the claims people make about our social problems?

SUMMARY

There are two major sociological definitions of the term *social problem*. One says that social problems are created by gaps between a society's ideals and actual conditions in that society. The other defines a social problem as a condition that a significant number of people consider to be a problem. The public's perceptions of social problems change from time to time. The major forces influencing these changes are social movements that try to bring about social change.

Over the years sociologists have developed a body of knowledge, theories, and methods that aid in the study of social problems. Basic concepts used by virtually all sociologists include role, norm, institution, class, culture, subculture, and society.

Sociologists approach the study of social problems from different theoretical perspectives. The two major approaches dealing with large groups and entire societies are the functionalist perspective and the conflict perspective. Functionalists see a society as something like an organism or machine in which all the parts usually work together for the common good. Every society has a set of needs that must be fulfilled if it is to survive, and all the components of a society have functions that they perform to meet these needs. But they may also have dysfunctions or harmful consequences for society. Social problems occur when a society becomes so disorganized that its basic functions cannot be performed as well as they should be. Conflict theorists see social order as a set of power relationships. Coercion, not shared values and beliefs, is the strongest cement holding a society together. Some conflict theorists emphasize class conflict, and others emphasize conflicts between people from different ethnic groups or between the genders. But they all agree that the oppression of one group by another is a basic cause of social problems. Conflict theory can also be taken to a global level to understand how rich nations are able to exploit poor nations and the impact such exploitation has both at home and abroad.

Feminist theory attempts to counterbalance the male-oriented view of the traditional sociological perspectives by describing the world and women's place in it from a woman's viewpoint. They argue that men's and women's lives are not only distinctly different, they are unequal as well, and that contemporary society is a patriarchy that benefits men at the expense of women.

The dominant social psychological perspective in sociology is known as interactionism. Interactionists explain our behavior in terms of the patterns of thoughts and beliefs we have. They place particular emphasis on the importance of the way we define ourselves (self-concept) and the way we define our social environment (definition of the situation), both of which are in large measure learned from our interactions with others.

Theory is an important guide, but it becomes effective only when applied to facts. Social scientists use four principal methods to gather data to test theories and uncover the facts. Public records and statistics provide social scientists with a rich source of data so that they do not have to collect it themselves. The case study is a detailed examination of specific individuals, groups, or situations. Surveys put questions to cross sections of the population. Experiments usually try to duplicate the social world in a laboratory so that the various factors being studied can be carefully controlled.

Even those who never do research on social problems should be able to interpret and judge the claims of others. There are at least four commonsense methods for evaluating speeches, books, and articles about social problems: (1) check the qualifications and biases of the author; (2) check the biases of the people who pay for the author's work; (3) check the publishers of magazine articles and the special interests of the audience listening to a speech; and (4) check the content of the speech or article and the logic of the arguments the author uses to support a point.

QUESTIONS FOR CRITICAL THINKING

One of the most vital sociological skills is the ability to take a general understanding about the way society operates and apply it to our own personal lives. List the two or three most serious problems facing you in your own life. How do the social forces examined by the different sociological perspectives influence those problems? Is one sociological approach better than the others at helping you to understand those problems? If so, why?

KEY TERMS

behaviorism	globalization
biosocial perspective	interactionism
case study	methodology
class conflict	norm
conflict perspective	patriarchy
culture	personality
definition of the situation	personality theories
deviant	role
dysfunction	sample
experiment	self-concept
feminist theory	sexism
function	social class
functionalist perspective	social disorganization

social institution   society
socialization   sociology
social movement   subculture
social problem   survey
social structure   world system theory

NOTES

1. See Robert K. Merton, "The Sociology of Social Problems," in Robert K. Merton and Robert Nisbet, eds., *Contemporary Social Problems*, 4th ed. (New York: Harcourt Brace Jovanovich, 1976).

2. Herbert Blumer, "Social Problems as Collective Behavior," *Social Problems* 18 (1971): 298–306; Malcolm Spector and John I. Kitsuse, "Social Problems: A Reformation," *Social Problems* 21 (1973): 145–159.

3. See Robert H. Lauer, "Defining Social Problems: Public Opinion and Textbook Practice," *Social Problems* 24 (1976): 122–130.

4. See Howard S. Becker, *Outsiders* (New York: Free Press, 1963).

5. Karl Marx, *Capital: A Critique of Political Economy* (New York: Random House, 1906).

6. Max Weber, *From Max Weber: Essays in Sociology*, ed. and trans. Hans H. Gerth and C. Wright Mills (New York: Oxford University Press, 1946).

7. See Harold R. Kerbo, *Social Stratification and Inequality: Class Conflict in Historical and Comparative Perspective*, 4th ed. (New York: McGraw-Hill, 2000).

8. See Emile Durkheim, *Division of Labor in Society* (Glencoe, IL: Free Press, 1947). For some classic works on functionalism, see Emile Durkheim, *The Elementary Forms of Religious Life* (New York: Free Press, 1965); Robert K. Merton, *Social Theory and Social Structure*, rev. ed. (New York: Free Press, 1957); and Talcott Parsons, *The Social System* (New York: Free Press, 1964).

9. See Marx, *Capital*; Max Weber, *The Theory of Social and Economic Organization* (Glencoe, IL: Free Press, 1947); and Randall Collins, *Conflict Sociology* (New York: Academic Press, 1979).

10. Karl Marx and Friedrich Engels, *The Communist Manifesto*, ed. Samuel Beer (New York: Appleton Century Crofts, 1955).

11. Patricia Madoo Lengermann and Jill Niebrugge-Brantley, "Contemporary Feminist Theory," in George Ritzer, *Sociological Theory*, 4th ed. (New York: McGraw-Hill, 1996), pp. 436–488.

12. George Herbert Mead, *Mind, Self, and Society* (Chicago: University of Chicago Press, 1934).

13. See, for example, Herbert Blumer, *Symbolic Interactionism: Perspective and Method* (Englewood Cliffs, NJ: Prentice Hall, 1969), and Tamotsu Shibutani, *Society and Personality* (Upper Saddle River, NJ: Prentice Hall, 1961).

14. For a good summary of contemporary interactionist theory, see John P. Hewitt, *Self and Society: A Symbolic Interactionist Social Psychology*, 6th ed. (Needham Heights, MA: Allyn & Bacon, 1994).

15. See B. F. Skinner, *About Behaviorism* (New York: Knopf, 1974).

16. See, for example, Albert Bandura, *Social Learning Theory* (Upper Saddle River, NJ: Prentice Hall, 1977).

17. W. I. Thomas, *The Child in America* (New York: Knopf, 1928), p. 572.

PART I

TROUBLED INSTITUTIONS

A NEIGHBOR AND HER FAMILY ARE EVICTED FROM THEIR HOME BECAUSE SHE LOST HER JOB AND can't keep up the payments. A man you know is beaten and robbed by a gang of local teenagers. A girl who used to live down the street gets pregnant and tries to kill herself after her parents berate her and her boyfriend walks out.

When such problems arise, we usually explain them in personal terms: "I thought that house was more than Mrs. Jones could afford." "Those boys are a bunch of thugs." "That girl was always a wild one." The goal of the sociological study of social problems is to look behind those personal stories to see the powerful social forces that lie at their roots. An understanding of our social problems must be built on an understanding of society itself. This book therefore begins with an examination of the basic institutions that are fundamental building blocks of our social life. Each institution has its own problems, and each has a major impact on the other problems we will discuss later. We start with an analysis of our political and economic institutions and the ways they operate together. Next we well examine one of the most basic social institutions of all—the family—and we finish with a look at our educational system.

PROBLEMS OF THE POLITICAL ECONOMY

Questions to Consider

What is the global political economy?

What are the consequences of the growth of multinational corporations?

Who runs the government?

What problems do our workers face today?

How has globalization affected our political economy?

What can we do to solve our political and economic problems?

Money and power—nothing is more central to the causes of our social problems or to their solution. Yet many of us see our economy and our government as part of two separate realms that only occasionally touch. While it can be useful to examine those two critical institutions separately, at some point we have to link them back together if we are going to understand the whole picture. In contemporary society economic power is political power, and vice versa. Government sets the rules of the economic game, acts as a referee, and makes countless decisions that shape the economic process, but at the same time even democratic governments are controlled and constrained by powerful economic interests in their society. Thus, instead of talking about separate economic and political systems, this chapter will consider them both as part of a single **political economy**—an interlocking system of economic and political relationships. Whether it is crime, racism, or the destruction of our environment, understanding our political economy is the key to understanding our social problems.

THE GLOBAL POLITICAL ECONOMY

The world is a vast and confusing place, and most people are familiar with only a small part of it. When problems crop up, we seek explanations by looking at familiar events close to home. Although some problems can be understood in terms of a single nation or even a single city, today's economic and political woes are world problems. No one can understand the causes of inflation, unemployment, or economic stagnation by looking only at a single nation in isolation from the complex international network of trade, production, and finance known as the **world economy**. Nor can we understand the decisions our governments make or the causes of international conflict without understanding the delicate balance of relationships that make up the world's political system.

Although all nations are part of the global political economy (also known as the **world system**), all countries do not have equal roles. The principal dividing line in the modern world is between the wealthy industrialized nations and the poor nations, often referred to as the **Third World** or the **less-developed countries** (LDCs). Although most of the world's products are manufactured in the industrialized nations, almost 80 percent of the world's people live in the poor nations.[1] Most of them make their living from agriculture and the export of raw materials. Although there is a growing industrial sector in many less-developed countries, their industries pay low wages and are often owned and operated by foreigners.

In contrast to the poverty of the Third World, industrialized nations have accumulated huge reserves of wealth, not just in terms of money but also in the things it can buy: highways, buildings, factories, power plants, public facilities, and, of course, an educated populace and a well-trained workforce. In between these two extremes are such nations as Thailand and South Korea, which have a higher standard of living and are more industrialized than most Third World countries, but are still far behind such nations as the United States and Japan.

The rich industrialized nations also dominate the world's political system. Many powerful international organizations such as the International Monetary Fund (IMF) and World Bank are completely dominated by the rich nations, particularly the United States. While the United Nations is a more democratic institution in that almost all nations of the world have some influence over UN programs and actions, only a small group of powerful nations dominate the Security Council, which makes the UN's most important decisions. The rich nations also have overwhelming military superiority over the armies of the Third World, and that combined with their enormous economic power often enables them to shape not only the foreign policies of the poor nations but also many of the domestic policies as well (see Chapter 11 for a discussion of the problems of the Third World).

While most Third World nations have struggled to improve their position within the global political economy dominated by the rich capitalist countries, some followed a different road and rejected the capitalist system altogether. Inspired by the ideology of Marx and Lenin, the governments of the communist nations took direct control of all their major economic institutions. They created planned economies in which there was little competition and the important decisions were made by government officials. Originally, the communist nations sought to keep out the influence of foreign corporations, and to industrialize themselves by following their own step-by-step development plans. While the old Soviet Union and some of the other communist nations had considerable success in completing the early stages of industrialization, none of them was able to reach the same level of affluence enjoyed by rich capitalist countries, and the challenge they posted to the capitalist economic system that dominated the world slowly faded away. In the past decade, most communist countries have made a radical shift in their economic direction—either abandoning **communism** altogether or mixing it with a strong dose of capitalism (as in China and Vietnam).

All this may sound as if the wealthy capitalist nations such as the United States and Canada have few economic problems, but that is hardly the case. To understand those problems, we must examine the nature of **capitalism** more closely. Although it is difficult to define it precisely, capitalist economic systems display three essential characteristics. First, there is private property. Second, a market controls the production and distribution of valuable commodities. Third, privately owned businesses compete with one another, each aiming to make the greatest possible profit. The classic statement of the theory of free-market capitalism was set forth in Adam Smith's book *The Wealth of Nations*, first published in 1776.[2] Smith argued that individuals will work harder and produce more when they work for personal profit. Private greed will be transformed into public good through the workings of a free market regulated only by supply and demand. The profit motive will drive manufacturers to supply goods that the public demands, and competition will ensure that the goods are reasonably priced. The market will regulate itself in the most efficient way possible as though guided by an "invisible hand"—if the government does not interfere with the free play of economic forces.

Although some economists and politicians still fervently believe in the principles set forth in Smith's writings, it is clear that no real economic system operates the way Smith said it should, and no nation has completely "free" markets. Smith himself realized that businesses can reap large profits by restricting free competition and raising prices: "People of the same trade seldom meet together, even for merriment and diversion, but the conversation ends in a conspiracy against the public, or in some contrivance to raise prices."[3] Since those words were written, the major corporations have grown to a colossal size that Smith could hardly have imagined, and as a result, their ability to control the marketplace has become a far greater problem. Moreover, markets are restricted in many other ways as well. The governments in capitalist nations all have numerous economic regulations and restrictions, sometimes to protect powerful special interests, sometimes to protect the public as a whole, and sometimes even to protect competition itself. They have also created welfare programs to help the most disadvantaged (which also helps discourage uprisings and political unrest), and the workers themselves have joined together into unions to demand higher wages and better treatment from their employers.

Even though no nations really live up to Adam Smith's ideal of the perfect capitalist economy, some are much stronger believers in the principles of **laissez-faire capitalism** that he advocated than others. On one side are nations such as the United States, which practice what is sometimes called **individualistic capitalism**. As the name implies, these nations tend to stress the importance of the individual over the group or community. The government's role in their economies is far greater than Adam Smith envisioned, but it is still significantly less than in other countries, and welfare benefits are generally lower. The government tries to encourage competition through the use of antitrust laws that restrict cooperation among the giant corporations, and the principal goal of the corporations themselves is to make a profit for their individual shareholders.

In contrast, the **communitarian capitalism** practiced in Germany and Japan is quite different.[4] Those nations are more skeptical about the value of unregulated competition, and protecting the long-term interests of the corporations and the people who depend on them is given greater priority than big profit margins. Corporations are allowed, and even encouraged, to cooperate with each other and to link themselves up into large corporate interest groups such as the Japanese *keiretsu*. The government itself plays a much larger role in directly guiding the economy of these nations: coordinating the actions of the large corporate groups, supporting various business activities, and trying to shape the overall direction of the economy. Workers also have a greater involvement in shaping corporate policy than is typical in the United States. This happens through a slow process of consensus building in Japanese corporations, and through powerful unions and "codetermination laws" that require corporations to bring the workers into the decision-making process in Germany. Underlying the structural differences between these two systems is an important cultural divide. As Lester Thurow puts it: "The essential difference between the two forms of capitalism is their stress on communitarian versus individualistic values as the route to economic success—the 'I' of America or of the United Kingdom versus 'Das Volk' and 'Japan Inc.'"[5]

QUICK REVIEW

What is the world economy?
What are the differences between communitarian and individualistic capitalism?

UNDERSTANDING OUR POLITICAL ECONOMY

The first step in understanding our political economy is to see it in its global context, but we cannot get very far in our efforts without also looking at its internal structures and the way they operate. In this section we examine the four key elements in the contemporary political economy—corporations, government, small businesses, and workers.

CORPORATIONS

If all the world's largest organizations, including its governments, were listed in order of size, half would be corporations. Such giants as General Electric, Exxon, and Wal-mart have hundreds of thousands of employees, and their assets are worth billions of dollars. Moreover, the largest corporations keep growing, both in absolute size and in the percentage of the economy they control. The ten largest American corporations alone had revenues of just under $1 trillion in 1999, making them twice the size of the total economy of Mexico, Australia, or the Netherlands, and almost three-fourths the size of the French and British economies.[6] This staggering concentration of wealth obviously gives these corporations enormous power to influence the government and to shape the way average people live their lives.

When the United States was first industrializing, several of the new corporate giants that sprang up seized monopolistic control of entire industries and were able to charge exorbitant prices unrestrained by any serious competition. As a result, the federal government and many individual states passed **antitrust laws** that outlawed **monopolies** (the control of industries by single firms), as well as any arrangements among competitors to work together to keep prices artificially high. While these laws did prevent most American industries from falling under the control of a single firm, they have failed in a number of other important ways.

Few of today's markets are controlled by outright monopolies (the Microsoft Corporation is one exception), but the markets for many important products and services, ranging from automobiles and gasoline to aspirin and broadcasting, are dominated by a few enormous firms—an arrangement known as **oligopoly**. About 60 percent of all the goods and services produced in the United States (not counting those produced by the government) are made in industries dominated by such oligopolies. Even in these restricted markets, one giant is often larger and stronger than any other, thus allowing it to have a considerable degree of market control. Although antitrust laws forbid collusion among the members of these oligopolies to rig prices or restrict competition in other ways, these laws have never been effectively enforced, and there is little doubt that such activities are still common. Wave after wave of corporate mergers have gone on largely unimpeded by government action. In 1999 alone, mergers in the communications industry totaled about $172 billion, along with $126 billion in the radio and TV industry, $63 billion among utilities, $59 billion among banks, $46 billion among oil companies, $31 billion among insurance companies, and $24 billion among drug companies.[7]

At best, antitrust laws have been only modestly successful at encouraging open competition, and in recent years they seem to be creating a new kind of economic difficulty for American firms competing in the world economy. While these laws have discouraged American firms from linking themselves together into cartels and corporate interest groups, their foreign competition faces no such restrictions. Not only do these foreign corporate groups provide many of their members with financial and technical support for their ventures, but they also relieve a great deal of the pressure for short-term profits that plagues many American companies. For example, most of the stock in major Japanese corporations is held by the other firms in their corporate groups, while private individuals hold a much larger share of American firms. Although the American system may sound like a better arrangement, private stockholders are primarily concerned with a corporation's quarterly profits and the dividends it allows them to pay out, while corporate stockholders are likely to take a much longer view of successful management.[8]

Who Runs the Corporations?   The modern corporation is a vast financial network. The relationships between a given corporation and its competitors, banks, subcontractors and suppliers, stockholders, directors and managers, workers, unions, and various local and national governments are extremely complex, and may change without warning. Moreover, researchers who try to determine who, or what, controls this network rarely have the cooperation of corporations. Because researchers must rely on secondhand data on this politically charged issue, their conclusions are often contradictory.

Current studies show that few major corporations are now controlled by an individual family, as were Standard Oil, Morgan Bank, or Du Pont, and many others 100 years ago. (The Ford Motor Company is one of the few remaining exceptions.[9]) Supporters of the American corporate system today claim that corporations are democratic institutions owned by many different people, and they point to the fact that tens of millions of citizens own stock in American corporations. However, studies show that although about 60 percent of the American people own stock, most own such a small amount of any individual corporation's stock that their voice is insignificant. (Each share of stock brings one vote in the affairs of the company, mostly through helping to elect the board of directors who oversee operations of the company.)

The biggest blocks of stock in major corporations today are owned either by a small group of wealthy individuals or institutional stockholders such as banks, insurance companies, and pension and investment funds. About 1 percent of the wealthiest and most powerful Americans control about 50 percent of family-held stock in American corporations.[10] The ownership of the other half of corporate stock is so widely dispersed that these small-time stockholders are unable to unite to offer much of a counterbalance to the power of that elite. Another powerful source of elite influence are the banks and other financial institutions that exercise great influence over corporate decision making through their power to grant or reject loans.[11]

What all of this means is that U.S. corporations—and in turn the U.S. economy—is run by a small group of people that can be called a "corporate class," or what economist John Kenneth Galbraith called the "corporate technostructure." He pointed out that most national and international corporations are no longer run by a single powerful person, such as Andrew Carnegie or John D. Rockefeller. Decisions are made by anonymous executives and managers who spend their entire careers gaining the technical skills and knowledge needed to manage a modern corporation. However, the managers of American corporations must still serve the primary interest of their stockholders—making profits—or they risk losing their jobs. David R. James and Michael Soref, for example, found that declining profits were the single major reason that corporate presidents lost their jobs, regardless of whether the firm was owned by a large number of stockholders or by a single individual.[12]

Corporate managers do not make their decisions simply on the basis of their knowledge and skills, however. High-level corporate managers are a distinct social class, and they act to promote their own self-interest.[13] If young managers are to get to the top, they must have more than just technical skills, ability, and drive. They must also accept the ideology and worldview of the corporate elite and support its interests. As C. Wright Mills put it back in the 1950s (when almost all corporate executives were males), "In personal manner and political view, in social ways and business style, [the new manager] must be like those who are already in, and upon whose judgments his own success rests."[14]

As can be seen from Table 2.1, U.S. corporate executives have been especially aggressive in pursuing their own interests, and now have by far the world's highest pay. But even the $901,200-a-year income is an underestimate because it does not include pay that comes in the form of stock options (which are prohibited in most other industrial nations). When the value of these stock options is included, it is estimated that the total pay for executives of the top 500 corporations was actually $10.6 million in 1998. Furthermore, the gap between the average worker's pay and that of top corporate executives has shown a staggering increase, from 40 to 1 in 1990 to 419 to 1 in 1998. This gap between the top executive and average worker is far greater than in any other industrial nation and rising fast. If the same wage increase that top executives received for the 1990s had been given to the average worker, their pay would have gone

TABLE 2.1   COMPARATIVE CORPORATE EXECUTIVE SALARIES, 1997

COUNTRY	SALARY	PERCENT OF U.S. SALARY
United States	$901,200	—
Australia	476,700	52.9%
Belgium	470,700	52.2
Canada	440,900	48.9
France	523,500	58.1
Germany	423,900	47.0
Italy	450,300	50.0
Japan	397,700	44.1
Netherlands	442,900	49.1
Spain	333,600	37.0
Sweden	340,700	37.8
Switzerland	465,200	51.6
United Kingdom	489,700	54.3

Source: Mishel, Bernstein, and Schmitt, *The State of Working America, 1999*, 1999, p. 213; Kerbo, *Social Stratification and Inequality*, 2000, p. 29.

from $29,000 in 1990 to $110,000 in 1998. Instead, however, average worker pay increased only slightly in the decade of the 1990s.[15]

Corporate Crimes and Abuses   In recent years most large corporations have expanded across national boundaries, setting up complex webs of sales, manufacturing, distribution, and financial operations. Although these firms are usually based in a single country, they are often transnational in organization and perspective. The growth of these powerful multinational corporations has generated tremendous controversy. Supporters see their rise as the first step toward world unity. They are convinced that by linking the economies of the world's nations, the multinationals are laying the foundation for a global government that will usher in a new era of peace and prosperity In contrast, critics of the multinationals see them as international bandits that exploit small countries and play large ones against one another.

The expansion of multinational corporations among industrialized countries has certainly created many problems of international control and regulation, but the worst abuses have resulted from corporate expansion into the less-developed countries of Africa, Asia, and Latin America. Although multinationals bring advanced technology

The symbols of powerful multinational corporations can be seen all over the world, and their expansion into weak and impoverished nations often brings with it the fear of foreign domination.

and encourage some types of economic development, the "host" nations often pay a heavy price. Foreign corporations wield tremendous political power in the poor countries in which they invest, and too often critical economic decisions are made by foreign corporate executives who have little concern for the welfare of the local people. Moreover, there are grounds for questioning how much economic benefit poor nations actually reap from foreign investments. Although there is considerable controversy about the issue, a number of studies have concluded that foreign investment produces only short-term economic rewards. Once the initial investment is made and the multinationals begin taking home their profits, these studies indicate that the economies of the nations with large foreign investments begin to fall behind the nations that rely on their own resources for economic development. Thus, in the long run, more self-reliant nations have greater economic growth.[16] It must be stressed, however, that not all poorer nations are harmed by the investments coming from powerful multinational corporations, and this is especially true for some of the Asian nations that have had so much foreign investment in recent decades. Thailand, for example, has reduced poverty from 50 percent of the population in 1960 to only 15 percent by the late 1990s, and China has seen its own economy boom.[17]

Even of we ignore the impact of globalization, the business world is sometimes described as a lawless jungle in which profits rule, and those who let ethics stand in their way are considered foolish and quaint. Although this is an exaggeration, there is ample evidence that the crime rate is high in the business world.

Everyone has had the experience of buying an article of clothing or an appliance that seemed to fall apart after hardly any use. Although the manufacture and sale of such merchandise do not violate the law, knowingly making false claims for a product is a type of **fraud**. There are countless examples of fraud in industries ranging from cosmetics to automobiles, but one of the most costly came from the savings and loan scandal that first came to light in the late 1980s. The virtual collapse of the savings and loan industry is estimated to have cost as much as $500 billion, much of it paid for by the taxpayers. Although estimates vary about what percentage of those staggering losses was caused by corporate crime, the evidence indicates that some kind of fraud or other illegal activity was involved in the majority of the savings and loan failures.[18]

Fraud is not just a matter of money, however; some fraudulent claims endanger the health or even the life of the consumer. The major pharmaceutical companies have, for example, frequently been caught making fraudulent claims about their products or concealing information to cover up their hazards. Two well-known examples are the painkiller known as Oraflex, which is thought to have killed 49 people and injured almost a thousand more, and the Dalkon shield contraceptive device, which is believed to have caused the deaths of at least 17 women and about 200,000 injuries.[19]

Price-fixing—collusion by several companies to cut competition and set uniformly high prices—is another common corporate crime. A survey of the heads of the 1,000 largest manufacturing corporations asked whether "many" corporations engaged in price-fixing. Among those heading the 500 largest corporations, a surprising 47 percent agreed that price-fixing is a common practice. An overwhelming 70 percent of the heads of the remaining 500 corporations agreed.[20] It is quite possible that price-fixing costs consumers more than any other kind of crime.

Many companies also use illegal practices to drive their competitors out of business. One technique is for a big company to sell certain products at a loss in order to bankrupt a small competitor. The company recovers its loss and increases profits by selling the products at much higher prices after the competition has been eliminated. Another technique is for a giant corporation to buy out producers of key raw materials and cut off supplies to its smaller competitors. As with most corporate crimes, the damage extends far beyond the immediate victims to the general public, who in one way or another end up footing the bill.

GOVERNMENT

Governments throughout the world have been growing rapidly since the beginning of this century. In 1929, the year of the great stock market crash, there were a little more than 3 million government employees in the United States; today there are over 19 million. Of course, the country's population also increased, but the percentage of the total workforce employed by the government still rose from 6.5 to around 16 percent. The often heard accusation that there has been runaway growth in the size of the government in recent years is false, however. There has actually been a small decline in the percentage of the labor force employed by the government since 1980,[21] and although there is some variation from year to year, the share of our national income that funds state and federal government hasn't changed much since the early 1970s.[22] Moreover, as we can see in Table 2.2, only Japan has a smaller government relative to the size of its economy than the United States, and both Japan and the United States are far behind European governments.

The influence of government on the daily lives of its citizens has grown along with its size. In past centuries, most centralized governments were distant and ineffective. Important decisions were made locally and were based on long-standing customs and traditions. Today, governments are much stronger, and they are less tightly bound by traditional restraints. Most of this growth in size and influence has been a response to

TABLE 2.2   COMPARING GOVERNMENT SIZE

GOVERNMENT SPENDING AS PERCENT OF GDP, 1995			
Country	*% of GDP*	*Country*	*% of GDP*
Sweden	66.4	Germany	46.7
Denmark	61.1	Spain	42.6
Finland	56.3	England	42.3
Belgium	53.3	Switzerland	36.7
Netherlands	52.8	Australia	36.2
France	50.9	**United States**	**35.8**
Italy	49.5	Japan	27.0
Austria	47.8		

Source: Organization of Economic Cooperation and Development, <http://www.oecd.org/puma/stats/govexp.htm>.

changes in other social institutions. For example, as the family became smaller and less stable, the government had to assume some of the functions once performed by families, such as ensuring some minimum financial support for the poor and the elderly. Similarly, as the contemporary system of industrial capitalism developed, it proved to be highly unstable, swinging from times of booming prosperity to deep depression. Even in the United States, with its deep suspicion of centralized authority, the federal government has been forced to get involved in regulating and directing the economy.

Who Runs the Government?   There is no more controversial topic in the social sciences than the question of who really runs the government. Most governments say they are democratic, but does power really reside in the people or is it in the hands of special-interest groups, an exclusive "power elite," or the government bureaucrats and officeholders themselves?

An enormous amount of research has been done on this critical issue over the years, and those who have studied it generally fall into one of three theoretical camps. Perhaps the most popular theory among sociologists is that of the **elitists**, who hold that government policy is shaped by a small and relatively unified group C. Wright Mills termed the "power elite."[23] Although the power elite contains both top government and business leaders, the lion's share of the power rests in the hands of corporate leaders who often dominate government decisions from behind the scenes. The **structuralists** agree with the elitists that the government reflects the interest of the few, not the many, but they differ about why that is so. They feel that the government is a more independent power group that is not under the total control of the power elite, but that the structure of the capitalist economy forces the government to protect the interests of the upper class or risk collapse of the whole system. A third group of theorists sees the government as being far more democratic. These **pluralists** are not so naive as to feel that the power to make key government decisions lies directly in the hands of the people, but they do feel that there is intense competition among many different interest groups and that no single elite predominates. As a result, the "will of the people" is usually served because it is able to tip the balance of power in the struggles among these competing interest groups.

In order to evaluate these theories, we must turn our attention to the actual operation of the political process. As most of us learned in our high school government classes, in an ideal democracy political power is shared equally by all citizens. Virtually no sociologists or political scientists feel that we actually have such a system, however. One of the major problems of any would-be democracy is the apathy of its citizens. Only about 49 percent of the voting-age population actually voted in the 1996 presidential election, and only 45 percent voted in the 1994 congressional elections.[24] The percentage of Americans voting in 2000, the closest election in U.S. history, was a bit higher, but not much above 50 percent.[25] Other forms of political participation, such as working in a political campaign or taking part in a political rally are even less common than voting. Of course, it is not necessary for all the citizens in a democracy to participate if those who do are representative of those who do not, but unfortunately that is not the case. Studies of citizen participation reveal a strange paradox. Those who most need the government's help are least likely to take part in the political process. People with higher incomes and better educations are much more

The unusual closeness of the 2000 presidential election brought public attention to the ways that the voting process still discriminates against minorities and poor people.

likely to be politically active, while the minorities and the poor are less likely to get involved.[26] Thus, it seems that wealth and education create the interest and the resources necessary for political participation.

Even those citizens who are interested in politics often find it difficult to decide where a particular politician stands on the issues. For one thing, politicians may try to conceal their opinions about controversial matters. In addition, the voters seldom get a chance to talk directly with candidates, relying instead on the mass media for information. Effective campaigners try to project a positive image in their advertising and television speeches, which often has little to do with the issues. Advertising agencies sell candidates in the same way they sell soap or deodorant. In a 30-second television commercial there is little time for serious consideration of political issues. Moreover, candidates of minor political parties and those without strong financial backing have little access to the media and are thus frozen out of the arena of serious political debate. To make matters worse, the media have been focusing more and more attention on politicians' personal lives and personal flaws rather than the real issues of public policy.

The media's influence, however, goes far beyond its role in political advertising and reporting the activities of the candidates. As Thomas R. Dye, a well-known political scientist puts it: "The media determine what the masses talk about. . . . Political issues do not just 'happen.' The media decides what are issues, problems, even crises, which must be acted upon."[27] Control of the media is, moreover, highly concentrated: Four huge media corporations account for 80 percent of the news and entertainment broadcasts on television. Most of America's 1700 or so daily newspapers receive news from the Associated Press wire service, and the 15 largest newspaper conglomerates account for over half of the total newspaper circulation in the country.[28]

One of the most important forces influencing legislators and other government officials is the so-called **special-interest group**—an organized group that has a stake in a particular piece of legislation. Big business, small business, labor unions, physicians, realtors—the list of special-interest groups could go on for pages. Of all the special-interest groups' many resources, money is often the most important. The price tag of the average congressional campaign is over 30 times higher today than it was in 1960, and most of the money comes from these special interests. Politicians inevitably claim that such contributions are merely a sign of support from those who favor their policies and have no influence on their votes, but few outside observers find such statements very convincing. It is too simplistic to say that most politicians overtly sell favors and influence for campaign contributions (although periodic corruption scandals show that this certainly does occur), but those millions of dollars often exert a dominating influence on the political process.

In addition to campaign contributions, special-interest groups also hire professional **lobbyists** whose job it is to influence lawmakers, whether by persuasive argument, personal friendship, or financial means. In theory, the ability of special interests to hire lobbyists and make campaign contributions that help elect sympathetic politicians wouldn't make much difference as long as supporters on both sides of important issues had roughly the same amount of money to spend, but that is clearly not the case. The corporations spend far more than the labor unions, the polluters spend more than the environmentalists, and big business more than small business. Obviously the poor and the underprivileged will never be able to spend as much money to advance their political interests as the wealthy do, just as "general interest" groups such as local communities and consumer advocates are unable to match the financial power of the big corporations whose policies they oppose.

Despite all the obstacles, average citizens do sometimes still band together into a social movement that wields significant power. One good example is the environmental movement. Although factory owners, land developers, and automobile manufactures saw nothing wrong with their polluting activities, a growing environmental crisis was obvious to average citizens when they looked around their communities. Activists began forming organizations and planning protests, meetings, and demonstrations. They eventually won sympathetic media attention, and came to wield significant influence on the political process.

Thus, the political process is complex and multifaceted, and although none of the major theoretical approaches has all the answers, some basic conclusions about the way the process operates do seem justified. First, numerous competing interest groups, including government officials themselves, take part in the struggle to shape government policy. These groups form shifting patterns of alliances on different issues: cooperating, competing, and compromising as called for by the political realities of their times. Second, although many diverse groups are involved in shaping political decisions, these groups are not equals. There is one group—made up of those who hold key positions of corporate power and/or great personal wealth—that is far more powerful than any of the others. In normal times, this elite dominates the decision-making process on most of the important questions of economic and foreign policy. Third, despite all this, it would still be wrong to say that average citizens have no political power. Throughout our history, people have often banded together in social movements, and on occasion they have been successful in forcing fundamental changes in government policies and even in the political process itself. Finally, there are concrete limits to what the government can do. In times of crisis, government may be forced to carry out policies for which no sector of society has much enthusiasm, and the demands of the global political economy limit the choices available to any individual nation, even a rich and powerful one.

The Government and the Economy   Although everyone recognizes the power and importance of corporations in our economic life, many people in the countries that practice individualistic capitalism underestimate the economic importance of the government. Although supporters of Adam Smith's laissez-faire ideology argue that the government should simply stay out of economic affairs and allow the free market to regulate itself, the governments of all industrialized nations are deeply involved in directing their economies. Actually, governments play two key economic roles in contemporary capitalist societies. First, as a major employer, government provides jobs and paychecks for millions of people who do everything from sweeping streets to flying jet bombers. Second, government regulates the economic activities of the private sector.

Some regulation occurs directly through the legal system—for example, when the courts decide civil suits involving private businesses or when the government brings legal action for the violation of antitrust laws. Government agencies such as the Federal Trade Commission and the Food and Drug Administration also play a major role in regulating the economic activities in a variety of different industries. While the government claims its regulations are designed to help promote the general welfare of society, consumer groups have long charged that these agencies usually end up serving the interests of the industries they regulate: "The regulatory agencies have become the natural allies of the industries they are supposed to regulate. They conceive their primary task to be to protect insiders from new competition—in many cases, from any competition."[29]

One problem is that the directors of these agencies often come from the industries they are supposed to regulate and return to those same industries when they leave the government. This "revolving door" between business and government obviously undermines the public interest. It brings in people who are more sympathetic to the interests of the corporations than to those of the public, and makes many regulators fearful of risking their economic future by offending corporations that might someday offer them a high-paying position. Moreover, even when officials try to do their best, the power of the corporations is so great that these small, underfunded agencies are often too weak to get the job done.

On the other hand, business groups often make the opposite criticism, charging that government regulation damages the economy by requiring a mountain of costly and time-consuming paperwork and placing unnecessary restrictions on their activities. As a result of these criticisms, several important industries have been **deregulated** in recent years. Unfortunately the results of deregulation have often been disappointing. Deregulation of the airline industry, for example, not only produced a drop in ticket prices, but also a decline in the safety and quality of service. Moreover, it touched off a wave of mergers, buyouts, and bankruptcies that has reduced competition and may once again lead to higher prices. Deregulation of the savings and loan industry had even more serious consequences. Once freed from government controls, many managers pursued speculative high-risk investments or fraudulent schemes to enrich themselves at their company's expense, and the result was the virtual collapse of the entire industry.

Government also has a variety of indirect means it can use to influence the economy. If the government wants to stimulate the economy to grow more rapidly, it can increase the size of its **budget deficit** (the difference between what the government takes in as taxes and other revenue, and how much it spends) or use its financial power to push down the interest rates charged on loans. As great as it is, however, the government's power is not unlimited. If it stimulates the economy too much, the result is likely to be a higher rate of **inflation** (price increases) and greater danger of a severe economic downturn in the future. If the inflation rate gets too high or the economy appears to be growing too rapidly, the government can reverse those policies and push up interest rates or reduce the deficit. Tax policies also have a tremendous impact on the economy, influencing the general rate of economic growth and providing special benefits or problems for specific industries. Whatever techniques the government uses, the average citizen now expects it to do everything possible to ensure economic prosperity. When the economy is in decline, the government is blamed and politicians have a difficult time getting reelected. Conversely, a prosperous economy is a great asset to incumbents running for reelection.

SMALL BUSINESS

Although overshadowed by the huge corporate and government bureaucracies, small businesses nonetheless play a key role in the economy. Numerically, small businesses have always been the majority. With the current limitations in the growth of government employment and the "downsizing" of many big corporations, small businesses play a key role in creating new jobs for the growing work force. The share of the work force that is self-employed has grown over 11 percent since 1973.[30] Estimates of the total number of American workers who are self-employed vary widely depending on the definitions and techniques used, but they range from about 8 to 13 percent of the work force.[31] Of course, most people in the small-business sector are not self-employed but work for someone else.

Although there may be more job opportunities in small business, working conditions are very different from those in the government or corporations. The main attraction of small business is the independence it offers to its many owner-operators; but most new businesses go bankrupt in their first year or two, and many of the entrepreneurs who succeed work long hours for a modest return. The employees of many small businesses share their boss's economic insecurity, but without the compensation of greater independence. In comparison with corporate workers, the employees of small businesses are less unionized and receive lower pay and fewer fringe benefits.

Although small businesses and corporations are often lumped together as part of the private sector, there are fundamental differences in the economic environment they face. As we have seen, the large corporations are often able to restrict competition, thus safeguarding their profitability. Even when they do face stiff competition, most major corporations have accumulated huge financial assets that can help see them through rough times. In contrast, small businesses generally struggle against a host of competitors and have very limited financial reserves to fall back on.

LESSONS FROM OTHER PLACES

OVERWORKED AMERICANS

When living and working in Europe, Americans are often confused at first by all the holidays and the short hours during which shops are open. Cash runs low and you run to the bank, only to find that it is closed for some holiday. Spain seems to have the most "bank holidays," but it may have been just my bad luck for running low on cash at all the wrong times. In Germany, almost all shops close early on Saturday afternoon. I am sure I have not been the only unlucky American arriving at Frankfurt Airport on Saturday afternoon, only to face an empty refrigerator in my apartment and no food stores open until Monday morning. After a while, Americans began to wonder, "When do these people ever work? Are they always off on a holiday?"

These questions, of course, are exaggerated. But there are official statistics to back up these impressions. Americans work more hours than people in any other major industrial nation. As of 1994, Americans averaged 1,896 hours per year, while Germans averaged 1,620 hours per year, with 1,752 for the British, 1,744 for Italians, and 1,755 for the French. The Japanese, formerly the world's foremost workaholics, logged in slightly less than the Americans in 1994 with an average of 1,880 hours per year.

During the late 1980s and early 1990s the Japanese government began a national campaign to get Japanese people to work fewer hours. Some estimates put the number of deaths from overwork—known as *karooshi*—as high as 10,000 per year in the early 1990s. The Japanese government also figured that if its citizens stop working such long hours, there would be more leisure time for Japanese consumers to spend money. There were posters in all the buses making the plea and major corporations were pressured to reduce worker's hours. One major corporation even decided to cut electrical power to its building to force managers and employees to leave.

During the early 1990s, however, many researchers didn't really believe the official Japanese figures showing that the Japanese worked fewer hours per year than Americans. Japanese corporations were trying to appear to be accommodating government demands to cut working hours just to keep the powerful Japanese ministry officials appeased, but many people kept running into evidence of noncompliance, such as a darkened Japanese office building with windows and blinds closed on holidays, but the desks occupied by employees working away with little desk lamps.

The number one rating for Americans is much more convincing now. Recent U.S. government data show that the average hours worked per week and year by Americans went up dramatically during the 1990s. From 1989 to 1999 the average American added 3.4 weeks per year to their already overworked lives. Just between 1995 and 1998 Americans increased their average work year by 70 hours.

—*Harold Kerbo*

*See Harold Kerbo and John McKinstry, *Modern Japan* (New York: McGraw-Hill, 1998); Harold Kerbo and Hermann Strasser, *Modern Germany* (New York: 2000); Juliet Schor, *The Overworked American* (New York: Basic Books, 1991); the *International Herald Tribune*, September 11, 2000.

Another important difference is political. Major corporations wield enormous political power and as a result can obtain many benefits and special favors from the government. Small businesses are much less influential, and therefore they pay higher taxes, receive fewer government benefits, and cannot expect a government bailout when they run into financial trouble. For these reasons, some economists refer to corporations as the monopoly sector of the economy and to small businesses as the competitive sector.

Perched between the corporate giants and the legions of "mom-and-pop" businesses are the medium-sized firms that are at the center of much economic innovation and technological development. Unlike small companies, these firms have the size and economic resources necessary to develop new products and market them effectively. Compared with the giant corporations, medium-sized firms have less cumbersome bureaucracies and are more subject to the competitive pressures of the marketplace. Because medium-sized firms are not large enough to dominate their principal markets, they face the same fate as small businesses: Be efficient and competitive, or go under.

WORKERS

Both the types of jobs and the kinds of people who work at them have changed radically in this century. Three major trends are apparent in this changing job market. The first—and perhaps most important—of these trends involves the sweeping changes in the role of women in the work force, which will be examined in Chapter 8. Second, the numbers of workers, owners, and managers of farms—once the largest job category— has steadily declined. Third, because of automation and increasing competition from foreign companies, there has been a shift of workers away from higher-paying manufacturing and production jobs and into lower-paying **service occupations** (jobs that provide a service to someone else rather than making a product or extracting a natural resource). Just since 1989, the United States has lost over 1 million jobs in manufacturing, mining, and construction while creating 10 times that number of new service jobs.[32] In addition to the growing number of self-employed workers we have already discussed, there has been an even sharper increase among temporary workers, whose numbers have more than tripled in the past decade and a half.[33]

These changes have brought great hardship to people from all walks of life but especially to the working class. Although a service job may sound more attractive than working in a factory, the reality is often quite different. Service work can be just as dull, menial, and repetitive as most factory work, and on the average the pay is only 70 percent as high. The result has been a growing income gap between the working class and more highly trained managers and professionals, along with the deterioration of entire towns that depend on failing manufacturing concerns.

It is easy to overlook the unemployed, but it should be remembered that those who are out of work are still part of the work force. The amount of **unemployment** goes up and down from one year to the next depending on the state of the economy. At the beginning of the twenty-first century, the United States was well into its longest economic boom in history. In recent decades unemployment generally ran between 5 to 8 percent, but in 2000 it reached its low point of 4 percent and has headed up since then.[34] Official unemployment statistics do not, however, count **discouraged workers** who have given up looking for jobs and those who are the victims of **underemployment**—that is, those who take part-time jobs when they want full-time work. If those two groups were added in, the unemployment figures would almost double.

Although government unemployment insurance provides some help, only people officially defined as unemployed are eligible, and even among that group the number who actually receive unemployment benefits has steadily declined as eligibility standards have been raised. When people do become eligible for unemployment benefits in the United States, they normally get less than 50 percent of their former wages, and even this normally ends after six months. In contrast, European nations provide far more support for the unemployed. For example, in Germany an unemployed person can receive up to 80 percent of his or her former wage up to two years after becoming unemployed, and thereafter up to 60 percent of the former wage for life.[35]

To make matters worse, the use of part-time workers has grown increasingly popular with employers. Since 1973, the percentage of workers holding part-time jobs has increased more than 11 percent.[36] The reason for this trend is clear: Part-time workers are cheaper. On the average, women who work part time earn 23 percent less per hour than full-time workers, and men receive almost 40 percent less; and they are both far less likely to receive medical or retirement benefits. Not surprisingly, more than one-fifth of part-time workers really want full-time work.[37]

Hazards on the Job   Mechanization of the workplace during the industrial revolution led to a progressive dehumanization of workers as they were forced to change their patterns of work to meet the demands of the machines they operated. Although work hours may not be as long as they were a century ago, many of today's factory workers still find their jobs tedious and trivial and see themselves as little more than cogs in a machine. Such feelings of **alienation** are so common that they have been given a name: the blue-collar blues. David J. Charrington's survey of worker attitudes found that "feeling pride and craftsmanship in your work" was one of the most highly desired characteristics of a job.[38] Yet technology is rapidly eliminating skilled craftspeople and replacing them with complex computer-controlled machinery. People displaced from such jobs often drift into low-skilled service industries; but even those who are retrained to repair and maintain the new equipment often lose the sense of pride that came from being directly responsible for producing a high-quality product.

The computer revolution has had an especially strong impact among the growing number of clerical workers. Computers were supposed to liberate office workers from the drudgery of performing the same tasks again and again, but so far that hasn't been the result. As in the early days of factory automation, computers have been used to break down jobs into smaller and simpler tasks. The use of computers has also tended to isolate workers from other employees, while at the same time, the new technology has increased employers' ability to scrutinize the actions of their workers. For example, workers who deal with the public on the phone often find that computer-generated reports show how many calls they answer and how long they spend with each customer, while supervisors randomly audit calls that exceed a given length. Moreover, repetitive movements required by some computerized equipment, such as cash registers that read bar codes, have caused huge increases in repetitive-strain injuries in the wrist and a host of eye and back problems.

Stress and alienation are not the only problems workers have to face on the job. Working for the wrong company or in the wrong industry can have fatal consequences. The Centers for Disease Control and Prevention estimate that about 17 workers a day are killed on the job.[39] In addition to the thousands of workers who die from workplace accidents, a much larger number die more slowly from the effects of occupationally caused diseases. The U.S. government estimates that there are 100,000 such deaths a year, but that figure is only an educated guess. Many workers who die from occupational diseases never know the source of their condition. Besides this huge death toll, at least 2.2 million workers a year are injured in occupational accidents, and many more are probably made ill by the work they do.[40]

It is clear that some employers simply do not care about the deaths and injuries they cause their workers. New procedures and techniques are constantly being developed by industry, but few employers take time to test them adequately before bringing them into the workplace. Over half a million chemicals are used in industry, but only a few thousand have been thoroughly tested to see if they are dangerous. And even when tests do show a chemical to be hazardous, some firms try to keep the results secret. For example, when an Italian scientist discovered that vinyl chloride (a popular plastic) causes a rare form of cancer that had been found among workers exposed to it, the Manufacturing Chemists Association joined with the European firm that sponsored the research in a coordinated effort to keep the findings secret. Confidential memos indicate that the manufacturers of asbestos followed the same policy and intentionally concealed the dangers of asbestos exposure from their workers. The ultimate death toll among these men and women is expected to be well over 200,000.[41]

Labor Unions   The early period of industrialization created misery among workers. Entire families labored in mines and factories. Industrialists paid subsistence wages, claiming that workers were lazy and would stop working if they were better paid. Working conditions were terrible, and deaths from occupational accidents were common. Workdays were long, often 14 hours or more, and holidays were few and far between. Conditions were so bad that Karl Marx proclaimed the workers would soon destroy capitalism in a violent revolution. But the workers did not respond with revolution; they responded with unionization.

Early labor unions faced bitter struggles with employers and the U.S. government, which supported employers' interests. In many places, unions were outlawed and organizers jailed; even when unionization became legal, organizers found themselves harassed at every turn. Unions gradually gained official recognition and acceptance, and as they won power, the conditions of the average worker improved. Unions eventually became a major economic and political force that was often critical to the success of politicians and business enterprises alike.

Yet despite the successes of the past, unions are in a serious decline. By the year 2000, only about 13 percent of the work force (excluding the self-employed) was unionized; that figure was close to 50 percent about 50 years ago, and it remains at about 40 to 50 percent for most European countries today. With dwindling labor union membership in the United States has come timidity and ineffectiveness. The average number of strikes a year has dropped to a fraction of what it was in earlier

Traditionally, the threat of a strike has been the unions' most effective weapon in their struggle for better pay and better working conditions. In today's anti-union climate, however, the number of successful strikes is far lower than it was in the past.

decades, and the wage settlements unions win are also far smaller than in the past.[42] Indeed, a growing number of strikes has resulted in the permanent replacement of the strikers with nonunion labor.

What caused this erosion of union membership and union power? Since union membership is highest in manufacturing and among **blue-collar workers**, a significant part of the decline in union membership resulted from a decrease in the importance of those occupations. Unions are now directing more efforts toward organizing government employees and **white-collar workers**, but resistance remains strong. Today's unions face other serious problems as well: On one side are the increasingly sophisticated technologies such as industrial robots that threaten more and more union jobs; on the other are the masses of the world's poor who will eagerly work for a fraction of union wages. Ironically, increasing their output through automation is one of the few ways workers in high-wage countries, such as the United States and Canada, can continue to compete with low-wage workers in the less-developed countries. As a result, the unions are often faced with the unpleasant choice of losing jobs to automation or to foreign labor. To make matters worse for the unions, their declining numbers have reduced their political clout, which has made it easier for business interests to win government bureaucrats and policy-makers to their side.

QUICK REVIEW

Who runs the corporations?
What are some of the main types of corporate crimes and abuses?
Describe the differences between the pluralist, elitist, and structuralist theories of government.
How has our work force changed?
Why has union membership declined?

GLOBALIZATION AND ECONOMIC CHANGE

To deal with our economic and political problems, we must understand their causes, and the first place to look is in the changing world economy. Modern world system theory has made it clear that for the last 500 years the competition between powerful nations for advantage in the world economy has been an ever more important force driving economic change. The industrial revolution and new machine technologies brought British dominance in the early 1800s. And further development of industrial technology, and especially assembly-line production, helped the United States win world leadership during the early twentieth century.

American economic dominance was enhanced even further at the end of World War II when all the major industrialized nations—except the United States and Canada—lay in ruins. The factories of North America emerged from the war undamaged, and their products were sometimes the only ones available. As Europe and Japan began to recover from the war, they were hungry consumers of North American goods. The United States became the world's dominant economic power, and the American dollar was virtually an international currency. During this boom, the level of income inequality in the United States declined and the poverty rate dropped dramatically from over 20 percent to 11 percent. It was a time of economic expansion benefiting almost all Americans.

The oil crisis of 1973 marked the beginning of a new and unsettling era in the American economy. An embargo by the Arab oil producers caused the price of oil to increase 400 percent that year, and the world economy went into shock. Inflation skyrocketed while unemployment increased and real wages plummeted. But America's economic problems did not disappear when the price of oil started to decline again. For the next two decades, the yearly increase in **productivity** (the value of the goods and services produced by each worker) dropped to less than half its earlier levels, average wages declined, and unemployment and inflation remained far higher than they had been in the past. For the first time, key American industries seemed unable to compete with products being pumped out by Japan, Germany, and the newly industrializing nations. American manufacturers were virtually driven out of the home electronics business, and they lost a sizable share of the market for such vital products as automobiles and machine tools. At the same time, the availability of cheaper labor in the poor nations led large American corporations to shift many of their manufacturing operations to other countries. Increasing competition faced by American workers drove wages down and unemployment up.

The government responded to this economic crisis with conservative economic policies. It forced a huge increase in interest rates, which slowed the economy, in hopes of bringing down inflation. Taxes were cut for the wealthy, and many regulations designed to control business activity were stripped away. Big corporations slashed their labor costs by attacking unions and laying off ("downsizing") millions of workers. Pressed by economic troubles on all sides, average families were still able to win a small increase in their real (after inflation) income, but only because a flood of women who had been staying home to raise their families entered the job market.

From the early 1990s until 2001, the American economy underwent another remarkable change. Unemployment and inflation both declined, and corporate profits skyrocketed. While American products did not seem markedly more competitive in terms of quality than they were in the 1980s, American productivity began increasing more rapidly, thus making American goods cheaper in the world market.

But while the stock market was booming, billionaires were multiplying, and top executives received fat increases in pay, the average wage for workers was going down. From 1989 to 1996, real wages declined by 7 percent. Poverty stood at 14 percent in the early 1990s, inching above 15 percent after the boom had been going on for two years. Americans were working more hours, and poverty rates were going up! In simple terms, the rich were getting richer—much richer—while the poor were getting poorer.

It was not until the late 1990s, almost eight years after the economic boom began, that the average person felt some small benefits. Real wages finally started moving up even though workers saw only a tiny fraction of the increases that top executives received. In 1997, the poverty rate finally started going down, reaching 11. 3 percent by 2000.

As one would expect from these trends, the gap between higher-income Americans and lower-income Americans has reached its highest level in 70 years, and perhaps the highest level in American history.[43] As the long economic boom finally ended in 2001 (around the same time as the September 11 terrorist attacks), the outlook for the average American became even more uncertain.

QUICK REVIEW

Describe the changes the American economy has undergone since the end of World War II. What have been the results for American workers?

DEMOCRACY, POWER, AND CORRUPTION

As we have argued throughout this chapter, economic and political problems are two sides of the same coin. Farsighted government policies could certainly have resolved or at least greatly reduced the problems we just examined. But despite the claims of some commentators, the problem is not the incompetence or stupidity of government officials, but the power of the special interests who profit from the status quo. So in one sense, many of our economic problems can be traced to the failure of democracy and the fact that the government acts in the interests of a powerful few and not the nation as a whole. Unfortunately, most people see this problem in personal terms: crooked politicians getting rich or getting reelected by dishonest means. It is far greater than that, however, for government corruption strikes right at the heart of democracy itself. The more control the influence-peddlers and special interests have over government policy, the less control the people have.

DEBATE

Is Freer World Trade and More Globalization the Way
to Economic Prosperity at Home?

Yes

Recent years have seen some important steps toward freer world trade—including the ratification of the North American Free Trade Agreement (NAFTA), which allowed Mexico to enter the free-trade zone that already existed between the United States and Canada, and the creation of the World Trade Organization, which is charged with insuring that no nation illegally impedes the free flow of goods and services in the world economy. But are such agreements really beneficial to our own economy?

The record is clear. Free trade is good for the world economy, and it is good for the individual nations that participate in it. When the United States passed the Smoot-Hawley Tariff Act in 1930, the ensuing trade war established new barriers to world commerce that were a major cause of the Great Depression. After World War II, however, the industrialized nations worked together to bring down their trade barriers, and the world economy flourished.

The reasons for this are simple. Freer trade gives the businesses of each nation larger potential markets, but also many more competitors. Thus, well-run businesses flourish while the incompetent go under. The result is a more efficient and more productive economy that benefits everyone.

Some people claim that freer world trade will help the Japanese, the Germans, or the Third World nations more than it will us, but there is no reason to believe that is true. Each nation has its own unique economic strengths and weaknesses. And it

Government officials can be corrupted in many ways that are completely legal. The biggest problem stems from our system of campaign financing. It is clearly a crime to pay a politician to vote for a certain bill or to perform some other political favor, but it is perfectly legal to give large campaign contributions to that same politician and then to ask her or him to vote in the way you want—as long as no one acknowledges that the contributions were made in exchange for the vote. The fact that our politicians must carry on a continual quest for financial gifts to pay for their election campaigns creates a built-in **conflict of interest** every time a bill favored by one of their major contributors comes up for a vote. Our whole system of campaign finance operates to take power away from the average citizen and concentrate it in the hands of the well-financed special interests. Moreover, the skyrocketing cost of operating the kind of media campaign essential to political success has made this problem worse year by year.

Although most conflicts of interest fall into the gray area between the unethical and the illegal, there is no question that outright **bribery** is still a serious problem. In earlier times, when only a small group of landholders could vote, the main problem was the bribery of the voters by politicians. In the 1757 race for the Virginia House of makes good sense to let each nation make the products it makes best and buy from someone else the products it is not good at making. Although some nations may be hurt if they can't produce anything that anyone else wants to buy, does anyone really think that is true of the United States or Canada? We will prosper in an open world market, and we should do everything we can to encourage its growth.

No

The world has changed, and the old responses to our economic problems simply don't work anymore. In the past, freer trade always benefited the most industrialized nations because their products were cheaper and better than those from other places. After World War II, for example, North American products were the best in the world, and the fewer restrictions there were on trade, the more money our businesses made.

But today things are different. There is far greater competition from such places as Germany and Japan, but the more critical problem is the Third World. In the past, Third World industries weren't much of a problem because they operated with inefficient management and outdated technology. But now multinational corporations bring the latest technology and management techniques to whatever country has the lowest labor costs. There are literally billions of workers in the Third World willing to work for a few dollars a week, and their numbers and their desperation are growing every day. Free trade is a boon to the multinational corporations and their stockholders, but it will drive millions of our workers into poverty and unemployment.

Free trade can flourish only in a free world. Until we can break the Third World nations' chains of poverty and despair and help them bring their runaway population growth under control, we must protect our workers with strong tariff barriers. We have no other choice!

Burgesses, for example, George Washington was accused of giving out 50 gallons of rum, 24 gallons of wine, 46 gallons of beer, and 2 gallons of cider in a district that had only 391 voters![44]

Today, of course, bribe money normally flows in the opposite direction. Political bribery is probably most widespread at the state and local levels, often involving zoning changes or the award of government contracts. But no one knows how common bribery at any level really is. There have, of course, been numerous scandals over the years, but how much bribery goes undetected is anybody's guess. Some even claim that investigators sometimes inadvertently create the crimes they are supposed to prevent. For example, in the so-called Abscam case FBI agents claimed to be working for an Arab sheik in need of some Washington favors. The agents handed out bribes to eight officeholders and subsequently arrested them. Critics of such "sting" operations (which are more commonly carried on against state and local officials) claim the agents are themselves creating crime by tempting honest officeholders to break the law; others feel that the relative ease with which they find officials who will take their bribes indicates a high level of government corruption.[45]

Although U.S. citizens still have the right to stand up and protest social injustice, people of all political persuasions are becoming concerned about the threat to civil liberties posed by the use of powerful new computer technology and the panicky attempts to root out terrorists that followed the September 11th attacks. The federal government maintains 910 different databases that contain billions of entries about its citizens.[46] They range from files on "subversives" and criminals kept by investigative agencies such as the FBI, the CIA, and military intelligence, to the files in the massive record-keeping systems of the Internal Revenue Service and the Social Security Administration. The Department of Justice alone keeps lists of persons involved in civil disturbances, members of criminal syndicates, narcotics addicts, criminal defendants, individuals wanted by the police, passers of forged checks, and aliens.

Clearly government agencies need many of these files if they are to do their work efficiently, but is such efficiency dangerous? What about the growing number of private firms that are keeping their own lists and selling them to whoever pays the price? What about the corporations that maintain lists of "disruptive employees" or political opponents? The prospect that all these files might be centralized is a frightening thought to anyone who values our civil liberties. It is now possible to establish a system that could, with the entry of a single identification number, reveal all the significant events in an individual's entire life. The power available to the controller of such a system would obviously be immense, as would its threat to our democratic freedoms.

QUICK REVIEW

How is democracy corrupted by the influence of the powerful?

RESPONDING TO THE PROBLEMS OF THE POLITICAL ECONOMY

There are a staggering number of proposals for dealing with the problems in our political economy, and we can discuss only a few of the most important. Perhaps the best place to start is with the effort to make the government more democratic, since that will probably be necessary before the government can be free to enact the kinds of economic reforms that are in the best interests of the entire nation. There are, of course, deep divisions about what kinds of economic reforms we ought to make, but there is considerable agreement that we must take a longer-term view and invest more in our future prosperity. On the other hand, however, economic growth is not enough. Environmentalists point out that we are already one of the richest nations on earth, but that enormous wealth has not seemed to make us much more happy, content, or secure. They therefore urge us to seek out ways to adjust to our changing world and to build a more sustainable society that allows us to improve our quality of life whether the economy is growing or shrinking.

BEING MORE DEMOCRATIC

As we have seen again and again in the pages of this chapter, the political deck is stacked in favor of the wealthy and against people who would challenge those already in positions of power. The obvious reason for this enormous imbalance is that those in office are in a far better position than their challengers to offer political rewards to big contributors. Political action committees, for example, contribute seven times more to incumbents than to challengers.[47] Current laws regulating campaign financing look good on paper, but they do virtually nothing to limit the ability of the wealthy to use their money to frustrate the will of the majority. The law limits direct contributions to a candidate's election committee, but the wealthy can still spend all the money they want to help a candidate as long as they do so as individuals or give the money to PACs that support their views. Presidential candidates are eligible for federal funds if they agree to a fixed spending limit, but there are no spending limits on federal money for other candidates. Even in presidential elections, individuals and PACs are once again allowed to spend an unlimited amount to support a candidate so long as they do so independently of the candidate's election committee. Moreover, there are virtually no limits on the donations to the Republican and Democratic parties, and this so-called soft money can also be spent for their presidential candidates. In 2000, the Democrats raised $199 million in soft money and the Republicans $211 million—a 56 percent increase from 1996.[48]

The fact is that the current system forces some politicians to sell their powers of office to the highest bidder and creates grossly unequal contests between candidates running for the same office. The best solution to this problem is to provide federal financing in all campaigns for national office, not just in presidential elections. This law would have to be written so that third-party candidates would be eligible for government financing along with candidates of the two major parties. If properly drawn, such a law could eliminate the injustices of the current campaign financing system. A related idea, intended to counteract the slick professional television commercials that tell so little about the real political issues, is to require the media to provide free time for all candidates to discuss their views in depth.

Another means of increasing democracy could be to limit government secrecy. There are good reasons for some government secrets. National governments must keep military and sometimes even economic information from potential enemies; local governments must not let speculators know that a certain piece of land is about to be purchased for public use. But the "secret" stamp used for these purposes can also be used to cover up official incompetence and, worse yet, crimes and violations of civil liberties. The cold light of publicity can do a great deal to restrain overzealous government officials, and that is the reason the Constitution prohibited Congress from making any law that abridges the freedom of the press. In effect, the press was given the duty of uncovering government secrets.

Making sure government bureaucrats inform the public about their behavior is not easy. One of the first attempts came in the Freedom of Information Act. This act requires U.S. government agencies to hand over any information they have about an individual citizen if that person requests it. Many government bureaucracies, however, respond to requests with months of stalling, and some charge fees for the information they furnish. Other agencies protect information they do not want the public to see by classifying it as secret. In response, Congress has added amendments to the bill, establishing a deadline for responding to requests for information, limiting the fees that can be charged, and providing for judicial review of classified material. This legislation gave the public much greater access to government records, but the bureaucracies continue to put up a determined resistance. The fact is that no bureaucrats or public officials want their activities subject to close public scrutiny, and that is doubly true when it comes to the domestic surveillance and covert operations that are the biggest threat to civil liberties. There is clearly a compelling need for stronger laws to limit government secrecy and protect the right of free political expression.

Another pressing need is for new protections for the privacy of citizens in this age of information. Tough new laws are needed to prevent the government (and private individuals and organizations) from snooping through its citizens' e-mail or keeping covert lists of which websites they visit or the material they choose to download onto their computers.

IMPROVING THE ECONOMY

The United States invests far less in its economic future for such things as basic **infra-structure** (roads, power plants, sewers, etc.) and new plants and equipment than Germany or Japan, and there is a growing consensus that Americans need to take a much longer-term perspective when making key economic decisions. While it is easy to say that we need to increase our investment in the future, there seems to be little will to actually do it. We cannot have our cake and eat it too: The only place to raise money for those investments is to save more and reduce our consumer spending—in other words, to lower our current standard of living. Perhaps we should learn from the long-range perspective taken by Native Americans, who consider a major decision by asking themselves what impact it would have seven generations in the future.

There are several possible ways to take a longer-term view and to invest more in the future. To start with, we could reform the tax structure to reduce taxation on investment and increase it on spending. For example, we could increase the tax rate on corporate profits and use the money to provide tax credits and other incentives to companies that invest in more research and new plants and equipment. Another idea would be to increase the tax rate on speculative investments, such as buying and selling commodities or real estate, and reduce the rate for productive investments, such as building an environmentally sound factory that creates new jobs.

More money and effort should be spent on education to improve the quality of our work force and to teach the growing population of poor and immigrant children the skills needed in a high-tech economy. The "digital divide" between Americans who can use computers and the other new technologies so essential in today's world economy and those who cannot is growing wider all the time. If new educational programs are not directed toward less-educated Americans, a growing portion of the American labor force will be unable to function effectively in the ever-more-demanding high-tech economy.

Another pressing need is to create better systems of mass transit and rebuild our decaying highways and railroads. The rate of American investment in basic infrastructure (roads, bridges, etc.) is less than half what it was in the 1960s, and we are outspent by all our major economic competitors.[49] In addition to their long-term benefits, many of these kinds of investments are also likely to create a considerable number of the kind of well-paying working-class jobs that are currently in such short supply.

Many proposals have been made to improve our productivity by restructuring workplaces and the corporations that organize and create them. One Japanese idea that is gaining growing popularity is known as **lean production**. Firms using this approach cut back their overlapping layers of management, use a smaller but more flexible workforce, and strive to develop a closer working relationship with parts and equipment suppliers. Another successful Japanese idea is to give workers more responsibility in the

Environmentalists argue that conversion to more environmentally sound technologies can create many new jobs, such as the one for the installer of this solar panel.

decision-making process. This approach not only fosters a greater commitment to the organization, but also takes advantage of the workers' intimate knowledge of day-to-day problems they face on the job. In the long run, however, workers are unlikely to show more commitment to their companies unless companies also demonstrate greater commitment to them by avoiding layoffs and showing a genuine concern for their welfare.

Advocates of **economic democracy** take such ideas a step further and propose programs to give workers more power over the decisions of top corporate officials as well. Past experience has shown that employees have a more cooperative attitude, accept necessary hardships, and work harder when they own a part of the company and share directly in its profits (or losses). It therefore seems logical that the government assist workers to take over the ownership of financially troubled firms and help workers start new cooperative enterprises.

In fact, the trend toward greater employee ownership is already under way. The number of employees participating in stock ownership plans has grown substantially in recent years. Although most of these plans fall far short of owning a controlling interest in the firm, several major corporations have been acquired by their employees in recent years—one of the most successful examples being the Avis car rental company.

A bolder approach would be to pass legislation, as Germany has, to require that worker representatives be included on the boards of directors of all major corporations. This "Works Constitution Act" requires all corporations to allow employees to elect a "works council" to represent their interests. By law, employees elected to the works councils have the right to examine the corporate books and must be consulted by management on any hiring or firing, change in the work process, working hours, or anything related to the interests of employees. Studies have shown that worker commitment to the company and worker productivity has increased as a result of these work laws in Germany.[50] Another useful addition to corporate boards would be a public representative who could speak for the interests of the nation as a whole. However it is implemented, advocates of economic democracy argue that a fairer and more efficient system would give workers a strong voice in controlling their own occupational lives.

Advocates of a more **sustainable economy** propose even more fundamental changes. Clearly, if we stand back and take a hard look at the global economy, it seems shockingly irrational. Every year we are using up more and more of our limited natural resources and pouring out ever-increasing amounts of toxic pollutants in order to produce a flood of consumer goods that add little or nothing to the quality of our lives. In fact, the relentless materialism of our consumer culture is more likely an overall source of suffering than satisfaction. Spurred by the ideals of the environmental movement, many people are coming to believe that the economy should be fundamentally restructured to make it more environmentally sustainable.

From a theoretical standpoint, it seems clear that we must find a more harmonious way to live with our environment, yet we often fail to take even the most obvious steps toward that goal. For example, it has been decades since the first "energy crisis," yet the United States is still so dependent on foreign oil that a new crisis in the Middle East could have the same or even worse consequences. Every year more and more gas-guzzling "sport utilities vehicles" clog the highways, the daily commute to work gets longer and longer, and new homes get ever larger, driving up both their heating and cooling costs. If we wanted to reduce this danger and cut the enormous environmental damage caused by our heedless consumption of petroleum, we could raise gasoline taxes and use the money to help communities develop local hydroelectric and solar resources, and we could conserve energy by using better insulation in our homes and working on more effective systems of mass transit.

A major underlying problem is that our economic system is structured to reward individuals who seek immediate short-term profits, while the costs of the long-term harm they cause are passed on to our entire society. But an even more fundamental difficulty lies in the values of our consumer culture that tell us that we can never have enough. The more riches we have, the more of the latest consumer products we own, the happier we will be. Social status comes more from what we own, than the quality of our character or the contribution we make to the welfare of those around us. Chapter 12 explores many proposals for building a more stable, sustainable society, but we will have to take a long, hard look at our economic values before we will be willing to carry them out.

It is important to remember that the quality of life is not measured solely by the economist's computations of average income or the standard of living. The quality of life can be improved regardless of the economic climate. Numerous suggestions for such improvements are discussed in this book, including proposals to make the workplace safer, reduce crime, improve the lives of the elderly and the poor, clean up the environment, and upgrade the educational system so that people can better understand the complexities of the world around them. Of course, all these things are expensive, but their overall cost is small compared to the benefits they bring.

QUICK REVIEW

What are the best ways to make the government more democratic?
How can we best deal with our economic problems?

SOCIOLOGICAL PERSPECTIVES ON PROBLEMS OF THE POLITICAL ECONOMY

Shrinking wages, foreign competition, the hardships of unemployment, and similar difficulties seem to be matters for technically trained economists, just as the corruption and inefficiency of the government may appear to be of primary concern to political scientists. To the sociologist, however, our economic and political ills cannot be understood in isolation from each other. It makes no more sense to study economic problems apart from their social and political background than it does to try to solve government problems without understanding their economic basis.

THE FUNCTIONALIST PERSPECTIVE

Functionalists see our political and economic systems as integral parts of a larger social system that operates something like a machine to meet the needs of its people. If the system functions efficiently to give the society what it wants, there are few problems, but sometimes the machine balks or strains. One part may run faster or slower than others, throwing the whole system out of balance; for example, we may produce too many goods of one kind and not enough of another, or government regulations may become too restrictive, thus blocking economic growth. A crisis may occur when the whole machine becomes disorganized and coordination throughout the system falters.

Functionalists blame the contemporary problems in our political economy on the rapid changes that have thrown the traditional system out of balance. It took hundreds of years for Western society to develop and perfect an economic system based on open competition among private individuals in a free market, but as the system became larger and more complex, its problems multiplied. Huge corporations sprang up and gained control of many vital markets, the government stepped in to regulate the economy, and powerful unions began to control the labor market. Thus, these new cogs destabilized the old machinery. Then, just as we were struggling to bring the system back into balance, major shifts occurred in the world economy that threw North American business into intense competition with dynamic new economies around the world. Under these conditions, many of the old ways of doing things no longer worked as they had in the past, and dysfunctional decisions followed. The breathtaking pace of economic and political change made it impossible to resolve old problems before new ones arose.

Most functionalists shy away from radical, far-reaching proposals for solving our problems, principally because they know that change brings new difficulties as well as solutions. Disruptive change in an unbalanced system makes a new balance even more difficult to achieve. Functionalists favor specific, limited cures for specific, limited problems, such as education and training for the unemployed, better law enforcement to deter corporate crime, and campaign finance reform to make our government more democratic. The basic goal of the functionalist is to reduce the disorganization in political and economic institutions and to improve the coordination between them and the rest of society. Only when this goal has been reached will the political economy function smoothly and efficiently.

THE CONFLICT PERSPECTIVE

Conflict theorists take a very different view of our political economy. Unlike functionalists, they do not consider society a unified whole based on a consensus about norms and values. Consequently, they do not say that the political economy performs either well or badly for the entire society. Rather, they believe that it benefits certain groups at the expense of others, and that who benefits, and to what degree, changes from time to time.

From the conflict perspective, society is composed of many different groups, each trying to take advantage of the others. Most problems arise because one group—or a coalition of groups—seizes economic and political power and uses that power to exploit and oppress other groups. In contemporary society, those with great wealth and top positions of corporate power dominate the political economy. They seek to maximize their profits by keeping wages low and workers docile. They invest their capital in whichever part of the world offers them the best return, regardless of the consequences for their own country. They use their wealth to control elected officials and in turn use the government to protect and advance their interests.

Thus from the conflict perspective, the underlying cause of most of the problems in the political economy is the exploitation of the common people by powerful elites. If those problems are to be solved, the masses must somehow gain enough power of their own to make the elites give up their advantages. According to the Marxists, the first step is for oppressed workers to develop "class consciousness," a sense of unity based on the realization that they are being exploited. Then the workers must organize themselves for political action and achieve change either through peaceful struggle—elections, protests, and strikes—or, if need be, through violent conflicts. Conflict theorists, whether Marxist or not, see the widening gap between the income of the haves and the have-nots as a direct result of the decline in power of the unions and the failure of political organizations to represent the interests of working women and men. They feel that if these trends are ever to be reversed, the common people must join together and demand that we create a more just society.

THE FEMINIST PERSPECTIVE

When feminists look at recent developments in our economy and the role women have played, they see two important stories. The first is the enormous flexibility women have shown in adapting to a historic change in their economic role. In earlier years, women's primary economic contribution was in the home: doing housework and taking care of children. But with the economic crisis of the 1970s, millions of women poured into the workforce to help their families make ends meet. As a result, the position of women in our society underwent a fundamental transformation, and both women and men are still struggling to adjust. Today, the average mother not only handles most of the traditional homemaking and child-care responsibilities, but she puts in many long hours working outside the home as well.

The second story is one of continuity, not change. Unfortunately, that continuity lies in the economic exploitation of women. Although record numbers of women have entered the workforce and many hold traditionally male jobs, the fact remains that on the average, a woman is still paid only 75 cents for each dollar her male counterpart earns.

The solution to this problem lies in an attack on the barriers of prejudice and discrimination that still keep women as second-class economic citizens. Changes in the educational system to encourage women to enter the highest-paying fields of study, tougher enforcement of anti-discrimination laws, and changes in the hostile attitudes many male workers have toward their female co-workers are just a few of the suggestions commonly made. In addition, the workplace needs to be made more "woman-friendly." Women still bear the major share of the responsibility of child rearing, and employers need to create more on-site day-care centers, allow more flexible working hours, and in general take a more supportive attitude toward the needs of their employees' families.

When feminists look at the political system, the first thing they see is the gross underrepresentation of women at all levels of government. In the United States, no woman has ever been president, vice president, speaker of the house, or chief justice of the Supreme Court. Only one woman has ever been the prime minister of Canada, and then for only a few months. A few European countries have better records, but there isn't a single country around the world in which women have an equal share of government power. Moreover, whether we look at top officials, elected representatives, or only middle-level bureaucrats, the story is still the same.

From the feminist perspective, this situation is a real tragedy, not only because it deprives women around the world of their basic human rights but, perhaps as important, because it deprives the decision-making process of the wisdom and common sense the world's women have to offer. Many feminists feel that this would be a more peaceful planet with more caring governments if women had their full political rights.

At least in the Western democracies, the official, legal barriers to women's political participation have been removed (although feminists point out that former slaves got the vote in the United States before women did). Today, feminists call for women and sympathetic men to ban together and force open the doors of the "old boys' club" that still dominates the political system. The majority of eligible voters in most industrialized countries are women, and feminists urge them to seize the power their numbers give them and work to create fundamental improvements in the way the old system operates.

THE INTERACTIONIST PERSPECTIVE

Because interactionists are concerned mainly with individuals and small groups, they rarely address large-scale problems of the political economy. Instead, they are more interested in the impact of this system on an individual's psychological makeup, attitudes, and behavior patterns, and in turn, the impact individual behavior has on the larger system. Interactionists and other social psychologists have found, for example, that unemployment has devastating psychological consequences for many workers. Feelings of boredom, uselessness, and despair are common, and some frustrated workers suffer much more serious difficulties. Studies show that the rates of such stress-related problems as high blood pressure, alcoholism, mental disorder, and suicide are significantly higher among the unemployed. Unemployed workers are also more likely to lash out at those around them. An increase in the unemployment rate increases the rate of child abuse and other family violence.

But the psychological damage caused by our political economy is not limited to the unemployed. Our competitive system encourages a strong achievement motivation that often leads to dissatisfaction and anxiety. When a large percentage of the population is oriented toward individual competition, the culture they share is likely to show many forms of innovation and creativity, but this system also promotes insecurity, fear, and aggression. Social psychologists have observed, moreover, that these burdens are not equally shared by everyone in a society. On average, the unskilled and downwardly mobile have far more social and psychological problems than other people. They are more likely to be hostile and withdrawn and to suffer from low self-esteem and bouts of intense anxiety.

Effective solutions to the psychological problems created by our political economy are not easy to find. One possibility would be to deemphasize the values of competition and achievement and to emphasize instead cooperation and mutual support. But despite the fact that such values have long been stressed in family and religious institutions, their application to society at large meets with strong resistance. This opposition seems to be based on the fear that reducing competitiveness will destroy initiative and creativity. Perhaps this is why more emphasis is placed on the clinical treatment of psychological disorders than on changing the economic and social conditions that produce them. Many interactionists nonetheless continue to argue that reducing economic insecurity, even in a competitive society, would improve the mental health of our entire population.

QUICK REVIEW

What are the differences in the ways a functionalist, a conflict theorist, a feminist, and an interactionist would explain our economic problems?
What are the differences among the main sociological perspectives about the problems of government and their solutions?

SUMMARY

Many people see our economy and our government as two separate realms, but in reality they are both part of a single political economy—an interlocking system of economic and political relationships. Another common mistake is to try to explain our problems by looking only at the familiar events close to home and ignoring the web of international relationships that make up the global political economy. The principal dividing line in the modern world is between the wealthy industrialized nations and the poor agricultural nations. All the rich industrialized nations practice one version or another of capitalism. Although no nation lives up to the ideals of the completely open, free-market system advocated by Adam Smith, the nations that come closest, such as the United States, are said to have a system of individualistic capitalism, while the systems that emphasize more economic cooperation and government involvement have what is called communitarian capitalism.

The corporation is a major force in the modern political economy. Although antitrust laws no longer permit most markets to be controlled by a monopoly (one corporation), many industries are dominated by an oligopoly (a few large corporations). There is considerable debate over who runs the corporations. Some people see stockholders as the owners and controllers, while others argue that power rests with corporate managers. Many charge that the multinational corporations are exploiting the poor and the powerless around the world, and it is clear that they often engage in criminal activities such as fraud and price-fixing in their own countries as well.

The government, like the corporations, has grown rapidly over the past century, and it also plays a key role in the economic system. It is not only a major employer but also is deeply involved in managing the economy. Social scientists strongly disagree about who actually runs the government. The elitists believe that a small, unified power elite is in control, while the pluralists see many more-or-less equal groups competing for power. Like the elitists, the structuralists also feel that the government works primarily in the interests of the privileged few, but not because of the direct involvement of individual members of the elite, but because the structure of capitalist societies forces the government to support the interests of the upper class. Many observers of all persuasions are concerned with the corrupting influence big money has on our political system and the threat new computer technologies pose to our civil liberties.

With the "downsizing" of many corporations, small business has come to play an increasingly important role in the creation of jobs. However, conditions are difficult for many small businesses. Competition is generally much more intense than in the corporate sector, financial reserves are often inadequate, and unlike the corporate giants, small businesses seldom get a government bailout when they get into trouble.

Recent times have seen a sharp decline in the number of workers in the old manufacturing industries, while service jobs have been on the increase. Unemployment and underemployment remain significant problems, and there are many dangerous hazards in the workplace. Unions were the key to the worker's ability to win higher wages and better working conditions in the past, but today their power is in serious decline.

The United States emerged from World War II as the leader of the global political economy and enjoyed two decades of booming prosperity that benefited all social classes. The reemergence of strong foreign completion sent the U.S. into a serious economic slump during the 1970s and 80s. Although things have improved since then, the benefits have gone to the upper classes while many average workers have continued to experience hard times.

Many proposals have been made for dealing with the problems of our political economy, including being more democratic, investing more in the future, and working to build a more environmentally sustainable society.

QUESTIONS FOR CRITICAL THINKING

There are many different ways we can evaluate our political economy. Economists tend to take the narrowest view and look simply at how much wealth it produces. Most sociologists think the question of how fairly wealth and power are distributed is more important than how much wealth there is. Environmentalists focus their attention on the sustainability of the political economy: How much damage does it do to the environment, and does it consume resources faster than they can be replaced? Finally, from the broadest perspective, we might ask whether our political economy contributes to the overall sense of well-being and happiness of the people or whether it leaves them frustrated and unfulfilled. Do your own evaluation of our economic system in terms of each of these four viewpoints.

KEY TERMS

alienation	lean production
antitrust law	lobbyist
blue-collar worker	monopoly
bribery	oligopoly
budget deficit	pluralist
capitalism	political economy
communism	price-fixing
communitarian capitalism	productivity
conflict of interest	service occupation
deregulation	special-interest group
discouraged worker	structuralist
economic democracy	sustainable economy
elitist	Third World; less-developed countries
fraud	underemployment
individualistic capitalism	unemployment
inflation	white-collar worker
infrastructure	world economy
laissez-faire capitalism	world system

NOTES

1. World Bank, *World Development Report, 2000/2001* (2000).
2. Adam Smith, *An Inquiry into the Nature and Causes of the Wealth of Nations* (New York: Random House, 1937 [originally pub. 1776]).
3. Ibid., p. 128.
4. Harold Kerbo and John McKinstry, *Modern Japan* (New York: McGraw-Hill, 1998), Chapter 4; Harold Kerbo and Hermann Strasser, *Modern Germany* (New York: McGraw-Hill, 2000), Chapter 4.
5. Lester Thurow, *Head to Head: The Coming Economic Battle Among Japan, Europe, and America* (New York: Morrow, 1992), p. 32.
6. Kerbo, *Social Stratification and Inequality*, pp. 190–191; World Bank, *World Development Report, 2000* (New York: Oxford University Press, 2000).
7. Thomas Mulligan, "Corporate Concentrations Paradox," *Los Angeles Times*, August 22, 1999.
8. See Thurow, *Head to Head*.
9. See Kerbo, *Social Stratification and Inequality*, Chapter 7.
10. Ibid.
11. See Beth Mintz and Michael Schwartz, *The Power Structure of American Business* (Chicago: University of Chicago Press, 1985).
12. David R. James and Michael Soref, "Profit Constraints on Managerial Autonomy: Managerial Theory and the Unmaking of the Corporate President," *American Sociological Review* 46 (February 1981): 1–18.
13. See G. William Domhoff, *Who Rules America? Power and Politics in the Year 2000* (Mountain View, CA: Mayfield, 1998).
14. C. Wright Mills, *The Power Elite* (New York: Oxford University Press, 1956), p. 14.
15. *Los Angeles Times*, August 30, 1999.
16. Volker Bornschier and Christopher Chase-Dunn, *Transnational Corporations and Development* (New York: Praeger, 1985); Glenn Firebaugh, "Does Foreign Capital Harm Poor Nations? New Estimates Based on Dixon and Boswell's Measures of Capital Penetration," *American Journal of Sociology* 102 (1996), 563–578.

17. Robert Slagter and Harold Kerbo, *Modern Thailand* (New York: McGraw-Hill, 2000); Harold Kerbo, *Exploiting the World's Poor? Globalization, Multinational Corporations, and Asian Economic Development*, forthcoming.
18. James William Coleman, *The Criminal Elite: Understanding White Collar Crime*, 4th. ed. (New York: St. Martin's Press, 1998), pp. 80–85.
19. Ibid., pp. 76–77.
20. For a review of this and other studies on price-fixing, see Coleman, *The Criminal Elite*, pp. 51–53.
21. U.S. Bureau of the Census, *Statistical Abstract of the United States, 1996* (Washington, DC: U.S. Government Printing Office, 1996), pp. 419, 421; U.S. Bureau of the Census, *Statistical Abstract of the United States, 1991* (Washington, DC: U.S. Government Printing Office, 1991), pp. 400–401.
22. Lawrence Mishel, Jared Bernstein, and John Schmitt, *The State of Working America, 1996–97* (New York: Sharpe, 1997), p. 102.
23. C. Wright Mills, *The Power Elite*.
24. Federal Election Commission, August 1997, <http://www.fec.gov>.
25. U.S. Bureau of the Census, Census Brief, "Too Busy to Vote" (Washington, DC: U.S. Government Printing Office, 1998).
26. Harold Kerbo, *Social Stratification and Inequality* (New York: McGraw-Hill, 2000), pp. 235–239; Frances Fox Piven and Richard Cloward, *Why Americans Don't Vote* (New York: Pantheon, 1988); U.S. Bureau of the Census, *Statistical Abstract, 1996*, p. 286.
27. Dye, *Who's Running America?* p. 125.
28. Ibid.
29. Morton Mintz and Jerry S. Cohen, *America, Inc.* (New York: Dial, 1971), p. 70.
30. Mishel, Bernstein, and Schmitt, *The State of Working America, 1996–97*, pp. 271–273.
31. Ibid., p. 271.
32. Ibid., p. 185.
33. Ibid., p. 268.
34. *Statistical Abstract of the United States, 2001*, p. 386; Kerbo, *Social Stratification and Inequality*, p. 15.
35. Kerbo and Strasser, *Modern Germany*.
36. Ibid., p. 258.
37. Ibid., pp. 257–261.
38. David J. Charrington, *The Work Ethic: Working Values and Values that Work* (New York: AMACOM, 1980).
39. Associated Press, "17 American Workers a Day Died on the Job During the 80s," *New York Times*, April 15, 1994, p. A8.
40. Coleman, *The Criminal Elite*, p. 10.
41. Ibid., pp. 70–71.
42. Harold R. Kerbo, *Social Stratification and Inequality*, pp. 240–243; Steven Greenhouse, "Strikes Decrease to a 50-Year Low," *New York Times*, January 29, 1996, pp. A1, A10
43. For all of these figures see, Kerbo, *Social Stratification and Inequality*, pp. 14–15 and Chapter 2; Mishel, Bernstein, and Schmitt, *The State of Working America, 1999*, p. 260; U.S. Bureau of the Census, *Poverty in the United States, 1999* (Washington, DC: U.S. Government Printing Office, 2000); U.S. Bureau of the Census, *Money Income of Households, 1999* (Washington, DC: U.S. Government Printing Office, 2000); *International Herald Tribune*, September 11, 2000; *Los Angeles Times*, August 30, 1999.
44. James William Coleman, *The Criminal Elite*, pp. 102–103.
45. Ibid., p. 45.
46. Thomas B. Rosenstiel, "Someone May Be Watching," *Los Angeles Times*, May 18, 1994, pp. A1, A12.
47. Theodore Caplow, *American Social Trends* (San Diego, CA: Harcourt Brace Jovanovich, 1991), p. 114.
48. Doyle McManus, "President Proposes End to 'Soft Money' Donation Loophole," *Los Angeles Times*, June 4, 1997, pp. A1, A16; data from Federal Election Commission Website, <www.fec.gov>.
49. Thurow, *Head to Head*, p. 161.
50. Lowell Turner, *Democracy at Work: Changing World Markets and the Future of Labor Unions* (Ithaca, NY: Cornell University Press, 1991); Kathleen A. Thelen, *Unions of Parts: Labor Politics in Postwar Germany* (Ithaca, NY: Cornell University Press, 1992); Kerbo and Strasser, *Modern Germany*, 2000.

CHAPTER 3

PROBLEMS OF THE FAMILY

Questions to Consider

How is the modern family changing?

Is divorce a social problem?

What are the causes of family violence?

Are children victims of their parents' problems?

How can the family be strengthened?

Donna Oakes works from 8 to 5 as a receptionist at a dental office in Concord, California. Every morning she gets the kids up and dressed, fixes their breakfast and lunch, and drops them off at school on her way to work. Her husband, Randy, is an insurance salesman, so he can usually take time off from work to pick them up and get them over to her mother's house. When Donna gets off work, she picks up the kids, and then it is time to fix dinner, try to help with homework, and drive the kids to their ball games and music lessons. Randy has to work a lot of nights, so they don't get to see much of each other except on the weekends.

Tasha Parker got pregnant with Jerome when she was 17. Jerome's father was immature and scared to death of responsibility, so Tasha ended up raising her son as a single mother. She dropped out of high school and was on welfare for a while. Times were hard then. She felt deserted by Jerome's father and ashamed to be getting a public handout. Even with a few odd jobs on the side, she never earned enough to get by on her own. She finally moved back in with her mother and finished high school. After two years as a secretary in the county clerk's office, she is earning enough to start making plans to move out again.

Our family system has been undergoing sweeping changes, and all the old expectations—from the assumption of male dominance to the idea that marriage itself "is forever"—seem open to question. The divorce rate has soared, and more and more women like Tasha Parker are having children without being married. With all the economic and social pressures of modern life, even two-parent homes like that of Donna and Randy Oakes just aren't the same as they used to be. Some take all this as a sign of the impending collapse of our family system, but that attitude ignores the many strengths of today's families. As we will see in this chapter, the family is certainly changing, but it shows no signs of disappearing. Most people in the United States eventually marry, and most who divorce marry again. Although it is easy to idealize the past, there is little reason to believe that families of former years were any happier than families are today.

FAMILIES AROUND THE WORLD

A family is usually defined as a group of people related by marriage, ancestry, or adoption, who live together in a common household, but like much else about the modern family, even its definition is a matter of debate. Shouldn't two people who have lived together for 10 or 20 years be considered a family—even if they have never been officially married? What if they were legally forbidden to marry because they are both the same sex? What about people who are legally married but have no emotional bonds, or people who have intense bonds but live separately? The interactionist perspective suggests a more flexible definition, one that seems better suited to today's diverse family landscape. In this approach, a family is simply any group of people that defines itself as a family.

Although some form of family is universal to all human societies, its structure and traditions vary enormously from one place to another. For example, some societies permit only one husband and wife, while others allow more. Anthropologist George P. Murdock's classic study of 565 societies found that about one-fourth followed the pattern of **monogamy** (only one husband and one wife at a time), whereas three-fourths allowed some form of **polygamy** (more than one husband or wife). However, while over 70 percent of all the societies studied allowed a husband to have more than one wife, he found only four societies that allowed a wife to have more than one husband.[1]

Another useful classification divides families into two types: nuclear and extended. The **nuclear family** consists of single parent or couple and their children. Although there are often close ties between the members of the nuclear family and the other relatives, nuclear families are independent, self-controlled units. When two people commit themselves to each other, the couple and their children become a separate family, usually living apart from the families in which they were reared.

Although the nuclear family is the most common in the world's industrialized nations, anthropologists have found that the **extended family**, which includes a much wider range of relatives than the nuclear family, is the ideal in most agricultural societies. Life in an extended family is very different from the life most of us know in the nuclear family. For one spouse at least, marriage does not represent a sharp break with the past, as it does in our culture. That spouse continues to live with his or her parents, as before. Although the adjustment is more difficult for the spouse who must move into a new family, husband and wife both remain under the authority of the older generation. They have little chance of controlling their own lives unless they live long enough to take over the responsibility for the entire family. On the other hand, each family member receives far more support and protection from the family unit. For example, many more adults are involved in the rearing of the children, so if something happens to one of the parents, there is always someone else to take over.[2]

Another important variation in the traditional extended family is whether the married couple live with the husband's family (called patrilocal) or the wife's family (called matrilocal). There are also important differences in the way people in these societies trace their descent. People in patrilineal societies follow the father's line of ancestry, while people in matrilineal societies follow the mother's line, and still others follow **bilateral** ancestry, seeing themselves as equally related to both sides of their family. Most agricultural societies are patrilocal and patrilineal with the oldest male considered to be head of the family and the family name following the male family line. In this type of family system, the newly married woman is expected to leave her family and move in with the family of her husband. However, this is not always the case, and some important differences in gender roles around the world are related to differences in family organization. In much of mainland Southeast Asia, for example, traditional agricultural people have had a matrilocal family system, meaning that daughters inherited the land and the new husband would move to the farm owned by the family of his new wife. These societies, however, were not matrilineal or patrilineal because there were no family names (only first names) until increasing contact with the West and Western economic and political institutions forced them to change. Even today, women in these traditionally matrilineal societies have more influence and better representation in the professions and the business world than in other Asian nations or even in many Western societies.[3]

QUICK REVIEW

What is the best definition of family?
What different types of families are there?

UNDERSTANDING FAMILY DIVERSITY

Before the industrial revolution transformed our social world, most cultures had a clear idea of what a "normal" family should be like. Of course, not every family could live up to those expectations, but there was enormous pressure to conform and the vast majority of people did. In preindustrial societies, the family was the basic unit of economic production, and it was very hard to survive outside of family bonds. Marriages were often arranged by parents or other family members, and the needs of the family were supposed to be placed above those of its individual members. Marriage was seen as a family duty, and divorce was often difficult or impossible. The father or oldest male was given authority over the family and its assets. Indeed, women and children were frequently seen as his property and were expected to respect and obey him.

The industrial revolution transformed Western family life. As production shifted away from the family farm, individuals gained more economic independence, and it became easier to live without family support. Today, marriage has become a matter of individual choice (except, of course, for same-sex couples who are not given the opportunity to marry in most places). Couples usually marry out of the desire for companionship and personal happiness, not because of duty to their families or economic necessity. The idealization of **romantic love**, which first became popular among the European aristocracy, was originally applied only to extramarital affairs. But with the changes brought by industrialization, it became a primary goal of marriage itself, and the process of mate selection came to focus on finding a compatible person and "falling in love." The underpinnings of the **patriarchal system** (a social system based on male domination) slowly eroded as more and more women took jobs outside the home. And family units themselves became smaller as birthrates dropped, the number of single parents increased, and fewer relatives outside the nuclear family lived in the home.

This relentless tide of social and economic change has produced a diverse mosaic of family patterns in modern society. Yet many people still have an idealized picture of the "normal" family handed down from the time when there was still a strong consensus about family issues. Perhaps best symbolized by the popular television comedies of the 1950s and 1960s, such as Leave It to Beaver and Father Knows Best, this ideal combines elements of the preindustrial family with many newer developments. The husband is the head of this idealized family, earning the money and making the major decisions. The wife stays home to take care of the house and, most particularly, the children, who are the central focus of family life. The family unit is stable, sex strictly confined to the married couple, and divorce hardly considered as a possibility. This ideal family lives in a large suburban house in a neighborhood filled with people very much like themselves.

Even in the 1950s, this ideal was only that—a goal our culture encouraged us to desire. The ability to live that lifestyle was always limited: The poor and ethnic minorities were largely excluded, and as time went by, this "typical" family became less common in the white middle class as well. In order to understand the wide diversity of today's families, we must turn our attention to the changing pattern of family life and the ways families differ along class and ethnic lines.

CHANGING FAMILY PATTERNS

Our family system has undergone rapid change since World War II, as it has in other industrial societies in Europe and Japan (see "Lessons from Other Places"). While many Americans still live in the kinds of nuclear families idealized in the old television shows, more and more are living in other kinds of family arrangements. One important trend is that people are staying single longer than they did in the past, so there are now more one-person households. In the past four decades, the average age for a first marriage has increased, and people are waiting longer after a divorce before remarrying. Industrial society's ever-increasing demand for education and training is one reason more marriages are delayed, but there are other important factors as well. Greater acceptance of premarital sex makes the single life more attractive, and the public's attitude toward singles has undergone a remarkable change. Nineteenth-century stereotypes of the lonely bachelor and the neglected spinster have been replaced by the new stereotype of affluent, carefree singles who often elicit envy instead of pity. Figure 3.1 (on page 72) shows how rapidly the number of singles has been growing, but this figure should not be misinterpreted. The majority of Americans eventually get married (though the number is in decline), but they are choosing to remain single for a somewhat longer part of their lives. In the past three decades the average age for a first marriage and the amount of time people stay single after a divorce or the death of a partner have both increased.[4]

Another important change in family size concerns children. In the past, it was almost scandalous for a couple to decide that they didn't want to have any children, but a growing number of couples are now making that choice; and although the vast majority of married couples do eventually have children, they are having fewer than they did in the past. The percentage of families with three or more children is only half of what it was in 1970, while the percentage of families with no children has increased substantially.[5] We will examine the reasons for this more thoroughly in Chapter 12, but there is little doubt that they are closely linked to the process of industrialization. Technology has helped to bring down the death rate, so it is no longer necessary to have many children to ensure that a few survive. And although children were an economic asset in a traditional agricultural society, they are often a financial burden in the industrial world.

One of the most important trends has been rapid growth in the number of **single-parent families**. In 1970, single-parent families made up about 11 percent of all American families, but by 1999, 28 percent of families with children had only a single parent in the home. Most of these single-parent families are headed by women (just over 80 percent), but the number of single-parent families headed by men more

LESSONS FROM OTHER PLACES

FAMILY CHANGE IN EUROPE AND JAPAN

While all industrial societies have experienced a sweeping transformation in their family structure, in some ways the United States has actually undergone fewer changes than most other places.* In Europe and Japan, far fewer people are getting married than in the United States. When they do marry, they do so later, seeming to delay marriage as long as possible. Moreover, the number of children born to each woman (called the total fertility rate) is dropping dramatically.

In 1970, about 8 percent of Americans between 30 and 34 years of age were single, compared to about 25 percent in 1999. The fertility rate in 1999 was slightly over 2 children per woman, which is just about the "replacement rate" necessary to keep the population stable. In European countries, however, from Germany to Italy and Spain, fewer and fewer young people are getting married. The average number of children born per woman in all of Europe is only 1.6, with many countries considerably lower. Surprisingly, Italy has the lowest rate in recorded history at 1.2. In Germany, about 40 percent of people between 20 and 60 years of age are not married. However, 25 percent of these Germans consider themselves part of a couple even though they do not live in the same household. In Japan, the change is even more dramatic. Just 40 years ago, well over 95 percent of young Japanese were married by their mid-20s. But now the number of singles has exploded and the fertility rate is just above 1.3 children per woman.

These changes have many interrelated causes, and they vary to some extent from country to country. A common theme is that more women are working outside the home, but are getting little extra help when it comes to child-care and domestic responsibilities. Another is the growing division between men who are more likely to hold traditional gender stereotypes, and women who expect a more egalitarian relationship. Japan, for example, still clings to an old system of marriage and gender relations that an increasing number of Japanese women do not find appealing. A recent Japanese government survey found that 25 percent of women in their 20s said they do not plan to marry or have children. The actual percentage of Japanese women in their late 20s who have not married has gone up from 30 percent to 50 percent in the past 15 years. This survey also found that 40 percent of Japanese women aged 25 to 30 had no boyfriend, while 50 percent of men in that age group said they had no girlfriend.

*See World Bank, *World Development Report*, 2000 (New York: Oxford, 2000); Harold R. Kerbo and John McKinstry, *Modern Japan* (New York: McGraw-Hill, 1998); Harold R. Kerbo and Hermann Strasser, *Modern Germany* (New York: McGraw-Hill, 2000). News summaries of recent reports can be found in the *International Herald Tribune*, July 11, 1998, October 10, 1998, August 15, 2000, February 11, 2000.

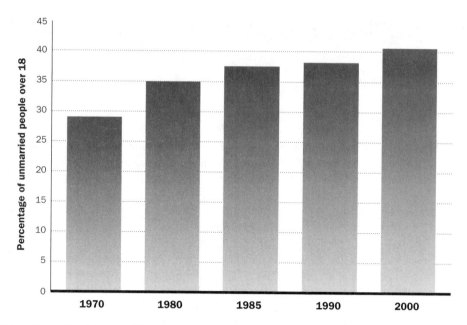

FIGURE 3.1   THE GROWING NUMBER OF SINGLES

The percentage of Americans who are single has steadily increased over the years.

Source: U.S. Bureau of the Census, *Statistical Abstract of the United States,* 1996 (Washington, D.C.: U.S. Government Printing Office, 1996), p. 54; U.S. Bureau of the Census, *Statistical Abstract of the United States,* 2000 (Washington, D.C.: U.S. Government Printing Office, 2000), p. 5.

than doubled between 1980 and 1999.[6] Although we will examine single-parent families more fully in the next section, the causes of this increase are not hard to find. The percentage of families headed by widows has declined, but there has been a sharp increase in the number of families with children that are headed by women who have been divorced or have never married.

Another major change has been in the economic role of married women in families with two spouses. In 1938, a national survey found that 75 percent of all Americans disapproved of a woman working if her husband could support her. But just 40 years later, another survey found a complete reversal of public opinion: 75 percent of those surveyed approved of wives holding a job.[7] Statistics also show that behavior has changed along with attitudes. In 1960, 32 percent of all married women were employed outside the home, but by 1999 this had increased to over 61 percent.[8] Since fewer than a third of all families have only a single male breadwinner, the typical American family is now a **dual-earner family**. It should be noted, however, that males continue to carry greater responsibilities as "breadwinners," both because they usually earn higher wages than their wives (see Chapter 8) and because a greater proportion of working wives than husbands are employed in part-time jobs.

Although there is little reliable information about trends in the number of gay and lesbian couples, there is a growing recognition that they comprise families just as much as their heterosexual counterparts. According to one estimate, about half of gay

Despite continuing discrimination in child custody and adoption cases, a growing number of gay and lesbian couples are choosing to raise children.

men and three-fourths of all lesbians live with a partner.[9] Philip Blumstein and Pepper Schwartz's wide-ranging study of American couples found that homosexuals who live together face many of the same problems as their heterosexual counterparts: the division of household labor, money, power, and love.[10] In addition, however, they must also face deeply entrenched prejudice. Aside from the sneers, insults, and even physical abuse often directed at them, gays and lesbians also confront institutionalized discrimination. The law denies legal marriage to homosexual couples (see the "Debate" on gay and lesbian marriages on page 74) and often shows a strong bias against them when it comes to adoption and child custody cases. Many employers, including the federal government, openly discriminate against gays and lesbians, and few offer fringe benefits such as health insurance or death benefits to their domestic partners.

CLASS AND ETHNIC DIFFERENCES

While these sweeping changes have affected all segments of our society, they have not affected them all equally. Moreover, there have always been significant differences in family structure among the poor, the middle class, and the wealthy, and between different ethnic groups. In order to understand the mosaic of the modern family, we must therefore look at the way families differ along class and ethnic lines. Before we do, however, a strong word of caution is needed. The descriptions that follow are only

DEBATE

SHOULD WE LEGALIZE GAY AND LESBIAN MARRIAGES?

Yes

Forbidding someone the right to marry the person they love is simply wrong. Tens of millions of gay and lesbian Americans are being denied this basic human right, and it has to stop! Many same-sexed couples do, of course, form families, have commitment ceremonies, and raise children together, but they can't get the legal and financial protection afforded married couples. Why? The answer is simple: hatred and bigotry.

One day we will look back at this time in history and be ashamed of the discrimination that is aimed at those who do not identify themselves as heterosexuals, much as many are now ashamed of the fierce discrimination so many have faced in this country because of the color of their skin. If it is wrong to discriminate against someone because of their race, gender, or ethnic group, then it must be wrong to discriminate against them because of their sexual orientation. This nation has a long history of denying basic human rights to members of unpopular groups. But we also have a long history of struggle to change prejudiced views and discriminatory practices. We must live up to the promise enshrined in our pledge of allegiance to provide "liberty and justice for all."

No

Marriage is a sanctified union between a man and a woman. Legalizing same-sex marriages will have many negative effects on this nation. It will undermine the religious values that many of our nation's people hold dear. This nation was founded on Christian ideals. The Bible clearly states that same-sex unions are sinful and most other major religions agree. Sanctifying same-sex unions will promote same-sex relationships. People in this nation look to our laws to uphold morality. Legalizing same-sex marriages will, in effect, tell this nation's people that there is nothing wrong with homosexuality.

People who promote the legalization of same-sex marriages appear to have an "if it feels good, do it" mentality, without looking to the future to see what kind of havoc this disastrous change would wreak on our family structure, our view of the family, and the sanctity of marriage. What will happen to our nation's children? They will grow up with a confused sense of gender roles and sexuality, and will not know the difference between right and wrong. Restoring traditional family values will keep this nation strong. We only have to look back in history to the Roman Empire to see what will happen if we don't promote heterosexuality in this country.

statistical generalizations, and many, many families do not fit the pattern typical of their group. It is important not to let such generalizations harden into fixed stereotypes or to begin passing judgment on whole groups of people because their family patterns do not conform to our own ideals.

Over the years, there has been a considerable amount of research on the ways family patterns differ among the classes, and the general tendencies have been well established.[11] The most easily defined differences concern basic demographics. Poor people and those from the working class generally marry younger than those from higher classes, and they tend to have slightly more children. Numerous studies have shown that there is a negative relationship between income and divorce: The lower the income, the higher the divorce rate. The same holds true of the birthrate among single women, which is higher for the poor than the affluent. As a result, single-parent families are most common among the poor and decline in frequency as income increases. In 1999, the overall rate of poverty for children under 18 years of age was 16.9 percent, while the rate of poverty for children under 18 years of age living in single-parent households was 41.9 percent.[12] Although single-parent families are most common among the poor, they have increased significantly among all social classes in recent times, decreasing slightly only since 1997.

Although there are many explanations for these differences, most sociologists see economic causes at their root. Poor and working-class people marry earlier because they have far less chance of going to college and therefore less reason to wait. Moreover, they often have more incentive to leave their parents' home, since it is likely to offer less privacy and comfort. The economic problems faced by low-income people are a major contributor to their high rates of divorce. Money is a major source of family conflicts among people from all classes, and the less money there is, the more severe the conflicts are likely to be. Similarly, poor women are more likely to have a child without being married because they are less likely to know men who earn enough money to fulfill the social expectations for a husband and father.

Another important difference concerns the nuclear family's relationship with the wider world. Because of their tenuous economic position, lower-class families pool resources with a wide network of people—lending money, helping with child care, sharing meals. In the working-class family, an extended kinship network involving parents, grandparents, and siblings plays an especially important role in providing financial support and encouragement. Middle-class people receive far more help from outside institutions and are therefore less dependent on friends and relatives. When they are sick, they have health insurance. There are professional therapists for emotional problems, day care and domestic help for the children. Among the upper class, the network of family ties takes on more importance than in the middle class, since it is a great source of prestige, wealth, and social connections.

The African American family has been the focus of a considerable amount of public attention in recent years, most of it centered on a single characteristic: the frequency of female-headed single-parent homes. In 1999, 63 percent of African American family groups with children were headed by a single female, compared to about 23 percent of whites.[13] One of the reasons for this is that single African American women have a higher birthrate than women from most other ethnic groups. During 1998, 69 percent of all African American babies were born to single women, compared to 42 percent of Hispanic babies and 26 percent of white babies.[14] This in turn relates to another important demographic fact: African Americans in general, but especially African American women, are less likely to marry than other Americans.[15] In contrast to well-publicized findings about the high incidence of single-parent families, the media have paid far less attention to research that emphasizes the enormous resourcefulness of African American families in the face of racial prejudice and hard economic conditions or the important role that extended families play in African American life.[16]

Although it is still a matter of some debate, several causes stand out for the distinctive demographic characteristics of the African American family. First and foremost, African Americans are much more likely to be poor than whites, and the number of single-parent families is much higher among poor people from all ethnic groups. Second, the prejudice and discrimination that have been aimed at African Americans for so many years have hit particularly hard at males. As William Julius Wilson has shown, a deteriorating labor market for young African American males has produced a significant decline in the number of desirable marriage partners for African American women.[17] Moreover, the high death rate among young African American males and the fact that they are more likely to be incarcerated than members of other groups means that there are simply fewer marriage partners available to African American women.[18]

Despite their increasing numbers, there has been far less research on Latino families in North America. Although it is widely thought that Latinos tend to have larger extended family networks and a tendency toward traditional gender roles, much more research on these issues is needed. One thing we do know is that there is a major demographic split among different Latino groups in North America. The family pattern of Puerto Rican Americans tends to resemble that of African Americans, with high birthrates among single women and a larger number of single-parent families. However, the demographics of Mexican and Cuban American families tends to more closely resemble the pattern among European Americans.[19]

QUICK REVIEW

Describe traditional family structure and how it has changed over the past century.
How does the family differ among different classes and ethnic groups?

FAMILY PROBLEMS

The modern family is certainly not in as bad shape as some commentators claim, but it is still plagued by a host of serious problems. In this section we examine five of today's most important family issues: divorce, births outside of marriage, violence, child rearing, and the inequalities of family life.

DIVORCE

The twentieth century saw a dramatic increase in divorce rates. In 1920 there was one divorce for every seven marriages in the United States. Fifty years later the rate had climbed to one divorce for every three marriages, and today there is almost one divorce for every two marriages. The divorce rate in the United States is now the highest of any major industrialized nation, while Canada's divorce rate is in a rather distant second place.[20] There has, nonetheless, been a decline in the divorce rate since its peak in the early 1980s.[21]

Who Gets Divorced?   In the nineteenth century, divorce was mainly for the wealthy. Great Britain and many American states required a special government act for each divorce, and the poor lacked the influence and money necessary for such decrees. Divorce is now most common among the poor, and the divorce rate declines as education and income increase. As we have seen, one reason for this is the intense economic problems low-income families must face. It is possible, too, that divorce is less frequent among the wealthy because the dissolution of a marriage requires complex and costly arrangements for distributing wealth and income among family members. On the other hand, the availability of travel, entertainment, and domestic help allows the wealthy to handle marital problems more easily.

Age is also an important factor in marital instability. A marriage between teenagers is almost three times more likely to end in divorce than a marriage between partners over 30.[22] The divorce rate also varies significantly among different ethnic groups. African Americans are about 18 percent more likely to be divorced than white Americans.[23]

Most divorces occur fairly soon after marriage. About one in five divorces occurs within the first year of marriage, and the second and third years are the most likely times for a divorce.[24] Considering the length of time it takes to get divorced in many states, this means that many couples begin divorce proceedings shortly after their weddings.

Why the Upward Trend?   The increase in divorce has caused considerable alarm among those who consider it a sign of personal failure or moral weakness. Sociologically, the increase in the divorce rate can be explained only by other social forces, not by the vices or virtues of particular individuals. In the past, marriage was considered a social obligation, and great pressure was placed on the partners to stay together. Divorce was seen as an immoral act, an affront to "decent" people. In fact, public sentiment was so strongly against divorce that it was forbidden in some countries and extremely difficult in many others. Today, divorce carries far less stigma. Since romantic love is now the primary reason people get married, it seems to follow that it is better to separate than to continue in an unhappy marriage.

As attitudes have changed, so have the laws. In 1969, California became the first state to pass a "no-fault" divorce law, and its example has been followed around the nation. Instead of the painful process of proving that one partner did not fulfill the conditions of the marriage contract, the no-fault law allows for divorce by mutual agreement, substantially reducing the time and legal costs required.

Another major factor in the increasing divorce rates is economic. In preindustrial societies, the family was the basic economic unit and people could not easily get by on their own, so divorce was a major economic crisis. As employment moved outside the home, it became far easier to leave an unhappy family situation. These changes have had a particularly strong impact on women. As more and more women began working outside the home, they became less dependent on their husbands and, thus, less likely to stay married to men they had grown to dislike.

Is Divorce a Social Problem?   Oftentimes divorce appears to be the only satisfactory solution to an impossible family situation. Nevertheless, many continue to see divorce as a sign of failure—an admission by the marriage partners that they lack the ability, trust, or stamina to continue an intimate relationship. Many of the problems confronting divorced people stem from such attitudes, and because the parties to a divorce often share them, they feel guilty and ashamed about the breakup of their marriage. Despite the high frequency of divorce, we have not yet developed effective means for helping newly divorced people make the transition to a different lifestyle.

Whatever social support a couple may receive, divorce is likely to cause considerable personal suffering. The termination of an intimate relationship and accompanying feelings of anger and guilt make divorce a painful experience for both partners, even if there are no serious clashes. For two reasons, divorce is likely to be especially difficult for the wife. First, since men generally earn more money than women, a divorce often increases the standard of living of the husband and lowers that of the wife. Second, if there are children, the woman is likely to assume most of the burden of their upbringing. On the other hand, divorced fathers who want custody of their children often find the courts biased against them. Many divorced fathers may find it difficult to maintain close contact with their children if their ex-wives remarry or move away.

Despite the difficulties divorced couples face, the greatest concern centers on the children. Studies of the children of divorce show high levels of fear, grief, sadness, and anger at what has happened to them. They are significantly more likely to drop out of school, be arrested for a crime, or become pregnant as teenagers. Although most children eventually learn to adjust to their new situation, a divorce can have long-lasting effects. People whose parents are divorced are more likely to become divorced themselves, and young adults from disrupted families are twice as likely to have sought out some kind of psychological counseling than children from intact families.[25]

All this does not necessarily mean that children are better off if conflict-ridden marriages are kept together, however. A study of more than 20,000 children by a research team headed by Andrew Cherlin concluded that children whose parents were divorced did indeed suffer significantly more behavioral and psychological problems than other children. However, many of their difficulties actually started long before their parents' divorce, as tensions and conflicts built up within the family.[26] Another study of 1,400 children found that persistent intense conflicts in the home were just as harmful as the breakup of a marriage.[27]

The debate about the effects divorce has on children is an emotional one, and unfounded claims abound on all sides of the issue. At this point, it seems fair to say that the scientific research points to two conclusions. When there are intense and persistent conflicts in the family or one parent is abusive—sexually, physically, or verbally—the children are likely to be better off after a divorce. However, when the partners are merely frustrated or unfulfilled, evidence indicates that the children are more likely to be harmed than helped by a divorce. Such conclusions are only statistical generalizations, however, and may or may not apply to any unique individual family.

Blended Families   The vast majority of people who divorce eventually remarry, and so one result of the increase in divorce has been the creation of a large number of **blended families** in which at least one of the partners lives with the biological children of the other. If these blended families form when the children are still young, the difficulties they encounter will probably be minor, but the older the children, the greater the problems are likely to be. If both partners bring children of their own into the family, conflicts and competition between them are almost inevitable, at least during the adjustment period. And whether or not the partners both have children, they often report difficulties disciplining the children of their spouses—a problem that tends to be particularly severe if the children have already entered adolescence. Research shows that there are higher rates of divorce among couples who have children from a previous marriage than among those who do not, and the highest rates are found among blended families with adolescent children.[28]

The question of whether a parent's remarriage is likely to be harmful to the children is another emotional issue that has been the subject of many conflicting claims. Numerous studies have found that when compared to children from intact nuclear families, stepchildren suffer more psychological problems, such as anxiety and depression, and have more behavioral problems and more trouble in school. However, most of the differences found were not large, and the evidence does not indicate whether stepchildren are worse off than those in single-parent families.[29] One of the most disturbing findings comes from Martin Daly and Margo Wilson, who concluded that children in stepfamilies were far more likely than children from intact two-parent families to suffer physical and sexual abuse.[30] There are numerous possible explanations for the difficulties stepchildren face. The addition of a new adult to the family can be extremely stressful for a child, especially after the painful breakup of the original marriage. Children often have trouble accepting a new parent when what they wanted was to stay with old ones. Blended families may also carry special financial burdens if the husband is supporting children from a previous marriage who are living with their mothers. Moreover, society as a whole is often unsure how to deal with the blended family; children in the same home not only have different parents but have different sets of aunts, uncles, and grandparents. And part of the problem may come from the stepparents themselves, who favor their biological children over those of their spouse or resent the demands their spouse's children place on them.

BIRTHS OUTSIDE OF MARRIAGE

The birthrate among single women has been rising for most of this century, but it soared upward in recent years.[31] The rapid increase is ultimately a result of the same social forces that have transformed so many other aspects of family life—weakening both the consensus about what kinds of behavior are acceptable and the mechanisms by which the rules used to be enforced. Among the more immediate causes, a rise in sexual activity among teenagers combined with failure to use appropriate contraceptive techniques stands out as the major contributor. Although American teenagers have about the same level of sexual activity as teenagers in Western Europe, Americans are less likely to use birth control, and consequently their birthrate is far higher. Another important factor is the growing unwillingness of young couples to marry because the woman becomes pregnant. Studies of births in past centuries, when birthrates among single women were low, show that about 20 to 25 percent of all weddings occurred after the conception of a child.[32] Today, the "shotgun wedding" (in which a pregnant woman's father threatens the man if he does not marry the virgin he has "spoiled") has gone out of style. Unwed mothers are still often condemned, but the stigma has decreased over the years.

In some ways, the social position of an unmarried mother in today's society is very similar to her divorced or widowed counterpart; but in other ways, her problems are likely to be more severe. She is more likely to feel deserted by the father of the child and to lack the emotional support she needs during the difficult months of pregnancy. But the greatest problem of unmarried mothers is that many are not ready for the responsibilities of parenthood. The vast majority of single mothers are under 25 when they give birth, and almost one-third of all such births are to teenagers.[33] These births are seldom planned, and the arrival of an unexpected and often unwanted child may have wrenching consequences for the young mother. Teenagers who become pregnant are more likely than their peers to drop out of school to either work at low-paying jobs or be unemployed. Their children have a higher rate of infant mortality and more serious health problems than those of other mothers. Moreover, families headed by unmarried women are far more likely to be poor because there are fewer working adults in the family, both because women earn less then men and because birthrates are highest among single women who have the lowest levels of education and the fewest marketable skills.[34]

VIOLENCE

Beatings, stabbings, and other assaults are common events in many families. Family violence ranges in severity from the spanking of a troublesome child to cold-blooded murder. (Although spanking a child is usually socially acceptable in the United States, it is still a form of violence and has actually been outlawed in many European nations.) Until quite recently, the problem of family violence remained hidden behind closed doors. Even now, most spouse beaters and child abusers escape punishment.

Violence between Husband and Wife   The relationship between husbands and wives is one of the strongest bonds in our society. It is deep, passionate, and sometimes violent. The exact amount of husband-wife violence is difficult to determine, but it is one of the most common forms of violence. More calls to the police involve family disturbances than all other forms of violent behavior combined.[35] In one of the most comprehensive studies of family violence to date, Murray A. Straus, Richard J. Gelles, and Suzanne K. Steinmetz found that about one-fourth of the husbands and wives they interviewed admitted that there had been violence between them at some time in their marriage. But the researchers themselves feel that their study may have underestimated the rate of husband-wife violence. They estimate that it actually occurs in some form in about half of all marriages.[36]

In many societies, such as those in the Middle East, husbands have traditionally had the legal right to physically punish wives who refuse to accept male authority. Although this practice is no longer approved of in Western culture, it still occurs. Moreover, many victims of spouse abuse find that the police are reluctant to be of much help. Battered women report that abusive husbands are merely given a lecture or taken to jail for the night and are soon back to their threatening ways. There appear to be

Violence is one of the most serious problems plaguing the contemporary family.

two major reasons for this leniency. First, most police officers are male, and they tend to hold a traditional view of gender roles. Even assaults that do serious physical harm to the victim are often seen as private matters that should be resolved by the married partners, not the police. Second, unlike the victims of other violent crimes, a significant percentage of the victims of spouse abuse drop the charges against their attackers, so some officers feel that even a vigorous enforcement effort is likely to produce few results. Growing public attention to this problem and increasing pressure from concerned feminist groups, however, are slowly bringing about a change in police behavior. Moreover, as women gain financial and social equality, they also gain greater power in the home, making it easier for them to demand an end to violence or to leave abusive husbands. Straus, Gelles, and Steinmetz found that families that make their decisions democratically have lower rates of both child abuse and husband-wife violence than families in which one member dominates the other.[37]

The effort of husbands to dominate their wives is, however, only one of many causes of family violence. Although their conclusions are highly controversial, several surveys show that wives are about equally likely to initiate a violent episode as their husbands. Most husbands are bigger and stronger, however, and the wives are far more likely to suffer serious injuries. Although wives are almost as likely to kill their husbands as husbands are to kill their wives,[38] it is widely believed that murderous wives are more likely than murderous husbands to be responding to long-term abuse. There is also a great deal of evidence that a "cycle of violence" can be passed down from one generation to the next. Children raised in violent homes learn that violence is a way to deal with frustration and anger and are therefore much more likely to be violent themselves.[39] (See Chapter 10 for a more complete discussion of the causes of violence.)

Child Abuse   No one really knows how many children are abused by their parents each year. For one thing, there is no clear line between "acceptable" punishment and child abuse. The majority of parents spank their children at some time or other. These parents are certainly not all child abusers. Yet severe and repeated spankings can be just as cruel as other forms of violence. Straus, Gelles, and Steinmetz found that 8 percent of the married couples with children they surveyed admitted having kicked, bitten, or punched their children, and 4 percent admitted having "beaten up" their children.[40] Estimates of the amount of sexual abuse vary even more widely. One comprehensive review of the literature found that estimates of females who were sexually abused as children range from 6 to 64 percent; the range for males was 3 to 31 percent.[41]

Although the figures are shocking, we probably use less violence against our children than our ancestors did. Traditionally, severe physical punishment was considered essential to the learning process. Many parents believed that "if you spare the rod, you spoil the child." In colonial America, a statute even provided for the execution of sons who were "stubborn and rebellious" and failed to follow parental authority. There is, however, no record of such an execution actually taking place. The amount of child abuse reported to the authorities has increased significantly. In 1997, for example, the Los Angeles County office of Children and Family Services reported a 20 percent increase in reported child abuse in a single year.[42] But such statistics probably reflect the growing awareness of the problem and a greater willingness to report it if it occurs, rather than an actual increase in the amount of abuse.[43] A comparison of the rates of child abuse in a survey first done in 1975 and repeated in 1985 found a 47 percent decrease during that ten-year period.[44]

David G. Gil's study of officially reported child abuse cases provides some interesting insights into the type of child who is most likely to be mistreated.[45] Contrary to popular opinion, children of all ages are abused. Abused children are much more likely to come from single-parent homes, and fewer than half of the abused children in Gil's sample were living with their natural fathers. Children from large families are also more likely to be abused. Gil found that the usual indicators of social class—income, occupational prestige, and education—are all negatively related to child abuse. In other words, the lower the parents' social and economic status, the more they tended to abuse their children. The children in Gil's sample were more likely to be abused by their mothers than by their fathers, in part because the fathers were not present in many homes. Many of Gil's findings, such as those concerning the sex and class differences in child abuse, were also confirmed by Straus, Gelles, and Steinmetz's survey mentioned earlier.

There are many explanations for child abuse. Psychologists tend to picture child abusers as people who have severe emotional problems. The typical child abuser is described as impulsive, immature, and depressed, with little control over his or her emotions. Social workers are inclined to see environmental stress as the most important cause of child abuse. They note that an unwanted pregnancy, desertion by the husband, or unemployment and poverty put special pressures on a parent that may result in child abuse. Moreover, with the average hours worked per year higher for American men and women than in any other country in the world (see Chapter 2), psychologists have found growing levels of stress among American adults. Social psychologists have also discovered that most child abusers learned that behavior when they were abused during their own childhood (see Chapter 10); that is, they themselves were beaten when they were young.

Many sociologists argue that child abuse is so common in America because the physical punishment of children is condoned and even encouraged. They call for laws that would make it a crime to inflict physical punishment on children, as has already been done in Sweden and some other European countries. It should be remembered, however, that child abuse can be psychological as well as physical—countless parents cause severe emotional damage to their children without ever being physically violent.

CHILD REARING

Raising children is the most critical function of the family. The vitality and even the survival of a society depend on how effectively the family does this job. The way we rear our children can affect many things about a society, such as the strength of its economy, the crime rates, and even its tendencies toward war or peace. In a sense, every society is only about 20 years from extinction, for if it fails to socialize its children for that length of time, it will cease to exist. Of course, this is extremely unlikely to happen, but it is clear that there are many dysfunctional families in which the relationship between parents and children is disturbed, and even "healthy" families often fail to socialize their children effectively.

Child rearing has never been an easy task, but it is particularly difficult today. Our nuclear family system gives parents almost exclusive responsibility for the support and upbringing of children. If one parent is unable to perform his or her duties, the family is almost automatically plunged into crisis since there are usually no other relatives in the household to help out. There is, moreover, a growing feeling among parents that our society has turned its back on its children. School lunch programs have been cut back, health care has become more difficult for poor families to get, and welfare benefits for mothers with dependent children have been reduced. In 2000, 16.2 percent of children under 18 were below the poverty line. This figure is down from 21.9 percent of children under 18 living below the poverty line in 1992, but it is still extremely high, especially compared to other industrialized nations. Figures show, for example, that European nations have poverty rates for children that are only one-third as high as in the United States.[46]

The increasing number of single-parent families (see Figure 3.2 on page 84) has made many of the problems of child rearing even more difficult. Financially, most single-parent families are always on thin ice, for the majority of them are headed by women, and women on the average earn far less money than men. Moreover, only 66 percent of children in single-parent families had parents who had finished high school, while this was the case for 85 percent of children living in two-parent households.[47] To make matters worse, single parents usually have to pay for child care out of their meager earnings. Child-support payments may help, but only a little more than half of all single parents have been awarded support payment, and about half of those receive only partial payments or nothing at all.[48] As a result, 28 percent of all single-parent families headed by women lived below the poverty line in 2000.[49]

Another common child-rearing problem in single-parent families concerns parental supervision and guidance. The plain fact is that single parents often do not

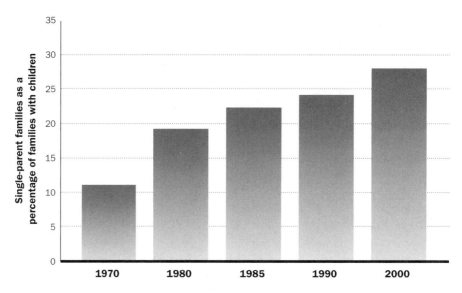

FIGURE 3.2   SINGLE-PARENT FAMILIES

The percentage of families with children that are headed by a single parent has shown a sharp increase in the past three decades.

Source: U.S. Bureau of the Census, *Statistical Abstract of the United States,* 1996 (Washington, D.C.: U.S. Government Printing Office, 1996), p. 62; U.S. Bureau of the Census, *Statistical Abstract of the United States,* 2000 (Washington, D.C.: U.S. Government Printing Office, 2000), p. 58.

have enough time to meet all the demands of their breadwinning and child-rearing roles and still maintain much of a personal life. As a result, their children sometimes do not receive as much guidance and emotional support as they need. After reviewing 50 different studies, L. Edward Wells and Joseph H. Rankin concluded that children from single-parent families are about 10 to 15 percent more likely to become delinquent than children from two-parent families with similar social characteristics.[50] The relationship between discipline and delinquency is not, however, a simple one. Studies show that parental discipline can promote delinquency when it is too strict as well as when it is too lax.[51]

Whatever its causes, there is strong evidence that children raised by a single mother (there is much less research on father-only homes) are at a disadvantage when compared to children from two-parent homes. In addition to the higher rates of delinquency already mentioned, children from mother-only homes score lower on academic achievement tests, get lower grades, and are more likely to drop out of high school. They have lower earnings as young adults and are more likely to be poor. They have higher rates of divorce, and women from mother-only homes are more likely to have a child without being married.[52] Remember, however, that these are only statistical generalizations and they don't paint an accurate picture of all single-parent homes.

A great deal of concern has also been expressed about the children of families in which both parents work outside the home, but although working mothers often bear extra burdens, the fear that maternal employment somehow harms children is apparently unfounded. After an extremely large number of studies and several comprehensive reviews of the literature, the general conclusion is that there are no major differences between the children of mothers who work and those who don't—at least in terms of the characteristics usually tested, such as intelligence, personal development, school achievement, and social adjustment. There is, however, some evidence of a slight weakening of the mother-child bond.[53]

Dual-earner families do have some special difficulties in raising their children, however. The biggest problem reported by working parents, whether single or married, is the lack of accessible high-quality child care. According to the Bureau of the Census, almost one-fourth of the preschoolers with working mothers are cared for in day-care centers, and about an equal number by family day-care providers or other unrelated persons. The other half of those children are more or less evenly divided between those who are cared for by their fathers and those cared for by other relatives.[54] The data indicate that at least 13 percent of the children from families with working mothers are given no adult supervision during some substantial part of the day, including 8 percent of grade school children.[55]

Even for the children who are supervised, however, there are still serious concerns about the quality of the care they receive. The Children's Defense Fund estimates that 43 percent of the day care provided for children outside the home is unregulated (that is, not supervised by a government agency), and other studies show that even licensed day-care centers often provide inadequate care. Not surprisingly, one survey found that about half of all the mothers with children in day-care centers said they would have picked a different center if one had been available.[56] Studies of family day-care providers indicate that they have their own serious problems. One study found that 41 percent of family day-care providers had no planned activities for the children and that only half the children showed signs of trust or attachment to the people who provided their day care.[57] Another serious problem with our current system of child care is the cost. The average poor family with a working mother spends almost one-fourth of its total income on child care.[58]

A clear indicator of the difficulties modern families have with child rearing is the increasing number of **runaways**. The General Accounting Office of the United States estimates that 1 million young people run away from home every year. Although most return within a few days, those who do not are likely to suffer serious hardships. Both males and females may turn to crimes such as prostitution and shoplifting to support themselves. They are also more likely to be the victims of sexual abuse, and their rates of alcoholism and drug addiction are extremely high. In some cases, however, the label of "runaway" that is applied to these young people is quite misleading. A substantial number are actually **pushouts** who are forced to fend for themselves because their families no longer want them.

WORK AND FAMILY INEQUALITY

Our ideas about the proper roles of wives and husbands have been undergoing some remarkable changes, and the redefinition of traditional roles has placed considerable stress on the modern family. In the past, each partner in a marriage generally had a clear-cut idea of what to expect from the other, but today a bride and groom can no longer assume that their conceptions of their respective roles coincide, and considerable compromise is required to resolve such differences. More women work outside the home and expect an equal share of the decision-making power within the family. Some husbands, socialized to see women as subordinates, consider these demands a threat to their masculinity, particularly if their wives have more success in their careers than they do. Even when both partners accept the ideal of sexual equality, career conflicts can still arise. For example, one partner may be offered an important promotion that requires a move that would be disastrous to the career of the other, or one parent may have to miss a critical assignment at work because of a sick child.

The dramatic increase in the number of wage-earning women often leads us to forget about the other essential type of family labor: housework. Although many people assume that having fewer children and the use of modern home appliances have greatly reduced the total amount of housework, that has not proved to be true. New expectations for sparkling dishes and dust-free tabletops have raised the standards that homemakers strive to meet. Some technological "advances" have in fact created more rather than less work. The classic example is the automobile, which produced a new category of household work (driving) that slowly demanded more and

Today, more couples are sharing childrearing responsibilities by allowing each member to perform the tasks he or she does best—regardless of sexual stereotypes.

more time. As the car became increasingly common, door-to-door peddlers, home delivery by retail stores, and house calls by physicians were sharply curtailed, and automobile-based suburbanization placed schools and jobs farther away from home. These changes transformed the car from a convenience to a costly necessity.[59] Many of the other labor-saving devices women worked for actually saved less time than was required to earn the money to pay for them. Despite the dreams of science fiction writers that technology would create a society in which most of us would not have to work at all, polls show that that the amount of leisure time available to the average American has actually declined in recent years.

The growing shortage of leisure time makes the division of labor in the family a particularly important issue. In general, men work more hours outside the home and perform automobile and home repairs and other heavy household tasks. Women tend to work fewer hours outside the home but generally do most of the work that needs to be done around the house, including child care, cooking, cleaning, and laundry. How fairly are the family burdens divided? Research shows that when the husband is the only wage earner, the wife works about the same number of hours in the house as he does on the job, but since he also does some work at home, the husband puts in more total hours of work than does his wife. In dual-earner families, however, a sharp increase in the wife's duties reverses this relationship: Although the husbands of working wives generally do a little more around the house and more services are purchased from outsiders, the total number of hours the wife must work is greatly increased.[60] Working mothers are especially likely to report feeling heavily burdened by their wide-ranging responsibilities.[61]

QUICK REVIEW

Describe the trends in divorce and the reasons for them.
Is divorce a serious social problem?
What are the special problems faced by blended families?
Why has the percentage of children born to single women increased so much?
What are the causes of family violence?
What are the most serious problems we face in raising our children?
How have the family roles and responsibilities of women and men changed?

SOLVING THE PROBLEMS OF THE FAMILY

In one sense there are as many responses to family problems as there are families. Because each family is unique, its members respond to their problems in unique ways. In another sense, however, family problems are institutional, and therefore they affect us all. Despite its weaknesses, the nuclear family system is very much in tune with the economic and social institutions of modern industrial society. For this reason, most reformers have chosen to direct their efforts toward strengthening the nuclear family rather than trying to reestablish the larger family units typical of the extended family system.

BETTER PREPARATION

One way of strengthening the nuclear family is to see that people are better prepared for partnership. Perhaps the easiest way to achieve this goal is simply to discourage people from taking a partner too early, so that they are older and more mature when they do try to form a lasting commitment. Census Bureau figures show that the average couple is about four years older at marriage now than couples were in 1956.[62] Publicizing the difficulties of forming a commitment too early might encourage this trend and stop some young couples from marrying, but it is far from certain that such a campaign would be effective.

Another approach is to prepare the young for family responsibilities through educational programs in high schools and colleges. Although such programs encourage realistic expectations about adult life and teach techniques for dealing with domestic problems, this approach has not been notably successful. A few hours of classroom instruction are not likely to change long-held attitudes and expectations about marriage.

All educational efforts do not have to change deep-seated attitudes in order to be successful, however. One of the most serious family problems is unwanted pregnancy among teenage girls. More effective sex education programs in the schools could go a long way toward solving this crisis; but to be effective, such educational programs must be combined with a well-publicized effort to provide unrestricted access to birth control services for teenagers who need them (see Chapter 12). Many people, however, advocate restricting rather than expanding young people's access to birth control. Attempts are also being made to restrict the availability of abortion to teenagers and mature women alike. Since about 45 percent of all teenage pregnancies end in abortion, the complete elimination of abortion in the United States could be expected to nearly double the birthrate among American teenagers.[63] (See the "Debate" in Chapter 5 for arguments for and against the prohibition of abortion.)

An increasing number of young couples are living together before deciding on marriage. While some people feel that this practice promotes stronger marriages and others feel it is harmful, the overall effects of this trend are still unclear. A four-year study by M. D. Newcomb and R. R. Bentler found no differences in marital satisfaction or divorce rates between couples who "cohabited" before marriage and those who did not,[64] and J. Jacques and K. J. Chason found no differences in the way couples described their marriages when they compared couples who had lived together before marrying with those who had not.[65]

REDUCING FAMILY CONFLICT

Ideally, the family is a cooperative, trouble-free unit that shelters its members from the stresses of the outside world, but real families seldom, if ever, achieve this ideal. Periodic episodes of tension and conflict are the rule, not the exception. Indeed, open disagreements and discussions are an excellent way of resolving the differences that inevitably develop among family members. Families that avoid conflict by ignoring unpleasant subjects or conflict-laden situations are weaker, not stronger, for it. As feelings of resentment build, such families are likely to break up or deteriorate into an empty shell, in which family members carry out the obligations of their roles

Family counseling has become an increasingly popular response to the problems that arise in contemporary family life.

but without mutual love, affection, or understanding. Thus, an open and honest airing of disagreements is an excellent way to manage family conflict and keep it within acceptable bounds.

Sometimes, however, differences become so great that they cannot be resolved within the family unit. Friends and relatives can be helpful, but there has also been a significant increase in the number of people seeking professional counseling for family problems. When there are fundamental conflicts between personalities, attitudes, or lifestyles, even the best professional counseling may prove futile, but counseling can be extremely helpful for couples with specific, limited problems. For example, the sex therapy pioneered by the famous research team of William Masters and Virginia Johnson has proved very effective because it deals with specific problems, such as impotence or frigidity, that respond to straightforward treatment.[66] Counseling programs are also being established to deal with family violence. A number of these programs have apparently achieved significant reductions in violence among their clients, but sufficient scientific evidence has not yet been collected to make a final judgment on their effectiveness.

CHANGING SOCIAL EXPECTATIONS

Professional help can be beneficial to troubled families, but many of our most serious problems are rooted in the way the family is defined by our society as a whole. Traditional family patterns have often served to subordinate women and deprive them of the power to control their own destinies. As a result, many women feel frustrated and angry about their position in the family, while traditional role expectations blind their husbands to the problem. Moreover, the traditional division of labor in the family may require both men and women to do work for which they are poorly suited. Some families that would function more smoothly if the husband stayed home to care for the children continue more traditional arrangements because of our social stereotypes of a "house husband" as a loafer or a "wimp." It therefore seems likely that the nuclear family system will be strengthened by the continuing growth of gender equality. In such families the division of labor is based on the skills and abilities of each partner rather than on their gender, and decision-making power and the workload are shared equally. Many families already function in this manner, but traditional standards lead some people to brand any deviation from the customary patterns as wrong and unnatural, and the entire family system is weakened by this attitude. Public opinion polls show that the ideal of gender equality is gaining increasing acceptance, although a significant number of people still strongly believe in the traditional standards.

In addition to the contradictions and inequality so common in contemporary culture's view of the family, popular culture also creates unrealistic expectations for both partners. Movies, television, books, and everyday conversation encourage us to look at partnership as a romantic adventure in which two people meet, fall in love, and "live happily ever after." Romantic love is given an almost mystical power to solve our problems and to provide our very meaning for living. Given such towering expectations, it is not surprising that even people in seemingly successful partnerships often feel dissatisfied and unfulfilled. In sharp contrast, cultures based on the extended family see marriage as part of a network of social obligations and commitments, and they view romantic love as a rather subversive force. The solution to our family problems is certainly not to abandon the ideal of romantic love and return to the old views. But we do need to temper our romantic ideals with the realization that a successful family also requires commitment, responsibility, and a lot of hard work.

HELPING PARENTS

Americans have always seen the family as something private and personal and none of the government's business. Perhaps for that reason, the United States lags far behind the European nations, and even its Canadian neighbor, in providing basic services for parents and their children. Unfortunately, the changes that have transformed the family—the breakup of the extended family, the huge increase in the numbers of mothers who work outside the home, and the explosive growth in single-parent families—have created serious new problems that demand government attention.

The kinds of birth-control programs discussed in Chapter 12 could significantly reduce the number of single teenage mothers, if such efforts won vigorous government backing. Whatever measures we take, however, the number of single-parent families is likely to keep increasing in the immediate future, and much more needs to be done to deal with their special problems. Women head most single-parent families, and an effective program to eliminate sexual discrimination in the workplace would go a long way toward reducing the acute financial problems experienced by many of these families. To reach all needy families, the government must also reverse the current trend and begin increasing rather than decreasing the welfare benefits for poor families, whether headed by one or two parents. The United States provides less support for poor families with children than any other industrial nation, and as a result has a far higher rate of childhood poverty.[67] (See Chapter 6.)

One program that would benefit many families is the creation of a network of government-supported preschool and day-care programs. In such countries as France, Belgium, Italy, and Denmark, the vast majority of children are already in some kind of state-funded preschool program. Not only could such broadly based programs be a financial lifesaver for low-income families, but increased government supervision could help ensure that the highest possible standards are met for the care of children from all economic backgrounds—thus helping relieve the nagging fears so many parents have about what is happening to their children while they are away at work. Opposition to such a plan has nonetheless been strong. Critics argue that government agencies are poor substitutes for parents and point to the bureaucratic indifference and coldness that are typical of many orphanages, institutions for delinquents, and schools. They fear that day-care centers will harm children by depriving them of parental love. Advocates of government-sponsored day-care centers respond that children in such facilities still have ample contact with their parents and that properly run centers enrich children's lives rather than deprive them. Moreover, they point out that millions of children are already in day care and would benefit from government funding and regulation of the industry.

Rather than restricting their aid to the poorest and most desperate families, 67 countries around the world, including Canada and all of northern and western Europe, provide some kind of direct payment, known as a child or family allowance, to help parents with their heavy financial burdens. In most countries, all families are given a monthly cash payment based on the number of children they have. Typically, the amount is between 5 and 10 percent of the average wage, but it is higher in some nations. Although wealthy families end up paying this money back in taxes, the family allowance can be a significant aid to middle- and lower-class parents.

QUICK REVIEW

What are the best ways we can respond to our family problems?

SOCIOLOGICAL PERSPECTIVES ON PROBLEMS OF THE FAMILY

Concern for the "decaying" family is nothing new. Observers dating back as far as ancient Greece have bemoaned the deterioration of the family, complaining of everything from youthful rebelliousness to a breakdown of traditional moral values. But these age-old complaints have taken on new urgency in our times. The rapid change that the family has undergone since the industrial revolution has touched off public anxiety and led to considerable debate among the proponents of the different sociological theories.

THE FUNCTIONALIST PERSPECTIVE

Functional analysis of human society has led many sociologists to conclude that the family is the most basic social institution. Not only is it found in one form or another in all societies, but no other institution is responsible for performing as many important tasks. Most of us begin and end our lives in the family context, and we are seldom far from its influence during the years in between.

Functionalists agree that the family's most vital function is to provide replacements for members who have died or are disabled. Such replacement has four aspects. First, the family provides for reproduction by creating a stable mating relationship that supports the mother during pregnancy and the children during the critical early years of life. Second, the family socializes the young. It is in the family that the child learns how to think, talk, and follow the customs, behavior, and values of his or her society. The family is therefore an important agency of social control. Third, the family provides support and protection for its children. The family must satisfy a wide range of emotional needs as well as physical needs for food and shelter. Fourth, the family is a primary mechanism of status ascription. Each child is given a social status on the basis of the family into which he or she is born. Thus, children of the wealthy are automatically upper class, while children of low-income families are assigned to the bottom rungs of the social ladder. The family also performs significant functions for adults. As a primary group of great importance, it provides emotional support and reinforcement and physical care in times of illness and old age. The family also transfers wealth from parents to young children and, later, from older children to aging parents.

Functionalists see the historical roots of our family problems in the social disorganization caused by industrialization and the Western value of individualism. The extended family is well suited to the agricultural societies in which it is most commonly found, but it doesn't work very well in modern industrial societies. Economic changes brought on by the industrial revolution broke up the extended family system and forced a shift to the nuclear family, though this has happened to a far greater degree in Western societies than in Asian societies such as Japan. Even cultures that never had a strong tradition of extended families underwent sweeping changes in their family systems. With the declining importance of farming, the family lost its role as the basic unit of economic production. Instead of a social duty and financial necessity, marriage became a voluntary state based on mutual love and emotional support. More recently, the increase in the number of women in the workforce and the ideal of sexual equality are bringing about another realignment of family structure. The resultant disorganization and the structural weaknesses caused by the small size of the nuclear family have made it increasingly difficult for the family to perform its functions efficiently. From the functionalist perspective, the present family system is in trouble because it has not had enough time to adapt to these ceaseless social and economic changes.[68]

Functionalists agree that the prosperity and even the survival of contemporary society depend on the strength of its family system. However, functional analysis does not lead to any single proposal for improvement. One possibility calls for other agencies—such as day-care centers and schools—to assume more of the family's functions, permitting the family to handle its remaining functions more effectively. Another approach is to promote trial marriages as a test of compatibility and easier divorce for marriages that fail. However, many functionalists fear that such proposals would contribute to the erosion of the traditional family and the vital functions it performs. These functionalists therefore recommend a return to the values associated with the traditional nuclear family, such as a stronger stigma on divorce and more restrictions on sexual behavior.

THE CONFLICT PERSPECTIVE

Many conflicts of values and attitudes affect the modern family. People who hold traditional values emphasize the importance of a stable family environment for child rearing and thus reject the idea of divorce; modernists see personal happiness as the most important goal of family life and believe that a child will suffer more from an unhappy home than from a "broken" one. Traditionalists are convinced that sexual relations should be restricted to the married couple; modernists advocate greater sexual freedom. Modernists condemn traditional attitudes toward women as exploitative and unjust, and they support full sexual equality; traditionalists are likely to believe that male dominance is based on innate differences between the sexes and that any other sort of family relationship is unnatural. Traditionalists see the increase in the number of families in which both parents work as a threat to children's welfare; modernists see women's increasing financial power as a positive development that may help create more egalitarian families and a more just society. Traditionalists insist that marriage and child rearing be strictly limited to heterosexual couples, while modernists feel that any committed couple who wish to marry should be allowed to do so.

Conflict theorists are also concerned about the effects that class conflict has on the family. The poor have significantly higher rates of divorce, births to single women, and overall family instability than do other classes, and conflict theorists attribute these conditions to exploitation of the poor by the upper classes. For instance, many men cannot get decent jobs because the financial pressures of a life of poverty and the low quality of local public schools prevented them from learning basic reading, writing, and mathematical skills. Because these men cannot provide their families with the standard of living our society has led everyone to expect, they come to see themselves as failures. This sense of failure may in turn lead to a host of other problems, including the breakup of the family, alcoholism, and violence against other family members.[69]

In the eyes of most conflict theorists, the solution to family problems will come only with greater equality, both within the family and in society as a whole. They recommend that the government undertake a vigorous program to eliminate occupational discrimination against women and minorities and make a serious effort to reduce unemployment and the overall levels of economic inequality in our society (see Chapters 2, 6, 7, and 8 for more details). They also support proposals for a nationwide system of government-funded day-care centers for children and shelters for the victims of physical abuse.

THE FEMINIST PERSPECTIVE

Friedrich Engels, the German political philosopher who co-authored *The Communist Manifesto* with Karl Marx, long ago wrote that the oppression of women in the family was the original form of human exploitation, and present-day feminists still agree. From the feminist perspective, the traditional family is an exploitative institution organized for the benefit of the husband at the expense of his wife. The husband has the power, prestige, and independence, while the wife has to do the dirty work and carry out the subordinate role. The traditional marriage ceremony commanded the wife to love, honor, and *obey* her husband, while no such demands are made on the man. Even the word *family* reflects this fundamental inequality, for it comes from the Latin word famulus, which means "servant"—among whom were a man's wife, children, and household workers.[70]

While almost all feminists agree about the exploitative nature of the traditional family, there is considerable disagreement about what we should do about it. A few reject the whole concept of family as an outdated carryover from patriarchal times, but most feminists envision a new kind of family structure based on complete equality between the sexes. Such radical equality might well involve the complete elimination of gender roles. But whether or not that occurs, the division of labor in the family would be based on the individual abilities and inclinations of the people involved and not on a set of stereotyped social expectations. Women would not be expected to be nurturant and compliant, men would be freed of the expectation that they be responsible for the lion's share of the financial burdens, and same-sex marriages would be as accepted as any other kind. Of course, such a family system could flourish only in an egalitarian society committed to eliminating sexism from its culture and discrimination from its economy.

THE INTERACTIONIST PERSPECTIVE

Interactionists pay particular attention to the process of socialization in the maintenance of a healthy society, and of course it is the family that usually performs that task. Interactionists have linked faulty socialization to problems ranging from mental disorders to juvenile delinquency. Clearly, some families socialize their children to play conformist roles, whereas other families encourage children to behave in ways that others consider indecent and even illegal. Problems in the process of socialization, however, are far more likely to arise from neglect and indifference or, in more extreme cases, from hostility and even violence that parents direct at their children. Interactionists point out that the kinds of responses we receive from our family during early socialization, whether positive or negative, are critical in forming the self-concept that guides our behavior.

For adults, the nuclear family's most critical social psychological role is to provide emotional support and comfort. The family is the only shelter many people have from the relentless demands of modern civilization; it is the one place where an individual can develop a sense of stability and belonging—and for that reason, dissension and conflict within the family can have devastating psychological consequences for all its members.

Interactionists point to several possible ways to create the kind of stable, emotionally supportive families that do an effective job of socializing their children and providing security and comfort for all their members. One common problem is that the ideal of romantic love is given so much importance in our culture that young people approach marriage expecting more of each other than either can possibly give. Too often they end up bitter and disappointed when their romantic fantasies fail to come true. More realistic expectations, encouraged by schools and the mass media, may be one way of solving the problem. Another approach to building more supportive families is to encourage a wider network of kin and friends to share the emotional burdens of family life. Such family structures might also do a better job of socializing children. With more adults involved in the socialization of each child, the harmful effects of an incompetent or abusive parent could be neutralized more easily.

QUICK REVIEW

Examine our family problems from the perspectives of the functionalist, conflict, feminist, and interactionist theories. What do you think are the strengths and weakness of each theory?

SUMMARY

The institution of family is found in all societies, but in many different forms. The two main types of family are the nuclear family, which consists of only a married couple or single parent and children, and the extended family, which usually includes many more relatives.

In the past, there was a strong consensus about what a "normal" family was, along with great social pressures to uphold those ideals. As the economy changed and the family farm lost its role as the primary unit of economic production, society developed a diverse mosaic of family patterns. The number of single people sharply increased, more wives went to work, and the average number of children in each family declined. Divorce became far more common, and there was a significant increase in the birthrate among single women. As a result, there was also a large increase in the percentage of single-parent families.

Many problems are associated with divorce, including personal stress, family instability, and increased difficulty in child rearing, but it is not at all clear that divorce is worse than the alternative of continuing a conflict-ridden marriage. Unmarried mothers who keep their children have many of the same problems experienced by other single-parent families, but because so many of these mothers are teenagers, they are generally less prepared for the changes a baby brings into their lives.

Although there are no dependable statistics, there is no doubt that violence is a common way of settling disputes between domestic partners and leads to a substantial number of injuries and homicides every year. Another form of family violence, child abuse, is even more dangerous because the victims are too young to take action to protect themselves. Many explanations of child abuse have been advanced, including emotional disturbances in the parents and the transmission of child abuse from one generation to the next through a process of learning.

Child rearing has always been a difficult task, but the instability of the modern nuclear family and the common lack of sufficient external support make it even harder. The single-parent family is likely to have the most serious problems because only one adult must carry all the burdens traditionally divided among at least two people.

Another source of strain in the modern family is the changing expectations about the behavior of husbands and wives. Increasing numbers of women have gone to work outside the home, and because there are now a variety of alternatives to traditional gender roles, the expectations of husband and wife may conflict. One common problem is that the burdens of housework are not fairly reallocated to take into account the time working women must put in on the job.

Many proposals have been made for resolving problems in the family. One approach would strengthen the existing nuclear family system through education, marriage counseling, and a reduction in unwanted births among teenage girls. Sexual equality and greater fairness within the marriage are also frequent suggestions. Many proposals have been made to help parents with the difficult task of child rearing, including greater financial assistance from the government and the creation of a nationwide system of government-sponsored day care.

Sociologists of the functionalist school are convinced that problems of the family are symptoms of social disorganization caused by rapid social change. Industrialization greatly weakened traditional family structure, but no consensus has emerged about what kind of family system should replace it. Conflict theorists note the many conflicting values and beliefs about modern family life and point to them as a major source of tensions. They also stress the notion that many problems, from divorce to family violence, arise because society allows the powerful to profit at the expense of the weak. Feminists believe the problems of the family arise from the suppression and exploitation of women, and they call for a family system based on complete equality of the genders. Interactionists are concerned about the nuclear family's role in socialization and about the long-term impact of the definitions, attitudes, and values we learn during this process.

QUESTIONS FOR CRITICAL THINKING

You don't have to watch TV very long or read a lot of books and newspapers to find out that people are very worried about the future of the family. Why are people so concerned? Look at the history and the current conditions of the family and draw your own conclusions about the future of the contemporary family.

In this chapter we have described many different family patterns—the patriarchal extended family, the traditional nuclear family, the egalitarian nuclear family, and so forth. Evaluate the strengths and weaknesses of each different type of family. Which type of family would you rather live in? Why?

KEY TERMS

bilateral
blended family
dual-earner family
extended family
monogamy
nuclear family

patriarchal system
polygamy
pushout
romantic love
runaway
single-parent family

NOTES

1. George P. Murdock, "World Ethnographic Sample," *American Anthropologist* 59 (1957): 664–687.
2. For an analysis of the preindustrial family, see Randall Collins and Scott Coltrane, *Sociology of Marriage and the Family: Gender, Love, and Property*, 3rd ed. (Chicago: Nelson-Hall, 1991), pp. 80–119.
3. Robert Slagter and Harold Kerbo, *Modern Thailand* (New York: McGraw-Hill, 2000).
4. U.S. Bureau of the Census, *Women in the United States: A Profile* (2000).
5. U.S. Bureau of the Census, *Statistical Abstract of the United States, 2000* (U.S. Government Printing Office, 2000), p. 51.
6. U.S. Bureau of the Census, *Statistical Abstract of the United States, 2000* (U.S. Government Printing Office, 2000), p. 58.
7. James C. Coleman, *Intimate Relationships, Marriage, and Family* (Indianapolis: Bobbs-Merrill, 1984), p. 335.
8. U.S. Bureau of the Census, *Statistical Abstract*, 2000, p. 408.
9. Joseph Harry, "Gay Male and Lesbian Relationship," in Eleanor Macklin and Roger Rubin, eds., *Contemporary Families and Alternative Lifestyles* (Beverly Hills, CA: Sage), p. 225.
10. Philip Blumstein and Pepper Schwartz, *American Couples: Money, Work, Sex* (New York: Morrow, 1983).
11. See, for example, Randall Collins, "Women and Men in the Class Structure," *Journal of Family Issues* 9 (March 1988): 27–50; Rayna Rapp, "Family and Class in Contemporary America," in Barrie Thorne and Marilyn Yalom, eds., *Rethinking the Family: Some Feminist Questions* (New York: Longman, 1982), pp. 168–187; Susan A. Ostrander, *Women of the Upper Class* (Philadelphia: Temple University Press, 1984); Lillian Rubin, *World of Pain: Life in the Working-Class Family* (New York: Basic Books, 1976); Collins and Coltrane, *Sociology of Marriage and the Family*, pp. 187–230; and Maxine Bacca Zinn and D. Stanley Eitzen, *Diversity in Families*, 3rd ed. (New York: HarperCollins, 1993), pp. 88–109.
12. U.S. Bureau of the Census, *Poverty in the United States*, 1999.
13. U.S. Bureau of Census, *Statistical Abstract*, 2000, p. 56.
14. U.S. Bureau of the Census, *Statistical Abstract*, 2000, p. 65.
15. William L. Rogers and Garland Thornton, "Changing Patterns of First Marriage in the United States," *Demography* 22 (1985): 265–279.
16. Robert Joseph Taylor, Linda M. Chatters, M. Belinda Tucker, and Edith Lewis, "Developments in Research on Black Families: A Decade Review," in Alan Booth, ed., *Contemporary Families* (Minneapolis: National Council on Family Relations, 1991), pp. 275–296.
17. William Julius Wilson, *The Truly Disadvantaged: The Inner City, the Underclass, and Public Policy* (Chicago: University of Chicago Press, 1987).
18. Taylor, et al., "Developments in Research on Black Families."
19. William A. Vega, "Hispanic Families in the 1980s: A Decade of Research," in Booth, ed., *Contemporary Families*, pp. 297–306.
20. Andrew L. Shapiro, *We're Number One: Where America Stands—and Falls—in the New World Order* (New York: Vintage, 1992), p. 36.
21. U.S. Bureau of the Census, *Statistical Abstract*, 2000, p. 101.

22. Collins and Coltrane, *Sociology of Marriage and the Family*, pp. 457–459.
23. U.S. Bureau of the Census, *Statistical Abstract*, 1996, p. 54.
24. Collins and Coltrane, *Sociology of Marriage and the Family*, p. 454.
25. David H. Demo and Alan C. Acock, "The Impact of Divorce on Children," in Booth, ed., *Contemporary Families*, pp. 162–191; Bacca Zinn and Eitzen, *Diversity in Families*, pp. 383–386; Collins and Coltrane, *Sociology of Marriage and the Family* (1991), pp. 475–477; Judith S. Wallerstein and Joan Kelley, *Surviving the Breakup: How Children and Parents Cope with Divorce* (New York: Basic Books, 1980); Barbara DaFoe Whitehead, "Dan Quayle Was Right," *Atlantic Monthly*, April 1993, pp. 47–84.
26. Andrew J. Cherlin et al., "Longitudinal Studies of Effects of Divorce on Children in Great Britain and the United States," *Science Journal* 252 (June 1991): 1386–1389.
27. James L. Peterson and Nicholas Zill, "Marital Disruption, Parent–Child Relationships and Behavior Problems in Children," *Journal of Marriage and the Family* 48 (May 1986): 295–301.
28. Jean Giles-Sims and Margaret Crosbie-Burnett, "Adolescent Power in Stepfather Families: A Test of Normative-Resource Theory," *Journal of Marriage and the Family* 51 (1989): 1065–1078.
29. Nicholas Zill, "Behavior, Achievement and Health Problems Among Children in Stepfamilies," in E. Mavis Hetherington and Josephine D. Arasteh, eds., *Impact of Divorce, Single Parenting, and Stepparenting* (Hillsdale, NJ: Erlbaum, 1988), pp. 325–368; James Brey, "Children's Development During Early Remarriage," in Hetherington and Arasteh, eds., *Impact of Divorce*, pp. 279–298; Mary Burnside et al., "Alcohol Use by Adolescents in Disrupted Families," *Alcoholism: Clinical and Experimental Research* 10 (1986): 274–278; Elsa Ferri, *Stepchildren: A National Study* (Atlantic Highlands, NJ: Humanities, 1984).
30. Martin Daly and Margo Wilson, *Homicide* (New York: Aldine de Gruyter, 1988).
31. U.S. Bureau of the Census, *Statistical Abstract*, 1996, p. 79.
32. William J. Goode, "Family Disorganization," in Robert K. Merton and Robert Nisbet, eds., *Contemporary Social Problems*, 4th ed. (New York: Harcourt Brace Jovanovich, 1976), p. 519.
33. U.S. Bureau of the Census, *Statistical Abstract*, 2000, p. 70.
34. U.S. Bureau of the Census, *Poverty in the United States*, 1999.
35. Andrea Dworkin, "Trapped in a Pattern of Pain Where No One Can Help," *Los Angeles Times*, June 26, 1994, pp. M1, M6.
36. Murray A. Straus, Richard J. Gelles, and Suzanne K. Steinmetz, *Behind Closed Doors: Violence in the American Family* (New York: Doubleday, 1980), pp. 37–60, 148.
37. Ibid., pp. 190–197.
38. Jan E. Stets and Murray A. Straus, "Gender Differences in Reporting Marital Violence and Its Medical and Psychological Consequences," in Murray A. Straus and Richard J. Gelles, eds., *Physical Violence in American Families* (New Brunswick, NJ: Transaction, 1990), pp. 151–166; Collins and Coltrane, *Sociology of Marriage and the Family*, pp. 417–418.
39. Joan Kaufman and Edward Zigler, "Do Abused Children Become Abusive Parents?" *American Journal of Orthopsychiatry* 57 (1987): 186–192; Byron Egeland, Deborah Jacobvitz, and Kathleen Paptola, "Intergenerational Continuity of Abuse," in Richard J. Gelles and Jane Lancaster, eds., *Child Abuse and Neglect: Biosocial Dimensions* (Hawthorne, NY: Aldine de Gruyter, 1987), pp. 255–276; J. Ross Eshleman, *The Family: An Introduction* (Needham Heights, MA: Allyn & Bacon, 1997), pp. 573–577; for a dissenting view, see Mildred Daley Pagelow, *Family Violence* (New York: Praeger, 1984), pp. 67–68, 223–257.
40. Straus, Gelles, and Steinmetz, *Behind Closed Doors*, pp. 190–197.
41. Stephanie D. Peters, Gail E. Wyatt, and David Finkelhor, "Prevalence," in David Finkelhor, ed., *A Sourcebook on Child Sexual Abuse* (Beverly Hills, CA: Sage, 1986), pp. 15–59.
42. "Child Abuse Reports Rise 20% at Agency," *Los Angeles Times*, November 18, 1997.
43. Richard J. Gelles and Jon Conte, "Domestic Violence and Sexual Abuse of Children: A Review of Research in the Eighties," in Booth, ed., *Contemporary Families*, pp. 327–360.
44. Murray A. Straus and Richard J. Gelles, "Societal Change and Change in Family Violence from 1975 to 1985 as Revealed by Two National Surveys," *Journal of Marriage and the Family* 48 (August 1986): 465–479.
45. David G. Gil, *Violence Against Children: Physical Child Abuse in the United States* (Cambridge, MA: Harvard University Press, 1970), pp. 98–99, and "Violence Against Children," *Journal of Marriage and the Family* 33 (1971): 644–648.

46. U.S. Bureau of Census, *Poverty in the United States*, 2000; Kerbo, *Social Stratification and Inequality*.

47. U.S. Bureau of the Census, *Children with Single Parents—How They Fare* (Washington, D.C.: U.S. Government printing Office, 1997).

48. Ibid., p. 385.

49. U.S. Bureau of the Census, *Poverty in the United States*, 2000; Kerbo, *Social Stratification and Inequality*.

50. L. Edward Wells and Joseph H. Rankin, "Families and Delinquency: A Meta-analysis of the Impact of Broken Homes," *Social Problems* 38 (February 1991): 71–93.

51. Larry J. Siegel and Joseph J. Senna, *Juvenile Delinquency: Theory, Practice, and Law*, 3rd ed. (St. Paul, MN: West, 1988), p. 246.

52. For a good review of this literature, see Sara McLanahan and Karen Booth, "Mother-Only Families: Problems, Prospects, and Politics," in Booth, ed., *Contemporary Families*, pp. 405–428.

53. Melissa Healy, "Study Says Day Care Affects Bonding but Not Learning," *Los Angeles Times*, April 4, 1997, pp. A1, A27; Glenna Spitze, "Women's Employment and Family Relations," in Booth, ed., *Contemporary Families*, pp. 381–404; Suzanne M. Bianchi and Daphne Spain, *American Women in Transition* (New York: Russell Sage, 1986); Cheryl D. Hayes and Sheila B. Kamermann, eds., *Children of Working Parents: Experiences and Outcomes* (Washington, D.C.: National Academy, 1983); Thomas C. Taveggia and Ellen M. Thomas, "Latchkey Children," *Pacific Sociological Review* 17 (1974): 27–34.

54. O'Connell Marin, *Who's Minding the Kids? Child Care Arrangements: Fall 1991* (Washington, D.C.: U.S. Government Printing Office, June 1994).

55. Harris, *Inside America*, p. 95; Susan Leach, "1.6 Million Kids in US Are Alone at Home," *Christian Science Monitor*, May 20, 1994, p. 8.

56. Mishel and Bernstein, *The State of Working America*, 1992–93, pp. 413–415.

57. Susan Chira, "Broad Study Says Home-Based Day Care, Even if by Relatives, Often Fails Children," *New York Times*, April 8, 1994, p. A9.

58. Mishel and Bernstein, *The State of Working America*, 1992–93, p. 414.

59. Joan Smith, "Transforming Households: Working-Class Women and Economic Crisis," *Social Problems* 5 (December 1987): 416–436.

60. Janice Peskin, "Measuring Household Production for the GNP," *Family Economics Review* (summer 1982): 10.

61. Harris, *Inside America*, pp. 39–40.

62. Sam Roberts, *Who We Are* (New York: Times Books, 1995), p. 45.

63. See Theodore Caplow, *American Social Trends* (San Diego: Harcourt Brace Jovanovich, 1991), pp. 55–56.

64. M. D. Newcomb and R. R. Bentler, "Cohabitation Before Marriage," *Journal of Marriage and the Family* 41 (February 1980): 597–602.

65. J. Jacques and K. J. Chason, "Cohabitation: Its Impact on Marital Success," *Family Coordinator* 28 (January 1979): 35–39.

66. William Masters and Virginia Johnson, *Human Sexual Inadequacy* (Boston: Little, Brown, 1970).

67. Harold Kerbo, *Social Stratification and Inequality*, Chapter 9.

68. See Nancy Kingsbury and John Scanzoni, "Structural-Functionalism," in Pauline G. Boss et al., *Sourcebook of Family Theories and Methods: A Contextual Approach* (New York: Plenum, 1993), pp. 195–217.

69. Keith Farrington and Ely Chertok, "Social Conflict Theories of the Family," in Boss et al., *Sourcebook of Family Theories and Methods*, pp. 357–381.

70. Roberts, *Who We Are*, p. 33.

CHAPTER 4

PROBLEMS OF EDUCATION

Questions to Consider

Why is an educated population so important to modern societies?

Does our educational system favor rich and middle-class children?

Do our schools do a good job of educating minority students?

Why don't our students score better on standardized achievement tests?

Why are our schools so violent?

How can we improve our educational system?

There was nothing very special about it. As in thousands of other cash-strapped school districts, New York City school officials recently decided to lay off a fourth-grade teacher from Public School 41 in Greenwich Village. The parents, of course, were shocked and upset, especially when they found out that Lauren Zangara's layoff would force a big increase in the average class size—from 26 to 32 students. What was different was that the parents banded together and quickly raised $46,000 to pay Zangara's salary. This seemingly generous offer raised a furor on the school board and left many difficult questions to ponder.

Most of us would agree that there is nothing more important to the future of society than the education of our children, so why do so many of our schools seem to be teetering on the edge of financial disaster? Most people would also agree that all children should get an equal chance for a good education whether their parents are rich or poor, so why is it that the wealthier kids always seem to get all the advantages? Is it fair for the parents of P.S. 41 (from the case study above) to pay for an extra teacher when the parents in many other city schools can't afford to do the same? The school board solved the problem at P.S. 41 in the most politically expedient way. They refused the parents' offer of financial support but found enough of their own money to return Zangara to her classroom. Most conflicts of this kind are not, however, resolved so easily, and the troubling question this case raises remains unresolved.[1]

One thing is clear—we place tremendous faith in education. We expect it to provide a guiding light for the young and to pass on the democratic traditions of our society. Education is seen as a path out of the slums for new immigrants and a ladder out of poverty for the sons and daughters of the disadvantaged; but it is also essential for the "good life" and professional careers so highly valued by the middle class. As technology becomes more sophisticated, even our hopes for our economic future are coming to rest on the quality of our educational system and its graduates.

While our goals and aspirations continue to grow, however, our educational institutions seem to be mired in one crisis after another. Several national reports have issued stinging attacks on the quality of American education, and some corporate leaders complain that our work force is not as well trained as those of nations like Germany and Japan. Every year we lose tens of thousands of good teachers, and many of our students become alienated and rebellious. The poor and minority groups charge that the system has shut them out, while many in the middle class have growing doubts about how well it is serving their needs.

The picture, however, is not quite so bleak. Although our high school students often do not score as well on standardized achievement tests as students in other industrialized nations, it is generally agreed that American universities are the best in the world, and North Americans are more likely to receive a higher education than the citizens of other industrialized countries. For example, while 27 percent of Americans had a university education in 1998, the figure for Germany was 14 percent and for France only 11 percent.[2] Moreover, the history of our educational institutions is one of continual expansion. In 1890, only 7 percent of children of high school age in the United States were in school; today, more than ten times that percentage actually graduate.[3] This growth has transformed education into a big business. Virtually every American receives some formal education, and most people spend a good portion of their lives in school.

What are the reasons for this enormous growth? In small traditional societies, education took place in the home and in children's informal day-to-day association with adults. Training for the few specialized occupations that existed was the responsibility of those who held the jobs, usually members of the same family. Customs and traditions were passed along from one generation to the next without the assistance of schools or professional teachers. In more complex societies, specialized educational organizations developed. In the beginning, these schools mostly trained priests and other religious officials, but secular education soon followed. But, until the nineteenth century, this education was reserved for aristocrats and a few of their important servants. The masses had little need to read or write, and some aristocrats saw any attempt to develop these skills in the lower classes as a threat to their power. It was only a little more than two hundred years ago that the British governor of the colony of Virginia condemned all popular education: "Thank God there are no free schools or printing . . . for learning has brought disobedience and heresy into the world, and printing has divulged them . . . God keep us from both."[4]

It was not until the end of the eighteenth century, when democratic revolutions took place in America and France, that the idea of education for the common people began to catch on. Education for the lower classes became more important as technological advances created the demand for a more highly skilled work force. In fact, historical research has shown that the increasing level of education in the United States was a major cause of its economic growth in the twentieth century.[5] An even earlier contribution to the popularity of mass education came from Protestant religious groups, which placed increasing emphasis on the need for everyone to be able to read the Bible. Yet progress toward equality has been slow, and children of the wealthy continue to receive more and better education than children of the poor.

QUICK REVIEW

Why have our educational institutions expanded so much in the last two centuries?

EQUAL EDUCATIONAL OPPORTUNITY FOR ALL?

In the past, the keys to economic success usually involved such things as the ownership of good farmland or the canny skills of the small-business owner. As formal education and professional training have gained importance, so has the issue of educational equity. Many have charged that our educational system fails to provide equal opportunity for all, and as a result, the poor, immigrants, women, and minorities don't get a fair shot at economic success. To understand this significant issue, we will first examine the role that social class plays in a student's academic achievement, then look at how good a job the educational system does meeting the needs of minority and female students.

SOCIAL CLASS AND ACHIEVEMENT

Grade school teachers and university professors alike can easily see that children of affluent parents tend to do better in school than children of the poor. In fact, numerous studies have found social class to be the most effective predictor of achievement in school.[6] Robert James Parelius and Ann Parker Parelius put it as follows:

> Whether we look at scores on standardized ability or achievement tests, classroom grades, participation in academic rather than vocational high school programs,

involvement in extracurricular activities, number of years of schooling completed or enrollment in or completion of college and professional school, children from more socioeconomically advantaged homes outperform their less affluent peers.[7]

There are two principal explanations for this difference. One focuses on the advantages higher-status children have because they come from home environments in which books, a large vocabulary, and an emphasis on achievement are common. The other holds that the schools themselves are often organized in ways that ignore the educational needs of the poor.

Family Background   Lower-class children live in a very different world from that of middle-class children. The homes of the poor tend to have fewer books, newspapers, and magazines, and the parents have less education. People with low incomes are less likely to read for entertainment; thus, children in low-income homes are less likely to be encouraged to learn that vital skill. Lower-class families are also larger and are more often headed by only one adult. Children in such families frequently receive less parental contact, guidance, and educational encouragement. Another factor is health: poor children are more likely to be undernourished than their middle-class counterparts, and they are sick more days a year.[8] And unhealthy children simply do not learn as well as healthy ones. On the other hand, some of the academic success of children from affluent homes stems from the fact that their parents have higher expectations. A number of surveys have shown that children from wealthy families have higher educational aspirations than children from poorer backgrounds.[9] One reason is that middle-class families are more likely to define the world in a way that sees a college education to be essential for future success and happiness. Some of this difference also reflects a realistic adjustment by poor children to the fact that they have less chance of getting a good education.

Children whose first language is something other than English face obvious obstacles in most North American schools, but language differences among different social classes also have an important impact on educational achievement. **Standard English** is more commonly spoken by African Americans with middle-class backgrounds, while those from the lower class are more likely to speak Black English dialects. Similar language differences are found among Americans from European backgrounds. People from the lower class tend to use short, simple sentences, while middle-class people use longer, more complex sentences containing more abstract concepts and a larger vocabulary. These differences give middle-class students, whatever their ethnic backgrounds, a big head start in their schoolwork and make it easier for them to understand their teachers.

The Schools   In addition to the obstacles in the home environment of many lower-class students, the school system itself favors the education of middle- and upper-class students. This fact is obvious, first of all, in the way schools are financed. Even a brief examination of the American system of school finance reveals glaring inequities both in how taxes are levied and in how they are spent. For one thing, there are great differences among the various states in the importance placed on education and in their ability to pay for it. For example, New Jersey spends almost three times as much money per pupil as Utah.[10] Moreover, the differences between local school districts within the same state can be even greater. Because property taxes are a major source of school funding, districts with expensive homes and other valuable real estate often receive much more revenue than poor districts. In Illinois, for example, the richest districts spend about six times as much per student as the poorest districts, and in New York, they spend almost eight times as much.[11] Moreover, such inequities can occur even when the rich school districts have a lower tax rate than the poor ones.

Defenders of the present system of financing point to studies that conclude that the amount of money spent per student has little direct effect on educational achievement.[12] There is certainly little doubt that a badly run school can spend a great deal of money and still achieve poor results, but such findings hardly justify the practice of making the disadvantaged pay higher property taxes than the rich while their children languish in understaffed and underfunded schools.

There have been some serious efforts to correct this inequitable system through the courts. Twenty-nine different states have had legal challenges to their systems of school finance, and 14 state supreme courts have ruled the existing systems unconstitutional and ordered basic reforms.[13] But because the U.S. Supreme Court has refused to get involved in this issue, the process of reform is a hit-or-miss affair. Some courts have upheld the method their state uses to fund public education even when it allocates more money to educate rich than poor children, and no challenge has yet been made in many other states. Moreover, such cases do nothing to rectify the great imbalance in school funding among different states.

Family finances also have an important effect on educational achievement. Despite the fact that public education itself is free, children from poor families simply cannot afford as much education as those from more well-to-do backgrounds. Students from poor homes are more likely to drop out of school and go to work. At the college and university level, the cost of tuition, books, and transportation puts extra pressure on poor students. Many highly qualified lower-class students must attend local community colleges that emphasize technical careers because they cannot afford a university education. Less-qualified upper- and middle-class students may go to expensive private universities to prepare for professional careers. Moreover, the financial pressure on college students has gotten substantially worse in recent years. Even after adjusting for inflation, the cost of a college education has more than doubled since the 1960s, and the last decade has also seen large cuts in the financial aid available to college students.

Of course, colleges and universities are not the only educational institutions that charge their students. Compared to other industrialized nations, the United States devotes a far higher percentage of its educational spending to private schooling.[14] About 13 percent of American children currently attended private schools.[15] The quality, the cost, and the philosophical orientation of these schools vary enormously, however. The most prestigious of them are the so-called **prep schools**, which offer a much higher quality of education than most public schools, but only to the children of families who can afford to pay the price (or the gifted few who receive scholarships). Thus, many of the finest primary and secondary schools are largely closed to poor, working-class, and even most middle-class children. Even less-prestigious and less-affluent private schools have a major advantage over the public schools: It is far easier for them to exclude troublemakers and low achievers and thereby isolate their students from disruptive influences. Public schools must try to meet the needs of all the young people in their communities, even those with social or academic problems.

Because children from upper-class families generally receive a better secondary education, they have easier access to the elite universities that lead students to top positions in government and corporations. Moreover, some less-qualified students from upper-class families are able to attend elite universities because of admission programs that favor the children of alumni and the children of big contributors to fundraising campaigns.

Aside from differences in the quality of schools, achievement is also affected by the expectations that teachers have for their students. Considerable evidence indicates that teachers expect less from lower-class students, in terms of both academic achievement and behavior, and that for some students those exceptions become a self-fulfilling prophecy.[16] Robert Rosenthal and Lenore Jacobson performed an interesting experiment to demonstrate this.[17] Experimenters gave a standard IQ test to pupils in 18 classrooms in a neighborhood elementary school. However, teachers were told that the instrument was the "Harvard Test of Inflected Acquisition" (which does not exist). Next, the experimenters arbitrarily selected 20 percent of the students' names and told their teachers that the test showed these students would make remarkable progress in the coming year. When the students were retested eight months later, those who had been singled out as intellectual bloomers showed a significantly greater increase in IQ than the others. As you might expect, these findings created quite a controversy when they were first published, and many similar studies have since been done. Most of them supported Rosenthal and Jacobson's findings, but some did not, and it is still not clear under exactly what conditions teachers' expectations are most likely to become a self-fulfilling prophecy.[18] One thing we do know is that lower-class and minority students are the ones most likely to be harmed by this process, for they are the ones for whom teachers hold the lowest expectations. For example, when D. G. Harvey and G. T. Slatin gave teachers pictures of students and asked them to evaluate their chances for success in school, the teachers reported the highest expectations for white students who appeared to be from middle- and upper-class backgrounds.[19]

More recent research has used the concept of **cultural capital** to help us understand these influences. Capital refers to something people own, and thus, cultural capital refers to knowledge and skills a person "owns" and especially "higher culture" from the upper-middle class. Research has shown that when working-class children have such cultural capital, such as "knows how to play the violin or cello," or "attends ballet classes," the status of these children goes up in the eyes of their teachers. Thus, acquiring cultural capital can help working-class student's improve their academic achievement because it increases the expectations of teachers.[20]

Even if lower-class students are lucky enough to attend a good high school, they still often do not get the same quality of education as their middle-class schoolmates. Most high school students are placed in one of several different "tracks" or "ability groups." The "most promising" are put into college preparatory courses, while others go into vocational or "basic" classes. There is considerable evidence that lower-class students are more likely to be placed in the vocational or basic track.[21] Tracking is supposed to be based on such criteria as academic record, performance on standardized tests, and the students' own feelings about college, but there is little doubt that the schools themselves have lower expectations for students from the lower classes. Even when there is no bias, a serious problem remains: Once students have been placed in a lower track, they will be exposed to less challenging material and teachers will have lower expectations of them. When isolated from college-bound students, even the best students in the lower tracks are less likely to want to go to college. Karl Alexander, Martha Cook, and Edward L. Dill found that students in a college-preparatory track were 30 percent more likely to plan to go on beyond high school than equally motivated and able students in nonacademic tracks.[22]

MINORITY EDUCATION

The history of minority education has not been a bright one (see Chapter 6), and African Americans have been the victims of particularly harsh treatment. During the era of slavery, they were seldom given any education at all. Only 50 years ago, most African Americans in the South were forced to attend **segregated schools** that were clearly inferior to those attended by whites. A landmark Supreme Court decision in 1954 recognized the fact that segregated schools were inherently unequal and declared them unconstitutional. In the turmoil that followed, intentional legal segregation was ended, but unlike **de jure** (legal) segregation, **de facto** (actual) segregation has been resistant to change. Although African Americans and whites were assigned to the schools nearest their homes regardless of race, most schools remained segregated because most neighborhoods were segregated.

To deal with this problem, the Court ruled that school districts must aim for racial balance in their schools, even when it is necessary to bus students long distances. Intense opposition from whites made school busing an inflammatory racial issue for two decades. At first, busing and other court-ordered **desegregation** programs proved effective, and the segregation of ethnic minorities sharply declined. But because of the migration of the middle class to the suburbs, the fact that many urban whites send their children to private schools, and a heavy influx of new immigrants, in many big cities too few white children remain to create truly integrated schools. As a result, many city schools have become **resegregated**. According to a study by the Harvard Project on School Desegregation, two-thirds of African American students in the United States attend schools in which most of the students are from minority backgrounds. Moreover, Latino students are even more segregated than African Americans. Almost three-fourths of Latino students in the United States attend predominantly minority schools.[23]

The debate over school integration has generated a great deal of concern about the effects of integration on students. The Coleman report, published in 1966, found that the quality of schools attended by African Americans and by whites was similar when measured by such factors as physical facilities, curriculum, and the qualifications of teachers.[24] The greatest influence on achievement was found to be the students' class background. Middle-class students did much better than students from the lower class. However, Coleman found that disadvantaged students did better when they were in the same classes with middle-class students. He concluded, logically enough, that the performance of lower-class African American children would improve if they were integrated in the same classes as middle-class white students.

The effects of desegregation on academic performance have been the subject of dozens of studies since the Coleman report was first published. These studies vary widely in methodology and overall quality and have reached contradictory conclusions. Rita E. Mahard and Robert L. Crain reviewed 93 different works on this topic, and after eliminating the poorly designed studies, they analyzed the others and came to some interesting conclusions. Desegregation did indeed improve the academic performance of African American students, but mainly in the primary grades, not in junior high or high school. Moreover, there seems to be an optimum ratio of white students to African American students, which varied in the different studies from 3 to 1 to 9 to 1. Finally, the most successful approach to desegregation was the so-called metropolitan plan, which integrated inner-city and suburban schools.[25]

In addition to the academic benefits, school integration may help reduce racism and create understanding among the nation's many diverse ethnic groups. Unless school administrators modify some of their traditional policies, however, minorities may be resegregated into different classes within an integrated school. For example, academic tracking often results in predominantly white college-preparatory classes and predominantly minority vocational classes. Well-intentioned bilingual and compensatory education programs may also result in the removal of minority students from regular classrooms for a large part of the day.[26] Thus, to realize the full benefits of an integrated education, it is necessary to do more than just integrate the schools. Administrators, teachers, and concerned parents must work to create an integrated and supportive environment within individual schools as well.

How well are minority groups doing in today's educational system? The answer is a complex one. As far as standardized achievement tests go, the conclusion is not very positive. A 1999 study released by the U.S. Department of Education shows that over the last 30 years there has been very little overall improvement in the gap between African Americans and whites on math, science, and reading scores.[27] With respect to years of school completed, however, the picture looks better. The gap between Americans of European and African descent has narrowed considerably in the last 30 years. For people 25 years old and older, 87.7 percent of whites, 77.4 percent of African Americans, 84.7 percent of Asian Americans, but only 56.1 percent of Latinos had graduated from high school in 1999.[28] When we look only at younger Americans—those most affected by recent changes in education—the picture is much more encouraging, as can be seen in Figure 4.1 on page 108. At the college level, however, a huge gap remains. In the 25-to-29 age group 33.6 percent of whites, but only 15 percent of African Americans and 8.9 percent of Latinos have completed a four-year college degree. Asian groups have, however, done extremely well, ranking considerably above whites at 51.3 percent.[29]

Why do Latinos rank lower than African Americans when they are both in a very similar socioeconomic position in American society? One important factor is language. Many Latinos come into English-speaking schools with little knowledge of that language, and many others are less proficient in English than their classmates who grew up speaking it, and that obviously creates a host of difficult educational problems. A second factor is immigration. There has been a heavy influx of new immigrants from Latin America, and they frequently come from low-income groups that have received an inadequate education in their own country. (See Chapter 5 for more details on these problems.)

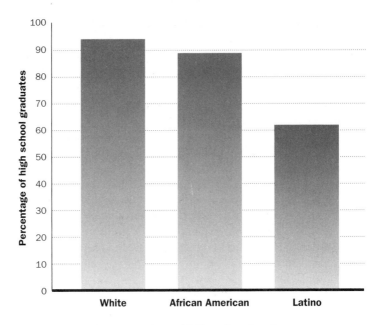

FIGURE 4.1   HIGH SCHOOL GRADUATES, 25 TO 29-YEAR-OLD AGE GROUP

African Americans and Latinos are less likely to finish high school than European Americans.

Source: U.S. Bureau of the Census, *Educational Attainment in the United States*, 1999 (Washington, D.C.: U.S. Government Printing Office, 2000), p. 12.

GENDER BIAS

In the past, our educational system openly discriminated against women and girls in much the same way it discriminated against minorities. The traditional attitude held that it was far more important to educate sons, who would have to go out and find jobs, than daughters, who would just stay home and take care of the house, and our educational system clearly reflected this bias. Boys were given more and better education than girls, and many of the top universities did not even admit women. While today's students may think this kind of blatant discrimination is a thing of the distant past, such practices actually continued until quite recently. Harvard University, for example, excluded women from its law school until 1950 and from its graduate business program until 1963.

Important progress toward gender equality has unquestionably been made since then. The most blatant barriers to equal educational opportunities for female students have been removed, and there has been a remarkable increase in educational achievement among women. In fact, young women are now actually better educated than young men. At the end of the twentieth century, a higher percentage of women aged 25 to 29 had graduated from high school (90 percent vs. 86 percent) and college (29.5 percent vs. 26.8 percent) than men.[30]

There are, nonetheless, many subtle forms of **sexism** that still remain and still affect the occupational chances of women today. The attitudes and behavior of teachers often reflect the same gender stereotypes that are found among other groups, and many times girls are subtly discouraged from pursuing "masculine" interests in subjects such as science and math. At least partially as a result, while more females graduate from college, they are less likely to be in the technologically oriented majors that often lead to the highest-paying jobs. In 1997, for example, only 17 percent of the students earning a BA in engineering were female. There have, nonetheless, been important improvements in this area as well. In 1971 less than 1 percent of the BAs in engineering went to females. The percentage of females graduates in business management increased from only 9 percent in 1971 to 59 percent in 1997.[31]

QUICK REVIEW

How does social class affect student achievement?
Discuss the history of ethnic discrimination in education and how we have tried to correct it.
What are the gender biases in our educational system?

THE QUALITY OF EDUCATION

The controversy about the quality of our educational system has jumped out of specialized journals and onto the political stage. Several prestigious national commissions have been highly critical of our schools, and there is a growing fear that American students are falling behind their counterparts in other countries. Such attention is certainly long overdue, but before we can go very far to make the schools more effective, we must first decide what they are supposed to do. Should they teach students to do well on standardized tests of academic achievement? Teach the skills of critical, independent thinking? Essay writing? Higher mathematics? Public citizenship? Or should they focus on students' social needs, such as preventing delinquency and drug abuse? In this section we will discuss some of the main issues in the current debate about our educational system. But remember that because the parties to this debate do not agree about the system's underlying goals, they tend to see its problems very differently.

AUTHORITY AND REBELLION

Our leaders are fond of talking about the need to teach children democratic principles and the ability to think for themselves. Most schools, however, are large bureaucracies that demand obedience to a rigid set of rules over which the students, and even most teachers, have little influence. Our schools have been compared to factories in which workers (teachers) turn raw materials (students) into finished products (educated citizens) under the strict supervision of the management (school administration); they have even been likened to prisons, with principals as wardens and teachers as guards. Although such comparisons can easily be taken too far, it is hard to see most schools as places that encourage creativity or individual initiative.

In one sense, the bureaucratic structure of our schools both reflects and requires **authoritarianism**. Students are required by law to go to school, where they are compelled to spend large amounts of time in classrooms and truancy is considered a form of delinquency. All bureaucracies require strict rules and regulations if they are to coordinate the activities of large numbers of people. Without such rules, school life would quickly degenerate into chaos; however, some observers believe that schools carry the emphasis on authority and obedience to harmful extremes. They argue that many schools are experiencing a problem common to bureaucracies—**goal displacement**. In this case, there has been a shift from education to the maintenance of order and authority as the primary goal of the schools. Many conflict theorists charge that there is thus a **hidden curriculum** in our schools: that along with reading, writing, and arithmetic, students are taught conformity and obedience to authority. Those who do not learn this lesson are doomed to failure in the educational bureaucracy, no matter how academically talented they may be.

While some criticize the authoritarianism of schools, others condemn what they see as chaos in the classroom. Numerous opinion polls have shown that the public believes "lack of discipline" to be the biggest problem in schools today. To most people this lack of discipline conjures up images of disrespectful students refusing to do their work or getting in fights on the school grounds. Of course, this is hardly a new problem, and students have been getting in fights as long as there have been schools. Unfortunately, there have been frequent reports of far more serious problems: drug dealing, students carrying weapons, and vicious assaults and rapes directed against students and even teachers. A survey of Los Angeles high schools in 1995 and 1996 found that 14 percent of their students had taken a weapon to school at least once, and 2.5 percent admitted taking a gun onto campus.[32]

Given the dramatic outbreaks of violence in our schools in recent years, such as the 12 students killed at Columbine High School in April 1999, the 5 killed at Westside Middle School in Jonesboro, Arkansas, in March 1998, and the 3 students killed at Heath High School in Kentucky in December 1997, it certainly seems that our schools are becoming more dangerous all the time. But such headline-grabbing incidents can actually confuse us about the realities of life in school today. Although they are certainly not as safe as we want them to be, schools are not the most dangerous places in America. In 1997, for example, students aged 12 to 18 were almost three times more likely to be the victim of a violent crime when they were away from school than when they were at school.[33] Though 20 percent of high schools in the United States reported at least one incident of serious violence to police in 1997, the rate of violent crime in America's schools actually came down slightly during the 1990s.[34]

In response to the increasing fear of violence in our schools, the federal government passed the Gun-Free School Act in 1994, which required schools receiving federal aid (which is almost all public schools) to expel for at least a year any student who brings a gun to school. But many states have gone well beyond the federal mandate and adopted "zero-tolerance" policies for all forms of weapons and drugs. While the supporters of these policies claim they are starting to bring down the rate of school violence, their inflexibility has produced many extreme reactions. For example, an 8-year-old Louisiana girl was suspended for a month because she brought her grandfather's gold pocket watch to school—and on the same chain was a one-inch knife that her grandfather used to clean his fingernails; and

The problem of maintaining order is a particularly serious one in poor inner-city schools. In this photograph, a school official is using a metal detector to check students for weapons.

a 13-year-old in Ohio was suspended for nine days for bringing a bottle of Midol to school.[35] Some schools in high-crime areas have even taken to using metal detectors to check students for weapons before entering campus. However, 64 percent of the students in the Los Angeles survey mentioned above said that metal detectors don't keep weapons off campus.[36]

Aside from the life-threatening violence, there has been a growing awareness of the problem of bullying in schools, in large part because of the Littleton, Colorado, shootings. The shooters were made fun of and victimized at school over a period of several years, and the final result was a violent rage that left a dozen people dead. Bullying occurs in all schools and has often been excused as normal behavior. Kids will be kids, after all. Bullying tends to be done differently by gender. For boys, much of the bullying and teasing centers on sexual orientation. Being called a girl, a sissy, a faggot, a queen, or a queer is a common way for boys to taunt other boys. Unfortunately, the consequences can be severe. Victims of intense bullying often drop out of school, see their academic performance drop, or succumb to depression. Gay and bisexual teenaged boys attempt suicide seven times more often than other boys their age, and the younger they are when they recognize their sexual orientation, the more likely they are to try. Bullying done by girls tends to center on appearance, especially on clothes. Again, bullying can have severe consequences on the victim. Underachieving, dropping out, life-threatening eating disorders, and depression are all common.

LESSONS FROM OTHER PLACES

EDUCATION IN GERMANY, THAILAND, AND JAPAN

In the mid-1990s, while I was living in Thailand and teaching at a Thai university, my Thai next-door neighbors had just returned from the United States, where both the mother and father had finished PhDs. At dinner I once asked their two daughters, aged 10 and 14, what they missed most about returning to Thailand after four years in the United States. Both replied immediately, "pizza." (I might note that a Pizza Hut opened in this university town in 1998, so they are most likely a bit happier.) I then asked them what they disliked most about being back in Thailand. Again, both replied immediately, "the homework!" It is clear that one of the major reasons that American students don't score as well on standardized tests is that they don't study as much.

But that isn't the whole story. I remember being surprised a few years ago while living in Tokyo when I opened a newspaper containing a front-page article titled "Japanese Education System Should Copy the United States." Considering that Japan has a much higher rate of literacy and high school completion, that Japanese high school seniors score higher than any other country in tests of math and science, and that (at that time anyway) there was almost no violence in Japanese schools, the title of the article seemed rather odd. But the report by a government commission studying Japanese education had a point; Japanese students' heads are filled with facts, figures, and dates, but their critical reasoning skills are usually poor. The Japanese educational system is far more geared toward passing exams than building skills in critical thinking and analysis. Most of the Nobel Prizes in science went to Americans in the twentieth century, in part because independent thinking and critical reasoning are important in American schools. Throughout the 1990s, the Japanese Ministry of Education instituted many changes in an attempt to overcome this lack of critical thinking, but so far with little success.

There are, however, other aspects of the educational systems in Europe and Japan that we may well want to emulate. While only half as many people in European countries graduate from four-year universities as in the United States,* they have very good systems of vocational education geared toward specific occupational skills. In Germany, for example, at the beginning of what would be the high school years for Americans, young people must go on either a college-bound track or vocational/apprenticeship school track. Students seeking to enter a good university

DECLINING ACHIEVEMENT?

It is estimated that at least 3 million Americans cannot read or write at all, and more than ten times that number are **functionally illiterate**—that is, their skills at reading and writing are so poor that they cannot perform many of the basic tasks go on to the famous Gymnasiums, which are more like junior colleges, during their last two (high school) years. For those who choose the vocationally oriented high schools, they receive the basics in math, science, writing, and language, but as they move to their final years of school they spend more of their school week in practical job training than in the classroom.

In Japan, there are high schools specifically oriented toward helping students pass the very difficult college entrance exams, and many students also spend may additional hours in private schools, generally called *juku*, to help improve their chances of getting into a good university. All of this means that typical college-bound students in Japan have little time left to themselves because of all the long hours of study. But Japan also has excellent "industrial high schools" which, like those in Germany, are specifically geared to train students for technical and industrial jobs, as well as the basics in math, science, and language.

As noted earlier in this chapter, several reports have shown that American corporations have higher labor costs and lower productivity in lower-level positions because so many workers lack basic skills. But while an educational system that included high-quality vocational training could help to solve this problem, there has been strong resistance to such proposals. Most American parents do not like the idea of their children being placed in a noncollege track at such an early age, and there is no question that it does restrict their life chances. It is very rare for a German or Japanese worker to change course in mid-life and go back to get a university education. Again, we must understand how American values of individual freedom and equality of opportunity restrict the options we might consider for reforming our educational system. Of course, the plus side is that the values of independence and individualism help Americans acquire critical thinking skills and make innovations that have given the United States an edge in the world economy during the last few years. A combination of the German and Japanese educational systems with the most positive aspects of the American system would be the ideal. But value preferences, as is often the case, restrict our options in such matters.

—*Harold Kerbo*

*Almost 50 percent of young Americans attend some type of college, as do about 35 percent of Japanese and 28 percent of Germans. But the actual completion rate of a four-year college degree is lower in every country.

Source: See Kerbo and Strasser, *Modern Germany* (New York: McGraw-Hill, 2000); Kerbo and McKinstry, *Modern Japan* (New York: McGraw-Hill, 1998).

necessary to daily life in an industrial society.[37] The demand for a more educated workforce has made the problem of illiteracy an increasingly serious one. The long-range trends have actually been toward an increase in the number of years the average person spends in school and a decline in illiteracy among native-born Americans.

Despite the fact that people are getting more years of education, there is growing concern that educational achievement has declined among secondary school students. One of the most worrisome statistics has been the poor performance of American students on standardized tests of academic achievement; for example, scores on the Scholastic Aptitude Test (SAT)—the most widely used college admission examination—declined about 7 percent from their peak in the mid-1960s until 1980, and since have come back only about 2 percent.[38] The U.S. Department of Education's "National Assessment of Educational Progress" reached similar conclusions. It found that test scores in reading, math, and science for young Americans had all improved in the latter years of the 1990s. That is the good news. The bad news, however, is that in no case are the test scores back up to the level they were in the late 1960s or early 1970s.[39] So overall, the data are quite mixed. Educational achievement may have improved a bit in the last few years, but it still has a very long way to go.[40]

Another serious source of concern comes from the comparison of American students with those from other nations. For example, when National Center for Educational Statistics compared the educational achievement of 15-year-olds in 32 nations in 2000, they found that the performance for American students in reading, math, and science was just about average.[41] However, the nations chosen for comparison included some much poorer countries such as Brazil, Latvia, Russia, and Mexico. In tests of geographic knowledge, young Americans rank dead last among the citizens of the industrialized nations. In fact, in one study, young people (aged 18 to 24) from Sweden, Mexico, Canada, Germany, Japan, and France knew more about the U.S. population than young Americans did.[42] Sadly, American adults of all ages don't do any better. In polls testing knowledge of international current events, Americans score lower than the citizens of any other industrialized nation.[43]

There are three common explanations for these educational problems. The first attacks the tests themselves, arguing that test scores don't accurately reflect how much students are actually learning; the second holds the schools responsible; and the third blames the problem on changes in students' social environment. Critics of the validity of these tests point out that some (but not all) of the decline in scores on college entrance examinations can be attributed to the increasing number of poor and minority students who are taking the tests. They also argue that the growing number of immigrants who do not speak English well has driven down test scores in our public schools. The critics also raise a more fundamental issue; such tests, they assert, focus on only one or two types of educational skills and should not be used to make an overall evaluation of educational achievement. The other side generally agrees that these tests do not measure all aspects of educational achievement, but they argue that the tests are a valid indicator of some critical skills. Moreover, they argue that there is no reason to believe American students do any better in the kinds of skills that are not tested than in the ones that are.

Those who blame the schools for the weak test scores attribute much of it to a decline in academic rigor. As more and more students come into school from unstable families, the schools have taken on numerous new tasks, from teaching about AIDS and family life to preventing drug abuse. A two-year study by the National Commission on Education and Learning concluded that American students spend only 41 percent of their school day on academic subjects such as math, science, and history. In their four

The Japanese students shown in this photograph are likely to go to school more hours a day, do more homework, and score higher on standardized tests of academic achievement than their American counterparts.

years of high school, American students spend less than half as many hours studying academic subjects as students in France, Germany, or Japan.[44] Moreover, many critics also charge that pressure not to flunk out disadvantaged poor and minority students has led to a watering down of academic standards and lower overall expectations. For example, surveys show that fewer than 40 percent of twelfth graders do an hour or more of homework a night.[45] Such softening of standards has often been covered up by the practice of grade inflation: assigning grades of A or B to students who have barely learned the subject at hand.

Whatever the shortcomings of the schools, experts agree that students' home environment has an enormous influence on how well they master their studies, and there are good reasons to believe that the environment of today's students is less conducive to educational achievement than it was in the past. For example, the average high school senior now spends almost three hours a day watching television.[46] A survey by the Educational Testing Service found that 13-year-old Americans were more likely to report watching a great deal of television and failing to do their homework than the 13-year-olds in any of the other countries studied.[47] Obviously, children who sit in front of television sets instead of playing basketball will not become good basketball players. Just as obviously, children who watch television instead of reading books will not become good readers and, consequently, will not learn to write very well either.

Teachers often complain that their students have been growing more rebellious and less interested in their studies, but it is difficult to determine whether such comments reflect a real change in students or just an idealization of the "good old days." There is, however, one good reason to believe that these complaints are accurate—the huge increase in the percentage of families in which there is only one parent or in which both parents work outside the home. These changes in family structure often reduce the amount of time and energy parents have to devote to their children, and it seems reasonable to assume that some students' behavior at school suffers as a result. These structural changes in the family may also mean that parents are not able to spend as much time assisting their children with their studies or getting involved in the educational programs of their schools.

QUICK REVIEW

Are our schools too authoritarian or too lenient?
What are the causes of low student achievement?

SOLVING THE PROBLEMS OF EDUCATION

The problems of education are economic and political problems as well. Some proposals for change call for a sweeping restructuring of society that goes far beyond our educational institutions. But educational problems are also bureaucratic problems, and other proposals for change call for improved efficiency in the existing school system and its teaching methods. Proposals to upgrade the educational system fall into two broad categories: recommendations for providing more equal educational opportunities for everyone and suggestions for improving the quality of education itself.

TOWARD EQUAL EDUCATIONAL OPPORTUNITY

Almost everyone agrees that there should be equal educational opportunity for all, but there is widespread disagreement about what equal opportunity means and how it can be achieved. Integration of students from different ethnic backgrounds into the same schools is often proposed as a solution to educational inequality. Another approach is to set up **compensatory education programs** to provide special assistance to disadvantaged students or programs to help fight gender inequality. Finally, many propose that we change the way education is financed so that the same amount of money is spent on both rich and poor students.

Effective Integration   For years the American government, particularly the judicial branch, has been trying to achieve racial and ethnic integration in the schools. Despite many advances, this goal has still not been met. Following court-ordered integration, unofficial resegregation often occurred as whites moved to the suburbs or enrolled their children in private schools. The metropolitan plan reduces resegregation by merging suburban school districts with inner-city school districts and then busing children within each district. One difficulty with this proposal is distance. Some suburban communities are so far from city centers that bused students would spend a large part of their school day in transit. Another difficulty is prejudice. The proposal does nothing to discourage white parents from putting their children in private schools, and in fact it might encourage more prejudiced whites to do so.

As an alternative, some districts have created voluntary desegregation plans that give students the right to attend any school they wish, provided it does not have a higher percentage of students of their ethnic group than their neighborhood school. A related idea is the creation of **magnet schools** with unique educational programs that attract students from all ethnic groups. The goal of these plans is to reduce "white flight" while still allowing minority and lower-class students to attend integrated middle-class schools if they wish. Critics of such plans argue that they are not likely to significantly reduce segregation because most students choose to attend their neighborhood schools, and most neighborhoods are still segregated to one degree or another.

Another approach encourages the integration of residential areas so that neighborhood schools are automatically integrated. In many ways this is the most appealing solution, for it provides the broadest possible opportunity for development of interracial friendships and cooperation. However, daunting obstacles stand in the way of efforts to create truly integrated communities. For one thing, a long history of prejudice and suspicion makes many Americans prefer to live in neighborhoods in which the residents have similar economic and ethnic backgrounds. Moreover, the poor and minorities simply cannot afford to live in affluent neighborhoods. One possible solution is to create more subsidized housing for low-income families in wealthy neighborhoods, along with tax incentives for affluent families who refurbish and live in older homes in lower-income neighborhoods. Specific proposals often run into intense opposition from wealthy homeowners, who fear that low-cost housing will decrease their property values, and from residents of low-income neighborhoods, who fear they will be displaced by more prosperous newcomers.

Compensatory Education   Another way to boost the educational achievement of the poor and minorities is to provide them with special programs and assistance. The most popular and widely known compensatory program of this kind is Project Head Start, which gives preschool instruction to disadvantaged children. The original research on the Head Start program indicated that it produced significant educational gains among its students, but follow-up studies found that most of the early benefits faded away by the time the children reached the second or third grade.[48] However, research on the Perry Preschool Program, which is very much like Project Head Start except that it spends about twice as much per student, has shown real long-term benefits. A study that followed a group of students from age 3 to age 27 found that those who attended the Perry Program earned more money, had more stable marriages, and were less likely to use illegal drugs than those in a matched control group. The researchers estimated that because of these benefits, the Perry Preschool Program saved taxpayers $7.16 for every dollar spent.[49] A related program under Title I of the Elementary and Secondary Education Act provides federal money to give extra help to disadvantaged students who are already in school. Over 5 million elementary school students are aided under this program, and its supporters credit it with helping make real improvement in the educational performance of poor and minority students. But critics point to studies showing that the benefits of elementary school programs do not carry over into high school.[50]

Compensatory education programs, such as the Head Start class shown in this photograph, are one of the best hopes for improving the educational achievement of disadvantaged students.

Research on both Head Start and Title I programs thus reaches much the same conclusion: These programs significantly improve the performance of the underprivileged students who are enrolled, but after they finish the program, the benefits tend to diminish.[51] The solution to this problem is obvious: Don't stop the programs after only a few years. Disadvantaged students should continue to receive extra help as long as they need it, which in many cases would probably be until their final years of high school. The difficulty with this proposal is, of course, money—but such an investment would pay enormous dividends in terms of a healthier, more competitive economy, lower rates of crime and welfare dependency, and, most important, a more just society.

A variety of educational opportunity programs have also been established at the college level. Generally, these programs make special provisions for the admission of disadvantaged and minority students who do not meet standard admissions requirements. They also provide tutoring and assistance to help these students stay in school. Although these programs have their critics, they have become an accepted part of most colleges and universities. One common problem is that such programs often fail to provide enough academic help after the disadvantaged students are admitted, so their graduation rate remains significantly lower than it is for other students. However, the greatest conflicts have arisen over special admissions programs for graduate and professional schools. Competition for places in these schools is intense, and white students complain that they are the victims of "reverse discrimination" because some whites are rejected in favor of less-qualified minority students. Supporters of special admissions programs argue that minorities have already been subjected to a great deal of discrimination and that **affirmative action programs** merely attempt to compensate for some small part of it (see Chapter 7).

The majority of the American public, however, is opposed to any kind of preference based on race or ethnic group,[52] and recent legislation and court rulings have undermined affirmative action in college admissions. A 1996 initiative in California banned such preferences, and the result has been a precipitous drop in the number of African Americans and Latinos attending the most prestigious University of California campus and graduate schools. The minority enrollment at its less prestigious campus were not, however, as severely effected. Court rulings in other parts of the nation have also created new obstacles to ethnically based affirmative action programs. Particularly important was *Hopwood v. the State of Texas*, which invalidated race-based admission criteria for the University of Texas's law school. One response to this trend has been a shift to programs that seek to provide better access to higher education to students from low-income families regardless of their ethnic background. This "racially blind" approach can still help to improve educational equality without violating strongly held public opposition to programs that are perceived to provide racial preferences.

Fighting Gender and Sexual Inequality   Although our schools have made significant progress in providing more equal opportunity for both genders, much remains to be done before full equality is achieved. The funding and attention given to male and female athletics, for example, remains highly unequal. Many schools, moreover, continue to tailor their curricula to reflect traditional gender stereotypes: nutrition classes for the girls and auto shop for the boys. More effort also needs to be made to convince girls that math and sciences aren't just "boys' classes" and that they too should get involved. The biggest challenge, however, is the teachers. Like most other people in our society, teachers have many stereotypes about what kinds of behavior are appropriate for girls and for boys and about how girls' and boys' abilities and interests differ. A comprehensive training program that sensitizes teachers to the negative effects of such stereotypes and teaches them how to keep such biases out of the classroom could help transform our schools from institutions that reinforce gender inequality to ones that actively promote equality.

There is also growing concern about the sexual harassment students often experience from other students. Of course, Title IX of the Educational Amendments of 1972, as well as the equal protection clause of the Fourteenth Amendment, already prohibit sexual harassment. All schools receiving federal funds are under the obligation to ensure that their students are protected from sexual harassment and discrimination. Unfortunately, that obligation has seldom been met. In 1999, the case of *Nabozny v. Podlesny* drove this point home. In his high school in Ashland, Wisconsin, Jamie was mock-raped in a classroom while 20 students watched. He was urinated on in a school bathroom, and he was kicked so severely that he required surgery to stop the internal bleeding. When notified of this harassment by Jamie and his parents, a school official simply said that he had to expect that sort of treatment because he was homosexual. Fortunately, the courts disagreed (although a federal judge initially dismissed the case); the school district eventually had to pay $900,000 in damages. Also in 1999, the Supreme Court decided in *Aurelia Davis v. Monroe County Board of Education* that school districts can be held liable if employees of the school are indifferent to complaints of peer-to-peer sexual harassment. But it is not just a matter of the attitudes of the teachers. One of the most critical issues is class size. When classes are large (over 25 students), it is much more difficult for teachers to be aware of the problems that are developing in class. Another essential task is to make teachers more aware of the damage such behavior causes and their obligation to help prevent it.

Reforming School Finance   As was pointed out earlier, schools in rich districts often receive much more money per student than do schools in poor districts. Although this problem could be dealt with by reforming the system of school finance in individual states, such an approach does nothing to rectify the huge inequalities among states. The only solution to that dilemma is much more federal funding. For example, if the federal government paid for all primary and secondary education, it could provide equitable funding for all schools. There is, however, a strong tradition of local control of the schools in the United States, and many people fear that national financing would mean federal control that would be unresponsive to the needs of local communities.

Although such concerns are certainly well grounded, there appear to be few alternatives to increased federal aid to education, even if it stops far short of complete financial support. When economic distress causes troubled school districts and financially strapped states to cut back on education, the result may be a vicious cycle in which poorer education creates a less competent workforce that, in turn, causes more economic problems. Federal money is needed to break this cycle. There is, moreover, another important reason for the federal government to get more involved: It is the only level of government that has the resources to significantly increase overall funding for education. It is worth noting that most funding for public education in other industrial nations comes primarily—and sometimes exclusively—from the federal rather than from local governments. The federal government pays only about 7 cents of every dollar spent for education in the United States today.[53]

IMPROVING THE SCHOOLS

The original Coleman report created a furor when it was first published in 1966 because it found that none of the measures of school quality it studied—funding, teacher qualifications, or physical facilities—had much effect on the educational achievement of the students. These results were widely interpreted to mean that "schools don't make any difference." Subsequent research has shown that those results were largely a product of the extremely narrow questions the researchers asked; in truth, their conclusions were highly misleading. For instance, Michael Rutter's study of London high schools found that schools had a critical impact on student achievement. Not surprisingly, the best schools were those that maintained high standards, required more homework, and had clear and well-enforced standards of discipline yet still created a comfortable, supportive atmosphere for students.[54] Coleman himself later acknowledged that schools do make a substantial difference. In a comparison of private and public schools, Coleman and his colleagues wrote that "the indication is that more extensive academic demands are made in the private schools, leading to more advanced courses, and thus to higher achievement."[55] In addition to the idea of requiring more work, reformers also propose reorganizing the school system and hiring better teachers.

Requiring More Work   One obvious way to improve academic performance is to raise the schools' requirements and make students work harder. In the 1960s, schools were heavily criticized for their bureaucratic rigidity, and the curriculum was loosened to allow more individual choice. Now, with increasing concern about scholastic achievement, electives are being replaced with tougher requirements for more academic courses. A related proposal is to increase the amount of homework so that students must meet higher standards in the courses they do take. A criticism sometimes heard from minority leaders is that tougher requirements force disadvantaged students who cannot compete to leave school and go out on the streets. Efforts to make our schools more rigorous must therefore be accompanied by the kinds of compensatory educational programs discussed in the last section; otherwise, the result is likely to be lower, not higher, academic performance among some groups.

Programs to raise academic standards and require more homework win at least verbal support from teachers and school administrators, but those groups often oppose another fundamental change that needs to be made—an increase in the amount of time students spend in school. The United States has one of the shortest school years of any major industrialized nation, and things are not much better in Canada. The average student in the United States goes to school about 180 days a year, while in Japan schools are in session for 244 days and in Germany about 210 days. Moreover, the average school day is only six hours in North America, while eight-hour days are common in other nations.[56] It is unrealistic to expect American students to compete with their counterparts abroad who have as many as 30 percent more school days a year. As far back as 1983, the National Commission on Excellence in Education recommended that the average school day be increased to seven hours and the school year be increased to between 200 and 220 days, but its conclusions have been largely ignored. So have similar recommendations by the National Commission on Education and Learning that were made in 1994 and again in 1999.[57] But in the long run, it is hard to see how North American students can remain competitive without this kind of reform.

Restructuring the Schools   The last two decades have been a time of ferment in our educational system, and there are literally dozens of proposals for restructuring our schools. One of the most popular among conservatives is the **voucher system**. (See the "Debate" on pages 122–123.) Under most versions of this plan, automatic support for existing public schools would be withdrawn, and parents would be given vouchers that could be "spent" at any school, public or private. Advocates of the voucher system claim it would stimulate competition among the schools and force schools and teachers to provide top-quality education or go out of business. Critics of these proposals, who include many of the nation's leading educators, say that such changes would create educational chaos: Tens of thousands of independent schools would spring up with enormous differences in quality, curriculum, and objectives. California's superintendent of public instruction described the voucher proposals as "dangerous claptrap" that would produce the same disastrous results as the deregulation of the savings and loan industry, and Wisconsin's superintendent likened this approach to "nuking" the public school system.[58] Liberals are also concerned that a voucher-based school system would promote an increasing fragmentation of our society as children go to schools that have only children just like themselves. Thus, the

---

DEBATE

Educational Vouchers: A Good Idea?

Yes

Parents have become increasingly concerned about the education their children are receiving in the public school system. Class sizes are too large, children aren't safe on the school grounds, and academic achievement is subpar. Too many children simply fall through the cracks in our present system. Moreover, many parents would prefer to send their child to a school that fits their religious or philosophical views if given the choice.

Educational vouchers will give parents a choice. Children in big cities who are trapped in dangerous ghetto schools will have a way out, and middle-class parents will have more control over their children's education. Using the voucher system will even the playing field. Parents can find a school that produces higher academic achievement and safer conditions. If parents are not pleased with the school their child is attending, they can shop around for a different school that better fits the needs of their child. This will create a healthy competition among schools, and those schools that are not performing well will either improve or go out of business.

The educational voucher system will make schools more accountable for the safety and academic achievement of their students. The voucher system will also give schools an incentive to be more economically efficient. Individual choice and competition to bring better service is the American way.

---

children of Christian fundamentalists, Muslims, Catholics, and progressive liberals, for example, would have little or no contact with each other at school.

A less radical proposal is to open the enrollment of public schools so that students can attend any school they want. The idea is that such programs cause a mass exodus from weak schools and force them to improve in order to get their students back. Left unanswered are the questions of how the good schools could physically accommodate all the students who would want to attend and what would happen to the teachers and facilities at the weaker schools.

One of the best-known success stories among school choice programs is in the East Harlem section of New York City. Starting in the 1970s, the district slowly developed a network of alternative elementary and junior high schools, each using its own unique educational approach. By the mid-1980s, reading scores in East Harlem had risen from the lowest in the New York City school system to about average. Improvements in other districts have caused the position of East Harlem schools to slip a bit since then, but they continue to produce impressive results for a district in which the overwhelming majority of students come from poor and minority backgrounds.[59]

No

School vouchers sound like a wonderful idea, but in fact considerable research shows that school vouchers will only serve to aggravate our educational woes. First, private schools can't provide better education for their students than public schools unless they spend more money per student. The students in many private schools do better on standardized tests because the schools accept only good students to begin with. Private schools that are paid for by government vouchers would have neither of these advantages.

Will our educational system be more cost effective under a voucher system? Again, the answer is no. Careful estimates show that educating our children with vouchers will actually cost billions of dollars more every year. Disseminating information, additional transportation costs, the numerous parallel administrative units, and the need for government supervision and the adjudication of problems are just a few of the reasons.

Some argue vouchers will give children in low-income neighborhoods an avenue to escape inadequate schools. Yet evidence drawn from the Milwaukee voucher experiment shows that parents who choose to use their vouchers have more education and higher socioeconomic status than those who do not. Sadly, a voucher system will therefore lead to greater socioeconomic and racial segregation of students. And that is not all. It will also lead to the segregation of students based on religion, ethnic background, and the political and educational views of their parents. In 1954, our Supreme Court ruled that "separate educational facilities are inherently unequal." It would be a tragedy for this country to reverse 200 years of educational progress by turning to a voucher system.

Baltimore tried an even more radical approach by turning nine public schools over to a private company to run for a profit. The company claimed that by cutting administrative overhead and staff salaries (but not teacher salaries) it could increase the amount of money actually reaching the classroom. After a year of operation, the company claimed that it had raised test scores in its schools by nearly a whole grade level. But when the National Federation of Teachers commissioned its own study, it was discovered that test scores had actually gone down, and Baltimore ultimately canceled the company's contract and reclaimed control of the schools.[60]

A proposal for educational reform that has been tested throughout North America calls for public schools to be made more accountable by making comparative evaluation of the performance of their students on standardized tests of basic academic skills. According to this concept, schools create a more rigorous curriculum that focuses on the basic skills of reading, writing, and mathematics, while student, teacher, and school performance is continually evaluated by standardized tests. Teachers whose students do better on the tests are rewarded while teachers with poorly performing students are penalized or removed. School principals and administrators are held accountable for the performance of the entire school in much the same fashion, and in addition the schools' rating is publicized so that parents can bring additional pressure on the schools or in some programs by removing their children from underperforming schools. Despite the increasing popularity of this approach, troubling questions remain. As more and more importance is given to standardized tests, teachers have been accused of "teaching to the test," that is, sacrificing the broader goals of education and focusing exclusively on the skills that improve test scores.

Moreover, many educators reject the idea that successful education involves nothing more than teaching students to excel at basic skills. Is it better, they ask, to produce creative, well-adjusted children or to turn out neurotic overachievers who ace standardized tests but lack essential social skills? Obviously, the matter is not that simple, but there are many alternative approaches that hold out a much broader ideal for education. The famous Summerhill "free" school, for example, encourages open expression and democratic principles among its students and allows them to focus their studies on whatever subjects interest them most,[61] and the Waldorf schools place as much importance on art and personal development as on basic academic skills.[62]

Finally, the most radical approach to restructuring our schools is advocated by supporters of the **home schooling** movement, who recommend that parents keep their children home and teach them themselves. Supporters of home schooling are generally critical of the quality of public education and feel that children's parents are likely to give them far more attention and concern than a professional teacher can. These parents also worry about the negative influence that close contact with other schoolchildren may have on their own child, and they object to some of the public school curriculum. Critics of home schooling point out that while some parents can do an excellent job of educating their own children, others cannot. Moreover, even the best home schooling is likely to provide only a narrow perspective that reflects only the personal viewpoints of the parents. These critics say that every child should have the right to hear a much broader range of views and perspectives and that social contact with other schoolchildren is essential for normal social development in our diverse society.

Better Teachers and Better Teaching   In the long run, nothing is more important to the schools than the quality and dedication of teachers. Recruiting and keeping the best possible faculty is therefore a vital task facing our schools. Unfortunately, we have not been doing a very good job of it. A 1996 report by the National Commission on Teaching and America's Future concluded that one-fourth of the nation's classroom teachers were not fully qualified and called the current state of teacher training a "national shame."[63] There is less prestige in being an elementary or secondary teacher than there was in the past, so one way to improve the quality of our teachers is to offer a substantial increase in pay to attract and retain high-quality professionals. In 1999 the average salary for an American teacher was only $40,600, far less than most other occupations that require a similar amount of professional training. America ranks last among major industrialized nations in how generously it compensates its teachers.[64] One proposal already implemented in some school districts provides additional merit pay for superior teachers. A related approach is to create "master teacher" programs in which a school's best teachers are given extra pay to provide counseling and assistance to other teachers.

Too little money, however, is not the only problem. Teachers also complain about the frustrations of working within a bureaucracy that is often more concerned about the smooth functioning of its schools than about education. Other sources of discontent are excessive paperwork and the conflict between the demand that they be classroom police officers and the need to be educators. It is no surprise, then, that teachers suffer such a high burnout rate. Fewer than one in five new teachers is still in the profession after ten years.[65]

Even streamlining the bureaucracy and increasing pay will not guarantee that schools can recruit enough top-quality teachers. Success will depend largely on society's attitude toward education. As Tom Hayden, chair of the California Assembly's Subcommittee on Higher Education, put it:

> The desire to teach is fostered in a social climate that supports the personal mission of helping others grow, of creating and sharing knowledge and pursuing a higher quality of life. Such values are not promoted in a climate of self-serving shortsightedness that lures people toward the quick fix, the fast buck, and the easy answer. Until a new emphasis on public service and social responsibility arises to balance narrow self-interest, the teaching crisis will remain difficult to resolve.[66]

Others see the solution to our educational problems in the use of new technology and especially the use of more computers in the classroom. With strong federal backing, there has been an explosive growth in the number of students with access to the Internet at school. In 1995, only about 8 percent of American classrooms were wired for the Internet, but by 1999 it was 63 percent.[67] There is little doubt that this rapid change will significantly improve the students' level of **computer literacy**, but it remains to be seen if the use of this new technology will help improve student performance in other more traditional areas of study such as reading or mathematics. Some of the new technologies can, in fact, even pose a threat to the quality of education. **Distance learning**, in which students earn credits over the Internet or by attending classrooms with only a video image of the professor, is become increasingly popular among administrators in higher education. But while such technologies can reach students who would otherwise be excluded and are big cost savers, many feel that distance learning provides a second-rate educational experience by reducing the traditional face-to-face interaction between professors and students and depriving students of contact with the rich diversity of campus life.

Valuing Learning   A strange paradox in American culture underlies many of the educational problems we have discussed in this chapter. Americans place tremendous faith in education in general, but at the same time they don't seem to value learning itself very highly. In European countries like France and Germany, and even more so in Asian countries such as Japan, South Korea, and Taiwan, intellectuals and scholars not only have great prestige but are a powerful political force. The same is often true in less-developed countries as well—two of the last three presidents of Mexico, for example, have had a PhD. In the United States, intellectuals are viewed with far more suspicion and kept on the margins of political life. But the problem goes far deeper than just politics. A student who scores at the top of the class in Japan is some kind of a celebrity in school, but the brilliant student in the United States is often seen as something of a "nerd." For boys, it is the star athletes who win the most admiration, and for the girls it is often those with the knockout good looks. International polls also show that Americans read fewer books and newspapers than people in other industrialized nations and are less informed about global events.[68]

In addition to the kinds of new programs and policies we have just discussed, the revitalization of American education will require cultural changes as well. The idea that there is some kind of contradiction between those who think and study and those who take action in the "real world" is nothing but an unfounded prejudice. Most of the world's greatest revolutionary leaders, from Thomas Jefferson to Mao Zedong, have been intellectuals as well. Earning a top score in the SAT is at least as difficult a task as winning a football game, and it is far more likely to lead to a successful career. But aside from any external benefits we may derive from education, it is vital to recognize the intrinsic rewards of learning itself in enriching our lives and the lives of those around us.

QUICK REVIEW

What can we do to give everyone more equal educational opportunities?
How can we improve the quality of the education our children receive?

SOCIOLOGICAL PERSPECTIVES ON PROBLEMS OF EDUCATION

There seems to be a virtually endless debate about the deficiencies of our educational system and what to do about them, and since the opposing sides do not even agree about the goals of a good education, the discussion often produces more confusion than consensus. A look at the problems of education from each of the major sociology perspectives can clarify the situation by linking criticisms of the educational system and proposals for change with the broader vision of society from which they arise.

THE FUNCTIONALIST PERSPECTIVE

Functionalists see education as a basic institution that must meet a growing list of social needs. Originally, the two principal functions of education were to teach students a body of skills and knowledge and to grade them on how well they had mastered their studies. Education also became an important channel for social mobility for talented students from disadvantaged backgrounds. As industrial societies became more diverse and education became virtually universal, schools took on an increasingly important role in transmitting values and attitudes as well as skills. They also assumed the important latent (hidden) function of reducing unemployment by keeping many young people out of the labor market. Finally, as the traditional family unit became more unstable, educational institutions were asked to take up some of the slack by launching programs to prevent delinquent behavior and to help deal with students' social and psychological needs.

Schools do much more than teach reading, writing, and arithmetic. One of their most important functions is to provide for students' social and recreational needs.

Many functionalists believe our schools have been given so many conflicting tasks that they are unable to do any of them very well, and as a result, their efforts to achieve one goal often conflict with other goals. For example, the time spent on drug education or "teen skills" can detract from the schools' academic programs, and attempts to modify the curriculum to prevent disadvantaged students from getting discouraged may lower the achievement of more gifted students. Functionalists also complain that many schools have become disorganized because of poor management and a lack of sufficient concern on the part of parents and the community.

All functionalists do not agree on how to make schools more effective, however. Many advocate the elimination of some of the new programs that have been introduced in recent years. Although such changes might well improve fundamental education, they are also likely to disrupt efforts to deal with other pressing social problems. Proposals for employing more effective teaching methods are also compatible with the functionalist perspective, but most functionalists argue that such reforms can work only if accompanied by a reorganization of the schools. For example, teachers must be rewarded for good teaching rather than for being efficient bureaucrats or for the length of time they have spent on the job. Finally, many functionalists advocate better planning and coordination with other social institutions in order to reduce the problem of unemployment and underemployment among the educated. But such a program must be combined with an effort to reduce the instability of our economic institutions, since it is extremely difficult to train students to meet the needs of an economy that is in a state of rapid and unpredictable flux.

THE CONFLICT PERSPECTIVE

Conflict theorists are not convinced that providing equal opportunity and encouraging upward mobility for the poor have ever been goals of our educational system. Rather, they argue that the schools are organized to do just the opposite: to keep members of subordinate groups in their place and prevent them from competing with members of more privileged classes. They point to the fact that free public education for all children is a relatively new idea and that even today many poor children must drop out of school to help support their families. Moreover, expensive private schools provide a superior education for children from the upper classes, whereas the public schools that serve the poor are underfunded, understaffed, and neglected. Conflict theorists also argue that the old system of officially segregated education and the current system of de facto segregation serve to keep oppressed minorities at the bottom of the social heap. Their general conclusion is that the social and cultural biases in the educational system are not an accident but rather reflect a social system that favors the powerful.

Conflict theorists also see the schools as powerful agents of socialization that can be used as a tool for one group to exercise its cultural dominance over another. For example, they argue that by demanding all students learn English, American schools serve to perpetuate the domination of those from one linguistic background over those from all the others.

From the conflict perspective, the best and perhaps only way to change these conditions is for the poor and minorities to organize themselves and reshape the educational system so that it provides everyone with equal opportunity but does not indoctrinate students in the cultural values and beliefs of any particular group. All children must be given the same quality of education that is now available in private schools; cash subsidies must be provided for poor students who would otherwise be forced to drop out of school; and special programs must be set up to provide extra help for children whose parents have a weak educational background. Nevertheless, most conflict theorists probably agree with Christopher Jencks, who concluded that the educational system can do little to reduce inequality without changes in the broader society. Even if there were complete educational equality and everyone were given a college education, social and economic disparities would remain. Such changes would not produce more interesting, highly paid professional jobs or reduce the number of menial, low-paying ones. Thus, educational and social change must be carried out together.

THE FEMINIST PERSPECTIVE

Feminists are deeply concerned about the role of schools in perpetuating gender stereotypes and failing to encourage the highest possible academic achievement from female students. From a feminist standpoint, an effective school system needs to do more than just eliminate obvious gender and ethnic discrimination; it needs to be an active agent for social change—encouraging full gender equality, not just in academic performance but in our social relationships as well.

Another feminist priority is to ensure that our children are in schools where they feel safe no matter what their gender, sexual orientation, or ethnic heritage. They understand that learning cannot occur when a student feels marginalized and threatened.

From this standpoint, it is important that prejudice, discrimination, and bullying behavior are eradicated from the schools. Feminists urge students and their parents to demand an end to this kind of behavior and take a stand strong and firm against the type of brush-off that they often receive from school administrators. They argue that administrators must be held accountable to enforce the laws that have been passed to prevent children from being marginalized and abused.

Many feminists also view the schools in the context of our broader social problems, and they see a vital role for the schools in helping relieve some of the enormous pressures on today's families. The standard of a six-hour school day for nine months of the year fit well with the rhythms of the farm, when children were needed as laborers during the summer harvest season and there was always somebody home after school. But in most of today's families, either both parents work or there is only a single parent in the home. So some feminists call for a new style of school that stays open 12 or 14 hours a day year-round, providing not only more academic work but also recreational and social programs. Feminists argue that such a program could improve the stability of our families, the security of our parents, and the academic achievement of our children.

THE INTERACTIONIST PERSPECTIVE

Interactionists are concerned with the vital role schools play in shaping students' view of reality. Many have commented on the possibility that the authoritarianism so common in our schools impedes learning and encourages undemocratic behavior in later life. Moreover, schools create serious difficulties for students who for one reason or another do not fit into the educational system. The schools show their students a world in which individual competition and achievement is of central importance, and this heavy emphasis on competition and the consequent fear of failure are disturbing to those students who are already anxious and insecure. Students who do not do well in school are often troubled by feelings of depression and inadequacy, and the failure to live up to the academic expectations of parents and teachers is a major contributor to teenage suicide. Many alternative schools, such as Summerhill and Waldorf, attempt to improve this socialization process by deemphasizing competition for grades and placing more importance on enhancing self-esteem. Of course, some children do poorly in such an environment and benefit from a great deal of discipline and an emphasis on obedience to authority. Authoritarian environments may, however, impede the ability of other children to learn and to function effectively; thus, it seems logical to provide the greatest possible range of educational alternatives so that the needs of each student can be met.

The finding that teachers' expectations have a huge influence on student achievement comes as no surprise to interactionists. Interactionists have long known that our behavior is shaped by the way we define the world, so if students are made to feel like high achievers, they will act like high achievers. Interactionists therefore call for teacher-training programs to encourage teachers to understand the critical importance of their role in influencing a student's view of the world, and they urge teachers to avoid branding students with negative labels that oftentimes become self-fulfilling prophecies.

QUICK REVIEW

What would a functionalist, a conflict theorist, a feminist, and an interactionist say about the problems of our educational system?
Which approach do you think is most useful?

Summary

Education was originally reserved for the elite. Today, however, it has become a big business, employing millions of teachers and administrators. Children from the lower classes generally do not do as well in school as children from the middle and upper classes. Poor children usually come to school with a variety of economic and cultural handicaps, and the school system discriminates against these children in a number of ways. Racial and ethnic discrimination in the American educational system go back to the days of slavery. Since the Supreme Court's decision outlawing school segregation, most legal (de jure) discrimination has been abolished. However, de facto (actual) segregation arising from segregated housing patterns is still widespread. In the same way that schools have helped to perpetuate ethnic inequality, they have often served to promote gender inequality.

Schools are always struggling to deal with the twin problems of authority and rebellion. If schools lack discipline, students run wild and education suffers; but if discipline is too strict, students learn antidemocratic values and attitudes, and rebellion and delinquency may increase. There is great concern about the quality of our educational system because of the decline in scores on college entrance examinations and because of North American students' relatively poor showing in international comparisons of academic achievement. Some critics argue that those tests are not a good measure of educational quality; others claim that the problem lies in the changing family environment of today's students; and still others hold the schools themselves responsible.

Many proposals for creating more equal education have been offered. These include programs to achieve more effective integration, to give special assistance to poor and minority students, and to promote gender equality, as well as reforms in school financing. Suggestions for improving the educational process itself include raising academic standards and requiring more homework, lengthening the school year, restructuring the schools to give teachers and local administrators more power, making education a more attractive career so that schools can hire better teachers, and increasing the cultural value we place on learning.

Functionalists argue that the educational system is not running smoothly and that solving the problems of education is mostly a matter of reorganizing schools so that they will operate more efficiently. Conflict theorists are prone to look beyond the stated goals of the educational system and argue that economic and political elites use the schools to help maintain the status quo and the privileges those groups enjoy. Feminists argue that the schools need to actively promote gender equality and institute programs to help relieve some of the pressure on today's families. Interactionists are concerned with the way the schools help shape their students' view of reality and with the harmful impact that negative labeling and an excessive emphasis on competition can have.

QUESTIONS FOR CRITICAL THINKING

Take a critical look at your own education. Were you one of the privileged students, or did you suffer from some kind of educational disadvantage? How good an education do you think you have received so far? How would you compare the quality of your education with that of a typical American student? This chapter discussed many different problems in our educational system. Which ones did you encounter in your own education?

KEY TERMS

affirmative action program	goal displacement
authoritarianism	hidden curriculum
compensatory education program	home schooling
computer literacy	magnet school
cultural capital	prep school
de facto segregation	resegregation
de jure segregation	segregated school
desegregation	sexism
distance learning	Standard English
functionally illiterate	voucher system

NOTES

1. Romesh Ratnesar, "Class-Size Warfare," *Time*, October 6, 1997, p. 85.
2. U.S. Bureau of the Census, *Statistical Abstract of the United States*, 2000 (Washington, D.C.: U.S. Government Printing Office, 2000), p. 830.
3. U.S. Bureau of the Census, *Statistical Abstract of the United States*, 1996 (Washington, D.C.: U.S. Government Printing Office, 1996), p. 158.
4. Quoted in Mavis Hiltunen Biesanz and John Biesanz, *Introduction to Sociology*, 2nd ed. (Upper Saddle River, NJ: Prentice Hall, 1973), p. 616.
5. See Pamela Barnhouse Walters and Richard Rubinson, "Educational Expansion and Economic Output in the United States, 1890–1969," *American Sociological Review* 48 (1983): 480.
6. See Harold R. Kerbo, *Social Stratification and Inequality*, 4th ed. (New York: McGraw-Hill, 2000), pp. 362–365.
7. Robert James Parelius and Ann Parker Parelius, *The Sociology of Education*, 2nd ed. (Upper Saddle River, NJ: Prentice Hall, 1987), p. 265.
8. See S. Leonard Syme and Lisa F. Berkman, "Social Class, Susceptibility and Sickness," in Howard D. Schwartz, ed., *Dominant Issues in Medical Sociology*, 2nd ed. (New York: Random House, 1987), pp. 643–649.
9. Kerbo, *Social Stratification and Inequality*, pp. 359–361.
10. U.S. Bureau of the Census, *Statistical Abstract*, 1996, p. 170.
11. William Celis III, "Michigan Votes for Revolution in Financing Its Public Schools," *New York Times*, March 17, 1994, pp. A1, A9; Bob Secter, "Gaps Between Rich, Poor Schools Ignite Legal Fights," *Los Angeles Times*, November 26, 1990, pp. A1, A20.
12. James S. Coleman et al., *Equality of Educational Opportunity* (Washington, D.C.: U.S. Government Printing Office, 1966); Christopher Jencks et al., *Inequality: A Reassessment of the Effects of Family and Schooling in America* (New York: HarperCollins, 1972); Harvey A. Averch et al., *How*

Effective Is Schooling?: A Critical Synthesis and Review of Research Findings (Upper Saddle River, NJ: Prentice Hall, 1974); Samuel Bowles and Herbert Gintis, *Schooling in Capitalist America* (New York: Basic Books, 1976).

13. Elizabeth Ross, "A Leveling of Granite State Schools," *Christian Science Monitor*, March 14, 1994, p. 10.
14. Lawrence Mishel and Jared Bernstein, *The State of Working America, 1992–93* (New York: Sharpe, 1993), p. 374.
15. U.S. Bureau of the Census, *Statistical Abstract*, 1999, p. 163.
16. See Parelius and Parelius, *The Sociology of Education*, pp. 293–296.
17. Robert Rosenthal and Lenore Jacobson, *Pygmalion in the Classroom* (New York: HarperCollins, 1969).
18. See Roy Nash, *Teacher Expectations and Pupil Learning* (London: Routledge & Kegan Paul, 1976); Parelius and Parelius, *The Sociology of Education*, pp. 293–296.
19. D. G. Harvey and G. T. Slatin, "The Relationship Between a Child's SES and Teacher Expectations," *Social Forces* 54 (1975): 140–159.
20. Kerbo, *Social Stratification and Inequality*, pp. 138–139, 232–233, 363.
21. See Jeannie Oakes, *Multiplying Inequalities* (Santa Monica, CA: Rand Corporation, 1990); Kerbo, *Social Stratification and Inequality*, pp. 362–363.
22. Karl Alexander, Martha Cook, and Edward L. Dill, "Curriculum Tracking and Educational Stratification," *American Sociological Review* 43 (1978): 47–66.
23. William Celis III, "Study Finds Rising Concentration of Black and Hispanic Students," *New York Times*, December 14, 1993, pp. A1, A11; William J. Eaton, "Segregation in U.S. Schools on Rise, Study Finds," *Los Angeles Times*, December 14, 1993, pp. A1, A22.
24. Coleman et al., *Equality of Educational Opportunity*.
25. Rita E. Mahard and Robert L. Crain, "Research on Minority Achievement in Desegregated Schools," in Christine H. Rossell and Willis D. Hawley, eds., *The Consequences of School Desegregation* (Philadelphia: Temple University Press, 1983), pp. 103–125.
26. See Janet Eyler, Valerie J. Cook, and Leslie E. Ward, "Resegregation: Segregation Within Desegregated Schools," in Rossell and Hawley, *The Consequences of School Desegregation*, pp. 126–162.
27. U.S. Department of Education, *National Assessment of Educational Progress* (Washington D.C., U.S. Government Printing Office, 2000).
28. U.S. Bureau of the Census, *Educational Attainment in the United States, 1999* (Washington, D.C.: U.S. Government Printing Office, 2000.
29. Ibid., p. 3.
30. Ibid., p. 204.
31. U.S. Bureau of the Census, *Statistical Abstract of the United States*, 2000, p. 194.
32. Richard Lee Colvin, "14% of Students Have Carried Weapon to School, Study Says," *Los Angeles Times*, March 10, 1997, pp. B1, B3.
33. Phillip Kaufman et al., *Indicators of School Crime and Safety, 1999* (Washington, D.C.: National Center for Educational Statistics, 1999); U.S. Bureau of the Census, *Statistical Abstract*, 1999, p. 221.
34. U.S. Bureau of the Census, *Statistical Abstract*, 1999, p. 172.
35. Tamar Lewin, "School Codes Without Mercy Snare Pupils Without Malice," *New York Times*, March 12, 1997, pp. A1, A13.
36. See John Devine, *Maximum Security* (Chicago: University of Chicago Press, 1996).
37. Irwin S. Kirsch, Ann Jungeblut, Lynn Jenkins, and Andrew Kolstad, *Adult Literacy in America: A First Look at the Results of the National Literacy Survey* (Washington, D.C.: Department of Education, 1993).
38. U.S. Bureau of the Census, *Statistical Abstract*, 2000, p. 177.
39. U.S. Department of Education, *National Assessment of Educational Progress, 1999* (Washington D.C.: U.S. Government Printing Office, 2000).
40. Ibid.
41. M. Lemke, et. al. *Highlights from the 2000 Program for International Student Assessment*, National Center for Education Statistics, December 4, 2001, <http://www.nces.gov>.

42. William Celis III, "International Report Card Shows U.S. Schools Work," *New York Times*, December 9, 1993, pp. A1, A8; Andrew L. Shapiro, *We're Number One: Where America Stands and Falls in the New World Order* (New York: Vintage, 1992), pp. 64–69.

43. Stanley Meisler, "Americans Get No Gold Stars for Current Events Answers," *Los Angeles Times*, March 16, 1994, p. A9.

44. National Commission on Education and Learning, *Prisoners of Time* (Washington, D.C.: U.S. Government Printing Office, April 1994).

45. Robert J. Samuelson, "Why School Reform Fails," *Newsweek*, May 27, 1991, pp. 62, 68.

46. Peter Applebome, "U.S. Gets Average Grades in Math and Science Studies," *New York Times*, November 21, 1996, pp. A1, A21.

47. Shapiro, *We're Number One*, p. 71.

48. Parelius and Parelius, *The Sociology of Education*, pp. 334–335.

49. William Celis III, "Study Suggests Head Start Helps Beyond School," *New York Times*, April 20, 1993, p. A9; see also John R. Berrueta-Clement et al., *Changed Lives: The Effects of the Perry Preschool Program on Youths Through Age 19* (Ypsilanti, MI: High/Scope, 1984).

50. David G. Savage, "U.S. School Aid: Looking for Results," *Los Angeles Times*, April 11, 1985, sec. 1, p. 1.

51. For an exception to this rule, see John R. Berrueta-Clement et al., *Changed Lives*.

52. Seymour Martin Lipset, *American Exceptionalism: A Double-Edged Sword* (New York: Norton, 1996), pp. 125–131.

53. See *International Herald Tribune*, October 11, 2000.

54. Michael Rutter, *15,000 Hours: Secondary Schools and Their Effect on Children* (Cambridge, MA: Harvard University Press, 1979).

55. James S. Coleman, Thomas Hoffer, and Sally Kilgore, *High School Achievement: Public, Catholic and Private Schools* (New York: Basic Books, 1982), p. 178.

56. Shapiro, *We're Number One*, p. 60; Michael J. Barrett, "The Case for More School Days," *Atlantic Monthly*, November 1990, pp. 78–106.

57. Dennis Kelly, "Panel: Extend School Year," *USA Today*, May 5, 1994, p. 53A; U.S. Department of Education, *National Assessment of Educational Progress* (Washington D.C., U.S. Government Printing Office. 2000.

58. Tom Morganthau, "The Future Is Now," *Newsweek*, *Special Edition on Education*, fall–winter 1990, pp. 72–76.

59. David L. Kirp, "What School Choice Really Means," *Atlantic Monthly*, November 1992, pp. 119–132.

60. Associated Press, "Baltimore Ends School Privatization Experiment," *San Luis Obispo Telegram-Tribune*, November 23, 1995, p. A6; George Judson, "Improved Schools at a Profit: Is a Private Effort Working?" *New York Times*, November 14, 1994, pp. A1, A12; William Celis III, "Hopeful Start for Profit Making Schools," *New York Times*, October 6, 1993, pp. A1, B3.

61. A. S. Neil, *Summerhill: A Radical Approach to Child Rearing* (New York: Hart, 1960).

62. Ronald E. Kotzsch, "Waldorf Schools: Education for Head, Hands, and Heart," *Utne Reader*, September–October 1990, pp. 84–90.

63. Elaine Woo, "Study Calls Poor Teacher Training a 'National Shame,'" *Los Angeles Times*, May 26, 1997, pp. A1, A5.

64. U.S. Bureau of the Census, *Statistical Abstract*, 2000, p. 169; Shapiro, *We're Number One*, p. 63.

65. Jonathan H. Mark and Barry Anderson, "Teacher Survival Rates: A Current Look," *American Journal of Educational Research* 15 (1978): 379–383.

66. Tom Hayden, "Running Short of Good Teachers," *Los Angeles Times*, June 24, 1983, sec. 2, p. 5.

67. U.S. Bureau of the Census, *Statistical Abstract*, 2000, p.173.

68. See Shapiro, *We're Number One*.

CHAPTER 5

HEALTH AND HEALTH CARE

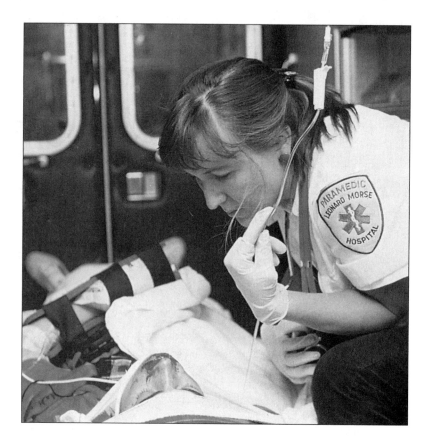

Questions to Consider

What are the most frequent causes of physical and mental disorders?

What are the special problems associated with mental disorders?

How well does the U.S. health care system work in comparison with other countries?

What are the ethical dilemmas posed by modern medicine?

How can the U.S. health care system be improved?

Gene Hays made a big mistake when he retired. He gave up his health insurance because he just couldn't afford the $500 monthly payments. Six months later his wife had a heart attack, and she has been in a coma ever since. Gene became one of those unlucky people who "fall between the cracks" in the health care system. Too young to qualify for Medicare (the government health care program for the elderly) and not eligible for Medicaid (the medical welfare program for the poor), the Hayses were on their own. Mr. Hays, who suffers from Parkinson's disease, together with his 93-year-old father had to take care of his wife when she came home from the hospital, managing the complicated medical equipment necessary to keep her alive. The costs were staggering. He soon used up all the savings they had accumulated for retirement, and he started selling off their other assets one by one.[1]

Illness and death are an unavoidable part of human life. Society nonetheless has a profound influence on our **health** and on the ways we cope with our illnesses. Countless people like Gene Hays are financially ruined by the cost of today's high-tech medical care, and millions more simply don't get the kind of health care they need. But our society has a great impact on our health before we ever get to the doctor. Society helps determine what kind of diet we eat, how many dangerous pollutants we are exposed to, how much stress we feel, and even how much we smoke and drink. Although most people don't realize it, our social groups even tell us when we are sick and when we are healthy. The visions that modern psychiatry interprets as a symptom of mental illness, for instance, may be seen as a special religious insight by some tribal people. The diarrhea and upset stomach that send us to the doctor are often accepted as normal conditions by people in poor countries. And when we do get sick, the availability, quality, and organization of health care help determine how quickly we recover—or whether we recover at all.

Overall, the world's people today are healthier and will live longer than those of any other generation in history. In the eighteenth century, the average life span in even the most prosperous nations was no more than 35 years. Dramatic declines in infant mortality and in deaths from contagious diseases have helped extend the average life expectancy in the industrialized nations to 75 years.[2] Although it is much harder to measure historical changes in mental health, the standards by which we judge it have certainly grown much higher. Only a century ago, conditions that would warrant serious medical concern today, such as depression or severe anxiety, were usually ignored. Only those who were unable to carry on a normal life were considered to be mentally disordered.

PHYSICAL ILLNESS

The great improvement in living conditions in the past century is the main reason people live longer today than they did in the past. A rising standard of living and increased agricultural production have meant better food, shelter, and clothing for the average person. The construction of sewer and water purification systems has sharply reduced waterborne disease. Although sophisticated and expensive medical procedures such as open-heart surgery have added little to the average life span, some medical breakthroughs, such as antibiotics and immunizations against contagious diseases, have been extremely important.

Not all changes that have transformed the world have been beneficial to our health, however. Stress, overindulgence, and environmental pollution can cripple and kill as effectively as typhoid or tuberculosis, and the ancient scourges of poverty, malnutrition, and warfare still plague humankind. We will begin our examination of contemporary health problems with a look at the way our lifestyle contributes to ill health; then we will explore the problems caused by physical injuries, environmental hazards, contagious diseases, and poverty.

UNHEALTHY LIFESTYLES

Most North Americans are far less active than their ancestors were. Laborsaving devices ranging from the automobile to the electric toothbrush have reduced the amount of physical effort required for daily living, and automation has created an increasing number of "thinking jobs" that demand no harder work than picking up a pencil or making a phone call. Medical research shows that regular exercise is essential to good health. Not only do people who exercise regularly report that they feel better, but exercise has been shown to reduce significantly the risk of heart disease—the leading cause of death in North America. In fact, a study of Boston men by Charles Rose and his associates found that the amount of exercise a person gets is one of the best predictors of longevity.[3]

Diet is another aspect of lifestyle that has a profound impact on health. Although there are many disagreements about what type of diet is most conducive to good health, there is a growing consensus among nutritionists about what is wrong with the way we eat. As the surgeon general's Report on Nutrition and Health concluded, North Americans eat too many fatty foods, such as red meat, and not enough fruits, vegetables, and whole-grain products. Our sugar consumption should be reduced and the fiber in our diet increased. Despite repeated warnings, however, North Americans' love of high-calorie food and our tendency to overeat have caused obesity to become a serious problem. Research shows that heart disease, high blood pressure, and diabetes are all associated with obesity, and the National Center for Health Statistics now estimates that one-third of all Americans are obese.[4]

Despite heated denials from the tobacco industry, there is no longer any doubt that smoking is a serious health hazard. It has been linked to a long list of diseases, including lung cancer, emphysema, ulcers, and heart disorders. The surgeon general's yearly reports on smoking state that, among other things, the death rate of smokers is 70 percent higher than that of nonsmokers the same age, and the death rate of heavy smokers (two or more packs a day) is double that of nonsmokers. A study in the *Journal of the American Medical Association* that looked at the underlying causes of fatal illness recently concluded that tobacco smoking causes almost one in every five deaths in the United States, making it America's number one cause of death.[5] Although there are some disagreements among researchers about the criteria for addiction, many feel that tobacco is more addictive than heroin, cocaine, or any other commonly used drug (see Chapter 9).[6] Growing concerns are also being raised about the effects of nonsmokers' exposure to tobacco. A report to the Environmental Protection Agency estimates that 53,000 Americans die because of "passive smoking" every year, and the EPA has declared secondhand smoke a "group A" carcinogen.[7]

Smoking is a personal choice, but stress seems to be an almost unavoidable part of modern life. The initial symptoms of stress, such as irritability, insomnia, and a queasy stomach, are usually minor, and a certain amount of stress may even be necessary to good mental health; but high levels of stress over long periods of time can lead to serious health problems. One study found that two-thirds of all air traffic controllers in the United States have peptic ulcers, probably as a result of the demands of a job in which a mistake may mean death for hundreds of people.[8] Stress is also associated with heart disease. A study of lawyers, dentists, and physicians found a strong correlation between the amount of stress associated with their specialty and their rates of heart disease; thus, general-practice lawyers had less heart trouble than trial lawyers, who had less heart trouble than patent lawyers. Interestingly, a study conducted by Columbia University found that workers such as waiters and telephone operators, who face heavy demands but have little decision-making control, are the most likely to have heart and circulatory problems.[9]

PHYSICAL INJURIES: SUICIDE, ACCIDENTS, AND VIOLENT CRIMES

Accidents are the leading cause of death among Americans from the time they are born until they reach middle age.[10] Common household accidents cause a huge number of injuries every year, but the most frequent type of fatal accidents involves motor vehicles. Fortunately, our society has become increasingly aware of these dangers. Legislation now requires automobile manufacturers to include such safety features as seat belts and air bags, and stronger efforts to combat drunken driving have also had considerable success (see Chapter 9). Lawsuits and consumer pressure have also forced the manufacturers of other products to improve their safety, and better educational efforts have taught people how to reduce their risks of harm. Overall, the death rate from accidents declined by more than one-third since 1970.[11] Rates of death and injury in the workplace have also declined. From 1992 to 1998 there was a 13 percent drop, down to 4.5 deaths per 100,000 workers.[12] Although accidents account for more deaths than suicides and homicides combined, the death rates from such intentional violence have shown some significant decreases in recent years.[13] (The causes of violent crime are discussed in Chapter 10.)

Suicide, which is actually more common than homicide, has very different causes and usually strikes a different type of victim. Unlike homicides or accidents, suicide is most common among elderly people and among whites rather than members of ethnic minorities. With the exception of some relatively rare acts of self-sacrifice, most people kill themselves because their lives seem so painful and unpleasant that they no longer want to continue living. What makes people feel that way? Emile Durkheim, the famous French sociologist, argued that the lack of supportive social groups leaves people aimless and unhappy, and he mustered an impressive battery of statistics to show that suicide rates are higher among those who are not part of such groups.[14] Psychologists, on the other hand, tend to focus on more individual characteristics, for example, a disturbed childhood or a mental disorder such as acute depression. Although they often seem irrational to others, suicidal individuals may actually be trying to achieve concrete goals by their attempts at self-destruction. A suicide attempt may be a way of calling for help or an effort to punish relatives or loved ones the victims believe have let them down.[15]

ENVIRONMENTAL HAZARDS

The pollutants that industries dump into the environment are more than just an ugly nuisance; they are killers. Air pollution has been found to be related to deaths from bronchitis, heart disease, and emphysema, as well as several types of cancer. An American Lung Association study concluded that between 50,000 and 120,000 deaths a year are linked to the air pollution caused by trucks and cars.[16] The Environmental Protection Agency estimates that exposure to radon gas causes 7,000 to 30,000 deaths a year.[17] And there is little doubt that the depletion of the ozone layer caused by atmospheric pollution is a major factor in the increase in skin cancer (see Chapter 12). The contamination of water with poisonous wastes, such as lead and mercury, has already taken many lives, and the list of new dangers grows daily. Over a thousand new chemicals are placed on the market every year, and most of the tens of thousands of chemical compounds already used by industry have never been thoroughly tested to find out how dangerous they are.

Not surprisingly, laborers who work directly with dangerous substances are at greatest risk. Steelworkers are 7.5 times more likely to die of cancer of the kidney and 10 times more likely to die of lung cancer than people in other occupations—but steelworkers are lucky compared with asbestos workers. Almost half of the 500,000 workers who were exposed to high doses of asbestos will die as a result: 100,000 are expected to die of lung cancer, 35,000 of asbestosis (another lung disease), and 35,000 of mesothelioma (an otherwise rare cancer of the linings of the lungs and stomach).[18] The Centers for Disease Control and Prevention estimate that about 17 workers a day were killed on the job during the last decade. A much larger number—perhaps 100,000 persons a year—die more slowly from the effects of occupationally caused diseases.[19]

CONTAGIOUS DISEASE

Cancer and diseases of the heart and circulatory system are the most frequent causes of death in wealthy industrial societies, but such killers are seldom the causes of ordinary health problems. Most common difficulties result from the relatively minor **contagious diseases** that are a seemingly inevitable part of daily life. A ten-year study of families in Cleveland, Ohio, found that common respiratory and intestinal diseases (colds, bronchitis, flu, and the like) accounted for 76 percent of all illnesses. The average person in this study had 5.6 respiratory and 1.5 intestinal diseases a year.[20]

Although these relatively minor ailments remain a continuing problem, great progress has been made against the death-dealing epidemics that once threatened humanity. Improvements in sanitation and water treatment have all but eliminated such waterborne diseases as cholera and typhoid from the industrialized nations and have sharply reduced their incidence in many poor countries. Vaccinations have had even greater success against other dread diseases such as polio and smallpox.

For a while it actually seemed that we were on the way to eliminating most of the contagious diseases that had threatened the human race for countless centuries. The tide has shifted, however, and it is obvious that the battle against these killers is far from over. Some of our current problems stem from simple neglect. For example, one in ten American preschoolers have not been vaccinated against polio, and that figure is about the same for measles and tetanus.[21] Although conditions in the Third World have improved, the struggle against contagious disease has never been as successful there as in the industrialized nations. Over 1 billion people in the world today lack safe drinking water; almost 2 billion have no access to proper sanitary facilities; and on the average there is less than 1 doctor for every 6,000 people.[22] As a result, diseases such as hepatitis, measles, malaria, and cholera take millions of lives a year. In addition, medical researchers have paid much closer attention to the diseases that affect people in rich countries. One study concluded that in 1996, about $3,274 was spent on AIDS research for every person who died from the disease, but only $65 was spent on malaria research for each fatal case of that disease.[23]

Another blow to our efforts to control contagious disease has come from the development of new strains of viruses and bacteria. One major problem is that many diseases eventually develop a genetic resistance to the antibiotics that are used against them. New strains of tuberculosis, malaria, and other contagious diseases are resistant to drugs that used to be highly effective against them. As a result, physicians must rely on more expensive medications that may not be as effective as the ones they replaced. This is a particular problem in the less-developed countries, where there is seldom enough money for even the most inexpensive drugs.

In addition to the antibiotic-resistant strains of old diseases, several entirely new (or at least previously unknown) viruses have emerged in recent years. The most dangerous of these is **human immunodeficiency virus (HIV)**, which causes **acquired immune deficiency syndrome (AIDS)**. Virtually unknown as recently as 1980, there were over 100,000 new cases of AIDS reported in the United States in 1993, and although the peak of the epidemic seems to have passed in 1999, there were still a little over 46,000 new cases.[24] The disease attacks the body's immune system, leaving it vulnerable to a host of other diseases. AIDS often lies dormant without symptoms for years, but once it becomes active, it is usually fatal. Current treatments can extend the life of the patient, but at present there is no known cure.

Fortunately, AIDS is not easily transmitted from one person to another; a direct exchange of body fluids is usually necessary. The most common forms of transmission in the industrialized nations are sexual intercourse and needle sharing among intravenous drug users.[25] In contrast, most AIDS cases in Africa (where the infection rates are the highest in the world) are transmitted through heterosexual activities such as prostitution. This is probably because Africans are in poorer overall health and are much more likely to be infected with other sexually transmitted diseases. (HIV is more easily transmitted to someone who already has another **sexually transmitted disease**.) In the last few years, the number of new cases of AIDS transmitted through homosexual contact has decreased in Western countries (although homosexual activity is still the most common way the disease is spread), while infection through intravenous drug use and heterosexual contacts has increased. The chances of contracting AIDS heterosexually remain low unless one partner is a bisexual male or an intravenous drug user.[26]

Despite the lack of a cure, new medical treatments have dramatically reduced the mortality rate among those who have AIDS in the United States—there was a 21 percent reduction between 1997 and 1998, and a 48 percent reduction between 1996 and 1997. Like many other diseases, AIDS is most widespread among the poor and

Because the AIDS epidemic first began among groups that were unpopular with large segments of the public, its victims and their supporters have had to band together and demand greater public attention to the problem.

minorities. The rate of infection among Latinos is more than double the rate for European Americans, and the rate for African Americans is seven times higher. Moreover, the differences are even greater among women and children from those groups.[27]

One of the most frightening things about the AIDS epidemic is the projection of how many people it will strike. The World Health Organization estimates 20 million people are already infected with HIV, and although the spread of the virus seems to be slowing in the industrialized nations, it is continuing unabated in the Third World. Unless a cure or an inexpensive treatment is found soon, the vast majority of those people can be expected to die from the disease, and the human impact of such an occurrence would obviously be staggering. Even the health care systems of the rich countries are ill prepared to deal with the flood of desperately sick AIDS patients, and things are far worse in the poor countries. Moreover, most poor nations have no social-welfare systems capable of coping with the growing number of orphans the epidemic is leaving in its wake.

There have been some significant new strides in treating AIDS sufferers, but until medical researchers can find a cure or an effective vaccine, the best way to combat this epidemic is by changing behavior. The two steps most likely to be effective are the use of condoms by all sexually active people who are not in a strictly monogamous relationship and an end to needle sharing by intravenous drug users.

It is hard for someone who doesn't know anyone infected with HIV to understand the suffering and depression AIDS can bring, and that is especially true when the victims are in faraway places where the epidemic is most severe. Cold figures can at least be helpful, even though they are sometimes so shocking that they are hard to believe. The epidemic is growing fastest in Asia, where there was a 70 percent increase in AIDS cases just between 1996 and 1998. But AIDS is likely to have its most devastating impact in Africa. Already it is estimated that each day more than 5,000 people die of AIDS-related illnesses in the African countries. It is anticipated that life expectancy in Africa will drop dramatically in the years ahead to as low as 29 years in some countries. (Life expectancy in the United States is now 77 years.) As of December 1999, over a quarter of the population of Botswana, Swasiland, and Zimbabwe were infected with the virus that causes AIDS, and the infection rate was around 20 percent in several other countries. This means that barring some unexpected medical breakthrough, many countries in Africa are likely to see a sharp drop in their population in the years ahead. There are already estimated to be 13.2 million African children orphaned by AIDS, and the number can only go up. In the next 10 years, the number of AIDS deaths in Africa will exceed all of those killed in both World War I and World War II, and it will be far greater than the 20 million people who were killed by the infamous bubonic plague that devastated Europe in the fourteenth century.[28]

POVERTY

There is overwhelming evidence that poor people have more health problems than those who are better off. The effects of poverty are obvious in the overpopulated agricultural nations. Lack of clothing, housing, and food takes a frightening toll; epidemic disease is commonplace; and 10 to 20 million people simply starve to death every year (see Chapter 11). The United Nations estimates that malnutrition causes 55 percent of the 12 million deaths of children under the age of 5 years that occur in the world every year.[29] The infant mortality rates in such countries as Iraq, Nigeria, and Pakistan are at least 10 times higher than in the United States, even though the United States itself has the highest infant mortality rate of any major industrialized nation.[30]

The problems of the poor are less visible in industrialized nations, but they are no less real. These problems include lower life expectancies, higher rates of infant death, and more contagious disease, heart ailments, arthritis, and high blood pressure. One study, which tracked over 1,000 poor people in California for 30 years, found that poverty is as bad for your health as smoking cigarettes.[31] African American children in the United States are twice as likely as white children to die in their first year of life, and a number of studies show that poor people and members of ethnic minorities are sick more days a year than the wealthy. African Americans are 39 percent more likely to die from cancer, 45 percent more likely to die from heart disease, and 150 percent more likely to die from diabetes than other Americans. An African American man in Harlem now has a shorter life expectancy than the impoverished citizens of Bangladesh. When asked about their health, poor people are about three times more likely to say that it is only fair or poor or that they have some serious chronic illness.[32] Research shows that there is a direct correlation between income level and death rates. The death rate for Americans with an income of less than $9,000 per year is 16.0 per 1,000 people for men and 6.5 for women. For those with more than $25,000 income per year, the death rates are only 2.4 for males and 1.6 for females.[33]

The relationship between poverty and poor health is not difficult to understand. About 25 million Americans cannot afford to keep themselves adequately fed and are therefore particularly susceptible to illness and disease. Their diet contains more cheap fatty foods, and poor people are more likely to be overweight. Lack of proper sanitation and protection from rain, snow, cold, and heat also take their toll. Reports of rat bites in slum areas number in the thousands each year. Moreover, daily life for the poor is stressful as they struggle to pay their bills and buy groceries. As Leonard Syme and Lisa Berkman put it, the poor have "higher rates of schizophrenia, are more depressed, more unhappy, more worried, more anxious, and are less hopeful about the future."[34] Finally, as we will see, the poor receive inferior care when they are sick.

QUICK REVIEW

How do unhealthy lifestyles contribute to physical illness?
How serious a health problem are accidents and environmental hazards?
What are the most deadly contagious diseases?
Why is poverty a health hazard?

MENTAL DISORDERS

Although there are deep disagreements about what is good mental health and what is **mental disorder**, there is no question at all that serious psychological problems are extremely common in our society. The best evidence we have on this issue comes from the National Comorbidity Survey headed by Ronald C. Kessler. The researchers asked a broad sample of 8,098 Americans aged 15 to 54 detailed questions about their mental health, and they reached some startling conclusions. Close to half the sample (48 percent) had experienced a mental disorder at some time in their lives, and in any given year, almost one-third suffer from a mental disorder. The most common problems were major depression, alcohol dependence, and various kinds of phobias.[35]

American men between the ages of 14 and 45 spend more time in the hospital for mental disorders than for any other cause, and only childbirth accounts for more days in the hospital for women of that age.[36] Yet most people who have mental problems never get to a hospital or receive professional help of any kind. The National Comorbidity Survey found that only four of every ten persons who had had a serious mental problem received any professional treatment.[37] The others turn to friends or to one of the dozens of new "pop psychology" books published every year, or they simply ignore their problems and hope that somehow the problems will go away. Even those who seek out professional help often find that the health care system is poorly equipped to meet their needs.

WHAT ARE MENTAL DISORDERS?

Few things are more frightening than the thought of "going crazy," but what does that expression really mean? Terms like mental illness or insanity may bring to mind images of a madman foaming at the mouth, struggling to break free of his straitjacket, or a disheveled woman babbling incoherently while she wanders the streets. Most mental disorders are neither bizarre nor dramatic, however; instead, they involve the common experiences of anxiety or depression.

Speaking generally, a person may be said to have a mental disorder if he or she is so disturbed that coping with routine, everyday life is difficult or impossible—but this definition, like most others, is vague. Exactly how do we determine whether individuals can or cannot cope with their everyday affairs? Or, for that matter, how can we tell if their circumstances are "normal" or so difficult that most people would have trouble dealing with them? Although many social scientists have attempted to define mental disorder more precisely, none of the definitions has received universal acceptance.

In the past, mental disorders were commonly believed to be caused by demons and spirits. "Treatments" such as flogging, starving, prayers and chants, and dunking the sufferer in boiling water were used to drive the devils out. As the scientific way of thinking gained strength, serious psychological disorders came to be seen as mental illnesses caused by the same natural forces as physical illnesses. Thus, the concepts and methods of modern medicine came to be used to diagnose and treat mental illness in the same fashion as, for instance, a sprained knee or the measles.[38]

A major alternative to the medical model holds that mental disorders represent problems of personal maladjustment. According to this perspective, mental disorders arise when someone is unable to deal effectively with his or her personal difficulties, and disturbed behavior is therefore caused by the same forces that govern other behavior. Therapists who use this approach do not look for symptoms of a specific disease; instead, they examine the patient's overall adjustment to his or her environment. Supporters of the personal-maladjustment approach point to two advantages it has over the medical model. First, it does not consider individuals in isolation from their environment, as a physician would when treating a broken leg or a "mental illness." Second, because abnormal behavior is seen to be produced by the same processes as normal behavior, this perspective discourages the assumption that mentally disturbed people are "freaks" or "lunatics." The personal-maladjustment approach has its shortcomings, however. Although it does not ignore the individual's environment, it still assumes that the individual—not the social order—is responsible for psychological disturbance. Yet some problems stem from an unlivable environment rather than an individual's deficiencies. In some circumstances, the healthiest individuals may actually be the ones who are not well adjusted to their social environment.

A more radical approach to mental disorders derives from **labeling theory**, which is discussed in Chapter 10. The idea is that there are really no objective standards by which to judge someone's mental health. From this perspective, the determination that someone is or is not mentally disordered is strictly a cultural matter, and what is considered mental illness in one culture may be perfectly normal in another. Thus, mental "illness" is really a form of social deviance. However, mental illness differs from other kinds of deviance in one important way—the rules that the mentally ill violate are so commonly accepted that most people don't even realize they are social rules. If a man stabs his wife to death while she is sleeping, he is labeled a murderer; if a woman sells sex, she is branded a prostitute. Most people condemn such behavior, but they still feel they understand why those people did what they did. People who do something we can't understand—refuse to come out of their room for months at a time or declare that they are Joan of Arc or Hitler—we label mentally ill.[39]

Because the social-deviance approach places responsibility for mental disorders on the environment rather than on the individual, the stigma of mental illness is removed. Therapists are encouraged to deal with the patient's family and personal environment rather than assuming that the patient is suffering from a personal defect or disorder. However, this approach has been severely criticized by experts who hold more traditional ideas about mental health and mental illness. These experts point out that the labeling approach neglects the disturbed individuals themselves and says nothing about the causes of the behavior that resulted in their labeling. Even if no one were labeled "mentally ill," people would still suffer from the same problems: their hallucinations, delusions, intense depressions, and anxieties would still be there. Further, the critics argue that labeling people who have mental problems is the only way we can identify those who need help.

In addition, both the personal-maladjustment and the social-deviance approach are often criticized for ignoring the ever-growing evidence about the biological basis of many mental disorders. If mental disorders are caused by some kind of biochemical abnormality, then it is easy to conclude that like physical illness, they are centered within the body of the patient. The defenders of the socially oriented theories, on the other hand, argue that while there are certainly biological differences in brain function among different individuals, it is society, not biology, that renders some types of behavioral tendencies a problem. For example, millions of American children who have trouble concentrating in class and following the rules in school are diagnosed as being "hyperactive" and prescribed various drugs to "cure" the problem. In traditional agricultural societies, where formal education in school is far less important, there is simply no such thing as hyperactivity. Similarly, when someone in contemporary industrial culture hears voices or has visions, they are often labeled mentally ill and given various drugs to try to cure their problem. In many tribal societies, on the other hand, such a person would be looked at as not having some kind of problem but a special gift for communicating with the gods and spirits.

CLASSIFYING MENTAL DISORDERS

Mental problems are as diverse as the people who suffer from them. In one way or another, every individual problem is unique; but those who work with the mentally disturbed have long sought a standardized system to help make sense out of these diverse problems. The most widely accepted classification is the American Psychiatric Association's *Diagnostic and Statistical Manual of Mental Disorders* (DSM). First published in 1952, this manual has been revised over the years, and critics charge that the changes have been motivated as much by political pressure and trends in public opinion as by new scientific knowledge. Changing public attitudes and pressure from gay activists resulted in the removal of homosexuality from the list of mental disorders in 1974, but less-organized groups, such as sadomasochists, remain on the list. Similarly, as the antismoking movement gained power, tobacco dependence was included as a mental disorder for the first time. Critics also point out that psychiatrists often use these diagnostic categories in inconsistent and contradictory ways. For example, in one study, 131 patients were randomly selected from a large mental hospital and rediagnosed by a team of evaluators. In the majority of cases, the new diagnosis did not agree with the old one. Only 16 of the 89 patients originally diagnosed as schizophrenic were given the same diagnosis by the research team.[40]

Despite its weaknesses, however, the DSM is still the best classification system we have. Although many categories of mental disorders are listed in the current DSM, three are far more common than the others (see Figure 5.1). The **mood disorders** most commonly involve some kind of depression. Of course, everyone feels sad at one time or another, but "major depression" involves not only a deep sadness but such things as fatigue, loss of appetite, low self-esteem, and a feeling of hopelessness. **Bipolar disorder**, on the other hand, generally involves alternating periods of depression and "mania" (a period when the victim is agitated, restless, and hyperactive.) **Substance abuse disorders** include problems resulting from the use of alcohol, tobacco, or illegal drugs. By some measures, the most common disorders of all are the **anxiety disorders**. Like sadness, anxiety is certainly a normal part of daily life. Anxiety disorders, however, involve severe and prolonged anxiety as well as irrational fears (phobias), panic attacks, obsessive thoughts and rituals, and posttraumatic stress syndrome (the debilitating consequences of a traumatic event such as being raped or being in a vicious military battle).

One of the most severe and persistent mental disorders is **schizophrenia**. Its symptoms include delusions, hallucinations, and disturbances in the thought process. Schizophrenia is, however, relatively rare. The National Comorbidity Survey found that less than 1 percent of the American population had ever suffered from this problem.[41]

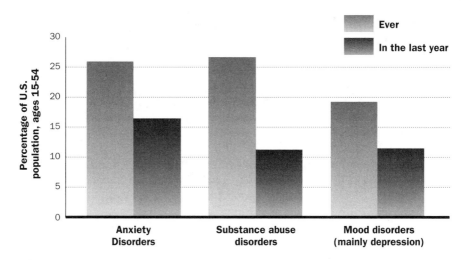

FIGURE 5.1   MENTAL DISORDERS

The most common mental disorders involve anxiety, depression, or substance abuse.

Source: Ronald C. Kessler, et al., "Lifetime and 12-Month Prevalence of DSM-III-R Psychiatric Disorders in the United States," Archives of General Psychiatry 51 (January 1994): 8–19.

THE DISTRIBUTION OF MENTAL DISORDERS

Sociologists have long been interested in the way mental disorders are distributed throughout society, both because of the inherent importance of the issue and for the clues it might offer about the causes of psychological disturbance. Starting in the 1930s with the research of Robert E. L. Faris and H. Warren Dunham[42] and followed by numerous others, including August B. Hollingshead and Frederick C. Redlich[43] and Leo Strole and colleagues,[44] sociologists have been particularly interested in the relationship between social class and mental health. After reviewing 44 studies on this subject, Bruce P. Dohrenwend and Barbara Snell Dohrenwend concluded that "analysis of these studies shows that their most consistent result is an inverse relation between social class and reported rate of psychological disorder."[45] In other words, the less money someone has, the more likely he or she is to have a mental disorder. The National Comorbidity Survey found that class differences were much more marked for disorders involving anxiety and fear than those involving depression.[46] Thus, it appears that a good-paying job and higher social status help reduce stress and anxiety but are less effective against feelings of sadness and depression. Many studies also show that, even though mental disorder is more widespread among poor people, the poor are less likely to receive any treatment.

The difference between being labeled a prophet and being labeled mentally disturbed depends on the reaction of the audience. This photograph shows the removal of the bodies of some of the 39 people who committed suicide at the urging of a flying saucer cult in San Diego, California. The members of the cult considered their leader a great prophet, but others said his role in encouraging this carnage was the act of a deranged mind.

Many sociologists also expected to find higher rates of mental disorders in the cities than in rural areas, but it did not turn out that way. For example, a study of the Hutterites—a religious group that lives in close-knit farming communities—concluded that their rate of severe mental disorder was roughly equal to the rate of hospitalization for mental disorder in New York State.[47] The most important difference was that the Hutterites usually cared for disturbed people in their homes rather than in hospitals. A comparative study by Eleanor Leacock found a high rate of psychosis in some decaying rural areas and a low rate in some relatively well-off urban areas.[48] It therefore appears that the characteristics of an individual's immediate community have more to do with mental health than does the number of people who live in it.

Men and women have roughly the same chance of experiencing some kind of mental disorder in their lifetimes, but there are some significant differences between the genders. A considerable body of research shows that women are more likely to suffer from disorders involving anxiety or depression, while men are more likely to have substance abuse problems. The National Comorbidity Survey also found that women are significantly more likely to have had three or more serious disorders during their lifetimes.[49]

Some researchers believe that these differences are the result of the physiological differences between women and men, but such figures are also influenced in several important ways by our gender role expectations. The elevated rates of anxiety and depression among women probably reflect the frustrations that come from the subordinate role many women are expected to play in the family and the workplace, as well as the conflicting demands modern society places on them. The difficulties men experience with alcoholism reflect, in part, the greater acceptability of heavy drinking among men. Moreover, the fact that men feel more pressure to conceal their emotional problems and "keep up a front" to the world may make drugs or alcohol seem to be the only way to cope with their psychological difficulties.

Marital status also has a bearing on one's likelihood of experiencing a mental disorder. Married people have the lowest rates of treatment for psychiatric problems, while rates for those who have never married are considerably higher for men but only slightly higher for women. Among the divorced, widowed, or separated, however, the rates are high for both sexes. Age is significant too. The National Comorbidity Study found that the rates of serious mental disorders were highest among 15- to 24-year-olds and declined steadily with age.[50] Although the survey did not include the elderly, it is generally recognized that they are much more likely to suffer from mental disorders that involve organic damage or deterioration, such as senility or **Alzheimer's disease**.

THE CAUSES OF MENTAL DISORDERS

Considering the amount of disagreement over the definition and classification of mental disorders, it is not surprising that there are many arguments about their causes as well. Although there are numerous theories, we will consider four of the most important—those based on biology, early childhood development, social stress, and labeling.

Biological Theories   Most psychologists and psychiatrists agree that some people have an inherited predisposition that makes them more likely to experience certain kinds of mental disorders, but there are enormous disagreements about the relative importance of heredity and environment. Some hold with the old axiom that "biology is destiny," while others argue that biological influences are of secondary importance and the real origins of most mental disorders lie in environmental factors.

Most of the earlier work by the biological theorists came from the study of schizophrenia. The most famous of these early studies was by Kallmann and Roth. They studied 17 pairs of identical twins (who have much greater genetic similarities than fraternal twins) and found that if one twin had schizophrenia, the other had the same problem 88.2 percent of the time.[51] However, the rate of concordance (if one has it, both have it) was only 22.9 percent for the 35 pairs of fraternal twins they studied. More recent studies have also concluded that close genetic relationships between identical twins are reflected in higher concordance rates. However, the differences found were not nearly as great as those reported by Kallmann and Roth. For instance, Hoffer and Polin found a concordance rate of 15.5 percent for identical twins and 4.4 percent for fraternal twins in a sample of almost 16,000 twins in the U.S. armed forces.[52] Of course, the concordance rate among identical twins may result from the fact that the physical similarity of identical twins leads their family and friends to treat them alike; but other research shows a higher concordance rate among identical twins even when they have been raised apart. Research also shows that a child is at greater risk of developing schizophrenia if one parent is schizophrenic and that the child's risk is significantly greater if both parents are schizophrenic. Moreover, such children are more likely to be schizophrenic even if they are raised away from their schizophrenic parents.[53]

There has also been considerable research into the biological roots of depression and related mood disorders. One team of researchers focused on a large Amish family in Pennsylvania with a very high incidence of bipolar disorder. After a careful analysis of blood samples, the researchers discovered genetic markers that indicated a difference in the DNA between those who had the disease and those who did not.[54] However, studies of people with the same problem from other groups have not found those same genetic markers.[55] Animal studies have led some researchers to believe that depression is linked to the deficiency of certain neurotransmitters, especially serotonin.[56] This conclusion is supported by the fact that drugs such as Prozac, which increase the body's level of serotonin, often relieve the symptoms of depression.

Although critics of the biological approach have been put on the defensive by the success that many of the new drugs have had in treating some forms of mental disorder, many nonetheless remain unconvinced that biological factors are as important as the advocates of the biological theories claim. They point out that the drugs are often ineffective and that even when biological treatments do work, that does not prove that the original problem was biological. Antidepressant drugs, for example, are often effective in treating depression caused by such social factors as the death of a child or the loss of a job. The critics have also raised numerous questions about the validity of procedures used in conducting twin studies, and they point out that nearly 90 percent of diagnosed schizophrenics have no close relatives with the disorder.[57]

Developmental Theories   Few experts doubt that social environment plays a major role in determining whether someone develops a mental disorder, but there are many different theories about how this influence is expressed. Details vary from one theory to another, but many of them borrow extensively from Sigmund Freud's psychoanalytic theory. Freud held that the unusual behavior of people who are mentally disturbed is merely a symptom of deeper unresolved conflicts locked in the unconscious mind of the patient. Freud believed that an individual's personality is formed during the early years of childhood and that the family is therefore the major force in personality development. If children experience serious emotional trauma, their psychological development may be impaired, leading to difficulties later in life. For example, traumas caused by the parents' negative reaction to infantile sexual behavior may create unconscious conflicts between the desire for sexual gratification and the desire for approval from parents and society. Freud treated mental disorders with **psychoanalysis**, a slow, detailed analysis of the patient's mental history. Freud's theories have been attacked on numerous grounds, from their lack of empirical scientific support to their seeming obsession with sexuality and their denigration of women, but they have nonetheless been extremely influential.

Many contemporary developmental theories see parental love and affection as the key to the normal maturation of a child. Children who are rejected by their parents may display a variety of psychological problems, including anxiety, insecurity, low self-esteem, and hostility. Parental standards of discipline are also important for proper development. Harsh, rigid standards may produce either a hostile and rebellious child or a passive, guilt-ridden one. Lack of discipline is thought to encourage antisocial and aggressive tendencies. Others feel that the children of overprotective parents develop "passive-dependent personalities."[58] Notice, however, that most of these conditions would not really qualify as mental disorders by most psychiatric standards.

Gregory Bateson and his associates developed a theory of schizophrenia based on what they called the **double bind**. This occurs when a parent gives a child two conflicting messages at the same time—for example, when a mother tells her son "I love you" but flinches or pulls away every time he touches her. Children who receive such conflicting messages are in a double bind; they desperately want to believe what their parents are saying, but they are constantly exposed to evidence that what is said is false. Thus, they may come to mistrust and misinterpret normal communications and eventually become seriously disoriented.[59]

On the whole, critics have not been kind to those who hold early parental influences responsible for major mental disorders. For one thing, they say that this approach is too vague about the exact conditions that cause mental disorders. Almost every family has some conditions that developmental theorists consider conducive to psychological disorder, but most children do not develop mental disorders. Moreover, many contemporary critics feel that this approach unfairly blames parents for everything that goes wrong with their children and that it produces unnecessary parental guilt and anxiety.

Social Stress Theory   While there is a great deal of skepticism about the old idea that child-rearing practices play a major role in the development of mental disorders, there is a growing recognition that traumatic events such as physical abuse or sexual molestation lie at the root of many serious psychological problems. In one study of female patients hospitalized for depression, over half acknowledged being sexually abused during childhood. A history of abuse was also correlated with the number and severity of depressive symptoms.[60] Similar results have been found in research on noninstitutionalized subjects. For example, a community survey of 3,125 women found that anxiety, depression, and phobias were significantly higher among those who had been sexually abused as children.[61]

A related approach known as **stress theory** is based on commonsense ideas about psychological problems. Simply put, the theory holds that each individual has a breaking point and that if stress builds up beyond this level, the individual will experience serious psychological problems. This theory is used by military psychiatrists to explain the symptoms of "battle fatigue"—a kind of mental breakdown that occurs among troops during periods of combat. It can also be used to account for the behavior of harried parents, pressured executives, and overworked students. Since sociologists have found that social stress is much greater among the poor than among the affluent, it is not surprising to find a higher rate of serious mental disorder in the lower classes.

The relationship between stress and mental disorder is, however, more complex than our simple illustrations suggest. A certain amount of stress is actually beneficial because it provides a challenge that motivates a person to respond in new and creative ways, but too much stress over too long a period seems to exhaust the individual's resources. The problem is to determine how much stress is appropriate and how much is harmful. People have different tolerance levels, so something that constitutes a healthy challenge to one person may cause serious psychological consequences in another.

Labeling Theory   Interactionists look at mental "illness" not as a medical condition but rather as a social role that is learned like any other role. Playing the role of being mentally ill offers many rewards to people who have trouble coping with their "normal" life or want to escape from unwanted personal or social responsibilities. Interactionists do not believe that most mentally disturbed people are "faking it" but only that their behavior is based on the social expectations of their society. According to labeling theory, which was created by the interactionists, people who have been declared mentally ill experience great pressure to act out that role. Their opportunities to play "normal" roles are reduced as friends shun them, prospective employers turn them away, and even their efforts to shed the label are taken as evidence of their instability. Everyone behaves as though the labeled person is sick; therefore, he or she eventually comes to believe it and acts that way. The "sick" role may even become attractive to some victims of labeling. It allows them to escape from responsibilities, stop worrying about other people's reactions to their behavior, and relax their battle against the label. The late British psychiatrist R. D. Laing went a step further, claiming that the people we consider disturbed are in fact the sanest ones among us and that it is really our society that is sick. To Laing, schizophrenia was a healthy attempt to deal with the sickness of everyday life: "Can we not see that this voyage (schizophrenia) is not what we need to be cured of, but that it itself is a natural way of healing our own appalling state of alienation called normality?"[62]

Not surprisingly, most traditional therapists and mental health experts vigorously deny the idea that mental illness is just a social label and argue that people who aren't unbalanced don't act in ways that everyone knows will get them labeled as mentally ill. Whatever labeling theory's weaknesses, however, there is increasing recognition that the labeling process does indeed have harmful effects on many psychiatric patients. For example, a study by Bruce Link found that labeled patients ended up with lower incomes and lower occupational status than people with the same background and the same psychological symptoms who had not been labeled.[63]

THE CONSEQUENCES OF MENTAL DISORDERS

Compared with people suffering from other health problems, those with mental disturbances face many special difficulties. As labeling theorists point out, there is a tremendous stigma attached to having a mental disorder, and that makes people reluctant to admit that they have a problem—oftentimes even to themselves. At best, people who suffer from mental disorders are seen as having some deep psychological flaw that makes them somehow inferior to those free of such problems. The more they show obvious behavioral symptoms, such as delusions or hallucinations, the more they are stigmatized and the more they are shunned by society.

The strong strand of individualism that runs through American society only makes things worse. No one blames the victim for getting cancer or having a stroke. No one tells them that they should "buck up" and handle the problem on their own or that they don't really need professional help. But that is exactly what those suffering from mental problems are told again and again. Because mental problems often do not have a clear-cut cause or obvious physical symptoms, many people think its victims are just being self-centered and blowing up minor difficulties out of proportion. Because virtually all healthy people have experienced depression, anxiety, and confusion, and then seen them pass away, they often don't understand that without help, those with mental disorders can remain mired in those states for months, years, or even for a lifetime.

But even if sound medical help is available, the disturbances in mood and behavior that accompany many mental problems often make it difficult for their victims to take advantage of it. Those with severe mental problems often have great difficulty making medical appointments, asserting their rights in our complex and impersonal medical bureaucracy, or taking prescribed medication on a regular schedule. In many cases, severe mental disorders make it difficult or impossible for their victims to even realize they have a problem, and obviously no one will seek out help if they don't know they have a problem.

In the past, mentally disturbed people who were unable to take care of themselves were usually committed to mental hospitals, where they at least received a basic minimum of physical care and perhaps some therapy. Today, there are far too few institutions to handle the need, and severely disturbed people are often left to wander the streets—or they are sent to prison for various kinds of minor violations of the law when they become a public nuisance.

QUICK REVIEW

What are the three views about the nature of mental disorder?

What are the most common types of mental disorder?

Among which groups is mental disorder most common?

What are the main theories about the causes of mental disorder?

What are the special problems faced by those with mental disorders?

THE CRISIS IN AMERICAN HEALTH CARE

The organization of America's health care system remains unique among industrialized nations. In response to ever-rising costs and the demand that competent health care be available to everyone, other industrialized countries have all adopted broadly based systems of government-supported health care. The United States, however, took a different course, creating a medical welfare system for the poor and the elderly but leaving the rest of the health care system in private hands. Direct payments by patients have been supplemented both by government programs and private insurance, which now pick up most of the tab, but these changes were not carried out in a systematic way.

How well does the American system work? Despite the efforts of some of the most dedicated and capable health care workers in the world, the problems of the American system remain serious and deep-seated, and many trends seem to be pointing in the wrong direction. Not only does the United States spend far more money per person than any other nation, but it also spends a much larger share of its total national income than any other industrial nation.[64] (See Figure 5.2) Yet despite spending almost $1 trillion on health care every year, the United States does rather poorly in a comparison of international health statistics. Although the United States is the world leader in many branches of medical research, its infant mortality rate is the highest of any major industrialized nation, and so is its percentage of low-birthweight infants. Overall, the United States ranks only fifteenth in average life expectancy. It would be wrong to attribute all these differences to the health care system alone; variations in lifestyle, diet, and environment are also important. Nonetheless, it is clear that the American system often fails its neediest patients, while at the same time its overall cost of health care continues to escalate out of control. (See "Lessons from Other Places" on page 154.)

FAILING THE PATIENTS: ACCESS DENIED

The American health care system offers some of the best care to be found anywhere on earth, but only for those who can pay for it. Those affluent enough to have good insurance coverage pay little or nothing in out-of-pocket costs for even the best medical care. While most middle-class Americans have some kind of private insurance, there are usually significant gaps in coverage. Some policies have little or no coverage for office visits or preventive care, while others require patients to make large deductible payments before the insurance company contributes. According to the

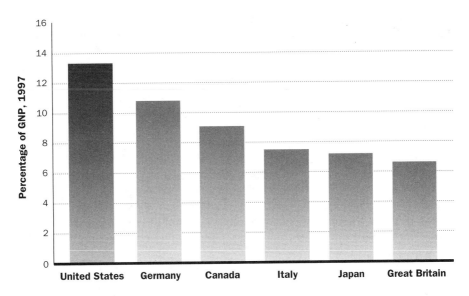

FIGURE 5.2   COMPARING HEALTH CARE COSTS

The United States has the most expensive system of health care in the world.

Source: National Center for Health Statistics, *Health, United States*, 2000 (Washington, DC: U.S. Government Printing Office, 2000), Table 114.

American Psychiatric Association, 98 percent of health insurance plans discriminate against those seeking treatment for mental problems by requiring higher out-of-pocket payments, allowing fewer doctor's visits and less time in the hospital, and even by denying coverage completely for some types of problems.[65] Most policies also limit the total amount the insurer will pay for any physical or mental illness. Thus, people with serious medical conditions may find that their coverage has run out or that their insurance company has canceled their policy and refuses to pay for any future treatment. Moreover, there have been numerous reports of insurance companies denying patients treatments they need when the costs are high. Some insurance companies, for example, classify established therapies as "experimental" in order to refuse coverage, or they demand that physicians use less costly treatments when the more expensive ones are known to work better.

Around three of every four Americans with health insurance are currently in some kind of **managed care** plan that monitors and controls the decisions health care providers make in order to keep costs down. Cost-conscious insurance companies provide financial incentives for general practitioners to limit the services they give to patients, and they require them to decide whether patients should be allowed to see specialists. Similar pressures are being felt by the physicians who work at **health maintenance organizations** (an origination that employs its own medical personnel and offers a complete range of health care services at a fixed rate). A 2000 Harris Poll found that 59 percent of Americans felt that HMOs (health maintenance organizations) compromised their quality of health care—a jump from only four years before when that

LESSONS FROM OTHER PLACES

HEALTH CARE IN THE UNITED STATES RANKED LOW
BY THE WORLD HEALTH ORGANIZATION

Americans working in Europe or Japan are often surprised by the excellent quality and low cost of their health care. While a professor in Japan, for example, one of your authors had complete medical insurance coverage from the Japanese Health Care system for his whole family at a cost of about $30 per month. A routine doctor's visit cost the patient only about $1. The situation in Germany, Switzerland, and most other European countries is similar. Even in a poorer country such as Thailand, our California students on study programs receive excellent health care at less crowded private hospitals for a fraction of the U.S. cost. A total bill for one of our student's six-day hospital stay in a private room with more than one doctor's visit per day, and many tests and several prescription drugs, was only about $1,500. A one-night hospital stay under similar conditions cost another of our students only $150. The other author of your text had an accident requiring emergency medical attention and several stitches while he was a visiting professor in Great Britain. There was no charge for the ambulance or the doctor care. They didn't even ask if he had insurance!

With this experience, we were not at all surprised that a new 2000 World Health Organization study of health care systems in countries all over the world ranked the United States—the world's richest country—in thirty-seventh place. France was ranked first, followed closely by Italy, Spain, Austria, and Japan. Surprisingly, the countries rated at the top spend much less per person on health care than the United States. Among the factors that hurt America's ranking was the high percentage of Americans who could not afford health insurance and did not qualify for any type of government health care assistance, a high infant-mortality rate, and a low life expectancy for an industrialized nation.

In many ways the United States has the most advanced high-tech medical care in the world. The world's rich and powerful often try to come to the United States for their medical care, and the other industrialized nations by no means have perfect medical care systems. But the simple fact remains that almost everyone in these countries receives reasonably good health care, while many American citizens cannot afford health care at all.

—Harold Kerbo and James Coleman

*For a summary of the report by the World Health Organization, see the *International Herald Tribune*, June 21, 2000.

figure was 39 percent—and the public's attitudes would undoubtedly be much the same about other forms of managed care. Similar opinions are found among physicians as well. One survey found that a majority of American physicians felt that managed care hurt their patients because of limitations on such things as diagnostic tests, the length of stays in a hospital, and the choice of specialists.[66]

Government health care plans also have glaring deficiencies. Government payments come primarily from two programs: **Medicare** and **Medicaid**. Medicare buys medical services for people 65 and older, while Medicaid is designed to help the poor, the blind, and the disabled. Medicare, a federal program, is relatively uniform throughout the nation. Medicaid, however, is administered by the states, and each state has its own standards of eligibility and levels of benefits. There are major gaps in the coverage of Medicaid, and they are growing wider year by year. When Medicaid was first established in the mid-1960s, it covered about 70 percent of those with incomes below the poverty line. Today, only about 43 percent of the poor are covered.[67] In addition, state and federal governments have been placing tighter limits on the assistance the poor receive. Some states have been creating more restrictive lists of the kinds of treatment they are willing to pay for, bringing charges that they are rationing health care for the poor. For example, the state of Oregon decided that medical procedures such as organ and tissue transplants were too expensive and that poor people who needed them would either have to get them from charity or do without. But the most common approach has been to limit access to care informally by making it difficult or unattractive for physicians and hospitals to treat welfare patients. For one thing, the states pay far less for most medical procedures than physicians and hospitals usually charge. On top of that, states often impose a bewildering array of bureaucratic barriers that must be overcome before a physician can actually be paid. As a result, many physicians simply refuse to accept Medicaid patients, and that means long waits for and rushed service from those that do.

Medicare coverage for the elderly is far less restrictive than Medicaid—almost everyone 65 and over qualifies. But Medicare still requires the elderly to make a substantial financial contribution of their own and excludes coverage for the costs of long-term care in a nursing home. A 1994 study by the American Association of Retired Persons estimated that despite Medicare coverage, older Americans spend about 23 percent of their total family income on medical care and that their out-of-pocket medical expenses had doubled since 1987.[68] Another problem is that the government's efforts at cost control have made Medicare payments fall further and further behind those of private health insurance companies. In the 1970s, Medicare paid about 85 percent as much as private insurers for the same medical procedures; today it pays only about 60 percent as much.[69] As a result, physicians and hospitals are becoming increasingly reluctant to treat Medicare patients. The failure to cover the cost of prescription drugs is an even more serious failing, since there has been an explosive increase in their cost in recent years.

Yet despite all these problems, those with some kind of private or government-sponsored heath care insurance are the lucky ones. Somewhere around 16 percent of the American population lack any health coverage at all, because they make too much money to qualify for welfare, don't have employer-provided insurance, and can't afford the cost of private insurance.[70]

As a result of all these problems, the poor and minorities often face severely restricted access to health services. Research shows that older whites are 3.5 times more likely to have heart bypass surgery than older African Americans and that African American kidney patients are only half as likely to receive a kidney transplant as white kidney patients. A study of patients on Medicaid found that they were less than half as likely as those with private insurance to receive several common surgical treatments; also the gap between the two groups has increased as the relative value of Medicaid payments has decreased over the years.[71]

In many ways, the problems with our system of dental care are even worse. Over 100 million Americans have no dental insurance. A minority child is three times more likely than a white child to lose a secondary tooth by the age of 17, and tooth decay in over half of Latino and African American children goes untreated.[72]

One poll found that almost one-fourth of Americans had put off some medical treatment in the last year because they could not afford it.[73] This situation is not only unjust; it is also foolishly shortsighted. When people delay medical treatment until their problems are so severe that they have no choice but to seek help, the total cost is likely to be far greater than that of timely preventive care. The cost of prenatal care denied to many poor women, for example, is far less than the hundreds of thousands of dollars often necessary to help their gravely ill infants.

RUNAWAY COSTS

Not only is the American health care system the most expensive in the world, the costs are going up year by year. In 1950, the United States spent 4.4 percent of its gross national product on health care; today that figure is around 13 percent.[74] The specter of runaway medical inflation led to a host of new measures by the government and the private insurance companies in the last decade to institute stricter cost controls. The rate of medical inflation dipped from 6.3 percent in 1995 to around 3 percent for the next few years, but by 2000 it was back above 4 percent.[75] Many experts believe that much of the cost savings from managed care have already been achieved, and they feel we can expect more sharp increases in the years ahead.

Why is health care so much more expensive in the United States than in most other countries? The most fundamental cause is the way the health care industry is organized and financed. Unlike most other countries, medicine in the United States is largely a private business organized for individual profit. The inefficient system of competing private health insurance companies that duplicate each other's services wastes billions of dollars in unnecessary overhead costs. Although estimates vary, private health insurers spend somewhere between $.26 to $.33 of every dollar they take in on administration, marketing, and commissions. In sharp contrast, the Canadian system of nation health care spends only 2 or 3 cents per dollar on overhead.[76] *Consumer Reports* estimated that the United States could save $200 billion a year by cutting down on administrative inefficiency and unnecessary medical procedures.[77]

Another reason America's health care costs are so high are the staggering salaries paid to many of the people who work in the medical field. Although we would like to think that the primary motivation for someone to become a physician is to help patients, physicians have kept their salaries so high that it severely restricts the access

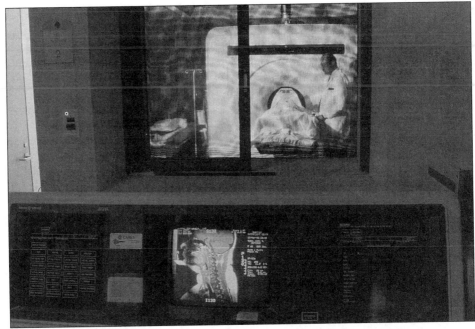

The development of complex and expensive new techniques has been a major factor in the rapid increase in the cost of medical care.

many people have to medical care. Most physicians choose to work in the affluent areas that offer them the best pay, while the inner-cities and poverty-stricken rural areas have a desperate shortage of all kinds of medical personnel. In 1997, the average physician made about $200,000 a year while the average surgeon made well over a quarter of a million dollars.[78] But the physicians look like paupers compared the executives who run the big medical corporations. One study that looked at the compensation of top executives in 17 health maintenance organizations in the United States found that they were paid an average of $42 million in cash and another $87 million in stock options in 1999![79]

The problem of runaway medical costs is not, however, in any way unique to the United States. One common problem among all the industrialized nations is that their populations are aging, and of course older people require more medical attention. A second factor has been the development of expensive new drugs and medical techniques. Such procedures as organ transplants are extremely costly and tend to drive up the overall price tag for health care. Some of the biggest increases have been in the cost of prescription drugs. A steady stream of powerful new drugs have come on the market in recent years, and the costs for their research and development can be staggering. Moreover, even though people can't buy their products without the approval of their physician, the big pharmaceutical companies have discovered that public advertising provides a big boost to sales both by increasing public interest and by discouraging physicians from prescribing less expensive generic drugs. Not only have the big pharmaceutical corporations consistently been at or near the top of the list of the companies with the highest return on their investment, but their top executives earn even bigger incomes than those who run health maintenance organizations. In 1998, the heads of the 10 largest drug companies earned an average compensation of $290 million each![80] Moreover, the fact that there are huge profits to be made in developing new drugs and medical procedures has diverted attention from less expensive, and often more effective, techniques of preventive medicine. As Jeffrey Klein and Michael Castleman put it, "The processes that drive medical research toward expensive treatments also turn it away from preventive measures that do not hold the promise of corporate profit."[81]

ETHICAL DILEMMAS

To most outsiders, the moral responsibility of the medical profession seems clear: to save lives and help patients be as healthy as possible. The increasing power of medical technology has created perplexing ethical dilemmas for which we have yet to find satisfactory answers, however. One such issue concerns the so-called heroic efforts physicians use to extend the lives of dying patients. Medical costs mount rapidly in the final weeks of a patient's life. One-third of Medicare's entire budget is spent on people in the last year of life. Most of us would say that cost should not be the standard to decide who lives or dies—but in a world in which millions of people starve to death every year, the money we use to keep one dying patient alive for another month could save a thousand hungry babies in the Third World. Is this fair? What about all the American babies who die because their mothers never received basic prenatal care?

Even if we ignore the costs, serious ethical issues remain. When people die, all their life-sustaining systems usually fail at about the same time, but medical equipment can take over the functions performed by the heart and lungs, thus keeping some gravely ill patients alive almost indefinitely. Although such patients are alive, the quality of their life is often pitifully low. They lie trapped in a hospital bed, connected by wires and tubes to a machine they totally depend on. If the patient wishes to continue under such conditions, there appear to be few ethical problems. In many cases, however, the patient is unconscious and unable to make any sort of decision. Some people now make out "living wills" that spell out how far they wish their physicians to go in using heroic means to extend their lives if they become gravely ill. Yet even the principle of self-determination implied in such wills is not universally accepted in our society. Many hospitals refuse to turn off patients' life-support machines even if they request it.

Oregon is the only U.S. state where physician-assisted suicide is legal. The law, first approved in 1994 and reaffirmed by Oregon voters in 1997, allows doctors to prescribe a lethal dose of drugs to patients with less than six months to live. In other states, a physician who helps a dying patient end a life of pain can be charged with murder. There is, however, growing support for legalizing "physician-assisted suicide"—that is, allowing physicians to assist patients to end their lives if the patients are too ill to do it by themselves. A Harris poll found that 73 percent of the Americans polled agreed with the statement "The law should allow doctors to comply with the wishes of a dying patient in severe distress who asks to have his or her life ended."[82] However, while the majority of Americans support making physician-assisted suicide legal under certain conditions, the terminally ill tend to resist using this option and prefer instead to use their final time preparing for death and being with loved ones. In Oregon, just 16 terminally ill patients took advantage of the new law in 1998 and 27 in 1999.[83] It is evident, nonetheless, that knowing the option of euthanasia or physician-assisted suicide is available gives great psychological comfort to those facing the imminent end of their lives.

Just as many perplexing ethical questions surround the beginning of life as its end. One of the most controversial ethical issues of our time is abortion. This difficult matter revolves around two separate issues that are often confused. On a personal level, the question is whether a woman is morally justified in deciding to have an abortion; and on the sociological level, the question is the role the government should play. (See the Debate "Should Abortion Be Legal?" on page 160.)

The abortion debate has been going on for decades, but advances in medical technology are also creating new dilemmas about human reproduction. The technique for artificial insemination has been used for decades to help women with infertile husbands. In contrast, the practice of **surrogate mothering**, in which a woman is hired to bear someone else's child, has raised a storm of protests. Although the surrogate mother signs a contract agreeing to give the child to its biological parents, bitter legal battles have arisen when surrogates have attempted to void those contracts and claim legal custody of the child. Obviously, there are no simple answers to these troubling ethical questions, yet society must somehow formulate social policies to guide the medical profession in making these ethical decisions.

QUICK REVIEW

How well does the United States do at providing health care for all its citizens?

Why is health care so costly in the United States?

What are some of the ethical dilemmas faced by our health care system?

SOLVING THE PROBLEMS OF MENTAL AND PHYSICAL HEALTH

There are two approaches to the problems of the sick. The first is to try to prevent health problems by changing lifestyles and eating habits, reducing pollution, and increasing the use of preventive medicine. The second aims at improving care for people after they become sick. The latter approach includes proposals designed to create equal access to health care, regardless of income, and to improve the overall quality of these services at less cost.

PREVENTIVE MEDICINE

The old saying "an ounce of prevention is worth a pound of cure" is as true today as it was a hundred years ago. As we noted earlier, improvements in sanitation and nutrition have saved more lives than all hospitals combined. Yet our health care system continues to emphasize treatment rather than prevention of disease. A delicate heart operation is much more dramatic than the dull business of educating people to avoid

DEBATE

SHOULD ABORTION BE LEGAL?

Yes

To deny a woman the right to have an abortion is to deny her control of her own body. The government has no right to force a woman to have a child she does not wish to bear. Those who demand that the government stop all abortions are urging us down the road to a totalitarian society in which the police and the courts control our most personal decisions.

Those who oppose abortion claim that a fetus is a fully formed human being and to abort it would be murder. Such claims lack any scientific support. A fetus is not an independent living creature and can survive only as long as it is attached to its mother's body. If it is murder to abort a fetus that cannot live on its own, then it is murder to practice birth control and cut off the unfertilized egg's chance of survival.

In addition to the obvious danger of giving the state authority over the private workings of our bodies, there is another important reason to keep abortion legal. The laws prohibiting abortion never stopped such operations. What they did do was to force hundreds of thousands of women to go to incompetent, untrained abortionists, and many of them paid with their lives. If the antiabortion crusaders are successful, the black-market abortionists will be back in business, and thousands of women will be their victims.

No

Abortion is murder, plain and simple. When a fetus is aborted, a human life is ended. An aborted fetus dies just as surely as a baby shot with a gun. A society that claims to respect human life cannot allow the continuation of this slaughter.

The supporters of abortion claim that the old antiabortion laws created a flourishing business in illegal abortions that injured or killed many of its customers. They are certainly right in pointing out the harm the illegal abortionists did to many of these women; but they ignore the harm that abortions—legal or illegal—do to innocent fetuses. The way to stop the black-market abortion business is not to legalize it but to demand tougher law enforcement to stamp it out.

There is another important reason to make abortion illegal again: to preserve the sanctity of the family and to reinforce our society's support of the fundamental value of human life. When society permits a mother to take the life of her unborn child, it tells us all that human life is a cheap commodity to be thrown away for the sake of mere convenience. Mothers should be required to carry their babies the full term necessary for their survival. Unborn babies have a right to life.

heart trouble through proper diet and regular exercise. Yet the second approach is both cheaper and more effective. In its broadest sense, **preventive medicine** includes a wide range of programs to encourage healthier living, including school courses in nutrition, personal hygiene, and driver training, as well as campaigns against excessive use of tobacco, alcohol, and other drugs, and to encourage exercise.

Preventive medicine has a long history in non-Western medical traditions. Wealthy Chinese commonly placed a practitioner of traditional medicine on a monthly salary to overlook the welfare of their families. The physician would make regular visits to check dietary and personal habits, dispense advice and medicines to help prevent illness, and generally keep abreast of the state of health of each family member. If anyone fell seriously ill, the payments were stopped until the physician had nursed the patient back to health.[84]

There is no question that Western medicine has made enormous progress in curing disease. Many critics charge, however, that today's physicians focus so intently on the symptoms of disease that they have forgotten the patients who suffer from them. Drawing heavily from the approach of traditional Chinese and Indian physicians, practitioners of holistic medicine focus on the patient's overall mental, emotional, and physical condition. The goal is not to cure the symptoms of disease but to improve the general state of the patient's health. Whether or not most medical practitioners utilize techniques of **holistic medicine** borrowed from non-Western traditions, they clearly need to pay more attention to their patients' lifestyles and mental outlooks and not just to the symptoms of disease.

Regular exercise is an important component of healthy living, and growing numbers of people are making an effort to incorporate more physical activity into their lives.

MEDICAL PERSONNEL

Although by most reckonings the United States has an oversupply of physicians in highly paid specialties, it clearly needs to train more general practitioners, pediatricians, and nurses. By restricting the number of students in overcrowded specialties such as surgery, medical schools could help move physicians into fields in which they are badly needed, especially general practice. Significant progress has nonetheless been made in one area: In 1996, almost 40 percent of medical school graduates are women, compared with only 5 percent in 1960.[85]

One thing we clearly need to do is to offer higher pay and more professional authority to nurses and other trained medical workers. Not only would this attract more people into the profession, but overall medical costs would decrease if nurses were allowed to perform more of the services now carried out exclusively by physicians. During the past two decades, the medical profession has been moving in this direction as the number of **physician's assistants** and **nurse practitioners** has grown. In fields such as pediatrics and women's health and internal medicine, nurse practitioners see patients very much as physicians do. But regulations concerning nurse practitioners vary greatly from state to state, and they have had to fight numerous battles with physicians, some of whom see advanced-practice nurses as a threat to their professional status.

RESTRUCTURING THE HEALTH CARE SYSTEM

As we have seen, America's health care system is in the midst of a deep crisis. Most Americans agree that reforms are necessary, and there seem to be two objectives that must be met: controlling costs and providing universal coverage. Unfortunately, this consensus quickly breaks down when it comes to specific proposals to achieve those goals. In an industry that accounts for roughly one-seventh of the economy, every proposal that would achieve significant improvements has run into intense opposition from powerful special interests.

In all the industrialized nations except the United States, the government has created a system of national health care with some form of universal coverage. The fact that the government pays most of the cost of health care does not make it "free," as is sometimes claimed. Obviously, citizens must be taxed or pay some other charge to finance those services. National health care nonetheless has three major advantages over the American system. First, it is usually more fair, since those best able to afford it can be made to carry a bigger share of the costs. Second, such systems provide far better service for the poor and prevent the impoverishment of middle-class people who develop expensive medical conditions. Third, national health care is cheaper.

All proposals for reforming the system of American health care must come to terms with two fundamental questions: how to organize the health care system and how it pay for it. From an administrative standpoint, the most efficient approach is a "single-payer system" in which one government agency pays all the bills for basic care, as in Great Britain or Canada. As we have seen, the overhead costs in such systems are far lower than in the current American approach, with its hundreds of competing insurance companies and numerous government programs. Not surprisingly, however, the insurance industry and large sections of the medical establishment have put up intense opposition to any effort to create a single-payer system despite it obvious advantages for the general public.

A second approach, put forth by President Clinton in his unsuccessful health care reform proposals, would be to encourage the existing insurance companies to band together in large "health care alliances" that would then compete with each other under general cost and procedural standards set by the government. Some supporters of this idea claim it would be even more efficient than a single-payer plan, but there is no hard evidence since it has never been tried in any other country. Moreover, the insurance industry is strongly opposed to this approach as well, and it mounted a very costly and very effective attack on the Clinton proposals when they were presented to Congress.

A third possibility would be to leave the current system as it is and just expand existing medical welfare programs or provide subsidies to enable more low-income people to afford private insurance. This approach, however, does little or nothing to contain the exploding cost of medical care and is not likely to gain much support from the middle class, since it would do little or nothing to help them with their heath care problems.

Some of the most bitter battles in the health care debate have concerned the best way to pay for universal coverage. There are three possible sources of money: direct payments by individuals, payments from employers, and general tax revenues. Not surprisingly, all the proposals for funding universal health coverage have run into strong opposition from one group or another. Some have proposed an "employer mandate" that would require all employers to provide insurance for their workers. Such ideas have, however, been fiercely attacked by small-business owners, who claim they simply cannot afford it. And obviously this approach would do nothing to help those without a job or who are self-employed. A second approach would put the burden on individual citizens by requiring everyone to maintain some form of health insurance. If their employers don't pick up the tab, individuals would be required to pay for it themselves. Even if the government provided a basic package of coverage at a fairly low cost, however, this approach still doesn't solve the problems of those too poor to afford insurance payments. A third approach is to use tax revenues to finance all health care or to subsidize those who can't afford it. The advantage of this approach is that it would place the burden of financing the health care system on those who are best able to pay. However, it would obviously require a major increase in taxes, and proposals to create such a system have run into the same kind of heated opposition as efforts to increase taxes for other purposes.

It should be clear from this discussion that the most difficult part of improving the health care system is political. None of the proposals is perfect, but there are several reasonable approaches that could provide both universal coverage and more effective cost controls than the current American system, which after all does very poorly in terms of cost and coverage in comparison with the health care systems of other industrialized nations. The critical task is to break through the logjam of opposition from the powerful special-interest groups—the insurance industry, pharmaceutical companies, the medical profession, and hospitals, among others—in order to create a system that serves the interests of society as a whole.

IMPROVING MENTAL HEALTH CARE

Of all the complex and difficult health problems we face, our health care system seems to do the worst job dealing with mental disorders. Time and time again victims are stigmatized and blamed for their illness in a way that would never happen to the victims of cancer or a heart attack, and as a result we are often reluctant to provide the full range of health care coverage that those with mental disorders need. As we have seen, insurance companies typically place special limits on how much treatment a patient can receive for a mental problem. The American Psychiatric Association advocates a concept known as **parity** which would require insurance companies to provide the same coverage for mental and physical disorders. The Mental Health Parity Act of 1996 required insurance companies to provide equal coverage for mental and physical disorders. But as is so often the case, this legislation was more of a political gesture than anything else, because it applied only to annual or lifetime cost limits and not to coverage of substance abuse patients, copayments, deductibles, or treatment limitations. But even if effective national legislation were enacted, it would be only a small step if it were not combined with some kind of system to provide universal health care because the same mental problems that cry out for treatment often cause their sufferers to lose their jobs and thus their health insurance.

In the past, most people with severe mental disorders were confined to mental hospitals—sometime for years on end. Critics strongly questioned the wisdom of sending psychologically troubled people to large, impersonal institutions in order to help them resolve their problems. For example, Erving Goffman's classic study of life in the "asylum" uncovered a host of difficulties that beset the institutionalized mental patient.[86] For one thing, patients often come into the institution with a sense of betrayal, believing that they have been tricked and manipulated by their friends and family. Upon admission, they are subjected to a variety of what Goffman called "degradation rituals" that strip them of their dignity and their identity. Familiar clothing and personal possessions are taken away; they are poked, prodded, and classified by medical personnel; and, worst of all, they are locked up and denied the freedom to move about as they please.

As a result of such stinging criticisms and the desire of politicians to reduce the costs of supporting these institutions, a widespread movement to deinstitutionalize mental patients developed. The goal was to treat people with mental disorders in community facilities and get them out of the large mental institutions, and the number of patients in mental facilities soon plummeted.[87] Critics of **deinstitutionalization** argue that it was merely a convenient justification for ignoring the problems of the mentally disturbed. It is estimated that about one-third of the nation's growing body of homeless men and women suffer from serious mental disorders. Former mental patients are commonly seen aimlessly wandering city streets, eating food from garbage cans, and sleeping in alleys and parks. These days, people with severe mental disorders are increasingly likely to end up in prison rather than in a mental hospital if they are unable to take care of themselves.

Although there seems little doubt that these people need more help than they are receiving, defenders of deinstitutionalization point out that the original intent of the reforms was never carried out. The idea behind deinstitutionalization was to treat fewer mental patients in hospitals and more in the community, but only a fraction of the community centers needed to support deinstitutionalized mental patients were ever built. So despite the problems created by the movement to deinstitutionalize mental patients, well-run community-based care is still considered by many to be the best way to treat all but the most severely disturbed individuals. Patients who remain in their communities during treatment avoid the shock of being taken out of their normal environment. They also escape the labeling, humiliation, and feelings of powerlessness that are bound to accompany institutionalization, as well as the painful readjustment period that follows it.

An effective community mental health center needs to offer at least five basic services: short-term hospitalization, partial hospitalization that allows patients to return home at night or on the weekends, outpatient therapy, emergency care for special problems, and consultations and educational services for the community at large. These centers would thus provide a broad range of services, many of which are likely to be unavailable from other sources. The major problem with today's centers is simply that there are not enough of them, and those that do exist are too often underfunded and understaffed.

Other kinds of community programs can also help meet the needs of people with mental health problems. For example, physicians, teachers, police officers, and others who are likely to come into contact with people who need mental health care should be taught the best ways of working with those individuals, and they should be familiarized with agencies that can provide help. Many private organizations can also help meet community mental health needs. For example, volunteers for hotline agencies answer phone calls from people in need of help, refer them to appropriate agencies, try to head off suicides, or merely lend a sympathetic ear.

QUICK REVIEW

What are the best ways to improve the health care system?

SOCIOLOGICAL PERSPECTIVES ON THE PROBLEMS OF HEALTH AND HEALTH CARE

Concern about ever-rising costs and the increasing gap between the high-quality health care that modern medicine can provide and the care that many people actually receive has made health care an important social problem. Social scientists of every persuasion have tried to explain why the social organization of health care is not better, given the fact that it is now a multibillion-dollar business and we have the knowledge and technology necessary to provide excellent services for everyone.

THE FUNCTIONALIST PERSPECTIVE

Viewed functionally, the jumbled health care system is a result of the rapid development of medical technology combined with changes in public attitudes about medical care. In the nineteenth century, medical knowledge was so limited that private doctors could handle almost all demands for health care. Rapid growth of medical knowledge and techniques greatly increased the kinds of services doctors could offer; because these services were effective, the demand for them boomed. People came to see good health care as a fundamental right, but the American system of health care was unable to adapt efficiently. The idea that health care is a commodity, to be bought the way one buys a sack of potatoes or hires a carpenter, is still with us, as is the conviction that medical care should be provided by a private practitioner and not by a corporation or a government bureau.

It is because of this lag, functionalists say, that the U.S. health care system is failing to do its job efficiently. Health care services are still sold privately. This individualistic "free-enterprise" system has been supplemented, in patchwork fashion, by a great variety of cooperative organizations: clinics, hospitals, group practices, and health maintenance organizations. It has also been supplemented by many new sources of funding: employers, unions, insurance companies, and a host of government agencies.

In short, the U.S. health care system is disorganized because it has grown rapidly and haphazardly, without proper planning. Obviously, the solution to this problem is reorganization, but functionalists do not agree on the form this reorganization should take. Some would have us return to complete free enterprise in the health care business. Such a system would allow physicians to sell their services at whatever price the market will bear, and those too poor to pay that price could turn to private charity or go without. Most functionalists, however, feel such a system would be too harsh and uncaring. Other functionalists believe that we should stick with the present system and work to streamline it and make it more efficient. They call for reallocating medical personnel, reducing fraud and malpractice, lowering costs, and training more nurses and other medical personnel in short supply. Still other functionalists argue that the best way to reduce the disorganization in the current system of health care is to create a centralized government-run system like those in Britain and Canada.

THE CONFLICT PERSPECTIVE

Conflict theorists see the U.S. health care system in a different light. They argue that its problems and deficiencies stem from the fact that it is designed to serve the needs of the rich and powerful (including doctors themselves) and thus neglects the needs of low-income groups. Health care is dominated by businesspeople with medical degrees who try to sell their services at the highest price. Because physicians have a legally enforced monopoly on medical services, they are in a position to rig prices. They sell their services at inflated prices that only the rich or well-insured can pay, and they oppose programs that would reduce profits or require physicians to provide cheap health care for the poor. Further, conflict theorists claim, physicians have created an aura of mystery about their profession in order to boost their occupational prestige and cover up their shortcomings. In this atmosphere, patients are not expected or allowed to judge the quality of their medical care—"the doctor knows best." Incompetents and profiteers are not weeded out because patients are kept in the dark about the true nature of the medical care they are receiving.

Sociologist Paul Starr's research has shown that the U.S. health care system's reliance on unrestricted **fee-for-service compensation** by insurance companies and government agencies was created by powerful interests in the medical industry itself.[88] According to Starr, the largest, most important health insurance company, Blue Cross/Blue Shield, was created to protect the interests of hospitals and physicians. Blue Cross, which originally covered only hospital expenses, was started in response to the financial crisis of U.S. hospitals during the Great Depression and was directly controlled by the hospital industry. Blue Shield, which originally covered doctors' expenses, was created and controlled by physicians. Starr also argues that the generous system of medical payments in the original Medicare legislation was put there as a result of pressure from the medical lobby.

Conflict theorists would resolve the health care problem by reducing the medical profession's control over the financing and organization of the health care system. This power would then be transferred to the government to ensure good medical care for all citizens, regardless of their ability to pay. Most conflict theorists call for government-financed health care without charge to individual patients. They also argue that such changes will come about only if those who receive inadequate health care organize themselves to counter the tremendous power of the health care establishment.

Finally, on a global level, conflict theorists point out that the medical professions are dominated by people from rich nations to the detriment of the world's poor. As in other occupations, the best and brightest medical professionals from poor countries often end up working in the rich ones that actually have far less need of their services. Medical and pharmaceutical research are also focused on the needs of those in the rich countries where the people can afford to pay for the new treatments they develop. While many pharmaceutical corporations manufacture drugs in less-developed countries, these drugs are primarily for export to people in rich nations. There are, of course, international health agencies, such as the World Health Organization, but conflict theorists point out that their resources are far too limited to deal with the overwhelming health problems of the world's poor.

THE FEMINIST PERSPECTIVE

Most feminists are more receptive to the conflict perspective than to the functionalist analysis of the health care system. But in addition to the exploitation of the poor and the working class by wealthy professionals, feminists also see a systematic repression of women. Until recently, women were grossly underrepresented in medical school, and they were excluded from many of the highest-paying and most prestigious medical positions. Not only is this unfair to the women who work in the medical profession, but the whole system has functioned to reinforce and support traditional gender stereotypes. The male doctors became powerful symbols of power and authority while the female nurses they directed carried out the subordinate roles. Generations of women went to male doctors and psychiatrists with their most intimate problems, and those medical professionals became a primary source of the male control of women's bodies and women's lives.

In addition, feminists argue that the current system of health care and medical research is focused more on needs of men than on those of women. Compare, for example, Viagra and RU-486. Viagra, a medication used by men with penile erectile dysfunction was not only approved and marketed fairly quickly in this country, but it is covered by most health care insurance policies. Yet birth control pills and other contraceptive methods are still not covered by many health insurance plans. Another example is RU-486, a highly effective abortion pill, which was not approved by the FDA until September 2000, after 17 years of investigation. Yet it has been used in France since 1988 and is widely available in Europe. RU-486 is unlikely to be covered by many insurance plans, and many doctors are reluctant to prescribe it for fear they will be targeted for violent attacks by anti-abortion groups.

Feminists obviously applaud the trends toward an increasing number of female physicians, but they argue that much more needs to be done. For one thing, women are still underrepresented in most of the highest-paying and most prestigious positions, and nurses are still paid far less than the physicians who give them orders. So, in addition to reforms to provide better medical care for the poor, feminists call for an end to the discrimination against women in medical careers and for new concern for the special health care needs of women and children.

THE INTERACTIONIST PERSPECTIVE

Although interactionists rarely deal directly with the organization of health care services, they have made significant contributions to our understanding of the health care field. They have shown, for example, that the socialization process in medical schools often has unanticipated consequences, making doctors into something less than the humanitarians many medical students set out to be. A crushing burden of work and isolation from people in other walks of life create a powerful sense of group solidarity among physicians, making it difficult for outsiders to exercise proper scrutiny of their behavior. Interactionists have shown that people learn to be "sick" (to play the role of sick people) just as they learn to be parents, factory workers, or lawyers. It follows that health care services sometimes make people sick rather than well.

Interactionists are also concerned with the ways we develop unhealthy habits and lifestyles. Attitudes toward exercise, diet, smoking, and drinking are learned from our primary groups and reflect the attitudes of our culture as well. Further, interactionists point out that unhealthful behavior is often encouraged by mass media, business, and even government. Expensive advertising campaigns designed to sell junk food, cigarettes, and alcohol are good examples. The competitive pressures of our economic system are also a major factor in the numerous health problems resulting from stress and tension.

Many interactionists believe that significant improvements can be made in public health through a concerted campaign of education and social change. First, there must be greater awareness of the damage caused by unhealthy lifestyles and poor diet. Second, there must be social changes that will encourage everyone to follow the principles of good health. The ideal of the successful, hard-driving achiever will have to be modified to permit a new emphasis on cooperation and mutual support. It is also important that businesses take greater social responsibility for the products they sell. A new social climate must be created in which it is no longer acceptable for corporations to spend millions of dollars advertising children's breakfast cereals that consist mainly of sugar, developing new cigarettes with more "sex appeal," or promoting other dangerous products.

QUICK REVIEW

How do the functionalist, conflict, feminist, and interactionist theories explain the problems of our health care system?

SUMMARY

In the past century, there has been a tremendous drop in the death rate. Though improved health care and new treatments for deadly diseases contributed to this decline, it was largely due to improvements in living conditions—better food, housing, and sanitation. While industrialization and technology have helped to increase food supplies and reduce epidemic disease, they have also created new health problems. The stress of modern-day living together with an unhealthy diet and a decline in physical exercise have increased the frequency of a variety of heart and circulatory diseases. Suicide, accidents, and violent crime are major health problems of a different kind. Occupational hazards, smoking, and environmental pollution are now major causes of death and injury. As the AIDS crisis has shown us, even the problem of epidemic disease is far from over. On the average, poor people and members of ethnic minorities have more health problems and a shorter life span than others. Many factors contribute to these problems, including stress and worry, dangerous occupations, poor diet, and inadequate medical care.

There are significant disagreements about the true nature of mental disorder. Some see it as mental illness, others as a problem of personal maladjustment, and still others as a label given to deviant behavior. The *Diagnostic and Statistical Manual of Mental Disorders* (DSM) is the most widely used classification system for mental disorders; its most commonly used diagnoses include mood disorders, substance abuse disorders, and anxiety disorders. Like physical illnesses, mental disorders are more common among the poor. There are many different theories about the causes of mental disorders, including the notions that they stem from an inherited biological predisposition, that they result from difficulties in early childhood development, and that they come from problems in the individual's environment. The victims of mental disorder suffer from a host of special problems including the stigma our society attaches to their problem and the special difficulties they have in getting effective treatment.

The American system of health care is unique among all the industrialized nations because it is organized and run as a private business. Despite medical welfare programs, poor people receive inferior care, and millions of Americans are not covered by welfare programs or private insurance. Moreover, many Americans who do have health insurance have found that it fails to cover all the services they need. The inefficiency and high overhead costs of the American health care system make it the most expensive in the world. In addition, such things as aging populations and the development of expensive new treatments are driving up medical costs around the world.

There are two general ways of dealing with the problems of the sick. One is to prevent health problems before they start. Another approach is to improve the quality of health care services for people who have become ill. This includes proposals for improving medical personnel, providing better mental health care, and perhaps most importantly for restructuring the health care system to provide universal coverage for all Americans.

Functionalists contend that the health care system is disorganized because the ways and means of delivering medical services have not adjusted to changes in the medical services themselves. Conflict theorists argue that because the U.S. health care system is controlled by medical professionals and the rich, it serves their interests and neglects the poor. Feminists point out that the health care system discriminates against women and perpetuates traditional gender stereotypes. Interactionists say that unhealthful lifestyles are learned, and they call for a program of education and social change to improve our way of living.

QUESTIONS FOR CRITICAL THINKING

Many sociologists believe that our economic and political institutions are critical forces in both causing and resolving our social problems. Is this true of our problems of health and illness? How have economic and political forces shaped our health care system? Does the system favor the rich at the expense of the poor and the uninsured?

KEY TERMS

acquired immune deficiency syndrome (AIDS)	Medicaid
Alzheimer's disease	Medicare
anxiety disorder	mental disorder
bipolar disorder	mood disorder
contagious disease	nurse practitioner
deinstitutionalization	parity
double bind	physician's assistant
fee-for-service compensation	preventive medicine
health	psychoanalysis
health maintenance organization (HMO)	schizophrenia
holistic medicine	sexually transmitted disease
human immunodeficiency virus (HIV)	stress theory
labeling theory	substance abuse disorder
managed care	surrogate mothering

NOTES

1. Jerry Bler, "Man 'Hit Cracks' in Wife's Care," *Fresno Bee*, March 2, 1994, p. A1.
2. Population Reference Bureau, *World Population Data Sheet*, 2001 (Washington DC: Population Reference Bureau, 2001.
3. See P. H. Fentem, "Benefits of Exercise in Health and Disease," *British Medical Journal* 308 (May 1994): 1291–1295; Gregory D. Curfman, "The Health Benefits of Exercise: A Critical Reappraisal," *New England Journal of Medicine* 328 (February 1993): 574–576; William L. Haskell, "Overview: Health Benefits of Exercise," in Joseph D. Matarazzo et al., eds., *Behavioral Health: A Handbook of Health Enhancement and Disease Prevention* (New York: Wiley, 1984), pp. 409–423.
4. Melinda Beck, "An Epidemic of Obesity," *Newsweek*, August 1, 1994, pp. 62–63; D. M. Hegsted, "What Is a Healthful Diet?" in Matarazzo et al., *Behavioral Health*, pp. 552–574.
5. Sheryl Stolberg, "Mortality Study Finds Tobacco Is No. 1 Culprit," *Los Angeles Times*, November 10, 1993, pp. A1, A33; Oakley Ray, *Drugs, Society and Human Behavior*, 3rd ed. (St. Louis: Mosby, 1983), pp. 183–205; U.S. Department of Health and Human Services, *Smoking and Health: A Report of the Surgeon General* (Washington, DC: U.S. Government Printing Office, 1979).
6. Philip J. Hilts, "Is Nicotine Addictive? It Depends on Whose Criteria You Use," *New York Times*, August 21, 1994, p. B6; Associated Press, "Koop: Tobacco Like Heroin, Cocaine," *San Luis Obispo Telegram-Tribune*, May 16, 1988, p. A1.
7. John Schwartz, "Secondhand Smoke Increases Health Risk, Study Finds," *Los Angeles Times*, May 20, 1997, p. A10; Sheryl Stolberg, "Science Stokes the Tobacco Debate," *Los Angeles Times*, May 26, 1994, pp. A1, A22, A23; Associated Press, "EPA Official Tries to Bury Smoking Report," *San Luis Obispo Telegram-Tribune*, May 30, 1991, p. B8.
8. Sidney Cobb and Robert M. Rose, "Hypertension, Peptic Ulcer, and Diabetes in Air Traffic Controllers," *Journal of the American Medical Association* 224 (1973): 489–492.
9. *New York Times*, April 3, 1983.
10. U.S. Bureau of the Census, *Statistical Abstract of the United States*, 2000, p. 93.
11. Ibid., p. 97; U.S. Bureau of the Census, *Statistical Abstract of the United States*, 1966, p. 95.
12. National Center for Health Statistics, *Health, United States*, 2000 (Washington, DC: U.S. Government Printing Office, 2000).
13. U.S. Bureau of the Census, *Statistical Abstract of the United States*, 2001, p. 80.
14. Emile Durkheim, *Suicide* (New York: Free Press, 1951).
15. See George Howe Colt, *The Enigma of Suicide* (New York: Summit Books, 1991).
16. Marlene Cimons, "Car Fumes Linked to High Medical Costs," *Los Angeles Times*, January 20, 1990, p. A18.
17. Associated Press, "Radon Tied to 30% Rise in the Risk of Cancer," *New York Times*, January 25, 1994, p. B8.
18. James William Coleman, *The Criminal Elite: Understanding White Collar Crime*, 4th ed. (New York: St. Martin's, 1998), pp. 70–71.
19. Associated Press, "17 American Workers a Day Died on the Job During the 80s," *New York Times*, April 15, 1994, p. A8; Coleman, *The Criminal Elite*, p. 10; Lawrence White, *Human Debris: The Injured Worker in America* (New York: Putnam, 1983), pp. 15–23.
20. John H. Dingle, "Ills of Man," in *Life and Death and Medicine* (San Francisco: Freeman, 1973), p. 53.
21. U.S. Bureau of the Census, *Statistical Abstract*, 1999, p. 149.
22. United Nations Development Programme, *Human Development Report*, 1994 (New York: Oxford University Press, 1994), pp. 134–135, 152–153.
23. Nicholasa D. Kristof, "Malaria Makes a Comeback, and Is More Deadly Than Ever," *New York Times*, January 8, 1997, pp. A1, A7.
24. *Statistical Abstract of the United States*, 2000, p. 138; *Statistical Abstract of the United States*, 1999, p. 148.
25. *Statistical Abstract of the United States*, 2000, p. 138.
26. Ibid.

27. National Center for Health Statistics, *Health, United States, 2000*, p. 8.
28. Information comes from the United Nations, World Health Organization, and other international health and aid agencies. Recently summarized reports from these agency reports can be found in the *International Herald Tribune*, July 6, 2000, October 5, 1999, December 13, 1999, and the *Los Angeles Times*, July 11, 2000.
29. See Harold Kerbo, *Social Stratification and Inequality* (New York: McGraw-Hill, 2000) p. 412.
30. Population Reference Bureau, *World Population Data Sheet, 2001*.
31. "Researchers Tracking 1,100 Californians over 30 Years Find Sustained Hardship Roughly as Damaging as Cigarettes," *Los Angeles Times*, December 25, 1997.
32. U.S. Department of the Census, *Statistical Abstract*, 1996, p. 96; Colin McCord and Harold P. Freeman, "Excess Mortality in Harlem," *New England Journal of Medicine* 322 (1990): 173–177; "Forgotten Americans," *American Health*, *Special Report*, November 1990, pp. 41–42; Leonard Syme and Lisa Berkman, "Social Class, Susceptibility, and Sickness," in Howard Schwartz, ed., *Dominant Issues in Medical Sociology*, 3rd ed. (New York: McGraw-Hill, 1994), pp. 643–699.
33. Kerbo, *Social Stratification and Inequality*, p. 38; National Center for Health Statistics, *Health, United States*, 2000, Table 35.
34. Syme and Berkman, "Social Class, Susceptibility, and Sickness," p. 644.
35. Ronald C. Kessler et al., "Lifetime and 12-Month Prevalence of DSM-III-R Psychiatric Disorders in the United States: Results from the National Comorbidity Survey," *Archives of General Psychiatry* 51 (January 1994): 8–27.
36. U.S. Department of the Census, *Statistical Abstract*, 1993, p. 126.
37. Kessler et al., "Lifetime and 12-Month Prevalence of DSM-III-R Psychiatric Disorders in the United States."
38. Robert C. Carson, James N. Butcher, and James C. Coleman, *Abnormal Psychology and Modern Life*, 8th ed. (Glenview, IL: Scott, Foresman, 1988), pp. 28–43.
39. See Thomas Scheff, ed., *Labeling Madness* (Upper Saddle River, NJ: Prentice Hall, 1975).
40. Alan A. Lipton and Franklin S. Simon, "Psychiatric Diagnosis in a State Hospital: Manhattan State Revisited," *Hospital and Community Psychiatry* 36 (1985): 368–373.
41. Kessler et al., "Lifetime and 12-Month Prevalence of DSM-III-R Psychiatric Disorders in the United States."
42. Robert E. L. Faris and H. Warren Dunham, *Mental Disorders in Urban Areas* (Chicago: University of Chicago Press, 1939).
43. August B. Hollingshead and Frederick C. Redlich, *Social Class and Mental Illness: A Community Study* (New York: Wiley, 1958).
44. Leo Strole, T. S. Langer, S. T. Michael, M. K. Opler, and T. A. L. Rennie, *Mental Health in the Metropolis: The Midtown Manhattan Study* (New York: McGraw-Hill, 1962).
45. Bruce P. Dohrenwend and Barbara Snell Dohrenwend, *Social Status and Psychological Disorder: A Causal Inquiry* (New York: Wiley, 1969), p. 165.
46. Kessler et al., "Lifetime and 12-Month Prevalence of DSM-III-R Psychiatric Disorders in the United States."
47. Joseph W. Eaton and Robert J. Weil, *Culture and Mental Disorder* (New York: Free Press, 1955).
48. Eleanor Leacock, "Three Variables in the Occurrence of Mental Illness," in Alexander Leighton, John Clausen, and Robert Wilson, eds., *Explorations in Social Psychiatry* (New York: Basic Books, 1957), pp. 308–340.
49. Kessler et al., "Lifetime and 12-Month Prevalence of DSM-III-R Psychiatric Disorders in the United States."
50. Ibid.
51. Franz Kallmann and B. Roth, "Genetic Aspects of Preadolescent Schizophrenia," *American Journal of Psychiatry* 112 (1956): 599–606.
52. A. Hoffer and W. Polin, "Schizophrenia in the NAS-NRC Panel of 15,909 Twin Pairs," *Archives of General Psychiatry* 23 (1970): 469–477.
53. Irving Gottesman, Peter McGuffin, and Anne E. Farmer, "Clinical Genetics as Clues to the 'Real' Genetics of Schizophrenia," *Schizophrenia Bulletin* 13 (1987): 23–47.
54. Janice A. Egeland et al., "Bipolar Affective Disorders Linked to DNA Markers on Chromosome 11," *Nature* 325 (February 26, 1987), pp. 783–787.

55. Miron Baron et al., "Genetic Linkage Between X-Chromosome Markers and Bipolar Affective Illness," *Nature* 326 (March 19, 1987), pp. 289–292; Stephen Hodgkinson et al., "Molecular Genetic Evidence for Heterogeneity in Manic Depression," *Nature* 325 (February 26, 1987), pp. 805–808.

56. Paul Wender and Donald F. Klein, *Mind, Mood, and Medicine: A Guide to the New Biopsychiatry* (New York: Farrar, Straus & Giroux, 1981).

57. Ibid.

58. For a review of this literature, see Carson, Butcher, and Coleman, *Abnormal Psychology and Modern Life*, pp. 115–124.

59. Gregory Bateson, Don D. Jackson, Jay Haley, and John Weakland, "Toward a Theory of Schizophrenia," *Behavioral Science* 1 (1956): 251–264.

60. Jeffrey Bryer et al., "Childhood Sexual and Physical Abuse as Factors in Adult Psychiatric Illness," *American Journal of Psychiatry* 144 (1987): 1426–1430.

61. M. Audrey Burnam et al., "Sexual Assault and Mental Disorders in a Community Setting," *Journal of Counseling and Clinical Psychology* 56 (1988): 843–850.

62. R. D. Laing, *The Politics of Experience* (New York: Ballantine Books, 1967), p. 127.

63. Bruce Link, "Mental Patient Status, Work, and Income: An Examination of the Effects of Psychological Labeling," *American Sociological Review* 47 (April 1982): 202–215.

64. National Center for Health Statistics, *Health, United States*, 2000, Table 114.

65. American Psychiatric Association, "Mental Health Parity—Its Time Has Come," 1999, APA Online, <www.psycho.org>.

66. Physicians for a National Health Program, "PNHP Data Update, September 2000," <www.pnhp.org/data-update0900.htm>; Debra S. Feldman, Dennis H. Novack, and Edward Gracely, "Effects of Managed Care on Physician Patient Relationships, Quality of Care, and the Ethical Practice of Medicine: A Physician Survey," *Archives of Internal Medicine* 158: 1626–1632.

67. Consumers Union, "The Crisis in Health Insurance," *Consumer Reports* 55 (September 1990): 608–617; U.S. Department of the Census, *Statistical Abstract*, 1999, p. 124.

68. Rosenthal, "Patients Share Bigger Burden of Rising Health Care Costs."

69. Robert Pear, "Medicare Paying Doctors 59% of Insurers' Rate, Panel Finds," *New York Times*, April 5, 1994.

70. U.S. Department of the Census, *Statistical Abstract*, 2000, p. 118.

71. Sonia Nazario, "Treating Doctors for Prejudice," *Los Angeles Times*, December 29, 1993, pp. A1, A36, A37; Douglas P. Shuit, "Black, Poor Medicare Patients Get Worse Care," *Los Angeles Times*, April 20, 1994, pp. B1, B4; Thomas H. Maugh II, "Surgery Study Finds Poor at a Disadvantage," *Los Angeles Times*, December 9, 1993, pp. A3, A36.

72. Physicians for a National Health Program, "PNHP Data Update, September 2000."

73. National Center for Health Statistics, *Health, United States*, 2001, Table 114. U.S. Department of the Census, *Statistical Abstract*, 1996, p. 834.

74. National Center for Health Statistics, *Health, United States*, 2001, Table 115.

75. Health Care Financing Administration, "The Clinton Administration's Comprehensive Strategy to Fight Health Care Fraud, Waste and Abuse," 1998, <http://www.hcfa.gov/facts>; Consumers Union, "The Crisis in Health Insurance"; Associated Press, "Health Insurers' Efficiency Is Questioned," *Los Angeles Times*, October 19, 1990, p. D6.

76. Consumers Union, "Wasted Health Care Dollars."

77. Consumers Union, "The $200 Billion Dollar Bottom Line," *Consumer Reports* (July 1992): 436.

78. U.S. Bureau of the Census, *Statistical Abstract*, 2000, p. 125.

79. Physicians for a National Health Program, "PNHP Data Update 2000."

80. Physicians for a National Health Program, "PNHP Data Update 2000."

81. Jeffrey Klein and Michael Castleman, "The Profit Motive in Breast Cancer," *Los Angeles Times*, April 4, 1994, p. B7.

82. Brad Knickerbocker, "Assisted-Suicide Issue More Active as Citizens Appear to Change Mood," *Christian Science Monitor*, May 2, 1994, p. 6.

83. *Denver Post*, February 24, 2000, p. 20A.

84. Daniel P. Reid, *The Tao of Health, Sex, and Longevity* (New York: Simon & Schuster, 1989), p. 233.
85. U.S. Bureau of the Census, *Statistical Abstract*, 2000, p. 194.
86. Erving Goffman, *Asylums: Essays on the Social Situation of Mental Patients and Other Inmates* (New York: Doubleday, 1961).
87. U.S. Department of the Census, *Statistical Abstract*, 1996, p. 129.
88. Paul Starr, *The Social Transformation of American Medicine* (New York: Basic Books, 1982).

PART II

THE PROBLEMS OF INEQUALITY

Most people say they believe in equality. Political leaders around the world never tire of calling on this value to rally support for one program or opposition to another. In North America, the ideal is not so much that everyone have a college education, a high income, and a position of political influence, but that they have an equal *opportunity* to achieve those things. But even when stated in this more qualified way, there is a huge gap between our ideals and the realities of our daily life. Each of the chapters that follow focus on a different kind of inequality, exploring the ways our society is structured to favor the members of one group over those of another. We begin with the problem of poverty because the issue of economic inequality is critical to understanding all the other problems discussed in this section.

CHAPTER 6

THE POOR

Questions to Consider

Who are the poor?

Why is the gap between the rich and the poor growing wider?

What is the underclass?

Are the poor to blame for their poverty?

What can we do to reduce poverty?

The poor in North America may not look like the starving masses in famine zones of the Third World, but their misery is just as real. In fact, poverty can be more difficult in a rich country than in a poor one. There is less shame in poverty in a nation like India because so many people are poor. In North America, poor people are not only constantly confronted by the wealth they are denied; they are also often blamed for their own suffering. Despite the appearance of widespread affluence, North America has some of the worst slums in the industrial world. Poor nutrition, nagging hunger, shabby clothing, and a crowded room or two in a deteriorating old building are all that many families can hope for. Yet when compared with the people of the European countries, Americans appear to have a remarkably callous attitude toward the poor, as if people were poor simply because they didn't want to work.

Although the poor are a minority in every sense of the word, they are a sizable one. According to government estimates, there were over 31 million poor people in the United States as the twentieth century ended, which was 11.3 percent of the entire population.[1] Such figures should, however, be viewed with a skeptical eye, for as we will see, there is considerable debate about how to determine whether someone is poor. Although the experts may not agree about exactly how many poor people there are, there is no doubt that the problem is an enormous one. And no matter how poverty is measured, there is also no doubt that the United States has a much larger percentage of its people living in poverty than any other industrial society.

THE RICH AND THE POOR: A WIDENING GAP

When news commentators and politicians talk about the problem of poverty, they seldom have much to say about those at the other end of the economic ladder, but wealth and poverty are two sides of the same coin. To understand the problem of poverty, it must be seen in the context of the social and economic inequality between those at the top and those at the bottom of society.

All the data show that there is a huge gap between the haves and the have-nots and that it has been growing steadily wider for over 20 years. There are two general ways of determining how great this gap actually is. One approach attempts to measure differences in income, and the other focuses on wealth. Although these two yardsticks are related, there are important differences between them. **Income** refers to the amount of money a person makes in a given year. **Wealth** is the total value of that person's assets: real estate and personal property, stocks, bonds, cash, and so forth.

The requirement that everyone report their income to the Internal Revenue Service makes it fairly easy to examine the distribution of income (except for the income that people hide from tax collectors), and the U.S. Census Bureau conducts annual surveys that are even more accurate measures of the changes in the distribution of income from year to year. These data show a society deeply divided along class lines. One of the best ways to visualize the distribution of income in a society is to examine how much of the total income from an "income pie" goes to the top 20 percent of people compared to how much of that total income in the nation goes to the poorest 20 percent. When we do this, as shown in Figure 6.1a, we see that the richest 20 percent of Americans receive just about 50 percent of all income, while the poorest 20 percent

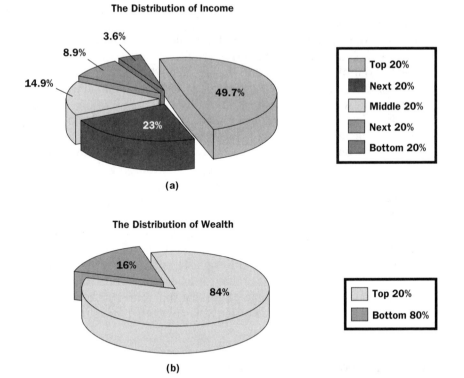

The Distribution of Income

3.6%

8.9%

14.9%

49.7%

23%

Top 20%

Next 20%

Middle 20%

Next 20%

Bottom 20%

(a)

The Distribution of Wealth

16%

84%

Top 20%

Bottom 80%

(b)

FIGURE 6.1   DISTRIBUTION OF INCOME AND WEALTH

Source: U.S. Bureau of Census, Money Income in the United States, 2000 (Washington, DC: U.S. Government Printing Office, 2001); Lawrence Mishel, Jared Bernstein, and John Schmitt, The State of Working America, 1998–1999 (Washington, DC: Economic Policy Institute), p. 262.

of Americans receive under 4 percent of this income.[2] In other words, in 2000 the top 20 percent of Americans received the same amount of income as everyone else combined. Thirty years ago, the top 20 percent received substantially less of the total income (43 percent) while the poorest 20 percent received more (5 percent). But when we look at the very top, the inequality figures are even more striking. By the end of the 1990s, top executives of the largest corporations in the United States received an average of $10 million in income and stock options, which means their income was over 400 times the wages of their average workers.[3]

Examining the distribution of wealth is more difficult. For one thing, it is not always clear how much a particular asset, such as a painting or a mansion, is actually worth; in addition, those with great wealth often conceal many of their assets from the scrutiny of outsiders. The U.S. Bureau of the Census does not even attempt to publish yearly reports on the distribution of wealth as it does for income, but in recent times it has been trying to estimate wealth inequalities every few years. All of these studies find that wealth is far more unequally distributed than income. As can be seen from Figure 6.1b, while the richest 20 percent of Americans held about half of all income, the richest 20 percent held over 84 percent of all wealth. Further, the richest 10 percent held almost 75 percent of all wealth in America, and the top 1 percent of people alone owned almost 40 percent of all wealth.[4]

Why is wealth distributed so much more unequally than income? There appear to be two principal reasons. First, lower-income people usually have to spend everything they make just to get by and are therefore less able to build up savings accounts, investments, or other assets. The debts of the bottom 20 percent of American families equal or exceed their assets, so they have zero net worth.[5] Second, wealth tends to be passed on from one generation to another. Poor people usually have poor parents and start out with nothing. On the other hand, wealthy people usually have wealthy parents and are much more likely to come into a substantial estate.

Although many Americans see their country as the land of opportunity and equality, international comparisons do not bear out this view. There is certainly far more economic inequality in the poor nations than in any of the industrialized countries (see Chapter 11). But the research indicates that of any developed nation, the United States has by far the highest poverty rate and the biggest gap between those on the top and those on the bottom, while Canada has slightly more poverty than European countries such as Germany and France.[6] The infant mortality rate—a common indicator of the amount of poverty in a nation—is also substantially higher in the United States than in Japan, Canada, and most western European nations.[7]

The old saying "The rich get richer and the poor get poorer" has not always proved to be true, but since the 1970s there has clearly been a significant widening of the gap between the haves and the have-nots. For example, between 1973 and 1995, the top 5 percent of American families saw their share of all income go up almost 30 percent while the bottom 40 percent of American families saw their share drop about 17 percent, and there was a similar trend in the concentration of wealth as well.[8] Since 1997,

Wealth and poverty are two sides of the same coin. The gap between wealth and poverty would narrow if income was more equally distributed.

after almost ten years of the longest economic boom in American history, lower- and middle-income groups in the United States finally made some modest gains in income, but the overall level of inequality in American society remains remarkably high.[9]

Many complex forces contribute to the growth of inequality of American society, but three stand out as particularly important. First, foreign economic competition and increasing industrial development in poor countries have placed the North American worker in direct competition with workers around the world who receive far lower wages. Managers and stockholders of multinational corporations, on the other hand, benefit from the profits made possible by lower labor costs, and incomes of engineers, scientists, and other professionals have increased substantially, since few people in the less-developed countries have the training necessary for such jobs. A second factor has been the use of technology to reduce or eliminate high-paying jobs for skilled laborers, as well as the corresponding increase in low-paying service jobs. The third cause of the growing inequality in American society is a political one. Since 1981, taxes on the rich have been substantially reduced, while government programs that benefit the poor and the working class have been cut to help make up the loss in revenue (see Chapter 2).

QUICK REVIEW

What are the differences between the distribution of wealth and the distribution of income? Why has the gap between the rich and poor increased?

MEASURING POVERTY

Even though everyone has a general idea of what **poverty** is, it is a difficult term to define precisely. Certainly, poor people lack many of the goods and services that others enjoy. They may have insufficient food, shelter, clothing, or entertainment, but how much is "insufficient"? Are people poor if they have no shoes, no bicycle, no car, or only one car?

Poverty is usually defined in one of two ways: absolute or relative. The **absolute approach** divides the poor from the nonpoor by using some fixed standard, usually the lack of money to purchase a minimum amount of food, shelter, and clothing. The **relative approach** holds that people are poor if they have significantly less income and wealth than the average person in their society.[10] Supporters of the relative approach argue that what is really important is not the fact that the poor have a low standard of living but that they are psychologically and sociologically excluded from the mainstream of society. Despite the appeal of such arguments, the absolute approach is nonetheless far more widely used both by government agencies and social scientists—perhaps because what most concerns the public is not the relative deprivation of the poor but their lack of basic necessities.

Every year the U.S. government sets a "poverty line" for families of different sizes. If a family's income falls below the line, they are officially considered to be poor. The poverty line was originally based on studies showing that the average low-income family spent about one-third of its budget on food. The Department of Agriculture's

Economy Food Budget was then multiplied by 3 to calculate the poverty line. Beginning at $3,000 in 1964, the poverty line for a family of four reached $17,761 by 2000.[11]

Although such numbers make the poverty line sound precise and objective, it is actually a rather arbitrary figure. A different approach to these computations could easily lead to a different figure, and there is considerable debate over whether the poverty line is too high or too low. Some conservatives feel that it is too high (thus overestimating the amount of poverty) because noncash welfare benefits, such as food stamps and Medicaid, are not counted as income. Advocates for the poor counter that the original calculation that a poor family spends one-third of its income on food did not include such benefits either (although it is true that benefits are higher now than they were in 1964). They argue that if we are going to count such welfare benefits as income, we must also deduct the taxes the poor must pay. In recent years, however, the Census Bureau has included all of these criticisms and each year provides different poverty rates; poverty rates that include the value of food stamps and estimates of the Medicaid value, as well as estimates that consider what the poor must pay in taxes. All of these additional poverty figures are fairly close, meaning that poverty rates do not differ much each year when these other things are also calculated.

Perhaps most important, however, is the criticism that the estimates of the cost of food, which is the base for calculating the poverty line, is far too low. The Department of Agriculture itself admits the Economy Food Budget it used was intended only as a temporary or emergency budget, not to meet long-term nutritional needs. But there is an additional problem that makes the poverty line lower than it should be to accurately reflect true costs of basic necessities such as food over the years. In 1969, the government stopped adjusting the poverty line on the basis of the rising cost of food and used a measure of overall inflation instead. Since then, the cost of necessities, especially housing, has gone up much faster than the consumer price index as a whole, meaning that families living at the poverty line are unable to buy as much of the things they need as they could in the past. In 1995, the National Research Council examined the way the poverty level was calculated and recommended an alternative measure that adds noncash welfare benefits, subtracts out-of-pocket child-care and medical expenses, and adjusts for changing consumption patterns (for example, Americans now spend proportionately less on food and more on other expenses such as housing). The result was that about 9 million more people were counted as poor than in the official figures.[12]

WHO ARE THE POOR?

One of the major reasons for trying to define who is poor and who is not is to discover which segments of our society experience the greatest poverty. Single-parent families, for example, have a much higher than average poverty rate, and their growing numbers have had a major impact on the problem of poverty. From 1970 to 1998, the percentage of all families with children that were headed by a single woman more than doubled, from 10 to 27 percent, and single mothers with children were the fastest-growing segment of the poverty population.[13] In fact, the majority of poor families with children are now headed by single women, and the poverty rate of such families is substantially greater than that of married couples.[14]

As of 2000, the official poverty rate for the United States was 11.3 percent of the population, but this rate differed substantially for various subgroups. Children are among those with the highest rates of poverty—16.2 percent of those under 18 fall below the poverty line. Interestingly, while poverty has been rising among the young, the Social Security program has helped bring it down among the elderly (10.2 percent in 2000).[15] Contrary to popular stereotypes, the biggest group of poor people in the United States are white (46.1 percent in 1999), not African American (25.9 percent) or Latino (21.8 percent). However, the percentage of the white population below the poverty line is considerably lower than it is for most minorities. For example, in 2000, 7.5 percent of all whites were poor, compared to 22.1 percent of African Americans and 21.2 percent of Latinos.[16] Family structure is also a very important influence on poverty. While 8.6 percent of all families were below the poverty line in 2000, families with both parents present were only about half as likely to be poor, while three times that percentage of female-headed families were below the poverty line.[17]

When we think about where the poor live, it is the crowded urban ghettos that spring to mind most quickly—but the percentage of people below the poverty line is almost as high in rural areas.[18] The vast majority of poor people do live in cities, but that is simply because our population as a whole is so highly urbanized. The suburbs, in contrast, have the lowest poverty rate—less than half that of the central cities or rural areas—but as our original suburbs have aged, they too have developed growing pockets of poverty.[19]

TRENDS IN POVERTY

Another important use for poverty statistics is to measure changes in the poor population. Official statistics indicate that poverty declined sharply in the 1960s—from over 22 percent of the total population at the start of the decade to around 11 percent in the early 1970s. The two main reasons for this improvement were the economic prosperity of the times and a strong government commitment to what was called the War on Poverty. As economic prosperity and the government's efforts to reduce poverty both faded, however, improvements disappeared and poverty again began to grow. The poverty level reached over 15 percent in the early 1980s, then dropped a bit. It returned to that level in the early 90s. After a long economic recovery, the poverty rate declined in the mid-90s. It stood at 11.3 in 2001. Although studies indicate that there is less poverty now than there was 40 years ago, they also show that many problems associated with poverty have been getting worse. There has, for example, been a sharp increase in the percentage of poor people who live in **extreme poverty**. In 1975 about 30 percent of poor people had incomes that were less than half the poverty line,[20] but today that figure is 38 percent.[21] And as we shall see, it is this group of the "poorest of the poor" who suffer most severely.

HUNGER IN AMERICA

Many people assume that hunger goes up and down with the cycles of the economy, but it is often just as affected by changes in government policy. Hunger and malnutrition were significantly reduced during the 1960s and 1970s, mainly because of the creation of the food stamp program during the late 1960s. Yet despite this reduction, hunger remained a major problem. During the mid-1980s, a Harvard University Medical School study estimated there were 12 million children and 8 million adults in the United States who could be considered hungry by standard medical definitions of hunger and malnutrition.[22] U.S. Department of Agriculture figures for 1993 to 1994 indicate there were 30 million Americans defined as hungry (skipping meals each month due to lack of money).[23] A national survey of major cities by the U.S. Conference of Mayors found that 86 percent reported increases in emergency food requests after the welfare cutbacks of 1996. They estimated food requests went up by 16 percent in 1997 despite sharply declining unemployment.[24] In late 1997, another study surveyed 11,000 charity agencies across the United States. It found that about 40 percent of those seeking emergency food had someone in the household employed full time. More than 66 percent of the people seeking food aid were employed, but they had incomes of less than $10,000 per year, which, as we have seen, is far below the poverty line. That same year, Congress nonetheless cut over $27 billion from the food stamp program.[25]

The most recent study of hunger by the Department of Agriculture, released in 2000, is most striking because it came after years of economic boom. It was estimated that more than 10 percent of Americans faced hunger at some time that year or were worried that their food would run out. The study also estimated that approximately 17 percent of America's children, about 12 million young people, did not get enough to eat. Female-headed households had the highest rate of hunger (at around 30 percent), followed by African American families (21 percent), and Hispanic families (20.8 percent). Finally, even during this long economic boom, the poor people experienced an increase in hunger between 1995 and 1999.[26]

QUICK REVIEW

What are the two different ways of measuring poverty?
What type of person is most likely to be poor?
What are the current trends in poverty?
How much hunger is there in the United States?

THE LIFE OF POVERTY

Being poor in a rich country has profound psychological and sociological consequences. In our materialistic society, people are judged as much by what they have as by who they are. Children of poverty lack so many of the things everyone is "supposed" to have that they often feel there is something wrong with them or their families. Poor people of all ages are constantly confronted with things they desire but have little chance to own.

The poor are deprived of more than just material possessions. In contrast to the rich and even the middle classes, those brought up in poverty often appear to speak crudely, with heavy accents and a limited vocabulary. They have less education, are less informed about the world, and are less likely to vote. Significant numbers of poor people cannot even read or write and so are cut off from much of mainstream culture.

LESSONS FROM OTHER PLACES

POVERTY RATES AND CONTRASTING VALUES

Americans who live in or even just visit European countries are surprised to see so few signs of poverty. After giving relatives a tour of Germany, for example, I have even had them ask, "So where do the poor people live?" It is hard for many Americans to believe that poverty is so much less common in most of Europe than it is here.

The figures we have seen elsewhere in this chapter back up these informal observations: Poverty rates in the United States are far higher than in any other industrial nation. But why is this true when America so rich? This question is even more puzzling when we realize that the United States also has a low rate of unemployment. Germany has a poverty rate that is less than half that of the United States, while the German unemployment rate was over 10 percent throughout the 1990s. Other major industrialized nations in Europe, such as France and Italy, are in the same situation. What is the cause of these seeming contradictions?

While there are many economic differences among the nations on both sides of the Atlantic, the main reason that Europeans experience less poverty is that they have more effective social-welfare programs. For example, estimates suggest that Germany would see 22 percent of its population living in poverty without various types of welfare and unemployment benefits. Thus, the German welfare system has been able to reduce poverty by more than 65 percent. France, Italy, Belgium, Denmark, the Netherlands, and Sweden all have similarly low poverty levels because of their welfare programs. The same studies show that the U.S. government reduces poverty by only 28 percent through its welfare benefits—and this was before the major cuts in welfare programs in 1996.

Public opinion polls show that Europeans are far more likely to demand that their government do something to pull its citizens up from poverty. Unlike Americans, Europeans still support expensive welfare and unemployment benefits even if the result is higher taxes and higher unemployment. In other words, Europeans generally recognize there is some trade-off between extensive welfare benefits and slightly higher unemployment rates, but their value preferences lead them to accept the trade-off.

Another important factor that helps keep welfare benefits low and poverty high in the United States is political. Only around 35 percent of lower-income Americans vote in most major elections, compared to a voter turnout of over 70 percent for higher-income Americans. Because lower-income Americans are less likely to vote, politicians favoring more welfare and unemployment benefits are less likely to be elected. In Europe, the differences in voting by economic class are much lower and therefore politicians are more concerned with fighting poverty.

—Harold Kerbo

Sources: Harold Kerbo and Hermann Strasser, *Modern Germany* (New York: McGraw-Hill, 2000); Kerbo, *Social Stratification and Inequality* (New York: McGraw-Hill, 2000), pp. 254–255, 260, Chapter 15; Lawrence Mishel, Jared Bernstein, and John Schmitt, *The State of Working America*, 1998–1999 (Ithaca, New York: Cornell University Press, 1999), p. 377; Everett Carl Ladd and Karlyn H. Bowman, *Attitudes Toward Economic Inequality* (Washington, DC: AEI Press, 1998).

Under these conditions, poor people can hardly avoid feelings of inadequacy, frustration, and anger. Some bottle up those feelings, contributing to psychosomatic illnesses and aggravating problems such as high blood pressure and ulcers. Others express hostility and anger in violent crime. The rates of murder, assault, and rape are all much higher among poor people than among the rest of the population.

Economic uncertainty is another important part of being poor. Even poor people who are lucky enough to have a permanent job ordinarily work in low-paying, dead-end positions that are the first to be cut in bad times. Others can find only temporary work or are unemployed. Welfare sometimes helps out, but, as we shall see, the benefits are meager, the bureaucracy demeaning, and welfare programs have been sharply cut back in recent years. To make this insecurity worse, the poor have far higher rates of family instability than others. The poor marry younger and have the highest rates of divorce, separation, family violence, and out-of-marriage childbirth. This pattern of inequality even carries over into matters of life and death. Although we hear a great deal about medical miracles such as organ transplants, most of these "miracles" are reserved for people with good health insurance. As a rule, the poor receive second-rate health care, a deficient diet, and inadequate shelter. Consequently, they catch more contagious diseases and have a higher rate of infant mortality and a shorter life span.

While these generalizations apply to all the poor to one degree or another, it is important to recognize that people who live in poverty are as diverse as those in any other class. While some are so desperately poor they starve or freeze to death, for others poverty is a short-term condition that is soon overcome. We will devote some special attention to three overlapping groups among this diverse population: the homeless, the underclass, and the working poor.

THE HOMELESS

We have all seen them—the bag ladies who push around everything they own in a rusty shopping cart, the disheveled men sleeping on park benches or above heating grates to keep warm, an entire family living in an abandoned car. Lack of protection from the elements is the most obvious hardship they face. In the summer they swelter, and in the winter some freeze to death. Even getting enough food to eat is a continual concern for many of the homeless. Because they are almost always on the streets, they are easy targets for criminals and thugs. Aside from a few overworked charity and welfare agencies, the homeless confront a society that seems indifferent to their plight. The police, to whom most of us would turn for protection, see the homeless as a nuisance who must be moved out or arrested when their numbers become too great.

No one is really sure how many Americans are homeless on any given day. The Census Bureau counted 228,621 homeless people in its nationwide tally, but that figure is generally believed to be far too low, and even the bureau itself says it never set out to count every homeless person.[27] The Urban Institute estimates that there are about 600,000 homeless; the Department of Health and Human Services says 2 million; and advocates for the homeless put the figure at about 3 million or more.[28] The one thing virtually everyone agrees about is that the number of homeless men and women has grown substantially in recent years.

The problem of homelessness has grown much more severe in recent years, and the sharpest increases have been among women and children.

Who is most likely to be homeless? According to a survey of 26 major cities by the U.S. Conference of Mayors, over half of all homeless people are African American, about one-fourth European American, and 13 percent Latino. Almost half of the homeless have some kind of alcohol or drug problem. Although one in five has a full- or part-time job, they simply can't afford a steady place to live. Perhaps the most disturbing finding of this survey was the number of homeless families. While single men used to make up the vast majority of the homeless population, a year-long survey conducted in late 1992 and 1993 found an equal number of people in families among the homeless.[29]

There are several reasons why homelessness appears to have risen even in years when poverty has not. The most popular explanation is that the deinstitutionalization movement, which sharply reduced the population of state mental hospitals, has left many severely disturbed patients to wander the streets without the outpatient services that were promised. Although there is little doubt that this policy has been a major contributor to the ranks of the homeless, it is not the only factor. Articles in magazines such as *Time*, *Newsweek*, and *People* have claimed that the majority of the homeless are mentally disturbed, but several studies have put the figure much lower than 50 percent. Most research suggests that somewhere around one-third of the homeless have mental problems.[30] A study of homeless adults in Texas concluded that "the most common face on the street is not that of the psychiatrically impaired individual, but one caught in a cycle of low-paying, dead-end jobs that fail to provide the means to get off and stay off the streets."[31] The federal government has contributed to the problem by sharply reducing the amount of money spent on subsidized housing programs over the past three decades. (See the Debate on pages 188–189.) Equally important is the fact that large increases in the cost of rental housing have simply priced many poor people out of the market. Over 1 million "flophouse" rooms have been torn down since 1970, and the average cost of rental housing has grown twice as fast as the average income of renters.[32]

THE UNDERCLASS

Originally coined by sociologist Gunnar Myrdal in the early 1960s, the concept of the **underclass** was picked up in a series of articles published in *New Yorker* magazine in 1981, and from there it jumped into the daily vocabulary of educated Americans. Like most such terms, it is defined differently by different people. Common to most of these definitions is the idea that the underclass comprises the bottom of the poverty class and the implication that its members are excluded from the economic and cultural mainstream of society.[33] Disagreements arise over the standards that define who is in the underclass and over how large a group it is. The broadest standard holds that the underclass consists of those who are trapped in long-term poverty. By that definition, the underclass would include between 40 and 60 percent of all poor people.[34] Another approach defines the underclass as the "poorest of the poor"—that is, those who have the lowest incomes. If we define extreme poverty as living on less than half the poverty-level income, then almost 4 in 10 poor people were in the underclass in 1999.[35] Finally, the most restrictive standard would include only those who live in neighborhoods that are overwhelmingly poor. Rough estimates based on the data from census tracts (which do not follow the boundaries of actual neighborhoods) place that number at a little under 10 percent of the poor.[36] Despite its usefulness, some sociologists have become uncomfortable with the concept of the underclass because of the sensationalistic way many journalists use the term. Herbert J. Gans, for example, writes that it is an "increasingly pejorative term that seems to be becoming the newest buzzword for the undeserving poor."[37]

However the term is defined, the underclass is, in the words of William Julius Wilson, "the heart of the problem of poverty."[38] Members of the underclass are much more likely to have been raised in poverty than the population of poor people as a whole. They are also far more likely to come from ethnic minorities, especially if we define the underclass as those living in overwhelmingly poor neighborhoods. By that definition, 65 percent of the underclass are African American and 22 percent Latino.[39] Members of the underclass tend to come from single-parent families with a poor educational background and a history of welfare dependency. A substantial proportion of the people in the underclass can't read or write and lack other job skills. In the past, such people could at least get menial work as manual laborers, but changes in the job market have left many of them now without any hope of meaningful work.

As a result of these factors, many members of the underclass are trapped in a self-perpetuating cycle of poverty that is extremely hard to escape. The fact is that mainstream society no longer has a use for them, and many people would rather they just disappear. Of course, they are not going to do that, and the frustration and hopelessness of life in the underclass extract a heavy toll. Compared with other Americans and

---

DEBATE

SHOULD THE GOVERNMENT PROVIDE FREE HOUSING FOR THE HOMELESS?

Yes

Many cities and towns provide temporary shelter for the homeless, but there are many more homeless people on the streets than the shelters can accommodate. Some people therefore propose that federal funds be provided to guarantee every homeless person a place to sleep if he or she wants one.

A new wave of homeless men, women, and children is flooding the nation, and we must do something more than just pick up the bodies after they freeze to death. Some people say that we should rely on churches and other private charities to handle the problem. Although such an approach may have worked in a nation of small, tightly knit farming communities, it is hopelessly inadequate in a complex urban society. The charities themselves openly admit that they do not have the money or the resources to solve this problem.

The government is the one organization that can provide adequate housing for our most needy citizens. The only question is whether or not these people deserve to be helped, and the answer is a resounding "yes." More fortunate people often look down their noses at the homeless and blame them for their own misery. But no one chooses to be born into the underclass, to have a mental disorder, or to fall victim to the disease of alcoholism. And even the most zealous ideologue would have a difficult time finding a reason to blame homeless children for their plight. The real reason so many wealthy people oppose aid to the homeless is simple greed. They would rather see

---

even most other poor people, members of the underclass have significantly higher rates of mental disorder, alcoholism, drug abuse, and suicide, and they are far more likely to fall victim to violent crime.

THE WORKING POOR

We usually assume that people are poor because they don't work or can't work. But this is becoming less and less true. For example, while 9.6 percent of American families were below the poverty line in 2000, the rate of poverty was still 7.6 percent among American families with one or more full-time worker. We have seen that just under 25 percent of female-headed families are poor. But even when the mother works, the rate of poverty for female-headed households is still 21.4 percent.[40] What these figures clearly show is that, in today's economy, even a full-time job does not guarantee a

these unfortunates die on the streets than pay another $25 a year in taxes. Surely we are a more generous and public-spirited people than that. Our values and our traditions demand that we take forceful action to solve this tragic problem, and it is time we stopped talking and got the job done.

No

As soon as we hear about a new social problem, the first thing some people want to do is rush in and start throwing money at it. But a gigantic new government program to house the homeless would inevitably prove as wasteful and ineffective as other welfare programs have been. For one thing, the government is so inefficient and hamstrung by political pressures that most of the money is likely to be wasted before it ever gets to the homeless. Even if enough free housing were created to put a roof over their heads, that would do nothing to solve the underlying problems that made them homeless in the first place. The alcoholics and the mentally disturbed would simply be suffering from the same conditions indoors rather than on the streets.

A free housing program for the homeless would be a financial monster. It would grow bigger year by year, and eventually we would be forced to abandon it. We might begin by providing housing only to those who are now homeless, but what about the poor people who are working at low-paying jobs and still paying rent? They would soon walk away from their old apartments so that they too could become "homeless" and claim a free place to live.

The solution to the problem of the homeless is for individual citizens to give more to the private charities that have already proved they can do an efficient job dealing with the problem. Setting up another huge government bureaucracy would only make things worse.

person that they and their children can stay out of poverty. Furthermore, the working poor make up one of the fastest-growing groups in the poor population. Since 1978, the number of full-time workers living in poverty has risen twice as fast as the overall poverty population.

How can so many people hold full-time or nearly full-time jobs and still be poor? The answer is simple: low wages. A study by the Bureau of the Census found that nearly one-fifth of American workers did not earn enough money to keep a family of four above the poverty line. And that was a 50 percent increase since 1979—a development the usually understated Bureau termed "astounding."[41] The math, however, is simple: In the year 2000, working 40 hours a week at minimum wage for 50 weeks per year did not bring a person up to the poverty line. Clearly, such low-wage jobs have been the fastest-growing segment of the labor market in recent years, and the employment prospects for young workers without high school degrees have been growing progressively worse.

QUICK REVIEW

Why has the number of homeless people increased so much?
What is the underclass?
Why are so many working people still below the poverty line?

UNDERSTANDING THE WELFARE SYSTEM

Before we examine the general causes of poverty, we must first take a look at the welfare system, which has become so much a part of the phenomenon of poverty in the past 100 years. The first step is to understand the public's attitudes toward the poor.

ATTITUDES TOWARD THE POOR

Attitudes toward poverty are remarkably different in North America than in European societies. Rejection of the European class system and the availability of a vast new land to conquer helped create a tremendous faith in the value of hard work and competition among North Americans. In this way of thinking, each individual is responsible for his or her own economic destiny. Most people believe that even in a period of economic depression and high unemployment, anyone who works hard enough can be successful. It is also generally held that "there is always room at the top" for capable and hardworking people, no matter how humble their origins.

Despite its attractiveness, this belief in individual responsibility has a negative side. If the rich are personally responsible for their success, it follows that the poor are to blame for their failure. "Poor folks have poor ways," the old saying goes. Joe R. Feagin has summarized the principal points in this **ideology of individualism** as follows:

1. Each individual should work hard and strive to succeed in competition with others.
2. Those who work hard should be rewarded with success (seen as wealth, property, prestige, and power).
3. Because of widespread and equal opportunity, those who work hard will in fact be rewarded with success.
4. Economic failure is an individual's own fault and reveals lack of effort and other character defects.[42]

Surveys show that this ideology is still a potent force in American life. When asked about the causes of poverty, most people respond with individualistic explanations that blame the poor themselves rather than with structural explanations that hold society responsible or with fatalistic explanations that blame such things as bad luck or illness. In one survey, for example, 58 percent of the respondents said that lack of thrift and proper money management is a significant cause of poverty, and 55 percent said that lack of effort by the poor is a very important cause of poverty.[43] Americans also show very little support for government efforts to guarantee welfare and/or jobs to keep everyone above the poverty line. In contrast, 50 to 70 percent of the citizens of the European nations believe such efforts are a good idea.[44]

THE HISTORY OF THE WELFARE SYSTEM

The ideology of individualism has had an enormous impact on the response to poverty in the United States. People receiving government assistance are often stigmatized as lazy or incompetent even when they are recognized as "truly needy." Frances Fox Piven and Richard A. Cloward argued that the growth of the modern welfare system resulted more from an attempt to silence the political discontent of the poor than from a desire to improve their living conditions, and their findings have been supported by several more recent studies.[45]

The origins of today's welfare system are to be found in the Great Depression of the 1930s, when unemployment rose dramatically and armies of the newly impoverished demanded assistance: "Groups of men out of work congregated at local relief agencies, cornered and harassed administrators, and took over offices until their demands were met."[46] Despite such determined protests, reforms were made grudgingly. Relief for the poor was still largely a local matter, but cities and counties proved unable to shoulder the financial burden. The federal government began to give small direct payments to the unemployed, but it soon shifted to work relief programs, which were more in tune with the ideology of individualism. With the coming of President Franklin D. Roosevelt's New Deal, a host of new government agencies were created to put unemployed Americans to work. Public opposition to these and other welfare programs nonetheless remained strong through the Depression. The most popular New Deal program that still survives, Social Security, is often seen more as a form of insurance than welfare.

The 1950s brought only modest increases in welfare support for the poor, but a "welfare explosion" occurred in the 1960s. From December 1960 to February 1969, the number of recipients of Aid to Families with Dependent Children (AFDC), the main welfare program providing direct financial aid to poor mothers until its elimination in 1996, increased by 107 percent.[47] Daniel Patrick Moynihan laid the blame for this increase on the deteriorating black family and on the general increase in female-headed families.[48] Piven and Cloward disagreed, maintaining that family deterioration made only a minor contribution to the growing welfare rolls and that the real cause was increased activism among the poor, who began to demand greater social support.

The 1960s also saw the launch of President Lyndon Johnson's War on Poverty, which included such programs as the Job Corps, the Neighborhood Youth Corps, VISTA, and Head Start. These programs have often been criticized because they were inefficiently organized and because some of them were aimed primarily at young urban males and neglected females, the rural poor, and the elderly. Yet despite all its faults, most researchers agree that the War on Poverty did help to reduce poverty significantly in the United States.

The 1970s did not bring any new initiatives against poverty comparable to those introduced in the 1960s, but progress continued. There was, however, a sharp reaction against welfare programs for the poor in the early 1980s, which was spearheaded by the newly arrived Reagan administration. Between 1981 and 1985, federal welfare spending dropped by 19 percent; about 400,000 families were cut from AFDC rolls with another 300,000 receiving lower benefits, food stamp rolls were reduced by about 1 million people, and 3 million children were cut from school lunch programs.[49] The continuing growth in the number of single-parent families and the proliferation of poverty-level jobs once again forced up the number of welfare recipients. Yet welfare benefits were far less generous than they had been 20 years earlier, and many states had begun experimenting with time limits and work requirements to try to force mothers with dependent children off the welfare rolls. (See Figure 6.2.) As a result, the poverty rate that had stayed around 11 percent of the U.S. population during the 1970s (despite poor economic conditions), began moving up in the 1980s to roughly 15 percent. Studies show that this increase in poverty during the 1980s and early 1990s was largely related to these welfare cuts during the Reagan years.[50]

The ideology of individualism has always fostered a tendency for Americans to blame the poor for their own poverty, and during the past two decades critics charged that welfare does everything from encouraging sexual promiscuity to undermining the economy. In one televised debate, a well-known conservative even blamed the welfare system for his lack of success in hiring a maid. Ignoring the complex sociological forces that trap so many people in poverty, these critics often presented a

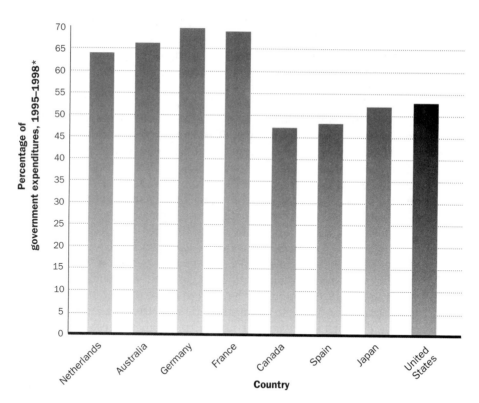

FIGURE 6.2 WELFARE

The United States spends much less on welfare programs than most other industrialized nations.

*Includes Social Security.

Source: United Nations Human Development Programme, *Human Development Report*, 2000 (New York: Oxford University Press, 2000), p. 300.

simplistic and unfair stereotype of welfare recipients as loafers who are living high at taxpayers' expense. This tendency to "blame the victims" for their misfortune reached new heights in a highly publicized book by Charles Murray and Richard Herrnstein. In *The Bell Curve*, they argued that poor people are biologically inferior to the affluent and that because their average intelligence is so low, government training or welfare programs for the poor are unlikely to do them any good.[51]

Ironically, those who attacked the welfare system ignored the largest welfare program, **Social Security**, because most of the benefits go to wealthier and more politically powerful recipients. (Social Security was supposed to be a kind of pension fund in which workers' contributions would be invested and the money returned to them when they retired, but the benefits are actually paid for directly by our taxes like any other welfare program.) Instead, the most bitter attacks were focused on AFDC—perhaps because although it was created with the intention of assisting children whose fathers had died or been disabled, the vast majority of recipients are single women who are divorced or have never been married. Or perhaps attacks on AFDC simply express hostility toward members of ethnic minorities, who were more likely to receive family assistance. The fact that there were so many unfair and unfounded attacks on the welfare system does not, however, mean that there were no reasonable criticisms. One of the biggest problems was that the welfare system was far too complex, too bureaucratic, and too wasteful. The government actually spent more money administering welfare programs (paying for welfare offices, case workers, and so on) than it paid out in benefits to the poor.[52] Another problem was that the old AFDC program tended to discourage welfare mothers from getting jobs: The money they earned was often deducted from their welfare checks, and they ran the risk of losing their Medicaid benefits if they earned too much. Another common criticism was that AFDC encouraged the breakup of families because it denied them assistance if an unemployed man lived in the home.

THE CURRENT WELFARE SYSTEM

As a result of criticisms, the welfare system put in place in the United States by the Social Security Act of 1935 came to an abrupt end in August 1996 when President Clinton signed the "welfare reform bill." The categories of welfare aid that existed in the past, such as AFDC, have not been entirely eliminated, but drastically altered. The biggest change is that each individual state now has the freedom to design its own welfare system without the strict federal guidelines that had existed since 1935. In essence, there are now 50 different welfare systems in the United States, and the variance in who can receive aid, how much, and for how long is extensive.[53] Moreover, in many states, like California, the welfare system is even more complex because each county has been given the task of designing its own welfare programs.[54]

Under this 1996 "welfare reform" the federal government did make a few important stipulations before giving individual states federal money. There had been work requirements for "able-bodied" recipients for many years, but these were made more strict—even requiring some mothers with babies just a few months old to find work or be cut off of welfare. The most important of these new requirements is the time limit on how long people can receive welfare. The basic commitment that the government

Welfare programs have never been as popular in the United States as they are in Europe, but in recent years welfare recipients have endured an unprecedented wave of political attacks.

should provide support for the needy has been eliminated: No longer will all "deserving people" who are hungry and poor be guaranteed some aid. According to federal rules, the time limits are two years for one stay on the welfare rolls and not more than 5 years of welfare in a lifetime—and many states have taken up the option to make these limits even shorter. What this means is that after the time limit runs out, it doesn't matter if someone is still poor and unemployed: They will be prevented from receiving further aid from what was once the main welfare program for poor people in the United States—AFDC. Some forms of limited aid, such as food stamps, may still continue, but the poor family's primary source of support is cut off.

In 1998, these time limits started becoming a reality across the United States. As we saw, there were reports of increasing numbers of people asking for emergency food, but the full impact of these sweeping changes is just starting to become clear. In a sense the U.S. government "got lucky." When the time limits on receiving welfare went into effect, the country was in the longest economic boom of the twentieth century and enjoying some of its lowest unemployment rates ever. The major question is what will happen now that the economy is slowing down again. What will happen to people with no more welfare eligibility and no job? Even with very low unemployment, most states have been reluctant to cut everyone off welfare who might have been out, and states have temporarily extended the deadlines for hundreds of thousands of people.[55]

Another consequence of the new limits on welfare assistance is just becoming apparent: The people who have been and will be kicked off of the welfare rolls will push down wages for all low-skilled workers in the United States. Surveys have already shown that this is happening in many states.[56] People desperate for food and shelter are working for lower wages than those currently employed who may lose their jobs to former welfare recipients.

Despite all the attention paid to programs that provide cash assistance to needy families, there are also several other important welfare programs. The other major cash program is **Supplemental Security Income (SSI)**, which gives financial assistance to poor people who are blind, disabled, or elderly. The federal government also has a variety of "noncash" programs that provide goods or services instead of money. The **food stamp program** gives recipients coupons that can be exchanged only for food, and **Medicaid** helps pay its recipients' health care bills. (Medicaid is only for poor people; **Medicare** is a more generous program for nonpoor over age 65.) Housing assistance is sometimes provided through rent subsidies and public housing projects that offer low rents to those poor enough to qualify. The states make a financial contribution to most of these programs, and state and local governments also supplement federal programs with short-term emergency aid and other benefits.

We know that the real (after-inflation) value of welfare benefits in the United States has been falling for more than two decades, and that the U.S. tax and welfare system already provides less help for the poor than any other industrialized nation.[57] The United States is the only industrialized country without a comprehensive national health system or some kind of **family allowance**. If current trends continue, if may be difficult to avoid some crisis among America's poor the next time we have a sharp economic decline.

QUICK REVIEW

What is the ideology of individualism?
Briefly describe the history of the American welfare system.
How did the 1996 reforms change the welfare system?
What are the main types of welfare assistance available in the United States?

EXPLANATIONS OF POVERTY

The economic base of some societies is so fragile that hunger is a daily reality for most people. Such extreme scarcity of food, clothing, and shelter is not characteristic of modern industrial societies or even most traditional ones. The poverty problem in these societies is one of distributing wealth rather than one of producing it. There are many explanations of economic inequality, but most fall into three overlapping categories: economic, political, and cultural.

ECONOMIC EXPLANATIONS

Much poverty can be traced to simple economic causes: low wages and too few jobs for those at the bottom of the social hierarchy. We have already seen that even a full-time job at the minimum wage doesn't pay enough to keep a family out of poverty, and a growing number of people are forced to take part-time or temporary jobs because they cannot find full-time work. In technologically advanced societies such as Canada and the United States, people without education and skills are finding it increasingly difficult to secure any kind of employment, and those who find work are likely to be employed in low-paying jobs. After controlling for inflation, the average earnings of men who did not finish high school have declined by almost one-fourth in the past two decades.[58] And this can only get worse with what is now called the "digital divide." With the increasing importance of computer literacy for all kinds of jobs, the less educated are likely to fall even further behind.

As we saw in Chapter 2, the average wages of all American workers declined significantly between 1973 and 1997, but the biggest decrease has been for those who get the lowest wages. For example, if we compare the top 10 percent of American workers with the bottom 10 percent, we find that the average wage earned by the lowest-paid workers declined by 17 percent in real terms, while at the same time the wages of the highest-paid workers increased by 5 percent.[59] Further, most of the new jobs added to the U.S. economy in recent times pay wages below the poverty line.[60] As a result of these changes, nearly one-third of all American workers received poverty-level wages in 1995, and by the end of the century there was only very slight improvement.[61]

Although the unemployment rate goes up and down with the business cycle (see Chapter 2), it has seldom dropped below 4 percent in the past four decades. Moreover, the official unemployment rate is not a very good measure of joblessness since it doesn't count those who have given up looking for work or those forced to take part-time jobs when they want full-time work. When those workers are added in, the picture gets far worse—in fact, the unemployment rate almost doubles. In addition to the overall national problem, many areas have a particularly high unemployment rate because of local conditions. For example, some regions depended on industries that are no longer competitive in the world economy. The slums of the central cities are especially vulnerable to a variety of forces that combine to create an unhealthy economic climate. Low income in these areas makes it tough going for businesses that depend on local residents for their customers. A high crime rate, lack of local services, and significant measure of fear and racism keep the wealthy away and discourage outside investment. At the same time, inadequate transportation and the long commuting distances to prosperous areas make it difficult for residents of inner-city slums to find work in other neighborhoods. For example, a study by James E. Rosenbaum and Susan J. Popkin found that poor women assigned to public housing in middle-class suburbs were much more likely to find jobs than those given housing in the central city.[62]

To add to their other problems, the poor often get less for their hard-earned dollars than do other consumers. Slum dwellers, for example, may pay more rent for a run-down apartment than people living in a small town pay for a house with a yard. More generally, because the poor are not mobile, it is difficult for them to shop around for sales and special values. They are obliged to patronize local merchants, who usually charge higher prices than those in affluent areas. Many stores in slum areas actively solicit sales on credit because the interest charges are more profitable than the sales themselves. If the customer cannot meet the installment payments, the merchandise is repossessed and sold to another poor customer.[63] When unexpected expenses occur, the poor must borrow money; but because they are not considered good credit risks, it may be impossible for them to get bank loans at standard interest rates. Instead, they must go to loan companies, which charge much higher interest rates, or to loan sharks, who charge exorbitant, illegal rates.

It is easy to look at all these difficulties as separate individual problems, but deeper roots in the basic structure of our economy link them all together. In an open capitalist society, the operation of the competitive market inevitably creates a huge gap between the rich and the poor. On the one hand, the market demands that employers pay the lowest wages and hire the fewest workers they can, or they run the risk of being driven out of business by more ruthless competitors. On the other hand, this same competitive struggle also stimulates the creation of enormous amounts of wealth, much of which goes to those who own and operate businesses. Although some workers who have skills or strong union organizations can demand better treatment, many others are inevitably left behind and sink into poverty. Of course, no capitalist economy operates in this completely unrestricted way. Governments in every capitalist nation have stepped in to help relieve some of the suffering caused by the harsh realities of the marketplace, both for humanitarian reasons and to prevent those at the bottom from rising up and threatening the whole system. But as we have seen, the U.S. government has done far less than any other industrial nation to reduce poverty and inequality.

POLITICAL EXPLANATIONS

Poverty is as much a political problem as a problem of economics or culture. How much poverty a country has (at least in the relative sense) is largely determined by the policies of its government. The United States has the highest poverty rate of any industrialized country because the U.S. government redistributes less money from the wealthy and the middle class to the poor.[64] For example, as we saw in "Lessons from Other Places" on page 184, government policies in European nations prevent high rates of unemployment from creating high rates of poverty. Inequality continues at such a high level in the United States because many Americans seem to have little concern about the poor, and those who do care are not politically organized. Politicians win votes by promising to eliminate crime and cut taxes, but few votes are won by promising to eliminate poverty. The ideology of individualism has convinced most Americans that the world is full of opportunities and that the poor deserve to be poor because they are too lazy or incompetent to seize those opportunities. As long as the poor are seen to be responsible for their own poverty, effective political action to change the conditions that cause poverty is unlikely.

Furthermore, as Herbert Gans has pointed out, poverty is valuable to the wealthy, and many powerful groups do not want it eliminated.[65] First, it ensures that society's dirty work gets done, for without poverty few people would be willing to do low-paying, unpleasant, and dangerous jobs. Second, the low wages the poor receive for their work subsidize the wealthy by keeping the prices of goods and services low and profits high. Third, poverty creates jobs for the many people who service the poor (such as welfare workers) or try to control them (such as police officers and prison guards). Fourth, the poor provide merchants with last-ditch profits by buying goods

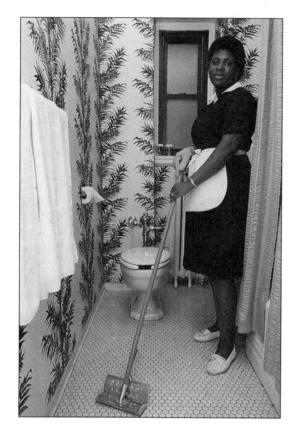

Conflict theorists argue that the wealthy want poverty to exist so they can be assured of a plentiful supply of cheap labor.

that otherwise would be thrown away: stale bread, tainted meat, out-of-style clothing, used furniture, and unsafe appliances. Fifth, the poor guarantee the status of the people above them in the social hierarchy. The poor provide a group that "respectable" people can brand as deviants—examples of what happens to those who break social rules. Thus, the fact that poverty helps make the middle and upper classes more comfortable creates powerful opposition to any program that is likely to significantly reduce it.

CULTURAL EXPLANATIONS

There are clear cultural differences among the social classes in all modern societies, and some scientists see these differences as a major cause of poverty. The foremost advocate of this position has been Oscar Lewis, who argued that some poor people share a distinct **culture of poverty**.[66] Lewis did not ignore the economic basis of poverty; his thesis was simply that a separate subculture has developed among the poor as a reaction to economic deprivation and exclusion from the mainstream of society. Once a culture of poverty has taken hold, it is passed down from generation to generation. Children who grow up in poverty acquire values and attitudes that make it very difficult for them to escape their condition.

According to Lewis, the family in the culture of poverty tends to be female centered, with the mother performing the basic tasks that keep the family going. The father, if present, makes only a slight contribution. Children have sexual relations and marry at an early age. The family unit is weak and unstable, and there is little community organization beyond it. Psychologically, those who live in the culture of poverty have weak ego structures and little self-control. Although Lewis did not use the term, most people living in the culture of poverty would clearly be part of the underclass.

Lewis studied a number of societies and concluded that the culture of poverty is international. It develops in societies with capitalist economies, persistently high unemployment rates, low wages, and an emphasis on accumulation of wealth and property. However, Lewis found a number of societies that have a considerable amount of poverty but no culture of poverty. India and Cuba, for example, have no culture of poverty because the poor are not degraded or isolated. Even in the United States, most poor people do not live in the culture of poverty. Lewis estimated that because of the influence of the mass media and the relatively low level of illiteracy, only 20 percent of the poor in the United States live in a culture of poverty.[67]

Most social scientists agree that poor people are more likely to have some of the characteristics described by Lewis, but there is much skepticism about claims that they have any special personality type or that they value work less than other groups. Some of Lewis's critics are not even so sure that a distinct lifestyle is passed from one generation to the next. Rather, it is argued by **situationalists** that each generation of the poor exhibits the same lifestyle because each generation experiences the same conditions: poor housing, crowding, deprivation, and isolation. Charles A. Valentine, for example, argued that the conditions Lewis described are imposed on the poor from the outside rather than being generated by a culture of poverty.[68]

QUICK REVIEW

Explain the economic, political, and cultural causes of poverty.

SOLVING THE PROBLEMS OF POVERTY

No one knows whether it is possible to create a classless society in which all people are economically equal in an industrial nation. Certainly no such society exists today. It does, however, seem possible to eliminate poverty in an absolute sense, even if some people remain richer than others. All industrial societies have made much greater progress toward this goal than the United States has, however, and some of the approaches to reducing poverty are discussed in this section.

MORE AND BETTER JOBS

Reducing unemployment and creating better-paying jobs is a continuing concern of governments around the world. As we saw in Chapter 2, at the beginning of the new millennium the United States was far ahead of all other industrial societies in producing jobs and pushing down unemployment. However, we know that unemployment always goes up again after such declines. When that happens, the easiest approach is to stimulate the national economy by cutting taxes and interest rates or by increasing the amount of money the government spends. The problem with this kind of "quick fix" is that it often drives up inflation and the national debt, and if carried on too long it may actually cause economic harm. Long-term improvements in the economy require the kind of basic structural changes described in Chapter 2. Unfortunately, reforms that aim to increase the rate of saving and investment, improve the educational system, and provide better government planning often have little political appeal; they are expensive and seldom produce results quickly enough to influence the next election. Such fundamental reforms are essential, however, if we are to make lasting progress in the struggle against poverty.

In the first years of the twenty-first century, however, the problem is not so much creating jobs, but creating well-paying jobs. The most obvious way to do this would be a substantial increase in the minimum wage, so that no one who works a full-time job year-round would still have to live in poverty. Critics of such proposals claim that they would create more unemployment. Although it is difficult to be sure how much of a problem that would be in today's economic environment, it would make good sense to combine an increase in minimum wage with the kinds of basic structural reforms that can help create more jobs.

Another approach is to create new education and job-training programs to give poor people the skills they need to land better jobs in today's global economy. European countries, for example, have much larger programs for **job retraining** than the countries of North America. The idea is a simple one: teach unemployed workers skills that are in demand so that they can find new jobs. While this approach is reasonable in this age of rapidly changing technology, it has basic limitations in times of high unemployment. If millions of unemployed and low-wage workers were all taught the latest skills, there still wouldn't be enough good jobs to go around under current economic conditions. So like the increases in minimum wages, such programs will be most effective if they are combined with an effort to create more jobs.

IMPROVING WELFARE

The welfare system has been attacked from all points of the political spectrum and, if the welfare reforms the conservatives have pushed through are to have any chance for long-term success, several things will have to be done. While few object to the goal of getting mothers off welfare and into gainful employment, progressives feel that those reforms are being carried out in a harsh and uncaring manner, and the overall objectives of the program are highly unrealistic. For one thing, a large number of welfare mothers are poorly educated and lack basic job skills. If they are going to have any chance to get a decent job, they will need education and training. That means that in the short run, an effective program will cost considerably more to set up and run than it saves. Yet the reform legislation actually cuts welfare spending. The second difficulty is providing enough good, low-cost day care for the participants' children while the mothers are in training or at work. Once again, this is going to cost more money than welfare programs are likely to be able to spend. The third problem is that the reform proposals are far too optimistic about the chances of these poor welfare mothers finding permanent jobs. In the past, even the most successful programs failed to find jobs for about one-third of the participants, and those who did find work often did not make enough money to get off welfare. For example, a study of 6,467 AFDC mothers who volunteered for a job-training and employment program found that only about half were still employed a year after the program was completed, and of those, only about one-fifth rose above the poverty level after two years.[69] A final drawback is that this approach is too negative. Although welfare mothers are threatened with the loss of their benefits if they do not find a job quickly enough, they are seldom given the understanding and respect they deserve for struggling to keep their families afloat.

Despite these difficulties, a well-designed employment program for welfare mothers could be a positive step if it avoids the kind of punitive approach based on stereotypes and misunderstanding that was so much a part of the 1996 welfare reforms. However, such a program must provide education and comprehensive job training and placement; even more important, it must make sure that poor children receive health care, proper nutrition, and good-quality supervision while their mothers are at work.

Another popular proposal for reform is to improve the system for keeping track of absent fathers in order to force them to contribute more to the support of their children. The advocates of such ideas claim that they can save taxpayers billions of dollars in welfare costs. Such an effort seems more likely to benefit mothers from more affluent backgrounds, however, since the fathers of children on welfare usually have few financial resources to contribute.

A different way to improve America's welfare system is through administrative reforms. As currently structured, welfare programs are administered by a patchwork of federal, state, and local agencies, and a tremendous amount of time and money that might be used to help poor people is spent on determining who is eligible for assistance. Such administrative waste would be drastically reduced if more welfare services were provided to all citizens, not just to those who can demonstrate special needs. Most other industrialized nations have taken this approach, relying far more heavily on **noncategorical programs**—social programs for which everyone is eligible. Canada, for example, provides all its citizens with medical care, a small retirement pension, and a family allowance for each dependent child, and similar programs exist in all the western European countries. Such an approach has three major advantages. First, the poor are not discouraged from working by the threat of losing their welfare benefits when they start to earn some money; second, welfare fraud is almost completely eliminated; and third, bureaucratic overhead is greatly reduced.

DISTRIBUTING THE INCOME MORE EQUALLY

One of the most important sociological functions of the welfare system is to transfer income from the middle and upper classes to the poor people who need it most. But even a well-funded welfare program is still likely to leave a tremendous gap between the haves and have-nots. Is a day's work by the CEO of an average U.S. corporation really worth 419 times more than a day's work by an average employee? The pay gap is far less in the other industrialized nations, as is the overall gap between the rich and the poor. There is no secret about how to create a more egalitarian society: The Europeans do it with a sharply progressive tax structure (one in which wealthier people must pay a higher percentage of their income in taxes) and more welfare support to the poor. Just a $1 increase in the minimum wage law could push hundreds of thousands of people above the poverty line. As we saw in Chapter 2, the United States has the lowest overall rate of taxation of any Western industrial power, and its taxes are particularly light on those with the highest income and the greatest wealth. For example, the first $1 million in inherited wealth is tax free. If we increased the taxes on those with the most wealth and highest incomes, we could reduce the taxes on those in the lower brackets and provide more government services (such as the system of national heath care discussed in Chapter 5), thus reducing the overall level of social inequality. Even assuming that all Americans below the poverty line in 2000 had no other income, the wealth of the two richest Americans could eliminate all American poverty. Because about half of all poor are in families in which there is an employed person, only about half of that wealth would actually be needed.[70]

ORGANIZING THE POOR

Any effective program to deal with the problems of poverty is likely to have a high price tag. Although we often give lip service to the ideal of equality, the government has usually been unwilling to put that ideal into practice with the kind of financial support it requires. As we have seen, most programs to help the poor were created only when the poor organized themselves and demanded a bigger piece of the economic pie. Amid the activism of the 1960s, for example, a number of poor people's organizations sprang up to press such demands and were able to win support from more broadly based groups. As a result, the welfare system was improved and poverty decreased. If the government is once again to take new action to deal with the plight of the poor, new organizations and new coalitions will have to be formed to push for change.

QUICK REVIEW

Discuss some of the best ways to deal with the poverty problem.

SOCIOLOGICAL PERSPECTIVES ON THE PROBLEMS OF THE POOR

Poverty has not always been seen as a social problem. Although concern for poor people has a long history, until quite recently poverty was considered an inevitable part of social life or the fault of the poor themselves—a lowly status deserved by the lazy and incompetent. The Great Depression of the 1930s, tragic though it was, helped show social scientists that the conditions of poverty are institutional matters determined by large-scale economic, political, and social processes. Social scientists now agree that poverty is a social problem rather than a collection of personal problems, even though they still have different views about its causes and solutions.

THE FUNCTIONALIST PERSPECTIVE

Functionalists consider the extremes of poverty and wealth common in most nations to be a result of malfunctions in the economy. In many parts of the world, rapid industrialization has disrupted the economic system, leaving it disorganized and unable to perform many of its essential functions. At first, people who lack job skills are forced into menial work at low wages, and later, with the coming of automation, they are not needed at all. Industrial products become outdated (horse carriages, steam engines, milk bottles), and unless rapid adjustments are made, people who manufacture those products lose their jobs. Training centers and apprenticeship programs may continue to produce graduates whose skills are no longer in demand. Discrimination, whether it is based on sex, age, race, or ethnic status, also wastes the talents of many capable people, and society is the loser.

Functionalists point out that the welfare system intended to solve the problem of poverty is just as disorganized as the economy. Administrators often show more concern for their own well-being than for their clients, and the first priority of many welfare workers has become the protection of their own jobs. Legislative bodies establish programs without enough funds to operate efficiently, and sincere welfare workers are drowned in a sea of rules, regulations, and paperwork. Inadequate communication systems fail to inform the poor about benefits to which they are entitled. Job training and educational programs are not coordinated with the needs of agriculture, commerce, and industry.

The best way to deal with poverty, according to the functionalist perspective, is to reorganize the economic system and the social service agencies so they operate more efficiently. The poor who have been cast out and neglected must be reintegrated into the mainstream of economic life. Members of the underclass must be provided with training and jobs so that they can resume their roles as productive citizens. They must also be given a new sense of hope based on the knowledge that the rest of society cares about them and is willing to help them overcome their poverty. Functionalists also recommend reforms to help stabilize the economic system so that it will not produce new poor people as others escape from poverty.

In general, however, functionalists are much more concerned about absolute poverty than about relative poverty. Many of them doubt that relative poverty (economic inequality) can or should be eliminated. Kingsley Davis and Wilber E. Moore, for example, argued that economic inequality is actually beneficial for society.[71] Their main point is that the desire for more money motivates people to work hard to meet the standards of excellence that are required in many important jobs. Without inequality of reward, the most capable people would not be motivated to train for or perform the demanding jobs that are essential to the economic system. It should not be concluded, however, that functionalists are convinced that the social system should remain unchanged or that the amount of economic inequality should not be reduced. The functionalist conclusion is simply that some inequality is necessary for the maintenance of society as we know it. In fact, Melvin Tumin has pointed out how high inequality and poverty is actually dysfunctional for society in many important ways.[72]

THE CONFLICT PERSPECTIVE

Conflict theorists start with the assumption that because there is enormous wealth in industrialized nations, no one in such societies need be poor. Poverty exists because the middle and upper classes want it to exist. Conflict theorists argue that the working poor are exploited: They are paid low wages so that their employers can make fatter profits and lead more affluent lives. The unemployed are victims of the same system.

Wealthy employers oppose programs to reduce unemployment because they do not want to pay the taxes to support them. They also oppose such programs because the fear of unemployment helps keep wages down and workers docile. Thus, conflict theorists argue that the economic system of capitalist countries operates to create and perpetuate a high degree of economic inequality. With changes in the balance of power between capitalists, labor, and other less-affluent groups, however, the extremely high level of inequality we find in the United States is not inevitable. European countries, for example, have lower levels of inequality and poverty, and workers and the less affluent have more influence on the political system.

Conflict theorists also note that wealthy and middle-class people are more likely than the poor to say that poverty stems from a lack of effort rather than from social injustice or other circumstances beyond the control of the individual. This application of the ideology of individualism enables the wealthy to be charitable to the poor by giving some assistance freely, while ignoring the economic and political foundations of poverty. Charity, including the government dole, blunts political protests and social unrest that might threaten the status quo. Moreover, some poor people come to accept the judgments passed on to them by the rest of society and adjust their aspirations and their self-esteem downward.

Conflict theorists view these adjustments to poverty as a set of chains that must be broken. They believe that the poor should become politically aware and active, organizing themselves to reduce inequality by demanding strong government action. In other words, political action is seen as the most effective response to inequality and, thus, to the problem of poverty. Most conflict theorists doubt that economic inequality can be significantly reduced without a concerted effort by poor people that gains at least some support from concerned members of the upper classes.

THE FEMINIST PERSPECTIVE

Feminists were among the first to point out what has been termed the "feminization of poverty"—that is, the long-term trend in our society for poverty to be more and more concentrated among women and children. While there are many causes for this trend, the most important factor is the changing economic organization of our families. While in the past most of our children were raised in nuclear families with men as the primary wage earners and women as the primary caretakers of the family, that is far less common today. The high divorce rate coupled with the growing number of unmarried women having children means that more and more women are raising children alone. Feminists point out that professions that have traditionally been open to women, such as teaching and office work, pay lower wages than occupations that are traditionally male, such as construction work. A more egalitarian salary structure would go a long way toward ending the devaluation of women in this country, and it would also make major strides toward lowering the poverty rate for women and children. Additionally, women still earn approximately 25 percent less than men earn for doing the same work requiring the same education today. Income inequality between the sexes must be ended in order for the downward economic spiral of our women and children to stop. Feminists also question the lack of accountability men often have for their children. For example, if a woman becomes pregnant and is unmarried, it is often expected that the woman raise the child by herself, without the financial or emotional support of the father.

She is also, of course, blamed for her poor judgment. The father, on the other hand, is often able to lead his life unchanged if he so chooses. Feminists call for a new approach that requires men to bear equal responsibility for the welfare of the children they father.

Feminists also argue that in addition to the kinds of general approaches advocated by the functionalists and conflict theorists, special attention must be given to the other problems of single mothers if we are to create an effective program to deal with poverty. There is, for example, a crying need for a nationwide system of government-supervised and subsidized day care—so that working women can be assured that their children are being properly cared for in their absence. A system of national health care in which basic medical services are seen as a right, not a privilege, would be another major step that would provide enormous benefits for poor families. Finally, more effort must be made to end occupational discrimination against women so that working mothers can earn wages high enough to keep their families out of poverty.

THE INTERACTIONIST PERSPECTIVE

Interactionists study the effects of attitudes and beliefs on behavior, pointing out that poor people learn to behave in the ways society expects of them. The values of those who live in the culture of poverty are passed on to their children, thus directing them into lives of poverty. For example, some claim that the children of the poor learn to seek immediate gratification and that, unlike middle-class achievers, they are not inclined to defer small immediate rewards so that long-run goals, such as a college education, can be reached. More generally, interactionists point to cultural differences in the ways poor people and wealthy people define their worlds. They note that even when new economic opportunities arise, poor people are often unaware of them or are psychologically and socially unprepared to take advantage of them. Thus, the differences in the ways the rich and poor see the world keep the poor at the bottom of the social ladder.

Interactionists also study the psychological effects of being poor in a wealthy society. The easy availability of television and other media encourages the poor to compare themselves with more fortunate people in a fantasy world. When they do so, many come to define themselves as failures. Some blame personal shortcomings rather than social forces that are beyond their control, and the outcome is likely to be low self-esteem, which in turn precipitates a variety of personal problems, ranging from drug addiction and mental disorders to delinquency and crime. Poor people may also come to define themselves as the victims of an unjust society. On the one hand, this attitude may contribute to a healthy social activism; on the other, it may create a sense of hopelessness or a desire for revenge against those who have taken advantage of them.

The interactionist perspective implies that poverty traps poor people psychologically, as well as economically and socially. We could eliminate this trap by eliminating absolute poverty (the lack of adequate food, shelter, and clothing) and by opening up more opportunities for the children of the poor, thus reducing overall inequality. Interactionists also agree that the poor must be encouraged to redefine their social environment. Even if avenues for upward mobility are created, little change will occur as long as the poor are convinced that they can expect nothing better than a life of poverty. Before they will be able to take advantage of any new opportunities, many poor people will also need help to change a self-image shaped by defeat and rejection.

QUICK REVIEW

How would a functionalist and a conflict theorist disagree about the causes of poverty?
What suggestions do feminists make for dealing with the problem of poverty?
How can poor people's definition of themselves trap them in poverty?

SUMMARY

Whether economic inequality is measured by income or wealth, there are large gaps among the rich, the middle class, and the poor that have grown much wider in recent years. Significant differences also exist in the cultural perspectives and lifestyles of these different groups. In cities the poor are trapped in run-down, crime-ridden neighborhoods, while the affluent have a multitude of opportunities from which to choose. Psychologically, the poor have to cope with feelings of inadequacy and inferiority because they lack the money and goods that everyone is "expected" to have. The families of the poor are more unstable, and poor people have more health problems and shorter life spans.

There are two common ways to measure poverty. The relative approach holds that people are poor if they are significantly less well-off than the average person in their society. The absolute approach, which is used by most government agencies, defines poverty as the lack of the essentials of life, such as sufficient food, shelter, and clothing. According to the official figures, the poverty rate decreased in the late 1960s and 1970s, only to increase again in the 1980s and early 1990s with cuts in poverty programs and a changing economy. In the past few years, poverty rates have once again taken a dip. A look at the distribution of poverty shows that the young are more likely to be poor than the middle-aged or the elderly, as are children from single-parent families and members of ethnic minority groups. The poverty rate is highest in the inner city and in rural areas and lowest in the suburbs.

There are many important differences among poor people. At the very bottom of the social heap are the homeless, who lack almost all the essentials of the lifestyle expected in our society. The underclass is composed of the long-term poor who are shut out of the mainstream of society. The working poor are those who hold down jobs but earn too little to be above the poverty line.

The ideology of individualism, which stresses personal responsibility and self-reliance, has made Americans far more likely than citizens of other industrialized nations to blame the poor for their own condition. Nonetheless, the Great Depression of the 1930s forced the government to deal with the acute problems of poverty. Programs and benefits generally kept increasing until the 1980s, when there was a sharp conservative reaction against the welfare system. The welfare reforms enacted in 1996 are the latest in a series of efforts to cut the welfare rolls and force mothers on welfare to get jobs.

There are many explanations for poverty. In some societies the economic base is so weak that many people must go hungry, but in modern industrial societies there is more than enough to go around. The immediate causes of poverty in industrial societies are such problems as unemployment and low wages, which can in turn be traced back to the basic economic structure and the competitive demands of the capitalist marketplace. In order to relieve such economic problems, governments all over the world have programs to reduce poverty and redistribute wealth to their less fortunate citizens, but because the rich and the powerful oppose effective measures to eliminate poverty, the government's actions inevitably fall short of that goal. Another explanation for poverty is based on Oscar Lewis's idea that some nations develop a "culture of poverty" with distinctive characteristics.

There are numerous proposals for reducing poverty. First, more and better jobs could be created by improving the economy, providing job training, supporting better education, and raising the minimum wage. Second, welfare programs could be improved by eliminating bureaucratic waste and inefficiency, providing day care and education to help mothers on welfare find employment, and providing basic necessities such as health care to all citizens regardless of income. Third, the poor could organize themselves to push for government programs that really meet their needs.

Functionalists see extremes of poverty and wealth as the result of a breakdown in social organization. Conflict theorists are convinced that poverty thrives because the wealthy and powerful benefit from it. Feminists point to social changes that have forced more and more women and children into poverty. Interactionists are concerned with the problems created by being poor in an affluent society, and they note that the socialization of the poor often encourages them to develop attitudes and behavior patterns that make upward social mobility difficult.

QUESTIONS FOR CRITICAL THINKING

The problem of poverty, along with the welfare system necessary to help deal with it, has been one of the most controversial issues in U.S. politics in the past two decades. Most Americans say they believe that everyone should have an equal opportunity to succeed in life, but they also believe that people who work harder or are more capable deserve to be wealthier than others. So it comes down to questions of fairness: Do you think U.S. society provides equal opportunities for all its citizens, whether their families are rich or poor or whether they are male or female, black, white, or brown? Are people who work at low-wage jobs paid enough for their labor? Are those at the top paid too much? What about the issue of inheritance? Is the present system fair, or should the government put more taxes on inherited wealth so that more money would be available to help the underprivileged? (Currently, most inheritances are not taxed.)

KEY TERMS

absolute approach	Medicare
culture of poverty	noncategorical program
extreme poverty	poverty
family allowance	relative approach
food stamp program	situationalist
ideology of individualism	Social Security
income	Supplemental Security Income (SSI)
job retraining	underclass
Medicaid	wealth

NOTES

1. U.S. Bureau of Census, *Poverty in the United States*, 2000 (Washington, DC: U.S. Government Printing Office, 2001), Table A.
2. U.S. Bureau of Census, *Money Income in the United States*, 2000 (Washington, DC: U.S. Government Printing Office, 2001), Table C.
3. See *Los Angeles Times*, August 30, 1999.
4. Lawrence Mishel, Jared Bernstein, and John Schmitt, *The State of Working America*, 1998–1999 (Ithaca, NY: Cornell University Press, 1999), pp. 258–262; U.S. Bureau of the Census, *Household Wealth and Assets*, 1998 (Washington, DC: U.S. Government Printing Office, 1999).
5. Mishel et al., *The State of Working America*, 1998–1999, p. 278.
6. See ibid., p. 402; Harold R. Kerbo, *Social Stratification and Inequality*, 4th ed. (New York: McGraw-Hill, 2000), pp. 26–29.
7. World Bank, *Economic Development Report*, 2000 (New York: Oxford University Press, 2000).
8. Lawrence Mishel, Jared Bernstein, and John Schmitt, *The State of Working America*, 1996–97 (Armonk, NY: Sharpe, 1997), pp. 53, 283.
9. Kerbo, *Social Stratification and Inequality*, pp. 22–26.
10. Ibid., pp. 250–252.
11. U.S. Bureau of Census, *Poverty in the United States*, 2000, p. 5.
12. Mishel et al., *The State of Working America*, 1996–97, p. 299.
13. U.S. Bureau of the Census, *Household and Family Characteristics* (Washington, DC: U.S. Government Printing Office, March 1998), p. 1; U.S. Bureau of the Census, *Statistical Abstract* (Washington, DC: U.S. Government Printing Office, 1993), p. 61.
14. Mishel et al., *The State of Working America*, 1996–97, p. 317.
15. U.S. Bureau of Census, *Poverty in the United States*, 2000, Table A.
16. Ibid., Table A.
17. Ibid., Table A.
18. Ibid., Table A.
19. Ibid., Table A.
20. Mishel et al., *The State of Working America*, 1996–97, p. 307.
21. U.S. Bureau of the Census, *Poverty in the United States*, 1999 (Washington, DC: U.S. Government Printing Office, 2000).
22. Larry Brown, "Hunger in the U.S.," *Scientific American* 256 (February): 37–41.
23. See *Los Angeles Times* (November 20, 1994).
24. See *Los Angeles Times* (December 27, 1997).
25. See *Los Angeles Times* (March 11, 1998, and December 27, 1997).
26. U.S. Department of Agriculture, *Household Food Security Survey*, 1999 (Washington, DC: U.S. Government Printing Office, 2000).
27. Associated Press, "Count of Homeless Useless, Official Says," *Los Angeles Times*, May 10, 1991, p. A27.
28. Anna Mulrine, "Self-Help Urged for Homeless," *Christian Science Monitor*, December 7, 1993, p. 6; Mitchel Levitas, "Homeless in America," *New York Times Magazine*, June 10, 1990, pp. 44–45, 82–91.
29. Elizabeth Shogren, "Families Total 43% of Homeless, Survey Reports," *Los Angeles Times*, December 22, 1993, pp. A1, A16.
30. James D. Wright, "The Mentally Ill Homeless: What Is Myth and What Is Fact?" *Social Problems* 35 (April 1988): 182–191.
31. David A. Snow, Susan G. Baker, Leon Anderson, and Michael Martin, "The Myth of Mental Illness Among the Homeless," *Social Problems* 33 (June 1986): 407–423.
32. Ibid.; Marta Elliott and Lauren J. Krivo, "Structural Determinants of Homelessness in the United States," *Social Problems* 38 (February 1991): 113–131.
33. William Julius Wilson, "Studying Inner-City Social Dislocations" and Christopher Jencks, "Is the American Underclass Growing?" in Christopher Jencks and Paul E. Peterson, eds., *The Urban Underclass* (Washington, DC: Brookings Institution, 1991).
34. U.S. Bureau of the Census, *Poverty in the United States*, 1999 (Washington, DC: U.S. Government Printing Office, 2000).
35. Mishel et al., *The State of Working America*, 1996–97, p. 307.

36. Wilson, "Studying Inner-City Social Dislocations."
37. Herbert J. Gans, "Deconstructing the Underclass: The Term's Danger as a Planning Concept," *Journal of the American Planning Association* 56 (summer 1990): 271.
38. William Julius Wilson, *The Truly Disadvantaged: The Inner City, the Underclass, and Public Policy* (Chicago: University of Chicago Press, 1987), pp. 6–8.
39. Wilson, "Studying Inner-City Social Dislocations."
40. U.S. Bureau, *Poverty in the United States,* 2000, Figure 6.
41. U.S. Bureau of the Census, "The Earnings Ladder: Who's at the Bottom? Who's at the Top?" *Statistical Brief* (Washington, DC: U.S. Government Printing Office, March 1994).
42. Joe R. Feagin, *Subordinating the Poor: Welfare and American Beliefs* (Upper Saddle River, NJ: Prentice Hall, 1975), pp. 91–92.
43. See Kerbo, *Social Stratification and Inequality,* p. 264.
44. Ibid., p. 260; Everett Carl Ladd and Karlyn H. Bowman, *Attitudes Toward Economic Inequality* (Washington, DC: AEI Press, 1998).
45. Frances Fox Piven and Richard A. Cloward, *Regulating the Poor: The Functions of Public Welfare* (New York: Vintage, 1971); Michael Betz, "Riots and Welfare: Are They Related?" *Social Problems* 21 (1974): 345–355; Larry Isaac and William Kelly, "Racial Insurgency, the State and Welfare Expansion," *American Sociological Review* 45 (1980): 1348–1386.
46. Piven and Cloward, *Regulating the Poor,* pp. 61–62.
47. Ibid., pp. 184–185.
48. Daniel Patrick Moynihan, *The Politics of a Guaranteed Income: The Nixon Administration and the Family Assistance Plan* (New York: Random House, 1973).
49. Bob Drogin, "True Victims of Poverty: The Children," *Los Angeles Times,* July 30, 1985, pp. 1, 10–11; Kevin Roderick, "Case History of a 20-Year War on Poverty," *Los Angeles Times,* July 31, 1985, pp. 1, 8–9.
50. See Kerbo, *Social Stratification and Inequality,* pp. 254–255.
51. Charles Murray and Richard Herrnstein, *The Bell Curve: Intelligence and Class Structure in American Life* (New York: Basic Books, 1994).
52. Michael Harrington, *The New American Poverty* (New York: Holt, Rinehart and Winston, 1984), pp. 81–87.
53. See *Los Angeles Times,* August 21, 1997.
54. See *Los Angeles Times,* February 2, 1998.
55. See *International Herald Tribune,* October 2, 1998
56. See *Los Angeles Times,* February 8 and February 9, 1998.
57. Mishel et al., *The State of Working America,* 1996–97, p. 403.
58. Ibid., p. 169.
59. Ibid., p. 143.
60. Kerbo, *Social Stratification and Inequality,* p. 26.
61. U.S. Bureau of the Census, *Money Income in the United States,* 1999 (Washington, DC: U.S. Government Printing Office, 2000).
62. James E. Rosenbaum and Susan J. Popkin, "Employment and Earnings of Low-Income Blacks Who Move to Middle Class Suburbs" in Jencks and Peterson, *The Urban Underclass,* pp. 342–358.
63. See Paul Jacobs, "Keeping the Poor Poor," in Jerome Skolnick and Elliott Currie, eds., *Crisis in American Institutions,* 5th ed. (Boston: Little, Brown, 1988), pp. 134–140.
64. Mishel et al., *The State of Working America,* 1996–97, pp. 328–331.
65. Herbert J. Gans, "The Uses of Poverty: The Poor Pay All," *Social Policy* 2 (1971): 21–23.
66. Oscar Lewis, *La Vida* (New York: Random House, 1965).
67. Ibid.
68. Charles A. Valentine, *Culture and Poverty: Critique and Counter-Proposals* (Chicago: University of Chicago Press, 1968).
69. Elizabeth Shogren, "Welfare-Job Study Indicates Tough Task for Reform Plan," *Los Angeles Times,* April 26, 1994, p. A14; David Whitman, "The Key to Welfare Reform," *Atlantic,* June 1987, p. 25.
70. See *International Herald Tribune,* June 22 and July 14, 1999.
71. Kingsley Davis and Wilbert E. Moore, "Some Principles of Stratification," *American Sociological Review* 10 (1945): 242–249.
72. Melvin Tumin, "Some Principles of Stratification: A Critical Analysis," *American Sociological Review* 18 (1953): 387–394.

CHAPTER 7

THE ETHNIC MINORITIES

Questions to Consider

What are the most common patterns of ethnic relations?

What are the problems shared by ethnic minorities in North America?

What are the special problems unique to each minority group?

Why do most minority groups have such a high poverty rate?

What are the best ways to deal with the problem of ethnic inequality?

Laurencie Nyirabeza lives in the highlands of central Rwanda, a small African country that has been ripped apart by ethnic conflict in the last decade. She is angry and upset because one of her former neighbors, Jean Girumuhatse, has just returned from exile and moved back into her neighborhood. In the mid-1990s, there was a genocidal bloodbath in Rwanda in which the majority ethnic group, the Hutus, slaughtered somewhere between 500,000 and 1 million members of the Tutsi minority. It was during that explosion of hatred and violence that Mrs. Nyirabeza says that Girumuhatse beat her with a stick and hacked at her neck with a machete. Finally, she says, "This man threw me in a ditch after killing off my whole family." Mr. Girumuhatse admits killing a total of six people, but he claims that he was not responsible for his actions because he was only following the orders of his superiors in the Rwandan government. Mrs. Nyirabeza's granddaughter, however, says that he killed 27 people in her extended family alone. Mr. Girumuhatse may eventually be put on trial by Rwanda's overwhelmed legal system, but until then these neighbors will have to live side by side in a climate of ethnic hatred and fear.[1]

The violent face of ethnic relations—riots, beatings, and even outright murder—is familiar to anyone who watches the evening news. From Albania to Zimbabwe, ethnic conflict is a burning issue around the world. Virtually every nation with more than one ethnic group has had its clashes. Some have managed to achieve long-term stability; others have been ripped apart in an explosion of violence and hatred; but most have just muddled through with alternating periods of conflict and cooperation. Today, most of the wealthy industrialized nations have a relatively stable system of ethnic relations, and each one claims to treat all ethnic groups fairly. But just below the surface there is a seething caldron of ethnic injustice. For Muslims in France, Koreans in Japan, and African Americans, Latinos, and other minorities in the United States, society is often a hostile place. Jobs are scarce, pay is low, and people from the dominant groups show in a thousand different ways that they think they are better than you. Of course, things are far better in the United States than they were a century ago, but that is small consolation to those who face a wall of hostility and discrimination because of the color of their skin, their religious beliefs, or the way they talk.

ETHNIC GROUPS

We often watch in horror and amazement when the news brings us the bloody spectacle of ethnic violence from around the world. Long-simmering hatred in the Middle East and Northern Ireland are bad enough, but the disintegration of Yugoslavia into a bloodbath of ethnic violence and the genocide and mass exodus in Rwanda seem almost incomprehensible. The sad fact is that the same forces that caused these tragedies are at work in our own society as well. It is essential to understand what these forces are and how they operate: We will start with some basic terminology.

An **ethnic group** is usually defined as a body of people who share a common set of cultural characteristics or at least a common national origin.[2] What sets an ethnic group apart is its sense of being a common group and the belief that its members share a unique social and historical experience. As we can see from even a quick look at the evening news, people often form an intense loyalty to their ethnic group, and many are even willing to die for it. Part of the reason is that in an ethnically divided society, individuals' economic and social destinies are often tied up with those of their ethnic group. If their ethnic group is powerful, they are likely to reap economic rewards. If they come from a disadvantaged minority, they are likely to face a host of economic and social barriers. People often form a strong psychological identification with their ethnic group as well. Thus, any slight or injustice toward their group is seen as a personal attack on them, and the victories and achievements of their group are likewise a source of personal pride and psychological satisfaction.

The term **ethnic minority** is used in two different ways. Sometimes it simply refers to a small ethnic group that is outnumbered by the majority group in a society, but sociologists use the term in a more relative sense. To the sociologist, how many people there are in the group is less important than how they are treated. In this sense, an ethnic minority is an ethnic group that suffers prejudice and discrimination at the hands of the dominant group in a society.

Although a racial group is often an ethnic group as well, the two are not the same. A **race** is usually defined as a group of people who are perceived by others in the society as having a common set of physical characteristics, but the members of a race may or may not share the sense of identity that holds an ethnic group together. The concept of "race" as it is used in everyday speech is a social idea rather than a biological fact. Physical characteristics are biological in origin, but the way they are classified and the meanings they are given are socially determined. Among the more than 6 billion people in the world, there is a wide range of skin colors, body builds, hair types, and other physical features, and even the scientists who study racial types do not agree on a single classification system.[3] Indeed, now that the complete genetic code of humans has been deciphered, scientists are finding that in fact our old concepts of race have no biological meaning at all.[4] Race, therefore, is an idea constructed by people in order to place themselves in social categories.

People from all ethnic groups tend to see their own culture as the best and most enlightened. This attitude is known as **ethnocentrism**. Because values and behavior patterns differ from one culture to another, one's own culture naturally appears superior when judged by its own standards. Thus, ethnocentrism seems to be universal. All cultures show some prejudice against foreigners, who are commonly viewed as heathens, barbarians, or savages. **Racism** is usually defined as a belief in the superiority of one racial group to another, which leads to prejudice and discrimination. The main difference between racism and ethnocentrism is that the former is concerned with the physical differences among people and the latter with their cultural differences. Although racism is common throughout the world, it is not as universal as ethnocentrism. In many societies, people who share a culture and a religion do not consider the racial differences among themselves important. Where racism does exist, though, it is often more vicious and divisive than ethnocentrism. Two chilling examples are Hitler's mass executions of European Jews and Gypsies and the nearly successful European and American attempts to wipe out the native population of much of North America.

PATTERNS OF ETHNIC RELATIONS

It is easy to see from the world news that relationships among ethnic groups take a bewildering variety of forms. To help us make sense of this confusing picture, sociologists have constructed three models of the general patterns that ethnic relations usually take. When one ethnic group holds all the power and keeps the others under its economic and political control, the pattern is known as **domination**. Societies based on ethnic domination often impose varying degrees of segregation (the separation of the ethnic groups) in order to protect the privileges of the favored groups. In contrast, the ethnic groups in a system of **integration** are basically equal. They go to the same schools, work in the same businesses, and live in the same neighborhoods. In **pluralism**, different ethnic groups are still equal, but they are more separate and distinct. Children are likely to go to a school that places emphasis on teaching the traditions of their group, families live in their own ethnic neighborhoods, and adults work in businesses run by other members of their ethnic group. It is important to note that these are only general models, however. In real life, conditions of domination, integration, and pluralism occur together. It is the sociologist's job to figure out how strong each of these patterns really is in a particular society.

When two ethnic groups come into close contact for the first time, ethnocentrism and competition for resources often stimulate conflict. One group usually emerges as the winner, monopolizing political and economic power and discriminating against the subordinate group. The domination of African slaves by white Americans is an example. Politically, the displaced Africans were powerless, sharing none of the rights of other Americans. They had no weapons or organizations with which to fight their oppressors. Their work produced riches for plantation owners, but their lowly condition was far beneath mere poverty. They were isolated, rejected, and considered more animal than human. Although American slavery is an extreme case of ethnic domination, the same pattern is found again and again throughout the world.

When competing ethnic groups are evenly matched, a more pluralistic system is likely to emerge. The ethnic groups in a pluralist society maintain a high degree of independence. They identify with the larger society but control some of their own social and political affairs. Oftentimes, they live in different neighborhoods or different parts of the country and are therefore able to control their local schools, governments, and economic institutions. In actual practice, the relationships among many ethnic groups have elements of both domination and pluralism. For instance, French Canadians are usually considered part of a pluralistic system, but though they maintain a distinct identity and have a strong cultural tradition, they are dominated in some ways by English-speaking Canadians. Anglo-Canadians control the Canadian economy, and the English and American cultural influence is very strong throughout Canada.

An integrated society, like a pluralistic one, strives for ethnic equality, but the interests of one ethnic group are not balanced against those of another. Rather, ethnic backgrounds are ignored, and, ideally, all individuals are treated alike. In a truly integrated society, all people attend the same local schools, go to the same houses of worship, and vote for political candidates on the basis of merit alone. Of course, complete integration never occurs in an actual society, any more than does completely equal pluralism. As long as people living together define themselves as members of different ethnic groups, some degree of prejudice and discrimination will remain. Most societies that encourage ethnic equality through integration have therefore enacted various laws that prohibit discrimination and try to compensate its victims.

Each of these three systems of ethnic relations has its own sources of instability. A system of domination must keep minorities weak and divided. If the victims of exploitation organize themselves to demand justice, the balance of power is likely to change. Sometimes the result is a civil war filled with the kind of bloodshed and brutality that ethnic hatred so often brings. But peaceful reforms are sometimes possible if the dominant groups can be persuaded to look at the situation realistically. A pluralistic system can also lead to ethnic conflicts, especially if one group decides it is not treated fairly. In the extreme, separatist movements may divide the pluralist nation into two or more independent countries. This was the case in the division of India and Pakistan and later of Pakistan and Bangladesh. A similar process is possible in Canada, where some French Canadians want to create separate French- and English-speaking nations.

Just as pluralism can lead to ethnic conflicts and the eventual partition of a society, integration may lead to the gradual reduction or elimination of distinctive ethnic characteristics. Groups that live in close contact, watch the same television shows, eat at the same fast-food stands, and even intermarry are bound to grow increasingly similar as time passes. Today, many North Americans with European backgrounds have given up their separate ethnic identities, which were seen as so important just a couple of generations ago; and now simply call themselves Americans. Even racial differences may begin to fade after years of intermarriage, as they have in Mexico.

MELTING POT OR SALAD BOWL?

So far we have been describing the kinds of relationships that exist among different ethnic groups. Aside from what is, people are naturally concerned about what ought to be. In North America, it was traditionally assumed that minority groups should take on the culture of the dominant group in a process known as **assimilation**. Because immigrants were expected to conform to the standards of Anglo-American culture, this ideal is often known as Anglo-conformity. To be accepted, the immigrant had to learn English, convert to Protestantism, and adopt Anglo-American values and ways of life. African Americans and Native Americans, as well as whites who refused to adopt Anglo-American ways, were condemned to be permanent outsiders. They were not "real Americans."

Although there is still considerable pressure to conform to Anglo-American standards, it has weakened over the years. As more and more different ethnic groups came to North America, people began proposing ideals that were less one-sided. The most influential was the **melting pot theory**, which holds that the different immigrant groups that came to the United States have blended into a distinctively new culture. To this way of thinking, the assimilation of ethnic minorities is still a good thing but should be a two-sided process. Immigrants should be encouraged to adopt the culture of their new home, but the majority group should learn from the newcomers and change their cultural expectations accordingly. Critics of this view often complain that while the ideal of the melting pot may be fine, in reality it has been used as a justification for continuing to demand conformity to Anglo culture.

A third ideal, which is sometimes called the **salad bowl theory**, holds that North America works best as a diverse blend of "unmelted" subcultures. Although Mexicans,

Jews, Africans, Chinese, Puerto Ricans, Koreans, Europeans, Indians, Cubans, and other groups all share in many common elements of American culture, they are not all the same. These groups remain equally American, but each retains its own distinctive traditions. Advocates of the ideal of the salad bowl hold that melding together these diverse groups would not only destroy valuable ethnic traditions but would make the United States a far less interesting place. However, critics of this view argue that it is unrealistic to think that immigrants, who often come from poor nations, can keep their traditional cultures alive in the middle of an alien industrialized society. At best, they might hang on to a few of their traditional ways in segregated ethnic subcultures, but, the critics charge, the discrimination and conflict such a system breeds is far too high a price to pay for its meager benefits.

QUICK REVIEW

What is an ethnic group?
What is the difference between racism and ethnocentrism?
Compare and contrast the systems of domination, pluralism, and integration.
What ideals do the theories of the melting pot and the salad bowl hold out for American society?

ETHNIC MINORITIES IN NORTH AMERICA

HISTORICAL BACKGROUND

The Indians were the first Americans, and for that reason they are often referred to as Native Americans, although that term also usually includes Eskimos and Pacific Islanders (residents of other Pacific islands that are part of the United States). Contrary to popular stereotypes, not all Native Americans were nomadic warriors. In fact, there were many different native cultures. Some Native Americans were wandering hunters, but many others lived in stable farming villages. In some areas, Native Americans had highly advanced civilizations. In North America alone the native peoples spoke about 300 different languages.[5]

Three major groups of European colonists settled in North America: French, British, and Spanish. In the beginning, relations between the European immigrants and Native Americans were generally peaceful, and a lively trade developed, but the continued influx of colonists disrupted this early system of pluralism. Europeans came to dominate the eastern tribes and then slowly moved westward, first driving the native peoples from their lands at gunpoint, then restricting them to isolated reserves, and finally requiring even reservation Indians to obey their laws.

Conflict was not restricted to whites and Native Americans, for the European powers also were bitter enemies, fighting among themselves for power, money, and land. The British emerged as the victors in the lands north of what is now the U.S.–Mexico border. The boundaries of the newly independent United States steadily expanded, moving westward as Americans took over vast sections of land formerly held by Spain, France, and Mexico. This westward conquest meant, of course, that sizable European and non-European minorities were brought under the domination of the English-speaking majority.

The two North American nations took very different approaches to the problems of their native minorities. The treaties Canada signed with Native Americans were usually honored, and the government attempted to minimize stealing, looting, and pillaging by the white settlers. In tragic contrast, the U.S. government repeatedly agreed to treaties and then broke them as soon as white settlers demanded more land.[6] The loss of their land, the disruption of their economy, and the spread of European diseases almost led to the annihilation of the native peoples of North America. There was, moreover, an unofficial and sometimes semiofficial policy by the U.S. Army to kill as many Native Americans as possible. A Congressional hearing found that the most common method of killing Native Americans was slaughter by gunfire, when whole villages were destroyed. But there were other methods, such as distributing clothing known by the U.S. Army to be infested with smallpox to reservation Indians.[7] In 1500, between 12 and 15 million Indians lived in North America (excluding Mexico), but by 1850, only about 250,000 survived.[8]

After the resistance of the Native Americans was broken, they were subjected to cruel domination. Most Indian people were denied the vote, had to obtain passes to leave their reservations, and were prohibited from practicing their own religions, sometimes by force. Children were dragooned off to boarding schools where they were severely punished if they were caught speaking their own language.[9]

The French minority in Canada and the Spanish minority in the United States took divergent paths after they fell under Anglo domination. French Canada had a substantial population at the time of the English conquest, and it has maintained itself as a self-perpetuating community with little new immigration. Quebec has become an island of French in an English-speaking sea. In contrast, the Spanish-speaking population in most of the areas taken from Spain and Mexico was quite small. After the Gold Rush and the building of the transcontinental railroad, these people were overwhelmed by waves of English-speaking immigrants. However, later immigration from Mexico and other Latin American countries eventually led to significant increases in the Latino population of the United States.

In the first century following the American Declaration of Independence, most immigrants to the United States came from the Protestant countries of northern Europe, but from 1870 to 1920, immigrants increasingly arrived from the Catholic areas of Europe: Italy, Ireland, and eastern Europe, especially Poland. At first it was assumed that these immigrants would quickly assimilate into British Protestant culture; when they failed to do so, ethnic tensions and hostilities grew. In addition, nonwhite immigrants, principally from China and Japan, arrived on the West Coast to be greeted with even more prejudice and discrimination. A federal law passed in 1924 severely restricted immigration from southern Europe and stopped all immigration from Asia. This restrictive policy remained in effect until the Immigration Act of 1965 eliminated the quota system that favored people from European counties. As a result, a new wave of Third World immigrants has come to the United States during the last two decades.

The history of the Africans in North America is unique because they were brought in chains against their will. Slaveholders intentionally tried to extinguish their native culture: The African family system was broken up, and fathers were routinely separated from their children. Slaves who shared common cultural roots were systematically separated and forbidden to speak their own language. They were even forced to abandon their native religions and to become Christians.

Unlike other immigrants, Africans were brought to North America against their will. Most were put to work as slaves on southern plantations.

After slavery had been abolished, African Americans continued to be plagued by racism. Black political power blossomed briefly after the Civil War, but this fragile flower was soon uprooted. African Americans were systematically murdered, terrorized, and subjugated. Terrorist organizations, such as the Ku Klux Klan and the Knights of the White Camellia, drove African Americans back into their subordinate status. Slavery was replaced by a system of segregation that once again denied Americans of African ancestry their civil rights. The goal of **segregation** was to separate African Americans from the rest of society and force them to accept second-class citizenship. African Americans were required to attend separate schools, swim at different beaches, use different restrooms, and even sit in the back of the public buses; and a variety of ruses were used to deny them the right to vote and to participate in the political process.

The rigid segregation system in the southern states and the more informal segregation practiced in the rest of the country thrived for a hundred years. It was not until the 1950s and 1960s that the civil rights movement finally broke the back of legal segregation. With a new sense of political awareness, thousands of African Americans and their supporters from other ethnic groups, backed by Supreme Court decisions, organized, demonstrated, and demanded equal rights. Although the system of official discrimination has ended, racial prejudice and discrimination continue to be a fact of life for African Americans.

The new sense of black pride and political awareness that developed out of this struggle had an impact on other ethnic groups as well. Militant Latinos, Asians, and Native Americans organized and began echoing demands for "black power" with calls for "brown power," "yellow power," and "red power." In Canada, the Quebecois (French Canadians) also began to assert their cultural identity, and some demanded a new nation separate from Canada. The ethnic conflicts that were simmering in the 1960s quieted in the following years, but the grievances that caused them remain very much alive today.

INSTITUTIONAL INEQUALITY

To understand the problems ethnic minorities face today, the first thing most sociologists do is look at such questions as "What kind of jobs do they have?" "What is their average income?" and "What is their educational background?" The answers reveal a high degree of institutional inequality in North American society—in other words, members of most ethnic minorities are much more likely to be at the bottom than at the top of our institutional hierarchies.

Education   North American culture puts tremendous faith in education. Numerous studies have shown that people with more education are likely to have higher-paying and higher-status jobs. But African Americans, Latinos, and Native Americans receive significantly less education than others. In 2000, almost 85 percent of adult whites had finished high school, but only about 78 percent of African Americans and about 57 percent of Latinos had finished. Asians are exceptions to this pattern; taken as a whole, they actually have a slightly higher level of educational achievement than white Americans, but such broad generalizations obscure the fact some Asian groups, such as Laotians and Cambodians, fall far below the American average.[10]

The sources of this educational inequality are rooted in economic and cultural domination. For example, during the period of slavery, few African Americans received any schooling, and after emancipation they were put into separate schools of decidedly inferior quality. The civil rights movement and the Supreme Court eventually ended legal segregation. Although there is no longer a separate system of schools for blacks and whites, many students still attend segregated classes as a result of the segregated housing patterns of American cities (see Chapter 4 for more details).

In many ways the history of Native American education is even more dismal. Many of the early Indian schools were run by missionaries who were determined to "civilize" and Christianize the "heathen savages." The government-run boarding schools that eventually replaced the missionary schools were no better:

> The young Indian, torn from his family, was shipped to the school where his hair was immediately cut and where he was given a military uniform and taught close order drill. One of the prime objectives of the system was to teach him the English language as rapidly as possible. He was given demerits for speaking in his native language. Since the incoming student could speak no other language, great personal tragedies resulted, leading to high suicide rates.[11]

Many young Native Americans returning from boarding school were adrift: They did not fit into the white world, yet they were no longer comfortable in the traditional world of their parents.

The cultural assumptions of the white middle class are still built into today's schools, and that creates behavioral as well as learning problems for some minority students. For example, success in school depends largely on the student's ability to meet middle-class standards of discipline and self-control. Students from homes that allow free emotional expression and place few controls on behavior are therefore at a disadvantage. In addition, textbooks and other course materials are often culturally biased. Imagine Native American children's reaction on reading that traitors in their ancestors' struggle to keep their land are to be called "friendly Indians." Only recently have American textbooks acknowledged the contributions of ethnic minorities to U.S. society. Cultural biases are also institutionalized through language. Immigrant children are often required to do their schoolwork in English, whether or not they are fluent in that language. Obviously, children who must struggle to learn mathematics, science, and history in a language they do not fully understand are less likely than native speakers of English to get good grades or even to finish high school.

It should not be concluded, however, that all of the differences in educational achievement between ethnic minorities and the dominant group stem from the cultural biases built into the school system. For one thing, regardless of their ethnic group, poor children do not do as well in school as children from wealthier families, and ethnic minorities are more likely to be poor. Further, ethnic groups differ significantly in the value they place on education and in their family structure, and these differences affect achievement. Japanese Americans, as well as several other Asian groups noted for their cohesive family structure, have been very successful in school despite the barriers of language and racial prejudice.

Employment   Statistics show that members of minority groups are far more likely to have low-status and low-paying jobs. Whites are more than twice as likely as African Americans or Latinos to work as managers or professionals, and similar patterns are found in the distribution of income. In 2000, the average African American family earned only about 66 percent as much as the average white family, up only slightly from 61 percent in 1970. The average earnings of Latino were little bit higher, but the larger size of Latino families meant less money per person.[12] A look at poverty rates shows much the same story. In that same year, 7.5 percent of whites were below the poverty line compared to 22.1 of African Americans and 21 percent of Latinos (see Figure 7.1 on page 220).[13]

Much of this inequality can be explained by the educational differences already discussed: Because minorities have less education, they are less likely to qualify for high-paying jobs. Education is not the whole story, however, for minority employees tend to receive less pay than whites with the same level of education. On the average, an African American family headed by a high school graduate has about the same income as a white family headed by someone with only eight years of education. One cause for this difference was clearly shown in an experiment conducted by the Urban Institute. When equally qualified groups of whites and blacks applied for jobs in Chicago and Washington, DC, most applicants were treated equally regardless of race. But 20 percent of the time, whites were given preferential treatment over blacks, while blacks were given preferential treatment only 7 percent of the time.[14]

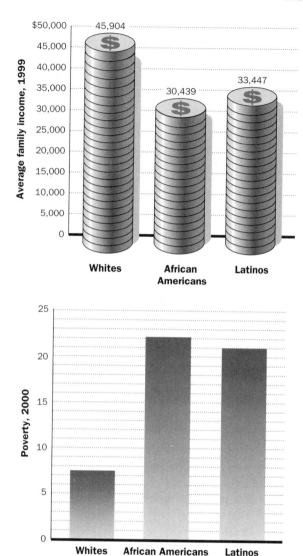

FIGURE 7.1   INCOME AND POVERTY

African Americans and Latinos have significantly lower incomes and more poverty than European Americans.

Source: U.S. Bureau of the Census, *Money Income in the* USA, 2000. (Washington, DC: U.S. Government Printing Office, Figure 1; U.S. Bureau of the Census, *Poverty in the* U.S., 2000 (Washington, DC: 2000), Table A.

A related problem arises from cultural discrimination. Despite the talk about equal opportunities for those with equal ability, many people are hired and promoted because of their personal relationship with an employer or manager. Generally speaking, it is mutual understanding and a common background that promotes such friendships. If the personnel manager and boss are white (which is likely to be the case), members of a minority group may be at a distinct disadvantage even if company policy prohibits job discrimination. A survey of America's 24 largest corporations found that 8 out of 10 African Americans and about half the members of other ethnic minorities felt that women and minorities were excluded from informal networks and work groups in their companies.[15]

Law and Justice   Discrimination has a long history in the American legal system. The U.S. Constitution did not explicitly mention race or slavery, but it nonetheless provided for the return of escaped slaves and held that a slave should be counted as two-thirds of a person for congressional apportionment and tax purposes. In 1857 the Supreme Court ruled that constitutional rights and privileges did not extend to African Americans:

> We think . . . that they [African Americans] are not included, and were not intended to be included, under the word "citizen" in the Constitution, and can therefore claim none of the rights and privileges which that instrument provides for and secures to the citizens of the United States. On the contrary, they were at that time considered as a subordinate and inferior class of beings, who had been subjugated by the dominant race, and whether emancipated or not . . . had no rights or privileges but such as those who held power and the government might choose to grant them.[16]

Even though such racist ideas are no longer part of the law, numerous studies have shown that African Americans are more likely than whites to be arrested, indicted, convicted, and committed to an institution. An analysis of Justice Department data, for example, shows that the racial difference in incarceration rates is huge and getting bigger. Today, about 1 in every 3 young African American men is either in prison or on probation or parole.[17]

Some criminologists say that these differences occur because African Americans are more often involved in serious and repeated offenses than whites. There is little doubt that the urban underclass has an extremely high crime rate and that its members are disproportionately drawn from the ranks of African Americans (see Chapter 10). Other social scientists, however, hold racial prejudice to be more important. They argue that the expectations of police officers, prosecutors, and judges that African Americans are more likely to be criminals become a self-fulfilling prophecy. Because African Americans are expected to commit more crimes, they are watched more closely, and therefore they are arrested and prosecuted more often. According to a report by New York State's Attorney General, blacks are more than twice as likely to be stopped by the police compared to whites, even when the higher crime rates in minority neighborhoods are taken into account. Although whites make up 75 percent of drug users in the United States, blacks account for 75 percent of the inmates with drug charges.[18]

Whether or not members of ethnic minorities are more likely to be arrested for their crimes, minority leaders are nearly unanimous in their complaints about excessive force and police brutality in their communities. One of the most infamous cases of police brutality in recent times was that of Rodney King. Several Los Angeles police officers were videotaped beating Mr. King as he lay helpless on the ground. As this shocking footage was shown again and again on television, this case quickly became

The problem of police brutality is a major concern in many minority communities. This photo shows a demonstration protesting the killing of an unarmed African immigrant, Amadou Diallo, by New York Police.

a national issue. In 1992, the officers involved were acquitted of the criminal charges against them by a jury without a single African American member; their acquittal touched off some of the bloodiest rioting in the history of urban America. Although the officers involved were later convicted on federal charges, this case remains a symbol of the failure of the American system of justice. Two more recent cases come from the other side of the nation in New York City. One notorious case was that of Abner Louima, a black Haitian immigrant, who was brutally tortured by New York police officers. Shortly thereafter, another political explosion occurred when an unarmed African American man, Amadou Diallo, was shot 41 times by four other members of the NYPD.[19]

PROBLEMS AND PROSPECTS

As we have seen, ethnic minorities in North America have many difficulties in common, but all ethnic groups have their own unique concerns and problems. In order to understand the mosaic of North American life, it is necessary to examine the largest ethnic groups separately.

Native Americans   Although they were the original residents of North America, native peoples are now far outnumbered by other groups. There are only about 2.4 million Native Americans in the United States, amounting to slightly less than 1 percent of the total population.[20] They nonetheless have a special status among the minorities of North America. While they share the economic problems experienced by most minority groups, no one else has signed legal treaties with the governments of the United States and Canada, and no other groups have reservations (lands granted to individual tribes by those treaties).

Indians who live on reservations have higher rates of poverty and unemployment and less education than other Indians. Moreover, many of the reservations offer inadequate housing, poor health care programs, and a lack of public facilities. Figures from Canada indicate that life expectancy for Native Americans is 8 years less than the national average, largely as a result of poverty and deprivation on the reservations. Yet the reservations give native peoples more political autonomy than other minorities have. Elected tribal governments have wide political and economic authority to regulate the affairs of their own people. Despite the fact that native peoples were given only the worst land in the most undesirable locations, many of these remote reservations have turned out to have considerable natural resources. One estimate holds that while native people own about 5 percent of the land in the United States, they have one-tenth percent of the known gas and oil reserves, one-third of the strippable coal, and half of the uranium reserves.[21] This situation has led to large economic disparities among the tribes that have rich natural resources and those that do not, as well as some bitter disputes among tribes over the control of reservation lands. Many tribes are also engaged in legal battles over lands they believe were given to them in treaties and then illegally taken away.

The biggest victory for native rights in recent times came in Canada. In November 1992, after years of negotiations, the Inuit people (often known as Eskimos) won voter approval for the creation of a new Canadian territory in which they predominate. The new territory, which was officially established in 1999, is known as Nunavut and contains almost one-fifth of all the land in Canada. Although this northern land is sparsely populated, over 80 percent of its residents are Inuit. The Inuit were also given direct title to some 136,000 square miles of land and a multimillion-dollar cash settlement.[22]

Despite the popular stereotype, most Native Americans now live in cities, not on reservations. While still earning considerably below the nation's average income, these urbanites are better off economically than those who remain behind, but at the price of growing separation from their traditional culture. Urban Indians are, for example, considerably less likely to speak a native language or practice a native religion than those who live on reservations.[23]

Europeans   Descendants of the European immigrants are, of course, the majority in North America, but within this large group there are many different ethnic traditions. Some writers divide the Europeans into two main groups: the Anglo-Protestants (Protestants of British descent) and the **white ethnics**, such as the Irish, Italians, Jews, and Polish. However, the term "white ethnic" is misleading, since Anglo-Protestants are obviously as much an ethnic group as any other. Over the years, religion has become one of the primary focuses of ethnic identity among European Americans, and the distinctions among Protestants, Catholics, and Jews are often more important than those based on the country from which their ancestors came.

Recent years have seen two contradictory trends among these groups. On the one hand, many European Americans responded to the minority activism of the 1960s and 1970s with an increased interest in their own ethnic traditions and a renewed identification with their ancestral homeland. On the other hand, the differences among European groups have sharply declined as immigrants have assimilated into the mainstream of American culture. Richard D. Alba's research shows, for example, that successive generations of Italian Americans have fewer and fewer distinctive cultural characteristics that set them off from other European Americans and that they have grown increasingly likely to marry outside their group.[24] Stanley Lieberson and Mary C. Waters find the same trends among other European ethnic groups as well.[25] Such data led Alba to conclude that these groups are in the "twilight of ethnicity." While it is unlikely that identification with different European nationalities is going to disappear any time in the near future, this kind of ethnic identity has become a voluntary personal choice, and a growing number of people descended from those groups see themselves simply as Americans.

It is a mistake, however, to look at this merely as a process of assimilation that has left the dominant group unaffected. Research by Andrew M. Greeley shows that many "white ethnic" groups now actually have higher educational achievement and income than white Protestants. Greeley found that the average income of Jews, Italians, the Irish, and Polish Catholics exceeded the income of Presbyterians, who were the most affluent white Protestants.[26]

There is, however, one group of Europeans in North America that has not followed this pattern of assimilation. Perhaps because of their long history on this continent or because they are heavily concentrated in the province of Quebec, where they are the majority, French Canadians continue to maintain a very different linguistic and cultural tradition from Anglo-Canadians. In fact, separatist feelings run so high in Quebec that the survival of a unified Canada has been in doubt several times in the last two decades.

Jews   Although the vast majority of Jewish immigrants to North America came from Europe, their special historical experience sets them apart from the European groups mentioned in the previous section. Jews have lived in Europe since ancient times, but their religious differences and distinct culture always distinguished them from the Christian majority. Through the centuries, they remained a distinct minority group that frequently suffered at the hands of the majority. European Jews were routinely discriminated against in both economic and social life, and on occasion they were the victims of violent assaults and even systematic attempts at mass extermination. Although many Jewish immigrants came to North America looking for a land of opportunity and a chance to escape European anti-Semitism, they encountered the same kind of prejudice they had always faced. Racist organizations such as the Ku Klux Klan condemned Jews along with African Americans; Jews were often stereotyped as greedy and clannish, and many prestigious universities established quotas to keep Jewish enrollment from growing too large. Nonetheless, the treatment of Jews in the United States has generally been better than in Europe. Research shows a decline in American anti-Semitism in recent decades, and some Jewish leaders, like those of many other ethnic groups, now worry about the loss of ethnic identity due to assimilation and intermarriage.

The roughly 5.5 million Jews in the United States account for about 44 percent of the world's Jewish population. American Jews are heavily concentrated in the big cities of the Northeast, especially New York, and in California. Although the Bureau of the Census does not collect systematic data on Jewish Americans as it does on most other ethnic groups, evidence shows that Jews have been remarkably successful in conquering the barriers of prejudice and discrimination. They now have the highest educational level and the highest income of any white group in the United States. One analysis of a list of the 400 richest Americans found that 23 percent were from Jewish backgrounds.[27] Their success has not ended the problem of anti-Semitism, however, and in some ways it may have intensified the tendency for frustrated and hostile individuals to blame their problems on Jews.[28]

African Americans According to the Bureau of the Census, as of the year 2000, 12.9 percent of all Americans were of African descent, making them the largest minority in the United States.[29] (See Figure 7.2.) For that reason and because they have always been singled out as the targets of special prejudice and discrimination, African Americans have come to symbolize the problems all ethnic minorities face in the United States. Not surprisingly, African Americans have often led the way in the struggle for ethnic justice in the United States.

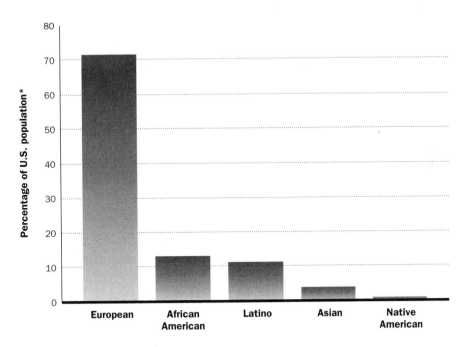

FIGURE 7.2 AMERICA'S ETHNIC POPULATION

African Americans are the largest minority group in the United States, but Latinos are not far behind.

*Estimate for the year 2000.

Source: U.S. Bureau of the Census, *Statistical Abstract of the United States,* 1999 (Washington, DC: U.S. Government Printing Office, 2000), p. 14.

But the African American community itself is now deeply divided between a growing middle class and the increasingly desperate poor. Since 1950, the number of African Americans holding white-collar jobs has risen much faster than their population as a whole, and the number of elected African American officials has shown even larger gains. African Americans moved into professional and managerial jobs in unprecedented numbers; they became increasingly important in the entertainment business; and they came to dominate several highly paid professional sports. Real family income and educational achievement went up, and infant mortality went down.

Yet as more affluent African Americans left the ghettos for the suburbs, conditions deteriorated for the poor who remained behind. Since the late 1970s, the percentage of African Americans living in extreme poverty (defined as family income of less than half the poverty line) grew from one-third of all poor African American people to almost half.[30] At least in part as a result of the "war on drugs," the already high rate of incarceration for African Americans has skyrocketed, increasing almost 30 percent since 1990.[31] Perhaps even more disturbing is that just over 69 percent of births to African American mothers were in single-parent families. This compares with just over 25 percent for white births and 40.9 percent for births to Hispanic mothers. As we saw in Chapter 3, however, there has been a large drop in births to black teenage mothers whether married or not—by 1999 there was a 38 percent reduction from the high point in 1990.[32]

The explanation for the crisis of the black underclass is not entirely clear, but William Julius Wilson argues that there are two major reasons.[33] First, there has been a major shift in employment away from the lower-skilled jobs many poor African Americans depended on. Second, the exodus of more successful African Americans to the suburbs led to what Wilson terms "concentration effects" that worsened the already serious problems in the ghettos. Wilson argues that the concentration of poor urban African Americans in homogeneous neighborhoods without a significant middle class intensified their social isolation and encouraged the decay of community institutions. In addition, many observers lay part of the blame on cutbacks in welfare benefits and other social programs of the last decade and a half and on the indifference of more wealthy Americans to the plight of the urban poor.

On the other end of the social scale, one of the most positive developments in the African American community has been the increasing ability of successful parents to pass their advantaged occupational status on to their children. In the past, when an African American achieved a high professional position such as doctor, lawyer, college professor, or high-level manager in business, their children still usually ended up in low-skilled and low-paying jobs. Now, the sons and daughters of successful African Americans are almost as likely to obtain high professional positions when they grow up as are the children of successful whites. On the negative side, this development has helped increase the rapidly growing gap between the high- and low-income families in the African American community.[34]

Latinos   Latinos are the second-largest American minority (about 11.4 percent), but because of heavy immigration and a high birthrate, they will probably outnumber African Americans in the near future.[35] Many outsiders think everyone who speaks Spanish is part of the same culture, but Latinos are actually a diverse group. Well over half of all Latinos in the United States are of Mexican origin. Most of them live in California, Texas, and the other states of the Southwest. Puerto Ricans are the second-largest group; their population is centered in New York City and the Northeast (and, of course, on the island of Puerto Rico, which is a commonwealth of the United States). Their poverty rate is about 50 percent higher than that of Mexican Americans, as is their percentage of single-parent families.[36] The third-largest Latino group is the Cubans, who are most heavily concentrated in Florida. Many well-educated middle-class Cubans came to the United States to escape the Cuban revolution, and as a result, Cubans are better off economically than other Latino groups in North America. However, more recent Cuban immigrants, often known as "boat people" because they arrived by sea in precarious small boats, tend to be from more disadvantaged backgrounds.

The constant influx of newcomers, who are often poorly educated and unfamiliar with the ways of American society, creates some serious problems for the Latino community. Many of these immigrants come illegally and because of their precarious status are subject to exploitation by unscrupulous employers who violate minimum wage and safety laws, knowing that these workers dare not turn them in. The problems of overcrowding, poverty, and lack of proper health care are also especially severe among new immigrants.

Spanish is the second most commonly spoken language in the United States. The large and rapidly growing Latino community has given rise to everything from Spanish-language newspapers and television networks to Spanish billboards and traffic signs. These changes have produced concern among some other groups that the nation will be permanently divided into separate English-speaking and Spanish-speaking societies. Such fears are unfounded: Latinos, like other immigrants, are certainly helping to reshape American culture, but there is no evidence that they are any less interested in moving into the mainstream of American life than the immigrants who preceded them.

Asians   Asians are the fastest-growing ethnic group in North America. The Asian population of the United States more than doubled between 1980 and 1990 and went up another 50 percent between 1990 and 2000. Asians now make up about 4.1 percent of the U.S. population.[37] But it is even more misleading to talk about Asian Americans as a single cultural group than it is for Latinos. At least most Latinos share a common language and some general similarities in cultural background. Today's Asian immigrants come from dozens of different countries that in many cases have little or nothing in common. A cross section of recent Asian immigrants might, for example, include everything from a Hong Kong shipping tycoon seeking a more stable economic climate, to a refugee from an isolated hill tribe of Southeast Asia, or a poverty-stricken peasant from Bangladesh.

As a group, Asian Americans have gained a reputation for being a kind of "model minority"—hardworking, well disciplined, and highly successful. While there is some truth to this image, such generalizations mislead as much as they inform. Studies do indeed show that Asians have a higher educational level, higher family income (although not necessarily a higher income per person), and lower rates of infant mortality than white Americans. For example, as of 1999, 37 percent of Asian Americans held high occupational status (managerial or professional) compared to 32 percent of whites. Yet the largest Asian American groups tend to have a "bipolar" occupational structure. In other words, Asian workers are clustered either in relatively high-paying professional jobs or in low-paying service jobs, with few in the middle of the occupational hierarchy. In 1999, the poverty rate for Asian children was 18 percent compared to 10 percent for white children.[38] Such generalizations also ignore the plight of the many new Asian immigrants and those from less successful Asian groups. A study by researchers from the University of California at Los Angeles found that while Asians as a whole have a relatively low level of welfare dependency, almost one-third of Southeast Asians in the United States receive welfare assistance. Among some groups, such as Cambodians and Laotians living in California, the welfare rate reaches as high as 77 percent.[39] Similarly, poverty rates among Asian Americans ranges from only 3.4 percent for Japanese Americans and 5.2 percent for Filipino Americans to 42 percent for Cambodian Americans and 32 percent for Laotian Americans. Americans of Chinese, Taiwanese, and Korean origins, on the other hand, have poverty rates about the same as whites (around 12 percent).[40] We should note that the Laotians and Cambodians who came to the United States after the Vietnam War were often poor "hill tribe" people who had to flee their country because they had helped the U.S. military. Only in 2000 did they finally received full citizenship status for their suffering during the war.

Many fear that the stereotype of Asian Americans as workaholic superachievers is also fanning the flames of racism and prejudice. Asian leaders complain that informal quotas are being used to restrict their admission to the most prestigious universities, that movies stereotype them in more blatant ways than any other minority, and that they often bear the brunt of the anger and frustration of workers who suffer from foreign economic competition. Japanese Americans have a special reason to fear such racism. Not only were they singled out for internment in U.S. concentration camps during World War II, but Japan's recent economic success has also made them easy targets for those seeking a scapegoat for America's economic problems. One study found that in 1993, 30 Asian Americans were killed in crimes that apparently had a racial motivation.[41]

Mixed Backgrounds   The traditional attitude among almost every ethnic group in North America is that their ways and their people are better than everyone else and that their children should marry only people "of their own kind." The strongest prohibitions have always applied to interracial relationships. Until relatively recently, interracial marriages were illegal in most states, but neither the law nor fierce social intolerance prevented millions of mixed-race babies from being born.

Traditional taboos about marrying outside one's ethnic group have slowly weakened but have not disappeared. Whether one's ancestors came from Italy, Germany, Ireland, or England has taken on less and less importance among white Americans over the years, and the vast majority of European Americans now have ancestors from several different countries. Although Jews maintain a more distinct ethnic identity, one survey found that half the marriages involving Jews are now interfaith marriages—compared to fewer than 1 in 10 a generation ago.[42] Similar trends are occurring among Asian Americans. About one-fourth of Chinese Americans under age 24, for example, marry someone from a different ethnic group. Even the marriage barriers between blacks and whites have shown signs of weakening. Although the total percentage of mixed-race couples remains small, it has quadrupled since 1970,[43] and interracial marriages are clearly growing more acceptable to the public. The Gallup poll found that 64 percent of those from age 18 to 29 approved of interracial marriages, while only 27 percent of those over age 50 did.[44]

Their mixed ethnic heritage doesn't usually pose much of a problem for the millions of Americans with ancestors from different European countries—provided their parents did not have unresolvable religious differences over their upbringing. People from mixed racial backgrounds, on the other hand, often run into much more serious difficulties. In some societies, they are in the unenviable position of being rejected by both racial groups. In America, children with a black and a white parent were traditionally considered black and were subject to the same discrimination and prejudice as other African Americans. Even today, most children of such mixed marriages identify themselves as African American, but that, of course, entails rejecting the ethnic identity and heritage of the white parent. Children from other kinds of racially mixed marriages often find that society doesn't know quite how to deal with them. As a result, there has been a growing movement to recognize people from mixed racial backgrounds as a distinct group. Advocates recently attempted to get the Bureau of the Census to list a "mixed" racial category along with its more traditional ones for the census in the year 2000. However, some African American leaders objected, fearing that the addition of a new category would reduce their overall numbers in the census count. The Bureau of the Census refused to add the new category, although the 2000 Census did allow people to check more than one racial group.

THE IMPACT OF IMMIGRATION

No other force has had a greater impact on the changing face of ethnic relations in North America than immigration. Recent years have seen not only a big increase in the number of immigrants but also a major shift in the countries from which they come. In the past, most immigrants came from European countries, but since the Immigration Act of 1965, things have changed. As recently as the 1950s, three-fourths of the immigrants to the United States were from Europe or Canada, but now about 85 percent come from Asia or Latin America.[45] Although exact figures are impossible to come by, there has also been a sharp increase in the total number of immigrants, with the last decade seeing the largest number of new immigrants in American history.[46] As of 2000, slightly over 10 percent of the U.S. population was foreign born. However, because the population of the United States is so much bigger than in the past, today's immigrants are still a smaller proportion of the total than they were at the peak of European immigration in the early decades of the twentieth century. The high point of immigration was 1910, when 14.7 percent of the U.S. population was foreign born.[47]

Unless there are major changes in government policy, this heavy influx of immigrants seeking to escape the poverty of the Third World is likely to continue. The Bureau of the Census estimates that whites will shrink from 83 percent of the population today to about 79 percent in the year 2020. Latinos will be the largest minority by then, making up over 16 percent of the population; African Americans will be next, at about 14 percent; and the percentage of Asians will have almost doubled to over 6 percent.[48]

The impact of this new wave of immigration is one of the most hotly debated issues in the field of ethnic relations. On the positive side, these new immigrants bring
willing hands and many skills that are needed in today's economy. Their distinctive cultural perspectives and overseas ties have proved vital to many businesses that compete in the global economy. (See "Lessons from Other Places" on pages 232–233.) On
the other hand, however, new immigrants often come into conflict with already established groups, and in hard economic times they may drive down wages and take jobs
from citizens who want them. Such problems are aggravated by the fact that the new
immigrants are not evenly dispersed throughout the country but rather are concentrated in only a few areas. Three-fourths of all foreign-born Americans live in just seven
states, and even within those states they are heavily concentrated in major cities such
as Los Angeles, New York, and Miami.

QUICK REVIEW

Briefly describe the history of ethnic relations in North America.
Describe the ways ethnic inequality is built into our educational, economic, and legal
institutions.
What are the special problems faced by each of the major ethnic groups in our society?
What impact has immigration had on the problem of ethnic relations?

EXPLAINING ETHNIC INEQUALITY

The first job of the sociologist facing an important social problem is to describe it as
precisely as possible. Although that is usually a lot harder than it sounds, the second
task—explaining the causes of the problem—is harder still. In the last section, we described the pervasive problem of ethnic inequality, and now we examine its causes. We
will focus our attention on three major factors that are the keys to solving this riddle:
conflict and competition, prejudice and discrimination, and class.

CONFLICT AND COMPETITION

If we go back far enough into the history of the relationship among different ethnic
groups, we almost always find a period of open conflict as the groups compete for
control of resources, power, and prestige. If the groups are roughly equal in strength,
there will probably be some equitable solution to their differences. If one group en-
joys significant advantages over the other, however, the weaker group is likely to be
stripped of its resources and forced into a position of subordination. For example, the
European settlers who came to North America had a far more technologically developed culture than the native peoples they encountered. The immigrants used that superiority to take Indian land and force Native Americans into a subordinate role in
the new European-style society they created.

Although the initial competition between ethnic groups often takes a military form,
it is likely to become more peaceful over the years. The military advantage of one group
is transformed into economic and political advantages. Members of the stronger group
seize resources from the weaker and then pass that wealth down to their descendants.

They also create political and economic systems that favor members of their own group. As time goes by, people may forget the origins of this inequality and come to see it as the natural order of things. Of course, things do not always happen this way. There are many examples of ethnic conflicts that result in seemingly endless rounds of bloodshed and military strife, and others in which the groups ultimately come to an equitable solution or forget the ethnic differences that once set them apart.

PREJUDICE AND DISCRIMINATION

Prejudice and discrimination are closely associated, but they are not the same. **Prejudice** refers to attitudes; **discrimination** refers to actions. Gordon Allport used the following definition in his classic study *The Nature of Prejudice*: "Ethnic prejudice is an antipathy based upon a faulty and inflexible generalization. It may be felt or expressed. It may be directed toward a group as a whole, or toward an individual because he is a member of that group."[49] Discrimination involves actual behavior: favoring one person or penalizing another because of that individual's ethnic status. It usually surfaces when members of a dominant group deny equal treatment to a subordinate group, but even the oppressed may discriminate against others when they have the chance. Although prejudice and discrimination usually occur together, this is not always so.[50] Sometimes we are prejudiced toward a person but reject discrimination because of moral conviction or the fear of legal penalties. On the other hand, economic and social pressures may lead us to discriminate against someone without feeling any prejudice.

Violence and terrorism, such as that practiced by the Ku Klux Klan, are common techniques used to protect the domination of one ethnic group over another.

LESSONS FROM OTHER PLACES

RACIAL AND ETHNIC DIVERSITY IN THE UNITED STATES: AN AMERICAN ADVANTAGE

We are always told that the United States is a nation of immigrants, and we have the most racially and ethnically diverse population of any industrial nation. But while we know these things, they often don't sink in until we spend time in other places. As a first-time visiting professor in Japan, I looked out over my class and thought to myself, "They are all Japanese!" Well, of course—but Americans are not use to such homogeneity. Calling the class roll the first day in Japan was easy compared to my experience in an American university classroom: They all had Japanese names! It is, of course, a very difficult task to read Japanese, but with a list of the students' names in one of the Japanese phonetic alphabets, it quickly became clear that they are all Japanese in origin and easy to pronounce. Back home it is always a tricky job to pronounce American names because they come from so many different places: Eastern and Western Europe, Asia, Latin America, Africa, and the Middle East.

My first day of class as a visiting professor in a German university provided a similar experience. Again my thought was, "They are all German!" This is less the case in Germany these days, especially with the increase in immigrants after the fall of the Berlin Wall and the European Union's new policy allowing young people to attend university in any of the EU member countries. But in 1991, I had only one student of Turkish ancestry and one student whose father was German and mother Mexican. Thinking as an American, I mentioned in class that she was Mexican German. The term was very amusing to my German students who have no concept like our "hyphenated Americans."

Given the problems of racism and ethnic conflict in American history, we often focus on the negative aspects of our racial and ethnic diversity. But looking around the world

Like other types of human behavior, prejudice and discrimination are not easily accounted for. Many influences come together to create them, and their origins cannot be found entirely in individual psychology or oppressive social institutions. Rather, psychological and social processes blend together, like prejudice and discrimination themselves.

Psychological Theories   Many psychologists believe that people with an **authoritarian personality** are the most likely to be prejudiced.[51] Such people are rigid and inflexible and have a low tolerance for uncertainty. They place a high value on conventional behavior and feel threatened when others do not follow their standards. Indeed, their prejudices help reduce the threat they feel when confronted by unconventional behavior. By labeling others as "inferior," "immature," or "degenerate," today, it becomes clear what a great asset our diversity is. For a few years in the mid-1990s a colleague and I conducted research on management-employee relations among Japanese and American corporations with operations in Thailand. Among other things, we examined relations between Japanese managers and Thai employees compared to relations between American managers and Thai employees. Because of their common Asian heritage, most people would assume that workplace relations between Japanese and Thais would be much better. We obtained more than 1,000 detailed questionnaires from Thai workers in American and Japanese corporations, and we conducted about 100 hours of personal interviews. Our findings were clear: Thai people prefer working for Americans, not for Japanese. The pay and benefits were almost identical among these corporations (and higher than the average for Thai corporations), and so were all the other factors that might have caused the differences in attitude.

Our research indicated that relations were better between Americans and Thais because American managers were more sensitive to cultural differences. To a far greater degree than Japanese managers, American managers had learned to respect and accommodate themselves to these differences. Coming from a very homogeneous society, Japanese managers have far more difficulty with the cross-cultural experience. Because the United States is the most diverse society of all industrial nations, many more Americans are ready and able to work with people from other nations and cultures around the world. This should certainly be recognized as a major American advantage in the increasingly global economy of the twenty-first century.

—*Harold Kerbo*

See Harold Kerbo and Robert Slagter, "The Asian Economic Crisis and the Decline of Japanese Economic Leadership in Asia," pp. 33–55 in Frank-Jurgen Richter (ed.), *The Asian Economic Catharsis* (Westport, CT: Quorum Books, 2000); Robert Slagter and Harold Kerbo, *Modern Thailand* (New York: McGraw-Hill, 2000).

authoritarians avoid any need to question their own beliefs and attitudes. The notion that this personality type is responsible for prejudice and discrimination has come under severe attack, however. Critics charge that the characteristics said to make up an authoritarian personality are not a unified whole but a number of unrelated traits given a single name, and that the concept of the authoritarian personality is just another label we can use to stigmatize people we dislike.

Another common psychological theory focuses on the use of minority groups as **scapegoats** for other people's problems: When people are frustrated and unhappy, minority groups can provide a safe target for their rage. The term *scapegoat* originates from a Jewish tradition. On Yom Kippur, the Day of Atonement, a goat was set loose in the wilderness after the high priest had symbolically laid all the sins of the people on its head. Ironically, the Jews themselves often became scapegoats in Western history. When plagues swept through medieval Europe, killing millions of people, rioters stormed into Jewish ghettos and burned them down, believing that Jews were somehow responsible for the epidemics. Six centuries later, when the Nazis set up their death camps, Jews were still being blamed for the troubles of Europe.

Cultural Theories   Prejudice and discrimination may be fueled by the desire to blame others for our problems—but both are learned. People do not need to have authoritarian personalities to have strong racial prejudice when they live in a culture in which such attitudes are the norm. Most prejudice is learned early in the socialization process. Children often adopt their parents' prejudices as naturally as they adopt their parents' language, and discrimination follows prejudice as regularly as night follows day.

Some of the most common prejudices are taken from **ethnic stereotypes** that portray all the members of a particular group as having similar fixed, and usually unfavorable, characteristics. The "happy-go-lucky Mexican," the "lazy Negro," and the "cunning Jew" reflect ethnic stereotypes that most of us have heard at one time or another.[52] In situations of ethnic conflict, **contrast conceptions** often develop; that is, people from two ethnic groups develop strong negative stereotypes about each other. For instance, while white racists in the United States perpetuate vicious anti–African American stereotypes, African American racists have developed their own stereotypes that depict all whites as greedy, selfish, and bent on subjugating African Americans.

Although the prejudice expressed in ethnic stereotypes is usually obvious, it can be quite subtle; for example, a white schoolboy living in an integrated neighborhood learns prejudice when he hears his mother say that it is all right for him to sleep overnight at the home of an African American friend because "that house is so clean you could eat right off the floor." An unspoken but potent prejudice is at the base of the mother's praise: African Americans are crude and dirty, but this family is an exception.

Structural Theories   Another important source of prejudice and discrimination can be found in the way a society structures its economic, political, and social activities. This form of bigotry is often termed **institutional discrimination** because inequality is built into the social structure and occurs whether or not the individuals working in that system are themselves prejudiced. For example, when Latino immigrants take civil service examinations, they are often at a severe disadvantage because English is their second language, and it is hard for them to do as well on a test written in English as those who grew up speaking that language.

There is ample evidence that the realities of economic competition lie beneath much prejudice and discrimination. If members of minority groups are excluded from elite colleges and professional schools, they obviously will not be able to compete with members of the dominant group in occupations requiring a high degree of training. In times of high unemployment, members of the dominant group can protect their jobs by making sure that minorities are the first to be fired and the last to be hired. It has long been noted that racial prejudice is highest among white working-class men who compete with African Americans for low-paying, unskilled jobs.

Members of the dominant group are not necessarily aware of the exploitation, however, because their stereotypes of ethnic and racial inferiority justify the inequalities in their society. Members of minority groups are seen to be poor because they are lazy or stupid, not because of the discrimination against them. Those in subordinate groups, of course, realize that they are being victimized, and their anger and resentment find expression in their own prejudices or may ultimately lead to revolutionary violence.

Racism and prejudice can also play an important part in class conflict. Racial animosities between African American and white workers in the United States have often been used to divide and weaken the working class. Many employers intentionally encourage racial conflicts to keep workers from forming a united front in their demands for higher wages and better working conditions. In the early part of the twentieth century, when most unions excluded African American workers, it was common for employers to bring them in as strikebreakers to end union disputes. The unions eventually realized that all workers were being hurt by these racial divisions and began recruiting African American members, although a more subtle racism still remains in many unions.

One of the most useful theoretical concepts for understanding the differences among ethnic minorities is that of **internal colonialism**. The idea is that minorities that are "conquered peoples" have a very different position in society than those who are not. Thus, a distinction is made between **colonized minority** and **immigrant minority**. Within the United States the category of colonized minority would include American Indians, African slaves and their descendants, as well as the descendants of the original Mexican population of what is now the United States. Immigrant minorities would include Asians, Latin Americans, and white immigrants such as Irish, Polish, and East European Jews. The colonized minorities have usually been more harshly treated, and they have experienced more prejudice and discrimination, which in turn leads to more social problems for the original victims of colonization and their descendants. This helps us understand why some immigrant groups are able to "make it" after a few years, while colonized minorities remain stuck in poverty, with less education and more social problems such as family disruption, crime, and substance abuse.[53] On the other hand, it is clear that immigrant minorities often bring much with them when they come to a new country such as the United States—they may bring wealth as well as social and human capital (in the form of education, occupational skills, and simply a strong family structure). For example, as Zulfacar found with Afghan immigrants to Germany and the United States, social capital in the form of a network of family and friendship ties in the new country are critical to achievement and economic success.[54] Research on Asian and Hispanic immigrants to the United States shows the similar effects of family and friendship ties.[55]

CLASS

In the late 1970s, William Julius Wilson published an influential book, *The Declining Significance of Race*, in which he argued that racial prejudice and discrimination are a less important cause of the problems of African Americans than they once were.[56] The principal source of today's problems is, according to Wilson, the fact that African Americans are trapped in a self-perpetuating cycle of poverty. Regardless of race or ethnic status, a person born into a poor family is more likely to be poor as an adult than someone from a middle-class family. Because of the history of discrimination, minority children are more likely to be born into poverty. Thus, the historical effects of the racism and discrimination that originally forced minorities into a subordinate position in the class system are seen to be more important than the discrimination they currently encounter. And just as the class system passes along the burdens of past discrimination to minority children, so the benefits of past favoritism are passed along to the descendants of the dominant groups.

Supporters of this theory can cite considerable evidence for their conclusion that class is now the key factor. Surveys show that racial and ethnic prejudice have been declining in recent years, and explicit laws have been passed against occupational discrimination. There is, as we noted, a vigorous and expanding African American middle class that seems to have been able to overcome the barriers of racism. There are also a substantial number of whites in the underclass who seem every bit as disadvantaged as the minorities (see Chapter 6). It is nonetheless important to recognize that although progress has been made in the fight against prejudice and discrimination, they are still powerful forces in American life. Members of minority groups must still deal with economic obstacles and social bigotry that European Americans seldom have to face.

QUICK REVIEW

What role do conflict and competition play in ethnic relations?
What are the different theories about the causes of prejudice and discrimination?
What role does social class play in the problem of ethnic inequality?

SOLVING THE PROBLEMS OF ETHNIC RELATIONS

Although true equality remains a distant goal, the history of the twentieth century shows significant progress toward racial and ethnic justice. Elimination of the oppressive segregation system in the United States was a major step forward, as was legislation outlawing discrimination in housing and employment. At least partially as a result, minorities have gained access to numerous high-level business and professional careers that used to be closed to them. Illiteracy rates among minorities have dropped, and their level of education has increased (see Chapter 4). Although racism and ethnic stereotypes remain, these prejudices are seldom publicly voiced by business and political leaders, as they once were; and public opinion surveys show that prejudice against minorities has significantly declined.[57]

Disturbing signs during the 1980s and early 1990s, however, indicate that hard economic times led to a deterioration of ethnic relations and that a new crisis may occur with the next economic slowdown sometime in the early twenty-first century. Whites have grown increasingly resentful of affirmative action programs designed to help win equality for minorities, and some politicians have used attacks on welfare recipients and street crime in thinly veiled attempts to make minorities the scapegoats for the nation's troubles. Factors including the loss of millions of manufacturing jobs in North America, the new influx of Third World immigrants, the exodus of middle-class African Americans from cities, and over a decade of government neglect have all contributed to ever-worsening conditions in the inner cities.

Even the many people working to solve these serious problems often disagree about the ultimate goals. Should we work toward a melting pot that merges us all into a single new group, or should the goal be to achieve true equality among a salad bowl of distinct ethnic groups? While this is a significant philosophical issue, it is important to remember that no matter which approach we prefer, the goal is the same—justice and fair treatment for all—and the proposals that follow all aim to achieve it.

POLITICAL ACTIVISM

Most of the government's actions to help minorities have come about only because of organized political pressure. The segregation system that denied those of African descent the rights enjoyed by other Americans was not declared unconstitutional until almost a hundred years after the Civil War. Even then, a tremendous political effort was necessary to win the implementation of that decision. The **civil rights movement**—a coalition of activist African Americans and liberal whites—used nonviolent demonstrations, marches, and sit-ins to demand an end to segregation. Despite their eventual success, many African Americans became increasingly frustrated with their failure to win full equality. The black power movement came to reject integration as just another form of domination. Its leaders demanded separation of the races, but on an equal basis. As the movement turned increasingly violent, it was repressed by force, and most of its leaders were killed or jailed.

Political activism has proved to be the most effective tool for winning social justice for minority groups. This photo shows a protest march in Boston led by the late Dr. Martin Luther King, Jr. Such protests were part of the civil rights movement that brought an end to legal racial segregation in the United States.

The spirit of minority activism nonetheless lives on. However, the activists, many of whom now hold government office, are generally working within the system. Native American activists, for example, have been particularly successful in using legal actions to win back the rights granted in government treaties. They won the right to fish in Puget Sound and Lake Michigan and won legal title to lands in North Dakota, Maine, and Rhode Island. In the last decade, Native Americans have also been among the most militant of all ethnic groups, directly confronting the political system. This militancy is perhaps best symbolized by armed confrontation between Mohawk warriors and army troops near the small town of Oka, Quebec, in the early 1990s. Although this incident began as a conflict over an attempt to put a golf course on a tribal burial ground, it soon escalated into a direct challenge to the authority of the government. However, violent confrontation has not proved to be the most successful tactic in the struggle. Inuit people won the creation of their huge new territory through 15 years of methodical negotiation with the Canadian government.[58]

The success of black political activism can be seen in the growing representation of African Americans among the nation's officeholders. The number of African Americans holding elected office was more than five times higher in 1994 than it was in 1970.[59] Yet despite such advances, an increasingly conservative political climate has meant that efforts of minority leaders have been largely devoted merely to defending the victories won in the past.

REFORMING THE EDUCATIONAL SYSTEM

Many people feel that the best way to compensate for the lingering effects of past discrimination and to help break the vicious cycle of poverty is through better education. In the early 1970s, the hottest issue in the field of education was whether to pursue that goal through integration, as the advocates of mandatory school busing proposed, or through pluralism, as supporters of neighborhood schools recommended. Today, the focus has shifted to finding the best ways to improve the academic performance of poor and minority children regardless of the makeup of their school's student body. Many different proposals have been made, and many experimental programs have been carried out, but the most promising approach is probably the most obvious one—to provide extra tutoring and other special programs to help overcome the barriers that poverty and prejudice place in the way of a good education (see Chapter 4).

Another important issue concerns the education system's responsibility to help reduce prejudice and discrimination. Until the wave of minority activism in the 1950s and 1960s, textbooks and teaching materials often contained blatantly racist stereotypes—or simply ignored ethnic minorities altogether. Great improvements have been made since then, but critics charge that our educational system still presents a **eurocentric** view of the world. In other words, they charge that the curriculum and the general orientation of our schools and universities still have a European slant, and they largely ignore the perspectives of those from Africa, Latin America, and Asia. These critics therefore call for **multicultural education** to reflect the background and perspectives of all Americans. Such proposals have met strenuous opposition from those who see them as a threat to European cultural traditions, and teachers who are not trained in the new approach see it as a threat to their jobs. A related proposal calls for secondary schools and universities to require students to take classes in ethnic studies to help them understand the perspectives, problems, and concerns of people from other groups.

FAIR EMPLOYMENT

The idea that everyone deserves an equal opportunity to make a living has a great deal of popular support, but implementing this idea has been difficult. Civil rights activists of the 1960s succeeded in winning the passage of a broad Civil Rights Act, which forbids discrimination by unions, employment agencies, and businesses employing more than 25 workers. But the problems in enforcing the law have been immense, as it is extremely difficult to prove why someone was not hired or promoted. The laws forbidding discrimination have now been supplemented by **affirmative action** programs, which require a positive effort to recruit and promote qualified members of minority groups. Employers can no longer defend themselves by claiming that a decision not to hire someone was based on some criterion other than ethnicity: They must prove they are not discriminating. If the percentage of minority employees is significantly lower than their percentage in the work force, companies must accept goals for minority employment and set up timetables stating when these goals are likely to be met.

These procedures have created a powerful white backlash. Conservative critics charge that the ratios are not goals but quotas and that affirmative action programs really call for **reverse discrimination** (discrimination against white males). Some more liberal critics also charge that the benefits of affirmative action have mainly gone to minorities from the middle and upper class because the members of the underclass who need the most help lack the necessary qualifications for most jobs. Resolution of these conflicts will be extremely difficult. It is true that affirmative action programs give preferential treatment to some members of minority groups and that therefore some whites are discriminated against; but it is also true that minorities still face far more discrimination than whites do even now.

The Supreme Court has yet to resolve these difficult legal issues. Originally, the Supreme Court upheld the constitutionality of most affirmative action programs. But as more conservative judges have been appointed to the Court, it has become more skeptical of affirmative action programs that are not intended to rectify a proven history of past discrimination, and one federal circuit court in the Southwest even ruled against the constitutionality of all affirmative action. Overall, it is still not clear which kinds of affirmative action programs are constitutional and which kinds are not. In 1996, California voters waded into this issue, passing an initiative that banned affirmative action for the state government and its contractors. The federal government, especially the executive branch, has continued its support for most affirmative action programs.

Laws that merely prohibit employment discrimination against minority groups do not seem able to do the whole job; therefore, some affirmative action procedures must be continued if equality of opportunity is to be achieved, but there is considerable disagreement about how to do so fairly. Opinion polls show that the public is deeply divided about this issue. Even among whites, about two-thirds tell pollsters that they support "affirmative action programs provided there are no rigid quotas." But if you ask those same people whether women or minorities should be given preferences to make up for past discrimination, large majorities say they are opposed. There is, nonetheless, overwhelming support for laws that ban discrimination based on ethnicity or gender.[60] (See the Debate on pages 242–243.)

ECONOMIC JUSTICE

No social problem stands alone. The dilemmas of ethnic relations are interwoven in complex ways with other social problems. Solutions to the problems discussed in other chapters of this book would go a long way toward alleviating ethnic conflicts as well. Perhaps the foremost issue among them is the lack of economic equality. As we saw in Chapter 6, the gap between the rich and the poor has been growing significantly wider in recent times. When the problem of poverty gets worse, minorities are most strongly affected, since they are most likely to be poor. Thus, programs to reduce unemployment, retrain unskilled workers, provide good-quality health care, reduce poverty, and shift the tax burden to those best able to carry it are as essential to achieving ethnic justice as programs specifically attacking prejudice and discrimination.

QUICK REVIEW

How can our educational system deal more effectively with the problems of ethnic inequality?
What is affirmative action, and why is it so controversial?

SOCIOLOGICAL PERSPECTIVES ON PROBLEMS OF ETHNIC MINORITIES

Public concern about ethnic inequality waxes and wanes with the political climate. Interest in equality is particularly intense in times of change, when old patterns of ethnic relations are breaking up and there is conflict over what direction to take in the future. In the United States, ethnic relations raised the most public concern during the Reconstruction period after the Civil War and again during the era of the civil rights and black power movements that marked the end of the segregation system a hundred years later. At both times, ethnic inequality became a pressing social problem because an old system of ethnic relations was deteriorating and a new pattern was taking shape. Even during the most stable periods, however, the problem of fairly managing ethnic relations in such a diverse society is never far below the surface.

THE FUNCTIONALIST PERSPECTIVE

Functionalists believe that shared values and attitudes are the cement that holds a society together. The more disagreement there is over basic values, the more unstable and disorganized a society is likely to be. Although the various ethnic groups in

North America have come to share many values over the years, significant differences remain, and these differences are an important source of conflict. North America lacks the unity, consensus, and organization essential to a harmonious society. Although efforts of the largest ethnic groups to dominate the others have become less and less successful, neither pluralism nor integration has replaced domination. Society is disorganized, unable to muster its people to work together for the common good.

From the functionalist perspective, ethnic discrimination is both a cause and an effect of contemporary social disorganization. The failure to give minorities full equality wastes valuable human resources and generates ethnic hostilities that reduce economic production and undermine political authority. These hostilities, in turn, contribute to prejudice and discrimination as different ethnic groups come to see one another as enemies.

To functionalists, the best response to these problems is to reduce discrimination by reorganizing our social institutions. Unity is the objective, whether it is achieved through domination, pluralism, or integration. Integration is the ideal, however, because an integrated society is likely to have the fewest conflicts. Functionalists ask for an attack on discrimination in housing, education, criminal justice, and elsewhere, arguing that an effective reform movement will increase support for "the system" among ethnic minorities while at the same time maintaining the allegiance of the majority.

THE CONFLICT PERSPECTIVE

Conflict theorists see the history of ethnic relations in North America as one of conflict and oppression. European colonists fought with each other and with the Native Americans. Eventually, English-speaking whites conquered most of the continent, but conflict did not end there. As new groups settled in the "promised land," some were assimilated. Those who refused to give up their ethnic identity were shunted into inferior positions: employees rather than employers, police officers rather than judges, farmhands rather than landowners, blue-collar workers rather than white-collar workers, and so on.

From the conflict perspective, the history of all ethnic relations is the history of a struggle for power. When one group is more powerful than others, a system of domination develops in which weaker groups are exploited for the political, social, and economic advantage of the dominant group. When power is more equally distributed, pluralism develops. Whether ethnic groups are in a relationship of domination or equality, there is no guarantee that the system will remain stable. Social change is primarily a process by which one group grows stronger at the expense of others. Those who have power want peace and stability; those who are out of power want conflict and change. Institutionalized discrimination is thus a technique for keeping the dominant group in power and protecting it from its competitors.

Conflict theorists assert that ethnic equality can be achieved only through struggle. A group that has improved its status is, by definition, a group that has seized more political and economic power. Conflict theorists argue that political change is often necessary to bring about economic change in such things as employment,

DEBATE

ARE AFFIRMATIVE ACTION PROGRAMS FAIR?

Yes

Affirmative action programs are designed to encourage employers to hire and promote women and minorities if they are underrepresented in the workforce. Under such programs, women and minorities are hired instead of equally qualified white males in order to compensate for past and present discrimination.

In a perfect world, we would not need affirmative action. Personnel decisions would be made on the basis of each individual's abilities and qualifications, without regard to ethnic group or gender. But we all know that things don't really work that way. Centuries-old prejudices will not simply vanish because the law tells everyone to stop discriminating. Even with current affirmative action programs, women and minorities still get lower pay and have fewer chances for advancement than white males. Without the government's pressures to meet affirmative action goals, the situation would be far worse. Affirmative action merely provides a small counterweight to a system that still treats women and minorities as second-class citizens.

Critics claim that laws prohibiting discrimination are all we need to ensure fair treatment for all. Unfortunately, it is extremely hard to prove to a court that you were the victim of discrimination because employers can always think of some excuse to explain their decision. All affirmative action does is to shift the burden of proof to the employers to show that they are not discriminating. After all, employers are the ones with the money to hire lawyers to make their case in court.

Even if we could wave a magic wand to end all discrimination tomorrow, we would still need affirmative action programs to compensate for the effects of past discrimination. Remember that Africans were brought to this land in chains. For generations they were brutalized, tortured, and even killed at the "master's" whim; their family structure was shattered and their culture destroyed. Women from all ethnic groups were themselves in a slavelike position. Traditionally, a woman was considered to be the property of her husband, whom she must "love, honor, and obey." She

education, housing, and health care. The key to increased power is organization for political action. A small ethnic group that is unified can wield much greater power than its numbers would suggest. In a democratic society, political change can be achieved by outvoting and outmaneuvering one's opponents according to the established rules of the game. Political change can also be achieved by attacking the established rules in demonstrations and protests that may threaten—or that may provoke—violence. Both techniques are being used in ethnic struggles in North America and around the world, and conflict theorists counsel those who would couldn't vote, she couldn't hold a responsible position, and her husband had complete control of all her property (if she was even allowed to own any). The effects of this kind of brutality and discrimination are passed on from one generation to the next. Their consequences will never go away unless we take affirmative action to correct them, and fairness demands that we do.

No

Two wrongs do not make a right. It was wrong to discriminate against women and minorities in the past, and it is wrong to discriminate against males with a European background today. Of course, supporters of affirmative action claim that such programs are not discriminating against white males but just correcting for past discrimination, but what else do you call it when an employer refuses to hire the most qualified candidate because of his race and gender? Racism is still racism even when the victims are white. Sexism is still sexism even when the victims are males.

Under current affirmative action laws, the daughter of a black television star with $100 million in the bank would be given preference in employment over the son of a homeless alcoholic who happened to be white. How can you call that fair?

The supporters of affirmative action say that simply banning discrimination is not enough to bring about true justice in our society, but society cannot fight racism and sexism by means of a law that requires employers to discriminate on the basis of race and sex. There are many far better ways to correct social injustices—for example, the government could work to improve the terrible schools in urban slums, provide job retraining for the unemployed, and create jobs. Of course, such projects cost money, and it is far easier for politicians simply to pass a law requiring employers to give special preferences to the groups that are pressuring them to act. Programs that seek to aid the poor and disadvantaged make this a stronger society by helping to bring those people (the majority of whom are minorities and women) into the mainstream of social life. Programs that give special privileges to someone only because of race or sex make this a weaker society by fostering a sense of injustice and feelings of hostility among members of different groups. Fairness demands that the law resolutely condemn all forms of discrimination, including that against white males. Affirmative action laws are based on pure hypocrisy and must be repealed.

change the system to study the historical record of the successes and failures of such efforts.

THE FEMINIST PERSPECTIVE

Feminists have often commented on the similarities in the social position of women and minorities in our society. Both groups have been put down in derogatory stereotypes, subject to widespread occupational discrimination, and often excluded from the mainstream of our cultural life. Women's groups also share a common interest with minority activists to protect the affirmative action programs that have benefited both groups over the years. Feminists also recognize that white women still hold a privileged position relative to women of color. White women are, for example, far more likely to be born into wealth and privilege than women of color, and they are also more likely to have the kinds of social connections that are often vital to economic success. So while strongly opposing discrimination of all sorts, many contemporary feminists are calling for special attention to the problems of women of color who suffer from the double discrimination of sexism and racism.

Feminists also call upon women and pro-feminist men to continue to educate people about the harm that ethnic and gender stereotyping causes and to encourage people to look closely at their own lives to discover and uproot stereotypes and prejudiced attitudes that have crept into their system of beliefs during the socialization process. While there are certainly many people who hold overtly prejudiced attitudes and intentionally discriminate against ethnic minorities, the bigger problem is that most people have prejudiced attitudes but are unaware of them. While these people do not see themselves as racists or as advocates of some theory of racial superiority, they still perpetuate the unspoken belief that their group is better than others, and that ethnic minorities should try to measure up to them.

THE INTERACTIONIST PERSPECTIVE

Interactionist theory holds that individuals develop their concept of personal identity from their interactions with the people around them. When members of a minority group are constantly insulted, demeaned, and harassed, they are bound to be affected. Some internalize these feelings, resulting in low self-esteem and feelings of personal inadequacy. The victims of such prejudice are also more likely to develop other personal problems, such as alcoholism and drug addiction. For example, the rates of addiction to heroin and crack cocaine among African Americans and Latinos are much higher than the national average, and alcoholism is an especially severe problem among Native Americans. Another common response by members of minority groups is to reject forcefully such ethnic stereotypes and those who believe in them and to assert their own value and importance. Still others try to avoid the effects of prejudice and discrimination by isolating themselves in segregated ethnic communities.

The interactionists' proposals for reducing ethnic discrimination and prejudice fall into two broad categories. Those in the first category are based on the fact that whatever is learned can be unlearned. Included here are recommendations for more ethnic contact and communication and for a direct attack on ethnic stereotypes in the media and in schools. By showing people from different ethnic groups as they actually are, and not as stereotypes depict them, we can break down the barriers to communication and understanding.

The second category includes proposals that attempt to go to the roots of the problem by recommending long-term changes to reduce ethnic competition and conflict. More contacts and communication among ethnic groups will enable people to overcome their prejudices, but research shows that these contacts must be among ethnic groups of relatively equal social status who are working together for a common goal rather than competing with one another for survival. In other words, interactionists say that prejudice and discrimination will decrease as the fear of economic competition decreases.

Interactionists also point out that grouping people into common categories on the basis of such characteristics as skin color and type of hair is simply a cultural tradition, and one that has caused enormous social problems. It therefore follows that the best solution to the "racial problem" is to abandon those traditional attitudes and adopt the more scientifically supportable view that all people are members of a single human race.

QUICK REVIEW

What are the differences between the ways conflict theorists and functionalists look at the problems of ethnic relations?

What are the similarities between the social position of women and minorities in our society?

What solutions do interactionists propose for our problems of ethnic relations?

SUMMARY

Throughout history, tension and conflict have existed between different ethnic groups that live in close contact with each other. People who share a sense of identity and togetherness tend to be ethnocentric, believing that their ways of doing things are better than those of other groups. Ethnocentrism becomes racism when it is based on the idea that people with certain physical traits are superior to others and deserve special privileges.

The relationship among ethnic groups usually follows one of three general patterns. Domination exists when one ethnic group holds power and is thus able to exploit another group or groups. When two or more ethnic groups have roughly equal power so that each controls its own affairs, a system of pluralism exists. Finally, when two or more ethnic groups blend together and share power, customs, and social institutions, the relationship is known as integration.

North American society has promoted several different ideals for ethnic relations. Originally, all other ethnic groups were expected to assimilate and to conform to the Anglo-American cultural pattern. A second, more recent, ideal is that of the melting pot, which holds that different ethnic groups should merge together to form a single new culture. Finally, there is the ideal of the salad bowl, which encourages ethnic groups to retain their cultural distinctiveness.

Historically, North America has seen the conquest and domination of the Native Americans, French, Spanish, and Mexicans by English-speaking peoples. Domination also characterized relations with African slaves and with most newly arriving immigrant groups. That domination has met increasing challenges. Some ethnic groups have won more equal status with the old dominant group, while the differences among other groups have slowly decreased as they have become more integrated. Nonetheless, our society still shows a high degree of inequality. Whether in education, jobs, or housing, the members of most minority groups still lag behind the national average. Each of the major ethnic groups in North America— Native Americans, Europeans, Jews, African Americans, Latinos, and Asians—also has its own special characteristics and problems, and each contains several distinct subgroups.

There are many possible explanations for the problem of ethnic inequality. The historical cause is competition among ethnic groups in which one group wins a dominant position and forces the others into a subordinate status. A second major factor is prejudice and discrimination, which, in turn, have psychological, cultural, and structural causes. Finally, there is the influence of class and the fact that a life of poverty or of privilege tends to be passed down from one generation to the next.

Many suggestions have been made to deal with the problems of ethnic relations. Greater political activism by members of minority groups and their supporters is often considered an important starting point for reform. Changes in the schools to include the perspectives of ethnic minorities is a common suggestion, as is a greater commitment to compensatory education programs designed to correct the damage done by poverty and discrimination. An end to bias in employment and promotion is another obvious need. Finally, many programs designed to help poor people can do a great deal to foster greater ethnic justice as well.

According to functionalists, North American society is disorganized and unable to muster its many ethnic groups to work in harmony for the common good; but conflict theorists see institutionalized discrimination as an intentional way of protecting the economic and political power of the dominant groups. The key to increasing the power of minority groups, in their view, is political activism. Feminists see many similarities in the position of women and minorities in our society and call for special attention to the needs of women of color. Interactionists point out that prejudice and discrimination are learned and that both are associated with the fear of competition. They recommend more contacts and communication among ethnic groups and a reduction of economic competition.

QUESTIONS FOR CRITICAL THINKING

Back in 1944, the famous Swedish sociologist Gunnar Myrdal called ethnic relations "the American dilemma"—because of the fundamental contradiction between the American creed of justice and fair play for all and the realities of a society rife with prejudice and discrimination.[61] Myrdal was convinced that, in the long run, the higher values of the American creed would win out over the forces of hatred and bigotry. Do you think he was right? How much progress have we made since 1944? How much further do we have to go?

KEY TERMS

affirmative action

assimilation

authoritarian personality

civil rights movement

colonized minority

contrast conceptions

discrimination

domination

ethnic group

ethnic minority

ethnic stereotype

ethnocentrism

eurocentric

immigrant minority

institutional discrimination

integration

internal colonialism

melting pot theory

multicultural education

pluralism

prejudice

race

racism

reverse discrimination

salad bowl theory

scapegoat

segregation

white ethnic

NOTES

1. Philip Gourevitch, "The Return," New Yorker, January 20, 1997, pp. 44–54.

2. Richard T. Schaefer, Racial and Ethnic Groups, 5th ed. (New York: HarperCollins, 1993), pp. 7–10.

3. Ibid., pp. 10–14.

4. See International Herald Tribune, August 24, 2000.

5. Richard T. Schaefer, Racial and Ethnic Groups, pp. 148–184.

6. Nancy Oestreich Lurie, "The American Indian: Historical Background," in Norman Yetman and C. Hoy Steel, eds., Minority and Majority: The Dynamics of Racial and Ethnic Relations, 4th ed. (Boston: Allyn & Bacon, 1985).

7. Murray Wax, Indian Americans (Upper Saddle River, NJ: Prentice Hall, 1971), pp. 17–18; Dee Brown, Bury My Heart at Wounded Knee: An Indian History of the American West (New York: Holt, Rinehart and Winston, 1970.)

8. Schaefer, Racial and Ethnic Groups, p. 150.

9. Lurie, "The American Indian," p. 179.

10. U.S. Bureau of the Census, Statistical Abstract of the United States, 2002 (Washington, DC: U.S. Government Printing Office, 2001), p. 139.

11. Joseph H. Cash, "Indian Education: A Bright Path or Another Dead End?" in Editors of the Winston Press, Viewpoints: Red and Yellow, Black and Brown (Groveland Terrace, MN: Winston Press, 1972), p. 14.

12. U.S. Bureau of the Census, Money Income in the United States, 2000 (Washington, DC: U.S. Government Printing Office, 2001), Table A.

13. U.S. Bureau of the Census, Poverty in the United States, 2000 (Washington, DC: U.S. Government Printing Office, 2001), Table A.

14. Seymour Martin Lipset, American Exceptionalism: A Double-Edged Sword (New York: Norton, 1996), p. 138.

15. Jim Schachter, "Unequal Opportunity: Minorities Find that Roadblocks to the Executive Suite Are Still in Place," Los Angeles Times, April 17, 1988, sec. 4, p. 1.

16. Quoted in Charles E. Reasons and Jack E. Kuykendall, eds., Race, Crime and Justice (Pacific Palisades, CA: Goodyear, 1972).

17. Fox Butterfield, "More Blacks in Their 20s Have Trouble with the Law," New York Times, October 5, 1995, p. A8.

18. *International Herald Tribune*, February 16, 2000; *New York Times*, March 12, 2000.

19. *New York Times*, March 12, 2000.

20. U.S. Bureau of the Census, *Statistical Abstract*, 1999, p. 14.

21. Richard T. Schaefer, *Sociology* (New York: McGraw-Hill, 1989), p. 253.

22. David Pelly, "Birth of an Inuit Nation," *Canadian Geographic* 116 (4) (April 1994): 23–25.

23. S. Dale McLemore, *Racial and Ethnic Relations in America*, 3rd ed. (Boston: Allyn & Bacon, 1991).

24. Richard D. Alba, "The Twilight of Ethnicity Among Americans of European Ancestry: The Case of Italians," in Richard D. Alba, ed., *Ethnicity and Race in the U.S.A.* (Upper Saddle River, NJ: Prentice Hall, 1988), pp. 134–158.

25. Stanley Lieberson and Mary C. Waters, *From Many Strands: Ethnic and Racial Groups in Contemporary America* (New York: Russell Sage, 1988).

26. Andrew M. Greeley, *Religious Change in America* (Cambridge, MA: Harvard University Press, 1989).

27. Lipset, *American Exceptionalism*, pp. 151–152.

28. See Schaefer, *Racial and Ethnic Groups*, pp. 395–426.

29. U.S. Bureau of the Census, *Statistical Abstract*, 1999, p. 14.

30. William Julius Wilson, "Studying Inner-City Social Dislocations: The Challenge of Public Agenda Research," *American Sociological Review* 56 (February 1991): 1–14.

31. Ronald J. Ostrow, "Sentencing Study Sees Race Disparity," *Los Angeles Times*, October 5, 1995, pp. A1, A17.

32. U.S. Bureau of the Census, *Statistical Abstract*, 1999, p. 14.

33. Wilson, "Studying Inner-City Social Dislocations."

34. Harold Kerbo, *Social Stratification and Inequality*, 4th ed. (New York: McGraw-Hill, 2000), pp. 344–346.

35. U.S. Bureau of the Census, *Statistical Abstract*, 1999, p. 14.

36. Theodore Caplow, *American Social Trends* (San Diego: Harcourt Brace Jovanovich, 1991), pp. 191–193.

37. U.S. Bureau of the Census, *Statistical Abstract*, 1999, p. 14; U.S. Bureau of the Census, *Statistical Abstract*, 1993, p. 18.

38. U.S. Bureau of the Census, *The Asian and Pacific Islander Population in the United States, 1999* (Washington, DC: U.S. Government Printing Office, 2000).

39. Nancy Rivera Brooks, "Study of Asians in U.S. Finds Many Struggling," *Los Angeles Times*, May 19, 1994, pp. A1, A25; Ashley Dunn, "Southeast Asians Highly Dependent on Welfare in U.S.," *New York Times*, May 19, 1994, pp. A1, A17.

40. Kerbo, *Social Stratification and Inequality*, p. 301.

41. Katherine Imahara, Stanley Mark, and Phil Tajitsu-Nash, *Audit of Violence Against Asian Pacific Americans: Anti-Asian Violence, A National Problem* (Los Angeles: National Asian Pacific American Consortium, 1994).

42. Barry A. Kosmin, *Highlights of the CJF 1990 National Jewish Population Survey* (New York: Council of Jewish Federations, 1991).

43. Richard T. Shaefer, *Racial and Ethnic Groups*, pp. 27–28, 367–369.

44. Lynell George, "Cross Colors," *Los Angeles Times*, March 27, 1994, pp. E1, E2.

45. Ronald Brownstein and Richard Simon, "Hospitality Turns into Hostility," *Los Angeles Times*, November 14, 1993, pp. A1, A6–A7.

46. Peter Skerry, "Has Immigration Collided with the Welfare State?" *Los Angeles Times*, May 1, 1994, pp. M1, M6.

47. U.S. Bureau of the Census, *Statistical Abstract*, 2001, p. 45.

48. U.S. Bureau of the Census, *Statistical Abstract*, 1996, pp. 18, 19.

49. Gordon W. Allport, *The Nature of Prejudice* (New York: Doubleday, 1956), p. 10.

50. Robert K. Merton, "Discrimination and the American Creed," in Robert M. MacIver, ed., *Discrimination and National Welfare* (New York: Harper & Row, 1949).

51. T. W. Adorno, E. Frenkel-Brunswik, D. J. Devinson, and R. N. Sandord, *The Authoritarian Personality* (New York: Harper & Row, 1950).

52. See Judith Andre, "Stereotypes: Conceptual and Normative Considerations," in Paula S. Rothenberg, ed., *Racism and Sexism: An Integrated Study* (New York: St. Martin's Press, 1988), pp. 257–262.

53. Robert Blauner, *Racial Oppression in America* (New York: Harper & Row, 1972); Alfredo Mirande, *Gringo Justice* (Notre Dame, IN: University of Notre Dame Press, 1987); Mary G. Powers and William Seltzer, "Occupational Status and Mobility Among Undocumented Immigrants by Gender," *International Migration Review* 32 (1998): 21–55. James W. Ainsworth-Darnell and Douglas B. Downey, "Assessing the Oppositional Culture Explanation for Racial/Ethnic Differences in School Performance," *American Sociological Review* 63 (1998): 536–553.

54. Maliha Zulfacar, *Afghan Immigrants in the USA and Germany: A Comparative Analysis of the Use of Ethnic Social Capital* (Munster, Germany: LIT Verlag, 1998).

55. Jimmy M. Sanders and Victor Nee, "Immigrant Self-Employment: The Family As Social Capital and the Value of Human Capital," *American Sociological Review* 61 (1996): 231–249.

56. William Julius Wilson, *The Declining Significance of Race: Blacks and Changing American Institutions* (Chicago: University of Chicago Press, 1978).

57. See Lipset, *American Exceptionalism*, pp. 129–130.

58. Julie Gozan, "Land to the Inuit," *Canadian Geographic* 13 (9) (September 1992): 7–8.

59. U.S. Bureau of the Census, *Statistical Abstract*, 1996, p. 284.

60. Lipset, *American Exceptionalism*, pp. 125–127.

61. Gunnar Myrdal, *An American Dilemma* (New York: Harper, 1944).

CHAPTER 8

GENDER AND
SEXUAL ORIENTATION

Questions to Consider

What are the differences between male and female gender roles?

Are the gender role exceptions rooted in biology or culture?

Is sexual orientation rooted in biology or culture?

How do we learn gender roles?

What forms does discrimination based on gender and sexual orientation take?

How can gender inequality and discrimination against gays and lesbians be reduced?

When the guerrilla army known as the Taliban first marched into Afghanistan's capital a few years ago, it seemed like just one more turn in the endless wars that had been raging in that country for two decades. But for the women of Afghanistan, it was anything but business as usual. Fueled by an extremist interpretation of their Islamic faith, these young and often illiterate soldiers imposed a virtual reign of terror on the women in the territories they controlled. In a country where women often had to keep the economy running while their husbands fought wars, the Taliban suddenly decreed that no women could work outside their homes. Girls were thrown out of school and denied an education, and even adult women who were veiled from head to foot in the traditional Afghani costume were forbidden to leave their homes without a male relative to accompany them. Finally, the Taliban decided it was immoral for male doctors to see female patients. They decreed that no female patients could be treated at any of the major hospitals—leaving thousand of desperate women without proper medical care.

Jamie Nabozny had a horrible time in middle school. He was verbally harassed, pushed around, and he was even the subject of a mock rape. Why? Because he was gay and didn't hide his sexual orientation from the other students. By the time he was in high school, his classmates had beaten him up and urinated on him at school. He went to the school administrators to complain again and again, but they never intervened to stop the abuse. It became so bad that Jamie attempted suicide three times; ultimately he dropped out of high school when he was in the eleventh grade. (His story does have a happier ending, however, for when he was 21 a jury awarded him almost $1 million in damages in his suit against the school district.)

These two stories took place on opposite sides of the world, and the abuse they describe had very different victims, but they actually have much in common. They are both rooted in the intolerance and bigotry that arise when someone is perceived to violate our social expectations about the way women and men are supposed to behave. Sociologists call these expectations **gender roles**, and they are the key to understanding what may well be the most basic inequality in contemporary society.

GENDER ROLES

Like actors on the stage, each of us plays many roles. The list is almost endless—parent, child, student, worker, pedestrian, automobile driver, shopper, consumer. Gender roles are assigned to us on the basis of our biological sex. (Although the terms are not always used consistently, sex usually refers to biological characteristics and gender to social characteristics.) These roles contain sets of expectations for both what we are supposed to do and what we are not supposed to do. A woman who spends hours coloring her hair and applying just the right makeup before going out meets our gender role expectations; a man who does the same thing violates those expectations.

Gender roles are assigned early in life. Children quickly learn that they are girls or boys and act accordingly. Nevertheless, adult gender roles are complex, involving both personality and behavioral characteristics. Women are traditionally expected to be passive, warm, and supportive. In contrast to men, who are expected to suppress their feelings, women are encouraged to express emotions openly. Men are supposed to be active, independent, and self-controlled, while women are thought to be more dependent and in need of emotional support. A man's role centers around his work and his responsibilities as breadwinner and provider of financial security. The traditional role of women, on the other hand, is to run the home and rear the children.

The movement of women out of the home and into the workplace has shaken the old notions about the natural differences between the sexes. In the past, people who did not fit the expectations for their gender were shunned and ridiculed. Today, some argue that the healthiest individuals display both strong masculine and strong feminine characteristics and that the new ideal should therefore be a single **androgynous** one combining traits traditionally assigned to both genders.[1] Others hold that the distinction between masculine and feminine characteristics is harmful and should be abandoned altogether.[2] Nonetheless, these traditional roles and stereotypes are still a powerful force in our society, and their consequences will be with us for a long time to come.

NATURE OR NURTURE?

Where do gender roles come from? Why do we see such differences in the way men and women act? As with so many other issues in the social sciences, the answers to such questions reflect the long-running debate about the relative importance of nature (biology) and nurture (learning) in human behavior.

The two most significant biological differences between the sexes are clearly the greater size and strength of the male and the female's ability to bear and nurse children. In most physical contests, males have a clear advantage. Not only is the average male taller than the average female, but testosterone, a male sex hormone, promotes muscular development and strength. The female, of course, has a much closer biological tie with the process of reproduction. Childbearing is the exclusive domain of the female; and before the development of baby bottles, only the mother (or another lactating woman) could feed a child for the first months of its life. Because a sexually active woman in an agricultural society will become pregnant about once every two years without the use of contraceptives, the average woman in such societies was either pregnant or nursing a small child during most of her adult life.[3]

Despite the male's advantage in physical strength, females are clearly the healthier sex. Males are subject to a variety of sex-linked genetic defects, including hemophilia and color blindness. They are also more susceptible to some diseases, and they mature more slowly than females. Although slightly more male infants are born, their rate of death is significantly higher, and females have longer life spans in all modern societies.[4]

The relationship between sex hormones and behavior is a complex and controversial issue. Numerous researchers have attempted to show that male hormones are linked to such things as aggression and dominance, female hormones to mothering and nurturing behavior. Studies have been conducted of children exposed to high levels of male hormones in the womb because of a hereditary defect in the function of the adrenal gland (adrenogenital syndrome) and of children exposed to high levels of a female hormone (progesterone) given to mothers because of difficulties in pregnancy. In

Changes in lifestyle have significant effects on physique. Muscular strength used to be considered "unfeminine," but such attitudes are now changing.

general, these studies have found girls exposed to male hormones to be more "masculine" and males exposed to female hormones to be more "feminine." However, the interpretation of these results is far from clear. The cause of the lower levels of aggression and physical activity in the "feminized" boys may have been their mothers' problems during pregnancy and not the drug prescribed to deal with those problems. Similarly, the "masculinized" behavior of girls with adrenogenital syndrome may have been the result of cortisone (a drug that can cause hyperactive behavior in adults) often given these girls by their physicians, or it may have been the result of the expectation of parents and friends that they will be more masculine than other girls (at birth their genital organs may appear to be those of a male).[5]

Other researchers have sought to demonstrate a causal link between high levels of the male hormone testosterone and aggressive behavior in adult men, but such studies have produced mixed results. Some have shown a significant relationship between high levels of testosterone and aggression and hostility, but most have not. Even if a correlation between the two were clearly established, however, it would not prove that the hormone causes aggression. Numerous studies have indicated that testosterone levels are strongly affected by an individual's environment and emotional state. For example, researchers have found that a man's testosterone level goes up after he wins a tennis match and goes down after he loses one. Moreover, the practice of castrating prisoners or giving them drugs that neutralize male hormones has proved to have little effect in preventing violence.[6]

One of the most recent areas of interest is the difference in structure in female and male brains. Although there is a slight difference in average brain size and weight, most of the attention has focused on a difference in neural pathways originally discovered by two anthropologists who conducted autopsies on 14 human brains.[7] What they found was that a portion of the corpus callosum that connects the two hemispheres of the brain is, on the average, larger in women's brains than in men's brains. Although some scientists have used this structural difference to explain various differences in behavior between the sexes, at this point there is not enough evidence to say what, if any, impact differences in brain structure may have on actual behavior.

If gender roles are determined solely by biology, it is logical to assume that they should be the same in all cultures. Researchers agree that some degree of male dominance is a characteristic of most known societies.[8] Anthropological studies have shown, however, that there are enormous differences in the gender roles of different cultures, and historians have found that gender roles change within the same culture over time. For example, in many foraging societies (small societies in which people make their livings by gathering food from the land), both men and women are peaceful and cooperative. In other societies, such as the Mundugumor of New Guinea, both men and women are highly aggressive and competitive.[9]

Further evidence against the biological determination of gender comes from the study of people who have been raised as members of the opposite sex. This usually occurs because of a physical abnormality of the genitals, but it occasionally happens for other reasons as well. The general conclusion from this research is that a woman raised as a man will act like a man and that a man raised as a woman will act like a woman.[10] In other words, people act the way they are taught to act; their behavior is not predetermined by a biological program.

Two conclusions seem justified from the evidence. First, gender roles themselves are social creations. The gender roles we learn are determined by society, not by biology. Second, the gender roles that society creates are nonetheless strongly influenced by biological considerations. Men tend to be stronger and larger than women, and only women can bear and nurse children, so it is not surprising that men are assigned more activities that involve strength and travel or that women are more concerned with child rearing and the responsibilities of the home. The typical pattern of male dominance can be seen as a result of the greater physical strength of the male. The typical "family-oriented" female pattern can be seen as a consequence of childbearing and breast-feeding. As we will see in the next section, however, the influence of these biological considerations has been greatly diminished in modern industrial societies.

THE HISTORICAL DEVELOPMENT OF GENDER ROLES

Throughout human history, the roles of women and men have been shaped by the demands of their environment and their economic system. In the earliest societies, people lived in nomadic bands and got their food by gathering edible plants and by hunting animals. Judging by the foraging societies that still survive today, it appears that these early human cultures were highly egalitarian, with few fixed distinctions of status or wealth. Leaders would emerge in response to specific problems and then be absorbed back into the groups when the problems were solved. The economic contribution of both men—who did most of the hunting—and women—who focused more on gathering and child care—were essential to the survival of the group. Although some anthropologists feel that men's monopoly on the hunting of large animals gave them a source of prestige not available to women,[11] others hold that women provided other services of equal social value.[12] Despite such disputes, anthropologists generally agree that the relationships between the sexes, like other relationships in foraging societies, tended to be egalitarian.

A major change in human society occurred with the discovery that plants could be grown specifically for human use. In the earliest farming societies, women and men often shared the work of cultivating the fields, while women did most of the child rearing and men fought the wars (foragers generally do not engage in warfare). As farming technology was improved by irrigation and the use of the plow, men's responsibility for agricultural labor increased, and the status of women generally declined. The growth of the state further strengthened male dominance as men came to monopolize government and religious bureaucracies.[13]

The industrial revolution once again brought profound changes in human society and in the relationship between the genders. The ideal of the large extended family declined, and the nuclear family became the norm (see Chapter 3). Economic changes that rendered children a financial burden instead of an asset led to lower birthrates and a smaller number of children. Industrialization reduced the importance of physical labor, and women joined the workforce in increasing numbers.

This transformation of the family and the economic system had a significant impact on gender roles. Technological and social development sharply reduced the importance of the biological differences between the sexes; therefore, gender roles changed as societies industrialized. The male's greater size and strength meant much less in an age of machines and automation. The qualities necessary for economic success were related more closely to personality and intelligence than to physique and these qualities were possessed equally by women and men. At the same time, birth control, smaller families, bottle feeding for babies, and the great increase in life span meant that child rearing no longer took up most of a woman's adult life. Though there have been significant improvements in the status of women in industrial societies, cultural change lags behind technological change. The ideal of equality between men and women has gained increasing acceptance in the industrialized nations, yet the realities of women's lives still often include subordination and oppression.

GENDER SOCIALIZATION

Socialization is the process by which we learn the essentials of life in our culture. Customs, behavior, mores, values, how to speak, even how to think—all these are learned in the course of socialization. **Gender socialization** is part of this process. It is the way we learn the behavior and attitudes that are expected of the members of our sex. **Sexual stereotyping** starts almost from the moment of birth, when boys are wrapped in blue blankets and girls in pink ones. Girls' and boys' bedrooms are often decorated differently and contain different kinds of toys.

Gender role socialization begins almost from the moment of birth. As children grow older, boys are encouraged to develop "masculine" attributes, while girls are taught "feminine" qualities. By the time most people reach adulthood, gender role socialization has produced significant differences between women and men.

Researchers have found that boys are given a wider variety of toys than girls and that boys' toys are more likely to encourage activities outside the home.[14] The most important differences, however, are learned as children begin to master a language. For one thing, most languages require the speaker to make frequent distinctions between the sexes. The use of the words he and his or she and hers continually draws the child's attention to the importance of gender differences. In addition, the structure of languages conveys social assumptions about the nature of the differences between the sexes. The English-speaking child quickly learns that the male is given first-class status, while the female takes second place. For example, masculine pronouns and adjectives are traditionally used to describe people whose gender is unknown (e.g., "No person shall be compelled in any criminal case to be a witness against himself"). The term *man* or *mankind* is often used to refer to the entire human race. The male is primary in our language, the female a vaguely defined "other."[15]

As children get older, different expectations for boys and girls become even more obvious. The male role is more narrowly defined, and young boys come under intense pressure not to be "sissies" and not to "act like a girl." A boy who playfully puts on a dress and lipstick is likely to receive a hostile and even panicky reprimand from his parents. One root of these attitudes is the deep-seated **homophobia** (fear of homosexuality) in Western culture; another is the general devaluation of women's roles. Some argue that the training boys receive to repress their feelings of love for other males eventually leads to a repression of all emotional expression, and there is little doubt that most boys learn at an early age to reject and even fear the feminine.[16] With the coming of adolescence, however, it is girls who find their lives increasingly restricted by the demands of their gender role. While boys are allowed and even encouraged to "sow some wild oats," girls are usually denied such freedom. Not only are girls far more closely watched, but they quickly learn that appearing too assertive is believed to make them less attractive to the opposite sex and may threaten their prospects for marriage and a traditional family life.

From their earliest years, girls are taught the vital importance of personal relationships, and they are encouraged to develop the traits that promote them: empathy, expressiveness, and sensitivity to others. Boys, on the other hand, are urged to be self-reliant, assertive, and achievement-oriented. The results of this differential socialization are reflected in the relationships that girls and boys create. Girls tend to have fewer, more intense friendships, whereas boys form larger, less intimate groups.[17]

Boys generally have more trouble adjusting to school than girls. Boys mature more slowly, so they are often less able to live up to the expectations of the school than are girls of the same age. Since boys are given more encouragement to be independent and assertive, they also tend to find the docile, cooperative behavior expected of schoolchildren far more frustrating. As a result, boys are more likely to get into trouble in school.[18] Perhaps for this reason, studies of teacher-student interaction have found that boys get more attention, both positive and negative, than girls. As Myra Sadker and her associates put it, "Boys are the central figures . . . and girls are relegated to second-class participation."[19]

Research shows that teachers' expectations have a powerful influence on the way students perform in the classroom (see Chapter 4). This fact creates a serious problem for girls because most teachers accept the gender stereotypes so common in our society. Teachers expect a good male student to be active, adventurous, and inventive, whereas they expect a good female student to be calm, conscientious, and sensitive.[20] Several studies have concluded that teachers pose more academically challenging questions to boys, are more likely to praise them for the intellectual quality of their work, and are more likely to encourage their classroom participation.[21] Researchers have found that the content of books and classroom materials has improved considerably in the use of gender-neutral language and in the inclusion of more female characters, but boys are still more likely to be given the active, adventurous roles.[22]

The mass media also have a profound effect on the definition of our gender roles. Many studies show that television, movies, radio, books, and magazines all tend to reinforce gender stereotypes. Children's television programs, which are particularly important in the early socialization process, reflect the same stereotyped attitudes. Male characters are shown in such active and prestigious occupations as physicians, lawyers, and police officers, while women are more likely to be relegated to secondary roles such as mother, secretary, or helper. Commercials also reflect these biases. J. H. Feldstein and S. Feldstein found that boys are overrepresented in advertisements for every type of toy except dolls and that the girls who are shown are far more likely to be given only passive roles.[23] A recent advertising survey of the parenting magazines *Child* and *Parents* indicated that all of the boys shown were in an active role, and in every advertisement where a girl is shown, she is in a passive pose.[24] Even children's cartoons are stereotyped. One study found that male cartoon characters outnumbered female characters by three to one;[25] but beyond simply showing more males, the cartoons depict males as being more powerful and having a greater impact on their environment than females do.[26]

Of course, sexist stereotypes are not limited to children's television. The advertising aimed at adult audiences reveals the same bias. Women are used to attract attention to the sales pitch—perhaps wearing a bikini while sipping a drink, wearing a silk gown while slithering into a sports car, or staring seductively at a man who uses the right brand of cologne. The prime concern of the "good housewife" is the whiteness of her wash and whether she can see her face reflected in her dinner plates. In contrast, male voices are often used to convey authority and importance.[27]

Another concern is the powerful influence the media has on our ideals of what an attractive body is, and the devastating effects unrealistic expectations have on the self-esteem of many women and girls. In 1995, television was introduced to the island of Fiji. While "you've gained weight" had previously been a compliment in that society, only three years after the introduction of television to the island, the number of teenagers at risk for eating disorders more than doubled. In one study 74 percent of the teenaged girls surveyed said they felt "too big or too fat," and 62 percent said they had dieted in the past month. The Fijian girls who were frequent viewers of television were 50 percent more likely to describe themselves as fat and 30 percent more likely to diet than the girls who didn't watch as much television.[28]

The same stereotypes are found in prime-time entertainment as well. Despite an increasing number of well-placed female characters, a long-term study by the Annenberg School of Communications found that women are still greatly underrepresented on television.[29] On the average, the characters played by women are younger and therefore less authoritative than male characters.[30] Research shows that in addition to being young, female characters are disproportionately likely to be thin, attractive, and blonde. In fact, one study found that women on television were twice as likely to be blonde as the average American woman.[31]

Music videos, which have become so popular in recent years, are a new subject of research interest. The original research on this subject agreed that music videos reflected the "chauvinism of rock culture."[32] Women were shown primarily as sex objects—often scantily dressed and acting provocatively. The videos were also full of violence, usually by men against other men. One departure from the usual stereotypes was that when women were involved in violence, they were more often shown as the aggressors than the victims. Nonetheless, the overwhelming message was that women are sexual objects, not complete human beings. The recent popularity of a new style of band with strong, independent female members has led to a new approach in music videos as well. Although still containing a heavy sexual content, this alternative style shows women controlling their lives and sexuality and depicts women's experiences in a more positive light.[33] The alternative video remains just that, however, and most videos continue to focus on women as sex objects. It seems clear, despite some serious efforts at reform, that the media—children's programs, prime-time entertainment, movies, and music videos—still play a powerful role in socializing both women and men into traditional gender role expectations.

QUICK REVIEW

What are gender roles?
What part do biology and learning play in creating our gender roles?
How do gender roles differ in different types of societies?
What forces shape gender socialization?

SEXUAL ORIENTATION

Traditional gender roles also have strict expectations about our **sexual orientation**—the sex (or sexes) to which we are attracted. In Western culture, the "normal" female was supposed to be attracted only to males and vice versa, and those who engaged in **homosexuality** (sexual relationships with members of the same sex) or **bisexuality** (sexual relationships with members of both sexes) were often brutally punished. Like many other aspects of our traditional gender roles, however, this condemnation of everything but **heterosexuality** (sexual relationship with members of the opposite sex) is coming under increasing challenge. There is, moreover, the same kind of debate raging about whether sexual orientation is learned or hereditary as there is about other types of gender behavior.

NATURE OR NURTURE?

Until recently most social scientists believed that we learned our sexual orientation as part of the process of gender socialization. Classical psychoanalytic theory views homosexuality in males as the result of an excessively close relationship with the mother and a distant and rejecting father. Several empirical studies have found that **gay** (homosexual) males are indeed more likely to experience paternal rejection than heterosexual males. Surveys also show that **lesbians** (female homosexuals) report much more fear and hostility toward their fathers than heterosexual women.[34] However, it seems quite possible that this parental rejection is the *result* of the sexual orientation of the children, not the *cause*. In one of the few long-term studies of the same group of subjects, psychiatrist Richard Green found that a homosexual orientation begins long before adolescence and so might easily contribute to early parental rejection. Three-fourths of the "feminine" boys he studied went on to homosexual lives as adults, while only one of the "masculine" boys became involved in homosexual activity.[35]

Sociologically, homosexuality is explained by examining the conditions in which it is learned. Given the enormous range of sexual behaviors in the cultures of the world, it would actually be much harder to explain the absence of homosexuality in diverse societies, such as those of the United States and Canada, than to explain its presence. Although there is a strong social condemnation of homosexuality, it is actually encouraged in many other ways. For instance, when adolescents first begin to feel strong sexual urges, society forbids them to engage in heterosexual intercourse. Young males and females are not permitted to sleep or shower together, but these activities are acceptable for members of the same sex. The encouragement of marked gender differences, combined with the pressures of mate selection, may make association with the same sex less painful and embarrassing than association with the opposite sex. Some adolescents can carry on homosexual activities without arousing the suspicion of their parents, when heterosexual activities would be out of the question. Further, the widespread belief that one is either homosexual or heterosexual often causes individuals who engage in exploratory homosexual behavior to define themselves as homosexuals. Once such a self-concept takes hold, it is likely to persist, perhaps for a lifetime.

There is also evidence that we are born with a biological predisposition toward one sexual orientation or another. Since most people are heterosexual, researchers have tended to focus on the question of why homosexuals differ from the majority. Some evidence indicates that there may be a biological predisposition to homosexuality. One source of support for this contention comes from studies of twins. Numerous investigations have found that identical (one-egg) twins are more likely to show the same sexual preference than fraternal (two-egg) twins.[36] However, the problem with such studies is that identical twins are more likely to be treated alike by family and friends; thus, their similarities may be the result of environment, not heredity. A study published in 1993 found that gay men had a disproportionately large number of gay relatives on their mothers' side of their family, but not their fathers'—a pattern typical of hereditary characteristics such as color-blindness that are carried on the X (female) chromosome. In fact, those researchers believe they have found the general area on the X chromosome (but not the specific gene) that carries the predisposition for homosexuality.[37] Other support for the biological theory comes from Simon LeVay and several other researchers who have found some differences in brain structure between those who are homosexual and those who are not.[38] Despite such new evidence, however, there is little to suggest that homosexuality is entirely determined by biological factors. For example, biological theories do not explain satisfactorily the significant differences in the extent of homosexuality in various cultures and in various time periods, or the reasons some people are homosexual during one period of their life and heterosexual during others.[39]

THE GAY AND LESBIAN COMMUNITY

There is considerable disagreement about how common homosexuality actually is. The original Kinsey study found that about 10 percent of American men were mainly homosexual, and that figure has often been cited through the years. However, it is highly doubtful that Kinsey's figures are accurate, since he used prisons as a source of subjects, and prisoners are obviously more likely to engage in homosexual behavior than men who are allowed normal contact with women. It seems more likely that somewhere between 1 and 4 percent of American men are primarily or exclusively homosexual. For example, a federally funded study by the Guttmacher Institute released in 1993 found that 2.3 percent of men had engaged in homosexual activity in the last 10 years, and 1.3 percent said that they were exclusively homosexual. The National Health and Social Life Survey conducted by a team of researchers from the National Opinion Research Corporation found that 2.7 percent of its male respondents and 1.3 percent of its female respondents reported a homosexual experience in the last year.[40] Almost all the surveys are consistent in showing less homosexuality among women. Most estimates indicate that women are only about half as likely as men to engage in homosexual acts.[41] There is, nonetheless, anecdotal evidence that lesbianism has become increasingly popular among young college-educated women in recent years.

In the past, most homosexuals were forced to conceal their sexual preference, but an increasing number of gays and lesbians are now "coming out" and openly declaring their sexual orientation.

Unlike many other minorities, homosexuals can conceal their differences from the public if they choose to do so. There is even a common slang term—the "closet queen"—for gay men who disguise their sexual preference and pass as heterosexuals. Such deception creates great emotional stress, however, and discovery and possible blackmail are a constant danger. In recent times, there has been a growing trend among homosexuals to "come out of the closet" and openly participate in the homosexual community. **Coming out** means more than just publicly admitting one's homosexuality, however; it also means admitting it to oneself, and the powerful stereotypes condemning homosexuals in our society can make that extremely difficult.

In the past, gay and lesbian communities were largely hidden from public view, but they are now an acknowledged part of urban life throughout North America. Like many ethnic communities, the gay and lesbian communities provide a variety of services for their members. Perhaps most important is the supportive social environment that allows gays and lesbians to be themselves without fear of condemnation by the outside world. Clubs, restaurants, and bars that cater to homosexuals are important to life in the gay community. They are places for socializing and relaxing, and they serve as a place to meet people with the same sexual orientation. Some cities even have gay and lesbian "yellow pages" that help homosexuals patronize businesspeople and professionals from their own community.

There is a common belief that homosexuals are more likely to have a high income and be well educated than the general population, but few reliable data support such claims. It does, however, appear that gay couples have a higher average income than heterosexual couples; also it is generally agreed that gays and lesbians are more likely than others to live in big cities where it is easier to escape the prejudice against them. Homosexuals also tend to be more liberal politically, since many conservatives are openly hostile to the gay community. An exit poll of voters in the 1992 presidential election found that two-thirds of those who identified themselves as homosexuals said they were Democrats, a much higher proportion than in the overall population.[42]

Gays and lesbians share many common problems created by the prejudice against them, but their sexual attitudes reflect some of the same differences that exist between heterosexual men and women. Many studies show that gay men are more likely to have numerous sexual partners, while lesbians are more likely to form sexually exclusive couples. One thing gay and lesbian couples do share is a greater tendency toward egalitarianism, perhaps because both partners have undergone a similar pattern of gender socialization.[43]

Starting in the 1960s, homosexuals began making steady progress against the hatred and prejudice so often directed against them. The AIDS epidemic among gay men has, however, dealt a severe blow to efforts to liberate the homosexual community from the centuries of bigotry it has faced. Irrational fears that one might catch that fatal disease from casual contact with homosexuals led to a new wave of hostility and even violence toward gays. At the same time, gays themselves have come to live with the fear that any new sexual contact might lead to a fatal experience—or the even more frightening thought that they may already have an undetected case of the disease. Not surprisingly, the AIDS epidemic has produced major changes in behavior among male homosexuals. Many "bathhouses," which served as sex clubs, have been closed, and there has been a sharp decline in casual sexual contact. The frightening toll of the AIDS epidemic also helped galvanize the gay community into a new sense of awareness and solidarity. Even though the rate of infection is much lower among female homosexuals, the lesbian community has rallied to the support of AIDS sufferers. As a result, the gay and lesbian communities have shown considerably more solidarity in recent years than they did in the past.

QUICK REVIEW

What are the main theories about the origins of our sexual orientation?
What is the gay and lesbian community like?

DISCRIMINATION AND INEQUALITY

In many ways, our culture's network of gender roles and gender expectations is highly unjust. Women are victims of **sexism** (the belief that there are fundamental differences between the sexes that justify active discrimination) in much the same way that African Americans are victims of racism. Gays and lesbians are the targets of even more frequent and more vicious attacks, and even heterosexual men often suffer from the rigid expectations our culture places on them. Although it is true that there have been real improvements in recent times, these problems remain deep and profound.

GENDER DISCRIMINATION

In Western society, traditional male and female roles are not only substantially different but also highly unequal. As we have seen, the male is given the dominant position. In a sense he is the star actor, whereas the female often plays only a supporting role. The male is expected to have superior strength, greater stamina, higher intelligence, and better organizing ability. Psychologically, the male is trained to play the role of decision maker, whereas the female is encouraged to be submissive and obedient. This same **gender inequality** is reflected in our basic institutions. In education, employment, religion, and politics, women clearly are treated as inferiors.

Education   In the past, women faced open discrimination in almost every aspect of our educational system. Far more boys than girls were enrolled in primary and secondary schools, and most of the best colleges did not admit women at all. Changing cultural expectations and new antidiscrimination laws broke down most of these barriers, and great progress has been made. Today, more females than males graduate from high school and from college. As we saw in Chapter 4, for the 25- to 29-year age group, 26.8 percent of men have completed a four-year college degree or more compared to almost 30 percent of women.[44]

Yet men still retain some important educational advantages. For one thing, men receive 60 percent of professional degrees and doctorates.[45] There are also important differences in the majors women and men pursue. As we saw in Chapter 4, the past decade has shown a large increase in women who are majoring in fields such as computer science and biology. Still, more women major in the liberal arts and humanities, while more men major in science, mathematics, and engineering—fields most likely to lead directly to high-paying careers. Although the reasons for these differences are not entirely clear, several factors appear to be important. It seems that traditional gender-role stereotypes no longer stop females from pursuing an education, but women are discouraged from going into academic areas that are overwhelmingly dominated by males. For example, one study shows that the lack of female role models among faculty members in mathematics, science, and engineering subtly conveys the message to young women that those fields are not for them.[46] Women's preference for a more general liberal education may also reflect the fact that because women expect to carry more child-rearing responsibilities than their male counterparts, they may shy away from majors leading to demanding careers that would interfere with those responsibilities.

Employment   Women's role in the workforce has undergone a remarkable change. Sixty years ago, fewer than one-fourth of all adult women in the United States worked outside the home. Today, that figure has almost tripled, and the number of working women continues to increase.[47] Currently, almost 60 percent of U.S. women are in the labor force, compared to 53 percent in Canada, 50 percent in Britain, 53 percent in Sweden, 47 percent in Japan, and only about 30 percent in Italy.[48]

Although the gap between men's and women's pay has narrowed in recent years, there is still a large gap (see Figure 8.1). In 1975, women earned only about 60 percent as much as men, but by 2000 that figure was around 74 percent.[49] Unfortunately, the gap has closed mainly because of a decline in men's earnings rather than an increase in women's pay. An analysis by the Economic Policy Institute concluded that about two-thirds of the improvement was caused by a drop in men's wages and only one-third of the improvement actually reflected rising women's wages.[50]

Many women receive smaller paychecks than men because women enter lower-paying occupations and hold lower-ranking jobs within their fields (see Figure 8.2). The secretary seldom becomes a top executive or the nurse a doctor. Although there are now far more women in middle management, they remain more likely to be in dead-end positions (such as administering affirmative action programs or supervising the hiring process) than in the production and financial posts that lead to the top corporate jobs. Yet there are substantial differences in pay even among men and women who do the same type of work. Women in sales earn only about 45 percent as much as salesmen, and women professionals earn about 62 percent as much as their male counterparts.[51] Even with the same level of education, men consistently earn more than women. In 2000, the median income for males with only a high school degree was $27,666 compared to $24,967 for women. With a bachelor's degree, the median income for males went up to $49,178 compared with $35,408 for women.[52] After years of progress, about 2.8 percent of women are in top corporate positions in the United States compared to 3.3 percent of men.[53] Still, many successful women complain about an invisible "glass ceiling"—a kind of unseen barrier that seems to block them from rising to the top levels of power. A survey of female attorneys in the Los Angeles area, for example, found that 60 percent felt they received less-desirable case assignments than their male colleagues, and 75 percent felt they were held to a higher standard than the men.[54]

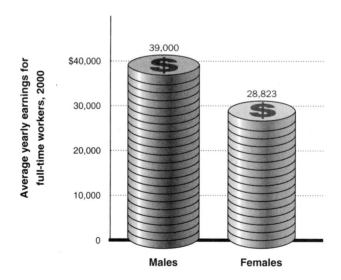

FIGURE 8.1   THE INCOME GAP

Working women still earn significantly less than men.

Source: U.S. Bureau of the Census, *Money Income in the United States*, 2000 (Washington, DC: U.S. Government Printing Office, 2001), Table 7.

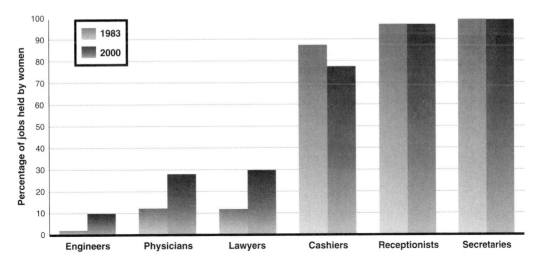

FIGURE 8.2   WOMEN AT WORK

Although the percentage of women in the professions has been increasing, most female workers are still concentrated in the lower-paying, less-prestigious jobs.

Source: U.S. Bureau of the Census, *Statistical Abstract of the United States,* 2001 (Washington, DC: U.S. Government Printing Office, 2001).

Employers traditionally justified such inequalities by claiming that men need higher pay because they must support their families and that women just work for "extra" money. Few employers openly use such rationalizations anymore, but they nonetheless persist in paying women lower wages. Some economists explain this income gap by pointing out that the average male worker has more years of experience than his female counterpart. Others argue that women are more likely to put the demands of their families ahead of their jobs. A *Time* magazine poll, for example, found that a happy marriage was the single most important goal for most young women, while young men rated career success as their number one objective.[55] Yet although such things are significant, sexism and discrimination are still extremely important factors. When researchers subtract the effects of the differences in education, type of job, and tenure on the job, the income gap is reduced but is still very significant.[56]

One hopeful sign for the future is that more and more college women are majoring in fields such as engineering, pre-law, and pre-med that used to be reserved almost exclusively for men. Indeed, there has been a significant increase in the percentage of women in all the professions. In 1983, only 5.8 percent of engineers were women, compared to 9.9 percent in 2000. For other professions the increases were 12.7 percent to 23.5 percent women in architecture, 15.8 percent to 27.9 percent among physicians, and 36 percent to 42 percent for university professors. However, the traditional "women's jobs" are still dominated by women. Women still make up 83.3 percent of elementary school teachers, 85.2 percent of librarians, 92.8 percent of nurses, and almost 72.4 percent of social workers—all lower-paying professions.[57] (See Figure 8.2)

Organized Religion   Organized religion throughout the world has usually (but not always) been a pillar of support for the patriarchal tradition. Both in religious doctrine and in church hierarchies, men have been given the position of power. Some Christians, following the story of Adam and Eve, place the blame for humanity's fall from grace and "original sin" on women. Christian-oriented organizations such as "The Promise Keepers" promote the position of males as the leaders of the family and the subordination of the wife to her husband's authority. In the Catholic Church, only males can be priests or high church officials such as bishops or the Pope. The Koran, the holy book of Islam, also gives men power and authority over women, for example, by allowing a man up to four wives, but limiting women to a single husband.

The problem is not simply that women are not given the opportunity to be leaders in many religious organizations—even though they are much more likely to participate in organized religion than men. Religion is also an important institution of socialization in our society. It helps teach children what is expected of them, and those expectations are very different for boys than for girls. The fact that young women are often taught to be a submissive "helpmate" to their husband may pave the way for them to accept their victimization in intimate relationships. When they turn to their religious elders for help, they are frequently counseled to forgive the abuser and to stay in the relationship. Studies show that women who turn to clergy for guidance stay longer with the men who have hurt them.[58] Paul Nejelski, an American judge, had this to say about his experiences on the bench:

> For me, in the last eight and a half years, (I have heard) thousands of cases. . . . Many involved violence against women. But certainly the most poignant were those where the violence was condoned or even encouraged in the name of religion. I wondered then, and I wonder now, at the institutionalized hatred for women found in parts of the major religions. Where religion should liberate and comfort, too often it is misused to enslave and torment women throughout the world.[59]

Yet despite such troubling problems, there have been many positive changes in recent decades. In many denominations, women are now being ordained as ministers or rabbis, and they are moving up into higher leadership roles. As the broader society has gained great awareness of how many women must endure violence and abuse in their home, many religious organizations are increasing the support they offer to battered women and changing the kind of counseling they give. In addition, there is a strong feminist movement within most organized religions that is working to change the gender inequalities that continue to exist.

Political Power   Politics has traditionally been considered a man's business. Women were not even allowed to vote in most democracies until the twentieth century. The few women who have gained top positions of power have often had the benefit of family connections to overcome objections to their sex: Pakistan's Benazir Bhutto, Sri Lanka's Chandrika Kumaratunga, and the hereditary European monarchs such as Britain's Queen Elizabeth II are good examples. The United States has never had a female head of state, and Canada's only woman prime minister, Kim Campbell, held that office for only about six months.

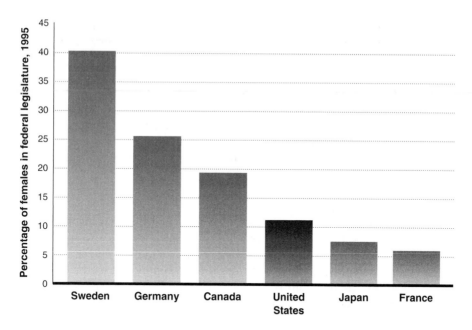

FIGURE 8.3   LAWMAKERS

Although the number of women lawmakers varies from year to year, the United States has never been among the leaders.

Source: United Nations Human Development Programme, *Human Development Report,* 1997 (New York: Oxford University Press, 1997), p. 152.

In 2001, only 13 women were in the U.S. Senate and 59 in the House of Representatives.[60] No woman has ever held a key position of power in the U.S. Congress, such as majority leader or speaker of the House, and women are still largely locked out of the inner circles of power in the White House—including, of course, the presidency itself. In the judicial branch, only two women in the history of the United States have ever been on the Supreme Court. Moreover, the story is much the same in other democratic nations. Women have the greatest representation in the Scandinavian countries and the lowest in France, the United States, and Japan, but they are greatly underrepresented in the legislative bodies of all the industrialized nations (see Figure 8.3).

Women nevertheless have enormous political potential. Most of the volunteer workers essential to political campaigns are women. Even more significant is the fact that women outnumber men and could outvote them if they voted as a bloc. Until recently, women voted much as their husbands did, but in the last decade, a significant "gender gap" between the voting patterns of men and women has developed. Polls show that women look more favorably on welfare programs and environmental protection and are more likely to oppose military spending and an aggressive foreign policy. In the last three presidential elections, substantially more women than men voted for the Democratic candidate. So far, the gender gap has not been a decisive factor in U.S. politics, but the potential is certainly there.

Social Life   Sexism in education, employment, and politics is obvious to anyone who cares to look. But women are also victims of less-conspicuous forms of discrimination that are woven into the fabric of our daily lives.

The Devaluation of Women   Women in our society are told in countless subtle ways that they are second-class citizens. Women are taught from childhood that beauty and sex appeal are the keys to happiness. Success comes not from their own efforts but from the ability to appeal to the "right man." Women are more likely to be admired as the wives and mothers of important people than as significant individuals in their own right.

Women are routinely expected to repress their desires and ambitions in ways that are seldom demanded of men. Studies of dual-earner families (in which both husband and wife work) reveal that it is usually the wife who must sacrifice her career if it interferes with that of her spouse. The working woman is also expected to carry more of the homemaking and child-rearing responsibilities in addition to her job.

Women are expected to repress their sexuality just as they are expected to repress their career ambitions. During the Victorian era, women's sexuality was almost entirely denied. Women were expected to keep themselves covered from their feet to their necks in what were often highly uncomfortable clothes. The "good" woman would never mention sex, and in fact, she was not even expected to enjoy it, but merely to put up with it for her husband's sake. Recent research shows that although the **double standard** for sexual behavior has weakened in recent years, it is still very much with us. Traditionally, young men were often expected to gain sexual experience before marriage, but women who do the same thing are condemned as "sluts." And those who berated an unfaithful wife often condoned a husband's infidelities with a wink.

Language and Communication   Until a few decades ago, no one seemed to pay much attention to the obvious inequity of calling the human race "mankind" or always using the masculine pronoun to refer to someone whose gender they did not know. Since then, feminists have made considerable progress in changing some of the most blatant linguistic inequalities. The use of gender-neutral terms such as police officer, humankind, and spokesperson has become far more common, and books are now more likely to use both masculine and feminine pronouns together or alternate between them. Nonetheless, our language continues to reflect (and thereby reinforce) the sexual inequalities of our society. Words associated with men tend to take on connotations of strength and power, while words associated with women are more likely to be linked with sex or family. Consider, for example, the difference between having a mistress and having a master or the difference between a governess and a governor.

More important than the words themselves, however, is the way they are used, and research on our patterns of communication reveals some striking gender differences. Studies of conversations between women and men reveal a clear pattern of male dominance. Men do more of the talking and interrupt women more often, and they are more likely to be successful in focusing the conversation on the topics they introduce.[61] Deborah Tannen argues that men and women also have different styles of communication and different objectives.[62] Women's conversations tend to have a more cooperative social character, while men are likely to be more competitive and individualistic. According to Tannen, men seek to dominate, while women seek to connect—a fact that she sees as underlying much of the misunderstanding between the genders.

Research shows that these same gender differences are also reflected in non-verbal communications. A man is more likely to invade a woman's personal space by touching her or standing close to her than the other way around. A man is more likely to stare at a woman, while the woman's response is often to avert her eyes. Research shows that, whether stared at or not, women smile at others more often than men.[63]

Sexual Harassment   The entry of women into the workforce in ever-greater numbers has focused attention on another kind of problem—**sexual harassment**. Since 1975, when the term was first used, a flood of complaints has come in from women who were the victims of unwanted sexual pressures at work. A survey of 13,000 federal employees found that 42 percent of the women reported experiencing some kind of sexual harassment on the job.[64] Even women in top executive jobs are not immune: One survey of women executives, whose salaries averaged almost $200,000 a year, found that 58 percent had faced sexual harassment on the job.[65] Sexual harassment has also become a major issue on campus; a growing number of students who have been the victims of unwanted sexual advances are recognizing their right to stand up and protest.

Although definitions of sexual harassment vary, it includes everything from unwanted sexual comments and gestures to direct physical assaults. There are two generally recognized types of sexual harassment. The first, which lawyers term *quid pro quo harassment*, includes sexual comments and advances aimed directly at a particular individual. This kind of harassment involves an implicit or explicit threat (e.g., loss of a job) if the victim doesn't go along, or a promise of a reward (e.g., a better grade) if the victim does go along. Obviously, a woman whose boss makes sexual advances is in a very difficult position. She must often choose between a physical relationship she does not want and a job she cannot afford to lose. The second type of sexual harassment is known as *hostile environment harassment*. This offense involves unwelcome sexual comments, gestures, explicit photographs, and other things that create an offensive or intimidating environment for female employees. This kind of harassment may be unintentional, or it may be part of an explicit effort by male employees to drive women out of jobs that they consider to be men's work.

Men's Problems   Women are not alone in suffering from gender stereotypes. Although the male role often has higher status, it is also more narrow and restrictive, and many men find the demand to repress natural "feminine" behavior a heavy burden. While women frequently complain about being only sex objects in the eyes of men, an increasing number of men are complaining that they are only "success objects" for women. Three-fourths of the young women, but only one-fourth of the young men, polled by *Time* magazine said that a well-paying job was an essential requirement for a spouse.[66] Obviously, three-fourths of all men do not have well-paying jobs. In fact, the income of the average man has dropped significantly in recent years, and the income of young men has been declining faster than that of any other group in our society.[67] Of course, men's incomes are still higher on the average, but these changes have placed enormous psychological pressure on many men, a pressure not felt by women. Success as a man has traditionally been defined by the ability to "bring home the bacon." The erosion of their incomes and their growing dependence on their wives' earnings to help make ends meet are therefore a serious blow to the self-esteem of many men. Not surprisingly, the suicide rate among men has shown a steady increase, and men are now over five times more likely than women to kill themselves.[68]

Another common complaint among men is that although they are being encouraged to take a greater role in child rearing, the deck is still stacked against them when it comes to child custody after a divorce. When both parents seek custody, many courts assume that the mother will make the better parent. Yet although the mother is usually given custody of the children, the father still has to pay to support them while being given only limited visitation rights. In addition, when the separation is a bitter one, many husbands complain that their wives have tried to turn their children against them.

Finally, the increasingly negative stereotypes of men have become a staple of the contemporary media. A study of 1,000 television commercials in which there was a negative portrayal of one side of a male-female interaction found that the male was cast as the "bad guy" in every case.[69] Today's media repeatedly stereotype men either as violent, sexually aggressive, and emotionally distant, or as fumbling nerds who are good for a laugh but not much else.

DISCRIMINATION AGAINST GAYS AND LESBIANS

No other minority group is subject to such open and blatant discrimination as gays and lesbians. One obvious reason for this is to be found in our legal system. Not only does the law fail to protect the basic civil rights of homosexual citizens in most states, but in many of them, homosexual activity between consenting adults is actually a crime. Historically, the Judeo-Christian tradition has condemned homosexuality as a vile sin, and lawmakers in Western nations have acted accordingly. During the Middle Ages, homosexuals were commonly tortured to death. In Britain, until 1956, homosexual activities were punishable by life imprisonment. The recent trend in the industrialized nations has, however, been toward greater tolerance. Britain repealed its most repressive laws in 1965, and most other European nations followed suit. Canada passed a law similar to Britain's in 1969, but some official harassment of homosexuals has persisted. The United States has lagged behind most other industrialized nations. Although a growing number of the states have legalized homosexual acts between consenting adults, many states still have **sodomy laws** (which forbid oral or anal sex), which threaten homosexuals with long terms of imprisonment. However, in states where homosexual activity remains a crime, the laws are not vigorously enforced. Only a few unlucky or unwise individuals are arrested, prosecuted, or punished. Moreover, the enforcement efforts that do take place are directed mainly against gay men. Lesbian activities are usually ignored.

Even where criminal penalties have been reduced or abolished, homosexuals nonetheless suffer from open legal discrimination. In some places the professions of law, medicine, and teaching are closed to homosexuals. The federal government of the United States openly discriminates against homosexuals in military service. After a major national controversy in the early 1990s, the U.S. military adopted the "Don't ask, don't tell" standard, which its supporters claimed was a major improvement for gays and lesbians in the military. In reality, the military continues its open discrimination against gays and lesbians under this new policy; it merely agreed not to fire homosexuals who keep their sexual orientation secret.

Another source of discrimination is the failure of the law to recognize same-sex marriages. This policy not only denies committed gay and lesbian couples the emotional satisfaction of having their bond officially recognized; more importantly, it denies them the right to tax breaks and health insurance benefits that are enjoyed by legally married heterosexual couples. In December 1996, a Hawaiian Circuit Court judge ruled that the state's law banning same-sex marriages was unconstitutional.[70] But this breakthrough was short lived. In 1999, a public referendum amended the Constitution to restore the ban on same-sex marriage. As of 2002, Vermont was the only state that allowed gay partners official recognition and many of the same rights as traditional married couples. Even there, however, such unions are still not legally defined as marriages. Underlying all these problems is the lack of legal protection for the basic civil rights of gay citizens, and thus employers and public organizations are allowed to discriminate against them openly.

The problems gays and lesbians face in our society, however, often go far beyond mere discrimination. No other group of this size is subject to the same kind of hatred and anger, which often lead to physical violence as well. A survey of 496 gay and lesbian youth from 12 to 19 found that over a third reported hearing homophobic remarks by the faculty or staff of their school and 40 percent said they did not feel safe in school.[71] Indeed, thousands of **hate crimes** (crimes directed at someone because of his or her ethnic group, gender, disability, or sexual orientation) are reported every year. Take the case of Matthew Shepard, a 21-year-old student at the University of Wyoming. On October 6, 1998, two motorcyclists found him tied to a fence in the country. His head and face had been slashed with a knife and his skull smashed in. The only reason for the brutal attack that ultimately cost Matthew his life was that he was gay. Then there was the case of Jack Gaither, who was beaten to death in February of 1999 by two Alabama men who claimed they were angry because Gaither had made a sexual advance toward them. In July of that year, the same story again unfolded in Alabama when Private First Class Barry Winchell was beaten to death with a baseball bat by another soldier because that soldier thought Private Winchell was gay.

QUICK REVIEW

How does our educational system discriminate against women?
Why do women receive lower pay and hold fewer political offices than men?
What kinds of sexism do women face in social life?
What problems do contemporary gender roles create for men?
How does our legal system discriminate against gays and lesbians?
What other kinds of discrimination and harassment do gays and lesbians face?

LESSONS FROM OTHER PLACES

GENDER INEQUALITIES AROUND THE WORLD

One of the most important things I have learned from spending time in other countries is the complexity of social arrangements. This is certainly the case with gender inequalities. We have seen that Germany has some of the best labor protection in the world, a low level of economic inequality, a short workweek, and extensive benefits from employers and the government. After living and working in Germany for a few months, however, I was surprised to find how women are disadvantaged in many ways when compared to American women. While unions and labor laws are strong, there is less legal protection for women in Germany. It is much more difficult to win a sexual harassment case, employers can specify that only men are to apply for job openings, and fewer women are in higher management positions than in the United States. There seem to be even more contradictions in Sweden. The pay gap between men and women is smaller in Sweden, and there are more women legislators. However, the "glass ceiling" keeping women from higher management positions appears to be stronger there.

Then there is the confusing situation among Asian nations. Women in Japan and South Korea certainly suffer from more obvious discrimination than women in the West. The gender pay gap is greater, and there are fewer women in high government and corporate positions. The vast majority of women who are employed outside the home are in jobs specifically categorized as "women's jobs," with little or no chance for advancement. Almost all of these jobs also require women to do traditional things, such as making and serving tea and coffee whenever they are asked to do so by men. (I must admit having some fun making tea and bringing it to women in my college office. I don't think it helped my standing with the older men, however!) I have seen college officials going through secretarial job applications and placing them in stacks according to how pretty the woman looked in the picture attached to the applications. All of this is quite legal.

On the other hand, Japanese women usually play a very powerful role in the family. During my first several months in Japan in the mid-1980s, I lived in a room rented from an upper middle-class family in Tokyo. Just as I had read about, the husband (a mid-level corporate executive) brought home his paycheck and his wife took it, and gave him a small weekly allowance. Businessmen know that women control the family finances in Japan, so, for example, stockbrokers try to sell stocks door-to-door when housewives are home. Major decisions about large purchases (such as a new car), investing money, or where children will be educated are made primarily by wives, not husbands.

After spending a couple of years in Japan I began spending more of my time away from the United States in Southeast Asia. Thinking I knew something about "Asia," I was surprised again. In my work in universities, most of the deans and university presidents I met were women. Conducting research on Japanese, American, and Thai corporations, I found that a very high percentage of top executives and board members of Thai corporations are women. Part of our research began to focus on how Japanese business executives in Thailand coped with having to do much of their business with women in top corporate positions!

One way to understand this complexity is to consider international rankings on gender inequalities, such as the United Nation's gender gap index. Some of the more interesting rankings are listed in the following table. The score for perfect gender equality is 0; negative numbers indicate how far women in each country are from gender equality in terms of such things as educational achievement, health conditions, income, and so forth.

COUNTRY	HDI* GENDER GAP	COUNTRY	HDI* GENDER GAP
Sweden	−5.7	Canada	−16.9
Norway	−9.9	Italy	−17.3
Denmark	−9.9	Austria	−17.9
Finland	−10.0	Germany	−19.7
New Zealand	−10.9	Switzerland	−21.5
France	−11.0	Japan	−22.4
Australia	−12.3	Singapore	−31.1
Netherlands	−14.8	Hong Kong	−32.3
Britain	−15.1	South Korea	−36.4
USA	−15.6		

*Human Development Index

There are some clear cultural groups in these rankings. The Scandinavian countries are all toward the top, the English-speaking countries are in the next group, with the German-language countries lowest among Western nations. The Asian nations ranked still lower. There are certainly many other factors that help make the mix of gender inequality a complex one around the world, but there are clearly some strong cultural forces at work.

—*Harold Kerbo*

Sources: Harold Kerbo, *Social Stratification and Inequality,* 4th ed. (New York: McGraw-Hill, 2000), Chapter 10; Harold Kerbo and Hermann Strasser, *Modern Germany* (New York: McGraw-Hill, 2000); Harold Kerbo and John McKinstry, *Modern Japan* (New York: McGraw-Hill, 1998); Robert Slagter and Harold Kerbo, *Modern Thailand* (New York: McGraw-Hill, 2000).

SOLVING THE PROBLEMS OF GENDER AND SEXUAL ORIENTATION

Like other social problems, an effective response to the problems of gender and sexual orientation must have many dimensions. On one level, we need to develop an understanding of the problems involved, and then we have to decide what needs to be done to improve things. But that is of little use unless we also join together and take political action to achieve those ends. Thus, sociological analysis and social action are intimately related. Effective social action must be based on an understanding of the problem. The results of that action will in turn provide information we can use to reformulate our plans and improve our understanding.

POLITICAL ACTIVISM

The problem of gender inequality has been the subject of intense debate in recent decades, but to understand the current controversy, we need to understand the history of the political struggles that created it. The beginnings of the women's movement in North America are usually traced to the nineteenth century with the drive to free the slaves. Many women who were involved in the abolitionist movement came to realize that they too were part of an oppressed group. These early feminists made wide-ranging demands for sexual equality, but the movement they created eventually came to focus on

The feminist movement has a long history in North America, dating back to the struggle for women's suffrage (the right to vote). Today's feminists are seeking complete equality between the sexes.

a single issue: women's right to vote. After years of struggle, these "suffragettes" built themselves into a powerful political force and won their battle for the vote; but after that success, the women's movement began to fade. It was not until the 1960s, when the civil rights movement was once again calling attention to the racial injustices of North American society, that the feminist movement was reborn.

The modern feminist movement has scored some remarkable successes. Women's liberation and sexual equality are now widely discussed, and more and more women are entering occupations that were formerly closed to them. Through effective court and legislative action, feminists have successfully attacked employment and promotion practices that discriminate against women. Government-sponsored programs now encourage employers to hire and promote more women and members of minority groups, and the overall gap between men's and women's pay has declined. Feminists have even made some inroads on the sexual biases built into the English language. Women now often identify themselves as Ms. rather than Miss or Mrs., and new sexually neutral words such as *chairperson* and *humankind* are replacing the traditional masculine terms. As we have seen in this chapter, however, we are still a very long way from full equality. The victories of the past have been won against the most obvious and direct forms of discrimination, and women must now face much more subtle forms of bias.

Although still much smaller and weaker, there is also a growing "men's movement" that has its own critique of today's gender problems. In general, the men's movement is sympathetic to the feminist perspective and its call to redefine gender relations. Advocates of the men's movement argue that current gender roles are just as harmful to men as they are to women, but in different ways. They particularly object to the ideal of masculinity that holds that "real" men must always be strong, self-controlled, and successful. The effort to live up to this impossible ideal (or at least to appear to live up to it) leaves many men feeling anxiety ridden and isolated. However, the men's movement does voice one major criticism of the feminists—what they see as their tendency toward "man bashing." That is, some supporters of the men's movement feel that feminists perpetuate negative stereotypes of men and blame men for problems that are actually created by historical forces beyond the control of any person or group.

Like feminists, the supporters of gay rights were also deeply influenced by the civil rights movement of the 1950s and 60s. They saw how much power oppressed people could wield if they banded together and demanded change. But unlike women and minorities, gays and lesbians had often been forced to hide their very existence. So as they saw the struggles other groups were waging to win their freedom, a growing number of gays and lesbians came "out of the closet" and courageously faced the bigotry and hatred directed against them. Gays and lesbians banded together to make t-shirts and banners and hold parades and demonstrations rejecting the bigotry directed against them, and proclaiming "gay pride." The supporters of gay rights also formed numerous political organizations and alliances to help them in their struggle. Today, there are literally dozens of different organizations in the gay rights movement, including the National Gay and Lesbian Task Force, the Gay and Lesbian Alliance against Defamation, the International Gay and Lesbian Association, Lambda Legal Defense and Education Fund, and the Gay, Lesbian, and Straight Educational Network.

FIGHTING DISCRIMINATION

Proposals for eliminating obvious discrimination against women often win wide support. Few people openly approve of such practices as paying women less money than men are paid for the same work, refusing to grant them financial credit or denying them jobs and promotions simply because they are women. The values of democratic society make it very hard to justify such practices, and many of the feminists' most important victories have been against this kind of discrimination.

As the most obvious forms of sexism are eliminated, however, the movement for social change must challenge more entrenched institutional structures, and further progress becomes increasingly difficult. For example, the law has long required employers to pay men and women the same wage for the same work, yet it remains perfectly legal to pay secretaries, nurses, and others in "women's jobs" far less than those in comparable jobs that are filled mainly by men. Proposals to require comparable pay for comparable work have run into fierce opposition because they threaten the interests of businesses that benefit from the low cost of women's labor. Although affirmative action programs, which force employers to take positive action to compensate for past injustices, have done much to combat gender discrimination in the last three decades, they too are meeting with increasing political opposition (see Chapter 7).

There are, nonetheless, several other useful ideas that have a wide base of support. Proposals to give tougher sentences to rapists and other sex offenders are extremely popular with the voting public, and the last two decades have already seen some significant increases in the average terms served by such offenders. The public is also far more aware of the physical abuse many women suffer from their spouses and boyfriends, and as public attitudes have changed, the approaches and priorities of the criminal-justice system have shown some significant improvements. Much more, however, remains to be done (see Chapter 10).

In today's political climate, women's greatest ally in the fight against gender discrimination is probably their own success. As more and more women hold key corporate and government positions, it is getting harder to practice the open discrimination that was the norm only a few decades ago. Many women are now banding together to form "old girls' networks" that in some cases rival or even surpass the "old boys' networks" from which women were traditionally excluded.

As we have seen, like many women and many ethnic minorities, gays and lesbians have also been organizing and demanding an end to such discrimination against them. But their task is an even harder one, since anti-gay discrimination is practiced completely openly, has wide public support, and is written into many state laws. Nonetheless, gay activists have won many victories. After a sustained debate, they persuaded the American Psychiatric Association to drop homosexuality from its list of mental disorders; television networks have been pressured to cancel programs that cast homosexuals in an unfavorable light; and boycotts have been launched against communities that have enacted antigay legislation. Starting with Wisconsin in 1983, activists have now been successful in winning passage of legislation banning employment discrimination against gays and lesbians in 12 states and well over 100 cities and counties including Los Angeles, Minneapolis, and

Seattle. Hawaii passed a bill allowing the partners in same-sex couples the same benefits as married couples in such areas as inheritance, worker's compensation, and health insurance, and Vermont has gone further in legally recognizing same-sex partnerships. Twenty-one states have enacted hate crime legislation that specifically protects gays and lesbians, and three others have laws that forbid crimes based on prejudice and bias without mentioning the specific categories of people to be covered. Pressure from the gay and lesbian community and its supporters have also been successful at getting many major corporations to add a ban on discrimination based on sexual orientation to their antidiscrimination policies. The majority of America's 500 largest corporations now have such policies, and the bigger and more successful the corporation, the more likely it is to have those policies in place.[72]

However, the movement has had its failures as well. The Hawaiian legislation just mentioned, for example, was passed along with a bill that put a constitutional amendment before the state's voters, which resulted in a ban on same-sex marriages. The U.S. Supreme Court has refused to forbid the prosecution and imprisonment of people for homosexual activities, even if those activities are conducted in private between consenting adults. Moreover, the gains of homosexual activists have often stirred counterattacks by religious fundamentalists, who have sponsored bills and constitutional amendments in several states prohibiting any legislation to protect gay people against discrimination.

CHANGING GENDER ROLES

Many feminists feel that despite its importance, fighting discrimination simply isn't enough to create real gender equality. As long as women and girls are socialized to be more supportive and compliant than men, they are likely to remain in subordinate positions with or without gender discrimination. And men who are socialized to be competitive, powerful, and always in control will continue to face the often devastating fear of failure they are bound to have since the ideal manhood taught to boys is unachievable. Yet proposals for restructuring gender roles have run into far greater opposition than those aimed at overt discrimination. Our attitudes and expectations about gender are formed early in life, and many people feel threatened when such basic assumptions are challenged. Many of the most vicious attacks on feminism can be seen as a response to this kind of insecurity. Despite the fear and hostility produced by rapid change, gender roles in industrial societies are nonetheless undergoing a revolutionary transformation.

The attitudes and assumptions parents bring with them into the family are one of the greatest forces shaping our gender role expectations, but social institutions such as schools, organized religion, and the media also play a critical role, and they are much more subject to social pressure. Although these institutions have made great strides in presenting powerful role models for women and girls, many of the old stereotypes still remain side by side with those new images. Stronger efforts to eliminate sexism in those social institutions are therefore critical to future success.

DEBATE

SHOULD WE CRACK DOWN ON SEXUAL HARASSMENT?

Yes

The problem of sexual harassment has reached crisis proportions, and we must take action before things get even worse. Sexual harassment is more than just the demeaning comments, the leering stares, and the snide remarks—although those are certainly bad enough. Every day countless women are pressured by their bosses, their male colleagues, or their teachers to engage in a sexual relationship against their will. Nobody knows how many women succumb to this pressure, but we do know the horrible consequences: anxiety, depression, fear, and plummeting self-esteem. Those women who hold out may not suffer as much psychological damage, but many pay for their integrity with the loss of a job or some other serious punishment.

Some claim that sexual harassment is inevitable in any society that allows free individuals to guide their own sexual behavior, but in fact just the opposite is true. Allowing people the freedom to make their own choices about their sexual behavior requires that we take strong action to end sexual harassment and coercion. Our society can never be free until women are free from this kind of degrading assault. We must end sexual harassment now, and only strong new laws and tough enforcement that treats the offenders like common criminals can do the job.

No

All the talk about sexual harassment is just the latest media fad. Of course, men sometimes say or do things that offend women, and women sometimes offend men. The fact is that in dating and sexual relationships, people inevitably have different goals, objectives, and dreams. Sometimes we experience unwanted sexual advances, and other times our own advances are rebuffed. Short of separating the sexes from all public contact and going back to arranged marriages, there is simply nothing we can do about it.

Of course, the government has a critical role to play in punishing rapists and other sex offenders, but it has already gone too far in trying to legislate away "sexual harassment." The current maze of rules and regulations in the workplace has already created an atmosphere of fear and suspicion. Male and female coworkers are often afraid to make a joke or to give a compliment or even a pat on the back. After all, how can one ever be sure that a friendly gesture won't be interpreted as an unwelcome sexual advance? One third-grader was even suspended from school for giving an innocent kiss to a classmate! The government has a vital role to play in many social problems, but when it intrudes into the most personal and private part of our lives, it is time to draw the line. Do we want to live in a free and open society or in a police state?

While it is impossible to say what roles will finally develop, there is no reason to suppose that sexual equality would mean that men and women would become socially identical. Some of the differences in behavior between men and women already have diminished, but the development of a "unisex" remains a prospect for the distant future, if at all. What does seem possible, perhaps even likely, is a further weakening of the rigid gender-role expectations of the past, allowing both women and men to act in ways that suit them as individuals instead of compelling them to conform to the stereotyped expectations for their genders.

Michael Kimmel, a leading researcher on masculinity, has this vision for the future of American manhood:

> The American manhood of the future cannot be based on obsessive self-control, defensive exclusion, or frightened escape. We need a new definition of masculinity for a new century, a definition that is capable of embracing differences among men and enabling other men to feel secure and confident rather than excluding them. A definition that centers around standing up for justice and equality instead of running away from commitment and engagement. . . . Profeminist men believe, as Floyd Dell wrote at the turn of the century, that "feminism will make it possible for the first time for men to be free."[73]

QUICK REVIEW

What are the best ways of responding to the problems created by discrimination based on gender and sexual orientation?

SOCIOLOGICAL PERSPECTIVES ON PROBLEMS OF GENDER AND SEXUAL ORIENTATION

THE FUNCTIONALIST PERSPECTIVE

Functionalists say that the problems with contemporary gender roles stem directly from the historical changes discussed earlier in this chapter. Traditionally, gender roles were based on biological differences between the sexes: Women were concerned primarily with child rearing and men with providing economic support. The changes brought on by the industrial revolution threw this arrangement out of balance, however. The decline in infant mortality and the spread of effective methods of birth control made it possible to depart from traditional roles. It was no longer necessary for women to devote most of their adult lives to the raising of children, and automation wiped out the importance of the male's greater strength for most types of work. However, attitudes and expectations about the proper role of women have changed much more slowly than social and economic conditions. This cultural lag is therefore the principal source of today's problems.

To resolve such difficulties, most functionalists suggest that expectations be made to conform more closely to actual conditions. Some advocate a return to the stable past, believing that too great a shift toward sexual equality is dysfunctional.

They argue that the traditional division of labor between men and women was highly efficient, enabling society to train people for specialized roles that meshed together in stable families. Other functionalists, however, advocate a redefinition of gender roles to bring them into line with current social conditions. Although these functionalists do not all agree on the exact form the proposed changes should take, they do generally accept the need for a shift toward full sexual equality and a reconstruction of women's roles to encourage economic competition and achievement. Along with this change, basic institutions would also have to be modified to eliminate sexual discrimination. The current family system, for example, would have to undergo extensive changes to accommodate new roles for both women and men.

Functionalists have generally had less to say about the discrimination against gays and lesbians. Functionalists do note that all societies have some kind of norms and standards that regulate sexual behavior. Although homosexual behavior is by no means universally condemned, where such norms do exist they have sometimes been held to function as a means to promote heterosexual behavior. The idea is that homosexual behavior is dysfunctional because unlike heterosexuality it does not lead to reproduction. However, given the huge problem of overpopulation the world is currently facing (see Chapter 12), it can also be argued that homosexuality is now actually a very functional way of limiting population growth.

THE CONFLICT PERSPECTIVE

Prejudice and discrimination against women come as no surprise to conflict theorists, since they see exploitation and oppression as universal human problems. Conflict theorists say that men first used their greater size and strength to force women into a subordinate position. Then, like any other dominant group, men created institutions that served to perpetuate their power and authority. Men gain economic advantages by paying women low wages and excluding them from positions of economic control and political power. Men also benefit from women's subordinate role in the family. The "good" woman, we are told, blindly serves her husband and obeys his will in the same way a domestic servant would. The traditional wedding vows reflect the strong social support for the subordination of women. Only the bride had to pledge to love, honor, and obey her spouse. Even the structure of our language serves to reinforce the belief in male dominance. Conflict theorists hold that the position of women in most societies today is similar to that of a subordinate ethnic minority, such as African Americans in the United States.

There are many indications, however, that the traditional male advantages are declining in importance. The superior strength of the male means little in a highly mechanized society. The real barriers to women's liberation are now the institutions and attitudes that were established in the days of unquestioned male dominance. An increasing number of women are coming to realize this fact, and they are organizing themselves to break these barriers. According to the conflict perspective, the feminist movement is thus both a reflection and a cause of the growing strength of women in industrial societies.

Conflict theorists see the oppression of gays and lesbians as a kind of cultural conflict. Supporters of the traditional norms that condemn homosexuality used to have unquestioned power and were able to openly practice the harshest kinds of discrimination and even to write their convictions into law. Those whose behavior differed from that of the dominant group were seen as criminals, harassed and abused in public, excluded from countless jobs and social activities, and often beaten or killed. Most gays and lesbians were forced to hide their sexual preference if they were to get by in the wider society. Today, as more and more homosexuals are openly admitting their sexual orientation and organizing themselves, they are gaining power and things are finally beginning to change. Conflict theorists advise all victims of oppression—whether it is because they are gays, lesbians, women, or ethnic minorities—to continue publicizing their grievances, and to join together in a unified movement. For the conflict theorist, social action is the road to social change and a just society.

THE FEMINIST PERSPECTIVE

Most feminists would agree with the conflict analysis given in the previous three paragraphs. In fact, conflict-oriented feminists were responsible for creating much of it, so there is no point in repeating it here. But although most feminists accept such a theoretical analysis, as in other social movements, there are significant differences among feminists about what to do now. Liberal feminists are the largest group in the movement, and their approach is the predominant one in groups such as the National Organization for Women (NOW). Drawing on the values of freedom and individual liberty that are central to the liberal tradition, these feminists call for a vigorous government attack on all forms of prejudice and discrimination: tougher legislation punishing discrimination in hiring and promotion, new initiatives against sexual harassment, legislation protecting gay rights, and longer sentences for rapists and other sex offenders. Liberal feminists also call for changes in the family, the schools, and the mass media so that people will no longer be socialized into rigid gender roles and narrow expectations about the proper sexual orientation, but will be allowed the freedom to follow their own unique individual paths. The liberal feminists nonetheless have their critics both inside and outside the movement.

Socialist feminists find common ground with many of the liberals in advocating a more generous and humane welfare system, but they also argue that the exploitation of women and sexual minorities arises from the capitalist system and that only fundamental changes in our economic institutions can liberate women. Thus, socialist feminists argue that it is necessary to do more than attack sexism. The racism and economic exploitation that lie at the root of the capitalist system must also be ended if we are to be truly free. Radical feminists, on the other hand, focus more on the social arena than the others, and they call for a "woman-centered" culture to replace the current pattern of **patriarchal** (male-dominated) homophobic society. To achieve this end, each woman must recognize her own value and strength and must band together with other women to reject the patriarchal system and create an alternative woman-based society.

THE INTERACTIONIST PERSPECTIVE

Interactionists see gender roles, sexual orientation, and the sense of identity we derive from them, as critical components of human personality. They are convinced that sexual identity develops in the early years of childhood in interaction with parents, peers, teachers, and the mass media. Once formed, these ideas and concepts are quite durable. Interactionists note that prejudice and discrimination against women and homosexuals arise from gender role socialization. Females are conditioned to be passive and dependent and are therefore less dominant than males, who are encouraged to be more aggressive and independent. Both sexes are often taught to see females as inferior and gays and lesbians as deviant.

Interactionists are convinced that gender roles and the inequality they promote can be changed if the process of socialization is changed. These theorists argue that girls should be encouraged to be more aggressive and that boys be urged to accept the passive, dependent side of their nature. Because parents have been socialized into traditional gender roles, persuading them to teach their children to behave differently is extremely difficult; but perhaps schools, which are an increasingly important influence in socialization, can be changed more easily. Feminists are already pressing to remove gender role stereotypes from schoolbooks and lectures and to promote higher educational and occupational aspirations for girls. The media have made some progress, but there is much more they could do to promote these changes. Showing men who do not live up to the code of heterosexual male dominance to be heroes equal to the "he-men" idealized in so many adventure films would be especially useful in promoting equality. Interactionists also hold that greater tolerance of human differences is desperately needed. No matter what characteristics and sexual orientation a culture attributes to the ideal woman or man, many people of both sexes will not live up to those standards. The nonconformist must often pay an enormous personal price for being a little different. There is no reason, aside from prejudice and bigotry, that society cannot recognize the full range of human diversity as a normal and healthy phenomenon.

QUICK REVIEW

What are the differences in the ways a functionalist and a conflict theorist see the problems of gender and sexual orientation?

What solutions do feminists recommend for the problems of gender inequality and discrimination based on sexual orientation?

What does the interactionist perspective say about gender inequality and sexual orientation?

SUMMARY

Gender roles (sets of expectations about the proper behavior for each sex) are basic components of individual personalities as well as of the larger social system. The male role has traditionally been centered on work and providing for the family. The male is expected to be more aggressive than the female and to have tighter control over his emotions. The female role has centered on child rearing and the family. Females are expected to be emotionally expressive, dependent, and passive. Gender roles show a wide range of variation among cultures, and in our culture, as in others, the behavior of many men and women does not fit the expected patterns.

Two important factors have influenced the development of gender roles: biology and culture. The fact that females bear and nurse children has had an obvious influence on the definition of gender roles, as has the fact that males tend to be larger and stronger than females. But gender roles are nonetheless cultural constants that vary greatly from one society to another. Some cultures assign what we consider "feminine" traits to both sexes, while others assign "masculine" traits to both.

In early foraging societies, relationships between men and women were generally egalitarian. With the coming of agriculture, the women's power declined because their contribution to food production was reduced. The economic and social conditions accompanying industrialization then neutralized many male advantages as mechanization made physical size and strength less important; and the sharp drop in infant mortality and the spread of birth control reduced women's child-rearing burdens.

Gender socialization is the process by which children learn the behaviors and attitudes expected of their sex. The family plays a critical role in this process. Parents begin treating boys and girls differently almost from the moment of birth. Schools reinforce the traditional gender roles learned at home. Teachers encourage high aspirations in boys and discourage them in girls. Radio, television, popular music, and motion pictures also convey sexual stereotypes.

The roles we assign to each sex clearly promote gender inequality, and the same inequality is reflected in our social institutions. Men are given the dominant position, and a variety of evidence reveals a clear pattern of discrimination against women in education, employment, politics, and social life.

Traditional gender roles also have strict expectations about our sexual orientation—the sex (or sexes) to which we are attracted. Contrary to popular belief, the differences among homosexuals, bisexuals, and heterosexuals are not absolute but are a matter of degree. Biological theorists feel that homosexuality is hereditary. Psychologists often argue that homosexuality is learned in the early years of childhood, and sociologists point out that strong prohibitions against adolescent heterosexual activity also encourage homosexual experimentation. In the past, most homosexuals concealed their sexual preference, but now many are "coming out," publicly acknowledging their sexual preference, and there are flourishing gay and lesbian communities in the big cities of North America. Despite recent improvements in the law, homosexuality still remains a crime in many places. Moreover, gays and lesbians are still subject to some of the most blatant occupational and social discrimination directed at any group in North America, and commonly face threats of violence and even death.

Functionalists see the problems of present-day gender roles as stemming from economic changes that upset the traditional cultural pattern, and they advocate a reduction in the gap between expectations and actual conditions. Conflict theorists are convinced that discrimination against women and homosexuals are problems that arise from domination and exploitation of oppressed groups by those who wield the power. They advise women and sexual minorities to organize themselves to gain power and to use it to build a more just society. Feminists generally agree with the conflict theorists, although there are several different schools of feminist thought about how society should be changed. Liberal feminists advocate a vigorous attack on all forms of discrimination; socialist feminists call for a fundamental restructuring of capitalist society; and radical feminists call for the creation of a more "woman-centered" social order. Interactionists are convinced that gender roles and sexual identity are learned in the process of socialization and that sexual inequality can be reduced by changing gender roles.

QUESTIONS FOR CRITICAL THINKING

The question of what the relationship between the sexes should be is a controversial one that often stirs deep emotions. Some people see traditional gender roles as preordained by God or biology, while others see them as repressive and unjust. Examine the traditional and the egalitarian pattern of gender relationships from a general sociological perspective. What are the overall advantages and disadvantages of each? Now, put those patterns into the context of an agricultural society and an industrial society. Why have gender roles grown more egalitarian as societies have industrialized? What directions do you see for the future?

KEY TERMS

androgynous	homophobia
bisexuality	homosexuality
coming out	lesbian
double standard	patriarchal
gay	sexism
gender inequality	sexual harassment
gender role	sexual orientation
gender socialization	sexual stereotyping
hate crime	sodomy law
heterosexuality	

NOTES

1. See, for example, Ann Ferguson, "Androgyny as an Ideal for Human Development," in Paula S. Rothenberg, ed., *Racism and Sexism: An Integrated Study* (New York: St. Martin's Press, 1988), pp. 362–371.

2. Sandra L. Bem, "Androgyny and Gender Schema Theory," in T. B. Sonderegger, ed., *Nebraska Symposium on Motivation: Psychology of Gender* (Lincoln: University of Nebraska Press, 1985).

3. Jane B. Lancaster and Chet S. Lancaster, "The Watershed: Changes in Parental Investment and Family Formation Strategies in the Course of Human Evolution," in Jane B. Lancaster et al., eds., *Parenting Across the Lifespan* (New York: Aldine de Gruyter, 1988), p. 191.

4. See Hilary M. Lips, *Sex and Gender* (Mountain View, CA: Mayfield, 1988), pp. 1–26.

5. Ibid., pp. 105–109.

6. Christine de Lacoste-Utamsing and Ralph L. Holloway, "Sexual Dimorphism in the Human Corpus Callosum," *Science* 216 (1982): 1431–1432.

7. Bruce Svare and Craig H. Kinsley, "Hormones and Sex-Related Behavior," in Kathryn Kelley, ed., *Females, Males and Sexuality: Theories and Research* (Albany: State University of New York Press, 1987), pp. 13–58.

8. Laurel Richardson, *The Dynamics of Sex and Gender: A Sociological Perspective* (New York: HarperCollins, 1988), p. 145.

9. Richard Borsay Lee, *The !Kung San: Men, Women and Work in a Foraging Society* (Cambridge: Cambridge University Press, 1979); Margaret Mead, *Sex and Temperament in Three Primitive Societies* (New York: Mentor, 1935); James A. Doyle, *The Male Experience* (Dubuque, IA: Brown, 1983), pp. 82–85.

10. Margaret L. Anderson, *Thinking About Women: Sociological Perspectives on Sex and Gender*, 2nd ed. (New York: Macmillan, 1988), pp. 49–52; John Money and A. A. Ehrhardt, *Man, Woman, Boy and Girl: The Differentiation and Dimorphism of Gender Identity from Conception to Maturity* (Baltimore: Johns Hopkins University Press, 1972).

11. Ernestine Friedl, *Women and Men: An Anthropologist's View* (New York: Holt, Rinehart & Winston, 1975).

12. See, for example, Eleanor Leacock, "Women's Status in Egalitarian Society: Implications for Social Evolution," *Current Anthropology* 19 (June 1978): 247–255.

13. Peggy Sanday, *Female Power and Male Dominance: On the Origins of Sexual Inequality* (New York: Cambridge University Press), 1981; Janet Saltzman Chafetz, *Gender Equity: An Integrated Theory of Stability and Change* (Newbury Park, CA: Sage), 1990; Richardson, *The Dynamics of Sex and Gender*, pp. 155–156.

14. Anderson, *Thinking About Women*, pp. 82–83.

15. See Richardson, *The Dynamics of Sex and Gender*, pp. 16–34; Simone de Beauvoir, *The Second Sex* (New York: Knopf, 1957).

16. Ruth E. Hartley, "Sex-Role Pressures and the Socialization of the Male Child," in Deborah S. David and Robert Brannon, eds., *The Forty-nine Percent Majority: The Male Sex Role* (Reading, MA: Addison Wesley, 1976), p. 236.

17. Leslie Brody, "Gender Difference in Emotional Development: A Review of Theory and Research," *Journal of Personality* 53 (1985): 102–149.

18. Richardson, *The Dynamics of Sex and Gender*, pp. 56–59.

19. Myra Sadker, David Sadker, and Susan S. Klein, "Abolishing Misconceptions About Sex Equity in Education," *Theory into Practice* 25 (autumn 1986): 220.

20. Beverly A. Stitt, *Building Gender Fairness in Schools* (Carbondale: Southern Illinois University Press, 1988), pp. 29–32.

21. Myra Sadker and David Sadker, *Failing at Fairness* (New York: Scribner, 1994); American Association of University Women, *How Schools Shortchange Girls* (Washington, DC: AAUW Educational Foundation, 1992); C. S. Dweck, W. Davidson, S. Nelson, and B. Enna, "Sex Differences in Learned Helplessness," *Developmental Psychology* 14 (1978): 268–276.

22. P. Purcell and L. Stewart, "Dick and Jane in 1989," *Sex Roles* 22 (1990): 177–185.

23. J. H. Feldstein and S. Feldstein, "Sex Differences on Televised Toy Commercials," *Sex Roles* 8 (1982): 581–587.

24. Kilbourne, Jean, *Deadly Persuasion* (New York: The Free Press, 1999) p. 142.

25. F. E. Barcus, *Commercial Children's Television on Weekends and Weekday Afternoons* (Newtonville, MA: Action for Children's Television, 1982).

26. N. S. Feldman and E. Brown, "Male Versus Female Differences in Control Strategies: What Children Learn from Saturday Morning Television." Paper presented at the annual meeting of the Eastern Psychological Association, Baltimore, April 1984.

27. See G. Metzger, "T.V. Is a Blonde, Blonde World," *American Demographics* (November 1992): 51; A. E. Courtney and T. W. Whipple, *Sex Stereotyping in Advertising* (Lexington, MA: Lexington, 1983); Richardson, *The Dynamics of Sex and Gender*, pp. 69–82; Claire M. Renzetti and Daniel J. Curran, *Women, Men and Society*, 3rd ed. (Boston: Allyn & Bacon, 1995), pp. 172–175.

28. Jean Kilbourne, *Deadly Persuasion* (New York: The Free Press, 1999), p. 135.

29. G. Berbner, *Women and Minorities on Television: A Study in Casting and Fate*, Report to the Screen Actors Guild and the American Federation of Radio and Television Artists, Annenberg School of Communications, University of Pennsylvania, 1993.

30. F. J. Fejes, "Masculinity as Fact," in S. Craig, ed., *Men, Masculinity and Media* (Newbury Park, CA: Sage, 1992), pp. 9–22.

31. Metzger, "T.V. Is a Blonde, Blonde World"; I. J. Silverstein, L. Perdue, B. Petterson, and E. Kelly, "The Role of the Mass Media in Promoting a Thin Standard of Bodily Attractiveness for Women," *Sex Roles* 12 (1986): 519–532.

32. B. L. Sherman and J. R. Dominick, "Violence and Sex in Music Videos: TV and Rock 'n Roll," *Journal of Communication* 7 (1986): 94–106; also see J. D. Brown and K. Cambel, "Race and Gender in Music Videos: The Same Beat but a Different Drummer," *Journal of Communication* 36 (1986).

33. See S. McClary, *Feminine Endings: Music, Gender, and Sexuality* (Minneapolis: University of Minnesota Press, 1991), pp. 94–106.

34. Ibid., pp. 24–28; A. P. Bell, M. S. Weinberg, and S. K. Hammersmith, *Sexual Preference* (Bloomington: Indiana University Press, 1981).

35. Richard Green, *The "Sissy Boy Syndrome" and the Development of Homosexuality* (New Haven, CT: Yale University Press, 1987).

36. See Gary F. Kelley, *Sexuality Today: The Human Perspective*, 6th ed. (Boston: McGraw-Hill, 1998), pp. 397–398.

37. D. H. Hamer, S. Hu, V. L. Magnuson, N. Hu, and A.M.L. Pattatucci, "Linkage Between DNA Markers on the X Chromosome and Male Sexual Orientation," *Science* 261 (1993): 261, 321–327.

38. Simon LeVay, "A Difference in Hypothalamic Structure Between Heterosexual and Homosexual Men," *Science* 253 (1991): 1034–1037; Kelley, *Sexuality Today*, p. 398.

39. Hilary M. Lips, *Sex and Gender* (Mountain View, CA: Mayfield, 1988), pp. 114–115; Philip Feldman, "The Homosexual Preference," in Kevin Howells, ed., *The Psychology of Sexual Diversity* (Oxford: Blackwell, 1984), pp. 20–22.

40. John Gagnon, Edward Laumann, Robert Michael, and Gina Kolata, *Sex in America: A Definitive Survey* (Boston: Little Brown, 1994), pp. 169–183; Boyce Rensberger, "2.3% of U.S. Men in Survey Report Homosexual Acts," *Los Angeles Times*, April 15, 1993, pp. A1, A17; Associated Press, "New Study Charts Men's Sex Habits," *San Luis Obispo Telegram-Tribune*, April 15, 1993, pp. A1, A12.

41. Gagnon, Laumann, Michael, and Kolata, *Sex in America*, pp. 169–183; James Leslie McCary and Stephen McCary, *McCarys' Human Sexuality* (Belmont, CA: Wadsworth, 1982), pp. 446–450; Reinisch, *The Kinsey Institute New Report on Sex*, pp. 139–140; Thomas H. Maugh II, "Sex American Style: Trend to the Traditional," *Los Angeles Times*, February 19, 1990, pp. A1, A22; Scripps News Service, "Sexual Revolution: Most of America Missed It," *San Luis Obispo Telegram-Tribune*, February 19, 1990, p. A1.

42. Kelley, *Sexuality Today*, p. 407; Bettian Boxall, "Statistics on Gays Called Unreliable," *Los Angeles Times*, May 1, 1994, pp. A1, A24–A25.

43. Joseph Harry, "Gay and Lesbian Relationships," in Eleanor D. Macklin and Roger H. Rubin, eds., *Contemporary Families and Alternative Lifestyles* (Beverly Hills, CA: Sage, 1983), pp. 216–234.

44. U.S. Bureau of the Census, *Educational Attainment in the United States*, 1999 (Washington, DC: U.S. Government Printing Office, 2000), Figure 3.

45. U.S. Bureau of the Census, *Statistical Abstract of the United States, 1999* (Washington, DC: U.S. Government Printing Office, 1999), pp. 204, 205.

46. Ann P. Parelius, "Mathematics and Science Majors: Gender Differences in Selection and Persistence," in Laura Kramer, ed., *The Sociology of Gender* (New York: St. Martin's Press, 1991), pp. 140–160.

47. See U.S. Bureau of the Census, *Women in the United States: A Profile, 2000* (Washington, DC: U.S. Government Printing Office, 2000).

48. U.S. Bureau of the Census, *Statistical Abstract, 1999*, p. 849; United Nations Development Programme, *Human Development Report, 1997* (New York: Oxford University Press, 1997), p. 209.

49. U.S. Bureau of the Census, *Money Income in the United States, 2000*, Table 7; U.S. Bureau of the Census, *Women in the United States: A Profile, 2000*, p. 1.

50. Lawrence Mishel, Jared Bernstein, and John Schmitt, *The State of Working America, 1996–97* (New York: Sharpe, 1997), pp. 147–148.

51. U.S. Bureau of the Census, *Money Income in the United States, 2000*, Table 7.

52. U.S. Bureau of the Census, *Money Income in the United States, 2000*, Table 7.

53. U.S. Bureau of the Census, *Women in the United States: A Profile, 2000*, p. 1; Erik O. Wright, *Class Counts* (Cambridge, England: Cambridge University Press, 1997), p. 337.

54. Donna K. H. Walters, "Barriers Still Persist, Women Lawyers Say," *Los Angeles Times*, March 10, 1994, pp. D1, D4.

55. Nancy Gibbs, "The Dreams of Youth," *Time*, Special Issue, "Women: The Road Ahead," fall 1990, pp. 10–14.

56. Harold Kerbo, *Social Stratification and Inequality*, 4th ed. (New York: McGraw-Hill, 2000), pp. 322–326.

57. U.S. Bureau of the Census, *Statistical Abstract, 2001*, p. 380.

58. Carol J. Adams, "'I Just Raped My Wife! What Are You Going to Do About It, Pastor?': The Church and Sexual Violence" in E. Buchwald, P. Fletcher, and M. Roth, eds., *Transforming a Rape Culture* (Minneapolis: Milkweed Editions, 1993).

59. Paul Nejelski, "Gender-Based Asylum in the United States: A View from the Trenches" in Courtney W. Howland, ed., *Religious Fundamentalisms and the Human Rights of Women* (New York: St. Martin's Press, 1999) pp. 247–248.

60. Associated Press, November 25, 2000.

61. S. McConnell-Ginet, "The Sexual (Re) Production of Meaning: A Discourse-Based Theory," in F. W. Frank and P. A. Treichler, eds., *Language, Gender and Professional Writing* (New York: Modern Language Association of America, 1989); C. Edelsky, "Who's Got the Floor?" *Language and Society* 10 (1981): 383–421.

62. Deborah Tannen, *You Just Don't Understand* (New York: Morrow, 1990).

63. N. Henley, M. Hamilton, and B. Thorne, "Womanspeak and Manspeak: Sex Differences and Sexism in Communication," in A. G. Sargent, ed., *Beyond Sex Role* (New York: West, 1985), pp. 168–185.

64. Theodore Caplow, *American Social Trends* (San Diego: Harcourt Brace Jovanovich, 1991), pp. 153–154; Carol McGraw, "Employers, Workers Act to Fight Job Harassment," *Los Angeles Times*, October 21, 1990, pp. A1, A30.

65. Nancy Rivera Brooks, "Gender Pay Gap Found at Highest Corporate Levels," *Los Angeles Times*, June 30, 1993, pp. A1, A20.

66. Gibbs, "The Dreams of Youth."

67. Mishel, Bernstein, and Schmitt, *The State of Working America, 1996–97*, p. 148.

68. U.S. Bureau of the Census, *Statistical Abstract, 1999*, p. 102.

69. Warren Farrell, "Men as Success Objects," *Utne Reader*, May–June 1991, pp. 81–84.

70. Susan Essoyan, "Hawaii Approves Benefits Package for Gay Couples," *Los Angeles Times*, April 30, 1997, pp. A3, A14; Susan Essoyan and Bettina Boxall, "Hawaii Ruling Lifts Ban on Marriage of Same-Sex Couples," *Los Angeles Times*, December 4, 1996, p. A1, A 19; Human Rights Campaign, February 2, 2001, <www.hrc.org>.

71. The Gay, Lesbian and Straight Education Network, "GLSEN's National School Climate Survey: Lesbian, Gay, Bisexual, and Transgender Students and Their Experience in School, 1999," <www//glsem/org/pages/sections/news/natlnews/1999/spep/survey>.

72. Human Rights Campaign, *The State of the Workplace for Lesbian, Gay, Bisexual, and Transgendered Americans*, 2000 (Washington DC: Human Rights Commission, 2000), p. 8.

73. Michael Kimmel, *Manhood in America* (New York: The Free Press, 1996), p. 333. Quotation from Floyd Dell, "Feminism for Men," *The Masses* 5 (20) (July 1917): 1.

PART III

CONFORMITY AND DEVIANCE

ALL SOCIETIES HAVE STRONG EXPECTATIONS ABOUT HOW THEIR MEMBERS ARE SUPPOSED TO behave. Until the 1960s, most sociologists simply accepted the dominant norms of their society, and they sought the causes of social problems in deviant behavior—that is, behavior that violates society's rules. While deviant behavior is unquestionably a major source of social problems, this approach has proved far too simplistic. Contemporary societies no longer have a single set of norms that almost everyone agrees with. Instead, we are confronted by a mosaic of fragmented subcultures and communities, each with its own unique standards and expectations. Conflict theorists have shown us another problem with the old approach: It automatically assumes that our laws reflect the best interests of society as a whole and ignores the fact that raw political power also plays a critical role in shaping our legal system. Finally, the horrors of World War II and the blind allegiance so many have shown to totalitarian dictators in the last century have proved that conformity can be as much a social problem as deviance. The chapters in this section therefore examine the problems of drug use, crime, and violence in light of this new, more complex understanding of the relationship between social norms and social problems.

CHAPTER 9

DRUG USE

Questions to Consider

Is drug use increasing or decreasing?

Which drugs create the most serious problems?

Why do people use drugs?

How does the law affect drug use?

How can we deal with the drug problem?

Scott Krueger graduated near the top of his high school class in upstate New York and moved to Boston to attend the Massachusetts Institute of Technology. As an engineering major and a member of the crew team, he had a lot of demands on his time, but he still decided to pledge the Phi Gamma Delta fraternity. During Greek Week of his freshman year, Scott went to a fraternity party and apparently downed the equivalent of 16 shots of alcohol in a single hour. After he passed out, his friends carried him down to the basement of their rambling frat house, and then they discovered that he wasn't breathing well. He was rushed to the hospital, where he was kept on life support systems for a few days until he died. Blood tests showed that Scott's alcohol level was 0.41—more than five times the legal driving limit of .08. The doctors said that he died either from an alcohol-induced thickening of the blood, which prevented oxygen from reaching his brain, or from choking on his own vomit.[1]

Few other social problems are surrounded by more myths and misinformation than drug use. The confusion starts with the very meaning of the term. Many people mistakenly believe that only illegal substances, such as heroin, cocaine, or marijuana, are drugs; but, as Scott Krueger's death shows, alcohol can be just as dangerous as illicit drugs, and so can tobacco. Nor is drug use confined to a few ragged deviants on the margins of society. Drugs are big business: Americans spend billions of dollars a year for coffee, tea, tobacco, and alcohol, and the manufacturers of these products have a respected place among the corporate giants of today's economy.

One of the most widespread myths is that we are in the midst of an exploding "drug epidemic." The truth is much more complex than that. The use of most illicit drugs increased rapidly in the 1960s and 1970s, but drug use declined sharply after its peak in 1979 and continued to drop until the middle 1990s. More recently the picture has been mixed. Between 1997 and 1999, illicit drug use dropped from 11 percent to 9 percent of 12- to 17-year-olds. However at the same time, illicit drug use went up from 14.7 percent to 18.8 percent for 18- to 25-year-olds.[2] Overall, legal drug use has declined. Between 1980 and 1994, the amount of beer and wine consumed by the average American dropped over 12 percent, and the consumption of distilled liquors such as whiskey and vodka declined by over one-third. Since then, alcohol use has continued to decline, though more slowly. Survey data from 1999 still shows that over half of all high school students consumed alcohol on a regular basis.[3] The decrease in tobacco smoking began even earlier. In 1965, over 40 percent of adult Americans smoked; today, only about 23 percent do. However, the picture is still a mixed one for the rate of smoking—among American high school students, in 1999, it was almost 35 percent.[4]

One common belief that is certainly not a myth is that the drug problem is widespread and extremely costly. According to the National Safety Council, about 60 percent of all drivers killed in automobile accidents had drunk enough alcohol to impair their driving skills. Alcohol abuse is estimated to cost $43 billion to $120 billion each year in lost workdays, medical expenses, and accidents.[5] Some of the most tragic problems occur among adolescents who turn to drugs to escape the intense emotional problems they face.

DRUGS AND DRUG ADDICTION

Addiction is a technical term that is difficult to define precisely. In the broadest sense, addiction refers to an intense craving for a particular substance, but this definition can be applied to almost any desire or craving, whether it is for ice cream, potato chips, or heroin. To avoid this confusion, drug addiction is sometimes erroneously defined as the physiological dependence that a person develops after heavy use of a particular drug. Most addicts, however, experience periods when they "kick" their physical dependence, yet their psychological craving continues undiminished, and they soon return to drugs. It is therefore more useful to define **addiction** as the intense craving for a drug that develops after a period of physical dependence.

Two essential characteristics of an addictive drug are tolerance and withdrawal discomfort. **Tolerance** is another name for immunity to the effects of a drug that builds up after heavy use. For instance, if someone takes the same amount of heroin every day for a month, the last dose will have much less effect than the first. If the user wants the same psychological effect at the end of the month, the dosage must be increased. **Withdrawal** is the name given to the sickness that habitual users experience when they stop taking drugs. Addictive drugs produce both tolerance and withdrawal distress. Drugs that produce tolerance but no withdrawal discomfort, such as LSD, are not addictive.

Drug addiction is not solely a physiological matter, however. Psychological craving supplements biological dependence. Moreover, the behavior of those who use drugs is influenced by cultural expectations that are quite independent of the drug's physiological effects. For example, anyone who drinks a large quantity of alcohol will pass out—a physiological reaction; but behavior of people who are drunk (but not dead drunk) varies greatly from culture to culture and even from group to group within a culture. For example, in some cultures people become more violent when they drink, but in other cultures such a reaction is rare.[6] A good example of the latter is Japan: Late at night there are many people coming home drunk from popular nightspots, but aggressive behavior is extremely unusual.

By examining such things as the percentage of users who become dependent on a particular drug, the difficulty quitting, and the relapse rate, researchers are able to rate how addictive different drugs are. When measured by such criteria, nicotine (a drug found in tobacco) is the most addictive, followed by heroin, cocaine, and alcohol. Second from the bottom is caffeine, and the least addictive of the commonly used drugs is marijuana.[7]

ALCOHOL

The use of alcohol is an accepted part of our culture. Businesspeople make deals over a bottle of expensive wine, college students escape the pressures of final exams with a keg of beer, restaurants offer champagne brunches and boast vast wine cellars, and neighborhood bars serve as social centers for many local residents. The fact that alcohol is so widely accepted and so widely used means that it creates more problems than other drugs.

Alcohol, like most other drugs, is rather harmless when used in moderation (except in the case of pregnant women), but it is extremely dangerous when used to excess. Alcohol is called a **depressant** drug because it depresses the activity of the central nervous system and thereby impedes coordination, reaction time, and reasoning ability. Large doses of alcohol produce disorientation, loss of consciousness, and even death. The psychological reaction to alcohol varies from person to person, but the physiological effects of alcohol clearly increase as the level of alcohol in the blood rises. The effects first become apparent when the concentration of alcohol in the blood reaches about 0.05 percent, and 0.08 percent is generally considered to be the point of legal intoxication. Extreme intoxication occurs between 0.20 and 0.30 percent. A user with over 0.4 percent blood alcohol is likely to pass out, and concentrations over 0.6 percent are usually fatal.[8]

Prolonged heavy drinking may generate a number of health problems. Alcoholic beverages are high in calories but have little other food value; for this reason, heavy drinkers sometimes lose their appetites and suffer from malnutrition. The harmful effects of excessive drinking on the liver are well known: The end result may be cirrhosis, a condition in which liver cells are destroyed by alcohol and replaced by scar tissue. Heavy drinkers are more likely than others to have heart problems, and there is evidence that they suffer from a higher rate of cancer as well. Drinkers may also be a problem to their children. Studies show that the children of alcoholic mothers have lower birthweights, slower language development, lower IQs, and more birth defects than other children.[9]

Alcohol will produce addiction if used in sufficient amounts over a long period. The so-called DTs (short for *delirium tremens*) are actually symptoms of alcohol withdrawal. These symptoms commonly include nausea, vomiting, and convulsions; sometimes they involve hallucinations and coma as well. Death from heart failure or severe convulsions occurs in about 10 percent of victims of the DTs. A much more common cause of death is the use of alcohol in combination with other depressant drugs. Many people have unintentionally killed themselves by taking sleeping pills after an evening of heavy drinking. Death occurs because two depressant drugs taken together have a synergistic effect; that is, the effect of the two drugs together is much greater than that of either drug taken alone.

When asked by survey takers, most Americans agree that heavy drinking is a serious problem in the United States, and one out of five persons questioned told the Gallup poll interviewer that drinking had been a source of distress in their own families.[10] It is doubtful that all the people who cause such problems should be considered alcoholics, but the term is often used so loosely that an uninformed person may call anyone who takes more than an occasional drink an alcoholic. For the purposes of this book, we will define an **alcoholic** as a person whose persistent drinking problem disrupts his or her life, interfering with the ability to hold a job, complete household tasks, or participate in family and social affairs. Statistics suggest that alcoholics can expect to die 10 to 12 years sooner than other people, and they are more likely to suffer from a variety of serious health conditions. Estimates of the number of alcoholics in the United States range from 8 to 25 million—more than the total number of users of most illicit drugs.[11]

One life-threatening problem associated with the use of alcohol is drunk driving. There are many different estimates about how many traffic fatalities are caused by drunk drivers every year, but it is a substantial number. What we do know is that the

Drunk driving continues to be a major social problem contributing to thousands of deaths and injuries each year.

percentage of the drivers in fatal crashes who were drunk has declined substantially in the last two decades.[12] In recent years, the victims of drunk drivers have banded together with other concerned citizens in such organizations as MADD (Mothers Against Drunk Driving) and SADD (Students Against Drunk Driving) to increase awareness of the problem and push for stiffer punishments. Public attitudes have grown less tolerant of those who drink and drive, and laws have grown increasingly tough as well. Forty-four states now have mandatory jail sentences for second-time offenders. In 2000, President Clinton, following the lead of several states that had lowered the level of alcohol in the blood that defines legal drunkenness, signed a bill making .08 blood alcohol level a nationwide standard.

Most countries in Europe as well as Japan have lower rates of drunk driving and fewer deaths than the United States, in spite of the fact that it is legal to drink at 16 years of age in these countries. These countries tend to have stricter laws and frequent police blockades to check for drunk drivers. However, the biggest reason for the lower level of drunk driving in these other countries is their good mass-transit systems. In short, people have alternatives to driving after they have been out drinking. But even in smaller towns in Japan, where mass transit is not as extensive as in the cities, they provide effective alternative forms of transportation. Taxis in the bar districts often have two drivers; one to drive the taxi and one to drive the customer's car home following the taxi.

In the most current surveys, a little more than half of all Americans say they have had at least one drink in the last month,[13] but as we have seen, the use of alcohol has been decreasing in recent decades. The prevalence of drinking also varies widely among different social and ethnic groups. Most studies indicate that more men than women drink, but the differences have narrowed as women have gained more freedom and taken on more financial burdens.[14] Whites drink more frequently than African Americans, and the prevalence of drinking is greatest among the college educated and those with higher incomes.

Drinking is a particular problem among college students. One survey found that 42 percent of college students had had a drinking binge (five or more drinks in a row) within the last two weeks. The stereotypes about drunken fraternity parties apparently have some basis in fact as well: Alcohol consumption is three times higher among students who live in fraternity or sorority houses than among others. Although female students still drink less than males, the biggest increase in recent years has been among women.[15] A similar problem occurs among high school students. During 1999, almost 50 percent of male high school seniors had admitted to binge drinking in the last 30 days, as had over 35 percent of the females.[16]

TOBACCO

Almost one in every four Americans over the age of 17 smokes cigarettes, as does one in every five between ages 12 and 17. Men smoke more than women, but the use of tobacco has been declining more rapidly among men.[17] About 70 percent of all smokers have more than 15 cigarettes a day, making tobacco one of the few drugs that addicts use nearly every waking hour of every day. Sales of tobacco, like those of alcohol, have been falling in recent years. Since 1985, the number of adult Americans who smoke has dropped almost 25 percent.[18]

The principal drug in tobacco is nicotine, which is clearly addictive. The average smoker takes in about 25 milligrams of nicotine a day and will begin to experience withdrawal when intake drops below 5 milligrams.[19] Symptoms include drowsiness, nervousness, anxiety, headaches, and loss of energy. Nicotine is a stimulant that raises blood pressure, speeds up the heartbeat, and gives the user a sense of alertness. However, nicotine also seems to have the contradictory effect of producing a feeling of relaxation and calm in some people. Some claim that this relaxation is due to the ritual of smoking and not to the drug itself, but the issue remains unclear.[20]

In 1964, the surgeon general's Advisory Committee on Smoking and Health issued its famous report concluding that smoking is hazardous to health, and since then the annual report issued by the federal government has painted an ever bleaker picture. Commenting on the particularly detailed 1979 report, the secretary of the Department of Health, Education and Welfare said that it "reveals with dramatic clarity that cigarette smoking is even more dangerous—indeed, far more dangerous—than was supposed in 1964."[21] In issuing the 1988 report, the surgeon general took another major step, forcefully acknowledging the addictive properties of nicotine and its similarity in that regard to heroin and other illegal drugs.[22] A study published in the *Journal of the American Medical Association* in 1993 concluded that tobacco smoking is implicated in almost one of every five deaths in the United States, making it America's number one cause of death.[23] The most common estimate is that tobacco smoking kills about 400,000 Americans every year.[24]

DEBATE

SHOULD SMOKING BE OUTLAWED?

Yes

The evidence is clear. Tobacco is a deadly killer. Tobacco kills more people than alcohol, heroin, marijuana, cocaine, amphetamines, and barbiturates combined. Deaths from guns and even from automobiles don't even come close. In fact, it is the number one cause of death in this country.

Numerous programs and policies have been tried to stem its deadly tide. Minors were forbidden to buy it. A health warning was placed on every pack. Television and radio ads were banned. The government issued endless reports warning of its dangers. Smoking was forbidden in many offices and public buildings. Yet after all this, one in every four adults still smokes. The fact is that this drug is highly addictive, and once people start smoking, many of them can't stop. The only cure for this deadly plague is the total prohibition of all smoking. That way addicts will be forced to quit and young people will no longer be tempted to start the deadly habit.

The opponents of prohibition claim that it will not stop smoking but will simply create the same kind of black market for tobacco that there is for other illegal drugs. Such arguments overlook one critical difference between tobacco and most other drugs: Most tobacco addicts smoke virtually all day long. Once tobacco is prohibited and people are arrested for smoking in public, they simply would not be able to keep up that kind of consumption unless they stayed home all day. Tobacco is an addictive drug that is turning billions of dollars in profits for the corporations that produce it, while killing hundreds of thousands of people every year. If not for the political influence that money has brought the tobacco corporations, this drug would have

---

Cigarette smoking has been linked to cancer of the larynx, mouth, and esophagus, as well as to lung cancer. Other diseases linked to smoking include bronchitis, emphysema, ulcers, and heart and circulatory disorders. The babies of women who smoke weigh less than other babies and have slower rates of physical and mental growth.[25] Even nonsmokers are at risk if they live or work in a smoke-filled environment. A 1991 report by the Environmental Protection Agency (EPA), which some of its own officials tried to cover up, estimated that 53,000 Americans a year die from **passive smoking**. In 1993, the EPA declared secondhand smoke a "group A" carcinogen.[26] A 1997 study by a team of Harvard researchers concluded that continued exposure to secondhand smoke nearly doubles the risk of heart disease.[27] (See the Debate above.)

been prohibited years ago. We must act to end this legalized murder. We must ban tobacco now.

No

Although a small number of alarmists are trying to whip the public into a frenzy, the fact is that millions of Americans enjoy smoking and have no desire to quit. A democratic government simply has no right to tell its citizens how to live their lives.

Look at the historical record. Prohibition didn't work for alcohol, and it won't work for tobacco either. After alcohol was prohibited, a huge black market sprang up and made millionaires out of organized criminals. There was an unprecedented wave of gang violence as bands of organized thugs fought to control that vast new illegal market. Moreover, prohibition did not even stop people from drinking. The same thing would happen today if tobacco were banned. Gangs and organized criminals would get rich, and the battle for control of the multibillion-dollar tobacco market would touch off a wave of violence and bloodshed, the likes of which this nation has never seen. Millions of average Americans would be turned into criminals overnight, and before long a new deviant subculture would spring up to meet the needs of tobacco smokers. As selling and transporting tobacco products became increasingly difficult, producers would be certain to develop more and more potent products that bring a higher price and are easier to conceal. Just as opiate prohibition eventually spawned the heroin market, so new "supertobaccos" would soon be on the market, and they would make our current problems with cocaine look like kid stuff.

Tobacco prohibition would be a national disaster. It would turn millions of upstanding citizens into criminals, put billions of dollars into the pockets of the real criminals, violate our most basic civil liberties, and on top of it all, it wouldn't even do much to stop the use of tobacco. How can anyone seriously suggest such an utterly misguided policy.

If smoking is so dangerous, why do so many people smoke? One reason is that cigarette smoking is addictive and most smokers find it difficult to stop. But what about the substantial number of young people who begin smoking every year despite medical warnings? Youthful rebelliousness is certainly part of the reason. Another factor is the tobacco industry's success in establishing an association in the public mind between smoking and maturity, sophistication, and sexual attractiveness. Cigarette manufacturers spend about $4 billion a year advertising their products, and smokers in those ads are invariably young and good-looking. The surgeon general's 1994 report on smoking concluded that the money the tobacco industry spends on advertising and publicity is contributing to an increase in smoking among the young.[28] As overall sales of cigarettes have decreased in recent years, the tobacco industry has responded with ever more sophisticated marketing campaigns targeted at specific groups. The popularity of smoking among women reflects the special efforts the tobacco companies have made to encourage them to smoke, and similar campaigns have been directed at African Americans and Latinos. Not surprisingly, rates of lung cancer and other respiratory diseases have shown an alarming increase among these groups in recent years.[29]

MARIJUANA

Marijuana is the most widely used illegal drug. At the end of the 1990s, more than 1 in 3 Americans acknowledges having tried marijuana, but only about 1 in 20 is classified as a current user (that is, reported using the drug at least once within the previous month).[30] Marijuana use is most frequent among those between 18 and 25 years of age, and use drops off sharply after age 35. Marijuana use increased greatly during the 1960s and 1970s, but as with most other drugs, marijuana smoking has decreased significantly since then. However, marijuana use is on the increase again among high school students, with about 21 percent of seniors classified as current users in 2000.[31]

The health hazards of marijuana are still the subject of an emotional debate that has often had more to do with politics than with scientific research. Numerous claims made about the damage caused by marijuana have later proved to be false. The current evidence indicates that the main health hazard in marijuana use is the risk of cancer and other lung problems caused by inhaling the smoke. Studies show that the way marijuana is usually smoked (deep inhalations that are held for a long time) makes it more damaging than tobacco, puff for puff.[32] However, this effect is offset by the greater number of cigarettes smoked by tobacco users. Two or three "joints" a day is heavy marijuana use (and because marijuana is usually shared among a group of people, each user actually smokes less), whereas many heavy tobacco users smoke more than 50 cigarettes a day. There is also evidence that marijuana may harm a user's unborn baby, and pregnant women should not use the drug. Thus, those who claim that marijuana is harmless are wrong: There are clearly significant health hazards involved in the excessive use of marijuana. However, on the whole, marijuana is probably less dangerous than most other widely used recreational drugs, including alcohol and tobacco. Marijuana has also proved to be a useful treatment for several medical conditions—for example, increasing appetite among AIDS patients suffering from "wasting syndrome" and nausea following chemotherapy—and there is a growing movement to legalize the medical use of marijuana. In 1997, California voters approved an initiative to do just that, and several other states have since followed suit.

The psychological effects of smoking marijuana are strongly influenced by the social environment and the expectations of the users. Howard S. Becker found that users must learn from their peers how to identify the effects of the drug before they actually get "high."[33] Descriptions of the drug's psychological effects vary considerably from one person to another. Typical effects include relaxation, increased sensitivity, and hunger. Studies show that a marijuana "high" impairs reaction time and coordination; therefore, it makes driving or operating other machinery more dangerous.[34]

OPIATES

The opiates are a group of natural (opium, codeine, morphine, and heroin) and synthetic (meperidine, methadone, OxyContin) depressants, all of which are highly addictive. Users rapidly develop a tolerance and must continually increase their dosage to get the same effects. Although the intensity of opiate withdrawal varies with the amount taken and with the individual involved, withdrawal seldom causes the screaming agony depicted in so many books and movies. Withdrawal distress usually resembles a bad case of the flu accompanied by a feeling of extreme depression. In some cases, however, it can be much more severe.

Opiate addiction has serious consequences for the health of the addict. Ironically, most of these problems come not from the drug itself but from the way in which it is used. The opiate addict's lifestyle, as well as impure drugs and infected needles, produces most of the severe health problems. Addicts often share the same needles without proper sterilization, and this practice spreads disease. In the past, hepatitis, a dangerous liver infection, was the most serious risk, but intravenous (IV) drug users are now stalked by a much more deadly disease: AIDS. About one-third of all new cases of AIDS are now among IV drug users (rather than being sexually transmitted), and a majority of the addicts in some cities are believed to be infected with the virus.[35] Overdose is another threat to the addict's survival and is a major cause of death among young males in many American cities. In many cases, however, death can more properly be attributed to the combination of opiates with other depressant drugs, such as alcohol.

Despite all the publicity, heroin use is actually quite rare. Only 1 of every 1000 respondents in a recent federal survey acknowledged having used heroin in the last month.[36] However, the Colombian drug cartels that dominate the cocaine market have been moving into heroin sales, and there has been a significant decrease in the cost and an increase in the purity of street heroin. As recently as 1985, the average purity of street heroin was about 5 percent; today, it averages as much as 37 percent.[37] As heroin use increases, some observers are becoming concerned about a new heroin epidemic, particularly if the price remains low enough to allow recreational users to smoke or sniff the drug rather than inject it.

Well over half of all heroin addicts in the United States live in its three largest cities, with the heaviest concentration in New York City. Addiction is an urban phenomenon in Canada as well, with its major center in Vancouver. Despite some increase in heroin use among the middle class, most addicts are young males from the poorest segments of society. However, not all opiate users fit these stereotypes. There are more addicts in the medical profession than in any other occupation,[38] and at least one new synthetic opiate, OxyContin, was first used for recreational purposes in rural areas. Because of OxyContin's popularity in the rural parts of New England and Appalachia, it is sometimes known by the nickname "hillbilly heroin."

PSYCHEDELICS

The physical effects of the most popular psychedelic drugs, such as LSD (lysergic acid diethylamide), mescaline, and MDMA (methylenedioxymethamphetamine), are generally minor. However, taken in large doses, they produce some of the most sweeping psychological effects of any drugs, including profound changes in emotion, perception, and thought. The psychedelics rank only third in popularity among the illicit drugs, but after years of decline, their use has been increasing.

Mescaline was probably among the first psychedelic drugs used in North America. The consumption of the peyote cactus (which contains mescaline) was apparently an important element in some Native American religions long before Europeans came to the continent. But LSD is the best known of the psychedelic drugs. A tiny dose of the colorless and tasteless drug produces a tremendous psychological effect that is highly unpredictable. Some users report an intensely beautiful experience, whereas others find it the most frightening experience of their lives, and still others swing from one extreme to the other on the same "acid trip." Aside from such profound emotional changes, LSD also produces hallucinations and perceptual distortions. Colors and smells often appear more intense under the influence of these drugs. Although some have charged that LSD produces brain damage and birth defects, there is little evidence to support this claim.[39]

The greatest dangers of such psychedelic drugs are psychological rather than physical. The "bad trip"—a terrifying experience that often throws the user into a panicky state—is always a possibility, especially among inexperienced users. Such bad trips have apparently brought on serious mental disorders in some susceptible persons. The average dose of LSD used today is only one-fourth to one-half of what it was during the drug's first wave of popularity in the 1960s, and as a result, the intensity of the psychological effects and the likelihood of a bad trip are both reduced.[40] Because the environment is so important in determining whether a psychedelic experience is wonderful or terrifying, many users take the drug with a "guide" who understands the effects of the drug and can help point them in the right direction.

SEDATIVE-HYPNOTICS

Sedative-hypnotics, such as barbiturates and tranquilizers, depress the central nervous system. In moderate doses, these drugs slow down breathing and normal reflexes, interfere with coordination, and relieve anxiety and tension. Speech becomes slurred, the mind clouded. In larger doses, they produce drowsiness and sleep. Medically, these drugs are used to produce two effects: relaxation (sedation) and sleep (hypnosis). The psychological effects of many of these drugs are similar to those of alcohol. Indeed, the state of intoxication produced by barbiturates (the sedative-hypnotic most commonly used by recreational drug users) is often indistinguishable from alcoholic drunkenness. Like alcohol, these drugs are addictive; repeated doses produce a growing tolerance, and heavy use can create severe withdrawal distress. In fact, abrupt barbiturate withdrawal is fatal for about 1 in every 20 persons. As already mentioned, another serious danger with the sedative-hypnotics is the risk of overdose if they are combined with each other or with alcohol.[41]

AMPHETAMINES

Amphetamines are a group of synthetic **stimulants** that includes Benzedrine, Dexedrine, and methedrine. These drugs were once widely marketed as "diet pills," although physicians are now much more likely to use other methods to help patients lose weight. Amphetamines reduce the appetite, increase blood pressure, and step up the rate of breathing. In moderate doses they generate heightened alertness, even excitement. Continuous heavy doses of an amphetamine produce a psychosis-like state that is often indistinguishable from schizophrenia. Fear and suspicion are common symptoms, and fits of violent aggression may occur. Hallucinations, delusions, and general confusion are also common. Repeated use of amphetamines leads to tolerance; withdrawal symptoms, mainly severe depression, also occur.

Most amphetamine users take the drug in pill form, but some inject it directly into the bloodstream, producing a brief but extremely intense high or "rush." Such heavy use takes a tremendous toll on the health of the users who often go on "runs" lasting several days, during which they often do not eat properly or sleep at all. Long-term users lose their hair, their teeth, and a large portion of their normal body weight, and amphetamine-induced psychosis becomes increasingly severe.[42] There is evidence that the crackdown on the cocaine trade has caused some users to switch to amphetamines— lower-priced drugs that are relatively easy for black-market chemists to produce.[43]

COCAINE

Cocaine is a natural stimulant derived from the leaves of the coca plant, which Peruvians have chewed for at least 1,500 years. Until 1906, it was a major ingredient of Coca-Cola and a number of patent medicines. The effects of cocaine are similar to those of amphetamines, but there are two differences: first, cocaine is a powerful local anesthetic, and second, the effects of cocaine do not last as long. Cocaine users often repeat their doses every hour or so as the effects wear off. Heavy cocaine users may experience the same personality changes and psychotic episodes as heavy amphetamine users, but the most frequent psychological effect is irritability and depression that occur after the drug wears off. The easiest way to avoid those discomforts is, of course, to take more cocaine, and compulsive use of the drug is a widespread problem. Many wealthy cocaine users report having spent hundreds of thousands of dollars on their drug habit.

Most users sniff cocaine powder into their nose through a tube or straw. Heavy users who "snort" cocaine in this way often suffer damage to the nasal passages and have a constant runny nose. Smoking cocaine has become popular because it produces an intense and immediate high, but it also has the potential to cause severe lung damage as well as a host of other serious health conditions. Street cocaine cannot, however, be smoked unless it is chemically treated in a process known as freebasing. In response to the rising popularity of freebasing, dealers introduced "crack": a special form of cocaine that comes in a small "rock" that can be smoked immediately without further chemical treatment. The enormous success this new product found among hard-core users created a crisis in many inner-city neighborhoods as gang wars broke out between groups trying to control the lucrative trade in crack.[44]

In the early part of the twentieth century, cocaine use was concentrated mainly among poor African Americans, but the demographics of cocaine use have changed dramatically. In the 1970s and early 1980s, cocaine became known as a "rich man's drug" because of its high cost and its popularity among some middle-class professionals. However, the popularity of crack in the underclass, as well as more negative attitudes about cocaine in the middle class, reshaped the demographics of cocaine use once again. Surveys indicate that cocaine use has plummeted in the last few years.[45] However, such studies generally miss large segments of the underclass, and it is quite possible that their behavior is not following the national trend.

STEROIDS

Anabolic steroids are synthetic drugs similar in structure to the male hormone testosterone. Steroids, along with a wide variety of related drugs, are unique among the drugs discussed here because they are taken not for their immediate psychological effects but for building muscle and increasing athletic performance. (Steroids also have legitimate medical uses, but it is their use as a performance booster that makes them a social problem.) Although there is no evidence that simply taking the drug produces athletic benefits, it does heighten the effectiveness of training programs designed to enhance muscularity and strength. Such benefits carry a heavy price, however, which may include elevated cholesterol levels, high blood pressure, heart problems, irritability, liver damage, and sterility. In males, heavy steroid use may cause atrophy of the testicles, and in females, heavy use may cause development of some male characteristics such as a deeper voice and more body hair. Steroid use by adolescents may also disrupt normal growth patterns. Thus, young steroid users who seek to build muscle may also be stunting the growth of their skeletal systems.[46]

Although steroids and numerous other performance-enhancing drugs are banned by virtually all reputable athletic organizations, including the International Olympic Committee, their use is still extremely common. In the ultracompetitive atmosphere of today's sports, many athletes feel they need every advantage possible. There are numerous reports that coaches as far down as the high school level have ignored the rules and encouraged their athletes to take these drugs. In some cases, coaches even act as drug dealers by providing steroids to their athletes. There is also disturbing evidence of increasing steroid use among teenage boys—both for improved athletic performance and for muscle building. A 1990 survey by the Department of Health and Human Services estimated that about 3 percent of the boys in grades 7 through 12 have taken steroids.[47]

CLUB DRUGS

The "rave"—an all-night dance party with choreographed light shows and music with a pulsating hypnotic beat—has become increasingly popular in the United States and around the world. Not only was a new style of music associated with the growth of the rave scene, but so were the use of several new drugs. Scientifically, these so-called "club drugs" can be classified as psychedelics or depressants, but it is useful to consider them separately because they tend to be used in the same setting to attempt to produce a trance-like euphoria in conjunction with the dancing and music.

The most popular of these drugs is MDMA, usually known as "ecstasy" when sold on the streets. The use of ecstasy first gained popularity in Europe, where it is an integral part of the rave scene. In the last few years, its use has shown explosive growth among partygoers in the United States as well. The 2000 report of the Monitoring the Future project, which does annual surveys of American students, found that while the use of most drugs had remained steady or declined since the mid 1990s, MDMA was rapidly increasing. In 2000, 8.2 percent of high school students had used MDMA at least once—almost double the figure for 1996.[48] The drug is also the center of controversy between some psychiatrists, who believe that it is a useful therapeutic tool because of its reputation for encouraging feelings of friendship and openness among its users, and drug enforcement officials, who have succeeded in banning its use. One of the most serious problems associated with the use of ecstasy is that there are many extremely dangerous counterfeit drugs sold under its name. The problem has gotten so bad that there is now a campaign to provide free testing services so that partygoers can know if the drug they are taking is really MDMA.

GHB (gamma hydroxybutyrate) is another popular club drug. GHB is a central nervous system depressant and has been used to stimulate muscular growth in the same way as anabolic steroids. Low to moderate doses produce a relaxed state similar to ecstasy, but excessive doses can result in nausea, seizures, and even coma. It has also gained some notoriety as a "date-rape drug," used to dose unwitting victims in order to make it easier for an attacker to force them into having sex. GHB was widely sold as a health supplement until 2000 when the federal government listed it as a controlled substance.

Another club drug, Ketamine, is known on the streets as "special k" or just "k." Ketamine was developed in the 1970s as a medical anesthetic and is often used in veterinary clinics for surgeries on animals. In addition to the depressant effects one would expect from an anesthetic, ketamine also produces hallucinations or dream-like states similar to LSD and the other psychedelics. Overdose can cause heart attacks, coma, and even death, and Ketamine is much more dangerous when used in combination with other depressants.

QUICK REVIEW

What are the definitions of addiction, tolerance, and withdrawal?
What are health dangers associated with each of the most commonly used drugs?
How do the physical effects of those drugs differ?

WHY USE DRUGS?

Researchers seem to be fascinated with the question of why people use drugs. Tremendous effort has gone into the investigation of this topic, much of it on the assumption that if we can find out why people take drugs, we can find ways of preventing them from doing so. Most of this research has been on the social-psychological level, but we will also examine some structural theories in the section on theoretical perspectives at the end of this chapter.

BIOLOGICAL THEORIES

Many observers believe that drug problems are caused by the nature of the drugs themselves: Once someone takes too much of a drug, he or she becomes addicted and is simply unable to stop. Although such theories are probably most popular with the general public, biological explanations of drug problems have also won increasing attention from scientists over the last two decades. For example, a Danish study found that 65 percent of people whose identical twin was an alcoholic became alcoholics themselves, compared with only 25 percent of nonidentical twins. Although much of this difference may stem from the fact that identical twins are treated more similarly than are fraternal twins, some studies indicate that alcoholism in adopted children correlates more closely with the alcoholism of biological parents than with the alcoholism of adoptive parents.[49] In one of the best-known biological theories of alcoholism, E. M. Jellinek argued that it is not voluntary behavior but a disease with a consistent pattern of symptoms.[50] Some studies have attempted to find the exact biochemical reason that one person is more susceptible to alcoholism than another. The evidence shows that alcoholics have higher levels of a chemical known as acetaldehyde that is produced by the metabolic breakdown of alcohol in the body. However, some researchers hold that these high levels of acetaldehyde are the result, not the cause, of alcoholism. Others argue that people who are better able to metabolize alcohol are more likely to become alcoholics. Because they have a higher tolerance to the effects of alcohol, such people drink more heavily, and their metabolism, in turn, produces more of the chemicals that create the physical addiction to alcohol.[51]

We must nonetheless be careful not to let the impressive findings of biological research lead us to unwarranted conclusions. Although there apparently is a genetic predisposition toward particular drug problems in some individuals, drug use is still a learned behavior, created and controlled by society. There are no alcoholics or heroin addicts in cultures where the use of those drugs is unknown or is practiced only in tightly restricted ritual situations. Drug problems are much more severe than they were two centuries ago because of the wrenching changes brought on by industrialization, not because there has been a genetic change in our population. Although biological theories cannot explain the historical changes in drug consumption or the reasons drug problems are so much worse in big cities than in traditional small towns, they do help us understand why one person develops a drug problem while another person with similar experiences and background does not.

BEHAVIORAL THEORY

Psychologists have done extensive studies of the effects of drug use on animals, and they have found that animals can be trained to use drugs and that some become habituated. Behaviorists argue that such experiments show that drug use is learned through a process of conditioning. Taking a drug often provides a reward (positive reinforcement), and when experimental animals or humans use a drug and find it pleasurable, they are likely to use it again.

Alfred Lindesmith, on the other hand, turned this behavioral theory on its head.[52] Rather than being attracted to an enjoyable experience, he said, the addict is trying to escape the unpleasant experience of withdrawal distress (negative reinforcement). According to Lindesmith, addicts so frequently use drugs to relieve withdrawal discomfort that they begin to associate the drug with the relief it brings. They continue to use drugs even when there is no physiological dependence because they associate drug use with the elimination of discomfort and pain.

Critics complain that the basic idea behind behavioral theory—that people use drugs because they find them pleasurable and continue to use them because doing so prevents withdrawal distress—is nothing new. But whether the concept is old or new, there is little doubt about the importance of this kind of reinforcement in developing and maintaining a drug habit.

PERSONALITY THEORIES

Many psychologists have tried to explain drug problems by investigating users' personalities. However, there is no general agreement among psychologists about the personality characteristics of addicts and drug abusers. Drug addicts have been classified as narcissists, psychopaths, sociopaths, dependent personalities, immature, schizophrenic, neurotic, and character-disordered, to list only a few of the labels used.

The most common theory is that alcoholics and drug addicts have weak personalities and low self-esteem and therefore turn to drugs to try to escape their problems. G. E. Barnes, for example, argues that there is an "alcoholic personality" that displays such characteristics as "neuroticism, weak ego, stimulus augmenting [a hypersensitivity to the environment that results in fear and anxiety], and field dependency [a passive-dependent orientation to life]."[53] Because these traits may be a response to alcoholism rather than its cause, psychologists also talk about a "prealcoholic personality." The characteristics that are believed to lead to alcoholism include impulsivity, gregariousness, and nonconformity.[54] Isador Chein and his associates reached similar conclusions about their sample of heroin addicts.[55] They found that heroin addicts have major personality disorders originating in the addicts' early family histories. The mother was usually the most important parental figure to the child, and the father was usually cold or even hostile. Children from these homes were found to be overindulged or frustrated and were uncertain of the standards expected of them. These conditions were said to produce such personality traits as passivity, defensiveness, and low self-esteem.

Critics of these studies charge that they are little more than a reflection of the popular stereotypes that condemn people who suffer from drug problems. They argue that heavy drug users have as many diverse personality characteristics as any other group of people, that the findings of these psychologists are based on their own prejudices, and the fact that addicts with inadequate personalities are more likely to seek psychological treatment. Support for this position comes from an unusually comprehensive 40-year longitudinal study of 660 young men drawn both from Harvard University and from an inner-city slum. Although the study found a strong correlation between alcoholism in parents and children, no personality differences were found between those who became alcoholics and those who did not.[56]

Despite the weaknesses in these theories, there is no question that personality plays an important role in an individual's decision to use a drug. After all, there are wide differences in drug use among people in the same environment, even when they have similar risk factors in their family backgrounds. It is too simplistic, however, to assume that there is a single type of personality that leads to drug problems. Rather, a great number of learned behavior patterns and personality traits interact in a given environment either to promote or to discourage drug use.

Drugs are used in many social settings. According to interactionist theory, people use drugs because of the attitudes and values they learn in their daily contacts with other people.

INTERACTIONIST THEORY

Most social psychologists see drug use simply as one more behavior pattern that is learned from interaction with others in our culture. They observe, for example, that most people in our society who drink alcohol do so not because they have some personality defect or a biological urge to drink but because drinking is a widely accepted cultural pattern. Most children see adults drink, and they learn attitudes, beliefs, and definitions that are favorable to alcohol use. When such children reach adulthood, they are likely to use alcohol just as their parents did.

Interactionists hold that the use of illegal drugs is also culturally learned, although in a slightly different way. Because the dominant culture encourages negative attitudes toward illegal drugs, some contact with a drug subculture is necessary before most people start using such drugs. The longer and more intense a person's contact with a drug subculture, the greater the likelihood that he or she will accept attitudes and definitions that are favorable to drug use. A person who actually begins to use an illicit drug is likely to grow closer to other drug users and to become more deeply committed to the values of the drug subculture. In fact, some people use drugs for the companionship of other drug users as much as for the effects of the drugs themselves.

The key point in interactionist theory is that drug use is determined by individuals' attitudes toward drugs, the meaning drug use has for them, their overall worldview, and their system of values—all of which are learned from interaction with people in a certain culture or subculture. Drug users, according to interactionist theory, quit only when their attitudes and values change and the drugs involved are redefined in negative terms.[57] Labeling theorists point out that such changes are much more difficult when a drug user has been publicly labeled as an "addict," "alcoholic," or "junkie." Those who have been branded in this way often find that they are excluded from contact with groups and individuals who might support their attempts to reform.

QUICK REVIEW

Compare and contrast the biological, behavioral, personality, and interactionist theories about the causes of drug use.

DRUG CONTROL IN NORTH AMERICA

The European colonists who came to North America brought their drinking customs with them. Before 1700, most drinking was moderate and socially accepted. The most common beverages were beer and wine. Strong religious and family controls limited drunkenness and disorderly conduct. However, as the westward expansion continued, drinking patterns changed. The traditional restraints of family and religion were less effective among rugged pioneers, and heavy consumption of distilled spirits became commonplace. This type of drinking, often accompanied by violent, destructive behavior, was the first alcohol problem to gain widespread social attention. At the same time, total abstinence was becoming more popular among farmers and people in more established rural areas.

By the nineteenth century there were two different drinking patterns among Americans: Rural middle-class people were largely abstainers, while settlers on the frontier and the thousands of immigrants in the big cities tended to be alcohol users. Three waves of state prohibition laws swept the United States as people from small towns tried to impose their customs on urban drinkers. The last wave resulted in the passage of the Eighteenth Amendment to the Constitution in 1919, which prohibited the manufacture, sale, and transportation of intoxicating liquors. This amendment was repealed in 1933 by the Twenty-First Amendment.

Just as the drive against alcohol intensified in the nineteenth century, so did the drive against the use of other drugs, particularly opiates. At that time, opium was sold legally in over-the-counter patent medicines as a cure for everything from diarrhea to whooping cough, and most habitual users were middle-aged, middle-class women who were no more involved in crime or deviant behavior than anyone else.

By the turn of the century, however, the wave of negative publicity had changed the public's attitude, and opiates came to be seen as "dope," not medicine. All nonprescription use of the drugs was prohibited in Canada in 1908 and in the United States in 1914.[58] This prohibition produced a sharp drop in the number of opiate users. However, users who were unwilling or unable to quit were placed in a very difficult position. They found themselves labeled "dope fiends" and were virtually forced to associate with smugglers and other criminals to obtain supplies of the drug. This small group of opiate users was the beginning of the subculture of opiate addiction that was to become such a problem in the years ahead. As the price of illicit opiates steadily rose, so did users' need for money. The method of consumption changed from drinking opiated medicines to injecting morphine and finally heroin. Within a few decades after opium prohibition, the modern junkie emerged: predominantly young, predominantly male, and often deeply involved in crime.[59]

Although shorter-lived, alcohol prohibition had similar consequences for American society. The Volstead Act, which amended the U.S. Constitution to prohibit the manufacture or sale of "intoxicating liquors," went into effect in January 1920 and was finally repealed in December 1933. While prohibition law was in effect, Americans witnessed an unprecedented wave of crime and gangsterism. The drinking public was not willing to give up alcohol, no matter what the law said. They turned to illegal sources of supply, thus creating a huge illicit market for alcohol. Members of organized crime and many independent operators jumped into the alcohol business, and speakeasies (illegal bars) sprang up in every city.[60]

Marijuana was the last major drug to be prohibited during this "era of temperance." As late as 1930, only 16 states had laws prohibiting marijuana use, and these laws were not vigorously enforced. A single government agency, the Federal Bureau of Narcotics, played the key role in bringing about the prohibition of marijuana in the United States. This agency was set up to enforce opium prohibition in 1930, and its director became convinced that marijuana use was a form of wrongdoing that should be under his jurisdiction. Accordingly, the bureau began an intensive program of lobbying for the prohibition of marijuana. It also circulated a number of phony horror stories about the effects of marijuana, but virtually no one challenged the bureau's distortions and outright lies. In 1937, Congress passed the Marijuana Tax Act, which was designed to stamp out use of the drug, and every state eventually passed an outright prohibition of its own.

Most of the newer drugs that became popular among recreational users in the twentieth century were created by the pharmaceutical corporations, and many were initially promoted with erroneous claims that they were less addictive than their predecessors. Heroin was synthesized in 1874 and first placed on the market by Bayer Laboratories in 1898. It was widely promoted as a safe substitute for codeine and a cure for morphine addiction. The first barbiturate was clinically tested in 1903, and by the 1930s barbiturates were in common use. Although references to barbiturate intoxication and withdrawal convulsions were made as early as 1905, it was not until 1950 that a controlled study was done to prove their addictive properties. As barbiturates were coming to be recognized as a major drug problem, methaqualone (often known by the brand name Quaalude) was falsely advertised as a safe substitute. LSD was first created in 1938. Although it was never promoted as a prescription drug, Sandoz Laboratories did give LSD samples to scientists from 1953 to 1966 in hopes of finding some commercial use. Moreover, it has now come to light that the Central Intelligence Agency and the U.S. Army conducted secret experiments with LSD during this period—experiments that included dosing unsuspecting citizens with the drug to test its effectiveness as a combat weapon.[61]

Of course, pharmaceutical companies never sold these drugs directly to recreational users on the black market. Drugs legally produced for the prescription market are often diverted into the black market, however, and once a particular drug gains popularity with recreational users, illegal laboratories soon spring up to meet the demand.

The main focus of the "war on drugs" was increased law enforcement, as shown in this photo of a narcotics arrest in Miami.

During the second half of the 1980s, American society began to focus on the problem of drug abuse more intensely than ever before. Drug use became a powerful public symbol for a host of social ills from the decline of the work ethic to the decay of the traditional family structure. In the frenzy that followed, politicians from all sides of the political spectrum seemed to be competing to outdo each other with their condemnations of drug users, and the federal government launched what was probably the biggest antidrug campaign ever. This so-called "war on drugs" involved many programs, but its principal focus was tougher enforcement. Unprecedented media attention and billions of dollars were devoted to the antidrug campaign, and prisons were soon overflowing with drug offenders (see Chapter 10). Supporters of this enforcement effort have claimed that it was responsible for the decline in drug use previously noted. This seems unlikely, however, for as we have seen, drug use was going down well before the big increases in drug enforcement funding, and the use of tobacco and alcohol (obviously not affected by the crackdown) declined along with the use of the illicit drugs. Rather, most sociologists would attribute these changes to the aging of the population and to a predictable counterreaction to the excesses of the 1960s and 1970s.

In the last few years, there have been some signs that the tide may once again be shifting. Several states have approved voter initiatives that permit the medical use of marijuana, and in 2000 the bellwether state of California passed a voter initiative that mandated drug treatment, not imprisonment, for first and second convictions on drug use charges. The penalties for drug dealing, however, remain unchanged.

LESSONS FROM OTHER PLACES

FIGHTING DRUGS IN GERMANY

If you walk around major cities in Germany you can see that, as the statistics indicate, Germany has much less poverty, street crime, and other social problems such as illegal drug use. But Germany does have a drug problem. In Germany's big cities there are areas where drug addicts congregate, sell and use drugs, and often sleep on the streets. One such area is a beautiful riverside park that is not far from the central train station in Frankfurt.

The German controversy over what policies will most efficiently deal with drug abuse will sound quite familiar to Americans. Conservatives, including the Christian Democrats, favor an abstinence strategy that aims at a controlled use of alcohol, nicotine, and prescription drugs, on the one hand, and the prohibition of all other drugs (whether "soft" or "hard") on the other. Conservatives frequently talk about "fighting drug use" that is "endangering social order," while their counterparts, the liberals, argue for "preventing addiction" and avoiding the "consequences of criminalizing drug use." The liberals, including large parts of the Social Democratic and Green Parties, advocate more tolerance by measures such as liberalizing laws against soft drugs and allowing the controlled use of hard drugs by addicts. While conservatives seem to have a stronger fear of the dangers of drug use, liberals see some drug use as inevitable and focus on the damage caused by harsh drug-enforcement policies.

The controversy over drug policy heated up in December 1990 when representatives of all the political parties and some other organizations met with then Chancellor Kohl to launch a fight against drug abuse. This National Drug Prevention Plan followed the American model for a "get tough" approach, and it resulted in more convictions and tougher sentences for drug offenses. Much to the frustration of the advocates of this approach, the number of hard-core users has almost tripled since the implementation of the plan. The official count of the number of addicts is at 150,000, while some estimates go as far as 200,000 to 300,000. There are now believed to be some 6 million Germans under 40 years of age who have had some experience with illicit drugs—that is about one of every three people in that age group. The proportion who use drugs on a regular basis over a longer period of time ranges between 18 and 20 percent.

Source: Harold Kerbo and Hermann Strasser, *Modern Germany* (New York: McGraw-Hill, 2000).

QUICK REVIEW

Summarize the history of the efforts at drug control in North America.

SOLVING THE DRUG PROBLEM

During the past two decades, the United States has been experiencing what sociologists sometimes term a "moral panic" about the use of illicit drugs. Many Americans see the spread of illicit drugs as a new plague the reflects the moral decay of modern times. If we look at the problem in historical perspective, however, we see that it is really nothing new and that we have already gone through several cycles of rapidly growing drug use followed by eras of "temperance" and declining use. For example, Daniel Patrick Moynihan points out that in the early nineteenth century "distilled spirits in early America appeared as a font of national unity, easy money, manly strength, and all-round good cheer. . . . It became routine to drink whiskey at breakfast and to go on drinking all day."[62] In 1830, the average American drank five gallons of distilled liquor a year—almost five times more than we do today. But by 1840, a vigorous temperance movement had brought consumption down to two gallons a person.[63] Americans disagree on just how serious our current drug problems are. What we can say is that we currently appear to have just completed another cycle, with big increases in the 1960s and 1970s and declining usage since then. Some recent developments may signal the beginning of another upward cycle, but they may not. Much will depend on the wisdom of the policies we pursue in the coming years.

PREVENTION

Most people agree that the best way to deal with drug problems is to discourage young people from using drugs in the first place—but how do we do that? One common approach is to try to frighten them by presenting horror stories in "drug education" classes. However, such attempts seriously underestimate the awareness and intelligence of our youth. Sooner or later they discover that they have not been told the whole truth, and they may come to doubt even the accurate information they have been given about drug problems. A more reasonable approach is to present the best factual information available, regardless of whether or not it is likely to discourage students from using drugs. Critics of educational programs argue that so much talk about drugs in the classroom excites some teenagers' interest in trying them. Education programs need not, however, be administered exclusively by the schools. Another approach that has been widely used is to run public service advertising about the problems caused by drugs, and a further step would be to prohibit all advertising for drugs such as alcohol and tobacco.

Others believe that prevention programs are doomed to failure because such programs pursue an unrealistic goal. These critics think that a certain amount of drug use is inevitable in our complex and insecure society, and the goal therefore should be to encourage moderation, not total abstinence. Most research indicates that moderate drug use does not usually cause serious psychological or physical problems. For example, a University of California study that tracked 739 young people from junior high until young adulthood concluded that the harm caused by drugs depends largely on the level of use. No measurable harm was found from moderate drug use, but as use increased, so did its damage.[64]

Many people therefore advocate more balanced educational programs that allow students to make a rational choice based on all the available information. In this view, the best way to prevent drug problems is to accept a certain level of use but encourage the creation of clear social standards about how much is too much. Researchers have found, for example, that the rate of alcoholism is low among Italians (and Italian Americans) even though their per capita alcohol consumption is significantly higher than in most countries. Italian culture does not condemn drinking but contains clearly defined norms that limit alcohol consumption to mealtimes and other social occasions. On the other hand, alcohol use was not part of the traditional culture of Native Americans, and their high rate of alcoholism today is often attributed to the weakness of the norms regulating alcohol use.[65]

TREATMENT

The treatment approach, like prevention, tries to discourage drug use. The difference is that treatment programs attempt to help people stop using drugs after they have already developed a problem. A variety of treatment programs have been tried, but no single program works for everyone. Many drug users go through several programs before kicking the habit.

Individual psychotherapy has proved to be one of the least successful approaches to drug problems.[66] Drug use is a social phenomenon, and no matter how much psychiatric care drug users receive, strong social support is usually needed to help them give up the drug habit.

Aversive therapy, a treatment based on the principles of behavioral psychology, is designed to discourage drug use by teaching the patient to associate the effects of the drug with some unpleasant sensation such as an electric shock or nausea. Aversive techniques are widely used to discourage smoking, but they have been less successful with other drugs, such as alcohol and heroin.

The most successful treatment programs involve group support. Alcoholics Anonymous (AA) is one of the oldest such groups and is now a worldwide organization. Treatment takes the form of meetings at which members describe their troubles with alcohol and the help they have found in Alcoholics Anonymous. Members are encouraged to call on one another for help when they feel a desire to start drinking again. The AA program is religiously oriented, but its success seems to derive primarily from its system of encouraging each member to try to reform others, thus reinforcing the reformer's own nondrinking behavior. There are also successful nonreligious programs, such as Rational Recovery (RR) and the Secular Organization for Sobriety (SOS), which follow the same principles but emphasize individual responsibility instead of reliance on a "higher power," as AA does.[67]

More intensive than AA-style programs are the **therapeutic communities**, in which patients live together in a special house or dormitory for long periods of time. The first of these communities was Synanon, founded in Santa Monica, California, in 1958.

Many social scientists believe that treatment programs, such as the one shown in this photo, are the most effective way to deal with the problems created by the abuse of alcohol and other drugs.

Synanon members were ex-users who maintained strict discipline, prohibited all drug use, and helped each other avoid drugs. Frequent group sessions were held in which members discussed their problems and criticized individuals who failed to live up to the expectations of the group.[68] Although Synanon has changed drastically in recent years, other therapeutic communities, such as Phoenix House, which now has about 15 percent of all the beds in the nation's therapeutic communities, still follow its original principles.[69]

Most therapeutic communities claim high rates of success, but few researchers have conducted rigorous studies to support those claims. One major drawback is that these programs appeal only to drug users who can accept their ideology and discipline. It has been estimated that only 10 to 25 percent of drug users who join these communities finish their program—but most of those who do so remain drug free.[70] Another problem with some therapeutic communities is that those who complete the program successfully may have difficulty leaving. Many become "professional ex-addicts" working in halfway houses or other drug programs.

LEGAL REPRESSION

When the use of a particular drug comes to be seen as a problem, the most common response is a legal one—prohibiting the manufacture and sale of the drug and punishing the users. This approach has been tried with almost all psychoactive drugs used in North America except caffeine and nicotine. The assumption is that people will not use drugs if there are simply none available or if they are threatened with jail, but it is difficult to evaluate the success of this approach. For example, opiate use declined sharply after it was declared illegal, but marijuana use has increased enormously since its prohibition. Supporters of this approach argue that its failures are due to a lack of tough laws and enough money to enforce them.

While it seems fair to conclude that the prohibition approach usually does reduce (but not eliminate) the use of the condemned drug, the matter is a good deal more complex than that. For one thing, the cost of effectively repressing a popular drug may be far more than society can afford. As the drug becomes more scarce, the price is driven up, and drug dealers have more money to offer in bribes and corruption (a key reason for the frequent failure of this approach). Political factors also obstruct the enforcement effort. For example, evidence has emerged showing not only that the Central Intelligence Agency has been involved with drug-dealing schemes to help finance its secret operations, but also that several presidential administrations have intentionally ignored drug-running activities by their allies in volatile Third World countries. Even if the enforcement effort could somehow dry up the supply of illicit drugs, this approach would still have unintended side effects. A policy that completely removed all popular drugs from the black market, while continuing to allow almost unrestricted over-the-counter sales of alcohol and tobacco, seems likely to achieve little more than the substitution of one dangerous substance for another.

In the real world, of course, a black market would almost certainly remain, and that situation fosters the growth of organized crime. When a drug is prohibited by law, legitimate businesses are forced out of the market. The demand for the drug is still there, however, and criminals organize to meet it. Because such criminals have no competition from legitimate enterprise, legal prohibition guarantees them huge tax free profits. The classic example of this process was the prohibition of alcohol in the United States during the 1920s and early 1930s. As many Americans sought new sources of alcoholic beverages, gangs of criminals began to supply them. The result was widespread gangsterism and disrespect for the law. Gang bosses such as Al Capone, who built his illegal empire by bootlegging alcohol, virtually controlled some American cities. Today, it is estimated that illegal drug dealers take in between $50 and $60 billion a year in the United States alone.[71]

In addition to organized crime, drug prohibition encourages the growth of deviant subcultures among users who band together to share their experiences and defeat government efforts to cut off supplies of their drug. Many marijuana users report that they originally were more attracted to the camaraderie and friendship of other drug users than to the effects of the drug itself. Finally, the enforcement effort poses a serious threat to civil liberties. Drug offenses seldom involve victims who call the police. Law enforcement agencies must therefore resort to such questionable techniques as the use of wiretaps, undercover agents, and spies to flush out violations. A final problem with prohibition programs is their cost. As a result of the antidrug campaigns of the last decade, there are now almost 300,000 Americans in prison for drug offenses, and the total cost of the enforcement effort runs about $20 billion a year.[72]

Of course, these criticisms do not necessarily mean that the enforcement approach should be abandoned, for the results may be judged to be worth the price. They do suggest, however, that it is far more preferable to reduce the demand for drugs through education and treatment.

INCREASED SOCIAL TOLERANCE

An alternative approach to the drug problem is to increase social tolerance. This approach includes a variety of proposals, ranging from reductions in penalties for some types of drug offenses to full legalization of all drugs. Advocates of such proposals claim that a less punitive reaction to drug use would reduce the negative side effects stemming from legal repression and, in the long run, reduce the need for treatment.

Legalization   Proponents of legalization believe that attempts at legal repression of drug use have been so disastrous that the problem can be solved only by taking the government out of the business of enforcing drug laws. If drugs could be obtained legally, it is argued, their attractiveness as "forbidden fruit" would decrease. Further, legalization would take the profit out of drug distribution, thus taking drugs off the street. Even if this approach failed to reduce drug use, its advocates assert that it would still reduce the drug problem by reducing organized crime, destigmatizing drug users, undermining drug subcultures, and eliminating the need for addicts to commit crimes to pay for high-priced illegal drugs.

In practice, regulation by government agencies would undoubtedly continue, as it does in the case of alcohol. Minors would be prohibited from purchasing drugs, and taxation and standards for potency and quality could be regulated. Most proponents of legalization do not advocate over-the-counter sales for all drugs, however. In fact, marijuana is the only drug for which full legalization has widespread support. Those who advocate the legalization of all drugs often base their arguments on philosophical opposition to government interference in individuals' lives. The psychiatrist Thomas Szasz, for instance, feels that the decision to use a drug is entirely an individual matter in which the government has no legitimate concern.[73]

Decriminalization   A step halfway between prohibition and full legalization is **decriminalization**. Its advocates argue that penalties for possession and use of a given drug should be dropped, but that the sale of the drug should continue to be illegal. The aim is to stop punishing those who use drugs, since they are not hurting anyone else, and instead discourage use indirectly by forbidding sales. Critics of this policy point to the contradiction between allowing legal possession but penalizing sale or purchase. Its advocates fear that legalization would encourage a new wave of drug use, yet they want to reduce the repression of users, so they propose decriminalization as a compromise.

Decriminalization of marijuana use, or a reduction in the penalties for possession and use of marijuana, has at times been endorsed by American and Canadian commissions on drug use, the American Medical Association, and the American Bar Association. Eleven states decriminalized possession of small amounts of marijuana during the 1970s. The new wave of concern about drug abuse has reversed this trend, however, and the legal repression of marijuana use has grown more intense in recent years. Well over 300,000 people are arrested for marijuana offenses each year in the United States; and there are now about 15,000 persons in federal prisons for such offenses and perhaps twice that number in state and local jails.[74] However, some observers believe that the 1997 passage of the California voter initiative legalizing the medical use of marijuana in that state may mark another turning point in the public's view of marijuana use.

Maintenance Through **drug maintenance** programs, addicts or habitual users can be supplied with a drug while it is still prohibited among the public at large. The only legal maintenance program in the United States involves the distribution of methadone (a synthetic opiate) to heroin addicts, and there are now about 125,000 people in such programs.[75] Although methadone maintenance is often called treatment, it has little in common with real treatment programs. In essence, these programs simply provide a restricted legal supply of an opiate to people who otherwise would obtain opiates illegally. Supporters of methadone maintenance programs point to research showing a very substantial drop in criminal activities among addicts who participate.[76] They also argue that methadone has several advantages over heroin: Its effects last longer, it can be given orally, and it does not generate the intense high that is produced by heroin. However, many heroin addicts refuse to participate in methadone programs because they prefer heroin, and for that reason, some researchers argue that heroin should be used in maintenance programs as well. Critics of maintenance programs, including some ex-addicts, argue that methadone is just another narcotic and thus dispensing it to heroin users does nothing to solve their addiction problem.

The Dutch Approach Some advocates of a new approach to the drug problem point to the Netherlands as a possible model. Dutch drug policy is an interesting combination of four elements. The first is the official tolerance of "soft drugs" (marijuana and hashish—a condensed form of marijuana). Although sale is technically illegal, many cafes openly sell marijuana without fear of arrests or fines. The second is a tough enforcement effort aimed at the dealers of hard drugs, such as heroin and cocaine, which are often smuggled into Rotterdam, the world's largest port. The third element of Dutch policy is the decriminalization of all users. No one is jailed for merely using or possessing small amounts of any drug. Finally, the Dutch have made treatment and maintenance programs easily available to all addicts.

Since this program was begun, Holland has seen both a sharp decline in the number of heroin addicts and an increase in their average age (indicating that fewer young people are starting the habit). Equally impressive is the fact that the Netherlands never experienced the cocaine epidemic that created such a crisis in North America. Despite these successes, however, the critics of increased tolerance for drug users remain unconvinced. They argue that the Dutch experience is not applicable to the United States because the Netherlands has no large ethnic ghettos and has a much more generous welfare system that makes poverty far less severe. As the barriers to free movement among European countries have come down, the Dutch are also being faced with a problem known as "drug tourism"—an increasing number of people from countries with more restrictive laws coming to Holland to buy marijuana.[77]

QUICK REVIEW

Summarize the different possible responses to the drug problem. Which one seems the best to you?

SOCIOLOGICAL PERSPECTIVES ON DRUG USE

THE FUNCTIONALIST PERSPECTIVE

Functionalist theory does not attempt to explain the specific reasons why individuals do or do not use drugs. It concerns itself with the social conditions that have caused the tremendous increase in drug use in industrial society. Many functionalists assume that drug use is a means of escaping from difficult and unpleasant social circumstances. Consequently, drug abuse is seen as a response to other social problems, such as poverty, worker alienation, and racism. To these functionalists, the way to reduce substance abuse is to deal with its underlying causes. This is obviously no simple matter, but functionalists have numerous proposals for improvements, many of which are described in the other chapters in this book.

Other functionalists, however, look at the causes of drug use in a different way. They feel that the use of drugs is inherently pleasurable and that, despite the serious consequences, people will take them unless prevented from doing so. The steep increase in drug consumption in the twentieth century is seen as the result of the weakening of the family and religious institutions that formerly kept antisocial behavior in check. The most direct way to deal with the drug problem is therefore to strengthen these institutions. Many functionalists feel, however, that the historical changes that have occurred are irreversible and that industrial societies must rely on formal mechanisms of social control—that is, the criminal-justice system. These functionalists often criticize the disorganization of our system of justice. They argue that the inefficiency, inadequate funding, and payoffs and corruption that plague so many of our criminal-justice agencies must be halted if we are to solve the drug problem.

THE CONFLICT PERSPECTIVE

Some conflict theorists also assume that drug users are escapists and agree that drug use is caused by other social problems. However, they hold that these social problems, such as unemployment and poverty, stem from exploitation and injustice rather than from social disorganization. Like their counterparts among the functionalists, these conflict theorists advocate a direct attack on the primary problem—exploitation—rather than on drug use, which they view as a symptom of the problem. They argue that drug use will decrease only after a just society, free from racism, poverty, and oppression, is created.

Other conflict theorists strongly disagree, asserting that drug use itself is neither escapist nor a social problem. Rather, it is normal behavior that occurs in all societies around the world. According to these theorists, drug use becomes a problem only when groups who oppose drugs use the power of the state to force their morality on everyone else. The inevitable result of such actions is social conflict, violent repression of drug users, and a booming black market.

Most conflict theorists argue that people should not be jailed for using drugs if their behavior causes no danger to others. Conflict theorists also believe that the attempt to repress drug use creates secondary social problems, such as organized crime and a seething discontent with the legal system. Those who hold this viewpoint advocate a simple solution to the drug problem: Legalize the prohibited drugs and stop jailing people who have done nothing worse than refuse to accept the dominant society's idea of what is good for them. If drug users victimize others to support their habit, they should be sent to prison; otherwise, they should be left alone.

THE FEMINIST PERSPECTIVE

Feminists point out the strong link between gender role expectations and our drug problems. Drinking and smoking have traditionally been more acceptable among men than women, and women continue to have lower rates of drug use than men. As a result, women who are heavy drug users often go to great lengths to conceal their behavior, and in general the drug problem among women tends to be more hidden. The one group of drugs used significantly more often by women are psychoactive prescription drugs, such as tranquilizers. One explanation for this difference is that women are more likely to seek out psychiatric help for anxiety and depression, while men who may have the same psychological difficulties are more likely to self-medicate with alcohol and illicit drugs. But the use of such prescription "medicine" also allows women to avoid the definition of their behavior as drug use. Men, on the other hand, are likely to feel a stronger stigma in seeking help from a physician for their emotional problems than in heavy drinking. Thus, feminists advise that people trying to do something about the drug problem must be sensitive to the important differences between the genders if they are to maximize their chances for success.

Feminists are also concerned that the criminalization of drug users, especially women who are pregnant or who have children, worsens the situation of many families, while doing virtually nothing to curtail drug use. It would be better, they say, to make effective treatment widely available rather than to vilify and criminalize users. It is especially important to make excellent prenatal care, which would include effective drug treatment for women who need it, available to all women.

THE INTERACTIONIST PERSPECTIVE

Interactionists have devoted a great deal of attention to drug use, and we have already examined their theory that it is learned in social interaction like any other behavior. Another major contribution of interactionist theory is its emphasis on the critical importance of the way society defines drugs and drug use. In their view, our definitions shape the way we respond to our social problems and even determine whether or not we consider something to be a social problem. In the nineteenth century, for example, opiates were defined primarily as medicine, and although their use was widespread, it was not considered a social problem. As sensationalistic press reports began to associate opium smoking with the unpopular Chinese minority, attitudes changed. Once the opiates came to be seen as dope, not medicine, they were soon prohibited, and we saw the growth of what might be termed the "junkie subculture." Interactionists point out that similar changes now appear to be happening in the definition of tobacco smoking. What used to be considered chic and sexy is increasingly being defined as dependence on an addictive drug. As more restrictions are placed on tobacco smoking, interactionists urge antismoking activists to learn from the mistakes of the past and avoid the prohibitionist policies that proved to be so disastrous for alcohol and the opiates.

QUICK REVIEW

What are the differences between the recommendations of conflict theorists and those of functionalists for dealing with the drug problem?
What are the differences in the drug problems of men and women?
Why do interactionists say that the way society defines drug use is important?

SUMMARY

Many people have mistaken ideas about drug use. For example, it is widely believed that because alcohol and tobacco are legal, they are not drugs, but there is actually little difference between these drugs and the illegal ones. Another misconception is that drug use is a new epidemic that is sweeping through our society. Surveys and sales figures indicate that total drug use has actually gone down in the last 20 years, although there has been an increase in drug use among teenagers since the early 1990s.

Physical dependence occurs when a user takes enough of a drug to produce a tolerance and when the user will become sick when it is withdrawn. Addiction is the strong craving that often develops after a period of physical dependence.

Alcohol is the most popular recreational drug, and it also creates the most problems for society. It is a depressant and is addictive if used in excess. Tobacco is another widely used legal drug. Cigarette smoking has been shown to be highly dangerous, yet large numbers of people start smoking every year. Although its popularity has declined in recent years, marijuana is still the most widely used illegal drug. Opiates are all highly addictive, and their use is associated with an extremely dangerous lifestyle. Mescaline and LSD are two of the most popular psychedelic drugs, and both produce powerful psychological changes. Sedative-hypnotics have effects similar to those of alcohol. They are frequently prescribed by physicians, but there is also a flourishing black market for many of these drugs. Amphetamines are stimulants, and excessive use can produce a psychotic state as well as considerable physical damage. Cocaine is a natural stimulant with effects similar to those of amphetamines. Some of the newest arrivals on the drug scene are the so-called club drugs such as MDMA (ecstasy), GHB, and Ketamine, which combine psychedelic and depressant effects.

Biological theories hold that some people have an inherited predisposition toward alcoholism or drug addiction. Behavioral theory sees drug use and addiction as products of conditioning: People use drugs because they find the experience to be rewarding, and addicts continue to take drugs because they want to avoid painful withdrawal. Personality theorists argue that individuals who use drugs have inadequate or impulsive personalities. According to interactionist theory, drug use stems from attitudes, values, and definitions favorable to such behavior, often learned in drug subcultures.

The original colonists had relatively few problems with drugs. Later, heavy drinking patterns developed among single men on the frontier, while farm families began to give up drinking. Several prohibitionist movements swept North America in the early twentieth century and resulted in the banning of alcohol, opiates, and marijuana. Prohibition of these drugs fostered drug subcultures among some users, who were branded as criminals.

Proposals for dealing with the drug problem fall into four main categories. The first consists of prevention programs designed to stop people from getting involved with drugs or using them to excess. The second approach is to treat drug users to help them quit using drugs. The most successful treatment programs use some form of group support. A third strategy calls for increasing legal repression of drug use. This approach discourages drug use but has damaging side effects, including the growth of organized crime and drug subcultures. A fourth alternative is increased social tolerance of drug use. Included in this category are legalization, decriminalization, and maintenance programs.

Most functionalists assume that drug use is a means of escaping from unpleasant social conditions that have arisen as society has become disorganized. Some conflict theorists also assume that drug users are escapists, but they are convinced that the tensions drug users seek to avoid stem from exploitation rather than from social disorganization. Other conflict theorists consider drug use to be normal behavior and argue that the problem lies in the state's attempts to repress it. Feminists point out the significant differences in the drug problem between women and men, and interactionists emphasize the critical importance of the way society defines the use of a particular drug.

QUESTIONS FOR CRITICAL THINKING

In the past decade or so, the public has often seen drug use as America's foremost social problem, but many critics have argued that the problem has been blown far out of proportion. How would you evaluate the importance of the drug problem compared with other difficult issues, such as poverty, warfare, violence, and racism? Why has the issue of illicit drug use been so popular among politicians? What effect have the media had on our perception of the drug problem?

KEY TERMS

addiction
alcoholic
aversive therapy
decriminalization
depressant
drug maintenance

individual psychotherapy
passive smoking
stimulant
therapeutic community
tolerance
withdrawal

NOTES

1. Debra Rosenberg and Matt Bai, "Drinking and Dying," *Newsweek*, October 13, 1997, p. 69.
2. See also, *Los Angeles Times*, September 1, 2000.
3. U.S. Bureau of the Census, *Statistical Abstract of the United States*, 1996 (Washington, DC: U.S. Government Printing Office, 1996), p. 148; U.S. Bureau of the Census, *Statistical Abstract of the United States*, 1999, p. 152.

4. U.S. Bureau of the Census, *Statistical Abstract of the United States,* 1996, p. 138; U.S. Bureau of the Census, *Statistical Abstract of the United States,* 1999, p. 153; U.S. Department of Health and Human Services, *Health, the United States,* 2000 (Washington, DC: U.S. Government Printing Office, 2000), Figure 26.

5. Richard G. Schlaadt and Peter T. Shannon, *Drugs,* 3rd ed. (Upper Saddle River, NJ: Prentice Hall, 1990), p. 45.

6. See Craig MacAndrew and Robert B. Edgerton, *Drunken Comportment: A Social Explanation* (Chicago: Aldine-Atherton, 1966).

7. Philip J. Hilts, "Is Nicotine Addictive? It Depends on Whose Criteria You Use," *New York Times,* August 21, 1994, p. B6.

8. Schlaadt and Shannon, *Drugs,* p. 175.

9. Jack H. Mendelson and Nancy K. Mello, *Alcohol Use and Abuse in America* (Boston: Little, Brown, 1985), p. 225.

10. Timothy J. Flanagan and Kathleen Maguire, eds., *Sourcebook of Criminal Justice Statistics,* 1989 (Washington, DC: U.S. Government Printing Office, 1990).

11. Schlaadt and Shannon, *Drugs,* p. 185.

12. B. Drummond Ayres, Jr., "Big Drop in Drunken Driving," *San Francisco Sunday Examiner and Chronicle,* May 22, 1994, p. A7.

13. U.S. Bureau of the Census, *Statistical Abstract,* 1996, p. 144.

14. Ibid., p. 146.

15. Associated Press, "College Boozing an Epidemic—Panel," *San Luis Obispo Telegram-Tribune,* June 7, 1994, pp. A1, A12.

16. U.S. Department of Health and Human Services, *Health, the United States,* 2000, Figure 27.

17. U.S. Bureau of the Census, *Statistical Abstract,* 1999, p. 153.

18. Ibid., p. 153.

19. Philip J. Hilts, "Visions of Nationwide Withdrawal," *New York Times,* April 27, 1994, p. B7.

20. Oakley Ray and Charles Ksir, *Drugs, Society, and Human Behavior* (St. Louis: Mosby), pp. 199–202.

21. Quoted in Matt Clark, "Slow-Motion Suicide," *Newsweek,* January 22, 1979, pp. 83–84; see also U.S. Department of Health and Human Services, *Smoking and Health: A Report of the Surgeon General* (Washington, DC: U.S. Government Printing Office, 1979).

22. Associated Press, "Koop: Tobacco Like Heroin, Cocaine," *San Luis Obispo Telegram-Tribune,* May 16, 1988, p. A1.

23. Sheryl Stolberg, "Mortality Study Finds Tobacco Is No. 1 Culprit," *Los Angeles Times,* November 10, 1993, pp. A1, A33.

24. See James William Coleman, *The Criminal Elite: Understanding White Collar Crime* (New York: St. Martin's Press, 1998), pp. 79–80.

25. Schlaadt and Shannon, *Drugs,* pp. 116–150.

26. Sheryl Stolberg, "Science Stokes the Tobacco Debate," *Los Angeles Times,* May 26, 1994, pp. A1, A22, A23; Associated Press, "EPA Official Tries to Bury Smoking Report," *San Luis Obispo Telegram-Tribune,* May 30, 1991, p. B8.

27. Denise Grady, "Study Finds Secondhand Smoke Doubles Risk of Heart Disease," *New York Times,* May 20, 1997, pp. A1, A10.

28. Marlene Cimons, "Teen-Agers Face Special Smoking Risk, Report Warns," *Los Angeles Times,* February 25, 1994, p. A19.

29. Barnaby J. Feder, "Increase in Teen-Age Smoking Sharpest Among Black Males," *New York Times,* May 24, 1996, p. A9; Jeff Bingaman, "Tobacco Has Dead Aim on Latinos," *Los Angeles Times,* February 11, 1990, p. M5; Donna K. H. Walters, "Cigarettes: Makers Aim at Special Niches to Boost Sales," *Los Angeles Times,* September 15, 1985, sec. 5, p. A3; Associated Press, "EPA Official Tries to Bury Smoking Report."

30. U.S. Bureau of the Census, *Statistical Abstract,* 1999, p. 152.

31. Monitoring the Future 2000, <http://www.monitoringthefuture.org>; see also U.S. Department of Health and Human Services, *Health, the United States,* 2000, Figure 28.

32. Eric Schlosser, "Reefer Madness," *Atlantic Monthly,* August 1994, pp. 45–63; Janny Scott, "Pot Takes a Hit in New Study of Health Dangers," *Los Angeles Times,* February 11, 1988, sec. 1, pp. 3, 36.

33. Howard S. Becker, *Outsiders* (New York: Free Press, 1963), pp. 41–58.
34. Schlaadt and Shannon, *Drugs*, pp. 258–259.
35. See William A. Rushing, *The AIDS Epidemic: Social Dimensions of an Infectious Disease* (Boulder, CO: Westview, 1995); Lawrence K. Altman, "Obstacle-Strewn Road to Rethinking the Numbers on AIDS," *New York Times*, March 1, 1994, p. B8; Schlaadt and Shannon, *Drugs*, p. 215.
36. U.S. Bureau of the Census, *Statistical Abstract*, 1999, p. 152.
37. Juanita Darling, "Colombians Up Quality, Lower Price of Heroin," *Los Angeles Times*, February 24, 1997, pp. A1, A6, A7; Robert Sabbag, "The Cartels Would Like a Second Chance," *Rolling Stone*, May 5, 1994, pp. 35–37, 43.
38. Ray and Ksir, *Drugs, Society, and Human Behavior*, pp. 342–359; James William Coleman, "The Myth of Addiction," *Journal of Drug Issues* 6 (1976): 135–141.
39. See Schlaadt and Shannon, *Drugs*, pp. 238–243; Ray and Ksir, *Drugs, Society, and Human Behavior*, pp. 336–337.
40. Peter Wilkinson, "The Young and the Reckless," *Rolling Stone*, May 5, 1994, pp. 29–32; Harry Nelson, "LSD Still on Some Minds," *Los Angeles Times*, March 25, 1991, p. B3; Schlaadt and Shannon, *Drugs*, p. 240.
41. Ray and Ksir, *Drugs, Society, and Human Behavior*, pp. 314–319.
42. Schlaadt and Shannon, *Drugs*, pp. 82–87.
43. See Anthony R. Lovett, "Wired in California," *Rolling Stone*, May 5, 1994, pp. 39–40.
44. Schlaadt and Shannon, *Drugs*, pp. 91–100.
45. U.S. Bureau of the Census, *Statistical Abstract*, 1996, p. 144.
46. Schlaadt and Shannon, *Drugs*, pp. 39–44.
47. Marlene Cimons, "Youth Steroid Use Believed Rising," *Los Angeles Times*, September 8, 1990, p. A2.
48. Monitoring the Future 2000, <http://www.monitoringthefuture.org>.
49. Sidney Cohen, *The Alcoholism Problem: Selected Issues* (New York: Haworth, 1983), p. 86; D. W. Goodwin, "Genetics of Alcoholism," in R. W. Pickens and L. L. Heston, eds., *Psychiatric Factors in Drug Abuse* (New York: Grune & Stratton, 1979).
50. E. M. Jellinek, *The Disease of Alcoholism* (Highland Park, NJ: Hillhouse, 1960).
51. Kathleen Whalen Fitzgerald, *Alcoholism: The Genetic Inheritance* (New York: Doubleday, 1985), pp. 1–21.
52. Alfred R. Lindesmith, *Addiction and Opiates* (Chicago: Aldine-Atherton, 1968), pp. 64–67.
53. G. E. Barnes, "The Alcoholic Personality: A Reanalysis of the Literature," *Journal of Studies on Alcohol* 40 (1979): 622.
54. Ray and Ksir, *Drugs, Society and Human Behavior*, p. 160.
55. Isador Chein, Donald Gerard, Robert Lee, and Eva Rosenfeld, *The Road to H* (New York: Basic Books, 1964).
56. George Vaillant, *The Natural History of Alcoholism* (Cambridge, MA: Harvard University Press, 1983).
57. James William Coleman, "The Dynamics of Narcotic Abstinence: An Interactionist Theory," *Sociological Quarterly* 19 (1978): 555–564; James William Coleman, "The Myth of Addiction," *Journal of Drug Issues* 6 (spring 1976): 135–141.
58. D. F. Musto, "The History of Legislative Control over Opium, Cocaine, and Their Derivatives," in Ronald Hamowy, ed., *Dealing with Drugs: Consequences of Government Control* (San Francisco: Pacific Research Institutes for Public Policy, 1987), pp. 37–71.
59. Coleman, "The Myth of Addiction."
60. See Randy E. Marnett, "Curing the Drug-Law Addiction: The Harmful Side Effects of Legal Prohibition," in Hamowy, *Dealing with Drugs*, pp. 73–102.
61. Ray and Ksir, *Drugs, Society, and Human Behavior*, pp. 314–319, 334–335, 377–380.
62. Daniel Patrick Moynihan, "Iatrogenic Government," *American Scholar* 62 (summer 1993): 354.
63. Seymour Martin Lipset, *American Exceptionalism: A Double-Edged Sword* (New York: Norton, 1996), pp. 271–272.
64. Janny Scott, "Debate Resurrected over Risks of Casual Drug Use," *Los Angeles Times*, August 10, 1988, sec. 1, pp. 1, 20.

65. See Marshall B. Clinard, *The Sociology of Deviant Behavior*, 4th ed. (New York: Holt, Rineha. Winston, 1974), pp. 412–419; Erich Goode, *Drugs and American Society* (New York: Knopf, 1972. pp. 147–148.

66. Roger Meyer, *Guide to Drug Rehabilitation* (Boston: Beacon Press, 1972), pp. 61–63.

67. David Gelman, "Clean and Sober—and Agnostic," *Newsweek*, July 8, 1991, pp. 62–63.

68. See Rita Vokman and Donald R. Cressey, "Differential Association and the Rehabilitation of Drug Addicts," *American Journal of Sociology* 69 (1963): 129–142.

69. Norman Atkins, "The Cost of Living Clean," *Rolling Stone*, May 5, 1994, pp. 41–42.

70. Ibid.; Meyer, *Guide to Drug Rehabilitation*, p. 72; Ray and Ksir, *Drugs, Society, and Human Behavior*, pp. 360–362.

71. Ethan Nadelmann and Jann S. Wenner, "Toward a Sane National Drug Policy," *Rolling Stone*, May 5, 1994, pp. 24–26.

72. Ibid.; U.S. Department of Justice, *Sourcebook of Criminal Justice Statistics*, 1999 (Washington, DC: U.S. Government Printing Office, 2000), p. 513.

73. Thomas Szasz, *Ceremonial Chemistry: The Ritual Persecution of Drugs, Addicts, and Pushers*, rev. ed. (Holmes Beach, FL: Learning Publications, 1985).

74. Schlosser, "Reefer Madness."

75. Atkins, "The Cost of Living Clean."

76. Ibid.

77. Marlise Simons, "Dutch Swamped by Flood of Drugs," *New York Times*, April 20, 1994, p. A7; Rone Tempest, "Drugs: Dutch Gain with a Tolerant Tack," *Los Angeles Times*, September 22, 1989, pp. A1, A10–11.

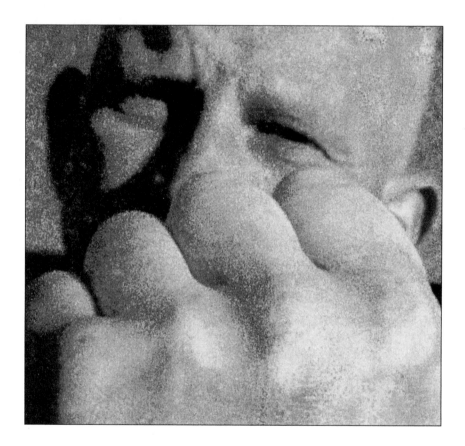

CHAPTER 10

CRIME AND VIOLENCE

Questions to Consider

What are the most serious types of crime and violence?

What do the statistics tell us about the crime problem?

What are the causes of crime?

How does society deal with crime?

What can be done to reduce crime and violence?

I got over it a little bit, but I still think about it. James was my best friend. . . .
He was lying there, shaking." Fourteen-year-old Alburto Dorner will never forget the afternoon he was walking with his best friend and a group of kids
pulled up and started shooting. James was shot 22 times before he died. He
had been in a fight with one of his assailants earlier in the day, and, as often
happens in tough neighborhoods, the loser came back for vengeance with his
older brother and some friends. The result was a cold-blooded murder.[1]

Every night the news is full of stories like this one—murders, rapes, and assaults—and
people are afraid. Home security has become a billion-dollar industry, and polls show
that most women and a good number of men are afraid to walk outdoors at night even
in their own neighborhoods.[2] The statistics say that one in every four American households is touched by crime every year, and the total of the resulting losses is staggering.[3] Yet despite enormous public concern, the average citizen is poorly informed
about the real nature of the crime problem. The public is often misled by sensationalistic reporting looking to sell newspapers or win TV ratings and by the claims of op-
portunistic politicians who inflame popular fears for their own political benefit. To
understand the crime problem more clearly, we will begin by examining the nature of
crime and violence. Next we will take a hard look at what the scientific evidence shows
us about the trends and distribution of crime, and then we will examine the various
theories about the causes of crime and violence.

THE NATURE OF CRIME AND VIOLENCE

Violence can be defined as any act that is intended to cause physical pain, injury, or
death to another. When most people talk about violence, however, they are usually
thinking only about the acts they dislike. When a criminal knocks an elderly woman
down, we call it violence, but when a police officer knocks down the criminal, we call
it necessary force. This chapter will focus on criminal violence, but it is important to
remember that there are many other types of violence as well.

Crime is usually defined as a violation of the criminal law. Thus, no matter how
indecent or immoral an act may be, it is not a crime unless the criminal law has listed it as such and provided a punishment for it. In practice, of course, it is not always
easy to tell whether a specific act is or is not a crime. The famous legal scholar Roscoe
Pound once pointed out that there is a great difference between "law on the books" and
"law in action." In other words, what the criminal law says and what police and the
courts actually do are often quite different. For example, some old laws—such as those
outlawing certain sex acts—remain legally valid but are almost never enforced, and
other laws, such as those making it a crime to go nude on a beach, are sometimes enforced and sometimes ignored. Even the most widely accepted laws are still enforced
selectively. This means, for example, that an act might be called burglary if it is committed by a poor person—especially one with a criminal record—but might be ignored if committed by the mayor's son.

Because of the confusing hodgepodge of different behaviors that are considered
crimes, much effort has gone into the attempt to classify them in some orderly way.

Legally, the most serious offenses are classified as **felonies** and the less important ones as **misdemeanors**. Generally speaking, the more serious the crime, the less frequently it occurs, and misdemeanors are certainly far more common than felonies. For example, the police are about 130 times more likely to make an arrest for drunkenness, disorderly conduct, or driving under the influence of alcohol than for murder.[4] For statistical purposes, crimes are usually classified as offenses against persons (**violent crime**), crimes against property (**property crime**), and crimes against public decency and order (**victimless crime**). This approach is useful for sociologists because it groups similar types of offenses together. We will begin by briefly examining the most important crimes in each category. But as valuable as these classifications are, it is sometimes more useful to focus on the differences in the criminals and the way they behave. We will end this section with a look at three broad types of offenses that are directed against both persons and property—juvenile delinquency, syndicated crime, and white-collar crime.

VIOLENT CRIME

Murder and Assault   Murder is not the same as homicide. **Homicide** is the killing of any human being; **murder** is an illegal homicide committed with what lawyers call "malice"—the intention of doing a wrongful act. Thus, the killing of enemies in wartime, killing in self-defense, and killing in lawful execution of a judicial sentence are all homicides but not murders, because they are neither malicious nor unlawful. **Manslaughter** is the unlawful killing of another person without malice. For example, if you intentionally run over and kill someone with your car, you have probably committed a murder; but if you kill someone while driving drunk or speeding, you would more likely be judged to have committed manslaughter, because there was no malice (intent to cause harm). Finally, if you accidentally killed someone but were observing all the appropriate driving laws, you would not have committed any crime at all.

An **assault** occurs when one person attacks another with the intention of hurting or killing the victim. There is little difference between some murders and some assaults. The fact that one victim of an attack got to a hospital in time to save her life and another did not may spell the difference between an assault and a murder. Most assaults do not involve deadly force, however. A punch in the belly is an assault; so is a slap in the face. The essence of assault is the intention to do harm. If your professor raises his fist at you in a menacing manner, you have been assaulted. You are also assaulted by anyone who takes a swing at you and misses. However, most states have laws that recognize a difference between "simple assaults" that produce relatively minor injuries and "aggravated assaults," which involve more serious harm to the victim.

Newspaper and television reports focus on dramatic crimes such as mass murders, "gang wars," and particularly brutal and vicious attacks, but such media coverage is seriously misleading. The fact is that few people are attacked or killed by demented strangers. We are actually far more likely to be killed by a relative, friend, or acquaintance. Indeed, the closeness of the relationship may add to the violence of the attack when someone feels betrayed or insulted.

Marvin E. Wolfgang's classic study of murder in Philadelphia found that only 15 percent of the 550 murders he analyzed occurred between strangers; almost 60 percent occurred between relatives or close friends.[5] More recent data show much the same picture.[6] Although the victims of assault are less likely to know their attackers than murder victims, a 1999 government study of all types of violent crime showed that 54 percent of victims knew their attacker.[7] One's chances of being assaulted or killed, therefore, depend more on one's relationship with relatives and friends than on the whim of some predatory stranger.

Alcohol is frequently an important contributing factor in murders and assaults, as it is for violent crime in general. Slightly over half of the inmates in prison for violent crimes report they were under the influence of alcohol or other drugs at the time of their offense.[8] Gender also plays a major role—both assault and murder are much more common among men than women. Not only are the large majority of the offenders men, but so are most of their victims. For all kinds of violent crime, the rate of victimization for women is only 75 percent that of men. However, a woman is six times more likely to be killed by someone she is romantically involved with than a man, and more than one-fourth of the women who are murdered in the United States are killed by their husbands or boyfriends.[9] Race and class also affect who falls victim to violent crime. The poor are twice as likely to be victimized as people from families with an income over $75,000, and African Americans are 25 percent more likely to be victimized than whites.[10]

Rape   Although the laws differ from place to place, **forcible rape** is usually defined as sexual intercourse forced on a person without consent. So-called statutory rape is not a violent crime; it is sexual intercourse between an adult and someone below the legally defined age of consent, which is usually 16 to 18 years old. Many jurisdictions now use the more appropriate term *illegal intercourse* for this offense.

Studies show that there are two distinct patterns of forcible rape. In the first type, rape arises from social interaction between friends or acquaintances, often on a spur-of-the-moment basis. This type of sexual assault is sometimes known as *date rape*; however, the term is misleading because this kind of offense occurs in many other circumstances as well. The other pattern of rape usually involves strangers. The rapist, often a repeat offender, actively seeks out a victim with the prior intention of raping her. The rapist may wait on a dark street for a lone woman to walk by, search for an unsuspecting hitchhiker, or break into a woman's home. Because the first type of rape is less likely to be reported to the police, it is difficult to determine which pattern is more common. Only about 28 percent of women who told the National Crime Victimization Survey (NCVS) that they had been raped or sexually assaulted said that their attacker was a stranger, but other research has not provided consistent support for this or any other conclusion.[11] According to the NCVS, about one-fourth of all rapes occur in the home of the victim and one-fifth in the home of a friend or relative. The rest occur in a variety of more public places.[12]

It is extremely difficult to measure the incidence of rape accurately. The NCVS puts the annual rate of victimization at about one rape or sexual assault for every 800 persons over the age of 12, but other research, using different methodology and different definitions of rape, has put the figure far higher.[13] Studies of college women, for example, have found that somewhere between 11 and 25 percent report having been forced to have sexual intercourse at some time in their life by a date or a boyfriend, and studies of high school students also show a high incidence of reported rape.[14] Whatever the exact number, the fear of rape has a profound effect on the way most women live their lives, forcing them either to severely restrict their freedom of action or to run the constant risk of victimization. As one woman put it: "I know what I can't do and I've completely internalized what I can't do. I've built a viable life that basically involves never leaving my apartment at night unless I'm directly going someplace to meet somebody. It's unconsciously built into what it occurs to women to do."[15]

Unlike the victims of other violent crimes, most rape victims are female. For every male who reported being the victim of a rape in the National Crime Victimization Survey, there were slightly more than 10 females.[16] The attackers, on the other hand, are overwhelmingly males. Fewer than 1 in 20 victims said that their attacker was female.[17] Thus, even most male victims are raped by other men. However, these figures greatly underestimate the number of men who are raped because they exclude the group with the highest rate of victimization: prison inmates. Although no one knows for sure, Stephen Donaldson, the head of a national organization dedicated to reducing prison rapes, estimates that 290,000 male prisoners are raped every year.[18]

Young women have the greatest risk of being raped, and the rate of victimization drops off sharply after age 24. In almost half of all reported rapes, the victim was under 19 years old.[19] The poor are also far more likely to be victimized than the wealthy. Those with family incomes under $7,500 a year are more than eight times more likely to report being raped than those with family incomes above $75,000.[20] Data from the National Crime Victimization surveys indicate that victims who physically resist their attackers are often successful in preventing the completion of the rape. The attacker completes the rape in only 32 percent of the cases in which the victim resists, but completes it in 56 percent of the cases in which she does not resist. However, resistance by the victim is also related to an increase in the probability of such injuries as black eyes and cuts.[21] Nonetheless, about 55 percent of rape victims who resisted their attacker said they believed it improved their situation, while only about 10 percent said it made things worse.[22]

Robbery   Although **robbery**—theft by force—is officially classified as a violent crime, in many ways it has more similarities with property crimes since it is actually a type of theft. Unlike most other violent crimes, robbery is seldom a crime of passion but is usually based on some measure of rational calculation. Perhaps for that reason, offenders and their victims are unlikely to know each other; most robbers would not select a victim who could easily identify them. Although the law doesn't require that a criminal actually use violence in order for a robbery to occur (threatening to use it is enough), robbery often results in the same kind of human carnage as other violent crime. Many robbery victims, especially those who attempt to resist an armed attacker, suffer serious injuries or death. About a quarter of all robberies in the United States involve the use of a handgun, around 40 percent of the attackers do not use any weapon, and most of the rest use a knife.[23]

PROPERTY CRIME

Although most people are much more worried about being the victim of violence than of a property crime, the latter is nearly ten times more frequent. **Theft**—taking the property of another—is by far the most common property crime. (Legally, this crime is called *larceny* in many jurisdictions.) Many thefts are related in one way or another to the automobile. According to FBI figures, stealing something from an automobile (or truck) is the most widespread type of theft reported to the police. Taking the whole vehicle is the second most common, and the theft of motor vehicle accessories such as stereos or wheels is third. Motor vehicle crimes are followed by thefts from buildings (such as homes or factories), shoplifting, and bicycle theft.[24]

Burglary is the unlawful entry into a structure with the intent to commit a felony. In most cases, the crime the burglar intends to commit is a theft, but it might also be a rape or assault. A burglary may also turn into a robbery if the burglar confronts the occupants and uses force to subdue them or take their property. (Remember that one action may break several laws at the same time—for example, burglary and theft are a common combination.) The most common targets of burglary are private homes and commercial businesses such as stores or offices. Although most residential burglaries are committed by strangers, a study by the Department of Justice found that in about 40 percent of the cases, the victims knew the offenders well enough to be able to identify them by sight.[25]

A **fraud** involves trickery and deception rather than just walking off with someone's property. Fraud is common in the business world, and offenses of this sort will be discussed in the section on white-collar crime. Off the job, the most common forms of fraud involve checks and credit cards. Contrary to popular belief, it is a crime to write a check when you know that you do not have sufficient funds to cover it. Finally, **arson** is the intentional burning of a structure or other property and is often part of some kind of insurance fraud. It is estimated that 30 percent of all losses from fires are caused by arson.[26]

The key to understanding these crimes is to recognize the diversity in the offenders' motivations and techniques. On one end of the spectrum are the "occasional criminals" who steal something only when they are short of money or happen to stumble on an especially attractive opportunity—a woman's purse sitting on the seat of an unlocked car or a store left untended while the clerk runs out to get some coffee. The occasional criminal is not usually very skilled and lacks a wide range of criminal contacts. At the other extreme are the highly skilled professional criminals, such as safecrackers and counterfeiters, who know the "fences" who pay the best prices for stolen merchandise, the lawyers who might be able to "fix" a case, and the latest anticrime technology. Amateur criminals usually commit crimes with a relatively small take—often stealing things for their own personal use or, in the case of juveniles, just to prove they have the guts to do it. The professional thief looks for the highest possible cash return and is far less likely to be deterred by such things as deadbolt locks or burglar alarms. The skills of professional criminals make it less likely that they will be caught for any one crime, but because of their repeated offenses, the odds are that their luck will eventually run out.

VICTIMLESS CRIME

In addition to crimes against persons and crimes against property, there is another category of crimes without a clear victim. These victimless crimes include such things as gambling, prostitution, and the use of illicit drugs (see Chapter 9). While some claim that marijuana smokers, gamblers, and the buyers of illicit sex are actually victimizing themselves, most of the people involved don't see it that way; for that reason these offenses are sometimes called crimes against public order and morality. With the exception of the use of illicit drugs, the public is generally far less concerned about the victimless crimes than about any of the other crimes we are discussing here. Perhaps as a result, laws prohibiting such activities contain many puzzling contradictions. For example, in most states, it is a crime to place a bet on a horse race with a bookie, but it is perfectly legal to bet at the racetrack. It is a crime to pay someone to have sex with you, but it is perfectly legal to have sex with someone and then give the person cash, a mink coat, or a new car. It is illegal to smoke marijuana, but it is perfectly legal to drink alcohol, which in most respects is a far stronger drug.

These crimes also present some unique problems for the criminal justice system. Since there are no victims to complain to the police, law enforcement agencies must rely on an elaborate network of undercover agents and informers. Moreover, syndicated criminals build huge criminal empires supplying the goods and services that the law forbids legitimate businesses to provide, and the enormous profits from such operations are often used to corrupt law enforcement officials.

SYNDICATED CRIME

From the yakuza of Japan to the South American cocaine cartels, **syndicated crime** is a worldwide problem. In North America, the most famous criminal syndicate is the Italian-Sicilian organization sometimes known as the Cosa Nostra or the Mafia, but this old-time criminal organization is being strongly challenged by new African American, Hispanic, Russian, and Asian groups. Although such criminal syndicates are more frequently referred to as *organized crime*, that term is misleading, since many other types of crime are also highly organized.[27] What sets syndicated criminals apart from other criminals is that they work together in large groups. As a result, they have far more power to threaten their enemies and to buy protection from law enforcement agencies. In fact, it is often said that large-scale syndicated crime would be impossible without the widespread corruption it creates.[28] In testimony before the U.S. Senate, representatives of the Central Intelligence Agency estimated that as much as half the money many criminal syndicates earn goes to pay off various officials.[29]

Criminal syndicates are, in many ways, very much like legitimate businesses (and as we will see, some legitimate businesses also have their similarities to the criminal syndicates). Like most businesses, they earn most of their income by selling goods and services to the public. The main difference is that the criminal syndicates sell illegal goods such as drugs and offer forbidden services such as gambling, loan sharking (providing loans at illegally high rates), and prostitution. In the beginning, a new criminal syndicate is usually run by violent young toughs who operate only in a small area. If the group grows and prospers, it is likely to come into greater contact with the legitimate world, seek to corrupt law enforcement, curry favor with politicians, and hide its profits in legitimate investments. Eventually, such syndicates may come to operate a number of legitimate businesses along with their criminal ones.

The latest concern of law enforcement officials is the growing links among criminal syndicates operating in different parts of the world. The drug cartels of Colombia, the traditional Chinese triads, the Italian Mafia, and new gangs in such places as Russia and Nigeria have begun to cooperate with their American counterparts to facilitate the sale of drugs, weapons, and other contraband. Many experts are afraid that these groups will forge closer ties in the years ahead. Even more disturbing are the efforts of syndicated criminals in Russia and other parts of the former Soviet Union to sell materials on the black market to make nuclear weapons. We do not know if any such deals have already gone through, but German police arrested a Russian smuggler in 1994 with a sample of weapons-grade plutonium, allegedly from a large cache being offered for sale.[30]

WHITE-COLLAR CRIME

There are white-collar criminals in every occupation, from accounting to zoology, and in every type of organization, from the corner grocery store to huge government bureaucracies. Unlike the victims of most other crimes, many of the victims of white-collar crimes do not even know that they have been victimized, and therefore they do not complain to the police or anyone else. As a result, the public is often unaware of how serious the problem of white-collar crime really is.

Edwin H. Sutherland originally coined the term to call attention to weaknesses in theories that say crime is due to personal pathologies or poverty (such theories obviously cannot account for most criminal activities among the upper classes). He defined **white-collar crime** as any "crime committed by a person of respectability and high social status in the course of his occupation."[31] There are two basic types of white-collar crime: **Organizational crimes** are committed by people who are acting on behalf of the organization for which they work; **occupational crimes** are committed solely to advance the personal interests of the criminal. For example, when employees embezzle money from a bank, the crime is occupational because the employees are obviously not working for the interests of their employer. But when an executive of a pharmaceutical company covers up negative findings from its research lab and claims that a potentially dangerous new drug is perfectly safe, it is an organizational crime because the offense was committed to benefit the company.

White-collar crimes cost more money and more lives than all other types of crimes put together. Although accurate tallies of the financial burden of white-collar crime are hard to come by, a conservative estimate places the yearly losses from 20 to 30 times higher than the losses from street crime. For example, the Department of Justice estimates that losses from conventional crimes cost the public $13 to $14 billion a year. That is a lot of money—but it is dwarfed by the sums involved in white-collar crime. The yearly losses from antitrust violation alone are estimated to be about $250 billion, and that is only one of hundreds of different types of white-collar crime.[32]

White-collar crime costs the public far more than any other type of offense. The man shown here (center), Nicholas Leeson, is believed to have made fraudulent trades that resulted in $1.3 billion in losses.

Most people do not think of white-collar offenses as violent crime, and it is true that these criminals seldom intend to injure or kill anyone. Nonetheless, the yearly death toll from unsafe products, worker safety violations, illegal dumping of toxic wastes, and other corporate crimes is far higher than that from murder. The cover-up of the deadly hazards of asbestos by its manufacturers will probably cost as many lives as all the murders in the United States for an entire decade. In addition to our lives and our money, white-collar criminals threaten something else as well: political freedom. Assassination of foreign political leaders, illegal surveillance and harassment of groups opposed to government policy, election fraud, and the political dirty tricks like the ones involved in the Watergate scandal are all white-collar crimes.[33]

Numerous studies have also shown that those charged with white-collar crimes are less likely to be prosecuted and convicted than those charged with comparable "street crimes," and when the defendants in white-collar cases are convicted, they receive lighter sentences.[34] Big corporations are the recipients of the greatest leniency. Take the case of the tobacco industry. It is estimated that in the United States alone, cigarette smoking kills about 400,000 people a year, and there is mounting evidence that the tobacco industry orchestrated an intentional effort to lie about its products and conceal their dangers from the public. Yet not a single tobacco executive has ever been charged with fraud or any of the other crimes the companies were apparently involved in.[35]

There are several reasons why white-collar criminals receive such lenient treatment. For one thing, their status and respectability make many people—including law enforcement officials—reluctant to believe the defendants are criminals; and, of course, if they are charged with a crime, they can afford the best defense available. In the case of corporate crimes, defendants can actually overwhelm many enforcement agencies, which are often underfunded and understaffed. Their enormous economic and political power also enables many corporate criminals to bring almost irresistible outside pressures to bear on enforcement agents. Even the laws themselves are often written to reflect the interests of corporate offenders and not the general public. Finally, the tens of thousands of victims of white-collar crimes such as false advertising and price-fixing lose only a few dollars each—so there is less public resentment than when a criminal strikes more heavily at a few individual victims. Indeed, many of the victims of white-collar crimes never even know they have been victimized.

JUVENILE DELINQUENCY

Adults who violate criminal laws are called criminals, while juveniles who do the same things are called *delinquents*. The difference between a criminal and a **juvenile delinquent** is not simply a matter of age, however. A substantial number of juvenile delinquents have never been accused of doing anything that would be unlawful if they were adults. Runaways, truants, and violators of curfew laws, for example, are delinquents only because they have broken laws pertaining to the behavior of juveniles.

Anthony Platt has shown that the concept of delinquency was created in the latter part of the nineteenth century by middle-class reformers he calls the "child savers."[36] Despite their good intentions, Platt argues, the child savers' efforts to create a special juvenile justice system to deal with delinquency introduced government controls over juveniles who did nothing more than violate middle-class standards of propriety. In the 1960s, civil libertarians began voicing strong objections to the practices of the juvenile courts. In theory, the juvenile courts were allowed to operate with fewer legal safeguards because they were intended to help, not punish, young people. Civil libertarians argued that juvenile courts were actually just as punitive as the adult courts. They eventually persuaded the Supreme Court, and juvenile courts are now run more like their adult counterparts. For instance, many states no longer define running away, incorrigibility, and other **status offenses** (juvenile offenses that do not violate adult criminal law) as delinquency. More recently, pressure from conservatives has led to increasing emphasis on punishment rather than rehabilitation for juveniles. The laws in many states have been rewritten to allow more young offenders to be tried as adults; the average sentence of those tried as juveniles has greatly increased; and the authorities are pressing charges against many juvenile offenders who, in the past, would have been released after a warning and a parent conference. Public opinion polls show that over 85 percent of Americans now believe that juveniles who commit serious crime should be tried as adults.[37]

Juvenile delinquency has probably been studied more carefully than any other category of crime. The principal explanations of crime were developed from the study of delinquency as well as adult criminality and are used to understand delinquency as well as crime. Nevertheless, juveniles have special problems and should not be considered merely young criminals. For one thing, the influence of the family on the lives of juvenile delinquents is certainly much greater. A number of studies show that children are much more likely to become delinquent if a parent is a criminal. Self-report studies show that children from all economic backgrounds commit minor acts of delinquency at about the same rate but that children from poor homes are much more likely to commit serious criminal acts.[38] Delinquency also occurs more often among children in single-parent families. After a careful review of 50 different studies on this subject, L. Edward Wells and Joseph H. Rankin concluded that the prevalence of delinquency was 10 to 15 percent higher among children from broken homes. However, it seems to make no difference whether the family is disrupted by a divorce or by the death of a parent.[39] Another unique problem of juvenile offenders is youth itself. In traditional cultures, everyone goes directly from being a child to being an adult, but in industrialized nations there is an extended in-between period of adolescence in which difficult demands are placed on young people. Adolescents are not considered old enough for marriage and family responsibilities of their own, yet they are too old to remain totally dependent on their parents. In a sense they are between two worlds and part of neither.

Finally, there is the problem of juvenile gangs. Adolescents all over the world form groups based on friendship and mutual interests. When these groups meet social approval, we call them clubs or organizations; but when the community condemns them, we call them gangs. Juvenile gangs of streetwise young toughs roam the streets of most urban slums and ghettos. The primary motivation of the "fighting gang" is to control their "turf" (territory) and defend their honor, sometimes by fighting to the death. The graffiti that cover so many urban neighborhoods are symbols to gang members—marking their territory and oftentimes issuing a challenge to rival gangs. Some of these gangs have long histories going back 30 or 40 years, and gang fights and killings have been a fact of life in some urban neighborhoods for generations. Some juvenile gangs, however, are more concerned with making an illicit profit than fighting gang wars, and they are more likely to resort to violence to protect their financial interests rather than their reputation in the neighborhood.

There is considerable disagreement among criminologists about how well-organized juvenile gangs are. Michael Gottfredson and Travis Hirschi argue that juvenile gangs have very little formal structure and are really just loose aggregations of friends and associates.[40] Martin Sanchez Jankowski, on the other hand, holds that gangs are highly organized, with clear leadership, many distinct roles, and sets of rules that are enforced by members.[41] Whichever form is most common, it is clear that juvenile gangs run the gamut: Some are so loosely structured that they soon fall apart, while others run well-organized illicit businesses, such as drug dealing or extortion rackets, operating very much the way adult criminal syndicates do.

QUICK REVIEW

Explain the ways criminologists classify different types of crimes.
Define each of the four major types of violent crime.
How do victim-offender relationships vary among the different violent crimes?
Define each of the most common property crimes.
What are the most common victimless crimes?
How does syndicated crime differ from crimes committed by single individuals?
Why do white-collar criminals get off easier than other criminals?
Why do kids join juvenile gangs?

MEASURING CRIME AND VIOLENCE

If we are to understand crime, we must measure it accurately, but that is much harder to do than it sounds. Criminals are often unwilling to talk about their activities, and the general public's knowledge about their own victimization is frequently inaccurate. For example, a homeowner who develops cancer may not know that the cause was toxic waste illegally dumped on a nearby lot, or a man who loses his wallet may mistakenly believe it was stolen.

Criminologists use four principal means of measuring crime, each with its own strengths and weaknesses. The first statistics available to criminologists were based on the crimes reported to the police. Since the 1930s, the FBI has published a summary of all the crimes reported to police agencies in the United States, and other industrialized nations now have similar publications. These FBI statistics, known as the **Uniform Crime Reports** or UCR, were virtually the only source of nationwide data on crime until the 1970s, when the federal government began conducting a yearly crime survey. This **National Crime Victimization Survey** (NCVS) asks a random sample of Americans to report information about any crimes in which they were the victim in the last year. Of the two, the NCVS is generally considered the more accurate because many victims are either afraid to report their problem to the police or simply do not want to take the time. The National Crime Victimization Survey's reports show about twice as much crime as the UCR.

Neither the victimization surveys nor the tallies of crimes reported to the police contain very much direct information about who commits those crimes. For that, criminologists often use arrest reports. Such figures give us a variety of information about the characteristics of people who are arrested (sex, age, ethnic group, etc.), but they have one major flaw. Everyone who commits a crime does not have an equal chance of being arrested, and therefore these statistics may not paint an accurate picture of the typical criminal. To try to solve this problem, some criminologists conduct what are called **self-report studies**. That is, they ask a sample of people to report anonymously on the crimes they themselves have committed. The obvious drawback to this approach is that, despite the assurance of anonymity, many people are still afraid to describe their criminal activities honestly—especially their more serious offenses.

IS THERE A CRIME WAVE?

Many people throughout the industrialized world are convinced that we are in the midst of a massive crime wave that is threatening our property and personal safety, but there is little scientific support for this view. The Uniform Crime Reports did show a steady increase in crime from the end of World War II until 1980. But the UCR declined from 1980 to 1984, rose until 1991, and has declined significantly since then.[42] Moreover, many criminologists believe the UCR may have made the trends in crime appear worse than they really were. Greater confidence in the police, quicker and easier ways of reporting crime, improved record keeping, and the growing popularity of theft insurance (which requires victims to report a crime in order to collect) have all tended to artificially increase the number of crimes that are reported. Some also believe that some police departments intentionally exaggerate the increases in crime in order to

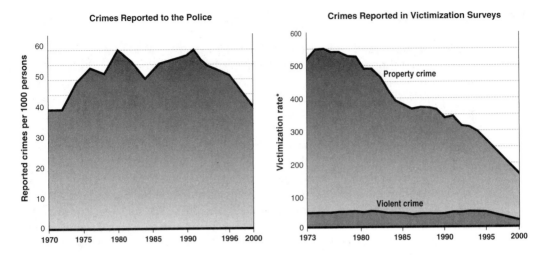

FIGURE 10.1   CRIME GOES DOWN

*Property crimes per 1,000 households; violent crimes per 1,000 persons age 12 or older.

Source: Federal Bureau of Investigation, *Uniform Crime Reports*, 2000 (Washington, DC: U.S. Department of Justice, 2001), p. 63; Bureau of Justice Statistics, *Criminal Victimization, 1973–1995* (Washington, DC: U.S. Department of Justice, 1997), Bureau of Justice Statistics, *Sourcebook of Criminal Justice Statistics*, 2000 (Washington, DC: U.S. Government Printing Office, 2001), p. 187.

justify their requests for more money and more personnel. On the other hand, data from the National Crime Victimization Survey show a steady decline in total crime since the mid-seventies when the survey first began. Property crimes measured by the NCVS have shown a continuous decline from 1974 to 2000. Overall, the crime rate declined by over one-third during that time. The rates of violence were less stable, increasing in some years and declining in others, but overall there was a 41 percent decrease between 1993 and 2000.[43] (See Figure 10.1.) Thus, there is good reason to believe that crime has been going down, not up, over the last three decades.

WHO COMMITS CRIME?

Criminologists agree that three variables—age, gender, and geographic area—all have an important influence on the incidence of crime. In the United States about four times as many men as women are arrested, and there are about 16 times more men than women in prison.[44] In many nations, such as the Islamic countries of the Middle East, gender differences are far greater. Of course, some of these differences may stem from the fact that the criminal justice system expects more men to be criminals and therefore watches them more closely. When the respondents in the crime survey are asked about the gender of the criminals who victimized them, however, their responses are generally consistent with the gender ratios in the arrest reports.[45] Over the past few decades, the difference in the arrest rate for women and men has declined. The biggest increases for women were in the nonviolent property crimes, such as larceny (theft), fraud, and embezzlement, for which 30 to 48 percent of the arrestees are now female.

There has been a big increase in the crime rate for women, but mostly for nonviolent offenses.

The change in the ratio of males and females arrested for violent crime, on the other hand, has not been very significant. And even for the nonviolent property crimes, there are still some important differences in the kinds of offenses committed by women and by men. The value of the "take" from women's crimes is generally much lower than from men's crimes, and women are more likely to act as single individuals rather than as part of an organized group.[46] (See Chapter 8 for an examination of the reasons men's and women's behavior often differs so sharply.)

Records of arrests and convictions show that teenagers and young adults have the highest crime rates. In the United States, the likelihood of arrest peaks in the 19- to 21-year-old age group and slowly declines after that. Contrary to the popular image of the violent teenage hoodlum, however, minors commit fewer violent crimes than young adults do. Thirty-three percent of people arrested for property crimes are under age 18, but minors make up only sixteen percent of people arrested for violent crime.[47]

Both victimization surveys and police reports also show that the highest crime rates are found in inner-city slums and that crime rates decrease as one moves out from the central city to the wealthier residential areas. Crime is lower in the suburbs than in the cities and lower still in the rural areas.

Most criminologists also believe that social class and ethnic group have a powerful effect on crime rates, but there is more controversy about this point. Arrest statistics show some significant differences among ethnic groups in the United States. Jews and Japanese Americans have lower-than-average arrest rates, while African Americans, Latinos, and Native Americans have higher-than-average rates. Although African Americans make up about 13 percent of the population of the United States, they accounted for about 30 percent of all those arrested at the end of the 1990s. The difference is even more pronounced for violent crime. In 1998, 53 percent of those arrested for murder, 37 percent of those arrested for rape, and 55 percent of those arrested for robbery were African Americans.[48] Official statistics also show that poor people are more likely to be arrested and sent to prison than those from middle- or upper-class backgrounds. Over two-thirds of the men and nine-tenths of the women in prison are from the poverty class or the working class. However, there is good reason to doubt that arrest and incarceration statistics are an accurate measure of the extent of crime among those groups, because poor people and members of ethnic minorities are probably more likely to be arrested and sent to prison for their crimes than others are. For one thing, money and influence often serve to protect someone from being arrested or incarcerated; a second factor is that ethnic stereotypes may lead the police to watch minorities more closely than members of other groups.

Most of the other data, nonetheless, point to the same conclusion as the arrest statistics. At one time, some criminologists claimed that the self-report studies did not indicate any consistent relationship between crime and social class,[49] but subsequent analyses have shown that to be true only for very minor offenses. Self-report studies that include serious offenses do reveal higher crime rates among the poor and minorities.[50] The victimization surveys also provide support for this conclusion. They show that the rates of victimization are highest in poor and minority areas, and the most probable explanation is that the crime rates are higher in those neighborhoods because more criminals live there.[51] According to studies of murder victims, African Americans are about seven times more likely to be murdered than other Americans, and we know from other studies that murderers and their victims are usually from the same ethnic groups. Further, when the NCVS asked respondents to identify the race of the criminals who victimized them, African Americans were selected in roughly the same proportion as we would predict from the arrest statistics.[52] There is still one serious weakness in our data, however. We have no good measures of the true incidence of most white-collar crimes because many of the victims of those crimes do not know they have been victimized. Since white-collar offenses are mainly committed by affluent individuals who are not from minority groups, it is impossible to be certain who has the highest overall crime rate. We can say that poor people and ethnic minorities commit more "street" crimes, such as murder, burglary, and theft, but that is all.

AMERICA: LAND OF THE VIOLENT?

The question of which nations have the highest crime rates and how we can explain the differences among nations is an extremely important one. Until recently the data we had was not very good, but more accurate data is now being compiled by such agencies as the United Nations and European Union Ministry of Justice.

Although a few less-developed countries such as Thailand and the Philippines report higher murder rates, the United States has by far the highest rate of any industrialized nation. According to the World Health Organization, the murder rate is five times higher in the United States than in Canada and seven-and-a-half times higher than in Europe. Data from the International Police Organization (Interpol) indicate that murder is three times more common in the United States than it is in Canada and five times more frequent than in Europe.[53] Although violent crime has declined in the United States in recent years while increasing in some European countries and Japan, the United States clearly maintains its position as the leader in murder among industrial nations.

The high level of violence in America is often seen as a holdover from the rowdy days of frontier expansion. According to this view, violence became a way of life as an unending stream of settlers fought among themselves and with native peoples for land and profit. However, Canada and Australia were also settled by rough pioneers, and the citizens of those countries have apparently not passed down a violent frontier tradition. The United States was unique, however, in its extensive use of slave labor, and slavery's legacy of racism and resentment is a major contributor to the pervasiveness of violence in this country. Furthermore, the United States is an extremely wealthy nation, but, compared with other Western countries, it has a bigger gap between the rich and the poor, as well as inferior welfare and social programs (see Chapter 6). Thus, those at the bottom of the social hierarchy tend to be more frustrated, desperate, and resentful of those who possess the wealth they are denied. Studies have shown that the higher the level of inequality in a nation, the higher the rate of personal violence and murder.[54]

With respect to nonviolent crimes, however, the United States is no longer the crime capital of the industrial world. Many European nations have begun doing their own victimization studies, and they don't show any marked difference between the United States and Europe in nonviolent crimes. Although the United States is on the high end for most types of crime, a few countries such as the United Kingdom and the Netherlands have slightly higher overall rates of crime.[55] It appears that while crime rates have been coming down in the United States in recent years, they have been going up in many European nations and Japan. (See "Lessons from Other Places" on page 340–341.)

QUICK REVIEW

What are the different ways criminologists measure crime?
What does the evidence tell us about whether crime is going up or down?
Which groups of people have the highest crime rates?
Why is there more criminal violence in the United States than in other industrialized nations?

THE CAUSES OF CRIME AND VIOLENCE

The birth of modern criminology can be traced to 1764 and the publication of the Italian nobleman Cesare Beccaria's book *On Crimes and Punishments*. The great English philosopher Jeremy Bentham applied Beccaria's ideas to legislation, and these two men became the leaders of what came to be known as the classical school of criminology. They thought that all people were guided by a rational desire to seek pleasure and avoid pain. According to the **classical theory**, people who commit crimes choose to do so. They weigh all the options and find that a crime will give them the most pleasure for the least amount of pain. This idea was regarded as a complete explanation of crime, and these early theorists saw no need for research on the economic, psychological, political, or social conditions associated with crime. The classical school

LESSONS FROM OTHER PLACES

THE UPS AND DOWNS OF CRIME AMONG INDUSTRIAL NATIONS

When it comes to crime and violence, the United States definitely has a bad image in the world. Any American living abroad for even a short time is almost certain to be drawn into a discussion about how dangerous America is compared to other places. Several of my students in Germany and Japan have told me they were reluctant to travel in the United States because of their fear of crime. Indeed, Americans living in Europe and especially in Japan feel much safer than they do at home. But statistics show that things have been changing.

To the shock of most Japanese and the foreigners living there, violent crime went up more than 50 percent during the 1990s. It increased 11 percent between 1998 and 1999 alone. And while the murder rate in Japan is still lower than in the United States, it has now surpassed some European countries such as Great Britain. In France the picture is much the same. Crime among teenagers and young adults in France increased 81 percent during the 1990s. Over 80 percent of French people now say that crime has reached alarming proportions. New data published by the United Nations shows that assault rates are about the same in Britain, New Zealand, and Australia, as in the United States, and only slightly lower in France, the Netherlands, and Canada.

Good sociologists, of course, want to know why these changes are occurring. Some of the theories of the causes of crime follow, but one obvious reason for these changes is the booming American economy of the 1990s. The longest economic expansion in its history, with jobs for almost everyone wanting to work, is almost certainly an important reason fewer people turned to crime in the United States. But while the U.S. economy was booming, European economies were doing badly. Many young Europeans came to feel rather hopeless when they looked at their economic future. Most

---

has been heavily criticized for its view of human beings as somewhat like rational calculating machines. Nonetheless, these ideas remain popular today. Like its classical predecessor, **rational choice theory** sees lawbreaking as the result of a rational choice by the criminal, but it uses a much more sophisticated analysis of the social structures that provide the context in which that choice is made.

BIOLOGICAL THEORIES

The first real challenge to the classical school was mounted by an Italian physician, Cesare Lombroso, and his supporters in the last quarter of the nineteenth century. The **positive school** of criminology rejected classical theory's assumption that crime was based on free choice. Its proponents felt that most criminals were biologically different from "normal" people and had easily identifiable physical traits such as

Europeans also cite the massive immigration from poorer areas of Europe and Northern Africa that occurred in the 1990s after the fall of the Berlin Wall. These poor immigrants came to find work in places where little work could be found, and some of them turned to crime.

The rapid rise of crime in Japan, however, seems more complicated. Yes, they too had had hard economic times throughout the 1990s. But in Japan we also saw a wave of youthful rebellion that was quite new to them. With their own growing sense of economic hopelessness, Japanese young people have become less willing to follow the older generation in its strict conformity to traditional Japanese ways. There is a rebellious youth subculture among people who never experienced the hunger or destruction of post–World War II Japan. These "new human beings" (shinjinrui) exasperate the older generation: They no longer even look like their parents. One of the most striking things about returning to Japan today, after living there for a couple of years in the 1980s, is all the blond, brown, and red hair on Japanese young people! In the 1980s, they would have been kicked out of school for coloring their hair, or for wearing their hair too long, or their dresses too short. That is certainly not the case today, at least in big cities like Tokyo. Along with these stylistic changes, Japanese scholars cite how such rebellion can lead to petty crime and some (usually mild) violence. Nonetheless, this new spirit of rebellion still doesn't approach what we see in the West, and Japan is still nowhere near the United States in its rate of serious violent crime.

—*Harold Kerbo*

Sources: United Nations, *Crime Survey*, 1999 (New York: United Nations, 2000); European Union Ministry of Justice, *Criminal Victimization in Eleven Industrialized Countries* (The Hague: Ministry of Justice, WODC, 1997); *Los Angeles Times*, February 27, 1998; *International Herald Tribune*, February 11, 2000; Thomas Rohlen, *Japan's High Schools* (Berkeley: University of California Press, 1983); Ikuya Sato, *Kamikaze Biker* (Chicago: University of Chicago Press, 1991).

sloping foreheads, small brains, overdeveloped jaws, and other apelike characteristics. Indeed, Lombroso believed that criminals were actually evolutionary throwbacks to our "savage" ancestors.

Although Lombrosian ideas about the physical characteristics of criminals have been discredited by the scientific community, other kinds of evolutionary theories are still used to explain violent behavior. Martin Daly and Margo Wilson, for example, argue that the basic motives and structure of the human psyche evolved to serve one evolutionary goal: the survival of our genes. Utilizing admittedly incomplete data, they argue that within the family we are most likely to kill those with whom we do not share common genes (for example, spouses and adopted children) and least likely to kill those who carry our genes (biological children). They see violence between strangers as rooted in the conflicts between males over access to the reproductive powers of females and the right to father as many children as possible. This "Darwinian psychology" raises some interesting new issues, but is still unable to account for the known patterns of violent behavior. For example, we are actually more likely to kill ourselves than to commit a murder; suicide obviously is an act that will greatly diminish our chances of passing our genes on to the next generation.[56]

Most of the current research in this area is concerned not with evolution but with the overall importance of biological factors as a cause of criminal behavior. The usual approach is to try to determine whether people who have a close biological relationship to a known criminal are themselves more likely to be involved in crime. One technique is to compare the criminal records of identical twins (whose genetic makeup is presumed to be identical) to see if such records are more similar than those of fraternal twins. Although most of these studies have found that to be the case, the interpretation of that fact is unclear because parents and friends tend to treat identical twins more similarly than fraternal twins.

A better methodological approach is found in studies that compare the crime rates of adopted children with those of their biological parents. Once again, most of these studies have found higher crime rates among adopted children whose biological parents were criminals than among those whose biological parents were not. Barry Hutchings and Sarnoff A. Mednick's study of 1,145 boys adopted in Copenhagen, for example, found that having a biological parent who was a criminal significantly increased a boy's chances of growing up to be a criminal, and the highest crime rates were among those boys whose adoptive and biological parents were both criminals.[57] Adoption studies have serious weaknesses, however. For one thing, adoption agencies do not randomly assign babies to adoptive parents, as research scientists would find more valid. Rather, they match up parents and children with similar characteristics, and the social environment of the adopted children may therefore be far more similar to that of their biological parents than the researchers assume. Another problem stems from the fact that adoption agencies screen out those they consider undesirable parents. Since people in homes with conditions that are likely to encourage criminality are not allowed to adopt children, adoption studies are bound to underestimate the impact of the home environment on criminal behavior.[58]

A general problem with the biological theories is that they have yet to determine exactly what inherited characteristics contribute to criminal behavior. James Q. Wilson and Richard Herrnstein speculate that low intelligence or an impulsive personality might be involved, but there is little conclusive evidence on the matter.[59] Criminality obviously cannot be directly inherited because crime is defined by legislators and politicians, and the definition of what is criminal and what is not is continually changing. It seems likely that inherited traits are often related to criminal behavior only by virtue of the fact that people have learned to react to others in different ways. For example, a student with high intelligence will be more likely to do well in school and thus receive praise and support from teachers, whereas a student with lesser abilities is far more likely to feel rejected and to rebel against school authorities. One of the biggest shortcomings of the biological theories is their inability to explain cultural variations in the amount of crime. For example, take the high rates of serious violent crime in the United States. Since we are a nation of immigrants, are we to say that the biology of Europeans, Asians, and Africans changed when they came to the United States, giving them higher rates of violent crime than people from their old country?

PSYCHOLOGICAL THEORIES

There is a widely held belief that many criminals, especially violent ones, are mentally disturbed. After a particularly gruesome murder has occurred, we often hear the comment, "A person would have to be crazy to do something like that." Although such statements express understandable shock and disbelief, they do not really tell us much about the causes of crime. Psychiatric examinations of convicted criminals show that only a small percentage are psychotic, and official records indicate that most psychotics are not criminals and have not attacked or harmed other people.[60]

Many psychologists and psychiatrists who examine convicted criminals have nonetheless concluded that criminals often have a **sociopathic personality**. This term is somewhat vague, but it refers to an inability to form close social relationships, combined with a lack of moral feelings or concern for others. Some psychiatrists think that this personality type is hereditary, but the most common explanation is that it develops in early childhood. The method of diagnosing a sociopathic personality is not at all standardized. For this reason, the labels "sociopathic" and "sociopath" can be applied to almost anyone. It appears that the idea of causation is often circular. People may be labeled sociopathic because they have broken the law, and then it is claimed that people break the law because they are sociopaths.

Standardized personality tests and rating scales have also been used to compare criminals and noncriminals. Although researchers have constructed scales that have been fairly successful at predicting criminal behavior, it isn't entirely clear what personality characteristics, if any, those scales are actually measuring. Three comprehensive reviews of studies of the most widely used personality test, the Minnesota Multiphasic Personality Inventory (MMPI), have all concluded that little evidence supports the claim that criminals have distinctive personality characteristics.[61] Recent research by Avshalon Caspi and his associates, on the other hand, found significantly higher rates of delinquency among juveniles who had a high tendency to feel negative emotions, such as anger and frustration, and had weak impulse control (a tendency to act impulsively).[62]

Gottfredson and Hirschi's **general theory of crime** combines the rational choice theory with the psychological notion that criminals lack self-control. Their theory holds that people commit crimes because they see them as the easiest way to get what they want. Given the right circumstances anyone can commit a crime, but those with weak self-control are much more likely to succumb to the temptation to violate the law. Thus, criminals as a general rule are impulsive and quick to act. Moreover, Gottfredson and Hirschi argue that such personality traits are largely the result of poor socialization by their families. Critics point out, however, that while studies have shown some correlation between measures of self-control and criminal behavior, it is not nearly as strong as Gottfredson and Hirschi's theory would lead us to expect. Moreover, their theory cannot explain the reasons corporate crime is so common (since business executives must be self-controlled to reach top decision-making positions) or the huge differences in crime rates between men and women (since studies have not found a significant difference in self-control between the genders).[63]

SOCIOLOGICAL THEORIES

There are dozens of sociological theories of crime and violence. In general, however, either they focus on the reasons an individual commits a criminal act or they examine the larger social forces that determine the overall rates of crime and violence.

The most common answer that sociologists give to the question of why someone becomes a criminal is that he or she has learned to act that way from others. One of the earliest and most influential of these learning theories is known as **differential association**.[64] This theory, developed by Edwin H. Sutherland, says that people become criminals because they are exposed to more people with attitudes and definitions that are favorable to a certain type of crime than are opposed to it. However, all associations and personal contacts do not have the same influence. The longer, the more frequent, the more intense, and the more important an association is to a person, the stronger its effect. Most criminal behavior, like most noncriminal behavior, is therefore learned in intimate personal groups and not from impersonal sources such as movies and television.

Numerous studies of violent behavior have shown that it is often learned from other family members. Murray A. Straus, Richard J. Gelles, and Suzanne K. Steinmetz found that men who grew up in families in which violence was prevalent were ten times more likely to beat their wives than men from nonviolent families.[65] A number of studies show that individuals who were abused as children are at greater risk than others to become child abusers when they grow up.[66] Two studies have found that even the physical punishment of children increases the probability that they will commit

Sociologists argue that criminal behavior is often learned from participation in a deviant subculture.

a violent crime as an adult,[67] and a long-term study found higher rates of arrest among people who were abused or neglected as children than among a control group matched for gender, race, and income.[68] Socialization into violence is especially pronounced for boys, who are expected to be tough, strong, and aggressive. Straus, Gelles, and Steinmetz summarized the literature on violence well when they wrote that "over and over again, the statistics . . . suggest the same conclusion. Each generation learns to be violent by participating in a violent family."[69]

Crime and violence are also learned from contact with **deviant subcultures**—that is, groups that have developed perspectives, attitudes, and values that support criminality. The more someone is involved with the members of such a subculture, the more likely he or she is to join in its criminal activities. Many sociologists consider the culture of poverty to be a deviant subculture, since many of its attitudes and values seem to encourage criminal behavior (see Chapter 6). The drug subculture and the subculture of juvenile gang members also have distinctive perspectives on the world, and both reject at least parts of the conventional morality embodied in the criminal law. For a girl or boy from the underclass who is a drug user and a member of a juvenile gang, committing a crime of one kind or another is almost automatic.

Labeling theory has added to our understanding of the way crime is learned by exploring the process by which people are branded as criminals and the effects such labeling has on them. Contrary to popular opinion, labeling theorists hold that branding someone as a deviant usually encourages further criminal behavior. For example, take the case of an adolescent boy whose "play" includes breaking windows and stealing hubcaps. He might consider such activities as akin to the fun of Halloween, but to most adults his behavior is delinquent, and they soon demand that he stop it. If he continues, there is a shift away from the definition of the acts as delinquent to the definition of the boy himself as delinquent. The boy, realizing he is being branded as "bad," draws closer to others with the same problem. The community responds with punishment, then counseling, and finally with commitment to an institution. The boy acquires a police record and eventually comes to define himself as he is defined by others: as a delinquent—and by this time an incorrigible one committed to a long-term criminal career.

There is little doubt that many types of criminal behaviors are learned, but critics claim that theories such as those previously mentioned, which are based on learning, have some serious weaknesses. For one thing, they are incomplete. Where do the behavior patterns that criminals learn come from in the first place? Differential association and labeling theory provide no answer. A second common criticism is that these theories are so vague and general that they can be used to explain almost anything, but they are difficult to prove or disprove scientifically.

Another group of sociologists see crime as normal and natural. If all people are born with an "aggressive instinct" or automatically commit crimes for some other reasons, it is not very useful to ask why they commit crimes. It is more reasonable, according to this way of thinking, to ask why people do *not* commit crimes. **Control theory** answers this question by saying that noncriminals are constrained by society and thus are prevented from breaking the law. Some control theorists emphasize the importance of the internal reins that society builds up in the individual through the process of socialization. They say it is a strong conscience and a sense of personal morality that stops most people from breaking the law. In this sense, Freud's psychoanalytic theory can be seen as a control theory. Other control theorists believe that what stops crime is the bond that individuals form to conventional social institutions. Still other control theorists have returned to the rationalistic assumptions of the classical school, arguing that most of us do not commit crimes because we are deterred by the criminal justice system and fear of legal punishment. These different versions of control theory are not mutually exclusive; in fact, the most convincing form of control theory sees all three types of controls working simultaneously.[70]

Critics point out that control theory, like learning theories, is extremely broad and virtually impossible to prove or disprove. Critics have passed particularly harsh judgment on control theory's assumption that people "naturally" commit crimes. Like the religious idea that human beings are evil by nature, it is an assumption that is almost impossible to study scientifically.

To understand the rates and distribution of crime, sociologists must link these individual explanations of crime to the larger social forces that shape contemporary society. For example, sociologists have been trying for generations to explain why there apparently is more crime among the poor than among the other social classes. Probably the most influential of these is Robert K. Merton, who developed what is often called **strain theory**.[71] Crime, according to this concept, is produced by the strain in societies that (1) tell people that wealth is available to all but also (2) restrict some people's access to the means for achieving wealth. Because lower-class people in such societies cannot legally obtain the things they are taught to desire, they may try to reach their goals by breaking the law.

Learning theorists, on the other hand, tend to emphasize the cultural characteristics of the lower classes that encourage crime. For example, Walter B. Miller argues that although the subculture of poverty may have originated from a process similar to the one described by Merton, strain and frustration are not the causes of the high crime rate in the lower class. Rather, the cause is the distinctive attitudes and values found among the poor.[72] Another explanation comes from control theorists, who feel that the punishments that keep most people from getting involved in crime are less effective on the poor because they usually have a weaker bond to conventional social institutions, and they have much less to lose in terms of material possessions and social prestige if they are caught breaking the law.

Of course, crime is not limited to the lower class. Another crucial sociological question concerns the reasons our society as a whole has such a high level of crime. To answer this question, many sociologists turn to the pioneering work of Emile Durkheim, who saw the roots of the problem in what he termed **anomie**, or normlessness. According to Durkheim and his contemporary followers, modern industrial society has become so diverse and impersonal that consensus about what is right and wrong has broken down, and many people no longer belong to strong supportive groups that regulate their behavior. As a result, there is not only more crime but more frustration and suicide as well.[73] On the other hand, supporters of **critical theory** argue that it is the capitalist economic system that is the root cause of our crime problem. According to this school of thought, capitalism fosters crime by encouraging, and even requiring, the exploitation of one group by another and by promoting the selfish quest for personal gain as if it were the inevitable goal of all human behavior.[74]

QUICK REVIEW

What role does biology play in criminal behavior?
What do psychologists say about the causes of crime?
Discuss and critically evaluate the most important sociological theories of crime.

CRIMINAL JUSTICE

The criminal-justice process reflects a conflict between two very different social goals. On the one hand, there is the need to stop crime and rid society of troublemakers. On the other hand, there is the need to protect, preserve, and nourish the rights and liberties of individuals. All societies pit these two needs against each other. Some are police states, in which the methods of crime control bulldoze citizens into submission. At the other extreme is chaos, in which individuals run wild. Democratic societies take a middle ground, tempering the need to repress crime with concern for the rights of their citizens. Even in democratic societies, few people agree on what the proper balance should be. Some North Americans favor what Herbert L. Packer called the **crime control model** of criminal justice, a program for the speedy arrest and punishment of all who commit crimes. Others advocate a **due process model** that tempers the rush to punishment with concern for human rights and dignity.[75] Speaking generally, those who fear the official abuse of power favor the due process model, while those who fear crime more advocate the crime control model.

THE POLICE

Police officers are on the front line of the criminal-justice process. They are much more visible than other criminal-justice personnel, and they have more contacts with the citizenry. They have become symbols of the whole system of justice. In addition to their symbolic importance, police officers are the gatekeepers for other criminal-justice agencies. They cannot possibly arrest all suspected lawbreakers. There aren't enough police, and even if there were, there wouldn't be enough courts to try the accused or enough jails to hold them. Equally important, it is not in the interest of justice to arrest everyone who has violated the law regardless of the circumstances. Thus, police officers must use a great deal of discretion in deciding how to carry out their duties, and those decisions, in turn, determine how much business there will be for the criminal-justice agencies down the line.

Contrary to popular opinion, only a small part of all the work done by a police department is directly concerned with fighting crime. For example, only 10 to 20 percent of the calls to most police departments require officers to perform law-enforcement duties, and most of the incidents an officer handles on any given day are not criminal matters.[76] Outsiders who have observed police activities confirm the idea that they function more as peace officers than law-enforcement officers.

Although most police work is routine, even boring, there is always an element of danger for the officer on the street. At least partially for that reason, police officers form tightly knit groups that stick together. The effort to protect fellow officers is vital on the streets but is a serious barrier to controlling police misconduct. Time and again, efforts to investigate charges of racism, corruption, and brutality run into a "wall of silence." As a result, no one can say how widespread this problem actually is, but there have been enough substantiated cases to know that **police brutality** is indeed a serious issue.

THE COURTS

After an arrest, police officers must take the suspect promptly before a lower-court magistrate (judge), who will decide whether the suspect must come back to the lower court for further proceedings and will set the conditions under which temporary release on **bail** can be granted. Under the American bail system, accused persons put up a sum of money to be forfeited if they do not show up for trial. In most courts, the accused with good credit or collateral can pay a relatively small fee to a bail bonder, who then provides the financial security (called a bail bond) necessary for release. The bail system clearly discriminates against the poor. The amount of money required is usually determined by the charge against the suspect, with little consideration for the defendant's personal finances. Poor people who cannot raise enough money stay in jail awaiting trial, sometimes for months, while the more affluent post their bail and go free.

Most people think that the defendant's fate is decided in a public trial, in which the prosecutor and defense attorney battle to prove their case. Actually, the trial plays a small part in the criminal-justice process. Most defendants make a deal with the prosecutor by agreeing to plead guilty in exchange for a reduction in the charges or some other consideration. This process, called **plea bargaining**, is much faster and cheaper than taking each case to trial. The state saves money, and the defendants receive more lenient punishment than they would have if they had gone to trial and been convicted. Critics from both the left and the right have nonetheless passed disparaging judgments on the process of plea bargaining. Civil libertarians complain that it takes the process of justice behind closed doors, where violations of defendants' rights are hidden from public view; they claim that innocent people are coerced into pleading guilty because they know that if they demand a trial and are convicted, they will receive much harsher punishment. Conservatives, on the other hand, complain that plea bargaining lets the guilty off with lighter sentences than they deserve.

After the defendants have pleaded guilty or have been found guilty, they are called back into court for sentencing. Until fairly recently, judges were given wide discretion in deciding how severe a sentence to hand down, but complaints about what were perceived to be excessively lenient sentences have led to much greater restrictions on judges' powers. In most cases, the judge must still decide whether to give the defendant probation or to sentence him or her to prison for the term prescribed by law, but even that power has been restricted by various laws requiring mandatory sentences for some offenses or for defendants with long criminal histories.

CORRECTIONS

Originally, prisons were nothing but places to hold criminals until society could decide how to punish them (for example, by fines, whipping, or execution). Prisons for the long-term confinement of inmates were originally established in order to achieve

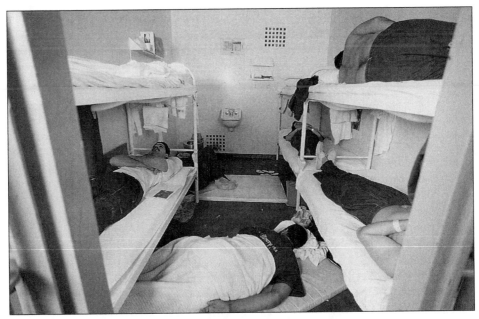

The prison population in the United States has exploded in the past decade and a half. As a result, prisons are becoming more and more overcrowded.

three goals, and they are still central objectives of today's prison system. The first is to get even (**retribution**). The public wants to make criminals suffer by depriving them of their liberty. The second is to scare potential criminals so much that they will be afraid to violate the law again (**deterrence**). The third is to protect the public from dangerous individuals by locking them up (**incapacitation**). In the 1940s and 1950s, an innovative new goal was added: to reform prisoners through such programs as job training and psychotherapy (**rehabilitation**). Unfortunately, this new objective often clashed with the prison's other goals. In most cases, prison officials adopted the language of rehabilitation (for example, penitentiaries became "correctional institutions"), but they continued to give the goal of reforming prisoners a low priority. As a result, few rehabilitation programs were effective, and many of them have been dismantled in recent years. However, prisons have proved no more effective at deterring crime than they have been at reforming criminals. Although it is a matter of some dispute, the most commonly cited figure is that about two-thirds of those released from prison commit another serious crime within four or five years.[77]

Despite such evidence of failure, America's prison population is growing at an alarming rate. The number of Americans behind bars has more than tripled since 1980 (see Figure 10.2 page 350). The United States now has a higher percentage of its population in jail than any other country in the world. When we consider both the prison population and those in more short-term jail confinement, there were almost two million people behind bars in the United States by 1999 and four-and-a-half million more on probation or parole. Even more disturbing is the fact that one in every three young African American men in the United States is either in prison or

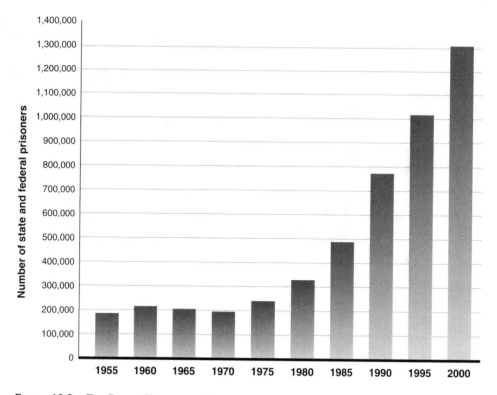

FIGURE 10.2   THE PRISON POPULATION EXPLODES

There has been a huge increase in the number of people in American prisons since 1970.

Source: U.S. Bureau of Justice Statistics, *Prisoners in* 1993 (Washington, DC: U.S. Department of Justice, 1994); Bureau of Justice Statistics, *Sourcebook of Criminal Justice Statistics,* 2000 (Washington, DC: U.S. Department of Justice, 2001), p. 488.

on probation or parole.[78] Prisons are becoming increasingly overcrowded, and living conditions have gone from bad to worse. Murder, assault, and homosexual rape are everyday events in our prisons, and mere survival has become the primary goal of many inmates.

Probation, which allows convicted criminals to remain in the community under government supervision, is the principal alternative to incarceration. In theory, probation officers work to help offenders stay on the right track, while keeping close tabs on them to make sure they do not return to crime. In practice, probation is seldom very effective in achieving either goal, primarily because probation officers are given such a huge number of cases to handle. A Rand Corporation study of 1600 probationers found that the majority are eventually arrested again for another offense; however, other research shows that people placed on probation are less likely to commit new crimes than are those who are sent to prison.[79] The most hardened and dangerous criminals are not given probation, however, so it is difficult to assess accurately whether current probation programs are really any more effective than incarceration at stopping crime.

QUICK REVIEW

What is the difference between the crime-control and the due-process models of criminal justice?

Describe the role the police play in the process of criminal justice.

What is plea bargaining, and why do so many people criticize it?

What are the four general goals of the correctional system?

SOLVING THE PROBLEMS OF CRIME AND VIOLENCE

Everyone seems to have an idea about how to stop crime. Politicians, police officers, criminologists, sociologists, and ordinary citizens propose one solution or another almost every day. Many of these proposals are contradictory, but it would seem possible to combine the best features of each in one comprehensive program. The following are a few of the most frequently suggested alternatives.

INCREASING PUNISHMENT

The United States punishes its criminals more severely than any other democratic nation. American criminals receive longer prison terms than criminals in other industrialized countries, and, as we have seen, a higher percentage of the U.S. population is in prison. Many Americans nonetheless believe that the solution to the crime problem is to get even tougher. (See the "Debate" on pages 352–353.) These proposals generally have two parts. First, they demand that punishment be made more certain, even if such a practice reduces legal protection against abuse of government power. Second, they demand that punishment be more severe, that prison terms be lengthened, and that more criminals be executed.

Such ideas are popular with the general public, and both kinds of proposals have been put into effect in the last two decades. Not only have prison sentences been significantly lengthened, but Supreme Court decisions have cut back on the legal safeguards granted by earlier, more liberal courts. Perhaps the harshest of these new policies are the so-called three strikes laws that mandate a life sentence without possibility of parole for a third conviction for a serious crime. Critics charge that it simply isn't fair to lock up a young man in his early twenties until he dies of old age, just because he was convicted three times for burglaries or robberies. Moreover, many worry that our prisons will have to devote an increasing share of their resources to geriatric care since they will never be able to release any of this new class of prisoners, no matter how little danger they pose to society.

Supporters of the "get-tough" policies that have been enacted in the last decade and a half claim that they are responsible for the drop in the crime rate; however, critics point out that most of the decline is the natural result of an aging population. While most criminologists will grant that get-tough policies can produce some short-term reductions in crime, many argue that in the long run they will do little to stop crime and may even increase it. Sooner or later almost all prisoners are released, and these criminologists argue that their experience in jail is likely to leave

DEBATE

WOULD PUTTING MORE POLICE ON THE STREETS HELP SOLVE THE CRIME PROBLEM?

Yes

Crime decreased during the 1990s but it is still a serious problem and could increase again. Changing the underlying sociological causes of crime is a good idea, but that would be an extraordinarily slow and difficult process. Proposals to imprison more criminals also make sense, but that approach is not only becoming prohibitively expensive, with more than one million prisoners now in the United States, it also runs the risk that long prison terms will turn inmates into more hardened and bitter criminals. A more realistic solution is to substantially increase funding for local police departments that agree to put more police officers on the street. While such a program would probably lead to an increase in arrests in the short run, the primary goal would be to prevent crimes before they occur. It is simply common sense that if there are more police officers on patrol, our streets and our property will be safer. It is especially important to have more officers walking a beat in the inner cities in order to bring residents some relief from the reign of lawlessness and terror still more common in ghetto neighborhoods.

In addition to reducing crime, an increase in the number of police will produce other benefits. Neighborhood police officers on patrol would provide a positive role model for children in slum neighborhoods, who too often see drug dealers and gang lords as the only local success stories. The new jobs created would help reduce unemployment problems, which have started to increase as we move into the twenty-first century. New officers could also provide other important services, including better

them bitter and hardened in their criminal ways. As Joan Petersilia, the author of a Rand Corporation report on California's get-tough policies, concluded: "The analysis suggests that the much higher imprisonment rates in California had no appreciable effect on violent crime and only slight effects on property crime."[80] Even more troubling is the threat such programs pose to civil liberties in a democratic society; and their costs are steadily growing ever larger so that many states are sacrificing other vital programs to help pay the bills for prisons. Critics pass particularly harsh judgment on the "war on drugs" that has sent huge numbers of nonviolent drug users into our prisons, where they are cut off from their families, their communities, and virtually all the other positive influences on their lives. We now send substantially more people to prison for drug offenses than for all violent crimes combined.[81]

traffic control and faster response to emergency situations. Perhaps most important, a more visible presence by the police will make our citizens feel safer and help end our paralyzing fear of crime that continues to exist even as crime has decreased. We need more police on the streets now.

No

Everyone realizes that the crime problem is still greater than it should be, but are we really willing to turn the United States into a police state in order to solve it? We already have a larger proportion of our population in prison than any other nation in the world, and an increase in the number of police would only make the political climate more authoritarian and oppressive. If the current trends continue, the majority of our adult population could end up either in prison or working for the military or the criminal-justice system. What kind of society would that be? What would remain of the individual freedoms we have fought so long to maintain? Who would dare to be different in a society with a police officer on every street corner and a prison in every neighborhood? Many people in ghettos already regard the police as an occupying army, and this kind of program would only make things worse.

The reason proposals to put more police officers on the streets are so politically attractive is that they offer a quick fix for the crime problem. Unfortunately, there aren't any quick fixes for problems as complex and deeply rooted as the phenomenon of crime in modern society. To solve this problem, we must attack its roots: racism, poverty, despair, and erosion of the family. If we solve these problems, the crime rate will come down on its own accord. If we don't solve these problems, all the police in the world won't do us any good. Turning America into a police state is not the way to solve the crime problem.

FOCUSING ON VIOLENCE

An alternative approach to criminal-justice reform would focus the most severe punishment on violent criminals, who virtually everyone agrees are the greatest threat to the public. Prison sentences would be significantly lengthened for such offenders as murderers, rapists, and business executives who knowingly endanger public safety. At the same time, prison terms for nonviolent property offenders could be reduced and greater reliance placed on restitution programs that force offenders to work to repay their victims. The primary response to drug users would be shifted from punishment to tolerance or treatment and therapy.

Another reasonable response to the problem of violence is to enact stronger gun control laws. Some opponents of this idea claim that criminals would simply use other weapons if guns were not available, but even if that were so, the evidence shows that guns are far more lethal than other weapons. A study of violence in St. Louis, for example, found that a person attacked with a small-caliber gun was almost twice as likely to die than one attacked with a knife, and gunshot victims were three times more likely to die if attacked with a larger-caliber weapon. Others claim that even tough gun control laws would not get most guns off the street. However, international comparisons indicate that the nations with the toughest gun control laws have the lowest level of gun ownership and the lowest percentage of criminals who use guns. In the mid 1990s there were about 200 million privately owned firearms in the United States, including 60 million handguns, and they killed almost 40,000 people a year in homicides, accidents, and suicides.[82]

Although the regulation of firearms in the United States is extremely loose and ineffective, public opinion polls starting as far back as 1959 have repeatedly shown that Americans favor more gun control. In 1999, an opinion poll found that 65 percent of Americans felt that controlling guns was more important than protecting the rights of gun owners, while only 30 percent felt that the rights of gun owners were more important. Polls also show that large majorities favor universal gun registration, mandatory safety locks, and an outright ban on assault weapons.[83] Why, then, aren't tougher laws passed? The major opposition comes from several powerful organizations—known collectively as the gun lobby—that are funded by sports enthusiasts and firearms manufacturers. Public opinion is apparently less influential than a well-financed and highly organized special-interest group such as the National Rifle Association.

Another controversial issue concerns the pervasiveness of violence in the media. After conducting an extremely large number of studies using a variety of different methodologies, scientists have reached a consensus that media violence encourages real-life violence.[84] As Jeffrey H. Goldstein puts it, "After nearly three decades of research social scientists are now almost unanimous in their agreement that portrayed violence increases aggressive behavior."[85] However, it is also widely accepted that government censorship of the media poses a fundamental threat to democratic institutions. Some way therefore needs to be found to get media corporations to be more responsible and reduce the huge amounts of graphic violence in the movies and on television without creating a new government bureaucracy to do the job. To date, public pressure has been to little avail. Nonetheless, organized minority groups have been successful in sharply reducing the racist stereotypes that were once common in the media, and if the public were concerned enough, there is no reason similar improvements couldn't be made in reducing gratuitous violence.

COMBATING WHITE-COLLAR CRIME

As we have seen, white-collar crime costs more money and more lives than all other types of crime combined, yet it receives a relatively low percentage of law enforcement resources. An effective program to solve the crime problem must therefore allocate far more time and more money to deal with white-collar crime. In theory, it should actually be easier to deter white-collar crime than common street crimes, because the typical offenders, especially when they are big corporations, are acting not out of irrational passion but from rational self-interest. If we increased the certainty and severity of punishment, it is likely that white-collar crime would show a significant decline. Because white-collar crimes are hard to detect and expensive to prosecute, there is a crying need for more investigators and more prosecutors. Tougher laws with mandatory penalties would also be a big help.

The greatest problem in combating white-collar crime is not that we don't know what to do, but that we lack the political will to do what needs to be done. Many corporate criminals have enormous wealth and power, and time and again they have been able to cripple the effort to bring them to justice. Individual white-collar offenders seldom have as much political influence as huge corporations, but they are still far less attractive targets for prosecution than the impoverished street criminals who have few social connections and lack the assets to put on a strong defense. An effective drive against white-collar crime will therefore require that the public put far greater pressure on the government to force it into action against these powerful offenders. The first step may well have to be an effort to reform the whole political system in order to reduce the dominating influence wielded by those with great wealth and positions of institutional power (see Chapter 2).

ATTACKING THE ROOTS OF CRIME

Proposals for punishing criminals, increasing our defenses against criminal activities, and employing social intervention are all concerned with preventing crime. Crime is prevented when perpetrators are afraid to commit new crimes. It is also prevented when criminals are killed or kept behind bars and when citizens lock up their valuables and themselves, thus frustrating people who would behave criminally. Finally, crime is prevented when the personal and social situations of criminals are improved or when the economic, political, and social order that generates high crime rates is modified so that it no longer does so.

Of these three approaches, social intervention has the greatest potential for producing a safer society. We have seen that crime is rooted in the economic, political, and social order. Most social scientists realize that it is foolish to leave this situation the way it is and then try to reduce crime by punishing criminals or defending against them. Such an approach is something like trying to cool down a burning house by turning on the air conditioner. Relying on punishment and defense are, however, easier than carrying out the sweeping social changes that have been proposed—reducing poverty, unemployment, and discrimination, for example—and attacking the whole complex of problems that has made life in the urban underclass more hopeless and more violent with every successive year. It is certainly no easy task to make such changes or to reshape the attitudes that glorify violence and define the "real man" as aggressive and domineering. In the long run, however, genuine crime prevention—changing the conditions that cause crime—is both the cheapest and most effective way to fight the crime problem.

QUICK REVIEW

Critically evaluate the most common proposals for dealing with the crime problem.

SOCIOLOGICAL PERSPECTIVES ON CRIME AND DELINQUENCY

THE FUNCTIONALIST PERSPECTIVE

Functionalists study crime rates rather than individual criminal behavior. They hold, generally, that a certain amount of crime is inevitable in any society because crime makes a contribution to social order. For instance, crime is said to promote the solidarity of the group, just as war does, by providing "common enemies" (in this case criminals). It is also argued that crime is functional because it provides an "escape valve" for the pressures arising from unjust laws or excessive conformity. Although some crime is natural and even healthy, too much crime is highly dysfunctional. Today most functionalists, like the general public, feel that current levels of crime pose a major social problem.

Functionalists argue that high crime rates in the industrialized nations have been caused by the hectic pace of social change in the twentieth century and the social disorganization it created. Old traditions have been shattered, but a new consensus has not developed to take their place. The weakening of such institutions as the family and the community has disrupted the socialization process and left many children without proper supervision and guidance. Increasing numbers of people find themselves socially isolated, and the bonds that are supposed to regulate and control our behavior are eroding. As a result, many people feel alienated from society and frustrated by the conditions of their lives. Some lash out in bursts of violence; others simply drift into criminal activity because society is too disorganized to prevent it.

To deal with these problems, functionalists often call for greater social integration and a return to the traditional values of the past. Many functionalists believe that crime and violence would be reduced if people were encouraged to commit themselves to primary groups such as the family, religious organizations, social clubs, and political groups. Functionalists also recommend a thorough reorganization of the criminal-justice system so that criminals can be dealt with more quickly and efficiently, as well as a greater effort by schools to deal with the problems that promote delinquency among their students. Much more difficult to carry out are their calls for a return to a more stable family system and the traditional values on which it was based.

THE CONFLICT PERSPECTIVE

Conflict theorists emphasize that both crime and the laws defining it are products of a struggle for power. They argue that a few powerful groups control the legislative process and that these groups outlaw behavior that threatens their interests. For example, laws prohibiting vagrancy, trespassing, and theft are said to be designed to protect the interests of the wealthy from attacks by the poor. Although laws against such things as murder and rape are not so clearly in the interests of a single social class, the poor and powerless are much more likely than the wealthy to be arrested if they commit such crimes.

Conflict theorists also see class and ethnic exploitation as a basic cause of many different kinds of crime. Much of the high crime rate among the poor is attributable to a lack of legitimate opportunities for improving their economic condition.

Exploitation of the poor and ethnic minorities creates a sense of hopelessness, frustration, and hostility. Such feelings often boil over into acts of violence that are aimed not only at the system that oppresses the underprivileged but also at their friends, relatives, and neighbors. More generally, conflict theorists hold that the greed and competitiveness bred by our capitalist consumer culture encourage crime among all social groups. Every day we are given countless subtle and not-so-subtle messages that wealth is the key to happiness and the measure of a successful woman or man. Thus, it is hardly surprising that even our richest citizens are often willing to break the law to enhance their fortunes and outdo their competition.

Conflict theorists believe that crime will be significantly reduced only if inequality and exploitation are also eliminated. Because that is obviously a distant goal, they advocate more limited responses to the crime problem as well. They ask, for example, that the police and the courts treat different classes and ethnic groups more equally. Thus, they want to see more attention given to white-collar crime, they support bail reform and programs to provide better defense lawyers for the poor, and they call for the elimination of class and ethnic discrimination in law enforcement. The repeal of laws that enforce one group's cultural dominance over another is also supported by many conflict theorists. Thus, they often support repealing laws prohibiting the use of marijuana, private sexual acts between consenting adults, and such activities as gambling.

THE FEMINIST PERSPECTIVE

Feminists have long been concerned with the role that violence plays in the exploitation of women, and their general conclusion is that violence has always been a principal means of establishing and enforcing male dominance. Although modern industrial societies have a legal prohibition against most forms of violence, feminists point out that the enforcement effort is often weak and ineffective. Some feminists feel that as industrialization and technological advances have eroded the underpinnings of male privilege, violence has become an increasingly important tool in keeping women "in their place." But whether or not violence against women has become more common, there is no doubt that some men use rape and physical brutality to degrade women who challenge their sense of superiority and to express their rage against women in general. As a result, fear of violence forces women to change their ways of living, acting, and dressing and thus deprives them of many basic freedoms.

Of course, women are not only the victims of crime; they are its perpetrators as well. Although the overall crime rate of women is still well below that of men, it has been getting closer. As women have gained more power and taken on more financial responsibility, their crime rates have gone up. Since the attack on gender inequality advocated by most feminists might accelerate this trend, feminists generally support many of the proposals made by conflict theorists to reduce the crime rate among all sectors of our society. They also call for the criminal-justice system to crack down on spouse abuse and the other kinds of violence men perpetrate against women so that society can create truly equal relations between the genders.

Feminists also call on schools to train teachers to recognize and prevent peer-to-peer bullying and sexual harassment. They argue that one of the most effective tools to end violence against women is to change male socialization so that bullying, sexual harassment, and violence are clearly unacceptable. Additionally, feminists advocate new programs in schools to teach adolescents how to maintain healthy relationships that have an equal balance of power in order to help end the relationship violence common among young people. Finally, feminists encourage women and pro-feminist men to continue to speak out against the attitudes in dominant culture that perpetuate the devaluation of women and the "rape culture" in which we live.

THE INTERACTIONIST PERSPECTIVE

Interactionists have probably been more focused on the causes of crime than the proponents of any of the other theoretical perspectives, and many of the theories we have already examined, such as differential association and labeling theory, have their roots in interactionism. Their general conclusion is that crime and deviance are not special or unique phenomena. Rather, they are learned in interaction with other people like any other behavior. People commit crimes because they learn attitudes and motivations that are favorable to crime. A boy who associates with other boys who believe that stealing is exciting is likely to adopt that attitude and start to steal. A woman who sees her coworkers getting rich by embezzling from their employer is more likely to do it herself.

If crime is learned, it follows that it can be unlearned, and interactionists advocate a host of proposals to modify criminal behavior. The media has become a powerful cultural influence in contemporary society, and some interactionists argue that it should be made to promote the ideals of cooperation and nonviolence and stop the glorification of mayhem and destruction so common in today's films, books, and television programs. Interactionists also urge those who are struggling with the crime problem to be sensitive to the critical role social learning plays in criminal behavior. For example, care should be taken to avoid mixing youngsters in with confirmed criminals as sometimes happens in juvenile halls and prisons, and programs intended to help offenders should seek to integrate them into primary groups that strongly discourage criminal behavior.

QUICK REVIEW

How do functionalists explain the high crime rates in industrialized countries, and what do they propose to do about them?

Critically evaluate the conflict theory about the causes of crime.

What is the sociological importance of male violence against women?

What proposals do interactionists make to deal with the crime problem?

SUMMARY

A crime is a violation of the criminal law. Violence includes any behavior intended to cause physical harm to a person. Murder is the unlawful killing of a human being with malice. Research shows that the victims and attackers in most murders are friends or relatives. An assault occurs when one person physically attacks another; it differs from a murder in that the victim does not die. Sexual intercourse forced on someone without consent is known as forcible rape. There are two types of forcible rape. The first kind occurs on a date or in the course of some other social contact; the second when the rapist simply selects a victim and attacks her (or him). Property crime includes a wide variety of offenses such as theft, burglary, arson, and fraud. Although robbery (theft by force) is officially classified as a violent crime, for sociological purposes it too is best considered a property offense. Offenses such as the use of illegal drugs, gambling, and prostitution are known as victimless crimes because there is no clear victim resulting from the crime. Offenses committed by highly organized groups of professional criminals are known as syndicated crime. White-collar crime is defined as a crime committed by a person of high status in the course of his or her occupation. Such crimes probably cost more and hurt more people than all other crimes combined. Juvenile delinquency includes a broad range of deviant behaviors committed by young people; some of the offenses would also be unlawful if committed by adults and some would not.

The Uniform Crime Reports, which analyzes the crimes reported to the police, and the National Criminal Victimization Survey both show that crime has been decreasing. The data show that crime is most common among males, young adults, and those who live in cities. For most types of crime, the poor and minorities are also the most likely to be the offenders; however, that is not true of white-collar crimes. International comparisons show that the United States has the highest rate of violent crime of any industrialized nation.

The classical school holds that criminals choose to violate the law because that is the easiest way to get what they want. Biological theorists see crime as rooted in human nature and often look to the process of evolution to explain it. Psychologists and psychiatrists argue that crime is caused by the personality of the criminals. Some sociologists hold that crime is learned from social interaction (differential association), while others see it as a result of society's failure to prevent it (control theory). Still other sociologists feel that our high crime rates are a result of the social and economic structure of contemporary society.

The police are the first to respond to most individual crimes, and how well they do their jobs has an enormous impact on the effectiveness of the rest of the criminal-justice system. If the police make an arrest, the suspects are usually held in jail until they can raise bail. If their case is not dropped, most defendants participate in a process called plea bargaining, under which they agree to plead guilty in exchange for some form of leniency from the prosecutor. In most cases, the judge sentences offenders either to prison or to a period of probation, during which they are allowed to remain free under official supervision. The huge increase in the inmate population of the United States has created serious overcrowding and deteriorating conditions in prisons.

There are many different proposals for dealing with the crime problem. Although the United States already has the highest percentage of its population in prison of any country in the world, some say we should get tougher still. Others propose focusing on violent criminals by lengthening their prison sentences but relying on other alternatives such as restitution and drug treatment for nonviolent offenders. Probably the most popular approach among criminologists is to attack the underlying causes of crime, such as poverty, unemployment, racism, and a deteriorating family structure.

Functionalists argue that the growing crime rate is but one symptom of increasing social disorganization. Conflict theorists emphasize the role of exploitation and inequality in promoting crime. Feminists see male violence against women as a major source of gender inequality. Interactionists argue that crime is learned like any other behavior.

QUESTIONS FOR CRITICAL THINKING

All democratic societies face a fundamental dilemma in dealing with the crime problem. On the one hand, there is a need to maintain order and repress dangerous or antisocial behavior. But on the other, there is also a need to protect individual freedom from the untrammeled power of the government. Every democratic government has to strike a balance between the need to repress crime and the need to protect civil liberties. How good a job are we doing of reconciling these two conflicting demands? Is our society more likely to dissolve into a sea of crime and violence or to evolve into a repressive police state? Is there some way to have more civil liberties and still reduce the crime problem?

KEY TERMS

anomie	murder
arson	National Crime Victimization Survey (NCVS)
assault	occupational crime
bail	organizational crime
burglary	plea bargaining
classical theory	police brutality
control theory	positive school
crime	probation
crime control model	property crime
critical theory	rational choice theory
deterrence	rehabilitation
deviant subculture	retribution
differential association theory	robbery
due process model	self-report study
felony	sociopathic personality
forcible rape	status offense
fraud	strain theory
general theory of crime	syndicated crime
homicide	theft
incapacitation	Uniform Crime Reports
juvenile delinquent	victimless crime
labeling theory	violence
manslaughter	violent crime
misdemeanor	white-collar crime

NOTES

1. Jimmie Briggs, "Childhood's End," *Village Voice*, February 18, 1997, p. 50.
2. Kathleen Maguire and Ann L. Pastore, eds., *Sourcebook of Criminal Justice Statistics*, 1995 (Washington, DC: U.S. Government Printing Office, 1996), p. 152.
3. Bureau of Justice Statistics, *Highlights from 20 Years of Surveying Crime Victims* (Washington, DC: U.S. Government Printing Office, October 1993).
4. Maguire and Pastore, *Sourcebook of Criminal Justice Statistics*, 1995, p. 410.
5. Marvin E. Wolfgang, *Patterns in Criminal Homicide* (Philadelphia: University of Pennsylvania Press, 1958).
6. Maguire and Pastore, *Sourcebook of Criminal Justice Statistics*, 1995, p. 361.
7. U.S. Department of Justice, *National Crime Victimization Survey*, 1999 (Washington, DC: U.S. Government Printing Office, 2000), p. 2.
8. Timothy J. Flanagan and Kathleen Maguire, eds., *Sourcebook of Criminal Justice Statistics*, 1990 (Washington, DC: U.S. Government Printing Office, 1991), p. 618.
9. U.S. Department of Justice, *Intimate Partner Violence* (Washington, DC: U.S. Government Printing Office, 2000) p. 10; U.S. Department of Justice, *National Crime Victimization Survey*, 1999, p. 6: Bureau of Justice Statistics, *Violence Against Women: Estimates from the Redesigned Survey* (Washington, DC: U.S. Government Printing Office, 1995), p. 4.
10. U.S. Department of Justice, *National Crime Victimization Survey*, 1999, p. 6.
11. Ibid., p. 8.
12. Bureau of Justice Statistics, *Violence Against Women: Estimates from the Redesigned Survey* (Washington, DC: U.S. Government Printing Office, 1995), p. 252.
13. U.S. Department of Justice, *National Crime Victimization Survey*, 1999, p. 6.
14. Elizabeth Shogren, "Survey of Top Students Reveals Sex Assaults, Suicide Attempts," *Los Angeles Times*, October 29, 1993, p. A22; McClatchy News Service, "Study of Sexual Abuse, Rape," *San Luis Obispo Telegram-Tribune*, November 29, 1993, p. A2; Sue Titus Reid, *Crime and Criminology*, 5th ed. (New York: Holt, Rinehart & Winston, 1988), pp. 234–235.
15. Quoted in Timothy Beneke, "Male Rape: Four Men Talk About Rape," *Mother Jones*, July 1983, pp. 13–22.
16. U.S. Department of Justice, *National Crime Victimization Survey*, 1999, p. 6.
17. Kathleen Maguire, Ann L. Pastore, and Timothy J. Flanagan, eds., *Sourcebook of Criminal Justice Statistics*, 1992 (Washington, DC: U.S. Government Printing Office, 1993), pp. 287, 290.
18. Stephen Donaldson, "The Rape Crisis Behind Bars," *New York Times*, December 29, 1993, p. A13.
19. U.S. Department of Justice, *National Crime Victimization Survey*, 1999, p. 6.
20. Ibid., p. 7.
21. Flanagan and Maguire, *Sourcebook of Criminal Justice Statistics*, 1990, p. 269.
22. Maguire and Pastore, *Sourcebook of Criminal Justice Statistics*, 1995, p. 240.
23. U.S. Department of Justice, *National Crime Victimization Survey*, 1999, p. 9.
24. Calculated from data in Robert J. Bursik, "The Dynamics and Distribution of Property Crime," in Joseph F. Sheley, *Criminology: A Contemporary Handbook* (Belmont, CA: Wadsworth, 1995), pp. 186–199, and Piers Beirne and James Messerschmidt, *Criminology* (San Diego: Harcourt Brace Jovanovich, 1991), pp. 97, 106.
25. See John E. Conklin, *Criminology*, 5th ed. (Boston: Allyn & Bacon, 1995), p. 73.
26. Beirne and Messerschmidt, *Criminology*, p. 116.
27. Ibid., pp. 204–238.
28. See Donald R. Cressey, *Theft of the Nation: The Structure and Operations of Organized Crime in America* (New York: HarperCollins, 1969).
29. John Dillin, "U.S. Probes Crime's Global Reach," *Christian Science Monitor*, April 22, 1994, pp. 1, 16.
30. Craig R. Whitney, "Germans Suspect Russian Military in Plutonium Sale," *New York Times*, August 16, 1994, pp. A1, A6.
31. Edwin H. Sutherland, *White Collar Crime* (New York: Dryden, 1949), p. 9.
32. James William Coleman, *The Criminal Elite: Understanding White Collar Crime*, 4th ed. (New York: St. Martin's Press, 1998), pp. 8–11.

33. Ibid., pp. 1, 9–10, 55–65.
34. Ibid., pp. 123–175.
35. See ibid., pp. 79–80.
36. Anthony M. Platt, *The Child Savers: The Invention of Delinquency* (Chicago: University of Chicago Press, 1969).
37. Maguire and Pastore, *Sourcebook of Criminal Justice Statistics*, 1995, p. 178.
38. Anthony R. Harris and Lisa R. Meidlinger, "Criminal Behavior: Race and Class," in Sheley, *Criminology*, pp. 115–144.
39. L. Edward Wells and Joseph H. Rankin, "Families and Delinquency: A Meta-analysis of the Impact of Broken Homes," *Social Problems* 38 (February 1991): 71–93.
40. Michael R. Gottfredson and Travis Hirschi, *A General Theory of Crime* (Stanford, CA: Stanford University Press, 1990).
41. Martin Sanchez Jankowski, *Islands in the Street: Gangs and American Urban Society* (Berkeley: University of California Press, 1991).
42. Maguire and Pastore, *Sourcebook of Criminal Justice Statistics*, 1995, p. 324; Federal Bureau of Investigation, *Uniform Crime Reports*, 2000 (Washington, DC: U.S. Department of Justice, 2001).
43. U.S. Department of Justice, *Sourcebook of Criminal Justice Statistics*, 2000 (Washington, DC: U.S. Government Printing Office, 2001), p. 187; Bureau of Justice Statistics, *Criminal Victimization, 1973–95* (Washington, DC: U.S. Government Printing Office, 1996), pp. 1, 4.
44. U.S. Department of Justice, *Sourcebook of Criminal Justice Statistics*, 1999 (Washington, DC: U.S. Government Printing Office, 2000), p. 349.
45. Darrell Steffensmeier and Emilie Allan, "Criminal Behavior: Gender and Age," in Sheley, *Criminology*, pp. 82–111.
46. U.S. Department of Justice, *Sourcebook of Criminal Justice Statistics*, 1999, 349.
47. Ibid., pp. 347–348.
48. Ibid., p. 350.
49. Charles R. Tittle, Wayne J. Villemez, and Douglas A. Smith, "The Myth of Social Class and Criminality," *American Sociological Review* 43 (1978): 643–656.
50. Delbert Elliott and Suzanne Ageton, "Reconciling Race and Class Differences in Self-Reported and Official Estimates of Delinquency," *American Sociological Review* 45 (1980): 95–110; Delbert Elliott and David Huizinga, "Social Class and Delinquent Behavior in a National Youth Panel: 1976–1980," *Criminology* 21 (1983): 149–177.
51. Bureau of Justice Statistics, *Highlights from 20 Years of Surveying Crime Victims*.
52. Harris and Meidlinger, "Criminal Behavior: Race and Class."
53. U.S. Bureau of Justice Statistics, *International Crime Rates* (Washington, DC: U.S. Government Printing Office, May 1988); United Nations Development Programme, *Human Development Report*, 1997 (New York: Oxford University Press, 1997), p. 213.
54. Steven F. Messner, "Societal Development, Social Equality, and Homicide: A Cross-National Test of a Derkheimian Model," *Social Forces* 61 (1982): 225–240.
55. United Nations, *Crime Survey*, 1999 (New York: United Nations, 2000); European Union Ministry of Justice, *Criminal Victimization in Eleven Industrialized Countries* (The Hague: Ministry of Justice, WODC, 1997).
56. Martin Daly and Margo Wilson, *Homicide* (New York: Aldine de Gruyter, 1988).
57. Barry Hutchings and Sarnoff A. Mednick, "Criminality in Adoptees and Their Adoptive and Biological Parents: A Pilot Study," in S. A. Mednick and K. O. Christiansen, eds., *Biosocial Bases of Criminal Behavior* (New York: Gardner, 1977); for a follow-up study with a different population, see Sarnoff A. Mednick, William Gabrielli, and Barry Hutchings, "Genetic Influences in Criminal Behavior: Evidence from an Adoption Cohort," in Katherine S. Van Dusen and Sarnoff Mednick, eds., *Prospective Studies of Crime and Delinquency* (Boston: Kluver-Nijhoff, 1983), pp. 39–57.
58. Janet Katz and William J. Chambliss, "Biology and Crime," in Sheley, *Criminology*, pp. 275–303.
59. James Q. Wilson and Richard Herrnstein, *Crime and Human Behavior* (New York: Simon & Schuster, 1985).
60. Edwin H. Sutherland and Donald R. Cressey, *Criminology*, 10th ed. (New York: Lippincott, 1978), pp. 158–191.

61. Karl Schuessler and Donald R. Cressey, "Personality Characteristics of Criminals," *American Journal of Sociology* 55 (1950): 476–484; Gordon Waldo and Simon Dinitz, "Personality Attributes of the Criminal: An Analysis of Research Studies 1950–1965," *Journal of Research in Crime and Delinquency* 4 (1967): 185–201; David Tennenbaum, "Research Studies of Personality and Criminality," *Journal of Criminal Justice* 5 (1977): 1–19.

62. Avshalon Caspi, Terrie E. Morritt, Phil A. Silva, Magda Stouthamer-Loeber, Robert F. Krueger, and Pamela S. Schmutte, "Are Some People Crime-Prone? Replications of the Personality-Crime Relationships Across Countries, Genders, Races and Methods," *Criminology* 32 (1994):163–191.

63. Michael Gottfredson and Travis Hirschi, A *General Theory of Crime* (Palo Alto, CA:Stanford University Press, 1990).

64. Sutherland and Cressey, *Criminology*, pp. 77–98.

65. Murray A. Straus, Richard J. Gelles, and Suzanne K. Steinmetz, *Behind Closed Doors: Violence in the American Family* (New York: Doubleday, 1981), p. 101.

66. See, for example, Reid, *Crime and Criminology*, pp. 240–246; and David G. Gil, *Violence Against Children: Physical Child Abuse in the United States* (Cambridge, MA: Harvard University Press, 1970), pp. 113–114.

67. Murray A. Straus, "Discipline and Deviance: Physical Punishment of Children and Violence and Other Crimes in Adulthood," *Social Problems* 38 (May 1991): 133–152; Joan McCord, "Parental Aggressiveness and Physical Punishment in Long-Term Perspective," in Gerald T. Hotaling, David Finkelhor, John T. Kirkpatrick, and Murray A. Straus, eds., *Family Abuse and Its Consequences* (Newbury Park, CA: Sage, 1988), pp. 91–98.

68. National Institute of Justice, *The Cycle of Violence Revisited* (Washington, DC: U.S. Government Printing Office, February 1996).

69. Straus, Gelles, and Steinmetz, *Behind Closed Doors*, p. 121.

70. See Walter Reckless, "A New Theory of Delinquency and Crime," *Federal Probation* 25 (1961): 42–46; Travis Hirschi, *Causes of Delinquency* (Berkeley: University of California Press, 1969); James Q. Wilson, *Thinking About Crime* (New York: Random House, 1975); and Marvin Krohn, "Control and Deterrence Theories," in Sheley, *Criminology*, pp. 294–313.

71. Robert K. Merton, "Social Structure and Anomie," *American Sociological Review* 3 (1938): 672–682.

72. Walter B. Miller, "Lower Class Culture as a Generating Milieu of Gang Delinquency," *Journal of Social Issues* 14 (1958): 5–19.

73. Emile Durkheim, *Suicide* (New York: Free Press, 1966).

74. See Gary Cavender, "Alternative Approaches: Labeling and Critical Perspectives," in Sheley, *Criminology*, pp. 339–367.

75. Herbert L. Packer, *The Limits of Criminal Sanction* (Palo Alto, CA: Stanford University Press, 1968).

76. Bureau of Justice Statistics, *Report to the Nation on Crime and Justice: The Data* (Washington, DC: U.S. Government Printing Office, 1983), p. 47; Eric J. Scott, *Calls for Service: Citizen Demand and Initial Police Response*, National Institute of Justice (Washington, DC: U.S. Government Printing Office, July 1981), p. 26.

77. See, for example, Allen J. Beck, *Recidivism of Prisoners Released in 1983*, U.S. *Bureau of Justice Statistics* (Washington, DC: U.S. Government Printing Office, April 1989); and John Wallerstedt, *Returning to Prison*, U.S. *Bureau of Justice Statistics* (Washington, DC: U.S. Government Printing Office, 1984).

78. Bureau of Justice Statistics, *Correctional Populations in the United States* (Washington, DC: U.S. Government Printing Office, 1995); Fox Butterfield, "More Blacks in Their 20s Have Trouble with the Law," *New York Times*, October 5, 1995, p. A8, U.S. Department of Justice, *Sourcebook of Criminal Justice Statistics*, 1999, p. 484.

79. Joan Petersilia, *Probation and Felony Offenders*, National Institute of Justice (Washington, DC: U.S. Government Printing Office, 1985).

80. Quoted in David S. Broder, "Population Explosion," *Washington Post*, national ed., April 25–May 1, 1994, p. 4.

81. Maguire and Pastore, *Sourcebook of Criminal Justice Statistics*, 1995, p. 567.

82. Wendy Kaminer, "Crime and Community," *Atlantic Monthly*, May 1994, pp. 111–120; Bob Herbert, "Deadly Data On Handguns," *New York Times*, March 2, 1994, p. A15; "Guns Gaining on Cars as Bigger Killer in U.S.," *New York Times*, January 28, 1994, p. A8.

83. *Sourcebook of Criminal Justice Statistics*, 1999, pp. 141, 142; *Sourcebook of Criminal Justice Statistics*, 1995, pp. 181, 191, 192.

84. National Institute of Mental Health, *Television and Behavior*, Vol. 1., *Summary Report* (Washington, DC: U.S. Government Printing Office, 1982); Surgeon General's Scientific Advisory Committee on Television and Social Behavior, *Television and Growing Up: The Impact of Televised Violence* (Washington, DC: U.S. Government Printing Office, 1972); George A. Comstock and Eli Rubenstein, eds., *Television and Social Behavior*, vols. 1–5 (Washington, DC: U.S. Government Printing Office, 1972).

85. Jeffrey H. Goldstein, *Aggression and Crimes of Violence*, 2nd ed. (New York: Oxford University Press, 1986), p. 39.

PART IV

PROBLEMS OF A CHANGING WORLD

N ONE OF THE PROBLEMS DISCUSSED IN THIS BOOK CAN BE UNDERSTOOD BY LOOKING AT ONLY a single nation, even one as large and important as the United States. Not only does a cross-cultural approach help put our own difficulties in perspective, but today's economic, social, and political problems are interlinked in ways that transcend national boundaries. The difference between the chapters in this section and those in the rest of the book is one of focus. In the earlier chapters, the focus was most often close to home, and international material was used primarily to help us understand our own problems and to point out some alternatives for dealing with them. The focus of the chapters in this section is more global, and the problems of the United States and Canada are treated as one case among many. In the chapters that follow, center stage is taken by the crisis of the less-developed nations and by the global problems with the world's environment and political economy.

CHAPTER 11

THE GLOBAL DIVIDE:
INEQUALITY, WARFARE,
AND TERRORISM

Questions to Consider

What are the economic differences between industrialized and less-developed countries?

How do sociologists explain the huge gap between the rich and the poor countries?

What are the causes of warfare, terrorism, and international conflict?

What can be done to make life better for all the world's people?

The images of our global crisis are becoming more familiar every day: the tiny famine victim with stick legs and bulging eyes, a desperate young mother begging for food, a crowd of refugees fenced off in a pen like cattle, the bloody carnage of a Third World battle field, a bombed-out city and its starving people. Bit by bit, media coverage is helping the people of rich countries to realize how fortunate they are. But the media cover only the most dramatic and desperate problems, so many people have a distorted concept of what life in the rest of the world is really like, and only a few know much about the causes of these global problems or what to do about them.

This chapter focuses on two interrelated problems of enormous importance: world poverty and political violence. Although most people don't understand the link between these two problems, it is clear that they go hand in hand. Researchers at the World Bank have recently concluded that some 90 percent of wars and political violence at the end of the twentieth century were related to world poverty,[1] and a recent poll of world leaders by the *International Herald Tribune* found that a large majority of them thought that the main threat to future world peace is the growing global inequality.[2]

Until recently, most Americans didn't seem very worried about the great issues of war and peace. Perhaps that was because the **Cold War** between the Soviet Union and the United States was finally over, and Americans felt protected by the world's most powerful military and the huge oceans that surround them. But all of that suddenly changed on September 11, 2001, when terrorists associated with Osama bin Laden's Al Qaida terrorist network launched their attack. They hijacked four huge American airliners, crashing two into the World Trade Center in New York and one into the Pentagon in Washington, D.C. They were thwarted by some brave passengers in what was probably an attempt to crash a fourth plane into the White House. Around 3,000 Americans were killed on that day—the most deadly attack on American soil in the history of the country. Suddenly Americans again came to realize the world remains a dangerous place. What they have yet to understand, however, is the link between such violence and the ever-growing division of the world's people between the rich minority and the poor majority. So before we look at the problems of warfare and terrorism, we will first turn our attention to this global divide.

GLOBALIZATION AND GLOBAL INEQUALITY

Each of the more than 175 nations on this planet has its own unique economic, political, and social institutions. At the same time, all these countries are growing increasingly interdependent. Some are fabulously wealthy, while others are mired in seemingly hopeless poverty. A few exercise awesome global power, while others are hardly noticed on the world stage. But it wasn't always this way. Only a few centuries ago people living in one part of the world had little or no contact with people living in other parts of the world. Now the ever-growing process of **globalization** has changed all that.[3] Today, goods, services, information, and people move around the world at an unprecedented speed. People in every part of the planet are becoming more dependent on the world economy for their livelihood, every nation is enmeshed in a complex web of political and military relations, and a global culture is beginning to emerge, especially among the more affluent members of the world community.

One of the best ways to make sense of the bewildering complexity of the modern world is to think of the nations of the world as making up a kind of international class system, similar in many ways to the classes found within individual countries (see Chapter 1). A century ago, the industrialized world, which comprises the "upper class," included only the United States and a few western European nations. Today it encompasses countries as far away as Japan and Australia. The countries in the "lower class," collectively known as the **less-developed countries (LDCs)**, or the **Third World**, are concentrated in the southern two-thirds of the planet, in Latin America, Africa, and much of Asia. Although they have some manufacturing industries, they are more likely to depend on agriculture and the sale of raw materials to get by.

Between these two extremes is a smaller group of nations, including South Korea and Mexico, that have characteristics of both kinds of societies. They are more industrialized and have higher standards of living than the poorest nations, but they are still a long way from the affluence enjoyed by the established industrialized powers. More often than not, these "middle-class" nations are counted as part of the Third World, but several more narrow terms are also used, including "moderately developed" or "newly industrialized nations." In addition, there are the numerous independent nations that emerged from the collapse of the communist empire in eastern Europe and the Soviet Union. Many of these nations have a well-educated population and a lot of heavy industry, but their standard of living is far below that of the developed capitalist countries in the global upper class and even below many of the newly industrialized nations of East Asia. It is therefore important to remember that the world is a complex place and that there is a broad spectrum of nations on both sides of the global divide.

Just as individuals occasionally move up or down in the class system of their nation, so the status of nations changes. Some of the countries in the world's "middle class" seem likely to become full-scale industrial powers; others do not. Several nations have been knocked out of the elite club of industrial powers by wars or internal chaos—but later rejoined it. Still other countries appear to be permanently stuck at the bottom of the heap.[4]

WEALTH AND POVERTY

Many people look at the differences between the industrialized nations and the Third World as simply a matter of money. When seen in these terms, the gap is certainly enormous. Statistics show that billions of people live in poverty around the world. Approximately 1.3 billion people are now living on less than $1 per day and another 2.8 billion people live on less than $2 per day. United Nations figures show that the top 20 percent of the world's population now receive 150 times the average income of the bottom 20 percent. Just 30 years before, the income gap was less than half that much.[5] In 1998, the average industrialized nation produced about $19,480 in goods and services for each of its citizens, while the less-developed countries produced only $1,450 per citizen—a difference of more than 17 to 1 (see Figure 11.1).

There are also major differences among the less-developed countries. The per capita income in the world's poorest region, sub-Saharan Africa, is less than one-fourth as large as it is in Latin America or in most parts of Asia.[6] But, as we will see, the differences go far beyond money. Moreover, dollars, marks, and yen are not necessarily the

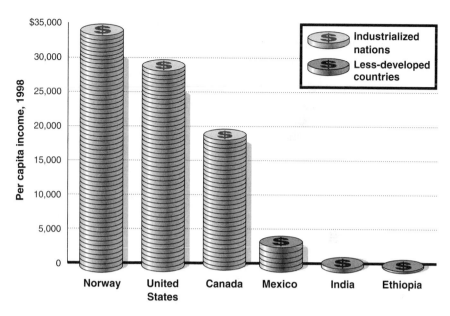

FIGURE 11.1 THE PRIVILEGED AND THE DEPRIVED

There is a huge gap between the income of the average person in industrialized nations and less-developed nations.

Source: Population Reference Bureau, *World Population Data Sheet*, 2000 (Washington, DC: Population Reference Bureau, 2000).

best way to measure wealth. The cost of living varies greatly between one country and another; so, for example, a dollar's worth of rupees may buy two or three times more goods in India than a dollar's worth of Euros does in Italy. To complicate matters further, many people in the poor nations depend more heavily on the barter system—trading one thing directly for something else they want—and goods that are informally traded seldom show up in official statistics.

Another way to compare different nations is to look at how much wealth they have accumulated. Some of this wealth is kept in dollars or yen, but more important are the physical assets of a nation—its roads and bridges, its power plants, its sewers and canals, its supply of housing, and its factories. The simplest way to make this comparison is just to look around. The industrialized nations are crisscrossed with telephone and electric lines and with highways full of cars and trucks. Their buildings are modern and are equipped with running water and indoor plumbing. Almost everyone has shoes to wear, and during the cold months most people have warm clothing.

In the less-developed countries, such comforts are far less common, and only a privileged few enjoy the affluent lifestyle taken for granted by so many North Americans. The less-developed countries have paved roads connecting their major cities, but the roads are likely to be much smaller than those in the industrialized nations and in a poor state of repair. Access to smaller towns is often only by footpaths or dirt roads that become very hard going when it rains. Most rural areas are further isolated by a lack of telephones and the electricity necessary to run radio transmitters. Even on major highways, the traveler will see far fewer private cars, and the trucks and buses are often dilapidated, noisy, and polluting. These motor vehicles must often share the road with a host of ox carts, horses, bicycles, and pedestrians.

Sanitation in the less-developed countries is often primitive, with open fields or shallow outhouses serving as the only toilets. In the cities and crowded villages, human waste may flow down the sides of streets in open sewers. Underground plumbing is now more common, but untreated sewage is usually dumped directly into rivers and lakes, which can create serious health problems. The quality of housing varies enormously. The wealthy live in sumptuous mansions with servants and all the latest conveniences, while in most big cities hundreds of thousands of people live on the streets with no permanent shelter; huge shantytowns of squatters have grown up on whatever vacant land is available. Since these squatters have neither the legal rights to the land they occupy nor the money to build homes, their structures are primitive affairs, often lacking electricity and plumbing, and providing little protection against the elements. In rural areas, most villagers at least have the legal right to live where they do, but construction techniques are still primitive—buildings often have walls of mud bricks and thatched or corrugated iron roofs—and the basic amenities are lacking.

Of course, not all poor countries are alike. Some are much poorer than others, and those have less hope of moving their people out of poverty.[7] One of the most fundamental problems in the poor nations is the absence of economic opportunities for their young people. Rapid population growth and a weak educational system mean there is almost always a large surplus of unskilled labor. In the past, these young people would have just gone to work on the family farm, but because so many more children now reach adulthood, there is often not enough land to support them all. To make matters worse, birthrates are the highest in the poorest countries and among the poorest people within each country. Young people from throughout the Third World are therefore migrating to the cities in search of work, but only the lucky find permanent jobs. Most become part of what is sometimes called the **urban subsistence economy**. They work a few temporary jobs, trade their labor for the help of other poor people, receive an occasional handout from the government or a relief agency, and in some cases turn to begging or even crime to make ends meet.

HEALTH AND NUTRITION

There is nothing more fundamental to the quality of life than good health, and the health statistics show the same global divide as the economic statistics. A baby born in a less-developed country is at least five times more likely to die in its first year of life than a baby born in a wealthy nation (see Figure 11.2). Overall, demographers say that the people of the industrialized world can expect to live 11 years longer than their counterparts in the poor nations.[8]

Many of the causes of these staggering differences can be traced to the poverty of the Third World; more specifically, poor sanitation, lack of clean drinking water, and enough food to eat. At the end of the twentieth century the United Nations' Food and Agriculture Organization estimated that 800 million people in the world are chronically undernourished, with another 2 billion people experiencing deficiencies

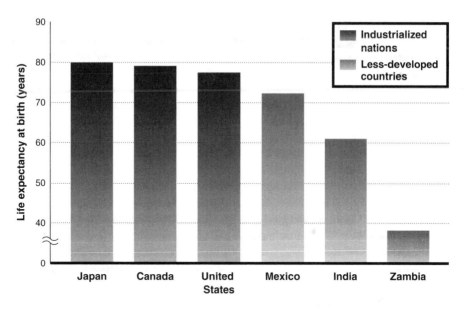

FIGURE 11.2   LIFE EXPECTANCY

People in the rich countries live longer than people in the poor ones.

Source: Population Reference Bureau, World Population Data Sheet, 2000 (Washington, DC: Population Reference Bureau, 2000).

in some crucial nutrients. UNICEF reports that malnutrition is a factor in about 55 percent of the 12 million preventable deaths that occur annually among children younger than 5 years old.[9]

These problems are caused by more than just lack of food. Lack of refrigeration and poor sanitation mean that a lot of food goes to waste, and the food itself is often a cause of illness. On the average, almost one in three people in the poor nations does not have access to safe drinking water, and in sub-Saharan Africa it is one in two.[10] Waterborne diseases such as typhoid and cholera, almost unknown in the wealthy nations, sweep through the less-developed countries in epidemic after epidemic, taking millions of lives every year. Another of the most lethal diseases, malaria, is transmitted by insects. The World Health Organization recently warned the world about the rapid increase in this global killer.[11] As with so many other problems in the Third World, poverty is a major contributor to the malaria problem because the poor nations often cannot afford the expensive mosquito eradication programs that are the best way to deal with the disease.

Although AIDS/HIV is not yet the number one killer among the world's diseases, its future looks ominous. The problem is particularly severe in Africa: over a quarter of the population in such countries as Botswana and Zimbabwe are believed to be infected and numerous other countries have double digit infection rates. The people in such poor countries simply cannot afford the expensive new drugs that can often hold infection at bay. Barring some new and inexpensive medical breakthrough, almost all of those currently infected can be expected to die from the disease.[12]

When people in the poor countries do get sick, they are often unable to find a doctor to help. There is only 1 doctor for every 5,833 people who live in the less-developed countries, but in the industrialized nations there is 1 doctor for every 341 people.[13] Even those lucky enough to find a doctor who will see them are likely to have their treatment hampered by shortages of everything but the least expensive medicines and equipment. Lack of medical care is particularly acute in the rural areas of most poor countries, where traditional healers often provide the only medical help available.

EDUCATION

Another major economic advantage of the industrialized nations is their high level of education. In most industrialized nations, less than 1 percent of the population is completely illiterate. But in the less-developed countries one in three people cannot read and write, and the majority of people are illiterate in the 45 countries the United Nations ranks at the bottom of its human development index.[14] Again, however, we must recognize the important regional differences among developing nations. In such Asian nations as Thailand and the Philippines the illiteracy rate is only about 5 percent while it is over 50 percent in Mozambique, Chad, and Haiti.[15] Workers in the industrialized countries are also far more likely to have specialized skills—for example, in word processing or automobile mechanics. The labor force in industrialized nations contains large numbers of physicians, engineers, scientists, and other highly trained specialists. Moreover, many of the skilled professionals the poor nations do produce migrate to industrialized countries, where wages are far higher. As computer skills are becoming ever more important in the global economy, a "digital divide" is emerging around the world even greater than the "digital divide" among the rich and poor within the developed nations (see Figure 11.3).

The system of universal education in rich nations also serves as a kind of social cement to help hold their people together. Children of widely different backgrounds acquire similar values and attitudes as they learn the history of their nation and read its literature. Mass communication contributes to the sense of national unity because people who read the same newspapers and watch the same television programs tend to develop a similar perspective on the world. In contrast, the perspective of most people in poor countries is much more local. They often know little of the history or politics of their country; many can't read the newspaper; and televisions, much less computers, are few and far between. To complicate matters, ethnic and linguistic differences are often far more pronounced in less-developed countries. Thus, these nations must deal with traditional ethnic animosities and suspicions without the benefit of the strong mass institutions that help hold the wealthy nations together.

WOMEN AND CHILDREN

Women suffer from prejudice and discrimination in every nation, but the problem is far more severe in the less-developed countries. Traditional agricultural societies usually have a high degree of gender inequality. Although all poor nations have undergone

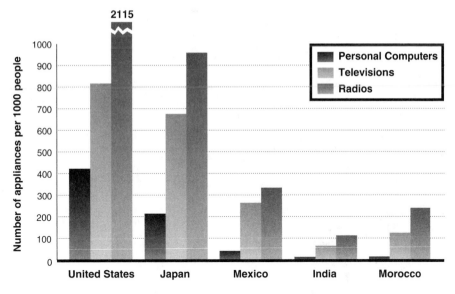

FIGURE 11.3   COMMUNICATIONS

Communication is much faster and easier in the rich countries than in the poor ones.

Source: U.S. Bureau of the Census, *Statistical Abstract of the United States*, 1999 (Washington, DC: U.S. Government Printing Office, 1999), p. 846.

some degree of economic development, the traditional attitude that sees women as second-class citizens remains strong. Female infanticide, inadequate care for child-bearing women, and the preference often given to male children when resources become scarce mean that there are considerably more males than females in the poorer nations of the world. (In industrialized nations, women normally live longer than men and thus outnumber them.) In the industrialized countries there are no overall gender differences in the literacy rate, but in the less-developed countries women are twice as likely to be unable to read and write as men. According to United Nations figures, 44 percent of the administrators and managers in the industrialized nations are women, but only 12 percent in the less-developed nations are women.[16]

The industrialized nations have made great progress toward the goal of giving women and men equal treatment under the law. In many parts of the world, however, equal treatment is not even recognized as a social goal, and women are commonly given second-class legal status similar to that of a dependent child. Property often passes from fathers to sons, and daughters do not receive an equal share of the inheritance. Husbands are commonly given the legal right to control the household property, and women find it difficult or impossible to get credit or establish financial independence. Women are expected to follow the orders of their husbands, and legal authorities seldom intervene to prevent a husband from beating a wife who disobeys him. In most Islamic nations, men are allowed up to four wives, but a wife is permitted only a single husband. In many places around the world, it is also far easier for a husband to win a divorce than for a wife.

The standard of living is far lower in the Third World than in the industrialized nations, and women and children are often the ones who suffer the most.

   The children of the less-developed countries also face a host of special problems. As in all societies, they are the most vulnerable to famines and plagues, and young children have far higher death rates than any other age group. The mortality rate among infants is about seven times higher in the less-developed countries than in the industrialized ones.[17]

   In agricultural societies, children were traditionally seen as a source of farm labor. When people in poor countries move to urban areas, they often send their children off to find jobs. There is a world of difference, however, between having children work on the family farm under the supervision of their parents and having children work for strangers in a factory or shop. For 1999, the World Bank estimates that about 19 percent of the 10- to 14-year-olds in low-income nations were in the labor force outside the home. In some places this rate was much higher; for example, in sub-Saharan Africa it was around 30 percent.[18]

   Such problems as poverty, warfare, and just too many mouths to feed have combined to force a growing number of children out of their homes to fend for themselves in the streets of the big cities. The United Nations Children's Fund estimates that there are about 30 million such "street children" in the less-developed countries,[19] but others have placed that figure much higher.[20] Life is hard for these children. They usually live in desperate poverty—begging, stealing, selling sex, or doing whatever work they can find. To make matters worse, they are often viewed with suspicion and hostility by the adult population. In Brazil, where such attitudes seem to be at their most extreme, thousands of these children have been murdered by police and vigilante organizations in the past decade.

SOCIAL STRUCTURE

Underlying the disparities in the quality of life are fundamental differences in the social structures of rich and poor societies. The class system, political institutions, and economic structures are all markedly different in the less-developed countries. For example, farming is only one of dozens of industries in the wealthy nations, but it is still the most common way people make their living in many parts of the world. Many of these nations depend heavily on the exploitation of natural resources such as petroleum, timber, copper, and uranium—if they are lucky enough to have them. A third major source of employment is low-wage jobs in industries that require large amounts of relatively unskilled labor. Sometimes the factories are owned by local businesspeople or governments, but more often they are branches of huge multinational corporations run from headquarters in one of the industrialized nations. As was already mentioned, rapid population growth and weak overall economies mean that there is a very large group of workers without steady jobs.

Another important difference between the rich and poor nations is their class systems. Both types of societies have a relatively small upper class that commands a disproportionate share of wealth and power. The industrialized nations also have a large middle class that has the skills necessary to keep the technological economy going. In less-developed countries, the middle class is much smaller and weaker, and the gap between the rich and the poor is far larger. For example, the bottom 20 percent of people in Germany and Japan receive from 8 to 10 percent of total income in the country, while the top 20 percent of the people received about 35 percent. Although income inequality is higher in the United States than in other industrialized nations, the gap is still wider in the Third World.[21] For example, in Brazil, Guatemala, Honduras, Columbia, Paraguay, South Africa, and Zimbabwe, the bottom 20 percent of people get about 2 percent of national income while the top 20 percent get more than 60 percent.[22] As in the wealthy countries, the disparities in wealth tend to be even greater than the disparities in income. In Mexico, for example, just 37 families control half the wealth, while millions live in severe poverty.[23]

Nations on both sides of the global divide also have significant differences in their political institutions. The most obvious is that the rich industrialized nations have stable democratic governments, while less-developed countries are much more likely to have some type of dictator or a small group of bureaucratic rulers who are not elected by the public. (Of course, many of these nations hold elections, but the results are rigged against the government's opponents.) Although there has been a trend toward more democracy in the less-developed countries, such governments are usually fragile affairs. Elected leaders often face a constant threat of a military coup or a disruptive outbreak of social violence if they make the wrong move.

Whether dictatorships or democracies, governments in the less-developed countries tend to be weaker and more unstable than their counterparts in the wealthy nations. Sharp ethnic and class differences and the lack of strong unifying institutions produce a high level of conflict in many poor nations. Popular discontent often leads to a succession of new governments that seem unable to get at the roots of the nation's problems or to an entrenched dictatorship that ignores public opinion. Significant parts of some countries are not actually controlled by their central government at all but by bands of organized rebels, as in the Tamil areas of Sri Lanka and the opium-producing regions of Burma. Even relatively stable governments are hopelessly outmatched by the military and economic power of the industrialized nations. No matter how independence-minded Third World leaders may be, they often find that their destiny is determined by decisions made in Washington, Tokyo, or Berlin.

QUICK REVIEW

What is the global class system?
Describe the differences between life in the industrialized countries and life in the Third World in terms of economic conditions, education, and health.
What are the special problems faced by women and children in the Third World?
What are the differences in social structure between rich and poor countries?

EXPLAINING THE GLOBAL DIVIDE

In the distant past, when all human societies were based on hunting and gathering, inequalities among the peoples of the world were fairly small. The transition to an agricultural economy greatly increased social inequality, but the beginnings of today's global divide can be found in the **industrial revolution** and the capitalist economic system that made it possible (see Chapter 2).[24] This new kind of society was based not on farming but on trade, commerce, and manufacturing, and as it took shape in western Europe, it stimulated one technological advance after another at an ever-quickening pace. The European countries used their technological superiority for political gains as well. They built a huge network of colonies (foreign territories under their political control) throughout the world. Even areas that managed to stay outside these colonial empires were often dominated by the economic and military power of the European nations. From the beginning of the colonial period (around the end of the fifteenth century), the standard of living of the European nations grew at an unprecedented rate, as wealth and resources poured in from their overseas empires. Most of the rest of the world, however, remained mired in poverty. Although European **colonialism** lasted well into the twentieth century, its days are now over. Nonetheless, the economic inequality between rich and poor nations is still growing larger year by year.[25]

Today's global inequalities clearly stem from the fact that some nations have undergone a full process of industrialization while others have not. The key question is why. In the early days of their colonial expansion, most Europeans simply assumed that their technological advantage was the result of their biological and religious superiority. Although such **ethnocentrism** is certainly still around, few social scientists take that attitude seriously. The effort to explain these differences scientifically has been a long and difficult process. Many of our greatest sociologists and historians have struggled with this crucial question, and even today, opinions remain sharply divided along political lines. In this chapter, we will examine two broad theories—modernization theory and world system theory—that both seek to explain this global divide. The aim of this section is to present each approach in a clear and coherent form, but it is important to keep in mind that there are many disagreements among those who support the same theory and that many social scientists freely combine insights from both approaches or hold to other theories altogether.

MODERNIZATION THEORY

This theory, which borrows heavily from the classic sociological work of Max Weber (1864–1920), was developed in the 1950s and 1960s by a group of functionalists who saw industrialization as part of a process of social evolution they called **modernization**.[26] According to this perspective, modernization is the result of the buildup of numerous improvements in the structure and function of social institutions. The most obvious are the countless technological innovations that have been made throughout the course of human history, but modernization also involves what economists call **capital accumulation**—that is, the buildup of wealth. The important thing is not so much amassing money, which is only a symbol of wealth, but increases in real assets (such as roads, buildings, and power plants) and improvements in the education and skill of the workforce. There are also important changes in the organization of society as its institutions become more specialized and more efficient. For example, in most agricultural societies, the extended family serves as school, employer, welfare agency, and punisher of deviant behavior—all rolled into one. As part of the process of modernization, a great deal of the responsibility for these functions is transferred to more specialized social institutions, such as the schools and the criminal-justice system.

Although modernization takes place as a result of the buildup of one improvement on another, this process does not necessarily occur at a steady pace. In fact, economist Walter W. Rostow has shown that industrialization in the Western nations took place in distinct stages, and he argues that all the less-developed countries will eventually follow this same road.[27] According to Rostow, all nations begin at the traditional stage, in which people cling to their old ways and are very reluctant to accept sweeping changes. As a nation enters the "takeoff stage," there is a slow but steady accumulation of wealth, assets, and skills until the nation reaches a kind of critical mass. Once it reaches this third stage, which Rostow terms the "drive for technological maturity," society undergoes a rapid process of industrialization and social change. A more stable balance returns in the fourth and final stage, when the society emerges as a mature industrial power. This process of transition is a tumultuous one, and Rostow held that the instability it causes may leave the developing nation vulnerable to communism or some other totalitarian system.

Why are some nations so much further ahead in the process of modernization than others? Max Weber pointed out several unique conditions in western Europe that helped make the industrial revolution possible. Weber argued that the spread of Puritan religions, which placed an enormous value on hard work and frugality, stimulated the accumulation of wealth necessary for industrialization. He also felt that the political disunity of Europe and the independence of its cities and towns prevented its feudal rulers from repressing the development of capitalism as they did, for example, in China.[28]

Contemporary modernization theorists tend to put the blame on the "traditionalism" of less-developed countries, which has made them resist the kind of changes necessary to create a modern industrial society. Rostow, for example, argues that less-developed countries tend to have a religious, rather than a scientific, cultural orientation, which makes it more difficult to develop and utilize modern technology. According to this view, people in less-developed countries often cling to their traditional ways of doing things and resist the innovations that inevitably go with the process of modernization. Rostow and other modernization theorists also cite the centralization of wealth and power in the hands of a small elite, the numerous restrictions on competitive markets, and the low overall level of education as other important barriers to modernization.[29]

WORLD SYSTEM THEORY

The perspective known as world system theory is one of the newest and fastest-growing theoretical schools in contemporary sociology. While modernization theory has its source in the functionalist perspective, world system theory is a conflict theory that can trace its roots back to Karl Marx. The immediate origins of this theory are often credited to Andre Gunder Frank's studies of Latin America,[30] but it was Immanuel Wallerstein who actually created world system theory.[31] Much of the inspiration for this approach came from a critique of modernization theory and what world system theorists saw as its ethnocentrism and its hidden bias in favor of the status quo. Some world system theorists nonetheless accept many of the points made by modernization theory, and many have also been heavily influenced by the works of Max Weber. Virtually all world system theorists agree, however, that modernization theory leaves out the most fundamental cause of Third World poverty—exploitation by rich industrialized powers.

This photo shows bombing by NATO warplanes in Northern Albania near the Kosovo border. World system theorists argue that the rich nations are able to dominate most Third World countries through economic means, but when that fails, they resort to military power.

The most fundamental insight of this new perspective is that industrialization does not take place in isolated individual nations, as modernization theory assumes, but within a complex web of international economic and political relationships known as the **world system**. In its beginnings, the modern world system was a rather small affair, limited to a part of northern Europe, but it eventually grew into the global financial and political network that now dominates the planet. At the center of the world system are the rich and powerful industrialized nations, known as the **core**. These core nations are surrounded by a much larger number of poor nations, called the **periphery**. The core nations exploit the periphery for its natural resources and cheap labor while using their own military and economic power to prevent peripheral nations from growing strong enough to challenge the interests of the core. Between these two extremes is the **semiperiphery**. Countries in this category are more industrialized than the peripheral nations but are far behind the core. Although they are still subject to the economic and political domination of the core, the semiperipheral nations are themselves able to exploit their poorer neighbors.

World system theorists disagree about how to classify the remaining communist nations. The most common view is that communism represented an effort by exploited nations to pull out of the world system and industrialize on their own, without foreign interference. The collapse of European communism is seen as evidence of how powerful the capitalist world system is and how difficult it is for any nation to challenge it. World system theorists argue that the former communist countries, such as Russia and the eastern European nations, are now back in the capitalist world system and once again in a subordinate role. Even countries such as China and Vietnam, which still claim to be communist, have realized they must play the capitalist game if they are to survive in today's global economy.

The historical record shows that the core is often led by a single **hegemonic power**—a dominant nation that is far stronger economically, militarily, and politically than the other core states. The first hegemonic power was Holland, followed by Great Britain and then the United States. However, the military and economic costs of protecting the world system impose a heavy burden on the hegemonic power, and many world system theorists argue that the United States is already slipping from its position of dominance, as Holland and Britain did before it.

According to world system theory, the fundamental cause of poverty in the peripheral nations is not that they are too traditional but that the core nations have forced them into a position of economic and political dependence. While modernization theory sees poor nations as simply places where economic development has yet to take place, world system theorists point out that peripheral nations have in fact undergone enormous social and economic changes. However, those changes have not been dictated by their own needs but by those of the core nations. Many poor countries have great natural resources, but it is the needs of the core nations that determine which minerals are to be produced and the price that such things as timber and petroleum will bring. Many poor nations have lush plantations, but their agricultural bounty is consumed by the people of the rich nations. Many poor nations have beautiful beaches and resorts, but they are full of wealthy tourists from the industrialized countries. Underlying all these inequities is the fact that many of the most productive assets in the poor nations are owned and operated by multinational corporations from the core nations.

Critics of world system theory complain that it is too ideological and that its supporters see only the bad side of capitalism. Such critics point out that both life expectancy and the standard of living in the Third World are actually much higher now than they were in the past. They argue that far from exploiting less-developed countries, industrialized countries are in fact helping them. Critics claim that if industrial capitalism had never developed in western Europe, the Third World would still be suffering from the extreme poverty and class exploitation typical of most agricultural societies. Defenders of world system theory respond that the standard of living as calculated by the economists is not a very good measure of actual conditions in the Third World. World system theorists argue that while monetary income may have gone up, the quality of life has declined as the traditional lifestyle of Third World people has been destroyed, and they say that conditions certainly would have been much better in the periphery without foreign interference.[32] (See the "Debate" on pages 382–383.)

EVALUATION

It may seem frustrating to students that the enormous amount of time and effort social scientists have spent analyzing global inequality hasn't produced more agreement about its causes. But behind the academic and political rivalry between these two theoretical camps, there are actually considerable areas of agreement. The naive version of world system theory would blame all the world's problems on the capitalist core nations, while naive modernization theorists see the "traditionalism" of the Third World as the cause of all its difficulties. More sophisticated members of both camps recognize that no single factor can explain the complexities of the modern world. Traditional values, the lack of capital, low educational levels, weak government, and the other factors cited by the modernization theorists have certainly played a major role in creating today's global divide, but so has the exploitation of poor nations by rich ones. To understand our current problems, we must look at both the internal conditions within individual nations that impede development and the world system of economic and political relationships in which those nations are embedded.

QUICK REVIEW

What impact did the industrial revolution have on global inequality?

Compare and contrast the ways modernization theory and world system theory explain inequality between groups of nations.

What are the strengths and weaknesses of the modernization and world system theories?

WARFARE AND TERRORISM

The rich nations of the world were horrified by the attacks on World Trade Center and the Pentagon in September of 2001, and they quickly united under American leadership to combat global terrorism. Tragically, there have been many other cases in recent decades in which even greater numbers of innocent people were massacred that the rich countries practically ignored. One of the worst cases was in the "killing fields" of Cambodia, where approximately 1.7 million people were murdered by the communist Khmer Rouge regime in the late 1970s. (See "Lessons from Other Places" on pages 384–385.) More recently there was the genocidal conflict between that raged between the Hutu and Tutsi in Rwanda and the attempt by Serbs of the former Yugoslavia to kill or drive off as many ethnic Albanians, Bosnians, and Croatians as they could in a policy chillingly called "ethnic cleansing."

Of course, world poverty and inequality do not create political violence all by themselves, but they are its prime breeding ground. Figures compiled by the World Bank show that between 1990 and 1995 about 90 percent of all cases of "civil war and strife" occurred in poor nations.[33] Contrary to popular stereotypes, such conflicts are not confined to any particular region of the world, but are spread out among all parts of the world that suffer from the problems of poverty. Also, it is not just a matter of how much people have, but of how fairly it is distributed. Measuring the gap between the rich and poor in countries and cities around the world, several studies have shown a significant correlation between inequality and levels of political violence.[34] It therefore seems obvious that any "war against terrorism" will not be successful if it aims merely to arrest, kill, or depose the leaders who support terrorism. Other bin Ladens will emerge. Something more basic must be done about poverty and global inequality, which are the breeding grounds for the terrorists. The pages that follow attempt to show us why so much genocide, terrorism, and warfare occur in our world today.

THE NATURE OF WAR

Although warfare goes back to the earliest recorded history, it is difficult to define precisely. Part of the problem is that the difference between war and peace is a matter of degree. Everyone will agree that World War II deserves to be called a war and that a typical murder does not, but what about an ethnic riot in which two groups throw rocks and insults at each other? What if they throw hand grenades and firebombs? To qualify as a war, such incidents must be organized and violent and must last over a reasonably long period of time. Thus, **war** may be defined as a protracted military conflict between two or more organized groups. This definition still does not tell us, however, exactly how long or how violent these conflicts must be to qualify as a war. Wars are classified in many different ways, but for sociological understanding, a simple division between **international wars** and **revolutionary wars** is most useful. The former are armed conflicts between the governments of two or more sovereign nations; the latter are armed conflicts between an official government and one or more groups of national rebels.

The Escalation of Military Violence   Throughout human history, periods of conflict have been the rule and peace the exception. Melvin Small and J. David Singer's study of warfare from 1816 to 1980 found only 20 years in which there were no international wars in progress.[35] The twentieth century alone saw two world wars and countless lesser conflicts. Even in the most peaceful times, the next war is seldom far away. There are so many international and national tensions, and the traditions of warfare are so deeply entrenched, that the world is likely to repeat this pattern for years to come.

DEBATE

Are the Rich Nations Exploiting the Poor Ones?

Yes

All you have to do is look around any Third World country. The evidence of victimization is everywhere. Children are sickly and malnourished while their parents are often tired and hopeless. Those who live in mud huts and crowded tenements are actually the lucky ones, for whole families often sleep in the streets. Most Third World cities are jammed with legions of unemployed young men and women who have little real chance of ever finding a steady job. Yet this poverty and deprivation occur in the shadow of the incredible abundance of the industrialized nations. The per capita income in the world today is far higher than it has ever been before, but most of that wealth stays in the hands of a privileged few.

Exactly how do the rich nations take advantage of the poor countries? First, Third World people are exploited for their labor. The Third World is now dotted with factories producing consumer goods for the rich nations. Wages paid by the multinational corporations that own most of these factories are pitifully low—often less than $1 a day. Not only are the hours long and the pay low, but the factories are hot, polluted, and dangerous. Hundreds of thousands of workers die every year because of working conditions that would never be tolerated in the wealthy nations.

Second, Third World nations are exploited for their natural resources. Their forests are stripped, their petroleum reserves pumped out, and their mineral deposits depleted in order to satisfy the core nations' voracious appetite for raw materials. Although the peripheral countries receive some money for these commodities, the economic monopoly of the industrialized nations enables them to keep the price of raw materials far below their real value.

Third, poor nations are forced to follow political and economic policies dictated by rich ones. Through the careful use of bribes, covert operations, and outright military force, the core keeps the poor nations from mounting an effective challenge to the world order that exploits them. In addition, a new form of exploitation is developing as the southern part of the planet becomes the dumping ground for toxic wastes and unsafe products manufactured in the core.

The next time someone tries to tell you how much good our corporations and our governments are doing in the Third World, stop and think about it for a moment. Picture Europeans and North Americans dying from the clogged arteries that come from overeating while millions of people starve to death in the Third World. Or picture a Third World dictator slaughtering his people with the guns, tanks, and aircraft supplied by his supporters in the core nations. The truth will soon become obvious.

No

It's human nature to try to find someone to blame for our problems. When we compare the poverty of the Third World with the affluence of the industrialized nations, it is natural to blame one on the other. When we place these problems in historical perspective, however, it is apparent that the industrialized nations have actually helped to improve the standard of living in the Third World.

The most useful comparison is not between the rich and poor nations of today's world but between the Third World today and the way most countries in Africa, Asia, and Latin America were before they were influenced by the industrialized powers. When seen in these terms, there is simply no question that the people of the Third World are far better off as the result of their contacts with the industrialized nations. Their average income and standard of living are much higher than they used to be. Even though most people in the Third World do not have all the latest technological innovations, they still have electric lights, radios, bicycles, and other inventions created in the industrialized nations. Health conditions have vastly improved—infant mortality has plummeted, and the average life expectancy in the Third World is probably double what it was five centuries ago.

Although there are a lot of complaints about "political meddling" in the Third World, the industrialized nations have actually been a vital force encouraging democracy and fighting communism and other totalitarian systems. Five hundred years ago, there wasn't a single democracy in the entire world; today, democracy is flowering even in many of the poorest nations.

The charges that the industrialized nations are exploiting the Third World are just ideological rhetoric intended for political purposes. When revolutionary leaders come to power and cut their nations off from "foreign influence," the people's standard of living goes down, not up. It is easy to complain about the low wages of the workers in the Third World. But the economic fact is that these workers are less educated and less productive than workers in industrialized nations. If their wages were raised too much, Third World factories would no longer be competitive with those in the industrialized nations. Besides, Third World workers employed by foreign multinationals are actually the lucky ones because they earn far more than they could in almost any of the other jobs available to them.

Of course, none of this means that the multinationals or the governments of the industrialized nations never take advantage of the people in the poor nations; the real world is not that simple. It is clear, however, that the industrialized nations have done far more to help than to hurt the Third World.

LESSONS FROM OTHER PLACES

THE KILLING FIELDS

I began making notes for this box one hot afternoon in December 2000 as I sat on a bench in Cambodia. Around me were many pits that had been excavated, still half full of earth. In front of me was a new pagoda about five stories tall and about 10 yards at its base. I was in the middle of one of the most infamous "killing fields" of Cambodia, *Choeung Ek*, about 10 miles outside of the Cambodian capital of Phnom Penh. Some 17,000 men, women, and children are believed to have been slaughtered there between 1975 and 1978. The bones of just under 9,000 of these people have already been dug up. The rest were in the ground somewhere under my feet as I wrote. The five-story memorial pagoda that faced me that day had glass on all four sides up to the top. Inside, the pagoda was piled to the top with human skulls. As I sat making notes, several hundred skulls were facing me—facing me as if eyes were still in the skulls, looking at me through the glass, wanting to know why the world had let this happen.

No one knows exactly how many men, women, and children were murdered by Pol Pot's Khmer Rouge army after they took power in Cambodia in 1975. Estimates run as high as 3 million, but most researchers agree that 1.7 million is the most accurate figure. This is below the estimate of 6 million Jews and "undesirables" killed by the Nazis, or the 9 million or so Africans who were killed by Europeans as they were being transported from Africa to the Americas as slaves. But Cambodia is a very small country and almost every family in Cambodia today has lost someone in the "killing fields." My driver/translator that day told me he had lost two uncles. Two young monks who befriended me a day earlier told me much the same; one monk had lost a sister and the other had lost an uncle.

Although the Nazi **genocide** (the attempt to wipe out an entire race or ethnic group in a particular area) is by far the most famous, numerous other genocidal conflicts have raged since the end of World War II. The massacres in Cambodia are just one more example. The most recent cases include the attempt by the Hutu of Rwanda to exterminate their tribal rivals, the Tutsi (about 800,000 were massacred), and the attempt by Serbs of the former Yugoslavia at "ethnic cleansing"—a euphemism they coined to describe their efforts to kill or drive out all the ethnic Albanians and Croatians from the lands they claimed.

How can people do such things? This question was certainly on my mind when I visited Cambodia. The people there are among the most polite, friendly, and gentle

Although history records a seemingly endless series of wars, the nature of those conflicts has changed significantly over the years. Traditionally, wars were limited. They usually aimed to achieve fairly narrow objectives, such as seizing part of a neighboring ruler's territory. A small group of military men, who were ordinarily from wealthy and privileged backgrounds, did most of the fighting. In fact, people one could find on earth. Only a small percentage of the Cambodian people were active in Pol Pot's killing, but that still means many of the normal-looking people walking the streets of Cambodia today must have been among the mass murders.

We cannot attempt a full answer to this important question here, but as we have been suggesting throughout this book, we have to look at several overlapping levels to understand the forces influencing human behavior. On a global level, there are the forces of political and economic change that bring people into conflict and make them fear for their future. Global economic depression and the treaty ending World War I that was so devastating to Germany helped fuel the rise of Hitler. In the case of "killing fields" in the Balkans in the 1990s, it was the fall of communism that had held the country of Yugoslavia together despite the presence of ethnic groups who had hated each other for centuries. In Cambodia, it was the political chaos caused by the fall of French colonialism and the war in Vietnam. The American government actually gave $150 million to support Pol Pot and the Khmer Rouge after 1979 because they were against Vietnamese communists.

On another level, there is the racism and ethnic hatred we explored in Chapter 6. The genocidal conflict between the Hutu and Tutsi in Rwanda, or the Serbs, Croatians, and Albanians in Yugoslavia are classic examples. Many similar ethnic hatreds are simmering on the back burner in other places waiting to explode into flames when the social conditions are right.

Finally, there is the psychological level. Actual people have to carry out the killings, but it seems hard to believed that anyone could do such things. Some of the most alarming research on this question was carried out years ago by Stanley Milgram. Milgram ordered subjects in his laboratory to give another person strong electric shocks that they thought could cause serious injury. He found that his authority alone was enough to get most of the research subjects to give electric shocks to a screaming victim. (In fact, the "victim" was working with the experimenters and was only faking it.) These people who went along and gave out what they thought were severe shocks were average Americans from all walks of life. In the same climate of fear and social chaos, it seems likely that many Americans would also be willing to follow the orders of a Hitler or a Pol Pot.

—*Harold Kerbo*

Sources: Stanley Milgram, *Obedience in Authority* (New York: Harper Colophon Books, 1974); *International Herald Tribune*, September 29, 2000.

these professional soldiers actually had far more in common with the enemies they fought than with the average men and women who watched the war from the sidelines. The behavior of soldiers in battle was often regulated by a code of gallantry, and those who did not conform ran the risk of losing honor in the eyes of their comrades.

Modern warfare, starting with Napoleon (emperor of France 1804–1815), has been marked by a steady escalation of violence. Modern warfare is often **total war**— an all-out national effort to kill or subdue enemy civilians and soldiers alike. Today's wars are no longer fought mainly by professional soldiers and privileged elites; most of the soldiers are average citizens, often drafted against their will. Civilians now play a key role in the military effort: manufacturing trucks and airplanes, producing oil, growing food. In modern warfare, victorious nations are usually those with the greatest productive capacity. It follows that civilians contributing to such production are prime military targets. Moreover, the tremendous range and destructiveness of modern weapons has expanded the combat zone to include most civilians.

Over the years, we have invented more and more efficient ways of killing our enemies at longer distances. The spear was replaced by the bow and arrow, which became the crossbow. The musket developed into the cannon, the rifle, and the machine gun. In World War I (1914–1918), the cannon and rifle were fused into the long rifle, a huge gun that enabled the Germans to shell Paris from a distance of 75 miles. The hand grenade of World War I became the bomb of World War II, dropped from high-flying airplanes 1000 miles from their base. The TNT bomb gave way to the atom bomb, and the bomber was replaced with the guided missile. Now, a modern military force can wreak destruction virtually anywhere in the world at any time.[36]

Some people consider this tremendous destructive power an instrument of peace. At a minimum, it makes total war less appealing, since even the victors are likely to suffer terrible devastation. Although modern nations are organized for total war, the wars that have occurred since the development of nuclear weapons have been confined to limited areas, as in Korea, Southeast Asia, and the Middle East. It appears that fear of a **nuclear war** has helped to head off full-scale global conflict. Nevertheless, the possibility remains that such limitations will someday be broken, and all-out nuclear war remains a real threat to human survival.

One of the main reasons that this threat remains so strong is **nuclear proliferation**: the spread of nuclear weapons to more and more nations around the world. At the dawn of the nuclear age, only the United States had these frightening weapons. Soon the Soviet Union, Britain, and France developed their own atomic bombs. For a few years, nuclear weapons were exclusively in the hands of the major industrial powers, but in the 1960s, China developed an atomic bomb, and China was soon followed by its neighbor to the south, India. Western experts believe that like China, India now has a considerable nuclear arsenal, some of which may be mounted on intermediate-range ballistic missiles. The next link in this chain was India's archenemy, Pakistan. When India resumed its nuclear testing in 1998, Pakistan set off its own series of atomic blasts in a new nuclear arms race in south Asia. It also seems certain that Israel has a large stockpile of nuclear bombs, although it refuses to admit that it possesses such weapons. There is, moreover, considerable concern that some of the more than 30,000 nuclear weapons or part of the huge stockpiles of weapons-grade nuclear material Russia inherited from the Soviet Union when it collapsed might fall into the wrong hands. And, several of the world's most belligerent and unpredictable governments, including Libya and Iran, are apparently working to develop their own nuclear capability.

It is becoming increasingly clear that the "peaceful" nuclear power plants and technical know-how that the United States, Canada, and other industrialized powers have sold to nations around the world have made it far easier for these nations to make nuclear bombs. As more nations develop their own nuclear weapons, it seems almost inevitable that someone, somewhere, will use them.[37]

The Consequences of War   Human history is filled with the carnage of war. Small and Singer concluded that there have been an average of 7.9 international and 6.4 revolutionary wars every decade for the last 165 years.[38] These wars have reaped a staggering toll in human lives—in the last two centuries over 150 million people were killed.[39] The battles of World War II alone are believed to have cost about 15 million lives, and when civilian casualties are added in, the total comes to almost 48 million deaths.[40] Although many Americans think that the world has been relatively peaceful in recent times, there have actually been another 40 million war-related deaths since the end of World War II.[41]

The dead are not the only victims, however. Every war leaves a human legacy of the maimed and crippled, widows and widowers, grieving parents, and orphans. Even the soldiers who escape physically unharmed often suffer psychological wounds that stay with them for the rest of their lives. The number of war causalities did drop somewhat after the Cold War, but the number of wars has been increasing again in recent years. During 2000, the National Defense Council Foundation estimated there were 68 countries experiencing severe civil unrest, drug wars, or international conflicts, up from 65 in 1999.[42]

Economically, the price tag for even a small war is astronomical. Property worth hundreds of millions of dollars has often been destroyed in a single day. Military technology has made it possible to transform a thriving community into a pile of rubble in a matter of seconds. Even if there were no loss of property, the costs of war are still enormous: Businesses fail; production of consumer goods slows down or stops; fields go unplanted and crops unharvested for want of labor. Many nations have plunged from affluence to starvation during a single war.

Even in times of peace, we pay a price for war. Almost 23 million people are currently employed by the world's armed forces, and in 1997, the nations of the world spent about $823 billion on their military (see Figure 11.4 on page 388). Of this amount, over one-fifth was spent by the less-developed countries, which, of course, often have trouble just feeding their people.[43] There are economists who argue that such enormous military outlays are beneficial because they create jobs and stimulate the economy. This might be true, but if it is, it also follows that much greater benefits would be reaped if the money were spent on goods and services that are economically useful. For example, a nation is no better off economically with 1,000 nuclear missiles than it is with 1, but a nation is much better off with 1,000 hydroelectric power plants than with only 1. Two of the nations that are often considered among the world's economic powerhouses, Germany and Japan, both have small armed forces and low military budgets.[44]

As heavy as all these military costs are, they are minuscule compared with those of a full-scale nuclear war. Such a war has never occurred, so it is impossible

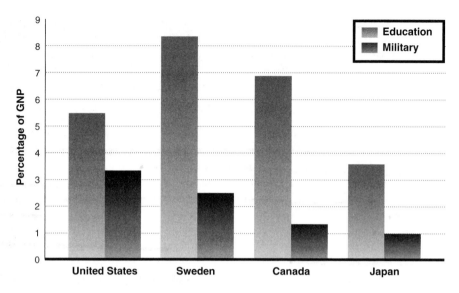

FIGURE 11.4   GUNS VERSUS BUTTER

In comparison with other industrialized nations, the United States tends to spend more on the military and less on education.

Source: World Bank, *World Development Report,* 2000 (New York: Oxford University Press, 2000), pp. 284, 307.

to be sure what would actually happen, but scientists have been able to make some educated guesses. The best source of data come from the only two atomic explosions that ever occurred in populated areas: the U.S. attacks on Hiroshima and Nagasaki. Those two bombs killed 110,000 people in the first seconds after the blast, and another 100,000 people died within a year. Tens of thousands more were severely injured, and people are still dying from the long-term effects of radiation poisoning. Despite this horrible toll, the bombs dropped on those two cities were small and primitive by today's standards. There are tens of thousands of nuclear warheads in the hands of the world's governments today, and some of them are over 4,000 times more powerful than the bombs dropped on Japan. Scientists estimate that a nuclear exchange involving only about one-third of those weapons would kill over 1 billion people in the first few hours. As clouds of radiation spread throughout the globe, entire species of plants and animals would die, along with 50 to 75 percent of the world's human population.[45]

Grim as this scenario is, many scientists believe that it may be too optimistic. Studies first published a decade ago and since subjected to intense scientific scrutiny indicate that an all-out nuclear exchange would create a huge cloud of dust and smoke that would cover the globe. Estimates based on studies of much smaller clouds released by volcanic eruptions suggest that some 96 percent of the sunlight normally reaching the northern hemisphere would be blocked out. The result would be a **nuclear winter** in which the average temperature, even in warm areas, would drop below

Nuclear war is the ultimate nightmare of human conflict. Although the end of the Cold War has greatly reduced the likelihood of the "doomsday scenario"—an all-out nuclear war between the United States and Russia—the probability that there will someday be a more limited nuclear conflict somewhere in the Third World seems to be increasing.

freezing for several months. The lack of sunlight and plummeting temperatures would have a devastating effect on the plants and animals that produce our food, perhaps changing the ecological system of the earth in an irreversible way.[46] The threat of an all-out nuclear war has, of course, been reduced since the end of the Cold War between the United States and the Soviet Union, but it is still a nightmare that has haunted humanity for half a century.

Many nonetheless feel that more limited military conflicts can still have beneficial effects. The most obvious is the overthrow of oppressive and unjust governments. For example, both Germany and Japan developed stable democratic states after their totalitarian regimes were destroyed in World War II. Although some argue that even the most ruthless dictatorship can be changed by nonviolent resistance, most people doubt that such tactics would have been successful against the bloodthirsty tyrants that fill the pages of the history books. Warfare can also promote the solidarity of a nation or some of the groups within it, and it has often been a stimulant to scientific and technological progress.[47]

There are, nonetheless, many other ways of acquiring the benefits of war without paying its staggering costs. Technology has, as we have seen, brought great increases in the costs of war and reduced its benefits. Since it is quite possible that no human beings would survive an all-out nuclear conflict, the ancient practice of warfare can only be seen as a menacing social problem of the greatest magnitude for the modern world.

TERRORISM

Although politicians and journalists talk with great authority about the problem of **terrorism**—especially since the September 11, 2001 attack on the United States—the concept is usually vaguely defined and its application charged with political bias. Even social scientists have had little success in agreeing on a definition. One review of the literature found over 100 different definitions, often with substantial differences in the kinds of acts they included.[48] Most students of terrorism would agree that it must involve violence used for political ends, but as it stands, such a definition is far too broad, for it would include everything from total war to everyday police work. Numerous attempts have been made to narrow the definition, but there is no agreement about the best way to do it. Many definitions include the additional qualification that the political violence must be aimed against a nonmilitary population. It is, however, doubtful that there has ever been a war in which civilians were not the target of some military violence, so the distinction between terrorism and warfare remains a vague one. Perhaps the problem is that terrorism is used primarily as an emotional label to brand political acts we dislike, so scientific definitions are largely beside the point. Groups we support are "freedom fighters," and those we oppose are "terrorists." From a sociological perspective, it would probably be better to dispose of the concept of terrorism altogether and simply consider such acts as one more form of political violence, but the term seems to have become too popular in the media and the political arena to ignore.

Despite the vagueness of its definition, it is possible to distinguish two general types of terrorism. The best known is **revolutionary terrorism**. It is used by groups trying to bring about major political changes in a particular country. Such groups believe that random terrorist attacks will create such chaos that the government they oppose will fall or at least will meet their demands. Terrorists often try to goad a government into taking extreme measures to combat them so that it will lose popular support. Underground groups also hope that their acts of violence will make the public more aware of their cause, enabling them to recruit more members and build stronger popular support. Some of today's more sophisticated terrorists openly cultivate reporters and other representatives of the media by granting special interviews, releasing prepared statements for the press, and holding open press conferences. Some terrorists even time their attacks to avoid other newsworthy events that might compete for media attention. Revolutionary terrorists often secretly receive the help of established governments that support their goals and objectives.[49]

The bloodshed of September 11th may well reflect the emergence of a new kind of revolutionary terrorism that occurs internationally rather then within a single nation. In one sense, the attacks led by Osama bin Laden were a classic example of revolutionary terrorism—a violent attack against innocent civilians in an attempt to overthrow an established political power. The difference was that bin Laden's group was not aiming to overthrow a single government but the entire world system of which the United States was merely the leader. Thus, his attacks cut across national boundaries. They were planned in Afghanistan, organized in Germany, and carried out in the United States.

Repressive terrorism is the opposite of revolutionary terrorism, in that its goal is to protect an existing political order. Although revolutionary terrorists receive most

Acts of revolutionary terrorism, such as the bombing of the federal building in Oklahoma City, are the focus of intense media attention. Repressive terrorism, on the other hand, is much more likely to be hidden from public view.

of the publicity, repressive terrorism is probably a far greater threat. Governments all over the world—from Iraq to Israel to the People's Republic of China—use violence to terrorize their political opponents and maintain their grip on power. Time after time, the opponents of Third World leaders mysteriously disappear and are never seen again. Torture and imprisonment without just cause are also common tools of repressive terrorists. One of the most extreme examples since the end of World War II occurred in the small country of Cambodia, where about 1.7 million of its citizens were killed in less than four years.[50] (See "Lessons from Other Places" on pages 384–385.) Although the scale of the violence in Cambodia was unusual, repressive terrorism is a fact of political life in many nations around the world.

Some experts fear that revolutionary terrorists might someday build or steal nuclear weapons. No one has ever carried out such nuclear terrorism, but it remains a disturbing possibility. For a group that has a supply of the right fuel, such as enriched plutonium, a nuclear bomb is relatively simple to build. With such a weapon, a band of revolutionary terrorists could gain enormous power. Even if they could only get less highly refined atomic material, a terrorist group could still wreak enormous damage by simply blowing it up with conventional explosives and sending a huge cloud of poisonous radioactive material into the air. Nuclear weapons are less suited to repressive terrorism; still, a government controlled by a small, unpopular minority might conceivably use such weapons against its own population. In the modern world, nuclear weapons are the ultimate source of terror.

QUICK REVIEW

What are the differences between revolutionary warfare and international warfare?
What is nuclear proliferation, and why is it such an important issue?
Discuss the costs of warfare.
Compare and contrast revolutionary and repressive terrorism.

EXPLAINING POLITICAL VIOLENCE

Many people believe that warfare is part of human nature. The same aggressive instinct that is said to make us violent is also said to lead inevitably to war. However, there is a great deal of evidence to indicate that this is not the case. Most important is the fact that the people of some cultures never go to war. As Marvin Harris, a noted anthropologist, put it: "Although humans may have aggressive tendencies, there is no reason that such tendencies cannot be suppressed, controlled or expressed in ways other than by armed combat. . . . There is no instinct for war. War is fought only to the extent that it is advantageous for some of the combatants."[51] The point is that warfare and violence are not the same thing. Humans may well have some kind of innate tendency to behave violently in certain circumstances, but that does not mean that we have an innate tendency to engage in organized warfare.

Another common approach seeks to find the causes of a particular war in the specific acts that set it off and the leaders who made the key decisions. It may be argued, for example, that if Hitler had not been born, World War II would never have happened. Since it is impossible to rerun history, there is no way of proving or disproving such claims. It does appear, however, that individual decisions have made the difference between war and peace in some cases. During the Cuban missile crisis of 1962, for example, the world seemed to be teetering on the brink of a nuclear war. The leaders of the United States and the Soviet Union made decisions that averted war, but one leader could well have plunged the world into a holocaust. Even so, this approach explains only the superficial causes of warfare. Certain social conditions must be present before war is possible. If the United States and the Soviet Union had not had enormous military machines and the willingness to fight, no conflict could have taken place, no matter what the decisions of their leaders.

In order to deepen our understanding of warfare, we need to understand the major theories about its causes. It will, however, be necessary to examine revolutionary and international wars separately, since they often spring from quite different roots. Although much less research has been done on terrorism, many of these theories work just as well in explaining the causes of terrorism as they do for warfare.

REVOLUTIONARY CONFLICT

Revolutions are romantic. They have given us some of the most dramatic episodes in human history. The revolutionary theme—a small group of freedom-loving patriots fighting against overwhelming odds—has captured the imagination of countless writers and artists. Even American cowboy stories show plain and simple folk in heroic struggles against land barons and railroad tycoons. Several theories help make sense of revolutions—but these theories are far from perfect. All the conditions that are said to cause revolutions are sometimes present in societies in which no revolutionary conflict takes place; and revolutions sometimes take place in societies that lack the important characteristics mentioned by theorists. The unique cultural traditions of individual societies play an important part in revolutionary struggles, as does the influence of individual leaders.

Exploitation and Oppression   One of the earliest and most influential theories of revolution was formulated by Karl Marx and Friedrich Engels.[52] They believed that the injustices they saw in the capitalism of their time would produce a worldwide revolution. As workers in capitalist nations sank deeper and deeper into poverty and personal alienation, they would eventually come to realize that they were being exploited by the owners of the factories in which they worked. The workers would then band together, overthrow their oppressors in a violent revolution, and create a classless utopia with liberty and justice for all.

The Marxist theory of revolution is almost 150 years old, and the revolutionary movement it predicted has not occurred. The revolutions fought in the name of Marxism in China, Russia, Cuba, and elsewhere did not happen the way Marx's theory predicted and did not produce anything like the communist utopia he described. Nevertheless, many Marxists and non-Marxists alike still believe that exploitation and oppression of the lower classes may eventually produce a revolutionary uprising. Far less accepted is Marx's idea that such a revolution will necessarily destroy capitalism and create a new, utopian economic system. Moreover, contemporary sociologists are likely to see a broader range of groups as the victims of exploitation and oppression. For example, in recent times it seems that ethnic oppression has been at least as common a cause of revolution as pure class conflict. Nonetheless, virtually all sociologists who have studied the subject agree that **class conflict** precedes many revolutions. Before a revolution, the various social classes come to view one another as hostile economic competitors. The English and French revolutions, for example, were fueled by the revolt of the merchants and traders against the feudal aristocracy.

Relative Deprivation   Considerable research since Marx's time suggests that it is relative poverty, not absolute poverty, that is most likely to spark a violent class conflict. According to **relative deprivation theory**, revolutions are caused by differences between what people have and what they think they should have.

James C. Davies, one of the leading exponents of this theory, presented some interesting data on several of history's most famous revolutions.[53] He concluded that "revolutions are most likely to occur when a prolonged period of objective economic and social development is followed by a short period of sharp reversal."[54] In other words, people were actually better off at the start of the revolutions he studied than they had been in previous decades. Apparently, improvement in social conditions creates an expectation of even greater progress. If a sharp downturn occurs, and the people are unwilling to reduce either their standard of living or their expectations, they will rise up against the government.

Institutions and Resources   Psychologically oriented approaches such as relative deprivation theory hold, in effect, that misery breeds revolt. However, more recent theorists have argued that, to understand why people rise up against their government, we also need to look at the imbalances in the social institutions of their society. Samuel P. Huntington, for example, asserts that the changes created as a country modernizes its economy throw its institutions out of equilibrium. As people become more educated, their desire to become involved in politics increases faster than traditional political institutions can accommodate, and the result may be a revolution.[55]

Charles Tilly responded to Huntington's theory by pointing out that the discontent caused by such institutional imbalances is unlikely to lead to a revolt as long as the discontented remain disorganized and lacking in resources. Arguing that conflict is a normal part of politics, Tilly felt that political violence is likely to occur only when dissatisfied groups are able to mobilize enough resources to mount a significant challenge to the existing government.[56]

Failure of the Government   Studies of the world's great revolutions show that the people who ran the governments that were overthrown had been doing a very poor job. Crane Brinton's classic study of the American, British, French, and Russian revolutions concluded, for example, that the old ruling class in all these societies was "divided and inept."[57] The authorities seemed to make the wrong decisions and then overreact or underreact to the beginnings of revolutionary ferment. Brinton also showed that these prerevolutionary governments were teetering on the verge of bankruptcy, although the economies of their societies were reasonably sound.[58]

Theda Skocpol, among other theorists, emphasizes the fact that governments do not always reflect the interests of the social elite of their society.[59] Often, the government and its top officials have special interests of their own that conflict with those of elite groups. For example, governments often become enmeshed in the game of international power politics, but the cost of war may threaten the welfare of substantial segments of the elite. When this occurs, the likelihood of an armed revolt is greatly increased, especially when elite groups have sufficient resources to mount a credible challenge to government forces.

Ethnic and Regional Conflicts   The collapse of the Soviet Union and the cooling of the great ideological conflicts that fueled the Cold War seem to have marked a turning point in the patterns of contemporary warfare. Ethnic hostility has become the leading cause of revolutionary violence, whether it be the Serbs, Croatians, and Muslims in the Balkans; the Hutu and Tutsi in East Africa; the Kurds and the Turks and Iraqis in western Asia; or any one of dozens of other regional conflicts.

Of course, ethnic conflict often led to violence in the past as well. History is full of examples of revolts by an ethnic group in one part of a nation against its central government, but the ideal of ethnic pride and autonomy seems to have taken on new force in recent times. Another major source of revolutionary conflict involves regional differences, which more often than not have an ethnic element as well. Regional differences were, for example, a major factor in the American Civil War.

When a rebellious ethnic or regional group wins control of one part of a country, these conflicts may be transformed into something more similar to an international war. Generally, if the rebels are successful, the nation is divided into two or more new countries, and future conflicts (which are extremely common in such cases) are then waged between sovereign nations. Sometimes, however, the rebellious group takes over the entire nation and reverses its relationship with the old dominant group, forcing it into a subordinate position.

INTERNATIONAL CONFLICT

The causes of revolutionary and international wars are usually quite different, but in some cases the internal conditions conducive to a revolutionary uprising may also contribute to an international war. For example, political leaders who are having trouble at home sometimes stir up an international conflict in an attempt to divert the people's attention from their domestic problems. It is said that "nothing makes friends like a common enemy," and such a strategy sometimes reunites a nation; but in the long run the internal problems reemerge, often aggravated by the strains of the international conflict.

Militarism   There are two faces of **militarism** that contribute to international wars. The first is glorification of war. International warfare is obviously more likely when a society sees it as a heroic show of strength or when young people see it as a path to personal fame and fortune. Although such attitudes are still common in the nuclear age, they seem to be on the decline in the wealthy industrialized nations. The growth of complex military technology has taken the glory out of person-to-person combat, and the fear of nuclear annihilation has quieted the cheers of civilians.

The second face of militarism is institutional. Many countries around the world, both rich and poor, devote a major portion of their wealth to military purposes, and their military institutions have become a powerful force in shaping national attitudes and priorities. Even when one of these nations has no aggressive plans, its military leaders demand huge "defensive" forces. In fact, as social support for war for its own sake has declined, there seems to have been an increasing concern with warding off foreign aggressors. Such desires are reflected in enormous military budgets and constant preparation for war. Nations that devote major parts of their economies to military purposes now claim that they are doing so merely for defensive purposes. The idea that the strength and integrity of a nation depend on military superiority over its competitors often leads a country to a frantic effort to build up its military forces faster than its enemies do. Such **arms races** usually increase rather than decrease a nation's sense of insecurity and have often led to major international conflicts.[60]

Nationalism and Ideology   Like patriotism, **nationalism** is a sense of identification with and devotion to one's nation. In the past, growing nationalism discouraged local wars by unifying petty feudal kingdoms into larger and more stable national units. In the modern world, however, nationalism all too often produces the opposite result.[61] Many wars have started over some petty incident that was interpreted as an affront to "national honor." Rational settlements based on fair compromise are difficult when nationalistic feelings are involved. After all, what wise politician would dare compromise his or her nation's honor?

Nationalism is also a critical part of the motivation for **imperialism**, the creation or expansion of an empire. As Quincy Wright pointed out in his classic study of war, some wars arise "because of the tendency of a people affected by nationalism . . . to acquire an attitude of superiority to some or all other peoples, to seek to extend its cultural characteristics throughout the world, and to ignore the claims of other states and of the world community."[62]

Nationalism is not, however, the only kind of ideology that can stimulate violent confrontations. Sometimes the conflict between secular political ideologies such as Marxism and capitalism has led to full-scale war—but religion has more often played this role. From the European Crusades to the conflicts in the Middle East in our time, the belief that one must protect and expand one's faith by force of arms has sent millions of people off to war.

Economic or Political Gain   Most wars are fought to achieve some kind of gain. One nation may attack another in an attempt to capture valuable natural resources, desirable land, cheap labor, or political control over a larger population. Sometimes an entire nation reaps advantages from its conquests, but more often only a small segment of a society benefits from a war. Some people—for example, high-ranking military officers and those who supply the arms and materials necessary to keep a war going—stand to gain from an outbreak of almost any sort of war. Other interest groups may profit from a war if it helps secure beneficial resources; exporters profit from the conquest of a new seaport, while farmers gain by winning access to valuable land or water. Although its political leaders gave various justifications, it is clear that Iraq's invasion of Kuwait in 1990 was prompted by the desire to gain a better port on the Persian Gulf and to seize Kuwait's rich oil fields. Similarly, the American-led invasion that freed Kuwait was justified on idealistic grounds, but it was motivated primarily by the desire to protect the industrialized world's supply of low-cost petroleum.

The enormous destructive power of modern warfare has nonetheless made it difficult for any nation to profit from an international war. Kurt Finsterbusch and H. C. Greisman put it as follows:

> Not only have the costs of wars increased greatly because of the vastly improved technology of devastation and the practice of total warfare, the benefits have also declined decidedly. Wars no longer gain booty, spoils or tribute; and they infrequently gain economic concessions.[63]

International Political Organization   In many ways, the most basic cause of international war is the way in which the world is politically organized. Our planet is divided into almost 200 sovereign states, most of which have their own military forces and a belief in their right to use them to protect or advance their national interests. With so many different governments and so many different armies, it is no surprise that international wars are frequent. Indeed, the threat of war is often just one more chip in the poker game of political bargaining among nations. In the famous words of nineteenth-century military strategist Karl von Clausewitz, "War is nothing but a continuation of political intercourse, with a mixture of other means."[64]

Despite appearances to the contrary, the nations of the world do not act like a pack of gunslingers in the Old West. There is a delicate and longstanding **balance of**

power among the nations in the world system. Although it is often claimed that peace is most likely when there is a balance of power, A. F. K. Organski and Jacek Kugler found just the opposite to be true.[65] According to their research, peace (or at least the absence of all-out wars among the world's major powers) is most likely when one power is clearly dominant and the others are afraid to challenge it, as was the case when Britain dominated the world system in the nineteenth century and when the United States was dominant in more recent years. Major wars tend to break out only when new nations feel strong enough to challenge the old leader.

QUICK REVIEW

Critically evaluate the main theories about the causes of international conflict.
Critically evaluate the main theories about the causes of revolutionary conflict.

SOLVING THE PROBLEMS OF GLOBAL INEQUALITY AND CONFLICT

Many social scientists and political leaders have a pet proposal they see as a solution to our global crisis; but just as there is no one cause of these problems, there is no single solution. This section will examine some of the most common suggestions, but there are still strong disagreements about the wisdom and the possible effectiveness of all these proposals. We will begin by exploring some ideas for reducing global inequality, since as we have seen, a major reduction in poverty is also likely to reduce warfare and political violence. Next, we turn to the proposals that take a more direct aim at encouraging world peace.

ECONOMIC DEVELOPMENT OF THE THIRD WORLD

Practically all Third World leaders say they are committed to **economic development**, but that phrase has different meanings for different people. One of the biggest issues concerns priorities and goals. Those who want to emulate the industrialized nations tend to focus on large-scale development projects in urban areas. Typically, local governments use loans, foreign investments, or their own funds to build modern factories like those in the core nations. Critics charge that expensive factories with labor-saving equipment make little sense in nations that are short on money but have vast resources of unused labor. Moreover, they argue that reliance on foreign investment ultimately produces an economy owned, operated, and controlled by foreigners.[66] Instead, many critics advocate building up simpler, "low-tech" industries that utilize inexpensive technology and local labor to turn out low-cost products. Others claim that the whole emphasis on industrialization is misguided and that the number one priority of governments in poor nations should be rural development. They argue that since the majority of people live in rural areas, an effort to increase farm production and prevent runaway urban growth will create the greatest benefits for the largest number of people.

Which ever approach they take, Third World nations need three things from rich countries in order to improve their economies and reduce poverty—access to their

The most effective foreign aid is often targeted to the specific needs of the recipient. This photo shows an American relief worker in Somalia.

markets, forgiveness of their international debt, and foreign aid. Most wealthy nations use a complex system of import taxes, quotas, and other restrictions to protect their own industries and limit the flow of goods from the low-wage countries of Africa, Latin America, and Asia. A sharp reduction or elimination of those barriers would provide a real boost to struggling Third World economies.

Although representatives of industries threatened by foreign competition in rich countries often make dire predictions about what will happen if trade barriers are removed, the impact on the core nations is likely to be relatively minor. A few industries that use simple technology and a lot of labor would be hurt, but poor countries lack the technology and skills to produce most of the high-quality products demanded by industrialized nations.

One of the most serious problems faced by the Third World is that many poor countries are saddled with debts so large that they cannot even pay the interest, much less the principal, and as a result they are falling farther and farther behind. In 1970, the external debt of all the less-developed countries was about $100 billion; today, it is more than $2.5 trillion. On the average, Third World nations now pay over 2.5 times more in interest on their debt than they receive in foreign aid.[67] In other words, more money is flowing from poor countries into rich countries than from rich to poor; and that is money the poor countries desperately need to overcome their poverty.

Many poor nations have been forced to turn to the World Bank and the International Monetary Fund as their only possible sources of capital to meet their debt payments. But in exchange for their money, international development agencies typically demand that national governments take harsh austerity measures to balance their budgets and reduce imports. The effects of these government cutbacks fall hardest on the poor—whatever meager government assistance they receive is reduced or eliminated while new economic policies drive their countries into recession. Many advocates for those poor nations argue that the loans should simply be written off as bad debts, so they can get a desperately needed fresh start.

It also seems clear that a serious effort on the part of the United States and the other industrialized nations to help alleviate the poverty of the less-developed countries should include a significant increase in the total amount of foreign aid and a change in the way it is allocated so that the assistance goes to the people who need it most. Nonetheless, foreign aid is no cure-all for the problems of peripheral nations. For one thing, the governments of some countries are so corrupt that foreign aid only enriches the local elites and does nothing for the poor, and handouts from foreigners can inadvertently create a vicious cycle of dependency. For example, food from core nations given to help feed the hungry often drives down the prices paid to local farmers, resulting in lower agricultural production and an even greater need for foreign aid the next year. Wherever possible, foreign aid should therefore be carefully targeted toward training, education, birth control, supplying credit to small farmers and businesses, and other specific development projects.

ARMS CONTROL AND DISARMAMENT

Advocates of arms control argue that the global competition among the nations of the world to gain military superiority over their enemies is a major contributor to warfare and political violence. They recommend a balanced reduction in weapons or, ideally, total **disarmament** and the elimination of all means for making war. Even proposals for relatively minor arms reductions are nonetheless likely to meet strong opposition. The most obvious obstacle is the lack of trust among the competing nations of the world; many fear that someone else will cheat and hide a secret cache of weapons. There is also an underlying economic and political issue that diplomats seldom openly admit: the opposition to effective arms control by what career army officer and U.S. President Dwight D. Eisenhower called the *military-industrial complex*—the armed forces and the civilian industries that supply their needs. This complex wields vast economic influence that comes from the hundreds of billions of dollars it spends every year, and its most basic financial interests are threatened by those who advocate arms control and disarmament.

Arms control agreements are most likely to be reached when the actual threat of war is lowest. In the decades following the end of World War II, when the Cold War between the United States and the Soviet Union was at its peak, and there was a serious danger of nuclear conflict, only a few minor treaties were signed. As the communists fell from power and the Soviet Union broke apart, several major agreements were finally reached. Thus, arms control treaties may not head off an impending conflict between enemy states, but they can play an important role in helping nations to stop seeing each other as enemies.

There is, however, another kind of arms control that does not require as high a degree of trust between avowed enemies: control of the international trade in military equipment. Industrialized nations now spend an average of about 2.4 percent of their national income on "defense," but the developing nations, which are far less able to afford it, spend just under 3 percent, and virtually all their sophisticated weaponry is imported from the developed countries.[68] If the arms-exporting nations got together and agreed not to sell sophisticated weapons to poor nations with totalitarian governments the world would be a far safer place than it is today. The Code of Conduct on Arms Transfers advocated by arms control groups would, for example, require that all signatories limit their arms sales to democratically elected governments that respect human rights and have civilian control of their military.

SOCIAL JUSTICE

As we have seen, feelings of resentment among exploited groups are a major factor in many uprisings, revolutions, and terrorist attacks. Although it is sometimes possible to reduce such resentment without major social reforms, the best way to prevent terrorism and revolutionary violence is to change the conditions of inequality that cause this resentment. This seems to be a rather obvious principle, but it is seldom followed, largely because most elites—whether national or international—are either unable or unwilling to do it. Some are unaware that their special status is unjust; others simply do not care. Entrenched elites are often indifferent to the need for compromise until it is too late. A stable government depends on its **legitimacy**: the consent of the governed, based on their belief that their leaders have a right to their position and are acting in an appropriate way. The more quickly a government moves to rectify grievances, the greater the legitimacy it will have in the eyes of its people, and the more peaceful and secure it will be.

As the world develops into a more tightly knit economic and political community, the causes of international war will increasingly come to resemble the causes of revolutionary wars. Vast inequalities in wealth between the north and south are creating a festering sense of resentment and hostility in the Third World that is the breeding ground for international terrorism. Citizens of the industrialized countries are beginning to realize that something must be done to improve the standard of living of the world's impoverished masses if we are to have a more peaceful world in the years ahead. Handouts of food and other essential supplies can help stave off immediate disasters, but they are obviously not a long-term solution. We have already discussed some proposals to help promote economic growth in the poor countries. Whichever approach is used, it is clear that the hunger and desperation so common in the world today fuel a political instability that is as much a threat to the wealthy nations as to the poor ones.

QUICK REVIEW

Critically evaluate the various proposals for promoting the economic development of the Third World and encouraging world peace.

SOCIOLOGICAL PERSPECTIVES ON THE GLOBAL INEQUALITY AND CONFLICT

Most sociologists are convinced that in order to deal with social problems effectively, we must first understand their causes and then formulate our response based on that understanding. As we have seen, functionalism (by shaping modernization theory) and conflict theory (through its influence on world system theory) have played a major role in explaining the deep divisions in today's world, and each approach implies a different program of action. Interactionists have given less attention to these problems, but they nonetheless have an important contribution to make to our understanding of global inequality and conflict.

THE FUNCTIONALIST PERSPECTIVE

Wherever functionalists look among the less-developed countries or in our international political relationships, they see the problems of social disorganization. Under pressure from rapid economic change, the extended family is breaking down and its traditional power is slowly ebbing away. There is a growing cultural lag as people cling to traditional attitudes that were useful in the past but have now become a serious drawback. For example, most people in less-developed countries still place much importance on having a large family, even though today's population explosion makes that an extremely dysfunctional attitude. Traditional religious beliefs are being challenged by secular ideas from the West and a rising tide of materialism. The educational institutions that foster the scientific worldview are often so weak that they do not even reach large segments of the population. Governments are ineffective and often look on their neighbors with hostility and suspicion. Economic institutions have not made a smooth transition from an agricultural to an industrial system, and often flounder somewhere between the two. A flood of immigrant villagers pours into cities that lack enough jobs, sanitation, and housing to support them. Government institutions are also weak and political violence is common. Thus, the functionalists see less-developed countries to be in a difficult state of transition from one kind of social and cultural system to another.

Since functionalists generally assume that less-developed countries will ultimately end up as Western-style industrial nations, they feel that the best way to help is to speed up the process of transition so these societies can regain their balance as quickly as possible. Functionalists therefore recommend a much stronger emphasis on education in order to teach people the skills necessary in an industrial economy. They advocate a strong program of family planning to help change dysfunctional attitudes favoring large families. Urban development programs must be launched to create enough housing for the expanding urban population. Since functionalists are not very concerned about the issue of economic exploitation, they often advocate more foreign investments by multinational corporations as a good way to spread modern attitudes and economic structures. The governments of less-developed countries need to be made more democratic so that they can gain the support of their population for the difficult reforms that must be made, and the world community must build some kind of rational legal system to prevent the devastating international wars that plagued the twentieth century.

Functionalist theory sees warfare and international conflict as an inevitable result of the world's political disorganization. From time immemorial, humanity has been creating political structures that are conducive to warfare. When there are so many large and small countries with so many conflicting interests, disagreements are bound to occur. The international organizations set up to handle these disputes simply cannot do the job.

This high degree of international disorganization actually makes war functional: It is often the only effective method for settling major international disputes. Warfare also provides short-term psychological and political benefits to individual nations, and it may function to keep a weak, divided society together for a time. For these reasons, we denounce warfare but nevertheless organize ourselves to retain it. It follows that the best solutions to the problem of international war are those that try to reorganize the world's political system. The primary need is for a program to replace our patchwork of international relations with a genuine world order based on international law enforced by some kind of worldwide government. This would obviously be no easy task, but it is hard to see how international violence can be eliminated without fundamental changes in the political institutions that create it.

THE CONFLICT PERSPECTIVE

Where the functionalists see disorganization, the conflict theorists see exploitation. In the past, the exploitation was obvious. When Europeans first colonized a new area, they would loot whatever gold and jewels they could find and then take over direct political control of the native peoples. Today, exploitation is more subtle, but conflict theorists are convinced that it is just as real. Peripheral nations now have their own governments, but conflict theorists feel that the armies and secret agents of the industrial powers are always waiting to punish any Third World leader who gets out of line. The people of peripheral nations are no longer forced to work as slaves in the mines and plantations, but they work for wages so low that they are barely better off than slaves. Foreigners no longer simply steal the wealth of peripheral countries—they buy it up at a fraction of its real value.

To conflict theorists, the answer to the problems of global inequality and conflict is a simple one—end the economic exploitation that victimizes so many of the earth's people. Exactly how that is to be done is a more difficult matter. Despite the failure of the communist government of the Soviet Union, many conflict theorists are still strong supporters of Third World revolutionary movements that seek to overthrow their local rulers. They urge revolutionaries to create new regimes, free from foreign influence, that represent the interests of all their people and not just a small elite. Conflict theorists also encourage Third World nations to band together in the struggle with industrialized nations. They point to the success of the Organization of Petroleum Exporting Countries (OPEC) in controlling the price of oil, and they call for the creation of similar cartels for other raw materials.

Many conflict theorists feel that the key to liberating the poor countries and establishing a more peaceful world lies in the core nations. They argue that because the multinational corporations are exploiting workers in the industrialized nations in much the same way they exploit the workers in the Third World, the two groups must join together to demand the creation of a more just world order that will benefit them all. Conflict theorists generally like the idea of some kind of a world government, but tend to be fearful that such an institution would be just one more instrument for rich countries to exercise their dominance over poor ones. This cannot, according to conflict theorists, be a peaceful world until it is a just one.

THE FEMINIST PERSPECTIVE

From the feminist perspective, the poor women of the Third World are the most exploited of all the exploited. Not only are their countries exploited by foreigners, but poor people within their countries are exploited by the rich, and poor women are exploited by their husbands and other male family members. As we have seen in this chapter, women of the Third World are denied the most basic human rights to control their own lives and are often treated as little more than domestic servants by family members.

Aside from its obvious injustice, this system also wastes the talents and leadership abilities of Third World women. Feminists therefore advocate the kind of female-oriented development projects that have proved not only to improve the status of women but to be one of the most effective techniques to stimulate economic development. One of the best examples is the Grameen Bank, which was started in Bangladesh but now has over a thousand branches around the world. The Grameen Bank specializes in making small loans to poor women in order to help them do such things as set up businesses or improve their farms. The bank prefers female clients because they have found that money loaned to women was more likely to be used to benefit the whole family and that women were more likely to repay their loans than men. The results of these modest loans have often proved to be revolutionary—not only improving the local economy but helping liberate women from the domination of their husbands.[69]

Feminists generally see the problem of warfare and political violence from a very different perspective than most other theorists. Since wars are organized and carried on primarily by men, many feminists focus on the question of why men are so much more warlike than women. Although some see biological roots to these behavioral differences, most feminists lay the blame on male gender role socialization. Young boys around the world are encouraged to "stand up for themselves" and not to be "sissies." In many cultures, the very definition of manhood involves the ability to successfully wield violent force. The aggressive, domineering male is the ideal, while the "wimp" is not a "real man." This process of socialization naturally leads men in positions of political power to resort to violence far more readily than they should, and the result is our ongoing epidemic of warfare and political violence.

Feminists propose two general responses to the problem of political violence. Public opinion polls show that women look far less favorably on military spending and an aggressive foreign policy than men. So one thing feminists propose is for women to band together and use their collective power to change the priorities and attitudes of the world's governments. A second tactic is to change the socialization practices that encourage warlike male attitudes. Once again, women are the key, since they usually have primary responsibility for child rearing. But their efforts must be supported by sweeping changes in our schools and in our media if they are to bear significant fruit.

THE INTERACTIONIST PERSPECTIVE

One of the interactionists' primary contributions to the study of global inequality has been through its efforts to understand the psychological consequences of modernization. Agricultural societies are characterized by mass poverty and a huge gap between the elite and the common people. Nonetheless, these tradition-bound societies provide their members with a sense of security and belonging seldom found in the industrialized world. Most people are born, live, and die in the same close-knit villages. The important transitions in life are all marked by religious rituals, and everyone holds a similar view of the world. Since poverty is the rule, not the exception, it holds no shame. The difficulty of social mobility and the absence of a profit-oriented economy minimize competition and the tensions it causes.

Sooner or later, the process of modernization shatters this traditional world. People leave their familiar village and move into an urban environment where few of the old rules seem to apply. Even if they can maintain strong family ties in this new world, the old sense of belonging is gone. The pressures of overpopulation and a changing economy create an intensely competitive environment in which those who fail may literally starve to death. Even those who remain in the villages are likely to find their lives changing in disturbing ways. Increasing levels of education and exposure to the media slowly spread the new commercial orientation, and economic dislocation and environmental deterioration make it harder and harder to make a living off the land.

Interactionists have also identified both individual and cultural characteristics that are conducive to warfare and political violence. Each culture champions a certain "ideal personality," and people are then encouraged in both subtle and open ways to develop personality traits consistent with this ideal. People growing up in cultures that place great importance on honor and pride are likely to encourage warlike national policies, as are people growing up in cultures that emphasize competition and individual aggressiveness. One's sense of nationalism or internationalism is also learned, as is the ethnocentric belief that one's own culture, religion, and social institutions are superior to all the others. Some people learn to identify so strongly with their country that any international setback is seen as a personal threat. Even Western religions often encourage us to conquer evil in an aggressive way. War allows people to identify enemies as evil and then win honor, glory, and a sense of righteousness by defeating them.

Solutions to these problems must come from the kinds of proposals advanced by the macro-level conflict and functionalist theories, but social psychologists make three additional recommendations. First, they urge the governments of less-developed countries to focus their efforts on improving the rural economy so that people can stay in their villages and avoid the wrenching psychological changes that accompany urban migration. Second, they advise the leaders of these nations to learn from the mistakes of the West, and do their best to maintain strong family and community institutions. Third, they encourage all the world's nations to promote the ideals of peaceful cooperation and humility and to discourage the aggressive attitudes that promote conflict and violence.

QUICK REVIEW

Compare and contrast the functionalist and conflict approaches to global inequality and conflict.

What do feminists see as the root causes of global inequality and conflict?

How do interactionists view the problems of global inequality and conflict?

SUMMARY

The nations of the world make up a kind of international class system, with rich industrialized nations at the top and a much larger group of what are often called less-developed countries below. The most obvious difference between these two groups of nations is in their wealth—in terms both of money and of accumulated assets such as buildings, roads, and factories. Because of runaway population growth and rapid urbanization, most cities in the less-developed countries have a large number of homeless people and huge shantytowns. Inadequate nutrition and contagious disease make the life expectancy far lower than in industrialized nations. Women are commonly denied the most basic rights men enjoy, and children face serious health and economic problems. Literacy rates are low, and because there is only a small middle class, the gap between the rich and the poor is usually a large one. Less-developed countries are also more likely to have deep ethnic divisions and ineffective governments.

The enormous difference between the wealthy nations and the poor nations developed in the modern era as some countries underwent a rapid process of industrialization while others did not. Modernization theorists see industrialization as a universal process that has simply taken place more quickly in some parts of the world than in others. Less-developed countries have made slower progress because they have clung to traditional attitudes and values that impede industrialization. World system theory, on the other hand, sees industrialization as a global process, not a national one. All nations are seen to be part of a single world system dominated by the industrialized nations (the core), which exploit the poor nations (the periphery).

War can be defined as protracted military conflict among two or more organized groups. Wars can be classified on the basis of the groups involved as international (between independent nations) or revolutionary (between groups within a nation). Since the nineteenth century there has been a steady escalation of the scale of violence in revolutionary and international conflicts. Terrorism involves attacks on civilians to gain political ends and is often used in situations that stop just short of full-scale war. The two main types are revolutionary terrorism, which aims to change an existing government, and repressive terrorism, aimed to protect it.

To understand the causes of warfare and terrorism, we must look at revolutionary and international conflict separately. There are many theories about the causes of revolutionary conflicts. One says that they stem from exploitation and the oppression of subordinate groups by a society's ruling elite. Another asserts that relative deprivation stimulates the discontent essential to a revolution. Other theories hold that revolutions occur when an imbalance exists in the institutions of a society, when dissatisfied groups are able to mobilize sufficient resources to challenge the existing government, or when the government weakens and loses its political support. A final theory notes that class and ethnic conflict and geographic divisions all contribute to revolutionary conflict.

Militarism and the buildup of armaments are major causes of international conflict. Ethnocentrism, when expressed in nationalism or dogmatic religious ideologies, may also encourage the conquest of other people. Plain greed cannot be ignored either: Some wars are fought more for profit than for anything else. Underlying all international conflicts is the nature of the world's political organization: The large number of heavily armed independent states, each determined to advance its own interests, makes political violence almost inevitable.

Many social scientists and political leaders have ideas about how to deal with the problems of global inequality and conflict, but there are strong disagreements about the wisdom and the possible effectiveness of each. We examined proposals to encourage economic development in the Third World, promote arms control and disarmament, and create true social justice.

Functionalists see today's global divide as the product of social disorganization in less-developed countries, and they recommend programs to speed up the transition to full industrialization in order to bring more stability to these societies. Conflict theorists see most of today's global problems as the direct result of European colonialism and the exploitative economic system that developed from it. They recommend an international effort by poor and working-class people around the world to create a more just international order. Feminists hold the women of the Third World to be the most exploited of the exploited, and see male socialization that encourages violence at the root of many conflicts. Interactionists point out that the destruction of the traditional way of life in agricultural societies has also meant a great deal more insecurity and anxiety for the average person. They urge the leaders of less-developed countries to work to keep their family and community institutions strong, and for all nations to promote more peaceful and cooperative attitudes among their people.

QUESTIONS FOR CRITICAL THINKING

When most Americans think about improving conditions in the Third World, they think of making those countries more like us. But is that really a good idea? What problems has our process of industrialization created for us? Is there some way developing countries can avoid repeating our mistakes? Would it even be possible for the whole world to consume as many resources and produce as much pollution as we do?

KEY TERMS

arms race	militarism
balance of power	modernization
capital accumulation	nationalism
class conflict	nuclear proliferation
Cold War	nuclear war
colonialism	nuclear winter
core	periphery
disarmament	relative deprivation theory
economic development	repressive terrorism
ethnocentrism	revolutionary terrorism
genocide	revolutionary war
globalization	semiperiphery
hegemonic power	terrorism
imperialism	Third World
industrial revolution	total war
international war	urban subsistence economy
legitimacy	war
less-developed countries (LDCs)	world system

NOTES

1. World Bank, *World Development Report*, 2000/2001 (New York, Oxford University Press, 2000), Chapter 3.
2. *International Herald Tribune* (December 20, 2001).
3. See Christopher Chase-Dunn, Yukio Kawano, and Benjamin D. Brewer, "Trade Globalization Since 1795: Waves of Integration in the World-System," *American Sociological Review* 65 (2000): 77–95; David Held, Anthony McGrew, David Golblatt and Jonathan Perraton, *Global Transformations: Politics, Economics, and Culture* (Palo Alto, CA: Stanford University Press, 1999).
4. See Harold R. Kerbo, *Social Stratification and Inequality*, 4th ed. (New York: McGraw-Hill, 2000), Chapter 13.
5. United Nations, *A Better World for All* (New York: United Nations, 2000); United Nations Development Programme, *Overcoming Human Poverty* (New York: United Nations, 2000).
6. Population Reference Bureau, *World Population Data Sheet*, 2000 (Washington, DC: Population Reference Bureau, 2000).
7. Ibid.
8. Ibid.
9. United Nations, *A Better World for All*; United Nations Development Programme, *Overcoming Human Poverty*.
10. United Nations Development Programme, *Human Development Report*, 1997 (New York: Oxford University Press, 1997), p. 165.
11. World Health Organization, *The World Health Report*, 1999; "Making a Difference" (Geneva, Switzerland: World Health Organization, 1999).
12. Population Reference Bureau, *World Population Data Sheet*, 2000.
13. United Nations Development Programme, *Human Development Report*, 1997, pp. 177, 204.
14. Ibid., pp. 146–148.
15. World Bank, *World Development Report*, 2000 (New York: Oxford University Press, 2000).
16. United Nations Development Programme, pp. 149–151, 172–173.
17. Population Reference Bureau, *World Population Data Sheet*, 2000.
18. World Bank, *World Development Report*, 2000, p. 279.
19. Robert M. Press, "More African Kids Take to the Streets," *Christian Science Monitor*, February 7, 1994, pp. 11–13.
20. Germaine W. Shames, "The World's Throw-Away Children," in Jackson, ed., *Global Issues 94/95* (Guilford, CT: Dushkin, 1994), pp. 229–232.
21. Kerbo, *Social Stratification and Inequality*, p. 27.
22. World Bank, *World Development Report*, 2000, p. 282.
23. Mark Fineman, "Anxious Mexicans Await Day of the Vote," *Los Angeles Times*, August 21, 1994, pp. A1, A10.
24. See Gerhard Lenski, *Power and Privilege* (New York: McGraw-Hill, 1966).
25. See World Bank, *World Development Report*, 2000 for some comparative statistics; and see L. S. Stavrianos, *Global Rift: The Third World Comes of Age* (New York: Morrow, 1981) for a comprehensive history of the development of the Third World.
26. See, for example, Talcott Parsons, *Societies: Evolutionary and Comparative Perspectives* (Upper Saddle River, NJ: Prentice Hall, 1966), and Wilbert Moore, *Social Change*, 2nd ed. (Upper Saddle River, NJ: Prentice Hall, 1974).
27. Walter W. Rostow, *The Stages of Economic Growth* (New York: Cambridge University Press, 1960).
28. For a contemporary discussion of these issues from a Weberian perspective, see Daniel Chirot, "The Rise of the West," *American Sociological Review* 50 (1985): 181–195.
29. See Walter W. Rostow, *The World Economy: History and Prospect* (Austin: University of Texas Press, 1980).
30. Andre Gunder Frank, *Capitalism and Underdevelopment in Latin America* (New York: Monthly Review Press, 1967).
31. See, for example, Immanuel Wallerstein's three-volume historical work, *The Modern World System* (New York: Academic Press, 1974, 1980, 1988).
32. For an excellent summary of world system theory and an analysis of its strengths and weaknesses, see Thomas Richard Shannon, *An Introduction to the World-System Perspective*, 2nd ed. (Boulder, CO: Westview, 1996).

33. World Bank, *World Development Report*, 2000/2001, p. 50.

34. Edward Muller, "Income Inequality, Regime Repressiveness, and Political Violence," *American Sociological Review* 50 (1985): 47–61; Judith Blau and Peter Blau, "The Cost of Inequality: Metropolitan Structure and Violent Crime," *American Sociological Review* 47 (1982): 114–129; Kirk Williams, "Economic Source of Homicide," *American Sociological Review* 49 (1984): 283–289.

35. Melvin Small and J. David Singer, *Resort to Arms: International and Civil Wars, 1816–1980* (Beverly Hills, CA: Sage, 1982), p. 293.

36. See Rudi Volti, *Society and Technological Change* (New York: St. Martin's Press, 1988), pp. 171–201.

37. Doyle McManus, "The New, Dangerous Dominoes," *Los Angeles Times*, May 8, 1994, pp. A1, A14; Bruce W. Nelan, "Fighting Off Doomsday," *Time*, June 21, 1993, pp. 36–38; David P. Barash, *Introduction to Peace Studies* (Belmont, CA: Wadsworth, 1991), pp. 126–127.

38. Small and Singer, *Resort to Arms*, pp. 293–294.

39. James F. Dunnigan and William Martel, *How to Stop a War: The Lessons of Two Hundred Years of War and Peace* (New York: Doubleday, 1987), p. 81.

40. Ibid., p. 239; Small and Singer, *Resort to Arms*, p. 91.

41. Mark Hatfield, "U.S. Needs Code of Conduct for Conventional-Arms Trade," *Christian Science Monitor*, April 15, 1994, p. 18.

42. *Los Angeles Times*, August 22, 1999; Associated Press, December 30, 2000.

43. U.S. Bureau of the Census, *Statistical Abstract of the United States*, 1999 (Washington, DC; U.S. Government Printing Office, 1999), p. 371; United Nations Development Programme, *Human Development Report*, 1997 (New York: Oxford University Press, 1997), p. 215.

44. World Bank, *World Development Report*, 2000 (New York: Oxford University Press, 2000), pp. 306–307.

45. G. Tyler Miller, *Living in the Environment: An Introduction to Environmental Science*, 5th ed. (Belmont, CA: Wadsworth, 1988), p. 128.

46. Ibid., p. 129; Barash, *Introduction to Peace Studies*, pp. 107–113.

47. See Quincy Wright, *A Study of War*, abridged by L. L. Wright (Chicago: University of Chicago Press, 1964), p. 85.

48. Peter C. Sederberg, *Terrorist Myths: Illusion, Rhetoric, and Reality* (Upper Saddle River, NJ: Prentice Hall, 1989), pp. 22–43.

49. See Harold J. Vetter and Gary R. Perlstein, *Perspectives on Terrorism* (Pacific Grove, CA: Brooks/Cole, 1991), pp. 87–104

50. Dunnigan and Martel, *How to Stop a War*, p. 247.

51. Marvin Harris, *Culture, People, Nature*, 6th ed. (New York: HarperCollins, 1993), p. 301.

52. Karl Marx and Friedrich Engels, *The Communist Manifesto* (Upper Saddle River, NJ: Prentice Hall, 1955). This pamphlet was originally published in 1848.

53. James C. Davies, "Toward a Theory of Revolution," *American Sociological Review* 27 (1962): 5–19; James C. Davies, "The J-Curve of Rising and Declining Satisfactions as a Cause of Some Great Revolutions and a Contained Rebellion," in Hugh Davis Graham and Ted Robert Gurr, eds., *Violence in America: Histories and Comparative Perspectives* (New York: Holt, Rinehart & Winston, 1958), pp. 547–576.

54. Davies, "Toward a Theory of Revolution," p. 5.

55. Samuel P. Huntington, *Political Order in Changing Societies* (New Haven, CT: Yale University Press, 1968).

56. Charles Tilly, *From Mobilization to Revolution* (Reading, MA: Addison Wesley Longman, 1978).

57. Crane Brinton, *The Anatomy of Revolution* (New York: Random House, 1965), p. 51.

58. Ibid., pp. 28–39.

59. Theda Skocpol, *States and Social Revolution* (Cambridge, MA: Cambridge University Press, 1978).

60. See Ronald J. Glossop, *Confronting War* (Jefferson, NC: MacFarland, 1987), pp. 66–68.

61. Ibid., pp. 58–65.

62. Wright, *A Study of War*, pp. 213–214.

63. Kurt Finsterbusch and H. C. Greisman, "The Unprofitability of Warfare in the Twentieth Century," *Social Problems* 22 (February 1975): 451.

64. Karl von Clausewitz, *On War*, trans. O. J. Matthkijs Jolles (Washington, DC: Infantry Journal Press, 1950), p. 16.

65. A. F. K. Organski and Jacek Kugler, *The War Ledger* (Chicago: University of Chicago Press, 1980).

66. See Volker Bornschier and Christopher Chase-Dunn, *Transnational Corporations and Underdevelopment* (New York: Praeger, 1985).

67. United Nations Development Programme, *Human Development Report*, 1997, p. 191.

68. U.S. Bureau of the Census, *Statistical Abstract of the United States*, 2000 (Washington, DC: U.S. Government Printing Office, 1999), p. 372; United Nations, *Human Development Report*, 1997, pp. 188–189, 215.

69. World Bank, *World Development Report*, 2000; Muhammad Yunus, "Helping the Poor to Help Themselves," *Los Angeles Times*, February 17, 1997, p. B5; Robin Wright, "Women as Engines Out of Poverty," *Los Angeles Times*, May 27, 1997, pp. A1, A6.

CHAPTER 12

ENVIRONMENT AND POPULATION

Questions to Consider

What is the human impact on our environment?

Are we running out of natural resources?

What are the causes of the environmental crisis?

Is there a population explosion?

What can we do to solve our environmental problems?

For centuries we have seen our environment as a boundless storehouse of wealth. Nature was to be conquered, tamed, and used in any way we saw fit. Until recently only a few people realized how fragile and limited our world really is. Now the damage done by exploitative technologies and the enormous growth of the human population are forcing this realization on us all. One by one the natural resources on which we have come to depend are dwindling away, and as they are used up, their by-products are fouling our land, air, and water, and disrupting the delicate web of life on which our very existence depends.

Western culture views us as special creatures, separate and apart from our environment. Humans are seen not as animals but as superior beings destined to rule over the planet and its lesser creatures. However, **ecology**—the study of interrelations among plants, animals, and their environment—shows us that humans are but one part of a complex network of living things. No human could live more than a few seconds if separated from the sheltered terrestrial environment with just the right proportions of water, oxygen, heat, and the other essential components that support our lives. Nor could we live more than a few days without the food supplied by the plants and animals of the earth. We cannot even digest our food properly without microorganisms that live inside our bodies. We are, in short, a part of nature, and our future depends on how well we take care of it.

The Human Impact on the Environment: Population and Technology

Early hunting and gathering people interfered very little with the ecosystems in which they lived. Their population was small, they used only a few simple tools, and muscle power was the main source of energy. As technology became more sophisticated and population grew, the human impact on the environment grew ever larger. With the invention of agriculture, we attempted to replace the delicate complexity of the natural environment with a narrow range of plants and animals that were best suited to supporting human life. Surplus food produced by agriculture made the development of cities possible, and with the cities came a host of new threats to the earth's ecological balance. Forests were cut down, rivers rechanneled, and tons of human waste dumped into the water and plowed into the soil. Some organisms were exterminated; others multiplied more rapidly than ever before. Humans soon became the single greatest force in changing the ecological balance of the planet. The process did not stop there, however. Industrialization with its countless new machines and technologies once again intensified the human role in shaping the course of environmental change. More forests were leveled, and huge cities were built and connected with a complex web of highways and railroads. Newly developed industries consumed energy and raw materials at an ever-increasing rate and in the process poured out an unending stream of **pollution**.

Aggravating all our environmental problems has been an explosion in the human population. The number of men, women, and children on this planet is now over 6 billion—twice as many as there were only a few decades ago. If the rate of population growth only 15 years ago had continued, the world's population would double in only 50 years. This would mean 12 billion people by 2050.[1] Fortunately, however, the world's population explosion has been slowing down, and most experts expect that birthrates will continue to decline. Instead of 12 billion people by 2050, the predictions are that there are more likely to be about 9 billion people.[2] Although that is certainly an improvement, most of those 3 billion new mouths to feed will be in the poor countries—those that often have trouble feeding the people they have now.

Many scientists wonder how long the earth can support such growth. To understand the problems caused by this **population explosion**, it is helpful to look at the history of world population in units of 1 billion people. It took all of human history until 1800 for the world's population to reach 1 billion, but the next unit of 1 billion was added in only 130 years (1800–1930), the unit after that in 30 years (1930–1960). The next billion people were added in 15 years (1960–1975) and the next in only 12 years (1975–1987).[3] (See Figure 12.1.) If this trend had continued, the world would soon have been adding 1 billion people every year and eventually every month.

Obviously, the world could not sustain such enormous population growth indefinitely. Fortunately, as we pointed out previously, the pace of population growth has slowed in recent years, and the last billion people took 13 years to add (1987–2000). Experts now expect the world's population to stabilize sometime in the next century. However, estimates vary widely as to when that will be and at what size. The crucial task facing the human race is to ensure that the population explosion is curbed by a rational program of population control and not by massive famines or devastating wars.

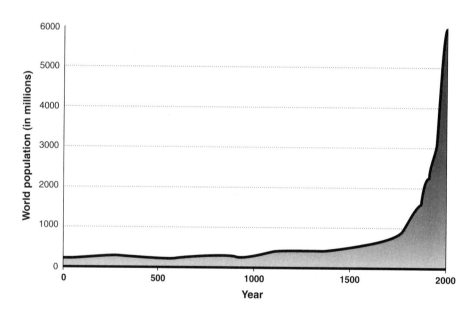

FIGURE 12.1   POPULATION

In the past three centuries, the world's population has been growing faster than at any other time in human history. There are now over 6 billion people on this planet.

Source: Population Reference Bureau, World Population Data Sheet, 2000 (Washington, DC: Population Reference Bureau, 2000).

The long-range forecasts are of course educated guesswork, but the population crisis is not a thing of the future. It is here now. Next year the world must house, clothe, and feed about 90 million more people. To make matters worse, the 208,200 who will be added in the next 24 hours will not be evenly distributed throughout the world.[4] Most will be born in the underdeveloped nations of Africa, Latin America, and Asia—in countries that are too poor to provide for the populations they already have (see Figure 12.2). Although these nations may seem alike to Western eyes, there are important differences among their population problems. The most immediate crisis is in the overcrowded nations of Southern Asia (including Bangladesh, India, and Pakistan), which already contain one-fourth the world's people, and in some of the rapidly growing states of sub-Saharan Africa (Africa south of the Sahara Desert). The current growth rate (excluding immigration) in Southern Asia is 1.7 percent and in sub-Saharan Africa it is a huge 2.6 percent per year.

The growth rate of the industrialized nations of Western Europe (0.1 percent), North America (0.6 percent), and Japan (0.15 percent) are much lower. Most other

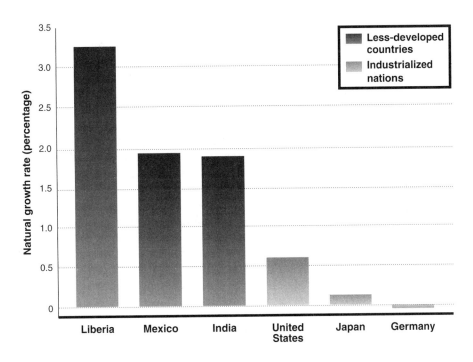

Figure 12.2 Population Growth

The population of the poor countries is growing much faster than the population of the rich ones.

Source: Population Reference Bureau, World Population Data Sheet, 2000 (Washington, DC: Population Reference Bureau, 2000).

areas of the Third World are somewhere in between. Eastern Asia is doing well (0.8 percent) because of China's successful population control program, while the growth rate is higher in Latin America (1.8 percent) and North Africa (2.0 percent).[5] But these continent-wide generalizations blur many important differences among nations. The Philippines, for example, has a growth rate of 2.3 percent a year, which is much higher than the average in Asia as a whole. At that rate, its population of 80 million will double in only 30 years. In 60 years, if its growth rate does not go down, the Philippines will have a population larger than the United States today, but with less than one-thirtieth the land area.[6]

There is, moreover, a different kind of "population time bomb" ticking in the wealthy countries with declining birthrates. One might think that such a decline is a positive trend given the rapid population growth in other parts of the world, but the situation is much more complicated. As birthrates have dropped, the population of elderly people has exploded leaving fewer and fewer people of working age. Adding this up, the question becomes, who is going to keep the economy running? Who is going to take care of all the elderly people? Major adjustments will be necessary if rich countries are to avoid a new kind of population crisis.

AIR POLLUTION

Few of us give a second thought to the invisible and seemingly inexhaustible ocean of air in which we live. But consider the fact that a person can live for weeks without food and for days without water but can survive for only a few minutes without air. We have been able to take our atmosphere for granted because rain and other processes naturally cleanse and renew it, but we are now dumping more pollutants into the air than can be removed by these natural processes. Air pollution is worst in the big cities, but because the ocean of air connects all parts of our planet, pollution has become a menacing global problem. On the local level, air pollution in the rapidly growing cities of the Third World has grown worse and worse while the air in many cities of the industrialized nations has actually improved. The average level of carbon monoxide in the air in the United States declined about 14 percent between 1985 and the mid-1990s, and ozone levels dropped about 12 percent. In more recent years, however, there has been little further improvement. Moreover, the United States still ranks substantially ahead of other industrial nations in carbon dioxide emissions per capita.[7] (See Figure 12.3.)

The single greatest source of air pollution in North America is transportation. Coal, oil, and natural gas used for heating and for generating electricity are also major contributors. Additional tons of pollutants are spewed into the air by paper mills, steel mills, oil refineries, smelters, and chemical plants. Even trash burning is a substantial cause of air pollution.[8]

The amount and kinds of pollutants in the air vary greatly from one area to another. The most common pollutants are carbon monoxide, hydrocarbons, sulfur oxides, nitrogen oxides, ozone, and tiny particles of soot, ashes, and other industrial by-products. The amounts of these pollutants vary in different industrial regions. Thus, areas that depend on oil for power have different pollution problems from those that use coal.

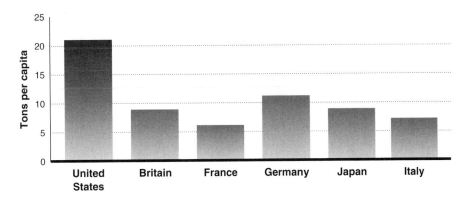

FIGURE 12.3 AIR POLLUTION

The United States emits more carbon dioxide per person than any other industrial nation.

Source: U.S. Bureau of the Census, *Statistical Abstract of the United States,* 1999 (Washington, DC: U.S. Government Printing Office, 1999), p. 839.

No matter which chemicals are involved, valleys and closed air basins are more likely to have air pollution than plains and mountains, where air can circulate freely. Air quality can become especially bad when a layer of warmer air moves over a layer of cooler air and seals in pollutants that would ordinarily rise into the upper atmosphere. This condition, known as a **temperature inversion**, is temporary, but while it lasts, it may create an intense bout of air pollution. Local winds also affect the distribution of pollutants, carrying them from one area to another. Finally, climate has an important effect on the kinds of pollutants that are present in different areas. For instance, sunlight acts on oxygen, hydrocarbons, and nitrogen oxides to produce new compounds collectively known as **photochemical smog**.

Air pollution is not merely a minor irritant that burns our eyes and clouds the skies: It is a major health hazard, contributing to many chronic diseases and killing a substantial number of people each year. Air pollution is believed to contribute to the deaths of at least 50,000 Americans every year, and it has been linked to such serious respiratory diseases as bronchitis, emphysema, and lung cancer. It is also a known contributor to several other types of cancer and to heart disease as well.[9] The effects of pollutants on an individual's health are, however, difficult to determine. For one thing, the various chemicals we release into the air combine to produce many entirely new substances. Further, all people living in a particular area are not necessarily exposed to the same amount of pollution. An executive who drives an air-conditioned car from her home to an air-conditioned office is exposed to less air pollution than a traffic officer who breathes smog all day long.

The damaging effects of air pollution are not limited to humans. Although there has been little research in this area, it appears that domesticated animals living in polluted areas suffer as well. It has also been shown that air pollution has harmful effects on trees, shrubs, and flowers. The orange groves of California and the vegetable farms of New Jersey, for instance, both suffer from smog damage.

Photochemical smog has made the air in many cities unhealthy, while the breakdown of the ozone layer in the upper atmosphere is increasing the risks of contracting skin cancer from exposure to the sun.

In many areas, chemicals from coal-burning power plants and other industrial sources combine with water in the atmosphere to produce **acid rain**. Not only do these rains harm plant life and eat away exposed metal surfaces and buildings made of limestone and marble, but they decrease the fertility of some soils and destroy life in streams and rivers. Acid rain has killed fish in hundreds of lakes in the United States, Canada, and northern Europe. Many scientists also believe that acid rain is one of the major causes of the decline in forest lands in industrialized nations. The control of acid rain poses a difficult international dilemma because pollution created in one country often rains down on another. For example, more than half the air pollution that causes acid rain in Canada comes from the United States.[10]

Air pollution is also creating some disturbing changes in the upper atmosphere, especially in the thin ozone layer that protects us from the harmful ultraviolet rays of the sun. Scientists have known for years that a group of chemicals—the chlorofluorocarbons (CFCs) used in air conditioners, refrigerators, Styrofoam containers, and many other applications—decomposes ozone. Many refused to take the threat to the upper atmosphere seriously, however, until a giant hole in the ozone layer, which opens up a few months every year, was discovered over Antarctica. As scientists began to investigate conditions in the upper atmosphere more closely, they were shocked to discover how rapidly the ozone layer has been thinning over the rest of the world as well. Between 4 and 5 percent of the ozone layer over North America, for example, has apparently been lost just since 1978. The Environmental Protection Agency now predicts an additional 200,000 deaths from skin cancer in the United States over the next 50 years, as a result of the increased ultraviolet radiation caused by **ozone depletion**. In addition to causing skin cancer, increased ultraviolet radiation causes cataracts and other eye problems, suppression of the immune system, harm to animals, and a decrease in crop yields.[11]

The first international response to this crisis occurred in Montreal in 1987, when 24 major nations met and agreed to cut their CFC production in half by the turn of the century. As the full scope of the threat became apparent, a larger group of nations met in Copenhagen in 1992 and set up a timetable to eliminate all production of CFCs, added other substances to the list of ozone-destroying chemicals, and set up a fund to help the poorer nations stop their use of CFCs.[12] Although progress has been made in reducing CFC emissions since the Copenhagen meetings, there has also been strong resistance to the effort to protect our ozone layer. It is estimated that between 10,000 and 20,000 tons of CFCs are sold on the black market every year.[13]

Of all the hazards of air pollution, perhaps the greatest potential threat comes from what is known as the **greenhouse effect**. The buildup of gases from the burning of various fuels and other human activities is changing the composition of the atmosphere. These gases are holding in more of the energy that comes to earth from the sun and are thereby raising the air temperature like the greenhouse of an orchid grower. The biggest problem is carbon dioxide, but methane and other gases also play a role. Worldwide, the air we breathe now contains about 25 percent more carbon dioxide than it did just a century ago, and the United States is by far the biggest polluter—contributing 22 percent of the world's total emissions of carbon dioxide.[14]

Although there is a great deal of controversy about the subject, most experts expect the greenhouse effect to raise the average temperature of the earth from 2 to 8 degrees Fahrenheit over the next century. Although that may not seem like much of a difference, the consequences could be devastating. For one thing, the increases will not be spread evenly over the planet: Some areas will have much greater increases, while a few places may actually experience cooler weather. More important, the changing temperatures will also change the pattern of rainfall, which could turn some major agricultural areas into dust bowls. Although some northern areas might see improved crop yield, the overall impact will be a decrease in food production, especially in the poor nations in the southern part of the globe. Moreover, as the temperature rises, the water in the oceans will expand and the polar icecaps will begin to melt. The result will be a higher sea level and the flooding of many low-lying coastal areas.

In sharp contrast to the response to ozone depletion, the world community has done little about the dangers of global warming. Although the developed countries said at the Earth Summit in Rio de Janeiro in 1992 that they would reduce their emissions of greenhouse gases, the Berlin Climate Summit in 1995 ended without any agreement to binding limits on these emissions; and the United States refused to sign any agreement. Yet another international conference was held in 2000, and once again international leaders failed to reach a consensus on what to do. The fact is that it is far easier to ban CFCs than to reduce our dependence on petroleum, coal, and the other fossil fuels that create so much of the global warming problem.[15]

WATER POLLUTION

Over two-thirds of the world's surface is covered by water. It is continually evaporating, forming clouds, and raining back to earth in a cycle that provides a seemingly endless supply of clean water. Perhaps it is blind faith in the enormous reserves of water and the natural purification system that has led people to dump so much garbage into lakes, rivers, and oceans. For some time the earth's water resources could tolerate such an onslaught, but with the population explosion and increased dumping of industrial wastes, marine animals and plants began to die in large numbers.

Organic wastes are important water pollutants. In small quantities, they are quickly broken down by waterborne bacteria, but if too much organic material is dumped into the water, the bacteria use up all the available oxygen as they decompose the waste. Fish and other complex organisms suffocate, and a barren body of water is left. Human waste is a major contributor to the problem, but so are the wastes from animal feedlots, oil refining, food processing, and textile and paper manufacturing. The U.S. Geological Survey takes regular water samples from America's rivers and streams, and the percentage of samples contaminated with a high level of fecal bacteria increased 13 percent from 1985 to 1995.[16]

Chemical fertilizers have much the same effect as organic wastes and cause similar damage. When rains wash nitrogen fertilizers into rivers and lakes, they stimulate the growth of huge "blooms" of algae. When these blooms die, they decay, using up oxygen the same way other organic pollution does.[17]

Our rivers, lakes, and oceans are also polluted by a host of poisons and dangerous chemicals that include everything from industrial solvents to pesticides. Not only do these substances kill wildlife and threaten our drinking water, but many of them become more concentrated as they move up the food chain. When fish eat plants exposed to toxic substances such as arsenic, mercury, and many pesticides, pollutants build up in their tissues. When these fish are eaten by larger fish, the toxins become still more concentrated, and so on. Because most of the fish we eat come from the top of the food chain, they are likely to have high levels of contamination. Moreover, no part of the world, however remote, is immune to the problem. The Inuit people, who live in what many mistakenly believe to be the pristine wilderness of northern Canada, eat large amounts of seal meat, fish, and other local game. Their diet exceeds the Canadian government's maximum limit for PCBs (a family of dangerous organic chemicals) 10 to 20 percent of the time, and the milk of Inuit mothers contains five times more PCBs than the milk of mothers who live in southern Canada.[18]

Even the world's great oceans are vulnerable to human pollution. This seabird is covered with oil from a ruptured petroleum tanker.

A study by the Environmental Protection Agency concluded that one out of every three American rivers was not in good condition,[19] and the situation in our coastal waters is even worse. About one-fourth of the coastal waters in the continental United States are closed to shellfishing, and the catch of other seafood has plummeted in many areas. Nonetheless, studies of chemical pollution in mussels and oysters found a small but steady decline since 1983.[20] Studies indicate that as many as 2 million seabirds and 100,000 marine mammals such as whales, dolphins, and seals die every year when they eat or become entangled in trash dumped into the ocean.[21] There are also periodic oil spill crises, usually caused by the wreck of an oil tanker. The Exxon Valdez, for example, dumped 11 million gallons of crude oil when it broke up off the Alaska coast.[22] As dramatic as such events are, at least an equal amount of oil reaches the oceans from land runoff and the intentional dumping of waste oil.[23]

To many people, the most important water is that coming out of the tap in their homes. Drinking water once commonly carried such dreaded diseases as cholera and typhoid, but modern water treatment has eliminated that risk. Now our drinking water is being threatened in another way: by chemical contamination. Dangerous industrial chemicals are seeping into the water supplies of many towns and cities, and underground water in many agricultural areas now contains a host of different pesticides. A study released by the Natural Resources Defense Council concluded that 20 percent of America's drinking water is not adequately treated for toxic chemicals, bacteria, parasites, and other pollutants and that 14 percent of the American population drinks from water systems that have been caught violating federal water standards within the previous three years.[24]

THE DETERIORATING LAND

Third World countries, faced with overpopulation and shortages of food and housing, once looked at the environment as a problem that only the rich can afford to worry about. In recent years, however, many of these poor nations have begun to realize that they are caught in the grip of an even greater environmental crisis than the one their industrialized neighbors face. The world's forests are shrinking at an alarming rate while the desert wastelands grow, and most of these changes are occurring in the less-developed countries. Every year, the world loses over 100,000 square kilometers of forest land. The problem is particularly severe in the Third World countries. The pace of deforestation in Brazil is almost double the world average, while in Venezuela and Indonesia it is more than triple.[25] More than half the world's tropical rain forests have been cut down just since 1945.[26] The problem is particularly severe in the great Amazon rain forest, which is by far the largest of tropical forest remaining in the world today. Although the rate of deforestation is lower than it was two decades ago, it has actually increased since the early 1990s.[27] At this rate there will be virtually no tropical forests in the near future, and if the rain forests are destroyed, millions of unique species of plants and animals will die with them.

Desertification—the transformation of productive land into desert—is a slower process. It is estimated that 20 percent of the earth's land surface is threatened by desertification; this threatened land is home to more than 80 million people.[28] Natural forces such as the periodic droughts that have recurred throughout history are an important part of this problem, but a great deal of the damage is being done by human beings. Desertification results from overgrazing by livestock, poor irrigation techniques that poison the soil with salts and alkalis, and desperate attempts to farm land that is not suited for agriculture.[29]

Deforestation is caused almost entirely by humans who log trees to get lumber and fuel and intentionally destroy the forests to make room for the farms and cities demanded by a growing population. Although conditions are worse in the less-developed countries, industrialized nations have serious problems of their own. Reforestation has allowed industrialized nations to slow down the loss of their temperate forests and in some cases reverse it. An estimated 7 million hectares of land are now planted with trees every year, but that is less than the area that is logged. Moreover, enormous damage has already been done. At one time, more than 80 percent of Europe was covered by forests, but as far back as 1800, only 14 percent of the land in Europe was still forested.[30]

The heavily mechanized techniques used by agribusiness do long-term damage to the soil, and North America is now facing a serious erosion problem. The impact of years of environmentally damaging plowing methods is adding up, and windbreaks, terraces, and antierosion ditches built during the 1930s are being torn out to make it easier to operate today's huge farming machines. The United States is now losing its productive soil seven times faster than natural processes can replace it. The problem is at its worst in the heavily farmed lands of the Midwest. Iowa, for example, is believed to have lost about half its topsoil.[31]

Another heavy burden on our beleaguered land is the huge quantity of solid waste produced by industry. Each year the United States generates about 1 ton of trash and garbage for every man, woman, and child in the country.[32] Some of this refuse is burned, thus adding to air pollution, but most of it is buried in landfills and dumps. This creates two problems. One is that an increasing number of ravines, gullies, valleys, and sloughs are being covered as the trash mounts up. Another comes from the disposal of plastic and other synthetic materials, which, unlike organic material, never decompose. Americans dump about 100 million tires and 38 billion bottles and jars each year.

As if these problems were not enough, new threats to the land are looming on the horizon. Population growth demands that more and more land be used for cities and for agriculture, and the shortage of energy and raw materials is leading us to use ever more environmentally destructive methods to obtain them. For instance, there are enormous reserves of coal in North America, and much of the fuel lies close to the surface. This makes it cheaper to extract, but the **strip-mining** technique that is normally used creates severe environmental damage. Strip mines are long, shallow valleys gouged out of the earth. After the coal has been removed, the dislocated earth is dumped back into the hole. Unless the topsoil is carefully replaced (an expensive and time-consuming process), the land will not be fertile again for centuries, if ever.[33] Perhaps the world's worst example of the hazards of strip mining come from the small island of Nauru, which used to be something of a Pacific paradise. After 90 years of strip-mining phosphate deposits, four-fifths of the island is now a barren moonscape of gray limestone pinnacles. Despite a considerable income from the mining industry, conditions on the island have grown so bad that the few remaining residents may have to move away.[34]

The growth of cities poses yet another threat to the ecological balance of our land. Great portions of the landmass of our planet are being covered by expanding cities and suburbs. These vast metropolitan areas are beginning to threaten the existence of the wilderness that supports so many different species of plants and animals. Many ecosystems have already been destroyed by urban sprawl, and the outlook for the future is not bright. If population growth continues at its present rate, only the most remote mountains and deserts will remain unspoiled.

CHEMICALS AND RADIATION

The human race is dosing itself with thousands of chemicals. The air we breathe and practically everything we eat or drink contains synthetic substances. Although many of these chemicals seem harmless enough, the fact is that we know almost nothing about most of their long-term effects. Recent history is full of examples of supposedly harmless food additives, drugs, and industrial wastes that were found to be serious health hazards. Only about 10 percent of the 70,000 chemicals in commercial use have been adequately tested, and about 1,000 new chemicals are introduced into the marketplace every year.[35]

The safe disposal of toxic wastes is a daunting problem. The United States alone produces an estimated 128 to 509 million tons of toxic wastes a year.[36] The United States has exerted considerable effort to deal with its toxic waste problems, but by and large its response has been inadequate. In 1980, Congress created a billion-dollar "superfund" to help clean up dangerous waste dumps. Though tens of thousands of sites are in need of immediate action, only a handful have been cleaned up. Even worse is the fact that over three-fourths of the superfund money has been spent on legal fees and administrative costs.[37] Critics have charged, moreover, that what little work was done was not done well. The EPA's approach to cleaning up most unsafe dumps is simply to move the dangerous chemicals to a different dump, which in some cases is no safer than the original site. The government has repeatedly been accused of dragging its feet on toxic-waste cleanups and, more generally, of supporting the interests of industrial polluters instead of the interests of the American public.

Radiation pollution is even more frightening than toxic waste, probably because we know so little about it. Small doses of radiation have no immediate effects. Moderate doses cause vomiting, fatigue, loss of appetite, and diarrhea. Death is practically certain for people exposed to high doses. However, no one knows much about the long-term effects of low and moderate doses of radiation. Studies of the survivors of the nuclear bombings of Hiroshima and Nagasaki show a high incidence of leukemia and other cancers, but it is not known exactly how much exposure is needed to produce cancer. There is ample proof that radiation causes genetic mutations, but again there is little information about how dangerous specific doses of radiation actually are.

The ultimate environmental disaster—nuclear war—was discussed in Chapter 11. But there is also growing alarm about the dangers of radiation from other sources, such as nuclear power plants and the factories that produce nuclear weapons. At present, such sources contribute little to the overall levels of radiation in the world, but environmentalists fear that nuclear pollution will increase as the world's nuclear plants continue to age. One major concern is the danger of a nuclear accident. There is little chance of a reactor erupting in a nuclear explosion, but if the cooling system of such a plant should fail, the tremendous heat of the nuclear reaction would melt the concrete and steel surrounding it, thus releasing enough radiation to wipe out an entire city. Nuclear power plants have elaborate safeguards against such meltdowns, and advocates of nuclear power argue that the probability of such an accident occurring is very low. The 1979 accident at the Three Mile Island reactor in Pennsylvania and the 1986 disaster at the Chernobyl reactor in the former Soviet Union have, however, convinced many people that serious accidents are far more likely than the public has been led to believe. Although the official death toll from the Chernobyl accident was originally only 32 people, it is now clear that figure was part of a sweeping effort by the government to cover up the real extent of the damage. The health minister of Ukraine estimated that 125,000 people have already died from the radiation released by the Chernobyl reactor, and the long-term effects of the massive radiation exposure have not yet peaked. The rate of leukemia in Kiev, the nearest large city, is four times higher than normal, and the overall death rate in northern Ukraine near the reactor has increased 16 percent. Moreover, the economic losses have been staggering—an estimated $358 billion—because of expenses such as the permanent relocation of 200,000 people (leaving another 4 million people still living on contaminated ground) and the destruction of 20 percent of the farmland of the republic of Byelorussia. It would be no exaggeration to say that the Chernobyl disaster was the worst accident of the twentieth century. But it was not until the fall of 2000 that the other nuclear reactors at Chernobyl were finally shut down for good.[38]

Even in the unlikely event that no other major accidents ever occur, the radioactive wastes generated by nuclear plants are deadly pollutants, and we have no effective way to handle them. The main problem is that these wastes remain dangerous for so long that scientists cannot agree on a safe disposal technique. For example, the EPA requires that spent fuel rods from nuclear plants be stored safely for 10,000 years—a staggering amount of time. The United States itself is only a little over two hundred years old. Currently, almost 50,000 of these old fuel rods are stored temporarily at U.S. nuclear plants because the federal government has yet to open a permanent disposal site. Even the temporary storage of nuclear wastes has proved to be inadequate: Hundreds of thousands of gallons of highly radioactive liquids have already leaked out of U.S. nuclear weapons plants, and it is becoming clear that the cloak of national security has been used to cover up horrible safety conditions that would never have been allowed at civilian facilities. Moreover, old nuclear power plants, whether civilian or military, are also a radiation hazard. Whatever techniques are ultimately developed to decommission such plants, the process is bound to be slow and costly, perhaps running as much as $1 to $3 billion for each plant.[39]

Another serious hazard in the use of nuclear energy is crime. Security is tight in most nuclear power plants, but this is a chaotic and uncertain world. The more this energy source is used, the more shipments of radioactive materials there will be, and the easier it will be for a terrorist group to steal them. Although it is difficult to turn low-grade nuclear fuels into atomic bombs, there is still great danger. The explosion of a conventional bomb placed next to some radioactive materials could spread a deadly radioactive cloud big enough to poison a large area. Moreover, some civilian nuclear plants use weapons-grade nuclear materials. **Breeder reactors** that turn uranium 235 into plutonium pose an especially serious problem. Unlike other nuclear fuels, plutonium produced by breeder reactors can be made into bombs. It is estimated that politically unstable Russia has 170 tons of military and civilian plutonium and 1,000 tons of highly enriched uranium that could be used in nuclear weapons.[40] The chance that terrorists and the nations that support them might seize some plutonium and hold entire cities for ransom is growing greater every year.

BIOLOGICAL DIVERSITY

One of the most serious consequences of our assault on the air, water, and land of this planet has been a sharp reduction in **biodiversity**—the number of plant and animal species living together in the ecosystems of the world. Although no one knows exactly how many species of plants and animals there are on earth or how many species humans have driven to extinction, it is clear that the pace of extinction has been increasing at an alarming rate. Just 20 years ago, in the mid-1970s, only a few hundred species a year were believed to have become extinct. Today, the number of extinctions is estimated to be between 10,000 and 50,000 a year and increasing rapidly. During the twentieth century, humans have killed off some 1 million species of plants and animals.[41]

The biggest threat to our wildlife is the loss of their habitat as we cut down trees, plow the land, and put up buildings, dams, and highways. Two-thirds of the original wildlife habitat in tropical Africa has been destroyed or severely degraded, and the picture is much the same in the rest of the world. One-third of the forests in the United States have been destroyed, as have half of the wetlands and most of the tall-grass prairies.[42] Commercial hunting and fishing have had a devastating impact on the populations of the most sought-after species, and, of course, the pollution problems we have just examined often have an even greater impact on wildlife than on our own species.

As disturbing as the statistics are, some people argue that the extinction of plant and animal species is a natural part of the process of evolution and that extinctions are nothing we need to worry about. It is true that the history of life on earth shows several other periods like our own in which a huge number of species met their end, but such arguments overlook the tremendous benefits biological diversity brings us. For example, a study by David Tilman and John Downing found that diverse ecosystems with many different kinds of plants and animals recovered from natural stress (such as severe drought) much more quickly than simpler ecosystems.[43]

Scientists are also coming to look at the many diverse species that currently live on this planet as a kind of storehouse of potentially useful biological material. Today, most of the world's food comes from domesticated versions of plants originally found in the tropics, and about half of all medicinal drugs have active ingredients extracted from wild plants.[44] The destruction of the rich biodiversity of the tropical rain forests might also destroy species that could provide the next "green revolution" in food production or the cure for countless dreaded diseases. Beyond all this, there is an intangible benefit derived from the rich parade of life on our planet. It might not hurt our food production or medical skills if there were no more elephants or sperm whales, but the world would surely be a poorer place for it.

QUICK REVIEW

What has the impact of human population growth been on our environment?
What causes smog?
What is the greenhouse effect, and what effects is it likely to have?
What are the major sources of water pollution?
How are we harming our land?
How effective have we been at disposing of our toxic wastes?
Evaluate the environmental consequences of using nuclear reactors to generate electricity.
Why has the world's biodiversity been declining so rapidly?

DWINDLING RESOURCES

Photographs of the earth taken from space have done much to further the cause of conservation. One look at a picture of that tiny blue-green globe hanging in the vast emptiness of space shows us how limited our world and its resources really are. Throughout most of human history, we have been acting as though the world were a rich mine to be exploited. We are just beginning to realize that there are only limited amounts of oil, coal, and uranium. When the supply is used up, there will be no more.

The United States, with less than 5 percent of the world's people, uses 25 percent of all the energy consumed each year.[45] All the industrialized nations combined hold only 25 percent of the world's people, but they use 80 to 90 percent of its resources. There is a growing feeling in less-developed countries that industrialized countries are using up the world's resources so rapidly that there will soon be nothing left. There is much talk about industrializing the poor nations so that they can stabilize their population growth and bring their standard of living up to those of the more fortunate nations. With current technology, however, the world's supply of oil and minerals cannot possibly support all the world's people in the style to which those in the wealthy nations have become accustomed.

ENERGY

Modern industrial society would be impossible without massive supplies of energy. If enough energy is available, most raw materials—iron, copper, aluminum—can be recycled; but most of our energy currently comes from sources that are not renewable: Once the supply is used up, it is gone forever. Fossil fuels (oil, coal, and natural gas) are nonrenewable: They took millions of years to form from organic materials deposited in the earth and cannot be replaced. Fortunately, we also have many sources of **renewable energy**: We can grow more wood and organic materials to burn in our fireplaces, and the supply of solar energy constantly renews itself, whether we use it or not.

Worldwide consumption of **nonrenewable energy** has grown at a staggering pace. As recently as the nineteenth century, the vast majority of the world's energy came from renewable sources. Particularly important were human and animal labor and the burning of wood and dung, but the industrialized world's appetite for energy grew so rapidly that it could not be satisfied by these renewable sources. By the beginning of the twentieth century, coal was the world's principal source of energy, and oil was just coming into use. Now the world gets over 60 percent of its energy from oil and natural gas, about one-fourth comes from coal, and all other sources contribute only about 12 percent.[46] North Americans are particularly heavy users of fossil fuels and consume more total energy than people in other nations (see Figure 12.4 on page 426).

Until 1973, oil was plentiful and cheap. The price had been steadily declining for years, and few people gave any thought to the possibility that we would ever run out of petroleum. Then, in 1973, the modern world was shaken by its first great energy crisis. War broke out in the Middle East, and Arab oil producers tried to stop all shipments to nations that they believed to be supporters of their enemy, Israel. At the same time, oil-producing countries quadrupled the price of oil. Although the oil boycott was soon ended, prices continued to rise, and economic shock set the industrialized world spiraling into a severe recession. Energy consumption in the industrialized world fell the following year but soon started to rise again.

A second major petroleum shortage occurred in 1979, after the Iranian revolution disrupted that country's oil production. A "panic" soon followed, causing long lines

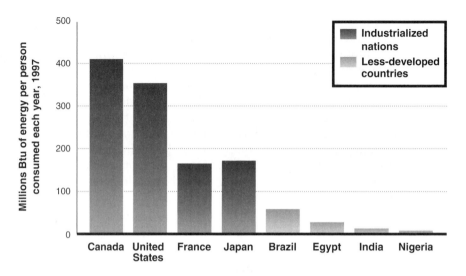

FIGURE 12.4   ENERGY

The people of the wealthy nations use far more energy than the people of the poor nations.

Source: U.S. Bureau of the Census, *Statistical Abstract of the United States*, 1999 (Washington, DC: U.S. Government Printing Office, 1999), p. 854.

of frustrated customers at gas pumps around the world. Many people came to see that the energy supplies so essential to the industrialized nations are dependent on a fragile international network of political and economic relations. But as the price of petroleum products dropped again over the following years, that important lesson seems to have faded from memory. For example, for many years the federal laws that required manufacturers to meet increasing fuel efficiency standards for their cars or face financial penalties produced a steady increase in the average miles per gallon new cars would get. But the growing popularity of trucks and huge "sport utility vehicles" (which are covered by weaker standards) means that the average fuel economy of new vehicles is now actually declining.[47]

No one knows how much longer the world's supply of oil will last. Experts disagree widely about how much oil remains to be discovered and the rate at which we are likely to consume it. World energy consumption increased 18 percent between 1990 and 2000. With global population growing at about 1.4 percent a year, and many poor nations starting to industrialize, projections are that energy consumption will increase another 25 percent in the next decade.[48] And of course that bring us that much closer to the day when the oil supply finally runs out. Heavy oils from tar sands and oil shale could provide some additional reserves, but they will be costly and environmentally damaging to develop. No matter what steps we take, however, it is quite clear that we are approaching the day when there will be no more oil at affordable prices.

The world's reserves of coal are much greater than its reserves of oil and natural gas.[49] As with petroleum, however, the actual amount of coal available for human consumption is a matter of economics. The size of the world's usable coal reserves depends on the cost of mining them and the amount of energy we must use to dig them up. Moreover, we should remember that coal, like oil, is fossilized organic matter. No matter how much we pay for it, no matter how much energy we use to mine it, and no matter how much land we destroy in the process, someday the supply will be exhausted.

Some people believe that nuclear power plants will be able to supply more of the world's energy as oil and coal are depleted. Nevertheless, it is highly unlikely that nuclear reactors, at least in their present form, can replace the energy now obtained from fossil fuels. For one thing, it takes enormous amounts of energy and labor to build a nuclear power plant, so a substantial portion of the energy produced by the plant merely replaces the energy consumed by its construction. With staggering increases in the cost of building new nuclear plants and doubts about their safety in the wake of the Chernobyl disaster, nuclear power seems to have reached a dead end in the United States. No new plants have been ordered since 1978, and numerous plants have been abandoned in various stages of planning and construction. Nuclear plants have a limited operational life, and many of the nuclear plants now operating in the United States will have to be shut down in the next decade. Germany has gone much further than the United States, however. During 2000 it became official Germany policy that no new nuclear power plants will be built in Germany and that all existing ones will be closed within a few years.

For the poorest one-third of the human population, the real energy crisis is the shortage of wood to burn. Over 3 billion people in the world still rely on wood as their primary source of energy for cooking and heating, and more than 1 billion of them do not have access to enough wood to supply their basic energy needs. Moreover, the supply of wood is dwindling every year. For many poor families, it now costs as much to heat their supper bowl as to fill it. About half of all the wood cut every year is used for fuel, and that has been a major contributor to the acute problem of global deforestation.[50]

Fortunately, there are other sources of renewable energy. For example, **Hydroelectric power**, generated by turbines turned by flowing water, is clean and efficient. New hydroelectric power stations are built every year, but the cost of transporting electricity limits their use. Currently, about 30 percent of North America's electricity bill pays for the production of hydroelectric power; the other 70 percent is for transporting the power from the generators to the consumers. However, breakthroughs in superconductivity may someday allow us to slash these costs by sharply reducing the amount of electricity lost from the wires during transmission. **Geothermal energy**—the heat of the earth's inner core—can be used to generate electricity and steam; thus, it is a possible substitute for fossil fuels. At present, however, this energy can be harnessed only in places with very special geological conditions. **Solar energy** is just beginning to make a major contribution to our energy supplies. The sun bathes the earth with an enormous amount of energy every day, and if that energy can be used efficiently, a clean substitute for coal, oil, and wood will be at hand.

RAW MATERIALS

Although humans were using the earth's mineral wealth long before they used petroleum, it does not appear that there will be a mineral crisis any time in the near future. Modern industry depends on about 80 basic minerals. About three-fourths are either abundant enough to meet all our needs or can be easily replaced. There are about 18 minerals that present more of a challenge. The known reserves of tin, zinc, and lead, for example, can meet demand for only a few more decades.[51] Although the known reserves are likely to increase, no one can say by how much. It is clear, however, that as high-grade deposits of these materials are used up, we will be forced to turn to deposits of ever lower quality, which are difficult to collect and refine.

The seas and oceans contain many minerals both in the water and on the bottom. If it were economically feasible to mine these resources, they would greatly boost the world's supplies of raw materials. Currently, it costs more to mine many of these minerals than they are worth, but technological advances are rapidly reducing the cost. As a result, there have been bitter political battles over the control of undersea mineral resources between the less-developed countries with extensive coastal territory and the wealthy industrialized nations with the technology required to exploit it.[52]

Unlike energy, most minerals can be recycled. A significant portion of the copper, lead, gold, silver, and aluminum being used today has been recycled at least once. Recycling most other raw materials is not profitable at present prices. As world stores are emptied, however, prices will rise, and recycling will look better and better—because it both conserves mineral resources and saves energy. An added benefit is that recycling can also reduce the production of solid wastes that are now choking our dumps and landfills. On the other hand, some industrial metals stay in use so long that only small amounts are available for recycling.

QUICK REVIEW

What is the difference between renewable and nonrenewable sources of energy?
What are the world's main sources of energy today? Are any of them in danger of running out?
What are our most promising sources of renewable energy?
Is there a shortage of minerals?
What are the benefits of recycling?

ORIGINS OF THE ENVIRONMENTAL CRISIS

Many ecologists and **demographers** (scientists who study human population) predict that an ecological disaster is on the way, most likely in the form of a devastating famine in the Third World. (See the "Debate" on pages 430–431.) Although not everyone is so pessimistic, there is no disagreement about the fact that we have been destroying the very ecosystems that sustain us. Such irrational behavior is not easy to explain. Its complex causes have roots stretching far back into history. Ironically, the same characteristics that have made humans such a successful species—

high intelligence and an enormous ability to manipulate the environment—have also contributed to the development of the technology and cultural orientation that are threatening many forms of life on earth.

THE POPULATION EXPLOSION

Many people believe that increasing birthrates are the cause of the population explosion, but overall birthrates have actually declined. The real cause is the decrease in death rates resulting from a longer average life span. Throughout most of human history, average life expectancy seldom exceeded 30 years. Under such conditions, a woman must have four children for two to survive to adulthood and have children of their own. That is just about how many children women in less-developed countries are having today (if we exclude China from those calculations), but the life expectancy in these countries is now about 66 years, and the result is an exploding population.[53]

The origins of the population crisis are thus to be found in the remarkable decline in death rates that began in Western Europe in the second half of the eighteenth century and later spread throughout most of the world. In the early years of the population explosion, European nations led the world in population growth. However, birthrates began decreasing in most industrialized nations in the latter part of the nineteenth century, reducing their rates of population growth. In poor agricultural nations, birthrates did not begin to decrease until much more recently, and they have not gone down nearly as rapidly as death rates in those countries. As

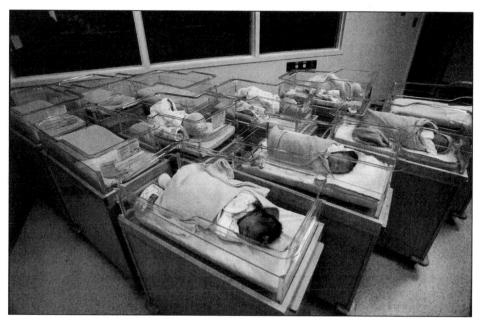

On the average, women in industrialized nations have only about half as many children as those in Third World nations, but infant mortality is much lower in industrialized countries.

DEBATE

Are We Headed for an Environmental Disaster?

Yes

Throughout history we have faced environmental challenges, but the unprecedented size of today's population and the ever-growing power of our technology have led some observers to predict an environmental crisis in the years ahead that will have devastating effects around the world.

Predicting the future is always a risky business, but there are so many signs warning of an environmental crisis that the only question is when, not if, it will occur. Never before in the history of this planet has a single species had such a devastating impact on so many other organisms. Humankind is driving thousands of species of plants and animals into extinction every year. We are replacing complex and diversified ecosystems with simple, artificial systems such as farms and urban neighborhoods; and it is a basic ecological law that the narrower the ecosystem, the more fragile it will be.

There are two main forces driving us toward disaster—overpopulation and pollution. The world is now choking with more than 6 billion people, but at the current rate of growth, there will be almost 100 billion people on earth in just two centuries. Of course, the world can't support that many human beings, and one of two things has to happen. Either we reduce our birthrates or increase our death rates. Despite all the talk and all the birth-control programs, we have failed to stop runaway population growth. Without a truly effective program of population control, only devastating plagues and famines can keep population growth in check.

As if the staggering increases in the size of the human population weren't bad enough, the average person is producing more and more pollution every year. Toxic chemicals and radioactive wastes are piling up in hundreds of thousands of sites around the world. Our rivers, lakes, and oceans are becoming toxic cesspools, and the fish they once supported are dying or taking in so many pollutants that they are dangerous to eat. The ozone layer is breaking down, and smoke from all the fuels we burn is clouding the air, poisoning our bodies, and transforming the weather in

a result, the patterns of world population growth have been reversed, and poor nations are now growing much faster than rich ones. In 2000, the growth rate in less-developed countries (excluding migration) was more than 17 times higher than in industrialized nations.[54]

Explaining these trends in world population has been one of the central tasks of modern demography. The most popular explanation is the theory of **demographic transition**, which attempts to put these changes in a long-term historical perspective.

unpredictable ways. Year by year, lush forests are shrinking while deserts grow. How much more evidence do we need? Unless we voluntarily make a radical transformation in our attitudes and in our way of life, a devastating environmental crisis will soon force us to do it.

No

Environmental problems are nothing new. Compared with the overwhelming difficulties our ancestors faced, we are actually far better off. Human history is a record of plagues, droughts, floods, and famines—all caused, in one way or another, by environmental forces. Life was precarious, and the slightest environmental disturbance could prove fatal. In contrast, today's environmental concerns are more a matter of aesthetics than survival. Certainly, trash dumps are unsightly, and unspoiled woodlands are more attractive than housing tracts, but such eyesores aren't much of a price to pay for our current standard of living.

Of course, some of the damage to the environment does create health hazards, but they are minor compared with the problems of the past. Otherwise, why would the average life span be going up year after year? In fact, the steady increase in human population that worries the environmentalists so much is actually proof that the human race is prospering. If things were really as bad as some scientists claim, the population should be declining, as it did in many other historical eras.

The alarmists who predict some kind of environmental disaster are basing their conclusions on emotion, not logic. They find a problem that is getting worse and then make wild predictions based on the assumption that it will never improve. Actually, most environmental problems are self-limiting. If a particular kind of pollution starts to cause a real threat, that very fact motivates people to do something about it. The more serious an environmental problem becomes, the harder we work to fix it. It is true that we face serious environmental issues today, but our difficulties can and will be resolved. In fact, the amazing technological progress of the last century has given us more power to shape our environment and tackle its problems than ever before. Far from an environmental collapse, the future holds the promise of unprecedented prosperity.

According to this theory, there are three distinct stages of population growth. In the first stage, which is characteristic of all traditional societies, both birthrates and death rates are high and population growth is moderate. In the second stage, the process of industrialization begins, and technological improvements bring a sharp decline in death rates. However, birthrates decline more slowly, and there is a population explosion. Finally, in the last stage, birthrates drop far enough to balance death rates, and population stabilizes.

Why does industrialization bring down death rates? For one thing, industrial technology increases the food supply, thereby reducing the number of deaths from starvation. Industrialization also prolongs life by giving people safer water and better diets, clothing, housing, and sanitation. Insecticides prevent epidemics spread by insects and thus increase life spans even more. As we noted in Chapter 8, improvements in medical technology also contribute to declining death rates. Vaccinations have brought numerous contagious diseases under control, and the discovery of antibiotics produced a cure for such killers as syphilis and pneumonia.

Although it takes longer, the economic changes industrialization creates eventually bring down birthrates as well. Children in agricultural societies make an important contribution to farm labor and usually support their parents when they grow old. In contrast, children in industrial societies are economic liabilities rather than assets. They make little economic contribution to the family, and they consume considerably more resources than their counterparts in agricultural societies. Thus, economic rewards no longer go to those with big families, but to those with small families. Changes in traditional gender roles are another factor in the lowering of birthrates. In industrial societies women have a far wider range of economic opportunities, and bearing and rearing children is no longer seen as their main social responsibility. More efficient methods of birth control have also helped bring down birthrates.

The theory of demographic transition has clear implications for the future of world population. According to the theory, the less-developed countries with rapidly growing populations are in the second phase of the demographic transition; once these countries become industrialized, their birthrates will come down and their population problems will be over. Critics point out, however, that this theory was based on population changes that occurred during the industrialization of Western countries; however, the situation in the less-developed countries is quite different than the theory implies. There is little doubt that industrialization was the direct cause of the decrease in the birthrates and death rates in Western nations (and in Japan as well). The decline of death rates in the less-developed countries has not been caused by industrialization but by the spread of foreign technology and know-how. Since the population explosion in the Third World started before the process of industrialization, it may take much longer for industrialization to progress far enough to bring the birthrates and death rates back into balance naturally (if indeed that ever happens).

EXPLOITATIVE TECHNOLOGY

More and more people are coming to realize that the magnificent technological advances that have made life so much more comfortable have a dark side as well. As we have seen, agricultural technology has brought havoc to the biosphere; industrial technology is polluting the environment; and military technology has for the first time in history given humanity the means to destroy itself. And even if we do not destroy ourselves directly with nuclear bombs, we may do so indirectly by disrupting ecosystems, food chains, and the whole life-supporting system.

Condemning technology as though it were separate from the humans who use it is both pointless and misleading. Every group of humans, from prehistoric times to the present, has used some form of technology to meet its needs for food, clothing, and shelter. Only a few of those technologies, however, have caused serious damage to the environment. The real culprit is **exploitative technology**, designed to produce the greatest immediate rewards without regard to the long-term consequences to the environment or the quality of human life.

This problem is nothing new. Although the earliest foraging peoples did little damage to their environment, the human race has been using exploitative technologies for thousands of years. Historians now believe that an environmental crisis caused by unsound farming techniques contributed to the collapse of many of the agricultural societies of the past; but the overall environmental damage done by industrial societies is far worse. For one thing, their technology is much more powerful and sophisticated, and, for another, they support many more people. Industrialization also brings about a qualitative change in the kind of technology we use. From nuclear radiation to the destruction of the ozone layer in the upper atmosphere, the cornucopia of modern science has produced problems undreamed of by our ancestors.

CULTURE

Rapid population growth and increasing use of exploitative technologies are the direct causes of the environmental crisis. Underlying them both are culturally based attitudes toward nature and humanity's place in it. As was already noted, one fundamental characteristic of Western culture is the idea that humans are superior to the natural world they inhabit. According to the Book of Genesis, humans were made in the image of God, who told them, "Be fruitful, and multiply, and replenish the earth and subdue it; and have dominion over the fish of the sea, and over the birds of the sky, and over every living thing that moves upon the earth." Western culture tends to see nature as a wilderness to be conquered and subdued by human effort. The art, literature, and folktales of the West repeatedly show people in a heroic struggle against the forces of nature.

The attitudes of most tribal peoples are quite different. In tribal cultures human beings are seen as part of nature. They are expected to live in harmony with their environment, not to subdue or conquer it. Native Americans, Australian aborigines, and many other traditional peoples see all of nature as sacred: the rocks, the trees, the mountains, the animals. To them, Europeans' assault on the environment is not merely unwise, it is sacrilege: the desecration of a holy place.

The attitude that nature is something to be subdued and exploited has been overlaid with newer beliefs in progress and materialism. The people of many ancient civilizations believed that the past contained some lost utopia, and they looked to the past for guidance in making important decisions. A radically different idea took hold in seventeenth-century Europe. In this new perspective the golden era lies in the future, when scientific progress will banish poverty, ignorance, disease, and perhaps even death itself. Thus, the faster technological development and economic growth take place, the sooner the new utopia will appear. Such optimism about the future has, however, been hard to sustain in a century that has seen the two most devastating wars in human history, the development and use of nuclear weapons, and the extermination of countless species of plants and animals. Many people, nevertheless, see little choice but to continue down the perilous path of "progress."

Although our faith in progress may be shaken, our materialism seems stronger than ever. Day after day we are bombarded with advertising telling us that we are what we own: A woman is judged by her clothes and jewelry, a man by the car he drives. A society that sees the road to happiness in wealth and the accumulation of material possessions is hardly likely to value the environment over the economic rewards its destruction may bring.

It is easy to see how these attitudes have led to our current crisis. We have mastered some living things but destroyed others. We have transformed the natural world in our quest for wealth and progress, but we have not conquered it. Sooner or later we will inevitably pay the price for abusing the web of life on which we all depend.

QUICK REVIEW

Discuss the causes of our environmental crisis.

SOLVING OUR ENVIRONMENTAL AND POPULATION PROBLEMS

Pollution, energy consumption, and runaway population growth are interdependent problems. Effective programs for dealing with one of them often aggravate the others. For example, devices that clean automobile exhaust and reduce air pollution also decrease fuel economy, thereby using up more of our limited oil reserves more rapidly. Exploiting new reserves of fossil fuel worsens environmental pollution as land, animals, and scenery are sacrificed for strip mines and oil wells, and the wastes produced by the fuel pour into the environment. On the other hand, ignoring the need for more energy retards the economy, thereby contributing to unemployment and possibly reducing food production. There is a way out of this trap, however. In a word, it is sacrifice. The fact is that there is no way to clean up the environment and conserve natural resources without changing the lifestyle of people in the industrialized nations. The challenge is to motivate people to make the necessary changes now, before a worldwide disaster forces much more difficult adjustments upon us.

POLITICAL ACTION

Despite the growing social activism of the 1960s, the environment can hardly be said to have been a political issue in North America during that decade. More than anything else, it was the observance of Earth Day on April 22, 1970, that first brought the environmental crisis to public attention. As a result of the unprecedented media attention this event received, membership in environmental organizations skyrocketed. The pressure from these groups and the publicity created by a seemingly endless string of environmental disasters helped win the passage of new legislation aimed at protecting North America's air, land, and water.

As environmentalists organized themselves and became a more effective political force, however, so did their opposition. From the smallest decisions over local land use to overriding global concerns about the greenhouse effect and the depletion of the ozone layer, environmentalists face powerful foes that reap huge profits from their environmentally destructive activities. Those profits in turn provide opponents of environmental protection with enormous financial resources to make campaign contributions, hire lobbyists, fund scientific research, purchase advertising, and pay for hundreds of other things that the defenders of the environment simply cannot afford. Moreover, environmentally destructive patterns of behavior are already deeply ingrained in modern society and will require a great effort to change.

There are, however, grounds for optimism in the fact that the world's people are becoming increasingly aware of the current crisis and the ways in which their prosperity and even their survival depend on the protection of our environment. As American pollster Louis Harris put it: "Poll after poll has come up with similar results. Whenever the public is asked about environmental issues, the returns point almost always nearly unanimously in one direction: deep worry, and concern about the ecological state of the country."[55] This same environmental concern has also been growing in other industrialized countries and even in less-developed countries. The Gallup International Millennium Survey found that four of five people were dissatisfied with the environmental conditions in their country. The majority of people in 57 of the 60 countries they surveyed felt that environmental protection was more important than economic growth, and in 55 of the 60 countries the people felt that their government was not doing enough to deal with environmental problems.[56]

If we are to preserve the natural environment for ourselves and generations to come, two important steps must be taken. First, a stronger effort must be made to educate people about our current crisis and to spread environmental awareness. Second, people from around the world must join more closely together and get involved in the political and social actions necessary to bring about meaningful change.

CONSERVING RESOURCES

There is no doubt that our existing resources can be used far more efficiently. Just as the necessities of life are used by one organism after another in various ecological cycles, so human society could reuse many of its essential raw materials over and over. To take a simple example, garbage could be used as fuel to run mills to make recycled paper; mill wastes could also be burned as fuel. Similarly, it is possible that community water districts will someday become closed systems, meaning that the water would be used again and again, never being discharged into an ocean or river. Some factories already have such closed systems. It is possible to envision larger closed systems designed so that no industrial material would ever be discarded as either waste or pollution.

Energy conservation can also stretch our natural resources. North Americans waste so much energy that significant amounts of oil, gas, and coal could be saved without lowering our standard of living. Sweden, for example, has a higher standard of living than Canada but only uses about half as much energy per person.[57]

LESSONS FROM OTHER PLACES

CONQUERING POLLUTION IN THE WORLD'S LARGEST CITY

With approximately 27 million people, Tokyo is by far the largest city in the world. With some 20 percent of the total population of Japan living in Tokyo, the city is the center of almost everything for the nation. Tokyo is the national capital, the financial center, industrial center, and cultural center. There are 828 people per square mile in Japan compared to just 77 for the United States. But this is rather misleading because Japan is a very mountainous country and most of the people are concentrated in two large flat areas around Osaka and Tokyo. As one would expect, therefore, Tokyo is packed. The traffic is jammed all day, and millions of people crowd onto the city's subways, trains, and buses for work every day. I had heard stories about the congestion, but until I experienced it, they were difficult to believe.

When I lived in Japan for two years in the 1980s there were, in fact, "pushers" employed by the train and subway lines to literally push people into the doors as the trains and subways took on passengers at each stop during the morning rush hour. Incredibly, people actually pop out of the subway doors when they open because of the pressure of people crowded inside the car. Despite all this, it all works surprisingly well. Tokyo's air is far less polluted than most major cities in the United States and its system of mass transit is a model of efficiency.

Such was not always the case, however. As Japan rebuilt itself from the ashes of World War II, there was little regard to the environment at first. By the 1960s, Japan had become one of the most polluted nations in the industrialized world. This all

Insulating homes, driving smaller cars at slower speeds, using more trains, buses, and bicycles, recycling the heat used in factories, and restricting the manufacture of energy-wasting gadgets—all are obvious ways of eliminating waste. Although some advances will require developing new, more efficient technologies, we must also find ways of persuading people to use the conservation measures that are already available.

BETTER TECHNOLOGY

Conservation can stretch our energy supplies, but new sources of energy will eventually be needed. We have already mentioned proposals for more nuclear, hydroelectric, and geothermal power stations. Some scientists are now proposing the development of power plants equipped with nuclear reactors using **fusion** (the merging of atoms) rather than **fission** (the splitting of atoms). However, nuclear fusion begin to change in the late 1960s. As the toll of deaths and injuries from industrial pollution mounted, a strong environmental movement emerged. Not long thereafter, Japan, which has no oil reserves of its own, was in another crisis caused by a world-wide petroleum shortage. These twin crises stimulated strong government action and by the 1990s Japan was one of the most energy-efficient countries in the world, with a much cleaner environment. Japan now uses less than half the energy per person as the United States. With virtually no oil production of its own, Japan still imports less oil than does the United States with its own huge oil reserves. And while the United States puts about 21 tons of carbon dioxide into the air per person each year, Japan's rate is only 9 tons per person.

One of the primary ways these goals were achieved was by expanding mass transit, thus reducing dependence on polluting autos. Autos have also been reduced by other government actions. In order to buy a car, for example, people living in Tokyo must show a city certificate proving they have a place to park it. Energy consumption was also cut through policies such as regulating the thermostat levels for heating in corporate and public buildings. Most importantly, energy consumption was reduced by simply raising taxes and making gasoline, electricity, and natural gas more expensive. Despite complaints by Americans today, the United States has the lowest energy costs of any industrial nation in the world, and produces the most air pollution.

—*Harold Kerbo*

Sources: U.S. Bureau of the Census, *Statistical Abstract of the United States*, 1999 (Washington, DC: U.S. Government Printing Office, 1999), p. 839; Harold Kerbo and John McKinstry, *Modern Japan* (New York: McGraw-Hill, 1998).

generates temperatures comparable to those of the sun, and no one knows whether it is possible to control such a powerful force or how safe such a source of power would be.

A growing number of scientists and concerned citizens are coming to see solar power as the best answer to the world's energy problems. Solar power units use the endless supply of energy from the sun, produce little pollution, and pose no threat of radiation or explosion. Solar energy is already being used to heat water, homes, and offices, and most experts are confident that more efficient technologies for storing and using the sun's energy can be developed. Considerable effort is being made to find cheap methods of turning sunlight directly into electricity through the use of **photovoltaic cells**. Other promising approaches use specially prepared ponds of water to trap solar energy or mirrors to concentrate it in a single location where it can be used to generate electrical power. There are also many indirect forms of solar energy that can be tapped for human purposes: power generated by wind, ocean tides, rivers, and dams all depend on the sun, and they all offer environmentally sound alternatives to our current dependence on burning fossil fuels. Such technology is an imitation of nature, since nearly all the energy in natural ecosystems ultimately comes from the sun.

CONTROLLING POPULATION GROWTH

Gaining control over the world's explosive population growth is one of the most urgent task before the human race today. If we fail, we will surely have to face our ancient enemies—famine, pestilence, and war—on a new and unprecedented scale. At present, the population of most industrialized nations is growing slowly or not at all, so our discussion will focus on the less-developed countries; however, the proposals and programs designed for poor nations can be modified to fit industrialized nations if the need arises.

Many political leaders in the poor nations who are interested in controlling population focus their efforts on industrialization, believing that attitudes toward the family and reproduction will change as the economy develops. As we have already shown, industrialization does bring about a demographic transition that ultimately results in slower overall growth. Many leaders insist that the population problem will take care of itself if we wait for this "natural" process to occur in the agricultural nations. Such expectations are, unfortunately, ill founded. The fact that industrialization has occurred in a few poor countries hardly means that it will occur in all of them. Moreover, even if all the poor nations of the world were somehow to industrialize, the demographic transition could not possibly occur quickly enough to limit the world's population to a manageable size.

There is, however, a growing consensus that one of the most effective ways to help stabilize population growth is to focus on the needs of women. The World Bank in its 2000 *Development Report*, for example, concluded that improving the status of women was the key to both economic development and population control.[58] In less-developed countries, women often live a very restricted life under the domination and control of their husbands and other relatives. They have few roads to status or social rewards other than bearing and rearing a large family. If a women can win power and prestige in other ways besides childbearing, then the pressures lessen to bear children as a means of winning social recognition. The power of women's labor can also provide a big boost to industrialization, thus making an indirect contribution to lower birthrates as well. Equal opportunities and equal status for women are revolutionary ideas in many Third World countries, but the success of that revolution would go a long way toward solving the problems of poverty and overpopulation.

A more direct approach is through population control programs. Most such programs try to encourage people to use birth control and limit the size of their families voluntarily. The assumption is that the birthrate will drop if couples have only the number of children they desire. To help achieve that goal, information and birth-control devices are usually given to the poor without charge. Such programs are called **family planning**, but the real objective is to cut the birthrate. Some countries support their family planning programs with publicity stressing the desirability of small families and

Voluntary family planning programs are common all over the world, but such programs have little chance of success unless traditional attitudes about the value of a large family are changed.

the dangers of overpopulation. In India, for example, the symbol of population control—a red triangle with the smiling faces of two parents and two children—can be seen in every village.

Such programs help reduce the number of unwanted children, but by themselves they are unlikely to achieve the kind of reduction in birthrates that the world needs to stabilize its population at a manageable size. For one thing, many family planning programs in the less-developed countries have been poorly organized and underfunded. There is a more basic problem, however. Publicity campaigns and speeches simply cannot change deeply rooted attitudes favoring large families. The most successful family planning programs have therefore been in countries such as South Korea, Thailand, and Taiwan, which have also been undergoing rapid industrialization.

The weaknesses in family planning programs have led some nations to provide additional incentives for parents to limit the size of their families: bonuses for couples with few children and penalties for those with many children. Some countries have even experimented with mandatory restrictions that require all families to limit the number of children they have. Of all the large Third World nations, the People's Republic of China has made the greatest progress in reducing its birthrate. China's powerful central government has put intense pressure on its people to abstain from premarital sex, to delay marriage and childbearing, and to use birth control and abortion. Couples who agree to limit their family to one child are given a single-child certificate, which entitles them to such benefits as priority in housing, better wages, a special pension, and preference in school admissions. As a result of such policies China's current growth rate is a below 1 percent a year—an extremely low figure for a poor agricultural nation. Yet these gains have not been made without considerable cost to personal liberty. Moreover, the new population limitation measures seem to have encouraged female infanticide and selective abortion as many families feel that if they can have only a single child it should be a boy who can take care of them when they get old. (In traditional Chinese culture, girls move in with their husband's family when they get married.)

CHANGING OUR LIVES

As is true for most important social problems, solving our environmental crisis will require both individual and collective changes. As individuals we may not be able to discover a new source of clean energy or solve the population problem, but we can commit ourselves to leading more environmentally sustainable lives. There is a long, long list of things we can do. A few quick examples include living as close to work or school as we can, walking or taking a bike when we don't need to drive, recycling our waste, boycotting products whose manufacturers show wanton disregard for the environment, and on a more fundamental level, dedicating ourselves to living a simpler life and taking no more of the world's resources then we really need. Of course, nothing we do as single individuals is likely to have a very large impact on this enormous problem, but such small individual changes add up and gain a kind of momentum of their own. If enough people start making these changes, the environment will improve.

QUICK REVIEW

Critically evaluate the different proposals for solving the environmental crisis.

SOCIOLOGICAL PERSPECTIVES ON THE PROBLEMS OF POPULATION AND THE ENVIRONMENT

The population explosion, pollution of the air and water, degradation of the land, and wasteful use of oil and other natural resources seem to be topics for engineers, biologists, and demographers to ponder; but environmental issues are also sociological issues. Sociologists take the broad view, repeatedly pointing out that social institutions are organized systems similar to the ecosystems of nature; that one must understand interacting physical, biological, economic, political, and psychological conditions if one is to understand collective human behavior; and that purposive human actions have unanticipated consequences. In short, sociologists try to teach people to understand that few human problems are as simple as they seem. The origins of the environmental crisis are to be found not in a few polluting industries but in the basic social organization and cultural outlook of the modern world.

THE FUNCTIONALIST PERSPECTIVE

Functionalists see today's environmental problems as latent dysfunctions of industrialization. Most of the technological advances that help society perform its basic functions easily and efficiently have had negative effects as well. The manufacturing, distributing, and consuming processes that make increases in our standard of living possible also produce undesirable by-products: pollution and resource depletion. Thus, the economic changes that helped create modern industrial society also threw the environment out of balance and created our current problems.

To many functionalists, the answer to our environmental problems is simple: The dysfunctions of the industrial economy must be reduced through more efficient pollution control and through new technological improvements that will produce more energy and use new raw materials. Thus, the environmental crisis is best solved by refining and improving our present way of doing things, not by making basic changes in our social and economic system. Most functionalists are therefore cornucopians: They believe that the solution to the problems of modern technology is more and better technology.

Other functionalists disagree, however, that the present industrial economy is inherently unstable because it depends on steady growth to maintain economic prosperity, yet it is using up the resources that are necessary for that growth. To this way of thinking, minor reforms cannot solve our environmental problems. Basic changes must be made because many of the central values of our social system have become dysfunctional. At one time, ideas about conquering nature and the importance of constantly increasing our personal wealth inspired the effort necessary for survival. Now, such attitudes threaten human existence itself because they ignore the long-term effects of the relentless pursuit of wealth by billions of people. The economic system is thus dysfunctional—it wastes resources and pollutes the environment in order to produce more than is necessary for the health and well-being of the people. To these functionalists, a solution to the environmental crisis will require major changes in our system of values and a reorganization of society.

Functionalists look at population growth in much the same way as our environment. When the world's population was small and there was no shortage of natural resources, the functions of population growth far outweighed its dysfunctions. Now the same social forces that promoted population growth in the past (when it was desirable), produce hunger, poverty, and social instability. For this reason, functionalists say, the population problem will be solved only when dysfunctional attitudes, values, and institutions that promote excessive birthrates are changed. Given time, the social system will reach a new balance. The critical question is whether this balance will come about as a result of famine, wars, or other disasters or because of well-organized programs to change traditional attitudes toward childbearing.

THE CONFLICT PERSPECTIVE

Conflict theorists see exploitation of the environment as just one more result of social exploitation. More specifically, conflict theorists hold that the economic structure of capitalist nations depends not only on the exploitation of the poor by the rich but also on an ever-increasing exploitation of the natural environment. Private businesses must win the competitive struggle for profits if they are to survive, and that places enormous pressure on them to use exploitative technologies to gain quick profits regardless of the environmental costs. Conflict theorists argue that if a firm carried out more responsible policies, it would be driven out of business by its less ethical competitors. One solution is obviously for the government to make firms pay for the environmental damage they cause. Conflict theorists argue, however, that the giant corporate polluters are so powerful that they have been able to block effective environmental programs that are clearly in the interests of the vast majority of the people.

This same pattern of exploitation occurs internationally as well and is a major contributor to the population explosion. According to conflict theorists, the wealthy industrialized nations are using their power to loot the poor nations of their irreplaceable natural resources, thus making the rich nations richer and the poor nations poorer. Now that the less-developed countries are finally trying to industrialize, they find that the cheap energy sources and raw materials that helped develop the wealthy nations are gone. Although exploitation of the poor nations has prevented them from industrializing (which eventually brings down birth rates), the spread of modern technology has cut death rates, thus creating runaway population growth.

Conflict theorists insist that to solve these problems, we must create a new kind of world system based on equality and respect for the dignity of all people. To stop the exploitation and destruction of our natural environment, we must reverse our priorities and put the welfare of humanity first and profits second. The competitive materialistic orientation that has produced such stunning economic achievements has also degraded us by making material possessions the measure of a person's worth. Conflict theorists argue that as long as this orientation and the economic system that fostered it continue, we will continue to brutalize both the environment and ourselves. But if we create a new mutual support and concern, our population and environmental problems will be easy to resolve.

THE FEMINIST PERSPECTIVE

To the "eco-feminists," the roots of our environmental crisis are to be found in the same patriarchal culture that has oppressed women for so many centuries. These feminists see a basic contradiction between the values of cooperation, nurturance, and mutual support that often predominate among women and the more competitive ideals of power and achievement often found among men. Because patriarchal culture places a one-sided emphasis on those masculine values, it has developed an exploitative relationship with the very environmental systems that keep us alive. Irreplaceable natural resources are wasted and huge amounts of toxic pollutants are dumped into the environment with little concern for the impact those actions will have on generations to come.

To the eco-feminists, the solution to our environmental crisis is obvious. There must be a fundamental shift in the values and perspectives of our culture. The cooperative nurturant values so central to most women's lives must now be given the same importance in our culture as a whole, while the cultural traditions that value aggressive, domineering behavior must be changed. Feminists urge women and men to band together to make fundamental changes in our culture and our economic system in order to forge a responsible, holistic relationship to the earth that supports us.

Feminists have also shown that the social restrictions placed on women play a critical role in the population problem. The cultures with the highest birthrates are also those that deny women equal access to education and jobs. When women are restricted to their family roles as mothers and as subordinates of their husbands, their whole social status and personal security derives from their ability to bear and raise children.

The feminist response to the population crisis is therefore obvious: Give women of the developing nations more rights and more freedoms. Following the urgings of the feminists, development workers have found that the most successful family planning programs are indeed those that focus on women—not just to provide birth-control technology, but to provide the education, economic assistance, and emotional support necessary to help women create a more powerful independent role for themselves. Not surprisingly, such programs have often proved highly controversial in traditional patriarchal cultures. The obstacles have not, however, proved insurmountable, because husbands also benefit from the extra income their wives are able to earn and from overall advantages of family planning.

THE INTERACTIONIST PERSPECTIVE

Sociologists from all theoretical perspectives agree with the interactionists that learned attitudes and values are at the root of our environmental and population problems. The belief in progress, in materialism, and in our superiority to the natural world are all important parts of the problem. Some interactionists hold that even more fundamental parts of our definition of ourselves and the world around us are also involved. Most of us see things in individualistic terms, doing whatever seems most likely to satisfy our personal needs. Such an approach works fine in many situations, but when a large group of people all follow the individualistic road to happiness at the same time, the result is likely to be chaos and confusion. Environmental resources are often held in common for use by many people, but it is in the individualistic interest of each to use as much of these resources as possible before someone else does. In a phenomenon often known as the **tragedy of the commons**, this individualistic pursuit of self-interest leads to the complete destruction of resources and long-term harm to everyone.[59]

Interactionists see the roots of the problem of overpopulation in the way traditional cultures define the world. Peasant farmers in traditional societies have a fatalistic attitude toward life. The idea of planning a family, let alone a world population, is alien to them. Fertility continues to be seen as a sign of virility and competence. A "real man" is one who has fathered many sons, and a "real woman" is one who has borne and reared them. Even in industrialized nations childless couples are sometimes pitied, and the inability to bear children may be reason enough for a husband to divorce his wife.

Such attitudes are learned, and interactionists tell us that if we are to deal effectively with our problems, these attitudes must be unlearned by an entire generation. As they are unlearned, new, more appropriate attitudes will have to take their place. Citizens of the twenty-first century must learn what tribal people have always known: that our survival as individuals depends on our concern for the interests of the community, that nature is to be regarded with respect and reverence, and that a lifestyle that attempts to achieve harmony with nature is more satisfying than one that attempts to conquer it. But such traditional attitudes must be combined with a new recognition of the necessity for limiting our population growth to manageable levels.

QUICK REVIEW

Compare and contrast the functionalist and conflict perspectives on the problems of environment and population growth.

What do feminists say about our environmental and population problems?

How do interactionists explain the causes of our environmental and population problems?

SUMMARY

The population explosion and the spread of industrial society have disrupted the delicate web of life on which human existence depends. Air pollution, for example, is a severe health hazard and is causing harmful changes in the world's weather and atmospheric conditions. Despite the world's enormous reserves of water, water pollution both above and below ground is becoming a serious concern. Organic wastes from human sewage and industrial wastes are water pollutants, as are the chemical fertilizers and pesticides used extensively in modern farming. Poisonous chemicals such as mercury and arsenic build up in the tissues of one marine animal after another, eventually reaching the humans at the top of the food chain. Overgrazing, logging, urban sprawl, faulty irrigation, strip mining, and poor farming techniques have combined to deface huge expanses of land. Over the years, forests have steadily shrunk as deserts, wastelands, and cities have grown. Moreover, chemicals used in business and industry are being dumped on the land, in the water, and in the air, and there is growing concern about radioactive wastes. One result of all these problems has been the extinction of many species of plants and animals and a sharp reduction in the biological diversity of our world.

The world is rapidly using up many of its irreplaceable natural resources. Oil and coal can meet the world's energy needs for only a limited period of time. Many key minerals and raw materials are also in increasingly short supply; however, given enough energy, most of them can be effectively recycled.

The complex causes of our environmental and population problems have roots stretching far back in human history. The population explosion has its origins with the industrial revolution that helped create dramatic reductions in death rates around the world. But while social changes created by industrialization eventually brought down birth rates as well, that has not occurred in the poor non-industrialized nations, thus creating runaway population growth. Technology has also become highly exploitative, using huge amounts of energy and natural resources and producing a large volume of pollution in the process. Underlying these conditions are three basic cultural attitudes: the belief in progress, the belief in materialism, and the idea that nature is something for humans to subdue and exploit.

Many different solutions have been proposed for our environmental and population problems, including united social action, conservation of resources, better technology, effective population control programs, and a concerted effort to live a more sustainable lifestyle.

Functionalists see environmental and population problems as latent dysfunctions of the industrial revolution, because the attitudes that inspired the explosion of economic growth are no longer functional. Conflict theorists see exploitation of the environment as part of a continuing struggle between the rich and the poor. They note that profits have been given a higher priority than human welfare, and they call for a reversal of these priorities. Feminists call for a strengthening of the traditional female values of cooperation and mutual support and for an end to the aggressive, competitive orientation that encourages exploitation of the environment. They also advocate an effort to provide new source of power and prestige for women aside from their roles as mothers and child rearers. Interactionists argue that the attitudes, values, and definitions that cause our problems are learned and that if we are to deal effectively with them, an entire generation of citizens must learn a new way to look at the world.

QUESTIONS FOR CRITICAL THINKING

Many sociologists believe that abuse of the environment will be the Achilles' heel of modern industrial capitalism. We keep using up more and more of our natural resources and pumping out more and more dangerous pollutants; in their view we are inevitably headed for an environmental catastrophe. The optimists, on the other hand, feel that newer and better technology will solve our environmental problems and allow us to continue on our present course without radical change. Considering what you have read in this chapter, what do you think our environmental future will be like? Do you think one of these two sides will be proved right, or are we likely to follow a middle course?

KEY TERMS

acid rain
biodiversity
breeder reactor
deforestation
demographer
demographic transition
desertification
ecology
exploitative technology
family planning
fission
fusion
geothermal energy
greenhouse effect

hydroelectric power
nonrenewable energy
organic waste
ozone depletion
photochemical smog
photovoltaic cell
pollution
population explosion
renewable energy
solar energy
strip-mining
temperature inversion
tragedy of the commons

NOTES

1. Population Reference Bureau, *World Population Data Sheet*, 2000 (Washington, DC: Population Reference Bureau, 2000).

2. World Health Organization, *The World Health Report*, 1999: *Making a Difference* (Geneva, Switzerland, 1999), p. 3.

3. Population Reference Bureau, *World Population Data Sheet*, 1994 (Washington, DC: Population Reference Bureau, 1994); John Balzar, "Doomsayers of Overpopulation Sound a New Jeremiad," *Los Angeles Times*, June 7, 1994, p. A5.

4. Calculated from U.S. Bureau of the Census, *Statistical Abstract of the United States*, 1999 (Washington, DC: U.S. Government Printing Office), p. 831.

5. Population Reference Bureau, *World Population Data Sheet*, 2000.

6. Ibid.

7. U.S. Bureau of the Census, *Statistical Abstract of the United States*, 1997 (Washington, DC: U.S. Government Printing Office, 1997), p. 234; World Bank, *World Development Report*, 2000 (New York: Oxford University Press, 2000), p. 293.

8. Ibid.

9. G. Tyler Miller, *Living in the Environment: An Introduction to Environmental Science*, 6th ed. (Belmont, CA: Wadsworth, 1990), p. 498.

10. Nick Middleton, *The Global Casino: An Introduction to Environmental Issues* (London: Arnold, 1995), pp. 114–126; Karen Arms, *Environmental Science*, 2nd ed. (Fort Worth: Harcourt Brace, 1994), pp. 451–452.

11. Mark Dowie, "A Sky Full of Holes: Why the Ozone Layer Is Torn Worse Than Ever," pp. 230–233 in John L. Allen, ed., *Environment 97/98* (Guilford, CT: Dushkin/McGraw-Hill, 1997); Marla Cone, "Ozone Hole Blamed for Frog Decline," *Los Angeles Times*, March 1, 1994, pp. A1, A20; Miller, *Living in the Environment*, pp. 501–503.

12. Arms, *Environmental Science*, p. 444.

13. Mark Dowie, "A Sky Full of Holes."

14. Singapore had a slightly higher rate of carbon dioxide emissions per capita, but Singapore is actually more of a city-state than a country with open land; see World Bank, *World Development Report*, 2000 (New York: Oxford University Press, 2000), pp. 292–293.

15. World Resources Institute, *World Resources 1996–97* (New York: Oxford University Press, 1996), pp. 313–325; Arms, *Environmental Science*, pp. 444–448; Miller, *Living in the Environment*, pp. 503–507; David E. Pitt, "Computer Vision of Global Warming: Hardest on Have-Nots," *New York Times*, January 18, 1994, p. B7.

16. U.S. Bureau of the Census, *Statistical Abstract of the United States*, 1996, p. 233.

17. Middleton, *The Global Casino*, pp. 155–170; Miller, *Living in the Environment*, p. 519.

18. Andrew Goudie, *The Human Impact on the Natural Environment*, 3rd ed. (Cambridge, MA: MIT Press, 1990), pp. 154–201; Mary Williams Walsh, "In Arctic, a Toxic Surprise," *Los Angeles Times*, June 18, 1991, pp. A1, A9.

19. Brad Knickerbocker, "'New Endangered' List Targets Many U.S. Rivers," *Christian Science Monitor*, April 21, 1994, pp. 1, 4.

20. William J. Broad, "Survey of 100 U.S. Coastal Sites Shows Pollution Is Declining," *New York Times*, January 21, 1997, p. B10.

21. Miller, *Living in the Environment*, pp. 529–535.

22. Agis Salpukas, "A New Slant on Exxon Valdez Spill," *New York Times*, December 1, 1993, pp. C1, C7.

23. Miller, *Living in the Environment*, p. 533.

24. Frank Clifford, "Study Finds Peril in Water Supply," *Los Angeles Times*, July 28, 1994, pp. A4, A26; Associated Press, "20% Drinking Inadequately Treated Water," *San Luis Obispo Telegram-Tribune*, July 27, 1994, p. A10.

25. *Statistical Abstract of the United States*, 1999, p. 856.

26. Arms, *Environmental Science*, p. 375.

27. World Resources Institute, *Global Trends*, January 2001, <www.wri.org>; Diana Jean Schemo, "Burning of Amazon Picks Up Pace, with Vast Areas Lost," *New York Times*, September 12, 1996, p. A3.

28. Arms, *Environmental Science*, pp. 304–305.
29. Ibid.; Middleton, *The Global Casino*, pp. 43–55.
30. Middleton, *The Global Casino*, pp. 28–42; Arms, *Environmental Science*, pp. 379, 382–383.
31. Middleton, *The Global Casino*, pp. 71–84; Miller, *Living in the Environment*, p. 225; Goudie, *Human Impact on the Natural Environment*, pp. 138–140.
32. U.S. Bureau of the Census, *Statistical Abstract*, 1993, p. 227.
33. See Branley Allan Branson, "Is There Life After Strip Mining?" *Natural History* 95 (August 1986): 30–36.
34. Philip Shenon, "Pacific Island Nation Is Stripped of Everything," *New York Times*, December 10, 1995, p. A3.
35. Miller, *Living in the Environment*, pp. 453–454.
36. Ibid., pp. 473–475; World Resources Institute, *World Resources 1996–97* (New York: Oxford University Press, 1996), p. 292.
37. Arms, *Environmental Science*, p. 404.
38. Nicholas Lenssen and Christopher Flavin, "Meltdown," pp. 119–126 in Allen, *Environment 97/98*; Carol J. Williams, "9 Years Later, Chernobyl Disaster Looks Worse," *New York Times*, April 27, 1995, p. A4; "Ukraine to Keep Chernobyl in Operation," *New York Times*, October 22, 1993, p. A6; Scripps News Service, "Tragedy of Chernobyl Keeps on Building in Byelorussia," *San Luis Obispo Telegram-Tribune*, March 27, 1991, p. D1; Associated Press, "Mystery Ailments Plague Chernobyl," *San Luis Obispo Telegram-Tribune*, April 22, 1991, pp. A1, A12; Michael Parks, "Chernobyl," *Los Angeles Times*, April 23, 1991, pp. H1, H6; Scripps News Service, "Chernobyl Worse Than Earlier Feared," *San Luis Obispo Telegram-Tribune*, April 28, 1991, p. A1.
39. Lenssen and Flavin, "Meltdown"; Miller, *Living in the Environment*, pp. 399–402.
40. Michael R. Gordon, "Russian Controls on Bomb Material Are Leaky," *New York Times*, August 18, 1994, pp. A1, A8.
41. Peter Raven, "A Time of Catastrophic Extinction: What We Must Do," pp. 175–178 in Allen, *Environment 97/98*; Miller, *Living in the Environment*, pp. 320–321; Arms, *Environmental Science*, p. 62.
42. Miller, *Living in the Environment*, p. 322.
43. William K. Stevens, "Study Bolsters Value of Species Diversity," *New York Times*, February 1, 1994, p. B7.
44. Miller, *Living in the Environment*, p. 318.
45. U.S. Bureau of the Census, *Statistical Abstract*, 1999, p. 853.
46. Ibid.
47. See Agis Salpukas, "What's Next, Tail Fins?" *New York Times*, February 15, 1996, pp. C1, C5.
48. U.S. Bureau of the Census, *Statistical Abstract*, 1999, p. 853; Population Reference Bureau, *World Population Data Sheet*, 2000 (Washington, DC: Population Reference Bureau, 2000).
49. Norman Myers, ed., *Gaia: An Atlas of Planet Management*, rev. ed. (New York: Anchor Books, 1993), p. 99.
50. Arms, *Environmental Science*, pp. 208–209.
51. Ibid., pp. 286–287.
52. See Miller, *Living in the Environment*, pp. 357–358.
53. Ibid.; John R. Weeks, *Population: An Introduction to Concepts and Issues*, 3rd ed. (Belmont, CA: Wadsworth, 1986), p. 55.
54. Population Reference Bureau, *World Population Data Sheet*, 1997.
55. Louis Harris, *Inside America* (New York: Vintage, 1987), p. 245.
56. *Gallup International Millennium Survey*, January 2001, <www.gallup-international.com>.
57. U.S. Bureau of the Census, *Statistical Abstract*, 1997, p. 847.
58. World Bank, *World Development Report*, 2000 (New York: Oxford University Press, 2000).
59. See Garrett Hardin, "The Tragedy of the Commons," *Science* 162 (1968): 1243–1248.

Glossary

absolute approach Defining poverty by dividing the poor from the nonpoor on the basis of an objective standard (e.g., income).

acid rain Rain with unusually high acidity produced by atmospheric pollution.

acquired immune deficiency syndrome (AIDS) A fatal disease that attacks the body's defenses against illness, caused by the HIV virus.

addiction The intense craving for a drug that develops after a period of physical dependence stemming from heavy use.

affirmative action program A program designed to make up for past discrimination by giving special assistance to members of the groups that were discriminated against.

alcoholic A person whose work, family, or social life is disrupted by drinking.

alienation (1) A feeling of estrangement from society and social groups. (2) A feeling of the loss of control over one's activities, especially one's labor.

Alzheimer's disease A disease that causes mental deterioration in older people.

androgynous Having the characteristics traditionally ascribed to both males and females.

anomie A condition in which social norms have broken down and no longer regulate individual behavior.

antitrust law A law designed to protect free competition in the marketplace.

anxiety disorder A mental disorder involving severe and prolonged anxiety, irrational fears, panic attacks, obsessive thoughts and rituals, or the debilitating consequences of some traumatic event.

arms race The escalating accumulation of military defenses in anticipation of enemy military buildup.

arson The illegal burning of a structure or other property.

assault An attack on a person with the intention of hurting or killing the victim.

assimilation A process by which a person takes on a new culture.

authoritarian personality The personality of someone who is rigid and inflexible, has a very low tolerance for uncertainty, and readily accepts orders from above.

authoritarianism An extreme belief in the importance of authority and the individual responsibility to submit to it.

aversive therapy   A form of behavioral therapy that uses punishment to discourage a particular behavior.

bail   A sum of money put up as security to be forfeited if a person accused of committing a crime does not appear for trial.

balance of power   The condition in which the military strength of the world's strongest nations or groups of nations is roughly equal.

behaviorism   A theory explaining human actions only in terms of observable behavior.

bilateral   A family system that traces its descent from both the husband's and wife's family line.

biodiversity   The range of plant and animal species living together in an ecosystem or on the planet as a whole.

biosocial perspective   A theory that explains social behavior by reference to biological traits.

bipolar disorder   A mental disorder characterized by extreme swings in mood.

bisexual   A person willing to have sexual relations with individuals of either sex.

blended family   A family in which at least one of the marital partners brings children from a previous relationship.

blue-collar worker   Someone employed in a job requiring manual labor.

breeder reactor   A type of nuclear reactor that produces plutonium, a fuel that can be used in nuclear weapons.

bribery   Giving money or some other reward in order to influence the way an official carries out his or her duties.

budget deficit   The amount of money the government spends in excess of the amount it receives in taxes and other revenue.

burglary   Unlawful entry into a structure with the intent to commit a felony.

capital accumulation   The buildup of wealth in a nation—including not only money but also its infrastructure and the skills of its labor force.

capitalism   An economic system characterized by private property, the exchange of commodities and capital, and a free market for goods and labor.

case study   A detailed examination of specific individuals, groups, or situations.

civil rights movement   The social movement in the United States that brought an end to the segregation system.

class conflict   The struggle for wealth, power, and prestige among the social classes.

classical theory   A theory that sees criminal behavior as the result of the rational choice of the criminal.

Cold War   The struggle for world domination between the capitalist and communist nations after World War II.

colonialism   A system in which one nation extends its political and economic control over other nations or peoples and treats them as dependent colonies.

colonized minority   A minority group that has acquired minority status through involuntary means, such as being captured and brought to a different country or having their home territory annexed by another group.

coming out   Openly admitting one's homosexuality for the first time.

communism   An economic system in which the government owns and controls all the major economic institutions.

communitarian capitalism   A capitalistic economic system that emphasizes the importance of the group or community over the individual.

compensatory education program   A special program whose goal is to help disadvantaged students reach educational levels comparable to those achieved by more privileged students.

computer literacy   The ability to use common computer programs and the Internet.

conflict of interest   The ethical dilemma that occurs when an officeholder's official duty and his or her personal interests would lead to different actions.

conflict perspective   A sociological approach that sees society in terms of conflicts and tensions between different social groups.

contagious disease   A disease spread from one person to another.

contrast conceptions   The strong stereotypes ethnic groups often develop about each other.

control theory   A criminological thesis holding that people commit crimes when social norms and other social forces no longer control them.

core   The wealthy industrialized nations that dominate the world system.

crime   Violation of a criminal law.

crime control model   A model of criminal justice that favors speedy arrest and punishment of anyone who commits a crime.

critical theory   A theory holding that the capitalist economic system is the root cause of the crime problem in modern industrial societies.

cultural capital   Knowledge of "higher culture" such as art and music that facilitates acceptance into high status groups.

culture   The way of life of the people in a certain geographic area, particularly their ideas, beliefs, values, patterns of thought, and symbols.

culture of poverty   A self-perpetuating subculture among some (but not all) poor people that traps them in poverty.

de facto segregation   Segregation of minority groups that results from existing social conditions (such as housing patterns) but is not legally required.

de jure segregation   Segregation of minority groups that is required by law.

decriminalization   The proposal that penalties for possession and use of a drug be abolished even if sales of the drug remain illegal.

definition of the situation   The meaning the actors give to a social situation in which they are involved.

deforestation   The destruction of the forests.

deinstitutionalization   The movement to reduce the number of patients treated in mental hospitals.

demographer   Someone who studies the distribution, density, and vital statistics of populations.

demographic transition   Changes in birthrates and death rates occurring during the process of industrialization.

depressant   A drug that slows the responses of the central nervous system, reduces coordination, and decreases mental alertness.

deregulation   Dropping government control over economic activities.

desegregation   Mixing of people of different races who were formerly kept apart by law or custom.

desertification   The transformation of productive land into desert.

deterrence   The strategy of preventing war by maintaining so strong a military force that other nations will be afraid to attack.

deviant   (1) An individual who violates a social norm. (2) An individual who is labeled as a deviant by others.

deviant subculture   A set of perspectives, attitudes, and values that support criminal or other norm-violating activity.

differential association theory   A theory holding that people become criminals because they are exposed to more behavior patterns that are favorable to a certain kind of crime than are opposed to it.

disarmament   Elimination of armed forces and weaponry, usually with a treaty.

discouraged worker   A person who has given up looking for work; not counted in unemployment statistics.

discrimination   The practice of treating some people as second-class citizens because of their minority status.

distance learning   Courses taken via the Internet or closed-circuit television.

domination   A social system in which one ethnic group holds power and uses it to keep other groups in a subordinate position.

double bind   A situation in which a parent gives a child two conflicting messages at the same time.

double standard   A code of behavior that gives men greater sexual freedom than women.

drug maintenance   A program providing drugs to addicts or habitual users.

dual-earner family   A family in which both spouses are employed.

due process model   A model of criminal justice that places more emphasis on protecting human rights and dignity than on punishing criminals.

dysfunction   The way a social phenomenon interferes with the maintenance of a balanced social order.

ecology   The study of the interrelationships among plants, animals, and their environments.

economic democracy   The control of economic institutions by the people who are involved in them.

economic development   Economic growth in the poor nations.

elitist   One who believes that nations are ruled by a small elite class.

ethnic group   A group whose members share a sense of togetherness and the conviction that they form a distinct group or "people."

ethnic minority   An ethnic group that suffers prejudice and discrimination at the hands of a larger dominant group.

ethnic stereotype   The portrayal of all the members of a particular ethnic group as having similar fixed, usually unfavorable, traits.

ethnocentrism   The tendency to view the norms and values of one's own culture as absolute and to use them as a standard against which to measure other cultures.

eurocentric   A view of the world or an educational curriculum that takes an exclusively European perspective.

experiment   A research method in which the behavior of individuals or groups is studied under controlled conditions, usually in a laboratory setting.

exploitative technology   Technology designed to produce immediate profits without regard to long-term consequences.

extended family   Members of two or more related nuclear families living together in the same place.

extreme poverty   Conditions of poverty among people who have less than half the poverty-level income.

family allowance   A welfare program that provides a small government allowance for every eligible family with children.

family planning   A population control program whose objective is voluntary reduction of the birthrate.

fee-for-service compensation   A form of payment in which a physician is paid a fixed fee for each service rendered.

felony   A serious offense, usually punishable by death or by confinement in a central prison.

feminist theory   An approach to understanding society and social behavior that focuses on the importance of gender and the inequalities based on it.

fission   Splitting of atoms to produce energy, as in a nuclear reactor.

food stamp program   A government program that provides vouchers that can be exchanged for food.

forcible rape   Sexual intercourse forced on someone against his or her will.

fraud   The acquisition of money or property through the use of deception.

function   The contribution of each part of society to the maintenance of a balanced order.

functionalist perspective   A sociological theory viewing society as a delicate balance of parts and holding that social problems arise when societies become disorganized.

functionally illiterate   Someone whose skills in reading and writing are so poor that he or she cannot perform many of the basic tasks necessary to daily life in an industrial society.

fusion   Merging of atoms to produce energy, as in the sun.

gay   Usually refers to male homosexuals, but sometimes to all homosexuals in general.

gender inequality   The differences in the economic, social, and political conditions of females and males.

gender role   A social role assigned on the basis of biological sex.

gender socialization   The process by which a person learns the behaviors and attitudes that are expected of the female or male gender.

general theory of crime   Gottfredson and Hirschi's belief that people commit crimes because of weak self-control.

genocide   A systematic attempt to distort an entire racial, ethnic, or political group.

geothermal energy   Energy derived from the heat of the earth's inner core.

globalization   The growth of a worldwide economic, political, and social system.

goal displacement   The substitution of a new goal or goals for the official stated objectives of an organization.

greenhouse effect   The trapping of heat in the atmosphere by gases produced by human activities.

hate crime   Illegal act directed at someone because of his or her ethnic group, gender, disability, or sexual orientation.

health   A state of physical and mental well-being.

health maintenance organization (HMO)   An organization in which a group of medical personnel offer a range of medical services to subscribers who pay a fixed monthly fee.

hegemonic power   The dominant nation in the world system.

heterosexual   One whose preference is for sexual relations with persons of the opposite sex.

hidden curriculum   The concepts that students must learn in order to succeed in school that are not part of the formal curriculum, such as obedience to authority.

holistic medicine   A medical approach that focuses on the overall health of the patient and not on individual symptoms.

home schooling   Educating students at home rather than in public or private schools.

homicide   The killing of a human being.

homophobia   The fear of homosexuality.

homosexual   One whose preference is for sexual relations with persons of the same sex.

human immunodeficiency virus (HIV)   The virus that causes AIDS.

hydroelectric power   Electric power generated by the movements of water.

ideology of individualism   The belief that each individual is personally responsible for his or her own economic success or failure.

immigrant minority   A minority group that has acquired minority status through voluntary immigration.

imperialism   The creation or expansion of an empire.

incapacitation   The prevention of crime by imprisoning criminals so that they cannot commit more crimes against the public.

income   The amount of money a person makes in a given year.

individual psychotherapy   Psychological therapy with a single patient and therapist.

individualistic capitalism   A capitalistic economic system that emphasizes the importance of the individual over the group or community.

industrial revolution   The change from an agricultural to an industrial society.

inflation   An increase in the overall prices consumers must pay for the goods they buy.

infrastructure   The basic physical necessities of modern society (e.g., roads, power plants, and sewers).

institutional discrimination   Discrimination against minority groups that is practiced by economic, educational, and political organizations rather than by individuals.

integration   A national system in which ethnic backgrounds are ignored and all individuals are treated alike.

interactionism   A theory that explains behavior in terms of each individual's social relationships.

internal colonialism   A theory of racism and discrimination that distinguishes between minorities who are "conquered people" and those who are not.

international war   Prolonged armed conflict between the governments of two or more nations.

job retraining   A program to teach workers new skills.

juvenile delinquency   Behavior by minors (usually defined as individuals below the age of 18) that is in violation of criminal law or the special standards set for juveniles.

labeling theory   A theory that sees crime, mental illness, and other types of deviance as labels applied to those who break social norms, and which holds that branding someone as deviant encourages rather than discourages further deviant behavior.

laissez-faire capitalism   An economic ideology that argues the government should stay out of economic affairs and allow the free market to regulate itself.

lean production   An approach to manufacturing that attempts to use the smallest possible amount of labor.

legitimacy   Consent of the governed based on a belief that those who govern have the right to do so.

lesbian   A female homosexual.

less-developed countries (LDCs)   Nations with a low level of economic development and a low standard of living; also called the Third World.

lobbying   The activities of special-interest groups aimed at convincing lawmakers to pass the kind of legislation they desire.

magnet school   A school with special enriched programs designed to attract students from all ethnic groups, thus encouraging integration.

managed care   A system of health care in which the treatments and services available to patients are tightly controlled to hold down costs.

manslaughter   The unlawful killing of another person without malice.

Medicaid   A U.S. program designed to help the poor, the blind, and the disabled pay for medical care.

Medicare   A U.S. program that pays for medical care of people over 65 years old.

melting pot theory   The belief that U.S. society acts as a sort of crucible in which people from around the world are blended together to form a new and distinctive culture.

mental disorder   A mental condition that makes it difficult or impossible for a person to cope with everyday life.

methodology   The study of how to do research.

militarism   (1) Glorification of war and combat. (2) Strong belief in "defense" combined with huge military expenditures.

misdemeanor   A minor offense, usually punishable by confinement in a local jail or by payment of a fine.

modernization   The process by which a nation moves from a traditional agricultural society to an industrialized state.

monogamy   The practice of being married to only one person at a time.

monopoly   The situation existing when a single corporation has gained complete control of a market.

mood disorder   A mental disorder involving severe disturbances in behavior and emotion.

multicultural education   Education that reflects the perspectives of many different cultural groups.

murder   The unlawful killing of a human being with malice.

National Crime Victimization Survey (NCVS)   A yearly survey of Americans that attempts to determine how many have been victimized by crime.

nationalism   A form of ethnocentrism based on a sense of identification with and devotion to one's nation.

noncategorical program   A welfare program with no restrictions on eligibility.

nonrenewable energy   A power source with a fixed supply that cannot be replenished.

norm   A social rule telling us what behavior is acceptable in a certain situation and what is not.

nuclear family   A married couple and their children.

nuclear proliferation   The spread of nuclear weapons to an ever larger number of countries.

nuclear war   Any war employing nuclear weapons.

nuclear winter   The sharp decline in average temperatures produced by dense clouds that would cover the earth after a major nuclear war.

nurse practitioner   A nurse who is trained to take full charge of patients' basic health care.

occupational crime   A crime committed in the course of the offender's occupation but without the support or encouragement of his or her employer.

oligopoly   The situation existing when an industry is dominated by a few large companies.

organic waste   Waste products with a biological origin.

organizational crime   A crime committed by someone acting on behalf of a larger organization, often his or her employer.

ozone depletion   The reduction in the protective layer of ozone in the upper atmosphere.

parity   Equal treatment.

passive smoking   Inhalation of secondhand tobacco smoke by nonsmokers.

patriarchy/patriarchal system   A society or social system dominated by men and run in their interests.

periphery   The poor nations of the world, which are subject to the economic and political domination of the core nations.

personality   The relatively stable characteristics and traits that distinguish one person from another.

personality theory   A theory holding that social behavior is determined by differences in personality.

photochemical smog   A group of noxious compounds produced by the action of sunlight on oxygen, hydrocarbons, and nitrogen oxides.

photovoltaic cell   A cell that produces electricity from the sun.

physician's assistant   Medical personnel trained to carry out particular medical services traditionally performed by physicians.

plea bargaining   A process by which a defense attorney and a prosecutor agree to let a defendant plead guilty in return for a reduction in the charge or other considerations.

pluralism   A national system in which several ethnic groups maintain a high level of independence and equality.

pluralist   One who believes that political decisions are made by changing coalitions of political forces.

police brutality   The use of excessive and unnecessary force by police officers in the performance of their duties.

political economy   The economic and political system of a community, nation, or group of nations.

pollution   The release of harmful substances into the environment.

polygamy The practice of having more than one husband or wife at a time.

population explosion The rapid increase in the human population of the world.

positive school A theoretical school in criminology that rejected the classical theory's assumption that crime was based on free choice.

poverty (1) The state of having an income below some specified level. (2) The state of having significantly less income and wealth than the average person in the society of which one is a member.

prejudice Antipathy, either felt or expressed, based on a faulty and inflexible generalization and directed toward a group as a whole or toward an individual because he or she is a member of that group.

prep school A private school designed to prepare students for college.

preventive medicine The theory or practice of staying healthy by maintaining good health habits.

price-fixing Collusion by several companies to cut competition and set uniformly high prices.

probation Suspension of the sentence of a person who has been convicted but not yet imprisoned, on condition of continued good behavior and regular reporting to a probation officer.

productivity The value of the goods or services an average worker produces in a given time period.

property crime A crime directed against property.

psychoanalysis Long-term therapy designed to uncover the repressed memories, motives, and conflicts assumed to be at the root of a patient's psychological problems.

pushout A child who leaves his or her family home because he or she is no longer wanted there.

race A group of people who are thought to have a common set of physical characteristics but who may or may not share a sense of unity and identity.

racism Stereotyping, prejudice, and discrimination based on race.

rational choice theory A theory that holds crime to be the result of the rational choice of the offender.

rehabilitation The process of changing a person's criminal behavior by nonpunitive methods.

relative approach Dividing the poor from the nonpoor on the basis of the wealth and income of the average person.

relative deprivation theory Holding that revolutions are caused by differences between what people have and what they think they should have.

renewable energy A power resource that is replenished through natural processes.

repressive terrorism Terrorism intended to protect the existing political order in a nation.

resegregation   A return to racial or ethnic segregation that occurs after official de-segregation problems have started.

retribution   The idea that the goal of the criminal justice process should be to make criminals suffer for their crimes.

reverse discrimination   Discrimination against white males.

revolutionary terrorism   Terrorism intended to bring about major political changes in a nation.

revolutionary war   Armed conflict between an official government and one or more groups of rebels.

robbery   The unlawful taking of another person's property by force or threat of force.

role   A set of expectations and behaviors associated with a social position.

romantic love   The powerful attraction that is expected to form the basis of marriage in most Western societies.

runaway   A child who moves away from his or her home without parental consent.

salad bowl theory   The belief that ethnic groups should maintain their distinct identity in a multicultural community.

sample   A cross section of subjects selected for study as representative of a larger population.

scapegoat   A person or group that is unjustly blamed for the problems of others.

schizophrenia   A mental disorder involving extreme disorganization in personality, thought patterns, and speech.

segregated school   A school in which students are separated according to their racial, ethnic, or class background.

segregation   The practice of keeping ethnic or racial groups apart.

self-concept   The image one has of who and what he or she is.

self-report study   A survey that asks respondents to report the crimes or other deviant actions they have committed.

semiperiphery   The partially industrialized nations that have characteristics of both the core and the periphery.

service occupation   A job that provides a service to someone else rather than making a product or extracting a natural resource.

sexism   Stereotyping, prejudice, and discrimination based on gender.

sexual harassment   Unwanted sexual comments, gestures, or physical advances.

sexual orientation   A person's identity as heterosexual, homosexual, or bisexual.

sexual stereotyping   The portrayal of all females or all males as having similar fixed traits.

sexually transmitted disease   A disease passed from one person to another during a sex act.

single-parent family   A family in which only one parent lives with one or more children.

situationalist   One who believes that the social characteristics of poor people are caused by their unique social situation and not by a culture of poverty.

social class   A category of people with similar shares of the things that are valued in a society.

social disorganization   The condition that exists when an institution is poorly organized and fails to perform its social functions.

social institution   A relatively stable pattern of thought and behavior centered on the performance of an important social task.

social movement   A group of people who have banded together to promote a particular cause.

social problem   (1) A condition that a significant number of people believe to be a problem. (2) A condition in which there is a sizable difference between the ideals of a society and its actual achievements.

Social Security   A government-administered old-age pension program whose formal title is Old Age and Survivors Insurance.

social structure   The organized patterns of human behavior in a society.

socialization   The process by which individuals learn their culture's ways of thinking and behaving.

society   A group of people in the same geographic area who share common institutions and traditions.

sociology   The scientific study of societies and social groups.

sociopathic personality   An antisocial person with a complex of personality characteristics including impulsiveness, immaturity, and a lack of concern for other people.

sodomy law   A law that forbids oral or anal sex. Sodomy laws are rarely enforced.

solar energy   A power source supplied by the sun.

special-interest group   A group of people who have a stake in a specific area of public policy.

Standard English   The English dialect spoken by the middle and upper classes.

status offense   A juvenile offense that does not violate the criminal law.

stimulant   A drug that arouses the central nervous system, increases the metabolic rate, and reduces drowsiness.

strain theory   A theory holding that crime is caused by the strain produced when societies tell people that wealth is available to all but nevertheless restrict access to the means for achieving wealth.

stress theory   A theory that holds that an individual will experience serious psychological problems if exposed to excessive levels of stress.

strip mining   A mining technique in which long strips of soil are dug up and processed.

structuralist   One who believes that the structure of capitalist society forces the government to support the interests of the privileged few.

subculture   A culture that exists within a larger culture and is influenced by it but has its own unique ideas and beliefs.

substance abuse disorder   A category of mental disorder applied to people who use excessive amounts of alcohol or other drugs.

Supplemental Security Income (SSI)   A program that gives financial assistance to those who are blind or disabled or have other special problems.

surrogate mothering   One woman bearing a child for another.

survey   A research method that asks people about their attitudes and activities, either in personal interviews or by means of questionnaires.

sustainable economy   A stable economy that does not exceed the carrying capacity of its environment.

syndicated crime   Crime committed by a group of individuals working together over a period of time.

temperature inversion   A condition in which a layer of warm air moves over a layer of cool air, sealing in pollutants that would otherwise rise into the upper atmosphere.

terrorism   Attacks against civilians to achieve political ends.

theft   Unlawful taking of property.

therapeutic community   A live-in community for drug treatment.

Third World   The poor agricultural nations of the world.

tolerance   (1) The immunity to the effects of a drug that builds up after repeated use. (2) The practice of ignoring behavior patterns that are personally objectionable.

total war   A war whose goal is unconditional surrender of an enemy nation and in which both military personnel and ordinary citizens participate.

tragedy of the commons   The destruction of common resources in the pursuit of individual benefits.

underclass   The lowest social stratum, made up of the long-term poor who are excluded from the mainstream of society.

underemployment   The problem suffered by workers who want full-time work but can find only part-time or temporary work.

unemployment   The problem suffered by workers who want a job but are unable to find one.

Uniform Crime Reports   A national summary of all the crimes reported to the police.

urban subsistence economy   The way of life of city dwellers in poor countries who make just enough to get by.

victimless crime   A crime in which the harm, if any, is not suffered by anyone except the offender.

violence   Behavior intended to cause bodily pain or injury to another; may be legitimate or illegitimate.

violent crime   Crime that involves physical harm or the threat of physical harm to an individual.

voucher system   An educational system in which the government gives students vouchers that can be used to pay for education at any school they or their parents choose.

war   A protracted military conflict between two or more organized groups.

wealth   A person's total economic worth (e.g., real estate, stocks, cash).

white-collar crime   Crime committed by people of respectability and high social status in the course of their occupations.

white-collar worker   A person employed in nonmanual labor, such as a business manager or office worker.

white ethnic   An American of European descent who maintains a distinct ethnic identity.

withdrawal   The sickness that a habitual drug user experiences when the drug is discontinued after a period of steady use.

world economy   The international system of economic relationships in which all countries participate.

world system   The network of economic and political relationships that links the nations of the world together.

world system theory   A sociological theory that holds the global political economy to be based on the exploration of poor countries by rich ones.

PHOTO CREDITS

INDEX